Supervision

MANAGING FOR RESULTS

NINTH EDITION

JOHN W. NEWSTROM

Professor Emeritus of Management
Department of Management Studies
Labovitz School of Business and Economics
University of Minnesota Duluth

McGraw-Hill Irwin

Boston   Burr Ridge, IL   Dubuque, IA   Madison, WI   New York   San Francisco   St. Louis
Bangkok   Bogotá   Caracas   Kuala Lumpur   Lisbon   London   Madrid   Mexico City
Milan   Montreal   New Delhi   Santiago   Seoul   Singapore   Sydney   Taipei   Toronto

McGraw-Hill
Irwin

SUPERVISION: MANAGING FOR RESULTS

Published by McGraw-Hill/Irwin, a business unit of The McGraw-Hill Companies, Inc., 1221
Avenue of the Americas, New York, NY, 10020. Copyright © 2007 by The McGraw-Hill
Companies, Inc. All rights reserved. No part of this publication may be reproduced or distributed in any form or by any means, or stored in a database or retrieval system, without the prior
written consent of The McGraw-Hill Companies, Inc., including, but not limited to, in any
network or other electronic storage or transmission, or broadcast for distance learning.

Some ancillaries, including electronic and print components, may not be available to customers
outside the United States.

This book is printed on acid-free paper.

3 4 5 6 7 8 9 0 VNH/VNH 0 9 8

ISBN-13: 978-0-07-354508-0
ISBN-10: 0-07-354508-2

Editorial director: *John E. Biernat*
Publisher: *Linda Schreiber*
Sponsoring editor: *Doug Hughes*
Editorial assistant: *Peter Vanaria*
Marketing manager: *Keari Bedford*
Media producer: *Benjamin Curless*
Senior project manager: *Laura Griffin*
Senior production supervisor: *Rose Hepburn*
Lead designer: *Matthew Baldwin*
Photo research coordinator: *Kathy Shive*
Lead media project manager: *Cathy L. Tepper*
Senior supplement producer: *Carol Loreth*
Freelance designer: *Kiera Pohl*
Cover image: © *Getty Images*
Typeface: *11/13 Times Roman*
Compositor: *GTS—New Delhi, India Campus*
Printer: *Von Hoffmann Corporation*

Library of Congress Cataloging-in-Publication Data

Newstrom, John W.
    Supervision: managing for results / John W. Newstrom.—9th ed.
        p. cm.
    Includes index.
    ISBN-13: 978-0-07-354508-0
    ISBN-10: 0-07-354508-2 (alk. paper)
    1. Personnel management. 2. Supervision of employees. I. Title.
HF5549.B52 2007
658.3′02—dc22
                                                                          2005052280

www.mhhe.com

Contents in Brief

Contents

Chapter 4   Problem Solving and Managing Information   81

Problems: Cause and Effect / Systematic Problem Solving / Decision Making:
Rational and Intuitive / Information as a Raw Material / Keeping the System Human

Part Three   Organizing, Staffing, and Training

Chapter 5   Organizing an Effective Department   111

Organizing for Effectiveness / Types of Organizational Structures / Authority, Responsibility,
and Accountability / Delegation for Leverage / Guidelines for Organizing

Chapter 6   Staffing with Human Resources   141

Forecasting Workforce Requirements / The Staffing Process / Interviewing Job Candidates / Making the
Selection Decision / Orientation Training / Minimizing the Potential for Absences and Turnover

Chapter 7   Training and Developing Employees   167

Training: Process and Purpose / A Training Partnership / Factors in Learning / Training Methods and Aids / Obtaining Results from Training

Part Four   Leading the Workforce

Chapter 8   Leadership Skills, Styles, and Qualities   195

Leadership Defined / Leadership Assumptions and Trust / Leadership Styles and Concepts / Selecting an Appropriate Style / Leaders and Followers

Chapter 9   Understanding and Motivating People at Work   221

The Importance of Individuality / A Powerful Pattern of Motivation / Satisfaction and Dissatisfaction / Achievement, Expectancy, and Equity / Motivation and Rewards / Motivation in the Work Itself

Chapter 10   Effective Employee Communication   247

The Communication Process / Methods of Communication / Nonverbal Communication / Communication Guidelines / Orders, Instructions, and Requests

Part Five   Working with Individuals and Teams

Chapter 11   Appraising and Developing Employees   275

Purposes of Appraisal / Factors and Format / The Appraisal Interview / Special Considerations / Legal, Financial, and Ethical Aspects

Chapter 12   Counseling and Performance Management   305

Problem Performers / Employee Counseling / Reducing Absenteeism / The Problems of Substance Abuse and Illness / Performance Management / Administrative Guidelines

Chapter 13 Building Cooperative Teams and Resolving Conflicts 337

Group Dynamics / Group Participation / Developing Cooperative Teams / Resolving Conflict in Groups / Securing Cooperation

Part Six Controlling

Chapter 14 Control: Keeping People, Plans, and Programs on Track 367

A Dual Role / Control Standards / The Control Process / Control Targets / Handling Employee Resistance

Chapter 18 Achieving Personal Supervisory Success 495

Managing Job-Related Time / Coping with Stress / Developing Personal Creativity / Becoming a Mentor and Coach / Personal Actions at Work

Part Eight Appendixes

About the Author

John W. Newstrom

John W. Newstrom is a respected teacher, widely published author, and consultant to organizations in the areas of training and supervisory development. He is a Professor Emeritus of Management in the Management Studies Department of the Labovitz School of Business and Economics at the University of Minnesota Duluth (UMD), where he taught courses in Managing Change, Training and Development, Organizational Behavior and Management, and Interpersonal and Group Relations. He was previously on the faculty at Arizona State University (ASU), and also worked at Honeywell Inc. He holds Bachelor of Accounting, MBA, and Ph.D. degrees from the University of Minnesota. He has conducted training programs on a wide range of topics for organizations in the healthcare, steel, taconite mining, consumer products, gas transmission, public utility, and paper products industries as well as for city governments and federal agencies.

Dr. Newstrom has published over 60 professional and practitioner articles in periodicals such as *Supervision, Academy of Management Executive, Workforce, Personnel Journal, Human Resource Planning, Business Horizons, Training and Development, Journal of Management Development, California Management Review, S.A.M. Advanced Management Journal, Training, Supervisory Management, Journal of Management, Journal of Occupational Behavior,* and *Academy of Management Journal;* he has served on the Editorial Review Boards of several management journals; and he is the co-author of 35 books, including *The Manager's Bookshelf, Organizational Behavior, Transfer of Training, Games Trainers Play, Leaders and the Leadership Process,* and *The Big Book of Team Building Games.* He is currently working on two more books, tentatively titled *The Fun-Minute Manager* and *Humor Works! 101 Funny Stories with Serious Lessons for Managers.*

His administrative experiences include being Chairperson of UMD's Business Administration Department, Director of the Center for Professional Development, Acting Director of ASU's Bureau of Business and Economic Research, and Chairperson of the Management Education and Development (MED) division of the Academy of Management. He has also served on (or as a strategic consultant to) the Boards of Directors of several organizations, such as the American Society for Training and Development, St. Louis County Heritage and Arts Center, United

Developmental Achievement Center, Duluth-Superior Community Foundation, Riverwood Healthcare Center, and Arrowhead Food Bank. He has held memberships in the Academy of Management, the Organizational Behavior Teaching Society, and the Society for Advancement of Management.

Dr. Newstrom has received many awards in recognition of his service to students and the community. He was the recipient of an "Outstanding Reviewer" Award from the MED division of the Academy of Management, the "Barbershopper of the Year" award from the Duluth-Superior Harbormasters, the "Outstanding Faculty" award from the UMD Student Association, the campus "Outstanding Adviser" award, and several "favorite professor" recognition awards at UMD. His highest honor occurred when he was named a recipient of the Horace T. Morse–University of Minnesota Alumni Association Award for "Outstanding Contributions to Undergraduate Education." Dr. Newstrom is also a member of the University of Minnesota's prestigious Academy of Distinguished Teachers.

On the personal side, John is married (to Diane, for over 40 years) and is the father of two college graduates (Scott and Heidi). He loves to hunt, work crossword puzzles, golf, work outdoors at his cabin in northern Minnesota, and vacation in Florida and Arizona. His favorite community service activities include being a frequent blood donor, co-leader of a Paint-A-Thon team for low-income persons, hospice volunteer, and "big brother" to a young boy. John also sings bass in a barbershop quartet, where he practices the art of *neoteny* (joyful living).

Preface

Today's work environment demands that supervisors do more than know how to supervise. They must manage to bring about results consistent with organizational goals and objectives. The ninth edition of *Supervision: Managing for Results* is written to help them do just that.

The Approach

The overall approach of this book continues to be guided by seven interlocking objectives:

1. To offer readers practical advice about how to handle real-life, on-the-job situations.
2. To recognize an ever-changing social and work environment.
3. To provide useful insights based on the job-tested experience of the author and his associates.
4. To cover all the vital aspects of supervision.
5. To reflect the latest professional concepts of supervisory practice and organizational behavior.
6. To employ the most effective techniques for helping readers enjoy and assimilate the material presented in the text.
7. To maintain a good-humored perspective on what continues to be one of the world's most demanding jobs.

With these objectives as a foundation, *Supervision: Managing for Results* provides a useful aid to a wide and diverse readership, which includes

- **Instructors,** who use it as a basic text in preparing their students for the complex world of supervisory management.
- **Students** of first-level management in business, industry, and government, who turn to it as a central source of information about the practice of supervision.
- **Supervisors,** who find it to be a complete reference guide of methods for dealing with people, managing their jobs, and planning their own advancement.
- **Managers,** who may gain from it an insight into the problems—human, technical, and personal—supervisors must face daily.
- **Training directors** and other human resource development professionals, who use this text for guiding the training of supervisors in the interpersonal and administrative skills of their jobs.

- **Members of self-managing teams,** who discover it to be a source for understanding the new roles they must play in the absence of a formal leader.

In This Edition

Supervision: Managing for Results reflects an extensive reexamination of every aspect of coverage. It provides readers with the very latest information and the most current points of view from authoritative sources. Throughout, there has been a rigorous updating—of data, language, legal interpretation, situations, and examples. Coverage includes applications to and examples from clerical, office, service, institutional, and government settings.

Several chapters, such as Chapters 2, 4, and 18, contain substantial amounts of new material. Others, such as Chapter 12, Counseling and Performance Management, and Chapter 15, Stimulating Productivity and Quality, have taken on a new thrust and focus. All chapters have been thoroughly updated to reflect the best thinking and most current solid practice in supervisory techniques.

Features new to this edition are:

- I have reorganized the material, based on reviewer comments, into 18 chapters and 8 parts. This has been done to streamline the flow of material and make the text more adaptable to semester-length courses.
- I have prepared and inserted 10 "Practical Guidelines for Supervisors" at the end of each chapter. The total of 180 prescriptions should provide a strong basis for supervisory success in their careers.
- I have increased the emphasis on ethical issues in supervision, adding additional "Ethical Perspectives" as well as thorough discussions of issues unique to some chapters.

This comprehensive text revision has also resulted in content enhancements in numerous areas, including the following:

- Ethical issues (many chapters)
- Fun at work (Chapter 2)
- Creativity (Chapter 4)
- Restructuring/downsizing (Chapter 5)
- Micromanaging (Chapter 5)
- Presenteeism (Chapter 6)
- Performance management (Chapter 7)
- Emotional intelligence (Chapter 8)
- Trust (Chapter 8)
- Caregiving (Chapter 8)
- Big Five personality traits (Chapter 9)

- Flow (Chapter 9)
- Goal settting (Chapter 9)
- E-mail usage (Chapter 10)
- Active listening and questioning (Chapter 10)
- Feedback seeking and feedback avoiding (Chapter 11)
- Empathy (Chapter 12)
- Just cause firings (Chapter 12)
- "In" groups (Chapter 13)
- Virtual teams (Chapter 13)
- High-reliability organizations (Chapter 14)
- Six Sigma programs (Chapter 15)
- GLBTs (Chapter 16)
- GenXers and Nexters (Chapter 16)
- Employee obesity (Chapter 17)
- Workplace violence (Chapter 17)
- Stress and spirituality (Chapter 18)

Unique Learning Techniques

This edition retains the three learning methods that differentiate *Supervision: Managing for Results* from most other texts in its field:

1. **An emphasis on inquiry learning,** in which readers are given a series of related questions and then are immediately provided with feedback in the form of answers. This approach helps raise the reader's curiosity and engage his or her intellect. It also reinforces understanding, targets key issues, and develops application proficiency in a manner similar to that of progressive or graduated learning. Additionally, the format enables readers to relate concepts to the problems and issues supervisors face daily at work. It also makes the text a convenient and invaluable resource for future reference on the job. See, for example, the comprehensive listing of hundreds of questions covered (cross-referenced to the pages on which they appear) placed on the Student Edition of the text's website, http://www.mhhe.com/newstrom9e.

2. **A sensitivity to readers' needs for high readability.** Although the text is well grounded in solid research and fundamental concepts, discussions of theory are minimized and the material is presented in a fast-paced manner. In addition, the text maintains a moderate vocabulary level, a manageable sentence length, and an active, engaging, vibrant style of writing.

3. **Practical advice in the form of dos and don'ts.** Based on a lifetime of experience and knowledge, the author is not afraid to offer straightforward advice about how to handle difficult situations. Especially in the sticky matters of interpersonal relationships, my intention is to provide current and prospective supervisors with

a useful starting point for their actions and responses, rather than leave them with a set of equivocating observations ("On the one hand . . . , but on the other hand . . ."). Where judgment is required, I present the pros and cons of each position and point in the direction of the weight of evidence and logic.

Chapter Features

Each chapter contains the following features:

- **A set of learning objectives,** which alerts readers to what they should know or be able to do as a result of reading the chapter. These objectives directly relate to concepts later discussed in the chapter.
- **Concept statements,** which precede and preview each numbered section within the chapter.
- **Thoughts to Ponder,** which highlight the current thinking on a relevant supervision topic.
- **Boxed features,** including Did You Know?, Quips & Quotes, and Internet Connections, that expand text topics and enliven the discussion.
- **Ethical Perspectives,** which raise difficult issues supervisors often face in today's complex world.
- **Job Tip Boxes,** which provide practical suggestions for readers to implement on the job.
- **Quick Tests** after each topic section, which help readers assess their understanding of the material covered and reinforce their learning and retention.
- **Definitions of Terms,** which are shown in the margin when a term is introduced.
- **Practical Guidelines for Supervisors,** which offer a set of prescriptions (do's and don'ts) for success.

A set of Review and Application learning aids appears at the end of the text material in each chapter. The Review aids include:

- **Key Concepts to Remember,** which enlarges on and summarizes each of the numbered concepts presented in the chapter.
- **Reading Comprehension,** which consists of 10 questions that probe the reader's understanding of the text material.

The Application aids include:

- **Self-Assessment,** with a self-scoring guide, which challenges readers to judge their skills, abilities, characteristics, and needs for improvement.
- **Skill Development, Role Play,** and **Group Exercises** are included in most chapters to help readers apply what they have learned.

- **Cases for Analysis,** three or more for each chapter, each calling for analysis and solution. These cases are numbered sequentially throughout the book for ease of identification and reference. Of special note are the cases that appear first in each chapter. These are uniquely structured in the *case-in-point* format—that is, each case presents the reader with five alternative solutions, often called "forced-choice" solutions. The reader is asked to rank the appropriateness of each alternative from first to fifth and to be prepared to defend those choices.

Teaching and Learning Resources

A *Study Guide* and an *Instructor's Resource CD-ROM (IRCD)* containing an *Instructor's Manual* supplement this textbook. The *Instructor's Manual* contains a number of useful instructional aids, transparency masters, and additional case studies for class or seminar use. The *IRCD* contains the ExamView Test Generator with True/False, Multiple Choice, and Completion questions. The *IRCD* also contains PowerPoint presentation slides for each chapter in the text.

DVDs

Several *Manager's Hot Seat* DVDs are included with the *Instructor's Resource CD-ROM*. These provide viewers with vivid opportunities to see, hear, and discuss supervisors' handling of difficult problems.

Acknowledgments

The author accepts full responsibility for the validity of everything that appears in this text. I am, of course, deeply indebted to my teaching colleagues and friends, former students, hundreds of professional peers, and thousands of practicing supervisors whose thoughts and actions have contributed directly and indirectly to this work. This resource could not have been developed and improved without them, and I regret that I cannot name them all. Three persons, in particular, deserve mention:

- I am grateful to my friend Gregory R. Fox, Vice Chancellor for Finance and Operations at the University of Minnesota Duluth, who prepared the *Study Guide,* the *Instructor's Manual,* and the test items for the *ExamView Pro* test generator for this edition (and several previous ones). Greg's experience as a supervisory trainer and (previously) as the director of the Duluth Center for Continuing Education adds considerably to the practicality, accuracy, and authority of the ancillary programs.
- I am forever indebted to the late Lester R. Bittel, Professor Emeritus of Management and a Virginia Eminent Scholar at James Madison University, for the masterful creation of early editions of this book, and for providing me with the opportunity many years ago to become a full-fledged partner with him in the authorship of it.
- I especially appreciate the never-ending support, encouragement, and love of my terrific wife, Diane E. Newstrom. She has performed innumerable book preparation tasks, provided the "quiet space" for me to work, and nurtured my heart and soul throughout over four decades of our partnership together.

I am also grateful to the following individuals for their reviews of the eighth edition of the text and the ninth edition manuscript. Their suggestions and comments helped immeasurably in creating useful improvements in the final product.

Vondra Armstrong
Pulaski Technical College
North Little Rock, Arkansas

Michael Bark
Wisconsin Indianhead Technical
  College
Ashland, Wisconsin

Eunice Glover
Clayton College
Morrow, Georgia

Carol Gottuso
Metropolitan Community College
Omaha, Nebraska

Mark Lampert
Los Angeles Valley College
Valley Glen, California

Dr. Ben U. Nwoke
Virginia State University
Petersburg, Virginia

Gary Marrer
Glendale Community College
Glendale, Arizona

Dr. William Recker
Northern Kentucky University
Highland Heights, Kentucky

Dr. Salvatore J. Monopoli
The Cittone Institute
Philadelphia, Pennsylvania

Leda Thompson
Arkansas State University
Mountain Home, Arkansas

Finally, the team effort provided by McGraw-Hill staff made this revision project particularly smooth for me. I thank Douglas Hughes, Peter Vanaria, Megan Gates, and Laura Griffin for their active "behind the scenes" roles in supervising this massive project. They must have read my book and its 180 Practical Guidelines for Supervisors, for they followed them superbly.

John W. Newstrom

Guided Tour

The ninth edition of *Supervision: Managing for Results* follows the same practical question and answer approach that has made previous editions successful yet provides updated material and new features for both students and instructors. Coverage within the text contains the most current points of view from authoritative sources and the very latest information. New pedagogical features, such as the Practical Guidelines for Supervisors, aim to expand the reader's exposure to real-life situations.

Objectives and Concepts

Each chapter opens with a list of Learning Objectives that outlines what skills the reader will learn. The chapter is then subdivided into five or six specific concepts that further develop the chapter's goals. Concept sections end with a Quick Test which allows the reader to apply what was just learned.

4

Problem Solving and Managing Information

LEARNING OBJECTIVES

After studying this chapter, you should be able to

- Recognize and define a problem or a potential problem.
- List the nine steps in problem solving and decision making that lead to the removal of a problem's cause.
- Discuss the rational and intuitive approaches to decision making and explain cost-benefit analysis, decision trees, and ABC analysis.
- Explain how unethical supervisors rationalize their behavior, and contrast that with a set of guidelines for helping supervisors make ethical decisions.

1

CONCEPT
Problems in organizations occur because of change, and are revealed by gaps between expected and actual outcomes.

Problems: Cause and Effect

What, exactly, is a problem?

A problem has several defining characteristics. In general, a problem is (a) an unsettled matter or disturbing condition (b) that raises puzzling questions about its specific nature and (c) demands resolution by decisive action; however, (d) its proper settlement is often clouded by difficulty, uncertainty, and doubt, and—as a consequence—(e) it may require considerable thought and skill to find an effective solution. A simpler and more useful definition, however, is this: A *problem* exists when there is a substantial difference between an expected condition (such as that spelled out by a performance standard or departmental goal) and the actual condition that has occurred or is now occurring. Further, *supervisory problems* usually require making a choice from among multiple options. Given this simpler characterization, studies show that supervisors may solve as many as 80 problems a day. If this figure is only half true, supervisors are called upon to find answers to, or render decisions on, 10,000 problems a year (40 × 250 days). Thankfully, the great majority of these problems are minor. Nevertheless, the figures are staggering and are of major concern to every supervisor.

As a practical matter, it is helpful to think of problems as falling into two classifications:

Current problems. These are ones that have already been observed or are occurring right now. Examples include merchandise that has spoiled, a valued employee who has quit, costs that are running out of line, and shipments that are not meeting delivery dates. These problems need immediate solutions to correct what has already happened or what is now taking place.

Potential problems. These lie in the near future. Nevertheless, you must be alert to their eventual presence. You will recognize them in such forms as how to finish a certain project on time, when to assign overtime, where to place the new copy machine, and when to tell employees about an impending change in their work schedules. It is important to identify such potential problems in advance. Then you can apply "preventive" problem solving to them.

Problems, and their solutions, are, of course, inseparably related to the management process. Problems arise all along the way. Supervisors must solve them when they plan, organize, staff, lead, and control. Otherwise, problems will interfere with the attainment of the department's goals.

Problems are often brought about by change. **How should supervisors deal with problems?**

Pedagogical Features

Throughout each chapter, certain features expand upon the ideas presented, including margin notes such as Internet Connection, Quips & Quotes, Did You Know?, and Ethical Perspectives. The Ethical Perspectives feature has been given an increased emphasis during this revision. Integral terms and definitions for understanding supervision techniques also appear in the margin.

5 Quality of Work Life

CONCEPT
Supervisors can improve the quality of work life when they *facilitate* the work of their employees, encourage feedback from them, and provide opportunities for them to have fun at work.

Facilitating. An approach to management in which a supervisor assists and guides employees in their efforts to perform their jobs rather than emphasizing orders, instructions, and control.

To what extent are supervisors responsible for dissatisfied employees?

Only to the extent that employees who ordinarily ought to be satisfied with their work begin to project a general dissatisfaction with it. One observer advises that when a state of "poor satisfaction" occurs, it may also be evidence of "poor management." Some organizations even make managerial bonuses dependent on the level of employee satisfaction in their unit.

What can supervisors do to improve the quality of working life?

There are two major approaches. The first stems from the view that improved productivity—greater output from the inputs of labor, materials, money, methods, and machines—results in measurable improvements in employee satisfaction. Workers get a feeling of achievement when they see accomplishments flowing from their efforts, and this provides a foundation for a better work life. Supervisors can help make this connection clear by telling employees how the fruits of higher productivity provide the resources for making work easier and freeing them to work on more motivating tasks.

The second appro[...]

Internet connection
www.hr.upenn.edu/quality
A comprehensive example of how a service organization—Penn State University—attempts to create a high quality of work life for its employees.

porary belief that a g[...] sion making at all le[...] essential. It may be [...] generations of mana[...] They divided jobs into[...] employees could spe[...] repetitive experts with low error rates. Howev[...] more educated, the majority of human bein[...] although not necessarily harder. As a consequ[...] opportunities to make the fullest use of the[...] when they are allowed to see how their ideas[...] efforts contribute to the overall objective. T[...] tions that enable each woman and man to n[...] contribution to the finished product or servi[...]

Quips & Quotes
A positive workplace atmosphere is worth developing, and not merely for its own sake; it may be the foundation of true organizational success.
Bronwyn Fryer

To most people, an improved quality of [...] their hours spent at work will not be waste[...] tions will be valued. They want to feel that, [...] more worthwhile as a result of working than[...] at all. The role of a supervisor is to help the[...]

38 PART 1 Supervisory Management

Did You Know

Obstacles to Creativity
According to a survey by The Creative Group, the most common blocks to creativity are tight deadlines, lack of inspiration, stress, and fatigue from working long hours. These obstacles can be reduced or avoided by setting aside time for brainstorming sessions, encouraging collaboration, monitoring burnout, and setting an atmosphere that encourages "business as unusual."
Source: "Time's Up," Training, May 2002, p. 24.

Creativity. The generation of new solutions to existing problems by using techniques to encourage "out of the box" thinking.

Ethical Perspectives

Prejudice and Bias
You cannot be completely free of the subjective elements of prejudice and bias. You are human! Be as objective and impersonal as possible with problems involving employees. What can you do to reduce your prejudice and bias?

They are harder to explain and defend, however, when they go wrong. More important, any decision is likely to be better if its goals are clearly understood. The logical approach helps strip away distractions and irrelevancies as well as minimize dangerous biases and prejudices (see Ethical Perspectives). Intuition often adds a valuable dimension by calling on an inner sense we don't clearly understand. Many authorities believe the best decisions come from the dual approach—a combination of logic and hunch, supplemented by creativity.

What is the importance of creativity in decision making?

In a nutshell, it is very important. Yesterday's solutions are often inadequate for today's unforeseen problems. Supervisors—and their staff of employees—must train their minds to "think out of the box." This involves looking at their situation from a unique perspective and then making connections that are not normally made by others. The resulting answers could be new combinations of previous approaches, or totally unexpected innovations. Effective creativity is a lot like the inquiry-based approach that forms a basis for this text—you ask questions, engage in critical thinking, keep your mind open to new ideas, and explore balanced arguments in a collaborative setting.

The key to *creativity* is to begin by asking what you hope to achieve (the new end result). The next stage involves mentally breaking out of old ways of thinking and acting—often by forcing yourself to use unique metaphors (e.g., an animal, a vegetable, or an athletic event) to stimulate new ideas. Once the creative ideas are out in the open, the normal analytical process can kick in. Examine the advantages of each idea, but also address the obstacles to implementing it. Finally, put one or more new approaches into practice. With practice and self-discipline, creativity becomes a useful habit.

What is meant by mathematical decision making?

Mathematical decision making refers to the use of certain mathematical, statistical, or quantitative techniques to aid the decision maker. These aids are very valuable in many instances, but they are only aids. The techniques do not make decisions. They arrange numerical information in such a way that it can be analyzed mathematically, but the executive, manager, or supervisor must make the final decision on the basis of an interpretation of the results. Further, the benefits of mathematical analyses are very dependent on the quality and relevance of the inputs received ("garbage in; garbage out").

90 PART 2 Planning and Problem Solving

When should you engage in group decision making?

Only when *all* these factors are in play:

- The work group can contribute information, know-how, and viewpoints that you need but don't have.
- You are truly ready to respect their opinions and prepared to act on their suggestions.
- You sense that such participation is needed to induce a commitment from the group to implement the decision.
- You've got adequate time.

Seeking help from a work team in making a decision involves the same considerations that were charted in Table 4-1 for problem solving. In any event, be forewarned that such a consultative approach should not be taken lightly. Employees who participate will be resentful if they sense that they are being manipulated. Their involvement in the process, while not necessarily at an equal level of authority with yours, must be absolutely genuine. Otherwise, the process will backfire and you will be worse off than you would be if you hadn't gotten them involved.

What can be done to make your decisions more effective?

Besides starting with a specific goal in mind and laying a foundation of facts and systematic analysis, there are two other kinds of insurance to which you can turn.

Pick your spots. Try to make decisions only where the potential for a payoff is great. You can identify this kind of opportunity by using ABC analysis (see Figure 4-4). The ABC analysis concept is based on an established economic fact: A vital few problems or opportunities for action account for the greatest loss or greatest gain. Most problems and opportunities are basically of little consequence. Statisticians call this the *80/20 principle.* It means that 80 percent of your problems will account for only 20 percent of your losses or profits. Conversely, 20 percent of your problems (the vital few) will account for 80 percent of your losses or profits. In ABC analysis, the vital few are called A items; the inconsequential many, C items; and those that fall somewhere in between, B items. If you were to examine all the items in your inventory, for example, it is a sure bet that a relatively few items would account for most of its value. A great many items, however, such as paper clips and erasers, would account for

Thoughts to ponder
Edward de Bono suggests that supervisors often get complacent about their thinking and problem-solving capacities, and fall into dangerous but avoidable ruts. They need to view the process as a deliberate skill that can be learned, and one that best uses a variety of approaches. He suggests that decision makers learn to wear any of six "hats" (roles) and shift between them as the need arises. Each of the six hats focuses attention on something different: facts and figures, feelings and emotions, errors in thinking, positive outcomes, a search for alternatives and their consequences, or subject definition and control.
Source: Edward de Bono, Six Thinking Hats, New York: Little, Brown and Co., 1999.

A new feature in the margin notes is the Thoughts to Ponder box, which highlights the current thinking on a relevant supervision topic.

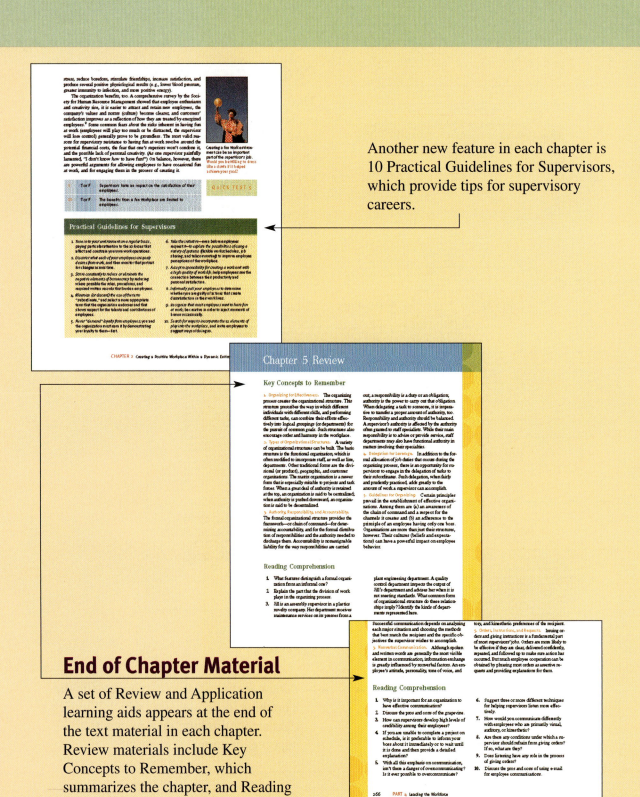

Another new feature in each chapter is 10 Practical Guidelines for Supervisors, which provide tips for supervisory careers.

End of Chapter Material

A set of Review and Application learning aids appears at the end of the text material in each chapter. Review materials include Key Concepts to Remember, which summarizes the chapter, and Reading Comprehension questions.

The Application section includes a Self-Assessment, as well as applied exercises such as Skill Development, Role Play, and Group Exercises. Finally, the Cases for Analysis section provides lifelike situations for readers to analyze and discuss. The cases that appear first in each chapter are in a case-in-point format, asking readers to rank the five alternative solutions.

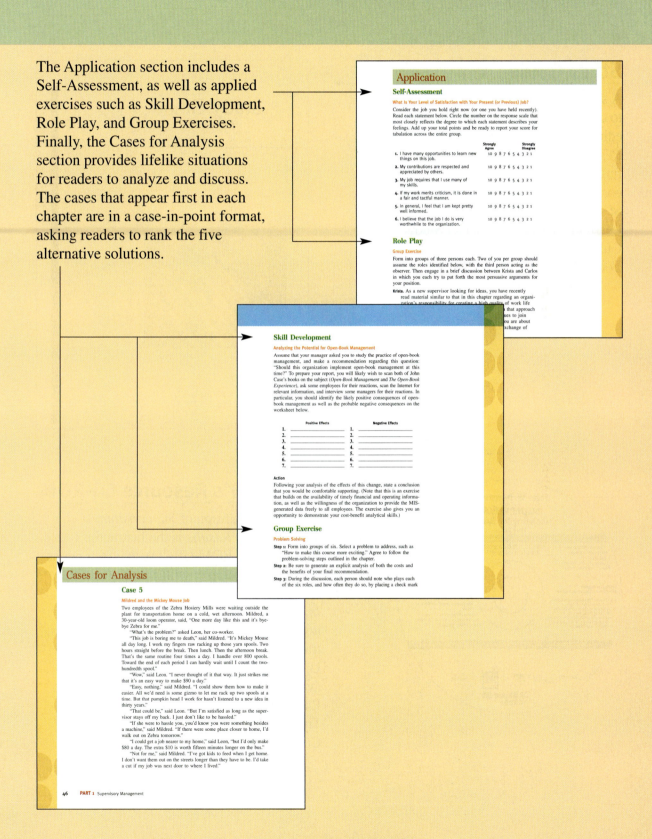

Application

Self-Assessment

What Is Your Level of Satisfaction with Your Present (or Previous) Job?

Consider the job you hold right now (or one you have held recently). Read each statement below. Circle the number on the response scale that most closely reflects the degree to which each statement describes your feelings. Add up your total points and be ready to report your score for tabulation across the entire group.

	Strongly Agree									Strongly Disagree
1. I have many opportunities to learn new things on this job.	10 9 8 7 6 5 4 3 2 1									
2. My contributions are respected and appreciated by others.	10 9 8 7 6 5 4 3 2 1									
3. My job requires that I use many of my skills.	10 9 8 7 6 5 4 3 2 1									
4. If my work merits criticism, it is done in a fair and tactful manner.	10 9 8 7 6 5 4 3 2 1									
5. In general, I feel that I am kept pretty well informed.	10 9 8 7 6 5 4 3 2 1									
6. I believe that the job I do is very worthwhile to the organization.	10 9 8 7 6 5 4 3 2 1									

Role Play

Group Exercise

Form into groups of three persons each. Two of you per group should assume the roles identified below, with the third person acting as the observer. Then engage in a brief discussion between Krista and Carlos in which you each try to put forth the most persuasive arguments for your position.

Krista. As a new supervisor looking for ideas, you have recently read material similar to that in this chapter regarding an organization's responsibility for creating a high quality of work life ... that approach ... ues to join ... you are about ... xchange of

Skill Development

Analyzing the Potential for Open-Book Management

Assume that your manager asked you to study the practice of open-book management, and make a recommendation regarding this question: "Should this organization implement open-book management at this time?" To prepare your report, you will likely wish to scan both of John Case's books on the subject (*Open-Book Management* and *The Open-Book Experience*), ask some employees for their reactions, scan the Internet for relevant information, and interview some managers for their reactions. In particular, you should identify the likely positive consequences of open-book management as well as the probable negative consequences on the worksheet below.

	Positive Effects		Negative Effects
1.	_____	1.	_____
2.	_____	2.	_____
3.	_____	3.	_____
4.	_____	4.	_____
5.	_____	5.	_____
6.	_____	6.	_____
7.	_____	7.	_____

Action

Following your analysis of the effects of this change, state a conclusion that you would be comfortable supporting. (Note that this is an exercise that builds on the availability of timely financial and operating information, as well as the willingness of the organization to provide the MIS-generated data freely to all employees. The exercise also gives you an opportunity to demonstrate your cost-benefit analytical skills.)

Group Exercise

Problem Solving

Step 1: Form into groups of six. Select a problem to address, such as "How to make this course more exciting." Agree to follow the problem-solving steps outlined in the chapter.

Step 2: Be sure to generate an explicit analysis of both the costs and the benefits of your final recommendation.

Step 3: During the discussion, each person should note who plays each of the six roles, and how often they do so, by placing a check mark

Cases for Analysis

Case 5

Mildred and the Mickey Mouse Job

Two employees of the Zebra Hosiery Mills were waiting outside the plant for transportation home on a cold, wet afternoon. Mildred, a 30-year-old loom operator, said, "One more day like this and it's bye-bye Zebra for me."

"What's the problem?" asked Leon, her co-worker.

"This job is boring me to death," said Mildred. "It's Mickey Mouse all day long. I work my fingers raw racking up those yarn spools. Two hours straight before the break. Then lunch. Then the afternoon break. That's the same routine four times a day. I handle over 800 spools. Toward the end of each period I can hardly wait until I count the two-hundredth spool."

"Wow," said Leon. "I never thought of it that way. It just strikes me that it's an easy way to make $90 a day."

"Easy, nothing," said Mildred. "I could show them how to make it easier. All we'd need is some gizmo to let me rack up two spools at a time. But that pumpkin head I work for hasn't listened to a new idea in thirty years."

"That could be," said Leon. "But I'm satisfied as long as the supervisor stays off my back. I just don't like to be hassled."

"If she were to hassle you, you'd know you were something besides a machine," said Mildred. "If there were some place closer to home, I'd walk out on Zebra tomorrow."

"I could get a job nearer to my home," said Leon, "but I'd only make $80 a day. The extra $10 is worth fifteen minutes longer on the bus."

"Not for me," said Mildred. "I've got kids to feed when I get home. I don't want them out on the streets longer than they have to be. I'd take a cut if my job was next door to where I lived."

Supplements

Study Guide

A student's Study Guide is available to complement and reinforce the ninth edition of *Supervision: Managing for Results.* The guide allows students to further apply their knowledge while continuing to study the fundamentals of supervision. The study aids include Learning Objectives, Chapter Study Guide Outlines, and Self-Check of Your Progress.

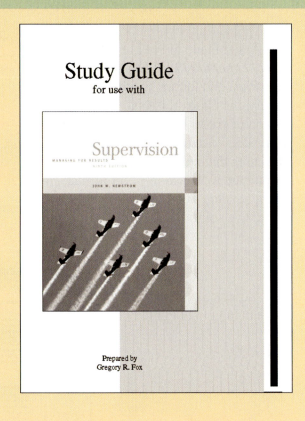

Instructor's Resource CD-ROM

New for this edition of *Supervision: Managing for Results* is the Instructor's Resource CD-ROM (IRCD), which contains all instructor supplements for the text. The IRCD contains an electronic version of the *Instructor's Manual,* which includes lecture notes, keys and commentaries, trigger cases, transparency masters, and lesson plans. Updated PowerPoint presentations are also available on the IRCD, as well as the ExamView Pro Test Generator with True/False, Multiple Choice, and Completion questions.

Hot Seat DVD

Several *Manager's Hot Seat* DVD vignettes appear on the IRCD to reinforce concepts presented throughout the text. In these vignettes, managers are presented with real-life situations, attempt to solve the problem, and reflect on their performance afterward.

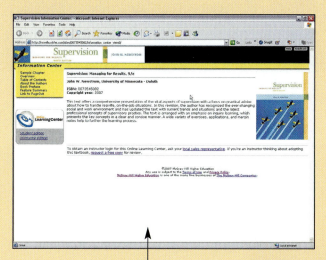

Online Learning Center

Also new for the ninth edition of *Supervision: Managing for Results* is the Online Learning Center (OLC), where both students and instructors can access supplementary materials over the Internet. The OLC contains an online test bank, materials from the IRCD, a comprehensive list of the 500+ questions that form the basis for the book, and PowerPoint presentations.

1

The Supervisor's Role in Management

LEARNING OBJECTIVES

After studying this chapter, you should be able to

- Identify the level of the supervisor's position in a management team.

- Describe the major competencies supervisors are expected to bring to their work.

- Discuss the resources supervisors must manage and the results obtained from them.

- Identify the key behaviors that are likely to positively affect employee attitudes and performance.

- Discuss the need for balancing a concern for output and a concern for the people who perform the work.

Management. The process of obtaining, deploying, and utilizing a variety of essential resources in support of an organization's objectives.

Manager. An individual who plans, organizes, directs, and controls the work of others in an organization.

Management process. Covers five key functions of planning, organizing, staffing, leading, and controlling organizational resources for the attainment of results.

Internet connection

www.amanet.org/index.htm
A Source for Management Development.
Access the American Management Association (AMA) site to see what this nonprofit organization provides in the form of educational forums and resources for managers.

What is management? Why is it important?

Management is the process of obtaining, deploying, and utilizing a variety of essential resources to contribute to an organization's success—both effectively and efficiently. Managers are deemed *effective* if they achieve their goals and *efficient* if they do so with a minimal amount of resources for the amount of outputs produced. One of the most important resources of an organization is its employees. *Managers* devote a large proportion of their efforts to planning, organizing, staffing, leading, and controlling the work of human and other resources. One clear distinction between managers and other employees, however, is that managers direct the work of others rather than perform the work themselves.

Where do supervisors fit in the management process?

They are an essential part of it. Supervisors perform exactly the same functions, to a greater or lesser degree, as all other managers in their organization—up to and including the chief executive. Each specific task, every responsibility, all the various roles that supervisors are called on to perform are carried out by the *management process* (Figure 1-1). This process is repeated over and over, daily, weekly, and yearly, and consists of five broad functions. From a supervisor's standpoint, each function has a particular significance:

Planning. This is the function of setting goals and objectives and converting them into specific plans. For a supervisor, the outcomes of planning include operating schedules, quality specifications, expense budgets, timetables, and deadlines. The planning process also establishes policies, standard operating procedures, regulations, and rules.

Organizing. In performing this function, a supervisor lines up all available resources, including departmental tools, equipment, materials, and—especially—the workforce. It is at this stage that the organizational structure of a department is designed and its work is divided up into jobs.

Staffing. This is the function by which supervisors figuratively put flesh on the organizational structure. Supervisors first figure out exactly how many and what kinds of employees a department will need to carry out its work. They

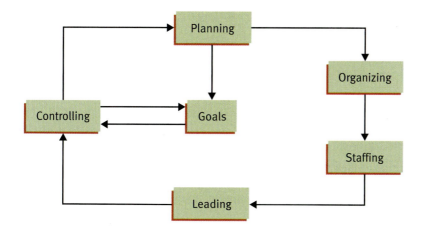

FIGURE 1-1
Functions in the management process.
Which function demands the most of a supervisor's time?

then interview, select, and train those people who appear to be most suitable to fill the open jobs.

Leading. This function gets the blood flowing in an organization. Supervisors energize the vital human resources of their department by providing motivation, communication, and leadership.

Controlling. Once departmental plans are set in motion, supervisors must periodically keep score on how well the plans are working out. To do so, supervisors measure results, compare them with what was expected, judge how important the differences may be, and then take whatever action is needed to bring results into line. Controlling is closely linked to planning (as Figure 1-1 shows), because control actions are guided by the goals established during the planning process.

In theory, supervisors perform the five functions of the management process in the order listed above. In practice, however, supervisors perform all the management functions in one way or another each time action is in order. They may find themselves shortcutting the management process sequence or turning back on it, inasmuch as each problem situation is unique and calls for its own solution.

Why is it called a process?

It is called a *management process* because it moves progressively from one stage to another in a fairly consistent sequence. In a fast-food restaurant, for example, a supervisor first plans the daily schedule, then organizes the tasks and resources, then assigns people to their roles, then directs the process by giving orders and instructions, and, finally, controls, or checks up on, results. In a typical office, a similar management process takes place as supervisors plan the workday, organize the work and the staff, direct others by communicating and motivating, and control by seeing that work procedures are followed properly.

Quips & Quotes

Peter Drucker's comment regarding the planning process: Trying to predict the future is like trying to drive down a country road at night with no lights while looking out the back window.

Management process. The major managerial functions of planning, organizing, staffing, leading, and controlling carried out by all managers in a repetitive sequence or cycle.

This process is carried on repeatedly, day by day, month by month, and year by year. For this reason many people refer to it as the *management cycle*.

Why is so much emphasis placed on the management process?

There are two reasons. First, the process serves to differentiate the work of managers from the work of nonmanagers. Second, the management process provides a valuable underpinning that guides the practice of management and its various approaches.

2 Supervisors Versus Managers

CONCEPT

The role of managers differs from organization to organization, but the supervisory role is clearly defined by federal laws.

Executive. A top-level manager in charge of a group of subordinate managers; this person establishes broad plans, objectives, and strategies.

Middle manager. A person who reports to an executive and who directs supervisory personnel toward the attainment of goals and the implementation of plans of an organization.

Supervisor. A manager who is in charge of, and coordinates the activities of, a group of employees engaged in related activities within a unit of an organization.

Are all managers alike?

No. Managers, and the work they do, differ somewhat by the organization they are in (for example, for-profit versus nonprofit organizations), the size of the firm, their industry, their country's cultural norms, their personal values and experiences, and especially their level in the organization's hierarchy. This latter difference is illustrated in Figure 1-2. At the top of an organization are its executives (often a chief executive officer—the CEO—and some vice-presidents). *Executives* are in charge of, and responsible for, a group of other managers. Executives establish a vision for the organization, define its mission, develop broad strategies, set objectives and plans, and implement broad policy guidelines. Then they motivate, direct, and monitor the work of the managers who report to them.

Middle managers plan, initiate, and implement programs that are intended to carry out the broader objectives set by executives. Middle managers motivate, direct, and oversee the work of the supervisors (and any other managers and employees) who report to them.

Supervisors are managers who normally report to middle managers. Supervisors are responsible for getting the "line" employees to carry out the plans and policies set by executives and middle managers. Supervisors plan, direct, motivate, and monitor the work of ***nonmanagerial***

Nonmanagerial employees.
Often referred to as <u>employees</u> or <u>associates</u>; workers who receive direction from supervisors and then perform specific, designated tasks.

employees at the operational level of the organization. Examples of line employees include production workers, bank tellers, short-order cooks, lab assistants, programmers, nurses, and thousands of other "hands-on" and knowledge (e.g., professional) workers. Some supervisors—about half the total—are called *first-level supervisors*, as they have only non-managerial employees reporting to them. Others are called *second-level supervisors*, because they supervise a combination of other supervisors and nonmanagerial employees.

In many organizations, the relative number of middle managers shrank significantly during the 1990s and the early twenty-first century. This was due mainly to a desire to cut administrative costs through the process of "restructuring," the increasing use of computer-based information systems to fulfill the middle manager's former role, a desire to "flatten" the organizational hierarchy, and the growing capacity and desire of many employees to take on greater responsibilities. As a consequence, supervisors now have greater challenges and expanded roles in planning and controlling their employees' work. In turn, supervisors have become increasingly dependent on the information provided by management information systems.

Legally, what makes a supervisor a supervisor?

The federal laws of the United States provide two definitions of a supervisor.

1. The Taft-Hartley Act of 1947 says that a supervisor is

    . . . any individual having authority, in the interest of the employer, to hire, transfer, suspend, lay off, recall, promote, discharge, assign, reward, or discipline employees, or responsibility to direct them or to adjust their grievances, or effectively to recommend such action, if in connection with the foregoing the exercise of such authority is not merely of a routine or clerical nature, but requires the use of independent judgment.

Assume that you have worked in a three-person office for several years. Recently, the supervisor of the unit retired. The manager came to you and explained that a "budget crunch" prevents the company from replacing the supervisor, but that you have been selected to assume some of the supervisory roles while still performing most of your previous duties. Your job will consist of about 70 percent technical tasks (as before) and about 30 percent supervisory tasks (including overseeing the work of the other two employees). You will receive the title of "Supervisor" and switch to a salaried position, but you will no longer qualify for overtime. According to the FLSA, is there a legal or ethical issue involved here? Explain.

The act specifically prohibits supervisors from joining a union of production and clerical workers, although they may form a union composed exclusively of supervisors.

2. The Fair Labor Standards Act (FLSA) of 1938 (or Minimum Wage Law) as amended set the tone for the above by defining a supervisor as

. . . an executive whose primary duty consists of the management of a customarily recognized department or subdivision; who customarily and regularly directs the work of two or more employees; who has the authority to hire or fire other employees or whose suggestions and recommendations as to the hiring or firing and as to the advancement and promotion or any other change in status will be given particular weight; who customarily and regularly exercises discretionary powers; and who does not devote more than 20 percent of his (or her) hours of work to activities which are not closely related to the (managerial) work described above.

The law also stipulates that supervisors be paid a salary (regardless of how many hours they work). This provision makes some supervisors unhappy, since it exempts them from the provision of the law that calls for overtime pay after a certain number of hours have been worked. Many employers, however, voluntarily recognize the reality of supervisory overtime by providing them with compensatory time off or other benefits.

The key thrust of these two laws was to make supervisors a key part of management.

Are supervisors permitted to do the same work as the people they supervise?

Within the 20 percent stipulation of the Fair Labor Standards Act, there is no law preventing this. Most companies with labor unions, however, have a contract clause that prohibits a supervisor from performing any work that a union member would ordinarily do (except in clearly defined emergencies, in which the supervisor would do as she or he sees fit).

This is a valid and practical point. Few companies want supervisors to do the work their other employees are hired to do. Supervisors are most valuable when they spend 100 percent of their time supervising. It makes little sense for a well-paid supervisor, for instance, to do the work of an employee who is paid at a lower rate.

Do employees ever do the work of supervisors?

Yes! An increasingly common trend, discussed in Chapter 13, is for members of self-managed teams to share many of the responsibilities (and perform many of the roles) that supervisors previously performed. This has resulted in a blurring of the supervisor-employee distinction and vastly increased the need for supervisors to become better coaches to develop these skills in their employees. Some observers even predict that the title *supervisor* will be replaced by *team leader* and other descriptors. Other commentators assert that supervisors play a more important organizational role than ever before. Whichever direction is true, much of the material in this book will be highly relevant to nonmanagerial employees as well as current supervisors.

QUICK TEST 2

| 3 | T or F | Supervisors are commonly considered middle managers but not executives. |
| 4 | T or F | Supervisors are the types of employees most likely to be downsized in a cost-reduction effort (restructuring). |

A Body of Knowledge from Which to Draw

3

CONCEPT

Supervisors become active in the management process by applying established management principles and practices to operating problems.

What does it take for a supervisor to become a manager?

Thinking and acting like one. Management is characterized by a professional—or disciplined—approach to the work environment. Individuals who move into supervision must begin to think in a systematic way. They need to approach their work positively, rather than passively. They should accept the responsibility of making things happen for the better in an organization. They shift their roles from those that entail just following orders, to those that require making task assignments, helping others solve problems, and making decisions. They become increasingly aware of their involvement in a complex system of organizational activities, and they act accordingly.

Where can one learn about management?

Newly appointed supervisors are not left alone without guidance. Fortunately, they have a vast background of management experiences to draw upon (see Job Tip.) First of all, supervisors can begin their new assignments by immersing themselves in the five responsibilities outlined for them in the management process. They can look next for guidance to a set of 10 basic management principles. And they can learn many "tricks of the trade" about effective supervision by interacting with a managerial *mentor*—an experienced person willing to engage in frequent dialogue to provide developmental guidance and support. Over a period of time, supervisors finally acquire a sense of the many factors at play in their spheres of influence. And from this sensitivity, they develop an invaluable flexibility. This enables them to do the right things at the right times for each situation they face.

How do management principles relate to the management process?

Management principles. A set of guidelines established by Henri Fayol and others for carrying out the management process.

They stem from the same source, according to Henri Fayol, an especially effective chief executive of a French mining company. Fayol was the first person to conceive of management as a separate "process of administration," consisting of several distinct functions and based on certain "principles." Fayol's writings (1916) led to the current generally accepted notion of the management process. His ***management principles*** as stated in those writings are acknowledged as widely applicable guidelines for carrying out the management process.

Exactly what are the principles of management?

They consist of a number of practical guidelines that many authorities think contain the "essence of management." Here, arbitrarily numbered, are the principles that appear to have the greatest value for today's supervisors:

Internet connection

www.brunel.ac.uk/~bustcfj/bola/competence/fayol.html
Fayol's Principles. Read more details about Henri Fayol and his principles of management, and compare them to the shorter discussion in the text.

1. Work should be divided so that each person will perform a specialized portion. In making a sailboat, for instance, one person will lay up the hull, another caulk, and another make sails. This ***division of work*** provides clarity in job assignments and helps workers increase their skill levels.

2. Managers must have the right (*authority*) to give orders and instructions, but they must also accept *responsibility* for whether the work is done correctly.

3. Managers are responsible for exacting *discipline* and building morale among members of their workforce, but they must reciprocate by offering something of value. Said another way, if you want loyalty and cooperation from employees, you must be loyal and cooperative in return.

4. An individual should have only one boss. Fayol called this **unity of command**. Experience bears this out: If an employee reports to more than one superior, confusion and conflict are likely to result.

5. Every organization should have only one master plan, one set of overriding goals. Such **unity of direction** is lost if the purchasing department, for example, slows down the production department's output by buying materials from a less costly but undependable supplier when the company's overall commitment is to ship orders on time.

6. Similar to the principle of unity of direction is Fayol's insistence that all individuals, especially managers, place their personal interests second to those of the total organization.

7. Pay and rewards (remuneration) should reflect each person's efforts and, more important, each person's contribution to the organization's goal. Each employee should be paid according to individual worth rather than at the whim of a manager who might be inclined to play favorites.

8. Orders and instructions should flow down a **chain of command** from the higher manager to the lower one. Fayol also said that formal communications and complaints should move upward in the same channel. In practice, however, it has proved to be a good idea to permit and encourage the exchange of work information sideways between departments as well. The real trouble seems to occur when a manager bypasses a supervisor with instructions to an employee or when an employee goes over a supervisor's head to register a complaint. This is known as *blindsiding*.

9. Employees should be treated equally and fairly. Fayol called this equity. It invites dissatisfaction and conflict among employees, for example, when a supervisor gives one employee a break while sticking to the rules for another.

10. Managers should encourage initiative among employees. Other things being equal, a manager who allows some flexibility on the part of subordinates is infinitely superior to one who cannot do so. This classic principle forms the basis for the modern practice of empowerment (to be discussed in Chapter 8).

Division of work. The principle that performance is more efficient when a large job is broken down into smaller, specialized jobs.

Unity of command. The principle that each individual should report to only one boss.

Unity of direction. The principle that there should be a single set of goals and objectives that unifies the activities of everyone in an organization.

Chain of command. The formal channels in an organization that distribute authority from top to bottom.

4 Many Competencies Required

CONCEPT

Supervisors must bring to their managerial work a broad range of technical and interpersonal competencies, along with certain personal characteristics.

How does a person become a supervisor?

Three out of four supervisors are promoted from the ranks of the organization in which they serve. Typically, they have greater experience, have held more different jobs in the organization, and have significantly more education (formal or informal) than do the employees they supervise. Usually, it is apparent that supervisors are chosen from among the best and most experienced employees in the organization. This isn't necessarily a good thing. Demonstrated knowledge and skill in the technology at hand is very helpful to a supervisor, of course. It says nothing, however, about the management skills that are needed, too. Just as many superior athletes fail as coaches while lesser athletes succeed, there is a similar pattern among supervisors who can't handle the interpersonal aspects of the job.

Other than the supervisors who rise from the ranks, about 10 percent enter the position directly from a college or technical institute or are specially prepared by a company-sponsored training program. Another 15 percent are hired into the position from another company or organization.

How long does the transition into supervision usually take?

The fact that someone is named to be a supervisor doesn't mean the complete change takes place overnight. The transition from worker to supervisor often moves through five overlapping stages over several months (or even years):

1. **Taking hold.** This is usually a short phase, where the focus is on learning how to run the department, establishing personal credibility, and beginning to build a power base.
2. **Immersion.** This lasts longer, while a supervisor gets to know the real problems of the department and becomes fully informed about the operations there.
3. **Reshaping.** During this period, a supervisor gradually rebuilds the department to fit his or her style, makes meaningful contributions

to operating procedures, and begins to place an "imprint" on the way of doing things.

4. **Consolidation.** In this phase, the supervisor works to remove deeply rooted problems while perfecting the changes made in previous periods.

5. **Refinement.** This is an opportunity for fine-tuning the operations, consolidating the gains, and seeking new opportunities for making improvements.

Management—at any level—is a challenging, yet rewarding job.
How can you best prepare yourself for a career in supervision?

What personal characteristics does higher management look for in selecting supervisors?

The job of supervision is so demanding that higher management tends to look for *super*people to fill the role. Most firms, however, establish a set of criteria against which supervisory candidates are judged. The most sought-after qualities in a supervisor include the following:

Job-related technical competence:
- Job knowledge
- Grasp of financial information
- Results orientation

Career-related skills:
- Problem solving
- Communication
- Leadership
- Teachability (rapid and willing learner)
- Ability to adapt to change
- Capacity to build a cohesive team
- Demonstrated ability to get along with people
- Capacity to present oneself professionally in public

Personal characteristics:
- Integrity and credibility
- Tenacity, dedication, and perseverance
- Flexibility
- Risk-taking propensity
- Willingness to take initiative
- Tolerance for stress
- Positive attitude
- Dependability and reliability
- Creativity
- Energy and good health

How do supervisory job roles differ from those at other levels of management?

They differ only in degree. Higher-level managers spend more time planning and less time directing, for example. The people who studied this matter came up with several useful conclusions. They first divided all the tasks and responsibilities we have listed so far in this text into three kinds of roles. *Roles* are the parts played by actors on a stage; they are also the real-life parts played by managers and supervisors in an organization. These three roles can be classified as those requiring the following:

- **Technical skills.** Job know-how; knowledge of the industry and its particular processes, equipment, and problems.
- **Administrative skills.** Knowledge of the entire organization and how it is coordinated, knowledge of its information and records system, capacity to interact with key constituents (often called stakeholders), and ability to plan and control work.
- **Interpersonal skills.** Knowledge of human behavior and the ability to work effectively with individuals and groups—peers and superiors as well as subordinates.

The observers then concluded that the role of the supervisor emphasizes technical and interpersonal skills most and administrative skills least. This emphasis tends to reverse itself with higher-level managers, as illustrated in Figure 1-3. Note the importance of interpersonal relations at all levels!

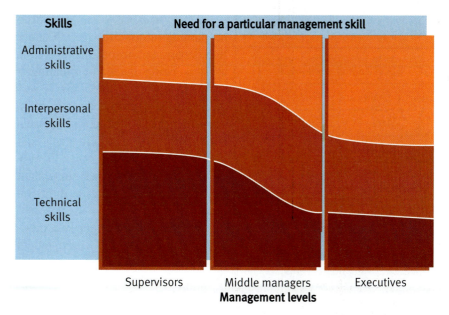

FIGURE 1-3
How the need for managerial skills varies at different levels of management.
Why are interpersonal skills so important to a supervisor?

What main supervisory behaviors are associated with results?

Though they vary somewhat from job to job and firm to firm, there are a number of regularly performed duties of the supervisory job that require attention. The broadest category could simply be called *performance management*. This is an ongoing process of clarifying and communicating performance expectations to employees, and then providing coaching and feedback to reinforce the desired actions. In addition, supervisors need to engage in personal time management, attend meetings and conferences, solve problems, provide training to employees, and handle a wide range of communications.

What two major end results are supervisors seeking?

The purpose of the management process is to convert the resources available to a supervisor's department into a useful end result. Said another way, a supervisor is in charge of seeing that inputs are transformed into outputs in his or her department, as illustrated in Figure 1-4. This end result, or output, is either a product or a service.

A *product* might be a pair of shoes, a loaf of bread, a bicycle, or steel strings for a guitar. Your product may be partially complete, so that it becomes the material resource for the next department in your factory. It may become the raw material for use in another manufacturing plant. Or, it may be ready, like a pair of shoes, to be sold directly to a consumer without further work performed on it.

Quips & Quotes

The most-desired management skill is good communication, followed by a sense of vision, honesty, decisiveness, and ability to build good relationships with employees.

Right Management Consultants

Performance management.
The ongoing process of clarifying and communicating performance expectations to employees, and then providing coaching and feedback to ensure the desired actions.

FIGURE 1-4

Measurement of supervisory performance.
Will more resources (e.g., more people, more money) necessarily assure better results?

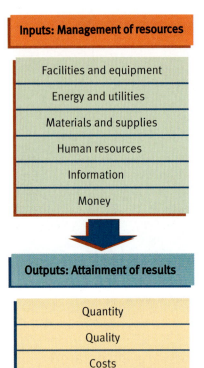

A *service* may be providing accounting information for a production department, inspecting a product as it is being made, or creating a schedule for others to follow. A service may be provided directly for a consumer, as in supplying an insurance policy or handling cash and checks for a bank customer. It may be maintaining machinery in a plant or washing windows in a shopping center.

Whether the endpoint is a product or a service, the management process is designed to make sure that the result is at least as valuable as the combined cost of the initial resources and the expense of operating the process. In a business enterprise a *profit* is made when the result can be sold at a price that is higher than the total cost of providing it. If the reverse is true, the business assumes a *loss*.

How is supervisory performance judged by higher management?

It is judged by two general measures: (1) how well you manage the various *resources* made available to you to accomplish your assignments and (2) how good the *results* are in terms of several criteria (see Figure 1-4).

Management of resources.   Resources are the things that, in effect, set you up in business as a supervisor. They include the following:

- **Facilities and equipment.** Examples are a certain amount of floor space, desks, benches, tools, production machinery, and computer terminals. Your job is to keep these resources operating productively and prevent their misuse.
- **Energy, power, and utilities.** Among these resources are heat, light, air-conditioning, electricity, gas, water, and compressed air. Conservation is the principal measure of effectiveness here.
- **Materials and supplies.** Included are raw materials, parts, and assemblies used to make a product and operating supplies such as lubricants, stationery, computer disks, paper clips, and masking tape. Getting the most from all your materials and holding waste to the minimum are the prime measures here.

- **Human resources.** This refers to the workforce in general and to your employees in particular. Your biggest job is to see that these people are present, trained, productively engaged, and challenged at all times.
- **Information.** Examples are the information made available by staff departments and found in operating manuals, in specifications sheets, and on computer screens. Your success often depends on how well you can utilize the data and know-how made available to you through these sources.
- **Money.** All these resources can be measured by how much they cost, although the actual cash will rarely flow through your hands. Nevertheless, supervisors are expected to be prudent in decisions that affect expenditures and often have to justify those decisions in terms of savings or other benefits.

Attainment of results. It follows that if you manage each of your resources well, you should get the desired results. Whatever your particular area of responsibility and whatever your organization, you can be sure that you will be judged in the long run by how well you meet these four objectives:

- **Quantity.** Specifically, your department will be expected to turn out a certain amount of work per day, per week, and per month. It will be expected that this will be done on time, to specifications, and within budget.
- **Quality and workmanship.** Output volume alone is not enough. You will also be judged by the quality of the work your employees perform, whether it is measured in terms of the number of product defects, service errors, or customer complaints.
- **Costs and budget control.** Your output and quality efforts will always be restricted by the amount of money you can spend to carry them out. Universally, supervisors are asked to search for ways to lower costs even further.
- **Management of human resources.** You will face many potential problems in the areas of employee turnover, theft, tardiness, absenteeism, discipline, and morale. Managing these dimensions of employee satisfaction and behavior will be a key element of your overall success.

| 7 | T or F | Most supervisors have risen to their positions from within the organization. |
| 8 | T or F | The most important skill set for supervisors lies in the administrative domain. |

QUICK TEST 4

5 A Concern for Both Work and People

Employee-centered supervision.
A method of supervision that places an emphasis on a genuine concern and respect for employees, and on the maintenance of effective relationships within a work group.

Task-centered supervision.
A method of supervision that places an emphasis on the job or task that employees are expected to perform to produce results.

Supervisory balance: What does it mean?

Simply this: Pay as much attention to interpersonal factors as to technical and administrative matters combined.

In other words, be as **employee centered** as you are **job** or **task centered** in your interests. Or, said still another way, spend as much time maintaining individual satisfaction, group cohesiveness, direction, and morale as you do pushing for productivity or task accomplishment.

It would be misleading to conclude that being nice is the answer to employee productivity. It isn't. As in sports, nice players often finish last. The important conclusion from research is that supervisors who focus on job demands to the exclusion of their interest in the welfare and the development of their people don't get the long-term results they are looking for. Conversely, supervisors who bend over backward to make work easy for their employees don't get good results either. It takes a balance between the two approaches, as shown in Figure 1-5.

What's a normal day in the life of a supervisor?

Many supervisors say that there is no such thing as a normal day. One thing is certain, however: A supervisor's day is full of interruptions. Estimates are that a typical supervisor handles from 50 to 80 problems a day. Thankfully, many of these problems are simple or short-lived. Nevertheless, solving problems quickly and systematically is the name of the game. Accordingly, anything supervisors can do to put order and system into their days is strongly encouraged.

FIGURE 1-5
Supervisors must balance their task-centered concerns with their employee-centered concerns.
How do those concerns differ?

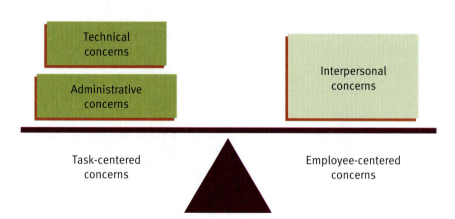

What kinds of pressures do new supervisors face?

Both internal and external forces bear on supervisors. Internally, a person who is promoted to a supervisory position makes a major transition from one mode of thinking to another. As an employee, an individual's concerns are with self-satisfaction in terms of pay, job satisfaction, and work-life balance. As a manager, the same person is expected to place the organization's goals above all other job-related concerns. This means that a supervisor worries first about meeting quotas, quality, and cost standards; second about the employees who do the work; and last about herself or himself. The difference in priorities is enormous, and requires a substantial realignment of thinking.

In addition to role differences, a new supervisor faces conflicting external pressures initiated by two groups. Higher managers have their expectations, and lower employees have their needs and demands. The supervisor takes pressure from both sides, much as a keystone in an organizational arch does (Figure 1-6). Without the keystone, however, the arch would collapse, and so the supervisor's role is highly crucial. The pressures felt can be handled best when a supervisor:

The supervisor's workday can be hectic. **How important is multitasking for supervisory success?**

- Admits the need for help, and seeks it from peers, boss, and employees.
- Provides a strong role model for employees by demonstrating good work habits.
- Anticipates both changes and crises, and prepares for them.
- Listens a lot and minimizes arguments with others.
- Learns to handle the inevitable stress from the job.

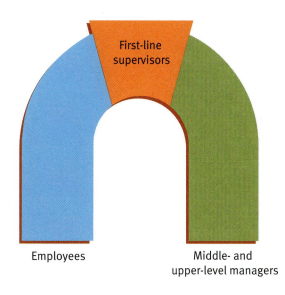

First-line supervisors

Employees

Middle- and upper-level managers

FIGURE 1-6

Supervisors as the keystone in the organizational arch. **What kinds of pressure will each group exert on the supervisor?**

| 9 | T or F | Supervisors should focus on their employees more than on the tasks to be accomplished. |
| 10 | T or F | Most days in the life of a supervisor are highly predictable and relatively interruption-free. |

Practical Guidelines for Supervisors

1. *Study the job of managing* and keep learning.

2. *Maintain a focus on your key tasks* (planning, organizing, staffing, leading, and controlling) despite the presence of daily crises.

3. *Recognize that your job*, although somewhat different in emphasis, *must mesh with the priorities, demands, and goals of higher management.*

4. *Find ways to involve employees* in key tasks and use their inputs.

5. *Follow the chain of command* whenever possible.

6. *Treat employees fairly.*

7. *Be patient* with your own developmental progress, remembering the stages of transition you probably will go through.

8. *Display integrity, consideration, energy, patience, and flexibility.*

9. *Find creative ways to achieve the multiple results you are accountable for with the inputs you are provided.*

10. *Strive for balance*—between being employee-centered and task-centered, between the pressures from employees and those from higher management, and between your work and your personal life.

Chapter 1 Review

Key Concepts to Remember

1. Members of a Unique Team. Supervisors occupy the vital first level of management that interacts directly with the workforce. Managerial work is different from nonmanagerial work in that managers, including supervisors, devote most of their time and energy to planning, organizing, staffing, leading, and controlling.

2. Supervisors Versus Managers. Supervisors are on the first rung on the managerial ladder. They usually direct multiple employees, can hire and fire, do not qualify for overtime pay, and have discretionary use of resources. Increasingly, they share some responsibilities with employees.

3. A Body of Knowledge from Which to Draw. Supervisors are expected to act professionally, think positively, and be rational as they solve problems. They draw from a vast body of accumulated knowledge about the management process and principles (such as division of work, unity of command, subordination of their interests to those of the organization, chain of command, and equity). These principles are general in nature and are subject to interpretation and judgment in their application.

4. Many Competencies Required. Supervisors often rise from employee ranks, and then go through a five-stage transitional process. To be able to learn and perform well in their roles, supervisors must bring to the position a wide range of skills, personal qualities, and technical competencies. The characteristics most often expected of supervisors include integrity, perseverance, stress tolerance, energy, and a positive attitude. They improve their effectiveness by developing their technical (know-how) skills, administrative (planning, implementing, innovating) skills, and interpersonal (communication, motivational, counseling) skills. Supervisors draw upon a variety of inputs to produce results that are measured in terms of quantity, quality, costs, and effective use of human resources.

5. A Concern for Both Work and People. In carrying out their responsibilities, supervisors must be careful not to be overzealous by either (a) pushing employees too hard for production or better service or (b) being overly protective of their employees. Supervisors face a variety of pressures and stresses in the workday, and must also learn to juggle competing demands from management and employees.

Reading Comprehension

1. There is one clear distinction between managers and their employees. What is it?

2. How many levels of management are there in a typical organization? At which level are supervisors found?

3. What characteristics of a supervisory management job are stressed by the two laws that define this position?

4. What is the purpose, or objective, of the management process?

5. Give a specific example of an activity that might be included in each of the five functions of the management process.

6. Why did Henri Fayol advise that an organization should have unity of direction?

7. Energy, good health, and self-control are among the characteristics looked for in a supervisor. Why are these qualities important?

8. Which two broad categories of performance are typically used to judge the effectiveness of supervisors at their work?

9. How is supervisory management similar to higher-level management? How is it different?

10. Why are supervisors advised to achieve "balance" in the application of their skills?

Application

Self-Assessment

How Good Are Your Supervisory Skills?

Read the following statements carefully. Circle the number on the response scale that most closely reflects the degree to which each statement describes you. Add up your total points and prepare a brief action plan for self-improvement. Be ready to report your score for tabulation across the entire group.

	Good Description	Poor Description
1. I am good at setting goals and working to achieve them on time.	10 9 8 7 6 5	4 3 2 1
2. I can define a problem and work it through to completion.	10 9 8 7 6 5	4 3 2 1
3. I enjoy assigning tasks to others and holding them responsible for results.	10 9 8 7 6 5	4 3 2 1
4. I am an attentive listener; I don't interrupt others.	10 9 8 7 6 5	4 3 2 1
5. I am able to stimulate others toward task achievements without offending them.	10 9 8 7 6 5	4 3 2 1
6. I am willing to criticize the work of others when their work is not acceptable.	10 9 8 7 6 5	4 3 2 1
7. I have consciously chosen a style of leadership that I will use.	10 9 8 7 6 5	4 3 2 1
8. I enjoy training people how to do things and coaching them to success.	10 9 8 7 6 5	4 3 2 1
9. I am good at explaining things to others in a clear fashion.	10 9 8 7 6 5	4 3 2 1
10. Once a goal is set, I strive hard to meet it on schedule.	10 9 8 7 6 5	4 3 2 1

Scoring and Interpretation

Scoring

Add up your total points for the 10 questions. Record that number here, and report it when it is requested. _____

Also, insert your score on the Personal Development Plan in the Appendix.

Interpretation

81 to 100 points. You seem to have a basic set of skills that are appropriate for supervisory positions.

61 to 80 points. Take a close look at some of your skills and discuss them with current supervisors and managers to see if they need improvement.

Below 60 points. Some of your supervisory skills may be substantially inconsistent with current organizational practices and could be detrimental to a career in supervision.

Identify your three lowest scores and record the question numbers here: _____, _____, _____.

Action

Write a brief paragraph detailing an action plan for how you might sharpen each of these skills. Then pay particularly close attention to the chapters that follow that provide key information about those topics.

Skill Development

Improving Your Capabilities

Assume that you want to become one of the best supervisors you know—one who is truly outstanding. According to an earlier discussion in this chapter, this might require strong capabilities in several of the following qualities. Identify three key people whose opinions you value and who have had an opportunity to observe you closely (e.g., your supervisor, your spouse, a co-worker). Ask each of them for specific suggestions for how you could improve in some of these areas:

1. Physical health _____
2. Personal energy _____
3. Ability to get along with people _____
4. Technical competence _____
5. Self-control under pressure _____
6. Dependability _____
7. Teachability _____
8. Communications _____
9. Problem solving _____
10. Leadership _____

Action

Commit yourself to a 1-month, 3-month, and 12-month plan of improvement by following these suggestions. At the end of each time period, return to the three people and ask them if they've seen any change in you on any of the 10 criteria.

Group Exercise

Reaching a Consensus

Step 1: Form small groups of about five persons each. Jointly consider Fayol's 10 principles of management as presented in the text.

Step 2: Arrive at a group consensus on which one of Fayol's principles you would rank as the highest (and the lowest) priority.

Step 3: On the list below, rank the 10 principles from 1 (highest priority) to 10 (lowest priority). Use each number from 1 to 10 only once.

Step 4: Present your results to the class, and discuss the reasons for any substantial differences among groups.

Principle (or Concept)	Group Rank
Specialization of jobs	_____
Authority of managers	_____
Need for discipline	_____
Unity of command	_____
Unity of direction	_____
Subordination of personal interest to that of the organization	_____
Pay according to individual worth	_____
Chain of command	_____
Equitable treatment of employees	_____
Encouragement of initiative	_____

Cases for Analysis

Case 1

The Brand-New Supervisor

Sheryl had just the kind of personality you'd like in a supervisor. She was focused, energetic, and friendly. She was brand new on the job, however. She had just received an associate degree in business from a nearby community college, where she had worked her way through as a teller at a local branch bank. Based on her good work there and her grades in college, the bank selected her to replace the retiring day supervisor of its eight-person data processing department.

From the start on her new job, things did not go quite right for Sheryl. For instance, almost immediately Sheryl spotted several inequities in the existing distribution of assignments. Accordingly, she prepared a more efficient—and more equitable—assignment schedule. She was disappointed, however, that her employees did not recognize how fair the new assignments were. Instead, they found all sorts of ways to make the schedule inoperable. Similarly, when Sheryl tried to show the operators some of the new techniques she had learned in college, they watched politely but continued to function as before. Then, after a few weeks, Sheryl discovered that the employees had arranged their own system of coffee and lunch breaks, without regard to the rules set forth in the bank's human resource manual. When Sheryl insisted that the employees conform to the rules in the manual, there was almost a rebellion.

Try as she might, things did not improve for Sheryl. The cruelest blow, however, fell at the end of Sheryl's first month on the job, when the bank manager called her into the office to review her progress. The manager said, "What's going on out there? I'm hearing all sorts of vague complaints from your employees. Furthermore, our records show that the output and quality from your department have fallen off sharply since you took over. What do you intend to do about it?"

Analysis

If you were Sheryl, which of the following actions would you consider most effective for you to take? Rank the alternatives on a scale of 1 (most preferable) to 5 (least preferable). You may add another alternative if you wish. Be prepared to justify your ranking.

_____ **a.** Ask for the bank manager's help and support in enforcing rules and changing the assignments in your department.

_____ **b.** Rethink your approach by placing an emphasis on establishing cooperative relations equal to what you now place on technical and administrative matters.

_____ **c.** Back off on the changes you have tried to initiate, and learn to "go with the flow."

_____ **d.** Make a concerted effort to build a better relationship with your staff, based on a mutual understanding of the department's goals.

_____ **e.** Crack down now on enforcing rules and assignments before you completely lose control.

Case 2

The Rejected Refrigerators

"You've got to get your department in order!" That's the word Dave received from his boss yesterday. Dave supervises a spot-welding department in an appliance manufacturing plant. His boss's complaint was twofold: Not only was Dave's department producing too many refrigerator bodies that were later rejected at inspection, but the cost of raw materials consumed by the department was also far more than expected. Dave couldn't understand the connection. He did know, however, that to speed up their production rates, his welders did damage a lot of raw materials. He also knew that often in their haste, the welders jammed the spot-welding equipment.

Analysis

a. How might there be a connection between the rejects and over-consumption of raw materials and jamming of the welding equipment?

b. What should Dave do to "straighten out his department"?

Case 3

Which Comes First—Departmental Performance or Employee Development?

Fred supervises the accounts receivable section in the accounting division of a public utility in the Northeast. He is a stickler for performance, and places a major emphasis on his staff's ability to meet monthly output quotas. Accordingly, he was disturbed when one of his more effective employees asked whether Fred could arrange her assignments so that she could learn something about billing operations in the division. "What do you want to do that for?" he asked. "I want to improve my chances for advancement," the employee said. "I'll have to think about it," said Fred. "I don't want to do anything that interferes with your meeting your production quotas."

Analysis

a. What do you think of the employee's request? Will it interfere with her output or productivity?

b. What answer do you think Fred should give?

Case 4

Too Much to Keep Up With

Tami, supervisor of the word processing section of a federal agency, was having one of those days. She had been pressing her staff of keyboard specialists to complete a major report in time for distribution to the press by the next morning. She was interrupted, however, by a call from the human resources department. "Would you come up here, please," said the personnel officer. When Tami arrived, she was irritated to find that one of her employees had registered a grievance related to Tami's continuing pressure for performance.

"Your handling of people leaves much to be desired," said the personnel officer.

"What am I supposed to do," responded Tami, "hold every employee by the hand all day? We've got work to do out there, and I expect each person to pitch in."

"Few people will complain about that," said the personnel officer, "It's the way you go about it that causes the trouble. You're getting a reputation for being too heavy-handed."

"I've got all I can do to keep up with the details of this job," said Tami. "Every day, I'm handling problems involving letter, memo, and report writing; telephone techniques; resource and reference materials; calculating, transcribing, and copying machines; and now this new baby—electronic filing. I was put into this job because of my know-how, wasn't I? Without it, the department would be in a hopeless mess. I can't help it if one or two employees are unhappy."

"It's more than one or two employees who are unhappy," said the personnel officer, "and it's up to you now to do something about it."

_____

Analysis

a. What do you think of Tami's view of her responsibilities as a supervisor?

b. What are her strengths and weaknesses as a supervisor?

c. What might Tami do to improve her overall effectiveness?

Quick Test 1	Quick Test 2	Quick Test 3	Quick Test 4	Quick Test 5	ANSWERS TO QUICK TESTS
1. T	3. F	5. F	7. T	9. F	
2. F	4. F	6. F	8. F	10. F	

2

Creating a Positive Workplace Within a Dynamic Environment

After studying this chapter, you should be able to

- Distinguish between a supervisor's work environment and that of higher-level managers.

- Identify the four characterizing features of work.

- Discuss the general expectations employees have for their jobs.

- Explain how and why different people have different perceptions of the nature of their work.

- List a number of ways in which supervisors can improve the quality of work life for their employees and allow them to have fun at work.

Ten Pressures to Cope With

CONCEPT

The unique environment in which supervisors work shapes their horizons, tends to restrict their options, yet provides opportunities for flexible and creative responses.

In what ways do the supervisors' worlds differ from that of their superiors?

Higher-level managers tend to be outward-oriented and focus on macro and longer-range issues. They are likely to be more influenced by forces and events outside the company or institution than by those within. Supervisors, in contrast, are more inside-oriented. They are more concerned with micro and short-range issues.

A company president or agency executive has concerns for things such as how to increase shareholder value, what the competition is doing, whether the company's creditors can pay their bills, how dependable suppliers are likely to be, sources of funding, and how to keep stockholders and the public satisfied. Higher-level executives are also concerned with general economic conditions, proposed government regulations, and public opinion.

Supervisors are concerned with, and restrained by, a number of more immediate factors. As shown in Figure 2-1, a supervisor's environment is characterized by 10 important factors. They include the following:

1. Technology, existing and changing, such as processes and equipment, emerging knowledge, and the way things are done in a particular company, department, or organization.
2. Legal restrictions, such as those affecting employee safety, health, rights to equal opportunity, fair pay, privacy, freedom from harassment and discrimination, accommodation of diverse backgrounds and values, and representation by a union.
3. Organizational policies and procedures, to which supervisors, as well as their employees, must conform.

FIGURE 2-1

Important factors in a supervisor's environment. **Which of these are most important?**

4. Pressures from above to meet the organization's goals for quantity, quality, and cost control.
5. Competition with other supervisors for scarce resources, such as employees, equipment, space, skills, and budgets.
6. A wide array of information that must be generated, processed, maintained, and utilized.
7. Rising expectations of employees for considerate treatment, meaningful work, work-life balance, and an opportunity to participate in decisions that affect them.
8. Globalization of business, requiring that a supervisor's operations be competitive with those that are thousands of miles—and maybe even an ocean—away.
9. Changes in the composition of the workforce, including more women and immigrants, an increasing number of older workers, the use of more part-time and temporary employees, and a shortage of applicants with the necessary technical skills.
10. Economic uncertainty that requires organizations to expand or contract their operations, or change structure quickly and efficiently.

Many of these circumstances are virtually uncontrollable, and they will become more powerful as time goes along. In addition, there is a greater emphasis on the *quality of work life* for employees—making work challenging and psychologically rewarding—and the need to help employees reach a better balance between work expectations and the pressures of a fulfilling home life.

Quality of work life. The idea that work can—in addition to being productive in a material way—be rewarding in a psychological way to the person who performs it.

How do time horizons differ?

Higher-level executives are, rightfully, more concerned with the long-term future than are supervisors. Executives, and most middle managers, are paid to plan for and create results that will happen next month or next year. Supervisors, who are on the firing line, have a shorter time horizon. A delay of 15 minutes in the arrival of operating supplies can loom large in importance when 15 employees are idled by it. Consequently, supervisors keep their eyes on hour-by-hour and day-to-day problems. For most supervisors, a "month from now" is a long look ahead.

JOB TIP!

Just as is the case for new U.S. presidents, the first 100 days on the job are key for supervisors. Here's some good advice for getting off on the right foot and avoiding crippling mistakes: Don't dis the actions of your predecessor; don't assume that you will be welcomed as a "savior"; think before responding to questions; keep your goals simple and understandable; spell out your expectations; listen to the employees; and give them prompt feedback on the ideas they propose.

When it comes to job responsibilities, what is expected of supervisors?

Supervisors' responsibilities encompass four—occasionally five—broad areas within an organization:

- **Responsibility to management.** Supervisors must, above all, dedicate themselves to the goals, plans, and policies of the organization. These goals are typically provided by higher management. It is the primary task of supervisors to serve as a "linking pin" for management to make sure that the goals are carried out by the employees they supervise.
- **Responsibility to employees.** Employees expect their supervisors to provide direction and training; protect them from unfair treatment such as sexual harassment; respect their privacy; and see that the workplace is clean, safe, uncluttered, properly equipped, well lit, and adequately ventilated. They also expect to be treated as intelligent and mature adults.
- **Responsibility to staff specialists.** The relationship between supervision and staff departments is one of mutual support. Staff people are charged with providing supervisors with guidance and help as well as with prescribing procedures to be followed and forms to be completed. Supervisors, in turn, aid the work of the staff departments by making good use of their advice and service and by conforming to their requests.
- **Responsibility to other supervisors.** Teamwork is essential in the supervisory ranks. There is a great deal of departmental interdependence. The goals and activities of one department must harmonize with those of others. This often requires the sacrifice of an immediate target for the greater good of the organization.
- **Relationships with the union.** Labor union and management views are sometimes in conflict, and the supervisor and union steward often see things differently. It is the supervisor's responsibility, however, to keep these relationships objective, represent the organization's interests, and not yield responsibility for the welfare of the organization and its employees.

QUICK TEST 1	1	T or F	Most supervisors need not be concerned with environmental issues such as technology, scarce resources, and legal restrictions.
	2	T or F	Supervisors may be called upon to sacrifice their own immediate targets for the greater good of the organization.

The World of Work

What is meant by *work*?

Webster's dictionary identifies several relevant aspects in these five definitions of *work*:

- Activity in which one exerts strength or faculties to do or perform.
- Sustained physical or mental effort valued to the extent that it overcomes obstacles and achieves an objective or result.
- Labor, task, or duty that affords one the accustomed means of livelihood.
- Strenuous activity marked by the presence of difficulty and exertion and the absence of pleasure.
- Specific task, duty, function, or assignment, often a part or phase of some larger activity.

Note the key words: physical, mental, effort, exertion, obstacles, difficulty, result, and means of livelihood. Note, too, the implication of work as a part of a larger activity and its age-old association with the absence of pleasure! An emerging definition of *work*, then, is an activity involving physical or mental effort to perform tasks and overcome difficulties to attain valued organizational results and a means of personal livelihood. Twenty-first-century supervisors need to try to combine work with pleasure for their employees, as measured by the degree of personal satisfaction they derive from their jobs or work environment.

Why do most people work?

For two relatively universal reasons: first, for the money it brings and for the necessities and pleasures that money will buy; second, for the satisfaction work can bring—from being with other people or from a sense of personal accomplishment.

Which reward is more important to most workers, money or job satisfaction?

That depends. Most of us want both, of course. But until each of us has a paycheck that is big enough for our own highly personal situation, job satisfaction may take a backseat. However, the need for money almost never disappears—especially for the millions of workers who are below the poverty level of income.

CONCEPT
The traditional world of work is characterized by various degrees of employee conformity, the exercise of authority by managers, the blending of personal interests with organizational goals, and the need for record keeping.

Work. An activity involving physical or mental effort to perform tasks and overcome difficulties to attain valued organizational results and a means of personal livelihood.

Did You Know

Workplace bullies, though hopefully rare in this enlightened age, exist in some organizations. They utter deliberate insults, make unreasonable job demands, falsely blame others for their own mistakes, are inconsistent in their application of rules, verbally harass individuals (most often women), and steal credit from deserving persons. The consequences include employee anxiety and stress, coupled with productivity declines and increased turnover. Workplace bullying is an archaic and unacceptable behavior!

In what ways does an organization affect the things people do?

Especially within organizations, four factors make work unique:

1. Rules, regulations, and procedures sometimes demand a degree of conformity in each employee's actions and thus limit free choice. Many independent people find it hard to channel their efforts into paths that are set by others. Modern supervision tries to keep rules to a minimum and stress the opportunity for self-control, especially when employees have previously demonstrated their capacity to act responsibly.

2. A chain of authority makes each person receive direction from and report to a boss, the boss in turn reports to another boss, and so on. In practice, this means that most companies are run by relatively few top-level managers. In organizations with many layers in the hierarchy, lower-level managers and employees at the bottom of the organizational pyramid often feel that they have little say in what happens. Employees may not have been asked to make constructive suggestions about how to run the business. Supervisors who invite help from employees tend to make the work more appealing to them.

3. Those who hold managerial responsibility are expected to place their personal interests behind those of the organization. It is no secret that some managers do not do so. Instead, they take care of themselves first and the company's resources, especially employees, later. Employees who work for this kind of manager may have very little job satisfaction and may expend their effort in complaints.

4. Much of what happens or is expected to happen is put into written records. Outside of work, most of our activities are loosely defined and rarely put into writing. Written documents—those that record the past and those that set goals for the future—are threatening to many people. They fear that no mistake will be forgotten and that every promise will be remembered. Because of so much formal communication, employees often feel more comfortable with supervisors who engage in easy, give-and-take conversation.

Bureaucracy. An organized system of work characterized by policies and rules, a chain of command, an emphasis on organizational goals, and many written records.

These four factors were first identified in the 1890s by the German sociologist Max Weber, who prescribed them for an "organized system of work directed by hired managers." He called this system *bureaucracy*.

QUICK TEST 2			
3	T or F	Most employees work for one thing and one thing alone—the money it provides them.
4	T or F	Most organizations no longer have policies, rules, or a chain of command.

Employee Expectations

How many people are truly happy with their work?

According to a number of authoritative studies, about 50 percent of all employees are reasonably satisfied with their jobs.[1] This doesn't necessarily mean that they are ecstatic about them; it just means that on balance the positives outweigh the negatives. These figures also show that African Americans and those in other cultural groups are not as satisfied as are whites and that females are less satisfied than males. Furthermore, factory workers tend to be less satisfied than white-collar workers. One of the clearest conclusions is that job satisfaction tends to improve with age. Younger people are by far the most dissatisfied with their work. Why is this? Perhaps because their expectations are much higher regarding the rewards of working. They have been raised in an era of abundance.

Despite some recent declines, the general level of job satisfaction is still high enough to give supervisors an even chance in attempting to move employees toward organizational and departmental goals.

What do today's workers expect from their jobs that is often lacking?

Something that challenges their skills and offers fair pay in return for extra effort. According to Daniel Yankelovich, a noted surveyor of public opinion and director of the nonprofit Public Agenda Foundation, most people can choose either to work hard or to just get by. Only one person in five, reports Yankelovich, says he or she does his or her very best. For one thing, workers assume that an increase in output may not benefit them, but only the consumers, stockholders, or management. Down deep, however, most employees will work harder and better, says Yankelovich and other observers, if the work they do makes sense to them and is truly appreciated by their bosses. In fact, 8 of 10 Americans say their jobs are too easy. They'd prefer a challenging job to an easy one where they merely "put in their time."

Supervisors can minimize both kinds of employee complaints. First, they can make sure that employees have enough to do, especially of the kind of work that capitalizes on their talents and skills. Second, supervisors can live up to their promises about promotions or relief from boring assignments for those who do commit all their energies to do a good job.

CONCEPT

Despite the constraints of a bureaucracy, the great majority of employees are reasonably satisfied with their work.

Thoughts*to*ponder

Easy Ways to Create Dissatisfaction

Adele Lynn suggests that there many ways for supervisors to destroy the spirits of employees at work. Worst of all, some supervisors aren't even aware that they are doing so. Topping her list of inappropriate actions are insincere gratitude, incongruence between promises and action, bullying of workers, and what she calls "celebrity egos." Other contributors to employee dissatisfaction are failing to follow through on promises, inequitable treatment across employees, and always finding someone else to blame for mistakes. Why would *any* reasonable supervisor act in these ways?

Source: Adele Lynn, *In Search of Humor: Lessons from Workers on How to Build Trust.* Belle Vernon, PA: BajonHouse Publishing, 1998.

Employees, workers, colleagues, cast members, crew members, team members, partners, associates? What should supervisors call subordinates, and why does it matter?

That depends. The dictionary term for an employed person, at any level, is *employee*. It has also been a common practice to think of employees at lower levels of an organization as *workers*. These two terms (employee and worker) have traditionally been used to differentiate lower-level, nonexempt employees from managerial (or exempt) employees. In recent years, however, a trend has emerged for designating employees—at whatever level—as *colleagues* or *team members* or *associates*. This reflects a recognition of the wisdom in considering the status of non-management employees as *collegial* (to be in partnership) with management. Wal-Mart stores, in particular, have popularized the use of the term *associates*. Not every organization, of course, uses this terminology. Progressive employers do, however, recognize that each employee—regardless of rank or designation—(1) shares a responsibility for helping an organization attain its goals, and furthermore, (2) has the potential to contribute not only the prescribed physical and mental effort but also ideas of value. Consequently, the term used should be selected with care, used consistently, and backed up by daily actions consistent with it. In short, it has to be more than a slogan.

QUICK TEST 3	5	T or F	The general level of job satisfaction is not extremely high among the workforce today.
	6	T or F	The vast majority of employees report that they do their very best on their jobs.

4 Understanding Employee Perceptions

CONCEPT

Individuals have differing perceptions of their work and differ in their responses to it.

What are the chances of developing a highly enthusiastic workforce?

Very slim. This is because of two important factors—individual differences and the role of perceptions. Extensive research on employee characteristics shows that they vary substantially—despite obvious similarities—in many ways. People differ in physical dimensions and appearance as well as in emotional and intellectual capacities, and this produces predictable differences in their desires for jobs and rewards. Each employee further develops a unique set of perceptions about the work itself (and his or her supervisor), affected by past experiences, mental models, and even trivial events. Therefore, it is likely that there will always be some dissatisfied employees (perhaps 1 or 2 out of 10), an equal proportion who are readily satisfied, and a broad group in between.

What are some key examples of employee perceptions at work?

Taken as a whole, today's employees are better educated than any workforce in history, and this leads to higher expectations. Applicants and subordinates are fully aware of their civil—and employment—rights. This leads to a widespread feeling that "I'm entitled." In fact, public law has legalized a great many *entitlements*, such as those related to equal employment opportunity, representation by a labor union, workplace adjustment for disabilities, family leave, due process, and privacy. One entitlement often leads to a demand for another, and seeing someone else receive an entitlement leads to a request for one's own ("Me, too!").

Entitlement. The perception by employees that they ought to receive certain benefits, protections, and privileges from their employer.

At the extreme, a mentality of entitlement leads some people to believe that society owes them a living, and a pleasant one at that. And any employee can become discouraged by the *downsizing* of organizations or the closing of plants that were once thought to guarantee secure employment for a lifetime. As a consequence, many employees have lost faith that hard work, dedication, and perseverance will assure job success or even job security. Towers Perrin, a respected consulting company, reports that less than half of all employees believe that they'll retire from their current employer. One explanation for this, however, is the diminishing level of *employee loyalty* (strong employee commitment to the employer), replaced by an increasing level of employee self-interest. Both employers and employees are asking, "What have you done for me lately?" and if the answer is shaky, either side is more willing than ever to cut the proverbial umbilical cord.

Downsizing. A reduction in the number of people employed by an organization, usually in order to respond to unfavorable economic conditions or in an attempt to improve efficiency.

It's no wonder, then, that so many employees place the burden of their need for job satisfaction on the supervisor. In turn, the supervisor needs all the skills and patience he or she can muster to motivate today's workers to perform at the levels that society—to say nothing of their employers—expects of them.

What causes employees to perceive similar kinds of work in such different lights?

The way people perceive things, including their jobs or the work they are asked to do, is influenced by five factors:

1. **Past experience with similar work.** If the work has been unpleasant with another company or a different supervisor, an employee

Your company is trying to improve the quality of work life for its employees, and it has begun offering new initiatives to do so. Specifically, the company is promoting the use of flexible work schedules and telecommuting. However, when you attended the companywide question-and-answer session today, you learned that (a) not all employees would be allowed to "flex" their schedules, and (b) telecommuting would be mandatory for some employees, optional for some, and unavailable for the remainder. The company also heavily promoted the organizational merits of such programs, while not mentioning the impact on employees at all. After some thought, you have concluded that the new policies on "flexibility" are unfair and unethical. Identify the ethical issues you would like to raise with your manager.

Flexible work schedule. A system by which employees can choose—and periodically change—the blocks of time in which they work.

Job sharing. The process of taking one job and splitting its duties into two so that the combined time and efforts of two persons will satisfy all the work demands.

may anticipate that the experience will repeat itself everywhere. The opposite will be true for a person whose experience with this work has been favorable.

2. **Assumptions about the motivation of others.** An unhappy person may blame her or his problems on the actions of aggressive co-workers or an unfair supervisor. For some unfortunate people, this becomes a guideline in dealing with *all* interpersonal relations. In contrast, a person who views others as supportive and friendly may perceive every work situation in that light.

3. **Expectations about what will happen.** "It's a foregone conclusion," we hear people say. This is based somewhat upon past experience and somewhat upon our beliefs about the motivation of others. Unfortunately, it reflects a rigidity of mind and the unwillingness of some employees to give a new job or a different assignment a fair try.

4. **The reliability of information.** Some employees make judgments about their work on the basis of what others tell them. This knowledge may be correct, or it may be unreliable hearsay or bitter prejudice. Supervisors can deal with this problem by providing accurate information upon which employees can then make valid decisions.

5. **The present state of mind.** All of us are subject to mood swings. If the supervisor proposes a new task, for instance, on a day when an employee feels good, the reaction is likely to be more positive than it would be if the idea were proposed on one of those inevitable "bad days."

Are there any programs or systems that can improve employees' perceptions of their work environment?

Yes. **Flexible work schedules** (sometimes called *compressed work-weeks*) can do this. As pressures rise for better use of the organization's facilities (space in particular), as workers wish to explore new lifestyles and pursue recreational interests, as the numbers of single-parent and dual-career households increase, and the cost and time associated with commuting rise, flexible work schedules can help. Many forms of these compressed schedules exist, with the more common ones being four 10-hour days or even the use of 12-hour shifts (three days one week and four days the next). Under *flextime* systems, employees have the chance to tailor their work schedules to their personal needs and reduce the number of commutes per week; employers benefit from fewer daily start-up and shut-down cycles and the broader band of hours available for customer service. Another flexible approach is **job sharing**, in which two people divide the duties in one job and split the total time at work according to mutually negotiated agreements with their supervisor.

Telecommuting has also become increasingly popular in recent years, with the availability of computers, voice mail, fax machines, and e-mail. Telecommuters work in their homes and usually have electronic connections with their place of work. They avoid the hassles of commuting, experience fewer interruptions, and can spend more time with family members. Employers like the results, too, as productivity often rises 10 to 20 percent, space needs are reduced, and new applicants become interested in the jobs available. Of course, not all jobs, and not all employees, are well suited for telecommuting. Supervisors need to make a special effort to provide resources, give clear instructions, keep telecommuters in the information "loop," be available for questions, and provide frequent feedback.

Telecommuting. Working at one's home, while being connected electronically to the employer's office.

7	T or F	Most employees are basically very similar in their thoughts, feelings, and perceptions.
8	T or F	Telecommuting provides substantial benefits for both the employee and the organization.

QUICK TEST 4

Millions of employees (telecommuters) now work out of their homes. **What challenges does this create for their supervisors?**

Quality of Work Life

Facilitating. An approach to management in which a supervisor assists and guides employees in their efforts to perform their jobs rather than emphasizing orders, instructions, and control.

To what extent are supervisors responsible for dissatisfied employees?

Only to the extent that employees who ordinarily ought to be satisfied with their work begin to project a general dissatisfaction with it. One observer advises that when a state of "poor satisfaction" occurs, it may also be evidence of "poor management." Some organizations even make managerial bonuses dependent on the level of employee satisfaction in their unit.

What can supervisors do to improve the quality of working life?

There are two major approaches. The first stems from the view that improved productivity—greater output from the inputs of labor, materials, money, methods, and machines—results in measurable improvements in employee satisfaction. Workers get a feeling of achievement when they see accomplishments flowing from their efforts, and this provides a foundation for a better work life. Supervisors can help make this connection clear by telling employees how the fruits of higher productivity provide the resources for making work easier and freeing them to work on more motivating tasks.

Internet connection

www.hr.upenn.edu/quality
A comprehensive example of how a service organization—Penn State University—attempts to create a high quality of work life for its employees.

The second approach arises from the contemporary belief that a greater involvement in decision making at all levels of the organization is essential. It may be hard to believe, but earlier generations of managers did just the opposite. They divided jobs into the smallest pieces so that employees could specialize in them and become repetitive experts with low error rates. However, as workers have become more educated, the majority of human beings *want* to "work smarter," although not necessarily harder. As a consequence, they often respond to opportunities to make the fullest use of their mental skills—especially when they are allowed to see how their ideas are used and the way their efforts contribute to the overall objective. They enjoy working in situations that enable each woman and man to make a demonstrably valued contribution to the finished product or service.

Quips & Quotes

A positive workplace atmosphere is worth developing, and not merely for its own sake; it may be the foundation of true organizational success.

Bronwyn Fryer

To most people, an improved quality of work life simply means that their hours spent at work will not be wasteful ones and their contributions will be valued. They want to feel that, somehow, their lives will be more worthwhile as a result of working than they would be with no job at all. The role of a supervisor is to help them see this.

What can supervisors do to make work more enjoyable?

Some basic (and easy-to-implement) approaches make for greater satisfaction among employees in general.

Offer employees an opportunity for "bottom-upward" feedback. This is a good way to find out what each person expects from work (and currently receives from it), even if it cannot always be fully provided.

View many supervisory functions as facilitating rather than directing. Few people want to be told how and when to do every little thing. Try to provide the kinds of information and resources an employee needs to get the job done—the right blueprint or specification, a key bit of useful guidance. A physical or mental assist, when needed or asked for, encourages employees to enforce their own discipline.

Stay flexible when and where you can. A supervisor whose department rules can't be bent to accommodate a worker's individuality on occasion makes employees feel hopelessly locked in. Keep to a minimum all directives that begin with the words *always* and *never*. Think in terms of *most of the time*, or *on the average*, when you will not permit this or insist on that. Be adaptable, not rigid.

Try to be a part of the total organization. Know your own superior as well as you can. Find out the company's basic objectives about costs, production, and quality. Understand the real intent of company policy toward employees. If you have this information, you will be in a better position to intercede for your employees. The supervisor who goes to bat for team members is often the supervisor an employee can face on a rainy Monday morning when there is a temptation to remain in bed.

Is it reasonable to allow employees to have fun at work?

Society encourages and provides many ways for people to have fun in their recreational lives. Play has a number of common elements, as seen in Figure 2-2. Many of these elements can be incorporated into the life of employees at work. A *fun workplace* is one in which supervisors encourage, initiate, and support a variety of playful and humorous activities. From the experiences of firms such as Southwest Airlines and the Disney Corporation, we know that employees *want* to have fun at work. A fun workplace is easily recognized by observing the presence of laughter, surprise, joy, and spontaneity; it means different things to various people; and it is relatively easy to create at work. We also know that there is a broad range of personal and organizational payoffs from a fun workplace, as discussed later.

Fun workplace. A work unit in which both employees and the organization benefit from the inclusion of playful and humorous activities.

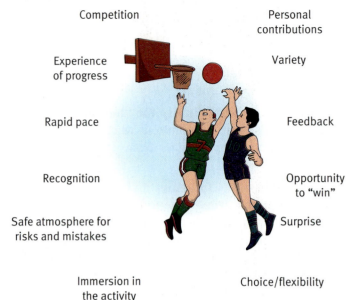

FIGURE 2-2

Typical elements of play.

Which of these can a supervisor apply to a work setting to help employees have fun there, too?

Competition

Personal contributions

Experience of progress

Variety

Rapid pace

Feedback

Recognition

Opportunity to "win"

Safe atmosphere for risks and mistakes

Surprise

Immersion in the activity

Choice/flexibility

What are the major ways in which organizations facilitate fun at work?

Literally hundreds of approaches have been used to stimulate fun at work. Key categories include unique ways to provide recognition for personal milestones (birthdays and anniversaries of hiring dates), hosting of special social events, public celebrations of professional and departmental achievements, games and friendly competitions, entertainment, and the use of humor in newsletters and correspondence. Specific tactics include costume days, cartoons tailored to employees, exaggerated job titles chosen by each worker, distribution of the "joke for the day," and the use of modified board games and TV show formats. There is no magic formula for success; the key is to be experimental, make it a continuous process, and involve others in coming up with new ideas. See the Internet Connection for a wide array of additional ideas.

Internet connection

www.playfair.com/fun or **www.junecline.com/funatwork**
Organizations like these provide a wide variety of practical ideas for having fun at work.

What are the benefits and risks of fun at work for employees? For the organization?

It is well known that employees like to work in an environment that satisfies their economic and security needs, makes them feel listened to, and provides personal recognition for their time, effort, and results. Beyond that, however, many employees value and appreciate the opportunity to relax and play a little, engage in laughter, have fun occasionally, and generally enjoy themselves at work. Unless the playfulness results in physical harm or personal feelings becoming hurt, fun at work can help decrease stress, reduce boredom, stimulate friendships, increase satisfaction, and produce several positive physiological results (e.g., lower blood pressure, greater immunity to infection, and more positive energy).

The organization benefits, too. A comprehensive survey by the Society for Human Resource Management showed that employee enthusiasm and creativity rise, it is easier to attract and retain new employees, the company's values and norms (culture) become clearer, and customers' satisfaction improves as a reflection of how they are treated by energized employees.[2] Some common fears about the risks inherent in having fun at work (employees will play too much or be distracted, the supervisor will lose control) generally prove to be groundless. The most valid reasons for supervisory resistance to having fun at work revolve around the potential financial costs, the fear that one's superiors won't condone it, and the possible lack of personal creativity. (As one supervisor painfully lamented, "I don't know *how* to have fun!") On balance, however, there are powerful arguments for allowing employees to have occasional fun at work, and for engaging them in the process of creating it.

Creating a fun work environment can be an important part of the supervisor's job. **Would you be willing to dress like a clown if it helped achieve your goal?**

| 9 | T or F | Supervisors have an impact on the satisfaction of their employees. |
| 10 | T or F | The benefits from a fun workplace are limited to employees. |

Practical Guidelines for Supervisors

1. *Tune in to your environment on a regular basis,* paying particular attention to the 10 forces that affect and constrain your own work operations.

2. *Discover what each of your employees uniquely desires from work,* and then monitor that portrait for changes across time.

3. *Strive constantly to reduce or eliminate the negative elements of bureaucracy* by reducing where possible the rules, procedures, and required written records that burden employees.

4. *Minimize (or discard) the use of the term* "subordinate," and select a more appropriate term that the organization endorses and that shows respect for the talents and contributions of employees.

5. *Never "demand" loyalty from employees;* you and the organization must earn it by demonstrating your loyalty to them—first.

6. *Take the initiative*—even before employees request it—*to explore the possibilities of using a variety of systems* (flexible work schedules, job sharing, and telecommuting) to improve employee perceptions of the workplace.

7. *Accept responsibility for creating a work unit with a high quality of work life;* help employees see the connection between their productivity and personal satisfaction.

8. *Informally poll your employees* to determine whether you are guilty of actions that create dissatisfaction in their work lives.

9. *Recognize that most employees want to have fun at work;* be creative in order to inject moments of humor occasionally.

10. *Search for ways to incorporate the 12 elements of play into the workplace,* and invite employees to suggest ways of doing so.

Chapter 2 Review

Key Concepts to Remember

1. Ten Pressures to Cope With. Supervisors face a different set of restraining factors in their immediate work environment than do higher-level managers. Specifically, a supervisor's horizons and options are greatly influenced by (a) technology, (b) legal restrictions, (c) organizational policies and procedures, (d) pressures for improved output, quality, and cost control, (e) competition with other supervisors for the organization's scarce resources, (f) the need to manage an enormous amount of information (or paperwork), (g) the rising expectations of employees, (h) globalization of business, (i) changes in the composition of the work-force, and (j) economic uncertainty. Additionally, supervisors need to be more concerned with day-to-day, short-term events than do higher-level managers, who are expected to be prepared much farther in advance for important changes in the external environment.

2. The World of Work. Work is a unique activity that is characterized, according to Max Weber, by (a) the necessity of employee conformity to rules, regulations, policies, and procedures, (b) the exercise of authority over others by managers, (c) the subordination of personal interests to the goals of the organization, and (d) the presence of written records for planning and control.

3. Employee Expectations. Most employees (50 percent or more) are reasonably satisfied with their jobs. Many good employees, however, would be better satisfied if their work required more of them and—as a result—was more challenging.

4. Understanding Employee Perceptions. Individuals perceive their work differently for different reasons. An employee's perception of the job is affected by past experience, assumptions about the intentions of others that will affect the situation, expectations about what will happen, the reliability of information about the job and its prospects, and the employee's present state of mind.

5. Quality of Work Life. Supervisors can help improve the quality of work life by maintaining a flexibility that accepts individual differences. Such supervisors also encourage "bottom-upward" feedback. Most importantly, these supervisors facilitate, rather than direct, the work of their employees. They also pay attention to the desire of their employees to have fun at work. Many opportunities exist for incorporating elements of play into the workplace, and the payoffs are substantial for both employees and the organization.

Reading Comprehension

1. Who might be more concerned with general economic conditions: a supervisor or a company president? With an employee's request for a less boring assignment? Why?

2. What factors distinguish a supervisor's work environment from that of a higher-level manager? Also, explain the difference in their time horizons.

3. List the four characteristics of a bureaucracy identified by Weber. Which is presumed to be the most threatening to most employees and why?

4. Contrast the work or job you have done for pay with a task you have done on a voluntary basis. Into which did you put more physical or mental effort? Why?

5. Think of persons you consider happy in their work. Describe one such person, the kind of work performed, and the kind of supervision provided.

6. Yankelovich says that only one person in five does his or her very best on a job. Why don't others do their best, too?

7. What's the difference between an employee's expectation of certain job conditions and a legal entitlement to them? Give some examples of the latter.

8. Ralph has been asked to perform a particularly nasty job. Surprisingly, he accepts it without hesitation, and he does it well. Ted, when given the same assignment, tries to duck it. When forced to accept it, Ted botches the job. What factors might explain the differing responses to this assignment?

9. Should a manager take total responsibility for creating and sustaining a fun workplace? Why or why not?

10. Have you ever had a job at which employees were encouraged to play, laugh, and have fun? What lessons can you draw from that experience?

Application

Self-Assessment

What Is Your Level of Satisfaction with Your Present (or Previous) Job?

Consider the job you hold right now (or one you have held recently). Read each statement below. Circle the number on the response scale that most closely reflects the degree to which each statement describes your feelings. Add up your total points and be ready to report your score for tabulation across the entire group.

	Strongly Agree		Strongly Disagree
1. I have many opportunities to learn new things on this job.	10 9 8 7 6 5 4 3 2 1		
2. My contributions are respected and appreciated by others.	10 9 8 7 6 5 4 3 2 1		
3. My job requires that I use many of my skills.	10 9 8 7 6 5 4 3 2 1		
4. If my work merits criticism, it is done in a fair and tactful manner.	10 9 8 7 6 5 4 3 2 1		
5. In general, I feel that I am kept pretty well informed.	10 9 8 7 6 5 4 3 2 1		
6. I believe that the job I do is very worthwhile to the organization.	10 9 8 7 6 5 4 3 2 1		

		Strongly Agree										Strongly Disagree

7. The expectations of quantity and quality of output are challenging, but fair and reasonable.   10 9 8 7 6 5 4 3 2 1

8. When I express ideas or make suggestions, they are listened to.   10 9 8 7 6 5 4 3 2 1

9. My pay is reasonably fair for the work that I do.   10 9 8 7 6 5 4 3 2 1

10. I have a lot of fun in my work.   10 9 8 7 6 5 4 3 2 1

Scoring and Interpretation

Scoring

Add up your total points for the 10 questions. Record that number here, and report it when it is requested. _____

Also, insert your score on the Personal Development Plan in the Appendix.

Interpretation

81 to 100 points. Congratulations! You seem to be reasonably well satisfied with your job.

61 to 80 points. There is clearly room for improvement. Set up a meeting with your boss to explore what might be done to provide more satisfaction at work.

Below 60 points. Your job lacks substantial opportunities for satisfaction, and this could cause other problems for you and the organization.

Identify your three lowest scores and record the question numbers here: _____, _____, _____.

Action

Begin thinking about the possibilities of changing jobs, changing employers, or taking a serious look at your overall attitude toward work and its rewards.

Skill Development

Building Loyalty

Loyalty is one's commitment toward someone or something. Conduct a mini-study on loyalty by talking to five employees. Ask them how committed they are to their employer today. Then talk to five managers, and ask them how committed their employees are to the organization today. Are the responses consistent? If not, why?

Employees' Comments	Managers' Comments
1. _____	1. _____
2. _____	2. _____

3. _____   **3.** _____
4. _____   **4.** _____
5. _____   **5.** _____

Action

Develop a basic plan for increasing loyalty among members of an organization's workforce. What are the five most important actions your employer could take to substantially raise the level of loyalty among its employees? List them below.

1. _____
2. _____
3. _____
4. _____
5. _____

Role Play

Group Exercise

Form into groups of three persons each. Two of you per group should assume the roles identified below, with the third person acting as the observer. Then engage in a brief discussion between Krista and Carlos in which you each try to put forth the most persuasive arguments for your position.

Krista. As a new supervisor looking for ideas, you have recently read material similar to that in this chapter regarding an organization's responsibility for creating a high quality of work life for its employees. You feel very comfortable with that approach and hope you can persuade some of your colleagues to join together in proposing it to higher management. You are about to meet with a colleague now for a preliminary exchange of ideas.

Carlos. As a new supervisor, you have been bombarded with ideas for improvement. Many of them seem overly simplistic or softhearted, and fail to consider the organization's need for good, old-fashioned hard work from employees. Krista has asked that you get together for a discussion to increase the quality of work life among employees, and you are going to try hard to persuade her to back down on that proposal. You are about to meet with her now.

Observer. You are about to overhear a conversation between two supervisors—Krista and Carlos—on the topic of quality of work life. Do not participate in the discussion, but take notes on the effectiveness of each person's argument, use of facts versus unfounded opinions, persuasiveness, listening skills, and overall communication skills. When they are finished, do not judge who "won" the argument, but simply give them both feedback for improvement in future conversations of this type.

Cases for Analysis

Case 5

Mildred and the Mickey Mouse Job

Two employees of the Zebra Hosiery Mills were waiting outside the plant for transportation home on a cold, wet afternoon. Mildred, a 30-year-old loom operator, said, "One more day like this and it's bye-bye Zebra for me."

"What's the problem?" asked Leon, her co-worker.

"This job is boring me to death," said Mildred. "It's Mickey Mouse all day long. I work my fingers raw racking up those yarn spools. Two hours straight before the break. Then lunch. Then the afternoon break. That's the same routine four times a day. I handle over 800 spools. Toward the end of each period I can hardly wait until I count the two-hundredth spool."

"Wow," said Leon. "I never thought of it that way. It just strikes me that it's an easy way to make $90 a day."

"Easy, nothing," said Mildred. "I could show them how to make it easier. All we'd need is some gizmo to let me rack up two spools at a time. But that pumpkin head I work for hasn't listened to a new idea in thirty years."

"That could be," said Leon. "But I'm satisfied as long as the supervisor stays off my back. I just don't like to be hassled."

"If she were to hassle you, you'd know you were something besides a machine," said Mildred. "If there were some place closer to home, I'd walk out on Zebra tomorrow."

"I could get a job nearer to my home," said Leon, "but I'd only make $80 a day. The extra $10 is worth fifteen minutes longer on the bus."

"Not for me," said Mildred. "I've got kids to feed when I get home. I don't want them out on the streets longer than they have to be. I'd take a cut if my job was next door to where I lived."

At this point Leon's bus arrived. "See you tomorrow—if you don't decide to quit," he said as he climbed aboard.

"Fat chance," said Mildred to herself. "What other choices do I really have?"

Analysis

If you were Mildred's supervisor, which of the following actions would you consider to be the most effective in handling Mildred's dissatisfaction with her job? Rank the alternatives on a scale from 1 (most preferable) to 5 (least preferable). You may add another alternative if you wish. Be prepared to justify your ranking.

_____ **a.** Demonstrate to Mildred that she is well paid for the work she does compared with the rates for other work in the mill.

_____ **b.** Ask what Mildred would do to make her job more interesting. Then try to incorporate her suggestions.

_____ **c.** Change the job so that Mildred would rotate assignments with co-workers doing related work in the same department.

_____ **d.** Ignore Mildred's complaints, since your attention may lead her to expect more than you can deliver.

_____ **e.** Suggest that, if Mildred is so unhappy, she should look for another job elsewhere.

Case 6

Hot Job, High Turnover

After Eileen H. graduated from high school in June, she spent most of the summer hanging around the public swimming pool during the day and with her friends in the shopping mall parking lot at night. By fall, however, her parents insisted that she find a job. The best she could get was a second-shift job at the local fiberglass boat factory. The work was difficult and disagreeable. The plant was hot, and the fumes from the plastic solvents were irritating. The pay was just above the minimum wage standard. The only thing really good about the job was her supervisor, Ray J. He was regarded by the boat plant workers as a "good guy." Ray was troubled, however, by the number of young people like Eileen who stayed on the job only a month or two before quitting.

Analysis

To reduce the chance of Eileen's leaving, Ray should

a. Make the work easier for Eileen.
b. Ask her for ideas about how to make the work more pleasant and fun.
c. Emphasize the value her job adds to the final product.
d. Try to get her a 50-cent-an-hour raise.

Circle the course of action you think would be most suitable, and be prepared to explain the reasons for your choice.

Case 7

The Disgruntled Customer Service Representative

"I expected to be moved to the day shift when I took this job," complained Aldo, a night telephone customer service representative for a credit card company. Aldo is married, and because his wife works nights, too, he had hoped that he could change shifts so that he could stay home with their two young children during the evenings. When Aldo's supervisor replied that there was little or no chance of his changing shifts, Aldo was greatly irritated. "I'm doing a first-rate job and have done so for six months. You told me when I was hired that I might make the change to days after I'd shown that I could do the job."

"I said that there was a possibility," said the supervisor, "but there are no openings available now."

"That's not true," said Aldo, "You've hired at least one day-shift worker since I've started here. I think I'm entitled to be switched right now."

Analysis

To handle this request with the most appropriate results, Aldo's supervisor should say:

a. "You're not entitled to anything. I'll give you a chance to change shifts only when and if it is convenient."
b. "No one is automatically entitled to fill a day-shift opening, but I'll try to fit you in the next time."
c. "Sorry, I forgot about you. I'll switch you to days right away, even if it means overstaffing that shift for the time being."
d. "Many factors affect how day-shift jobs are filled. I'll try to comply with your request, but only after giving consideration to all the factors involved."

Circle the course of action you think would be most suitable, and be prepared to explain the reasons for your choice.

Chapter References

1. Terence F. Shea, "For Many Employees, the Workplace Is Not a Satisfying Place," *HR Magazine*, October 2002, p. 28.
2. Evren Esen, Robert Ford, John Newstrom, and Frank McLaughlin, *Fun Work Environment Survey*. Alexandria, VA: SHRM Research Department, 2002.

Quick Test 1	Quick Test 2	Quick Test 3	Quick Test 4	Quick Test 5	ANSWERS TO QUICK TESTS
1. F	3. F	5. T	7. F	9. T	
2. T	4. F	6. F	8. T	10. F	

Setting Goals, Making Plans, and Improving Costs

After studying this chapter, you should be able to

- Differentiate among the various terms associated with the planning process.

- Discuss a supervisor's responsibilities for interpreting and implementing a company's policies.

- Create a relevant set of goals for a department supervisor.

- Explain the planning process and the differences between long-range and short-range plans and between standing and single-use plans.

- Understand how to select cost targets, assign priorities to them, and select appropriate strategies for cost reduction.

- Identify and evaluate the principal sources of cost-improvement ideas, list some positive approaches, and explain why some cost-improvement suggestions might be rejected.

- Discuss the reasons for employee resistance to cost-reduction programs and describe several ways for securing workers' support and cooperation.

Vision. A statement of an organization's ideal future.

Values. What an organization believes in and guides its practices by.

Mission statement. A statement that clarifies the nature and purpose of a business.

Strategies. The major methods for achieving an organization's vision and mission.

Aren't managers and executives paid to do organizational planning? Why should this chore be part of a supervisor's workload?

It's true that top managers bear the primary responsibility for setting an organization's direction. In particular, they provide the framework for a supervisor's efforts through the creation of a vision, values, a mission statement, and strategic plans. Further, managers are often aided in this process by planning and scheduling specialists. Let's take a quick look at the major elements of an organization's master planning process.

A corporate *vision* provides a dramatic look at what the entire organization might be like at a distant point in the future—perhaps 5 to 10 years out. It is a broad image of the desired state that lies ahead. A statement of corporate *values* lays out the beliefs and standards to which an organization must adhere. Examples might be adherence to cutting-edge technology, attaining superior quality, and providing outstanding customer service. A *mission statement* typically specifies what business the firm is in and what its primary areas of emphasis are. It answers the questions "Who are we?" and "What do we do?" From this, top managers develop a corporate *strategy* that sets the overall pattern for how the vision will be achieved and the mission fulfilled. Examples of corporate strategies include acquisitions of related companies, expanding existing products into new markets, diversification, and even downsizing. The key lesson is that *supervisors must custom fit their own units into these master planning pieces.* Supervisors, not executives, make the day-to-day assignments and adjustments needed to make a master plan effective. Without conscious awareness of what is going on above you, your planning efforts will be wasted.

Unless supervisors accept their share of this managerial responsibility, they will waste (a) time—because of avoidable delays; (b) materials and supplies—because of unwarranted haste, spoilage, or unnecessary accumulation of inventories; (c) machinery—because of operation below the optimum capacity; (d) space—because of overcrowding and poor coordination of incoming supplies and outgoing production; and (e) human resources—because of underutilization or improper assignments.

Internet connection

www.birnbaumassociates.com/developing-vision.htm
Vision versus mission. Access this site for a discussion of the contrasting but complementary nature of these two planning concepts.

How far ahead should supervisors plan their work?

Long-range plans should be handled largely by those in higher levels of management. As a supervisor, your target is necessarily much closer at hand. American Management Association studies show that supervisors spend 38 percent of their thinking time on problems that come up the same day, 40 percent on those one week ahead, 15 percent on those one month ahead, 5 percent on those three to six months ahead, and 2 percent on those one year ahead.

Check your own habits. If you feel you're too busy to worry about anything but today, chances are, you spend most of your time fighting fires that can be avoided by planning a week to a month ahead.

Typically, a supervisor is responsible for short-range (tactical) plans and higher executives for long-range (strategic) plans. In military language, tactical plans are those concerned with a particular engagement or skirmish or battle; strategic plans are those on which the major battle or entire war is based.

Plans, planning, policies, goals: What is the difference?

There are some subtle, but useful, differences among the terms. *Plans* are what come out of the *planning* process. Plans, or programs, are what you intend to do in the future. Before you can develop plans, however, you must set targets. These targets are called **goals** or **objectives**. After you have set these goals (that is the simplest term to use), you establish general guidelines for reaching them. These guidelines are called **policies**. Policies are, in effect, master plans that have been derived from organizational objectives. Only after policies have been set should the specific, operational plans be formulated. Operational plans include (a) **schedules**, which dictate what must be done as well as establish starting and finishing times, (b) **procedures**, which prescribe the exact methods to be used and sequence to be followed in carrying out a plan, and (c) **standards**, which prescribe the level (quantity or quality) of performance expected.

Finally, you may choose to lay down some *rules* and **regulations**. These will establish the limits (or controls) within which employees are free to do the job their own way.

Take this example. You are thinking ahead (planning) about what your department will do during the annual spring cleaning. You make a list of things you want to accomplish: filing cabinets cleared of all obsolete material, shelving cleaned and rearranged, equipment repaired and put in tip-top shape. These are your goals. Next, you establish some sort of policy. For example, cleaning will be done during normal working hours without overtime; discarding obsolete papers will conform to legal requirements; repairing equipment may be done internally or by an outside vendor. Then you lay out your own optional plan (schedule and/or procedures) of how the housekeeping will be done, when, and by whom. Then you clarify how everyone will know when he or she has done a

Thoughts*to*ponder

Robert Ramsey, a successful author and experienced supervisor, argues that many supervisors fail to plan. As a result, they are victims of their environment, not masters of it. He contends that planning is fun, puts you in control of your future, and marks you as a leader. Your plans motivate you and others to improve. As a result of good planning, supervisors spend less time putting out "fires" and have more time to set priorities and focus on important tasks. Planning, Ramsey concludes, is not a luxury but an essential part of a supervisor's job.

Source: Robert D. Ramsey, "Do You Have a Plan?" *Supervision*, March 2005, pp. 14–16.

Goals. Short-term and long-range targets (objectives) toward which an organization strives.

Policies. Broad guidelines that must be followed in pursuit of goals.

Schedules. Detailed date-and-time indications of how facilities, equipment, and employees are to be used to accomplish organizational goals.

Quips & Quotes

A good plan today is better than a perfect plan tomorrow.

General George S. Patton

FIGURE 3-1

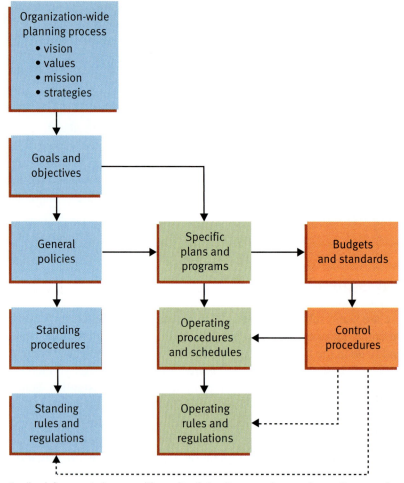

Feedback from control may modify results of standing procedures and operating procedures.

satisfactory job. Finally, you set down some firm rules or regulations for your employees: Only file clerks will make judgments about what paperwork will be discarded; before expenses are incurred, employees must check with you; employees who clean shelving must wear protective gloves. Figure 3-1 illustrates common relationships among these terms.

What is meant by *company policy*?

Company—or organization—policies are broad guidelines for action. At their best, these guides are a reflection of a company's objectives and a statement of its basic principles for doing business. In a major way, they represent a public commitment to employees, suppliers, customers, and the community. In a very practical way, however, they are intended as a guide for supervisors and managers for getting their jobs done. Many policies at the operational level give supervisors the opportunity to use their own best judgment in implementing them. Other policies are reinforced by firm rules and procedures that greatly restrict supervisory discretion.

Does policy apply only at high levels?

Policy is generally set by managers high up in the organization. But policy can be no more than a collection of high-sounding words unless the supervisor translates them into action.

Consider the following example of a disciplinary policy. Note how its formality decreases, and its action-orientation increases, as it works its way down from the executive suite to first-line action by the supervisors:

Company president: "Our policy is to exercise fair and reasonable controls to regulate the conduct of our employees."

Division executive: "The policy on attendance in this division is that habitual absenteeism will be penalized."

Area manager: "Here are the rules governing absences in this region. It's up to you supervisors to keep an eye on unexcused absences and to suspend any employee absent or late more than three times in three months."

Local supervisor: "I'm going to have to lay you off for three days. You know the rules. You took time off on your own without getting approval."

Note that no real action takes place until the supervisor puts the words of the policy into effect.

Is policy always in writing?

Far from it. Many rigid policies have never been stated in black and white, and many firm policies have never been heard from an executive's lips. But employees and supervisors alike recognize that matters affected by such policies must be handled in a certain manner and usually do so.

The existence of so much unwritten policy has led many authorities to conclude that all policy is better put into writing so that it may be explained, discussed, and understood. This is also the fairest way for employees. Nevertheless, many companies don't subscribe to this way of thinking, and their policies remain implied rather than spelled out. This can lead to genuine misunderstandings and more "exceptions" to policy.

Should a supervisor deviate from organizational policy?

No. That's a very dangerous thing to do. Policies exist for a good reason; they are set to guide action. It's a supervisor's responsibility to act within policy limits, although some firms encourage and give supervisory discretion.

Supervisors can influence a policy change, however, by making their thoughts and observations known to their manager, the human resources department, and top management. After all, supervisors are in the best position to feel out employees' reactions to policy, both favorable and unfavorable. You do your company a service when you accurately report employees' reactions, and that's the time to offer your suggestions for improving or modifying the policy. In a nutshell, provide your best input, and then agree to abide by the decision.

QUICK TEST 1			
	1	T or F	Supervisors are responsible for creating vision, values, mission statements, and strategies.
	2	T or F	Policies usually should be put into writing so that they will be more clearly understood and more consistently administered.

Goal Setting

CONCEPT

A supervisor's goals shape the targets toward which all of her or his plans and actions should be directed.

If a man (woman) knows not what harbor he (she) seeks, any wind is the right wind.

Seneca

Why must goals come before plans?

Because plans are the means to an end; goals are the ends you are seeking. Logically, then, you must first decide where you want to go and what you want your unit to accomplish. These are, of course, your goals or objectives. You should set them carefully and systematically. This can be done by following these seven steps:

1. **Consider the goals of the entire organization, not just those of your department.** Think about the needs and wishes of external customers—those the company serves with its products or services— as well as the "customers" your department serves internally.
2. **Assess the strengths and weaknesses of your department.** Ask how they will help or hinder you in trying to meet company goals and trying to serve external and internal customers.

3. **Look for areas of improvement.** Keep your mind alert to new opportunities, such as ways to improve quality or reduce costs. Don't restrict your thinking to what your goals were last year or how you met them. If you can forecast what may happen to change conditions next year, this will help focus your attention on goals that will be more meaningful in the months to come.

4. **Consult with those who will have to help you carry out your plans and those who can offer their support along the way.** Employees who are involved in setting goals are more likely to be committed to success in reaching the goals. Staff departments that are consulted in advance may direct your attention to potential pitfalls or to goals that will get the full measure of their support.

5. **Pick a relevant and reasonable set of goals.** These goals should meet two standards. They should (a) contribute to the organization's goals and (b) be attainable by your department, given its resources.

6. **Arrange your department's goals in a hierarchy of objectives.** That is, *prioritize them* by placing the most important ones at the top of your list and the least important at the bottom.

7. **Watch out for limitations.** Think about restrictions that may be imposed on you by your company or by the need to coordinate with or serve other departments. Your department cannot operate in a vacuum. It must base its plans on realistic planning premises.

With what kinds of goals are supervisors usually concerned?

Typically, the goals you set for yourself—or that are set for you, at least partially, as part of a company's overall objectives—are targets to be aimed at in the near future. They pin down your department's output, quality of workmanship, and allowable expenditures. Often, they also include goals in employee-related areas such as departmental attendance, labor turnover, and safety, as shown in Table 3-1. These goals may be stated in terms of tomorrow, next week, or next month, or as far ahead as a year. More often than not, the goals are *quantitative* (expressed as numbers, percentages, or dollars) rather than merely *qualitative* (described with words such as improve, maintain, good, or better). In short, results will be *measurable*.

In many companies and organizations, the degree to which you and your department attain your goals becomes the determining factor in what kind of raise you'll get or how good a job for which you can be groomed. This is one big reason why it is so important to lay out a detailed set of plans for meeting your goals.

TABLE 3-1   Typical Performance Goals for a First-Line Supervisor

Area of Measurement	Last Year's Record	Next Year's Goals
1. Number of new clients contacted	17 per month on average	20 per month on average
2. Complaints received	6 per month	Keep complaints to less than 5 per month
3. Workforce stability (turnover rate)	22% average	15% average
4. Absences	5%	5%
5. Tardiness rate	7%	2%
6. Overtime	Only on jobs okayed by sales department	Only on jobs okayed by sales department
7. Accidents	No lost-time accidents; 37 calls to health services for minor ailments	No lost-time accidents; reduce number of health services visits to 30 or less
8. Customer satisfaction	Average of 15 complaints per month	33% reduction in complaints per month received

How can goals be made more compelling?

There are four major ways. First, make sure goals don't focus on *activities*. Goals should be something to try to achieve, not just spend time on. They should also provide an opportunity for individual satisfaction when they are attained. Second, it is best to create a list of a *few* goals—but meaningful ones—on which you can focus your efforts. Don't try to impress others with a lengthy laundry list in an effort to demonstrate how many balls you can keep in the air at the same time, for you will almost surely fail to catch all of them.

Third, according to Professor Gary Latham and others, there are five key guidelines for making your statements of objectives more effective (and impressive to your manager!).[1] A goal should be characterized by the acronym *SMART*, as described here:

Specific. That is, goals should be clearly stated in terms, or numbers, that make their achievement concrete and detailed. It should be clear to any astute observer whether a goal was achieved by evaluating the results. Specific goals remove the ambiguity from the assessment process.

Measurable. It is tempting to state goals in terms of direction, such as "We will lower our absenteeism rate" or "We will improve productivity." Although trends like these can be detected, it is better to focus clearly on measurable outcomes with quantifiable ways to assess them, such as "Costs will be held below 97 percent of standard" or "Customer satisfaction surveys will average at least 4.5 on a 5-point response scale." The real value in this criterion stems from the well-known behavioral principle "Whatever gets measured, gets done." Employees are more likely to focus their efforts in domains where they know they will be evaluated.

Attainable. It makes no sense to set impossible goals; they must be achievable or they will haunt you later, when you are appraised against your accomplishments (or lack of them). But don't set easy goals, for they are not motivating to you or your employees. Effective goals should cause employees to stretch themselves and use their talents, creativity, and energies to attain them.

Relevant. The best goals are directly connected to the organization's mission and strategy, as discussed earlier. You should be able to state how each goal you set ties into, and contributes to, some higher-level goal of merit.

Time-oriented. The targeted outcome must always be related to a specific time period, such as "382 calls handled per day" or "5 percent reduction in turnover for the year." Managers (and employees) want to know *when* something will be done.

The fourth way to make goals compelling is to identify at least one *superordinate goal* for your work unit. These are overarching objectives that capture the hearts and imagination of employees, appeal to their emotions, require teamwork and mutual aid, and evoke a powerful commitment from them. For example, consider Rotary International's superordinate goal for its members: "Eradicate polio from the earth!"

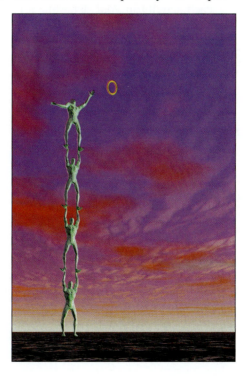

Superordinate goal. An objective that requires cooperation from others to achieve and appeals to both heart and mind.

Effective goals challenge employees and often require team effort to achieve. **What difficult goals have you set for yourself?**

3   T or F   After setting several goals, it is probably not important to prioritize them according to their relative importance.

4   T or F   Good goal statements should be measurable, general, time-oriented, and achievable.

3 The Planning Process

CONCEPT
The planning process should be systematic, yet it should allow for flexibility.

Once goals have been set, how does the planning process proceed?

In six steps (see Figure 3-2). Effective plans flow from clearly stated goals, such as those appearing in Table 3-1. Plans detail *how* goals will be achieved. These plans, however, depend upon your following a systematic planning process, just as you did when setting goals.

1. **Develop a master plan.** This should focus on your main objective. If, for example, the company's goal is to have higher-quality products or services, the master plan for your department should give this top priority.
2. **Draw up supporting plans.** This requires that you think about how each activity in your department can contribute to your master plan.

FIGURE 3-2
Critical steps in planning. **When should employees be involved in planning, according to the MBO process?**

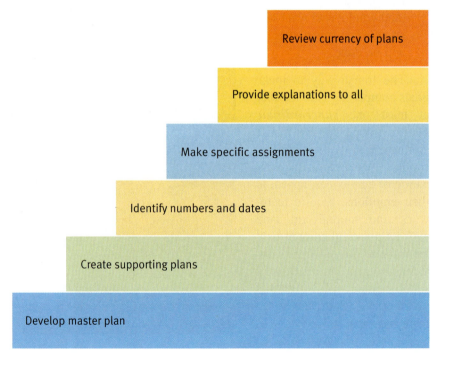

Review currency of plans

Provide explanations to all

Make specific assignments

Identify numbers and dates

Create supporting plans

Develop master plan

3. **Put numbers and dates on everything you can.** Plans work best when employees know how much or how many are required of them. Since plans are for the future—tomorrow, next week, or next month—times and dates are essential, too.

4. **Pin down assignments.** Plans are for people. Responsibility for carrying out each part of a plan or procedure should be assigned to a particular individual or team.

5. **Explain the plan to all concerned.** Plans should be shared. Their rationales should be explained and their goals justified. Employees who know *why* are more likely to cooperate.

6. **Review your plans regularly.** Circumstances and restrictions change. Your plans should be examined periodically to see whether they should be changed, too.

How does planning relate to management by objectives?

The process just described is the traditional way in which plans are created, but it has one major flaw—it fails to draw upon the knowledge and inputs of employees. For several decades now, many organizations have adapted their planning by using some form of the Management by Objectives (MBO) process. Although the steps in MBO closely resemble those in the basic planning process, there are a couple of very important differences. First, MBO explicitly invites employees to get involved in setting their own objectives; this creates a stronger sense of ownership for their goals. Second, employees are given considerable latitude in deciding *how* they will attain their goals; action plans draw upon their unique experiences and expertise. Third, the MBO process encourages frequent communications between supervisor and employee, and periodic mutual assessments of progress so that there will be "no surprises." In short, the major contribution of MBO is to make the planning process participative, and both sides gain from doing this.

Should a supervisor's plans be flexible or rigid?

They should be stated firmly and clearly so that everyone concerned can understand them and recognize their importance. They should not be so rigid, however, that they prevent your making changes to accommodate unexpected circumstances. A good plan should be flexible enough to anticipate and allow for an alternative course of action. Suppose, for example, you planned to start a new order or project on Monday, but the necessary materials are not on hand. Your plans should permit postponement of that project and the insertion of a productive alternative without delay.

Did You Know

Goal Setting Pays Off

A survey of a large sample of human resource managers concluded that employee performance increases by an average of more than 15 percent when supervisors help their team members set goals. The best goal statements are challenging, communicated, and accepted.

Source: Sara L. Rynes, et al., "Seven Common Misconceptions about Human Resource Practices: Research Findings versus Practitioner Beliefs," *Academy of Management Executive*, 2002, vol. 16, no. 3, pp. 92–103.

In what way are plans or programs usually classified?

They are usually classified according to their duration (long or short) and usage (standing or single-use).

Long-range plans are typically set by higher management and are expected to be in operation for one to five years.

Short-range plans are those with which supervisors are most concerned. These are usually based on operations of one year or less. At the department level, short-range plans may be in effect for a day, a week, a month, or a quarter.

Standing plans include just about any activity that goes on without much change from year to year. Standing plans cover general employment practices, health and safety matters, purchasing procedures, routine discipline, and the like.

Single-use plans are used only once before they must be revised. A plan for the development of a new software program is an example. It will be used only once.

Generally speaking, then, supervisors will follow short-range, single-use plans for day-to-day operations. But supervisors will also be guided by many standing plans that implement routine, relatively unchanging goals and policies.

Do these four types of plans cover both regular situations and crises, too?

Not necessarily. The plans discussed previously are designed mostly to handle relatively expected proceedings. But as we know, today's turbulent environment can produce a wide array of unpredictable and even unpleasant events—hurricanes, earthquakes, tsunamis, and terrorism. Not only might these tragic events affect a supervisor's operation, numerous other things can disrupt the workplace, including sudden demands by customers, dramatic actions of competitors, corporate mergers, a wave of employee illnesses, and "crash programs" dictated by higher management. Instead of "shooting from the hip" when these events occur, sharp supervisors will have done some contingency planning in advance to cover possible surprises. ***Contingency plans*** (also known as crisis plans or scenario plans) anticipate future situations (even if they are unlikely), lay out preventive measures where possible, take into account past similar circumstances, and specify probable responses. Such plans are best developed through dialogue (interpersonal or internal), in which supervisors are encouraged to think about what they would do *if* one of several events occurred. Contingency plans, then, are characterized by a matched set of "*If* this (premises) . . . then *this* (probable actions) . . ." statements.

Contingency plans. Special-purpose plans that anticipate crises and specify the probable responses to them.

Work projects—small or large—require careful planning and goal-setting.
What would likely happen if an organization had *no* goals?

What is a good way to evaluate your plans and projects?

Try using this six-point planning checklist (adapted from Rudyard Kipling's poem "Six Honest Serving Men"—what, why, where, when, how and who):

1. **What** is to be done? Spell out the objectives in terms of output, quality, and costs.
2. **Why** should this activity be done? Will it save money? Generate revenue? Add to customer satisfaction?
3. **Where** is this activity to be performed? At the workplace? In the field? Where is the finished product or service to be delivered? To the adjoining department, the shipping dock, the home office?
4. **When** must this activity or project be completed? Just as important, when must it begin? A starting date is often as vital to a plan's success as is its deadline. And this date cannot be determined without first having a reliable time estimate for doing the job. That way, if you know, for example, that it will take three days to complete a project that's due on Friday morning, you must start working on the project the first thing Tuesday morning.

5. **How** is this activity to be performed? Answers to this question should verify the job methods and equipment to be used and the procedures and sequences to be followed.
6. **Who** is to perform this work? This means not only that you must assign responsibility for this task; you also must specify the nature of the authority that goes with the job. That is, you must specify the extent to which that individual can control the resources needed to complete the task, such as tools, machinery, materials, and additional labor.

How do controls relate to plans?

Controls keep results in line with plans. When a plan is moving directly toward its goal, the track is kept clear. The supervisor need apply no control. But when actions stray from their planned targets, the supervisor must take corrective action to bring them back in line. When planning a department's goals, a supervisor must also plan its control limits, which provide the feedback needed to trigger corrective actions.

QUICK TEST 3			
	5	T or F	Supervisors are usually more concerned with short-range plans than with long-range ones.
	6	T or F	The major contribution of MBO is to make goals more measurable.

4 Cost-Improvement Strategies

CONCEPT
Organizations compete on many bases, but cost control is one of the most important, requiring carefully planned priorities.

Why is cost control so important today?

It has been critical for a long time, but sometimes it is neglected when the economy is booming. However, the recent spread of operations to sites around the world—often those with lower labor rates—has placed tremendous pressures on U.S. organizations (and their supervisors) to control costs. In addition, many mergers are arranged in the belief that there are substantial overlaps which, when eliminated, will produce higher net profits. The expectations of Wall Street analysts for ever-greater corporate earnings have caused wave after wave of downsizing, forcing the remaining supervisors to offer the same level of service with fewer employees. In short, the pressure to lower costs can be powerful and ongoing. Supervisors must learn to be cost-conscious, and demonstrate it when cost reductions are called for.

How sweeping are cost-reduction programs likely to be?

It depends. A strategy for cost reduction can be applied to the entire organization or confined to the operations of a single department. If it is organization-wide, the program is likely to be sweeping in nature and administered from the top down. If it is a departmental effort, the chances are that the strategy will be a piecemeal one. It will nibble away at costs under a plan conceived and implemented by the department's supervisor.

Supervisors will be expected to accept the disruptions and clear the path for changes dictated by large-scale, long-term cost-improvement programs. Usually, however, supervisors are concerned with modest, ongoing plans for cost reduction. The success of these plans, especially when initiated by the supervisors themselves, depends on how well they have been conceived and how creatively and persistently supervisors pursue them. As the hare and tortoise fable points out, "Slow and steady wins the race"—even the cost race.

Where can the most promising cost targets be found?

These usually emerge from a systematic search for the most obvious sources of expense, which include the following:

Product or service costs. Both total and unit costs.

Process, or operations, costs. All, or any part, of the department's operating procedures.

People costs. Both direct and indirect. The latter refers to labor costs that support the central operations of a line department—functions such as maintenance, material handling, inspection, housekeeping, and other service functions.

Equipment costs. Either in general or for a particular machine or device.

Materials costs. The materials that go into a product and, often just as important, the operating supplies consumed during the process or while providing the service.

Utilities costs. Power, fuels, water, and other utilities used by the department.

Communications costs. Telephone, facsimile, copying, mail, Internet connections, and so forth.

Information costs. Data collection, processing, retrieval, reporting, and analysis.

How should you set your cost-target priorities?

Approaches vary here. Short-term priorities are usually assigned to obvious "action-now" projects. Projects that take time to carry out, however, are usually held back for an assessment of what they might entail compared with their returns. On the basis of such an evaluation, targets can be picked and their priorities assigned according to ratings such as the following:

1. **Most obvious.** Sometimes the cost element that is most out of line is so obvious that you need search no further. Occasionally, this choice can be misleading; the true cause of the high cost may lie elsewhere, and the obvious element is only a result.

2. **Easiest.** The course of least resistance also is often the most tempting path to follow to achieve cost savings. A small savings that is quickly reaped with little effort cannot be ignored. Starting with a sure thing can be a good way to build momentum in a cost-reduction campaign.

3. **Crucial.** Sometimes a cost situation is so critical that it begs for immediate attention. If this is the case, it is probably wise to attack that cost target first. Otherwise, it may interfere with a more orderly progression toward long-term goals.

4. **Fastest payback.** Sometimes a company's financial policy dictates that the projects that pay back their investment fastest be given the highest priority. Certainly, for cost-reduction projects that do require significant investment, this is a sensible choice.

What is meant by a "belt-tightening" program?

This usually refers to a short-term plan, often dictated from above, to cut costs as rapidly as possible. Such an approach is negative in nature, in that it allows little room for creative cost "improvements." Instead, belt-tightening will emphasize any of the following approaches:

Stop spending—permanently. Costs are cut through the simple expedient of restricting spending to necessities only. Spending for frills, conveniences, and even improvements is stopped. Sometimes the halt can become a permanent way of life. In that case, a supervisor and staff must learn to operate frugally, always.

Find an alternative. Sometimes cost pressures stimulate the creative juices of individuals. Instead of buying an item, they make, lease, or borrow it. At the extreme, supervisors may have to learn to do entirely without a resource that they previously enjoyed. When financial times are tough, almost every expense item is fair game for the cost cutter's knife.

Postpone what you can. With this approach, spending is postponed, or deferred, until a later time when the pressure to cut costs is not so severe. Unlike stopping or doing without, postponing implies that the money *will* be spent, but at a later date. Deferred maintenance work is the most common of these postponed costs. This approach has a potentially serious flaw: Many times the money that must be spent to do the job later is greater than what might be needed now. A building that needs only one coat of paint this year may need total replacement of its siding in the future.

7	T or F	Attacking the "crucial" cost-reduction areas is likely to produce the fastest payback, by definition.
8	T or F	The least painful belt-tightening programs are likely to involve postponement of expenses.

QUICK TEST 4

Cost-Improvement Sources

5

CONCEPT
Cost-improvement ideas may be gathered from a variety of sources, but employees may not buy in to the techniques.

Who can provide the necessary cost-cutting ideas?

Three good sources follow, all close to home:

1. **You.** Build up a backlog of ideas the year round. Whenever you see, hear, or read about something that might work in your department, jot it down in a notebook or place it in a folder. Call these files your "idea banks." Later, when your attention is drawn to costs for any reason, check over your files to see what might be useful. (See especially Chapter 15 for ideas on improving productivity- and quality-related costs.)
2. **Your employees.** Employees probably know more about the ins and outs of the job than you do. If you encourage employees properly, they are likely to have ideas for cutting production costs or for reducing waste. (See the last question section of this chapter for ways to stimulate the flow of employee ideas.)
3. **Staff departments.** Once you have pinpointed a cost target, staff specialists, such as industrial engineers and systems analysts, can provide expert help. They can call on vast reservoirs of examples of how costs were reduced in similar target areas in other departments or other companies.

How helpful are cost-reduction committees?

Cost-reduction committees were the forerunners of quality circles. Quality circles changed the emphasis from relying mainly on the contributions

Continuous Improvement

Many organizations today engage in cost control through the process of **continuous improvement**. This approach sets aside the "crisis" orientation of many cost-reduction efforts, and encourages employees to search for a better way to do things (such as find less expensive methods or materials) on an ongoing basis. Employees and their supervisors are asked to break out of old habits and routines, take a positive approach to reducing costs (*expecting* to find room for improvement), correct errors and implement new ideas immediately, and take a critical view of existing practices. Many corporations, such as GE, Motorola, Pacific Bell, and Chase Manhattan Bank, have aggressively cut costs and saved expenses by implementing continuous improvement practices.

Continuous improvement. The ongoing process of searching for cost reductions (and process improvements) by taking a critical view of the present situation.

of experts and specialists to broadening participation to include small groups of well-trained and concerned employees. Members of quality circles are volunteers, and they contribute their ideas to work improvement as well as to cost reduction. Today, cost-reduction committees are often inseparable from quality circles, and these groups may go by many names. Regardless of designation, they rely on broad and informed participation that taps a large reservoir of people in the organization for ideas.

What are some positive ways to improve costs?

Compared with belt-tightening, the following six approaches to cost improvement tend to accentuate the positive. Each technique provides a different tool for cutting at the roots of cost problems. If one technique doesn't work, try another, or a combination of two or three.

Reduce waste. Where can you find waste in raw materials and operating supplies? How about people? Are you wasting their efforts? Are you getting the most from utilities, or are you wasting water, gas, or electricity?

Save time. Can you speed up or upgrade your equipment? Will time studies show you where time itself can be saved? Are you doing everything you can to get full use of your employees' time?

Increase output. You can cut cost rates—and improve productivity—by stepping up the amount of work put through your department. Sometimes there's a rhythm that goes with high production that's lost with lower production. Sometimes when you cut back, you need the part-time services of several different people, whereas if you increased output, the same people would be working 100 percent of the time. With the higher output base, unit cost rates would actually be lower.

Spend wisely. Cutting costs doesn't always mean that you stop spending. In fact, it's a popular and true expression that you have to spend money to make money. Often top management is more attentive to the need for wise spending during a cost-cutting campaign than at other times. So look for ways to spend money that will ultimately save money, such as on computerization or on replacement of slow equipment with newer, faster equipment.

Use space more intelligently. Space—for storage, manufacturing, and shipping—costs money. This cost goes on whether output is high or low. If you can figure out how to get more use out of the same space, you can cut costs.

Watch your inventories. It may make supervisors feel comfortable to know they have a big backlog of materials and supplies to use or to be shipped, but this is a very costly practice. Generally, it's best to stock as little as you can safely get away with, especially if supplies can be purchased and delivered quickly and reliably. This popular practice is known as *just-in-time inventory*.

Why is an apparent money-saving idea sometimes turned down by top management?

Mainly because the idea doesn't pay off quickly enough. It is exasperating, of course, for a supervisor to come up with an idea for saving $500, for example, only to have it rejected. Here's the way upper management may have evaluated the idea: Your plan will clearly save $500 a year, but its implementation will cost the company $3,000. This means that it will take six years for your idea to pay off. The cost of financing investments is so great that many companies have adopted the policy that a new machine or technology must pay for itself in five years or less. In fact, some companies insist on a payoff period of only one year!

Another factor is that your idea is often in competition for investment money with ideas suggested by other supervisors. Obviously, higher management will choose the ideas with the best and fastest payoffs.

Why do employees fear cost reduction?

Unless you can sell cost reduction to employees, they are likely to be indifferent at best, rebellious at worst. After all, to employees, cost cutting may mean loss of work, overtime, or their jobs. They feel that cost cutting threatens their security—or at least disrupts their work habits. In addition, employees often think that management itself throws away money through poor planning and downright misjudgment about what's really important—and that applies to supervisors, too.

Sitting as you do on the management side of the fence, you can understand the reason behind many moves that look wasteful to employees. But the tipoff for you is this: Employees frequently don't see the situation the way you do because *no one has taken time to make it clear*.

Your cue to selling cost reduction is to give employees the facts and help them see that cost cutting (or productivity improvement) helps them; it does not work to their disadvantage.

What is the best way to cut through employee resistance and build support for cost improvement?

It will take a long-range effort on your part and must be reinforced by sound planning and a genuine concern for employee welfare. The seven suggestions that follow will provide a firm foundation for your efforts:

1. **Talk to employees about cost reduction in terms of their interests.** You must see their point of view, or they'll never be able to see yours. In face-to-face conversations, show them how the company's

interest in profits relates directly to a worker's interest in higher wages and job security. Show that one can't be achieved without the other.

2. **Bring the cost picture down to earth.** Don't talk in global terms. If company sales have fallen off, talk in terms of its impact on the services produced in your department: "We processed 10,000 forms the first quarter, but our schedule calls for only half as many to be handled this quarter." If rising materials charges are a factor, pick up a product your employees make and tell them: "Last year, fabric for this item cost 50 cents; now it costs 60 cents—a rise of 20 percent."

3. **Set specific goals.** Don't say, "We've got to cut costs to the bone." Instead, suggest a specific program: "Our records show that costs must be lowered by 10 percent. We'll have to figure a way to improve our methods to do this." Or say, "Defective production that had to be scrapped cost us $1,200 last month. This month, let's get it down below $1,000."

4. **Invite participation.** Let employees know that you need their help in solving cost problems—and that help means more than passive cooperation. Tell them you *need* their ideas, too, and will welcome any suggestions.

5. **Explain why and how.** Spell out the reasons for each specific change. And remember that employees need your help, too, in deciding how to attain the cost-cutting goals you set.

6. **Train for cost improvement.** One of the key elements in quality circle programs is the training provided to employees in the techniques of problem solving and methods improvement. Try to incorporate these self-development elements into your cost-improvement training activities.

7. **Report cost progress.** Scorekeeping appeals to the achievement needs of many employees. Reports of progress toward cost goals (posted on bulletin boards, for example) stimulate competitiveness and self-motivation.

JOB *TIP!*

Tune in to the Rumor Mill

In today's electronic society, news—and rumor—travels very rapidly. Astute supervisors keep their ears tuned to the rumor mill and respond quickly to lay false rumors to rest. Employees may have heard exaggerated tales of impending cost cutbacks, retrenchments, or downsizings. Gather information, validate it, and share what you can with employees as soon as possible to diminish their fears. Above all, speak the truth to them, for they will judge your integrity through every word you speak, as well as by what happens later.

| 9 | T or F | Most employees are likely to welcome the opportunity to cut costs. |
| 10 | T or F | Good supervisory practices (e.g., goal setting, participation, training, explanations, and progress reporting) can help reduce potential resistance to cost cutting. |

Practical Guidelines for Supervisors

1. Obtain the vision, values, mission statement, and strategies for your employer and *review them regularly* to see where your plans fit in.

2. *Concentrate your planning efforts on the short term* (one week or less), but don't neglect to look into the future as well.

3. *Determine what your employer's essential policies are,* communicate them clearly to your employees, and be consistent, firm, and fair in their application.

4. *Set goals* for your operation that are specific, measurable, attainable, relevant, and time-oriented as well as stretching and motivational.

5. *Develop an array of action plans* that encompass both short- and long-term time perspectives.

6. *Involve employees in the planning process* to obtain the benefits of stronger ownership of the goals and commitment to their success.

7. *Accept the fact that cost control is a large part of your job,* and be prepared to respond to such initiatives with an array of creative approaches.

8. *Prioritize your brainstormed list of cost-cutting strategies* so that there is order and rationality in the steps taken under pressure for improvement.

9. *Learn to see the "big picture"* when making suggestions for cost reductions; remember that top managers look at things differently than you do.

10. *Accept the likelihood of employee resistance to cost-improvement measures;* invite their participation in helping you.

Chapter 3 Review

Key Concepts to Remember

1. Road Maps of an Organization. Planning is the process of systematically working out ahead of time what you and your work unit will do in the future. Good planning reduces needless waste of a department's resources. It is planning that establishes an organization's goals and standards and the policies that guide their attainment. Organizational policies, which are general in nature, are made increasingly specific as they move down the line in the form of rules and regulations. Supervisors are expected to act within the limits of these guidelines. Supervisory planning is mainly concerned with short-term objectives spanning a few days, a week, a month, or—at most—a year.

2. Goal Setting. Goals are usually arranged in a hierarchy. The goals of a supervisor's work unit should support those of the overall organization. The unit's goals should be specific and measurable, output- and time-oriented, and attainable within the limitations of the unit's resources.

3. The Planning Process. The planning process flows from the goals into the development of plans for implementing them. Plans must be supported by details, such as times and dates as well as the anticipated assignment of equipment, facilities, and people. Plans may be long range (more than one year) or short range (anything less than one year). There are standing plans, which cover procedures that remain in effect over a long period of time, and there are single-use plans, which cover operating schedules and budgets. MBO programs add a strong emphasis on employee participation in planning.

4. Cost-Improvement Strategies. Cost improvement efforts can be large scale and long term, or piecemeal and short range. Supervisors usually initiate the latter. The most promising cost targets are close at hand, including the costs of products or services, processing, people, equipment and tools, materials and supplies, utilities, communications, and information. Many cost-reduction programs are negative in nature, featuring several belt-tightening approaches, including stopping or postponing spending and finding an alternative.

5. Cost-Improvement Sources. Ideas for cost improvement come from supervisors, their employees, staff departments, and cost-reduction committees, including quality circles. Positive programs for cost improvement include reducing waste, saving time, increasing output, spending wisely, conserving space, and controlling inventories. Employees often are fearful that cost-reduction programs will bring about unpleasant changes and/or threaten their job security. Supervisors must struggle to modify these fears to obtain employee cooperation and support for cost and productivity improvements. This is accomplished by (among other things) honest, candid, factual communication and by inviting employee participation in solving cost-related problems.

Reading Comprehension

1. How do vision, values, the mission statement, and strategy concern a supervisor?

2. How are plans, goals, and policies related?

3. Why must establishing goals precede developing plans?

4. Identify each of the following as either a standing plan or a single-use plan: a department's monthly budget, a fire-drill procedure, this week's production schedule, the methods prescribed for filling out a purchase order.

5. How are plans and controls related?

6. When would it be wise for a supervisor to check with the boss before carrying out a particular policy?

7. A company's policy manual states, "It is our intention to listen with an open mind to employee complaints." What supplementary information might a supervisor need to better interpret that policy?

8. Compare a belt-tightening cost program with a cost-improvement program.

9. How are cost-reduction committees and quality circles alike? How are they different?

10. Which approach is more likely to stimulate employee cooperation in cost reduction? Why? (a) "Your jobs are threatened now by price-cutting competitors." (b) "You can help protect your jobs from price-cutting competitors if we can find a way to reduce our department's scrap percentage from 5 to 2 percent per month."

Application

Self-Assessment

How Good Are Your Planning Skills?

Read the following statements carefully. Circle the number on the response scale that most closely reflects the degree to which each statement describes you. Add up your total points and prepare a brief action plan for self-improvement. Be ready to report your score for tabulation across the entire group.

	Good Description									Poor Description
1. I can read the organization's vision, values, mission, and strategy and see how my department fits into that picture.	10	9	8	7	6	5	4	3	2	1
2. I know, and could explain to an employee, the difference between a policy, a procedure, and a regulation.	10	9	8	7	6	5	4	3	2	1
3. Once my plans are in place, I recognize the need for an associated set of controls.	10	9	8	7	6	5	4	3	2	1
4. I am familiar with the nature of policies and know when I could change them.	10	9	8	7	6	5	4	3	2	1
5. I could construct goals for my department that incorporate the suggested guidelines.	10	9	8	7	6	5	4	3	2	1

	Good Description	Poor Description

6. I can differentiate between standing and single-use plans. 10 9 8 7 6 5 4 3 2 1

7. I am effective at answering the six "W" questions in planning (what, why, where, when, how, and who). 10 9 8 7 6 5 4 3 2 1

8. I recognize that employees may resist my cost-cutting efforts, and I search for ways to reduce their resistance. 10 9 8 7 6 5 4 3 2 1

9. I actively seek to reduce costs through both direct (e.g., wise spending) and indirect (e.g., space-saving) methods. 10 9 8 7 6 5 4 3 2 1

10. I view cost control as resting on a "three-legged stool," with inputs from myself, my employees, and staff departments. 10 9 8 7 6 5 4 3 2 1

Scoring and Interpretation

Scoring

Add up your total points for the 10 questions. Record that number here, and report it when it is requested. _____

Also, insert your score on the Personal Development Plan in the Appendix.

Interpretation

81 to 100 points. You seem to have a basic set of planning skills.

61 to 80 points. Take a close look at some of your planning skills (those with lower self-assessments) and discuss them with a manager to see if they need improvement.

Below 60 points. Some of your planning skills may be substantially inconsistent with effective planning practices and could be detrimental to your success as a supervisor.

Identify your three lowest scores and record the question numbers here: _____, _____, _____.

Action

Write a brief paragraph detailing an action plan for how you might sharpen each of these skills. Pay particularly close attention to the related material in the chapter as you review the relevant sections there.

Skill Development

Goal Setting

Step 1: Pair up with another person. Working independently, each of you should develop (write out) a set of personal goals and associated action plans for the next year. Then exchange them with each other.

Step 2: Assess the degree (grade the product on A to F scales) to which your partner incorporated the following guidelines from the chapter regarding effective goals and plans.

Step 3: Share your evaluation of your partner's goals with him or her, and offer your feedback.

Step 4: Encourage your partner to revise his or her goals. Revise your goals on the basis of feedback from your partner. Discuss what you have learned from this exercise.

Grade	Incorporation of Chapter Principles
_____	Goals are based on an assessment of strengths and weaknesses.
_____	Goals fit into some larger system (e.g., one's family).
_____	Person consulted with others who are affected or can help.
_____	Goals are relevant and reasonable.
_____	Goals are arrayed in a hierarchy of importance.
_____	Goals clearly focus on output.
_____	The outcomes of the goals are measurable.
_____	Goals are targeted toward a specific time for completion.
_____	Goals appear to be achievable.
_____	Goals are specific and explicit.

Role Play

Responding to a Rumor

Triple-A Window Cleaning Service has been in operation for 20 years. It gradually grew in size, as more and more organizations became aware of the need for its service and its reputation for doing a good job at a reasonable price. Recently, however, a competitor sprang up—College Students Cleaning Windows—and the price for its services is about 15 percent less than that of Triple-A. A rumor has spread among Triple-A employees of cutbacks in its workforce unless drastic cost reductions are achieved. A meeting has been called by the owner of Triple-A to discuss the current cost situation and search for cost-reduction ideas. Divide into groups of five; each person should take one of the five roles shown below. All participants should read only their own roles before the meeting.

Justin (Triple-A's Owner). You are very concerned about the potential impact of the new competitor and fear that a significant loss of revenue will occur through loss of contracts unless you are able to initiate cost reductions of about 15 percent or make other operating improvements that justify your higher prices. You have called a meeting of your employees and are about to present the topic to them now. Prepare a mental plan for how you will conduct this meeting.

Abby. You are the newest and youngest employee of Triple-A, and therefore are worried about your future with the company. However, you are also attending college on a part-time basis, and have been thinking about applying for a job with a new company—College Students Cleaning Windows. If things really get bad here, you could always "jump ship" and switch companies.

Benito. You have the most seniority at Triple-A and therefore are not too concerned about the rumor of a cost-reduction program. As far as you are concerned, Justin (the owner) can go ahead and lay off a few of the newer employees; all they ever do is loaf and talk about the parties they have every night anyway!

Candy. You have recently read some material on the idea of "continuous improvement," and are intrigued by the possibility of finding ways to put it to work at Triple-A. You hope all the other employees will go along with your suggestions; this could be a fun experiment to liven up the workplace and make it more efficient, too!

Darren. You have read about cost-reduction programs at other organizations and are convinced that they always result in work speed-ups, job loss, insecurity for employees, and a negative work atmosphere. You are inclined to resist any cost-reduction program with all your energies.

Cases for Analysis

Case 8

The Disorganized Shipping Dock

Jackie J. is in charge of the shipping dock at the Black & White Dairy Products plant. Every day, she oversees the shipment of hundreds of pallet loads of milk-filled cartons, thousands of cases of ice cream and cottage cheese, and hundreds upon hundreds of boxes of butter packages. The daily routines in the shipping department run like this: The night before, Jackie is notified by a computerized dispatch order of the products to be shipped the next day. At that time, she is also given a tentative loading schedule for the 25 company-owned trucks and another for the 10 or more trucks that are expected from distributors and large grocery chains.

The following morning, Jackie directs her crews to begin removing the products scheduled to be shipped from where they have been stored in chilled "holding rooms." Using specially designed fork-trucks, her crews bring these products by pallet loads to a chilled and sheltered shipping apron. Such deliveries must follow a carefully planned sequence so that these perishable products will be exposed to blasts of outdoor temperatures for the least possible amount of time. If all goes right, the products arrive at the apron at the same time a truck backs in for that particular load. If the timing is wrong, considerable spoilage of goods can take place as they wait for the proper truck or are shunted aside to give priority to the next truck arriving.

To handle this complex schedule, Jackie supervises a crew of 15 employees: 10 fork-truck drivers; 3 "rovers," who perform a variety of labor-grade duties such as handling small or split loads by hand truck and cleaning up spills from broken cartons and leakage from milk containers; and 2 dispatchers, who coordinate the arrival of empty trucks and direct and verify their loading.

Lately, however, Jackie's department has not been running smoothly. For instance, there has been an unusual amount of breakage and spoilage on the dock. Jackie's boss made critical mention of this when the monthly spoilage report was issued. Then, too, hardly a day has gone by when there haven't been three or more trucks backed up waiting for loads that have not yet been brought up from the holding rooms. Repeatedly, the traffic manager has been on Jackie's back for this. There has also been an occasional misloading of a distributor's truck, which has necessitated either refunds or returns. The sales manager has made unpleasant remarks to Jackie about that.

When things didn't improve, Jackie decided that she had had enough. One Friday afternoon she called her crew together to find out what was going wrong. Here's what she heard:

"You never let us know until the last minute what is to be pulled from the holding rooms," said one fork-truck driver.

"When you issue the requests to bring stuff forward, you don't make it clear who should do it," said another.

"You have never made the load sequences clear to me," said one of the dispatchers.

"As to the trucks backing up," said the other dispatcher, "I thought you were coordinating truck arrivals."

"We could do a lot more to speed up loading if we knew beforehand what the small and split-load orders were," said the rovers.

Analysis

If you were Jackie, which of the following alternatives would you pursue to get things running more smoothly? Rank the alternatives from 1 (most preferable) to 5 (least preferable). You may add another alternative if you wish. Be prepared to justify your rankings.

_____ a. Consider that the majority of the crew's comments are more likely excuses for poor performance than valid suggestions for improvement.

_____ b. Bring the crew's comments to the attention of the traffic manager and the sales manager so that they can improve scheduling of the over-the-road truck drivers and clarity of orders with distributors.

_____ c. Ask the crew's help in preparing a master plan of operation that, over the long haul, will best fit the reality of shipping conditions.

_____ d. Clarify your daily plans so that crews will know the removal schedule in advance and what their particular assignments will be.

_____ e. Draw up and post a detailed shipping schedule each day; then advise the crew that it must be followed to the letter.

Case 9

Cora's Goals

The order-entry department of a large wholesale distributor owes part of its success to the careful planning done by its supervisors. The department's new computer system has caused some problems, but things generally have been running smoothly. Cora, the supervisor, is now establishing objectives for the coming year, and she wants to set reasonable, but measurable, goals for some important indicators of her department's operations.

The order-entry process consists of (a) accepting mailed or telephoned orders; (b) looking up or verifying the stock number, price, and current availability of each item ordered; (c) looking up the customer number; (d) adding the customer number and requesting a credit check if the customer is new; and (e) entering the customer number, items ordered, and quantities (as well as out-of-stock indicators, if applicable) on a computer terminal. The computer then automatically prepares packing lists, shipping labels, and invoices and makes appropriate entries in accounting records.

Analysis

Your assignment is to prepare a list of objectives for Cora and her department. Use Table 3-1 in the text as a model. Supply whatever numbers you think are reasonable and appropriate for the order-entry department. Among the items you should consider are processing time, costs, accuracy, overtime, lateness and absenteeism, employee turnover, and damage to equipment through misuse.

Case 10

The High-Flying Sales Staff

Trina's boss had a real head of steam. "Your department is too much. I've put up with a lot from them, but now they have reached the top of my list."

"That sounds great," said Trina, who supervised over a dozen of the division's best salespeople.

"Don't get funny with me," said her boss. "You know what I'm talking about. The list I had in mind was the company's big spenders. Of all the staffs in my division, yours is absolutely the worst when it comes to expense control. They have become too used to high living, and it's got to stop."

"Wait a minute," said Trina. "You're talking about a dozen of the best outside-sales people a distributor ever had. They bring in top dollar for the company."

"They may be good, but they're not that good," said Trina's boss. "Let me make it perfectly clear. Your department's expenses are way too high. I expect you to get them down to a reasonable level. And soon!"

"Okay," said Trina, "I'll get on it."

To herself, however, she said, "I'm sick and tired of taking the heat for those high-flyers on my staff. None of them give a hoot about what they spend or waste so long as they get the job done. I'll have to sit down with the whole gang of these artful dodgers now and straighten them out."

When Trina did sit down with her staff, here's what she told them:

"The division is throwing one of its cost-cutting tantrums right now, and I'm taking a lot of heat on your behalf. From now on, I want you to get your expenses back in line."

"Back in line with what?" asked one salesperson.

"Don't you worry about where the line is. I'll tell you if you step over it. Here's what I mean:

First of all, your auto expenses are way too high. I'm going to stop paying for your side trips to the seashore.

Second, you have been wasting our costly brochures by dumping them all over the territory as if there were no tomorrow. That's got to stop.

Third, you don't have to take every distributor's counter clerk out to lunch to make a sale. You know that's not necessary.

Fourth—" but she was interrupted.

"What do you want us to do," said another salesperson, "stop selling and sit around the office instead?"

"Kidding aside," said still another salesperson, "how are we to cut down on our expenses and still bring in the sales you expect?"

"That's your problem, not mine," said Trina. "You know what you've got to do. Do it!"

Time passed, and a couple of months later Trina was called into the boss's office. "I thought I told you to get your department's expenses in line," the boss said. "If anything, they are worse than ever."

Analysis

Why do you think that expenses in Trina's department did not fall back into line? What would you recommend that Trina do now?

Chapter Reference

1. Gary P. Latham, "A Five-Step Approach to Behavior Change," *Organizational Dynamics,* 2003, vol. 32, no. 3, pp. 309–318.

ANSWERS TO QUICK TESTS	Quick Test 1	Quick Test 2	Quick Test 3	Quick Test 4	Quick Test 5
	1. F	3. F	5. T	7. F	9. F
	2. T	4. F	6. F	8. T	10. T

Problem Solving and Managing Information

LEARNING OBJECTIVES

After studying this chapter, you should be able to

- Recognize and define a problem or a potential problem.

- List the nine steps in problem solving and decision making that lead to the removal of a problem's cause.

- Discuss the rational and intuitive approaches to decision making and explain cost-benefit analysis, decision trees, and ABC analysis.

- Explain how unethical supervisors rationalize their behavior, and contrast that with a set of guidelines for helping supervisors make ethical decisions.

- Describe a management information system and differentiate between data and information.

- Understand how supervisors can use information systems to implement open-book management.

- Discuss the impact on employees of management information systems and suggest ways to alleviate the stress associated with them.

Problems: Cause and Effect

What, exactly, is a problem?

A problem has several defining characteristics. In general, a problem is (a) an unsettled matter or disturbing condition (b) that raises puzzling questions about its specific nature and (c) demands resolution by decisive action; however, (d) its proper settlement is often clouded by difficulty, uncertainty, and doubt, and—as a consequence—(e) it may require considerable thought and skill to find an effective solution. A simpler and more useful definition, however, is this: A *problem* exists when there is a substantial difference between an expected condition (such as that spelled out by a performance standard or departmental goal) and the actual condition that has occurred or is now occurring. Further, *supervisory problems* usually require making a choice from among multiple options. Given this simpler characterization, studies show that supervisors may solve as many as 80 problems a day. If this figure is only half true, supervisors are called upon to find answers to, or render decisions on, 10,000 problems a year (40×250 days). Thankfully, the great majority of these problems are minor. Nevertheless, the figures are staggering and are of major concern to every supervisor.

As a practical matter, it is helpful to think of problems as falling into two classifications:

Current problems. These are ones that have already been observed or are occurring right now. Examples include merchandise that has spoiled, a valued employee who has quit, costs that are running out of line, and shipments that are not meeting delivery dates. These problems need immediate solutions to correct what has already happened or what is now taking place.

Potential problems. These lie in the near future. Nevertheless, you must be alert to their eventual presence. You will recognize them in such forms as how to finish a certain project on time, when to assign overtime, where to place the new copy machine, and when to tell employees about an impending change in their work schedules. It is important to identify such potential problems in advance. Then you can apply "preventive" problem solving to them.

Problems, and their solutions, are, of course, inseparably related to the management process. Problems arise all along the way. Supervisors must solve them when they plan, organize, staff, lead, and control. Otherwise, problems will interfere with the attainment of the department's goals.

Problems are often brought about by change.
How should supervisors deal with problems?

What causes a problem?

Change does. If everything operates exactly as it should, and the situation remains as it has been, very few problems will occur. Unfortunately, change, especially unwanted change, is always with us—and increasingly so in the 21st century. Changes occur in materials, technology and equipment, employee attitudes, specifications received from customers, the work space itself, and just about anything else you can imagine. The trick to **problem solving** is often the ability to spot the unwanted and unexpected change that has slipped into an otherwise normal situation.

Problem solving. A process of systematically analyzing gaps between expected and actual conditions to find and remedy their causes.

How can you recognize a problem or a potential problem?

A problem exists when there is a gap (or variance) between what you expect to happen and what actually happens (see Figure 4-1). Your budget, for example, calls for 2,200 insurance policies to be processed this week; the count at 4 P.M. on Friday shows that you completed only 1,975, a gap of 225 policies. Or you expected to hold the total number of employee absences in your department to 300 days this year; the total is 410, a gap of 110 days.

It is almost the same with potential problems. You know what you would like to have occur in the future: a project completed, a perfect safety record, fewer than 10 customer complaints. These are your plans. But when you look ahead at your procedures and the potential for mishaps, you think that your department will fall short of its targets—that

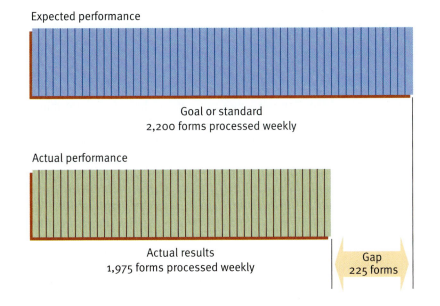

Expected performance

Goal or standard
2,200 forms processed weekly

Actual performance

Actual results
1,975 forms processed weekly

Gap
225 forms

Gap = a problem to be solved

FIGURE 4-1
How gaps between actual performance and goals, or standards, help to identify problems.
What causes gaps to occur?

there will be gaps. In a nutshell, you find problems by spotting a gap (deviation or variance) between actual and expected performance.

| 1 | T or F | A problem exists when there is a gap between what you expect to happen and what is predicted to happen. |
| 2 | T or F | Current problems require corrective action; potential problems require preventive action. |

2 Systematic Problem Solving

CONCEPT
Problems should be approached systematically, with the goal of removing their causes.

How are problems solved?

By removing whatever it is that has caused, or will cause, a gap between the expected (or desired) condition and the actual condition. That's the main idea, at least. Suppose, for example, that your hoped-for safety record of zero accidents is spoiled by three accidents in one week. You will want to (a) find their cause and (b) remove it.

Identifying and removing the cause or causes, however, is usually difficult and requires considerable examination and thought. There will be more discussion about the problem-solving process later.

What is the connection between problem solving and decision making?

Decision making. The part of the problem-solving process in which alternatives are evaluated and a choice is made.

The two processes are closely related (see Figure 4-2). A decision is always needed in the choice of the problem's solution. In many ways, problem solving involves ***decision making***. As you will see in a moment, any step along the way—planning, organizing, staffing, leading, controlling, and problem solving—that presents a choice of more than one course of action requires also that a decision be made. Take the safety record of three accidents again. A truly complete analysis of the problem might have suggested that the cause could be removed in three different ways. The supervisor, as decision maker, would have to choose among the three alternatives. One option might be judged too costly, the second not completely effective, and the third the best choice because it is relatively inexpensive *and* foolproof.

Should you approach problem solving systematically?

Yes. There are few exceptions to the rule that the best results come from a systematic approach. By moving from step to step progressively, you

1. State the problem clearly.	2. Collect relevant information.	3. List possible causes.	4. Select the most likely cause.	5. Suggest alternative solutions.	6. Evaluate alternatives.	7. Choose one solution.	8. Plan for implementation.	9. Implement and follow up.

Problem finding   Decision making

Problem solving

avoid the cardinal mistake in problem solving: jumping to a conclusion before you have fully explored all aspects of the problem. Here, as illustrated in Figure 4-2, is the fundamental approach to problem solving and decision making.

Step 1: State the problem clearly and specifically. Stay away from a general statement such as "We have a problem with quality." Instead, narrow it down and put figures on it if you can, as in "Between the first of the month and today, the number of rejects found at final inspection totaled 32, compared with our standard of 15 rejects."

Step 2: Collect all information relevant to the problem. Don't go too far afield, but do find data that may shed light on process changes, materials used, equipment function, design specifications, employee performance, and assignments. Much of the data will not tell you anything except where the source of the problem is not. If your information shows, for example, that there has been no change in the way materials have arrived or machinery has been used, good! You can then look elsewhere.

Step 3: List as many possible causes for the problem as you can. Remember that a problem is a gap between expected and actual conditions. Something must have occurred to cause that gap. Most particularly, something must have been changed. Is the present employee different from the former one? Was a power source less regular than before? Has there been a change, however slight, in the required procedure?

Step 4: Select the cause or causes that seem most likely. Do this through a process of elimination. To test a cause to see if it is a probable one, try seeing (or thinking through) what difference it would make if that factor were returned to its original state. For example, suppose a possible cause of rejects is that compressed air power is now only 75 pounds instead of 90 pounds. Try making the product with the pressure restored to 90 pounds. If it makes no difference, power irregularity is not a likely cause. Or perhaps you think that the new operator has

FIGURE 4-2

The problem-solving process. How problem solving and decision making overlap. **Why is using a systematic approach so important?**

Quips & Quotes

You're either part of the solution or part of the problem.

Eldridge Cleaver

misunderstood your instructions. Check this out with the operator. See if your instructions are, in fact, being followed exactly. If not, what happens when your instructions are followed? If the rejects stop, this is a likely cause. If the rejects persist, this is not a likely cause.

Step 5: Suggest as many solutions as you can to remove causes or overcome obstacles. There is rarely only one way to solve a problem. If the cause of an employee's absenteeism, for instance, is difficulty in getting up in the morning, this cause can be removed in a number of ways. You might change the shift, insist that the employee buy another alarm clock, make a wake-up telephone call yourself, or show how failure to get to work is job threatening. The point is to list as many "cause removal" suggestions as possible.

Some causes, of course, cannot be removed, as when the problem arises from an edict for change (such as "cut costs by 5 percent") received from above. If so, it is helpful at steps 3 and 4 to identify "obstacles to be removed" if the problem is to be solved. Then, at this step, look for ways to overcome the most difficult obstacles.

Step 6: Evaluate the pros and cons of each proposed solution. Some solutions will be better than others. But what does better mean? Cheaper? Faster? Surer? More participative? More in line with company policy? To judge which solution is best, you'll have to have a set of criteria like the ones just listed. Evaluation requires that you base judgments on facts. Consult the information gathered in step 2. Also, consult anyone who can offer an informed opinion about the criteria you have chosen.

Step 7: Choose the solution (or combination of solutions) you think is best. Yes, this—like what you did in step 6—is the decision phase of problem solving. In effect, you have weighed all the chances of success against the risks of failure. The strengths and benefits of your solution should exceed its weaknesses and costs.

Step 8: Spell out a plan of action to carry out your solution.
Decisions require action, and so you should indicate how to implement the solution. Pin down exactly what will be done and how, who will do it, where, and when. How much money can be spent? What resources can be used? What is the deadline?

Step 9: Implement the solution, and follow up. Decisions, by themselves, are quite passive unless they are put into action. Follow the steps specified in the solution, and then monitor the results to see if the problem initially identified has been eased to your satisfaction. Without taking this critical step, you will never be able to improve your problem-solving skills!

When should you solve problems on your own, and when should you go to others for help?

This depends on a number of factors. Table 4-1 shows how to look at the whole picture before deciding to handle a problem on your own

TABLE 4-1   Guide for Seeking Help in Problem Solving and Decision Making

Factors	1. You Decide Alone	2. You Consult with One of Your Employees	3. You Consult with a Group of Your Employees
Whose problem is it?	Yours alone	His or hers	The group's (ours)
Amount of time	None available	Have some time available	Plenty of time available
Expertise	You are fully expert	Expert advice is needed to fill gaps in your own knowledge	Yes, as for no. 2
Can others add anything to the decision?	No	Yes	Yes
Will you accept suggestions?	No, not likely	Yes, from someone you respect	Yes, from an effective unit
Will it help others to carry out the project if they are involved in the decision?	No significance; you will carry out the project yourself	Yes, helpful and essential	Yes, necessary and essential
Coordination of effort	Not needed; you will handle it all	Necessary with your superior or your employee	Needed and necessary among your employees
Learning value	No value to anyone else	Potential value to the employee	Potential value to your whole group

or to ask another person or a group of employees for assistance. Evaluate each of the eight factors before choosing one of the three approaches.

Where does ethics fit into the process of decision making?

It is almost a certainty that all supervisors will be faced with issues related to ethics at some time in their careers. The pressures to deviate from one's moral standards can be enormous, and they can come from superiors, peers, employees, or even one's own family. **Business ethics** is the capacity to recognize moral issues in the workplace, examine the situation objectively, apply relevant moral principles, and make fair decisions that will stand up to examination by others. Therefore, ethics goes beyond following the law; it concerns addressing right and wrong actions and protecting the dignity and rights of individuals both inside and outside the organization.

When some managers and executives get caught doing unethical things, they rationalize their behavior by pointing to factors beyond their control. (One famous comedian always used the line "The devil made me do it!") Guilty parties often contend that their behavior was necessary, not *totally* illegal, or just "part of the job." Sometimes they claim that no one was harmed by their actions, or the organization owed it to them, or they really didn't benefit personally. These excuses are generally invalid, without substance, and useless as legitimate defenses of their character.

Ethical supervisors, when faced with ethical dilemmas or even anticipating such issues, ask themselves many tough questions before coming to a conclusion: Who will gain? Should they? Who might be harmed? How can that be avoided? Which approach does the most good for the most people? Which approach is most defensible from a values perspective? What is right and fair? Which decision will stand up to public scrutiny? They also consult other peers and managers whom they trust to seek their input and perspectives. If they have done these things before making a decision, they can live with themselves, face their families with pride, and sleep well at night.

Business ethics. Having a set of moral values that one consciously develops, examines, and applies to business issues to produce fair decisions.

Quips & Quotes

Given the pressures of managerial life, therefore, ethics is easily pushed off the agenda.

Michael R. Rion

Internet connection

www.josephsoninstitute.org/MED/MED-5rationalizations.htm
Rationales for unethical actions. This site provides numerous arguments commonly given for engaging in unethical behaviors.

QUICK TEST 2	3	T or F	Problem solving is one part of the larger decision-making process.
	4	T or F	The first step in problem solving is to collect all relevant information.

Decision Making: Rational and Intuitive

How can you recognize the need for a decision?

Whenever there is more than one way of doing things, a decision is needed. Any kind of choice, alternative, or option calls for a decision. You might ask, "If this is so, why are so many decision opportunities overlooked?" The answer is that managers and supervisors alike get overly comfortable with the status quo, and even fixated on it. In effect, they say, "If it ain't broke, don't fix it." Such supervisors miss the point that there are always alternatives. There is always the choice to do something or not to do it, to speak or to remain silent, to correct or to let well enough alone, to improve a situation or to stick with the status quo. All too often a supervisor's decision is made by default. The supervisor does nothing because it is more comfortable that way. The tide of events carries the department until a crisis occurs. In reality, however, doing nothing represents a choice. It is a decision *not* to change, *not* to plan for improvement, *not* to anticipate a potential problem.

How systematic must the decision-making process be?

Most decisions should be approached systematically, but only up to a point, unlike the purely problem-solving steps. A systematic approach to decision making (often called the rational or logical approach) should be followed through step 6 (evaluating the pros and cons of each proposed solution) and well into step 7 (choosing the solution you think best). At that point, it may help to give some weight to your intuition before making the final choice. Decisions that affect the future, even if the future is only tomorrow, always contain a degree of uncertainty that logic cannot fully remove. In view of the limits of logic, many authorities believe that at this point you can often draw valuable insights from the part of your brain from which hunches, premonitions, unconscious thoughts, and creative ideas emerge. Intuition can also be useful at step 5, where you are trying to generate the maximum number of possible solutions.

Are decisions based on intuition as good as those based on logic?

If a decision works out well, it won't make any difference how it was reached. Many decisions based on hunches have proved to be correct.

Creativity. The generation of new solutions to existing problems by using techniques to encourage "out of the box" thinking.

They are harder to explain and defend, however, when they go wrong. More important, any decision is likely to be better if its goals are clearly understood. The logical approach helps strip away distractions and irrelevancies as well as minimize dangerous biases and prejudices (see Ethical Perspectives). Intuition often adds a valuable dimension by calling on an inner sense we don't clearly understand. Many authorities believe the best decisions come from the dual approach—a combination of logic and hunch, supplemented by creativity.

What is the importance of creativity in decision making?

In a nutshell, it is very important. Yesterday's solutions are often inadequate for today's unforeseen problems. Supervisors—and their staff of employees—must train their minds to "think out of the box." This involves looking at their situation from a unique perspective and then making connections that are not normally made by others. The resulting answers could be new combinations of previous approaches, or totally unexpected innovations. Effective creativity is a lot like the inquiry-based approach that forms a basis for this text—you ask questions, engage in critical thinking, keep your mind open to new ideas, and explore balanced arguments in a collaborative setting.

The key to *creativity* is to begin by asking what you hope to achieve (the new end result). The next stage involves mentally breaking out of old ways of thinking and acting—often by forcing yourself to use unique metaphors (e.g., an animal, a vegetable, or an athletic event) to stimulate new ideas. Once the creative ideas are out in the open, the normal analytical process can kick in. Examine the advantages of each idea, but also address the obstacles to implementing it. Finally, put one or more new approaches into practice. With practice and self-discipline, creativity becomes a useful habit.

What is meant by mathematical decision making?

Mathematical decision making refers to the use of certain mathematical, statistical, or quantitative techniques to aid the decision maker. These aids are very valuable in many instances, but they are only aids. The techniques do not make decisions. They arrange numerical information in such a way that it can be analyzed mathematically, but the executive, manager, or supervisor must make the final decision on the basis of an interpretation of the results. Further, the benefits of mathematical analyses are very dependent on the quality and relevance of the inputs received ("garbage in; garbage out").

How can supervisors make use of decision trees?

A *decision tree* is essentially a graphic portrait of steps 5 and 6 in the problem-solving process. It shows how each alternative solution forks into various possibilities. Suppose, for example, a supervisor is faced with a decision about how to treat Eduardo, an employee whose attendance has been very poor. One alternative (A_1) is to enforce strict discipline by laying Eduardo off for three days. A second alternative (A_2) is to provide constructive encouragement. A third alternative (A_3) is to try a little of both. Figure 4-3 shows how these alternatives work on a decision tree.

The supervisor can presume that there are only three ways Eduardo can react. He may respond only to strict discipline, he may respond only to encouragement, or he may respond favorably to both. The probable changes in performance from each kind of response are diagrammed, with outcomes

Decision tree. A graphic portrait of the possible outcomes of alternative solutions.

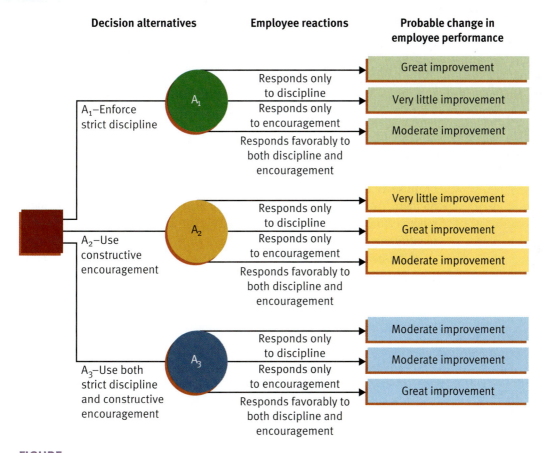

FIGURE 4-3

Example of a decision tree. Alternative outcomes of various applications of discipline versus constructive encouragement in trying to improve an employee's performance.

Does a decision tree replace or supplement the problem-solving process?

ranging from very little improvement to great improvement. Thus, the improvement in Eduardo's performance differs according to each decision strategy and each possibility of how Eduardo might respond to it.

Eduardo may react three different ways to the A_1 alternative. If he responds to discipline, there may be great improvement; if he responds only to encouragement, then there will be very little improvement. Or, if he responds favorably to both discipline and encouragement, there may be moderate improvement. Similarly, Eduardo may react three different ways to alternatives A_2 and A_3. The decision tree helps the supervisor visualize the various outcomes or possible changes in Eduardo's performance. On the basis of such an analysis, you may be better able to choose the alternative that has the best chance of being effective.

Even if you never construct a decision tree on your own, keep the concept in mind. It will add another dimension to how you think about alternative paths to choose from and their consequences.

What is meant by cost-benefit analysis?

It is not unlike the closing steps in problem solving and decision making. This is the phase in which you examine the pros and cons of each proposed solution. ***Cost-benefit analysis*** adds all the costs (both quantitative and qualitative, direct and indirect) of implementation and compares them with the projected value of the resulting product or services. This type of analysis has become a popular technique for evaluating proposals in the public sector. Take, for example, a proposal for a local government to offer a child care service to its residents. Typically, the benefits of such nonprofit services are hard to quantify; that is, it is hard to place a dollar value on them. Accordingly, many cost-benefit analyses include qualitative judgments of benefits as well as dollar estimates. These analyses also need to identify any *unintended* consequences of proposed solutions.

Cost-benefit analysis is similar to *input-output analysis*, which is an attempt to make sure that the cost and effort expended in carrying out a decision will at least be balanced by its outputs, or results. In business, when outputs exceed inputs, the result is a profit. If there is an excess of benefits over costs in nonprofit organizations, the excess is called a *surplus.*

Cost-benefit analysis. A technique for weighing the pros and cons of alternative courses of action.

What is a *programmed decision*?

Decisions that are spelled out in advance by a standard procedure or policy are said to be "programmed." That is, a supervisor has only to identify the problem correctly as one that has arisen before. There's no point in solving it a second time unless conditions have changed or new options are available. As a consequence, the supervisor simply applies the previous solution or the decision that is dictated by standard procedures and policies. By avoiding the necessity of having to "reinvent the wheel" each time the same problem comes up, a supervisor saves time and energy.

Programmed decision. A solution to a recurring problem that can be established for continual use every time the problem reappears.

Some problems occur so frequently that you can set up a routine decision for them. You must remember, however, that what worked before may not work again. It can be risky to follow past experience blindly without considering other possible solutions.

When should you engage in group decision making?

Only when *all* these factors are in play:

- The work group can contribute information, know-how, and viewpoints that you need but don't have.
- You are truly ready to respect their opinions and prepared to act on their suggestions.
- You sense that such participation is needed to induce a commitment from the group to implement the decision.
- You've got adequate time.

Seeking help from a work team in making a decision involves the same considerations that were charted in Table 4-1 for problem solving. In any event, be forewarned that such a consultative approach should not be taken lightly. Employees who participate will be resentful if they sense that they are being manipulated. Their involvement in the process, while not necessarily at an equal level of authority with yours, must be absolutely genuine. Otherwise, the process will backfire and you will be worse off than you would be if you hadn't gotten them involved.

What can be done to make your decisions more effective?

Besides starting with a specific goal in mind and laying a foundation of facts and systematic analysis, there are two other kinds of insurance to which you can turn.

Pick your spots. Try to make decisions only where the potential for a payoff is great. You can identify this kind of opportunity by using ABC analysis (see Figure 4-4). The ABC analysis concept is based on an established economic fact: A vital few problems or opportunities for action account for the greatest loss or greatest gain. Most problems and opportunities are basically of little consequence. Statisticians call this the *80/20 principle*. It means that 80 percent of your problems will account for only 20 percent of your losses or profits. Conversely, 20 percent of your problems (the vital few) will account for 80 percent of your losses or profits. In ABC analysis, the vital few are called A items; the inconsequential many, C items; and those that fall somewhere in between, B items. If you were to examine all the items in your inventory, for example, it is a sure bet that a relatively few items would account for most of its value. A great many items, however, such as paper clips and erasers, would account for

Thoughts*to*ponder

Edward de Bono suggests that supervisors often get complacent about their thinking and problem-solving capacities, and fall into dangerous but avoidable ruts. They need to view the process as a deliberate skill that can be learned, and one that best uses a variety of approaches. He suggests that decision makers learn to wear any of six "hats" (roles) and shift between them as the need arises. Each of the six hats focuses attention on something different: facts and figures, feelings and emotions, errors in thinking, positive outcomes, a search for alternatives and their consequences, or subject definition and control.

Source: Edward de Bono, *Six Thinking Hats*. New York: Little, Brown and Co., 1999.

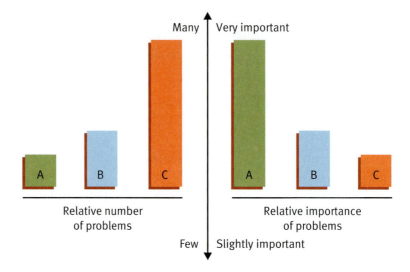

only a small portion of the inventory's total worth. Astute purchasing managers concentrate on the vital few items, not the trivial many. You should apply the same principles to your selection of problems and decisions to address.

Maintain your perspective. Statistically, problems fall in what is called a *normal distribution*, and so do the results of most decisions. We say, "You win some and you lose some." That's really what a normal distribution tells us. If you make 10 decisions, one or two will work out fine. One or two are likely to be "bombs." The rest will fall somewhere in between. Knowing this, you should keep the three guidelines on page 95 in mind when you make decisions. They will help you improve your "batting average."

JOB TIP!

Playing the Role

The next time you are participating in a group problem-solving meeting, make an explicit effort to play each of the following roles (as they seem appropriate). There are two keys to success: (1) being aware of *when* they are needed, and (2) having the *flexibility and willingness* to apply them. The six roles are

1. Data-gatherer—Solicit information, ideas, and opinions from others

2. Rational person—Provide key facts and relevant information

3. Emotion-injector—Express the depth and breadth of feelings on an issue

4. Uplifter—Offer your assessment of the benefits and advantages

5. Devil's advocate—Identify the costs, drawbacks, and disadvantages

6. Evaluator—Place everything in perspective, considering all inputs

The likely result will be wider respect for your contributions as well as better decisions from the group, and that is a win-win product!

1. Don't reach too high. Don't set your objectives at the very top; allow some room for mistakes.
2. Don't overcommit or overextend your resources on one problem; you may need them later for an unanticipated problem.
3. Always prepare a backup approach (often called plan B), a way to alter your course and attain at least part of the objective.

| 5 | T or F | A decision tree is a graphic portrait of the nine steps in the problem-solving process. |
| 6 | T or F | Unless the costs (inputs) exceed the benefits (outputs), there is little reason to proceed with a proposed solution. |

QUICK TEST 3

Information as a Raw Material

How long should a supervisor seek information to solve a problem or make a decision?

CONCEPT
Management information systems provide the basis for solving problems and making decisions.

Stop looking when the trouble and cost of obtaining the extra information exceeds its value. The rule is: The more critical and lasting the effect of the decision, the more you can afford to look for additional vital information. Don't spend two days hunting for background data on a purchasing decision, for example, if the item plays an insignificant part in your process and will be used only once or twice. However, it might pay to defer a decision to hire a full-time employee until you have made a reference check.

Do guard against using the absence of information as an excuse for procrastination. Some decisions are especially hard to arrive at and unpleasant to carry out. When you are faced with these situations, there is a temptation to procrastinate, and rarely does additional time or information add much to the quality of the decision. Therefore, *practice being decisive.*

Computers make it possible for organizations to develop enormous data banks.
How do managers at all levels use data banks?

The burden of information collection and analysis has become so enormous, however, that most organizations provide support with some form of management information system.

What is a management information system? Why has it become so important?

You may better understand a *management information system (MIS)* if you compare it to an accounting system. Like the traditional accounting system, it collects data from an organization's operations, sorts it out, analyzes it, and delivers consolidated reports to a manager for use in planning and control, problem solving, and decision making. The two systems, however, differ enormously in terms of the amount of data accumulated and the speed and complexity of the analytical process. A modern MIS is a network of computer-based procedures that provide timely and useful information for managers in carrying out their work.

The ultimate objective of an MIS is to tie together all of an organization's past and present data into a very large library with instant electronic recall. Managers at all levels draw from this library (called a *data bank*) any kind of information that aids short-range or long-term decisions. The goal is to create a fully integrated MIS system.

Should a distinction be made between data and information?

It may seem like hairsplitting, but MIS designers insist there are good reasons to distinguish between them.

Data can be described as merely facts and figures that, until processed, contribute little to decision making.

Information is data that has been processed for specific use by managers and supervisors in problem solving and decision making related to planning, organizing, staffing, leading, and controlling.

Where do supervisors fit into the MIS computer picture?

Supervisors become involved in computer operations in two basic ways:

1. You may simply be an *end user* of the MIS. If so, make the most of these outputs. Understand what they mean, what you are supposed to derive from them, and what kind of actions you are supposed to take on the basis of them. Should you make a correction today? Or can you wait until the next report before you get moving?

2. You may be a *prime source* of inputs. If so, find out specifically what information your department is sending to the computer.

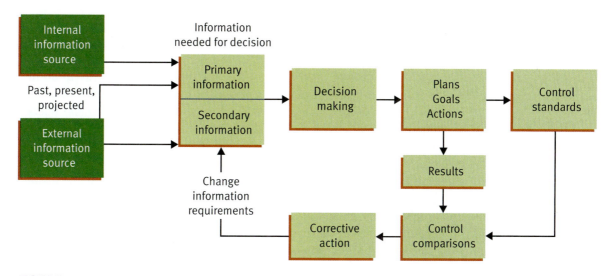

FIGURE 4-5

Basic components of a management information system.
What is the difference between primary and secondary data?

Exactly what form should data be in when they leave your department? Are the measures your employees are collecting exactly the same as those required for the computer?

Can supervisors supplement their management information systems with additional data?

Yes. Even if their parent organizations have an MIS, supervisors can and should develop their own concept of how information needed for decisions is gathered and routed to them. Figure 4-5 shows a basic management information system. *Primary data* is new information that is collected and analyzed for the specific purpose of running a particular operation. *Secondary data* is any useful information previously collected for another purpose and published by trade associations, business magazines, the U.S. government, or any other source outside the department.

Secondary data for your department may simply be the data you can gather from other departments in your own company, agency, or institution. However, since these data are uniquely tailored to your needs and interests, they provide a vital supplement to the information available from the MIS. Any information you can gather that is useful and cost-effective can potentially give you an edge over your competitors.

To make the MIS work, the supervisor could request the following: daily output figures from the shop clerk; weekly labor costs gathered from the time cards, processed by the payroll section, and recorded by the accounting department; and the weekly defects rate from the quality control department.

Should employees have access to information from the MIS?

Yes! According to author John Case and others, the best way to do this is through a program called ***open-book management***. Many companies are sharing a wide range of financial (e.g., sales, expenses) and operating (e.g., productivity data, absenteeism rates) information with employees. Along with "opening the books," they also train their workers to understand and use the data, emphasize how each employee's work can influence the financial results, empower employees to make decisions leading to improvements, post the key results conspicuously, and hold celebrations when milestones are achieved. Many organizations then provide bonus rewards to those employees whose actions have led to success and allow others to participate in the gain via stock ownership programs. Clearly, MIS systems have made open-book management possible.

QUICK TEST 4			
	7	T or F	Supervisors have a role to play in MIS systems as both sources and end users of inputs.
	8	T or F	For open-book management to work well, employees need to be trained in how to use the information wisely.

5   Keeping the System Human

How do management information systems affect people at work?

Computer-generated information has its good aspects and its unfavorable ones. Even these aspects draw conflicting responses. For example, consider these views:

1. **Systematic information and reports reduce job tensions and conflicts by making things more orderly.** There will always be conflict among people, jobs, and operations. The computer should lessen the intensity of conflict, however, because the interfaces will be fixed and predictable. Once an information issue is resolved between the production and the maintenance supervisors, it should be less bothersome, because it will arise in the same manner each time and can be anticipated.

2. **Systematization creates job dissatisfaction because it requires that individuals fit their work into a rigidly prescribed format.** Employees who dislike close supervision and control will feel the same way about any system that makes similar demands. Supervisors must do a better job than in the past of placing people in work that best suits their concept of job satisfaction.

3. **Systematization tends to make work monotonous because it reduces the opportunity to be creative.** If the job is one that is fully dominated by the system, this will be true. People who prefer routine to initiative may like it, however. For many jobs, the computer has just the opposite effect. It removes the routine and calls out for creative solutions to the problems it identifies.

4. **Systematization depersonalizes work; people serve the technology more than the technology serves people.** This is sometimes true at lower levels of employment. At skilled and managerial levels, however, the system takes over much of the tiresome work and allows people to devote a greater proportion of their efforts to work that matches their education, experience, and capabilities.

What can be done to make employees more receptive to MIS and to computers in general?

Management information systems and other applications of computer technology are with all of us to stay. Happily, employees coming out of high schools and colleges today are much more familiar with it than are those of previous generations. Nevertheless, there are several positive approaches that you as a supervisor should take.

Internet connection

www.personal.vineyard.net/dwright/luddite.html
Luddites—then and now. Check out the history of workers' fears of technology and how they still exist today.

1. **Try to reduce tension by allowing employees to bring their irritations into the open.** Tempers are likely to flare highest when a new system is being debugged. Suppose Helen says, "Nothing matters anymore except getting the data to the electronic monster on time." Try responding like this: "I agree that the computer now seems to be dominating our work in the department. Perhaps it won't be that way once we get used to it. After all, look how we adjust ourselves to the exact time for a TV show or a sports event. Let's stick with it and see if we can get the better of this situation."

2. **Acknowledge that it is only normal to be fearful of what the computer may do to jobs and job security.** Suppose Trang says, "When they introduced an MIS in another division of the company, six people in the payroll section were transferred to the sales order department, and not one of them likes it over there. What's going to happen when these MIS analysts finish up with us next

month?" Don't dismiss Trang's fear as something silly. Instead, agree that information systems have made changes in the company. And, yes, some of these changes have been hard to accept. But assure Trang that you will do whatever you can to make certain that higher management is aware of her present contributions. You will also look around to see where and how her talents can best be used if there is a change in her job.

3. **Focus your attention on trying to make sure people are assigned to the work they do best and like best.** Abe, Hillary, and Malcolm like routine work so that they can socialize to the maximum; assign them repetitive work that is less demanding mentally. Ella, Donna, and Vortek have strong creative qualities; assign them work that requires initiative. All six persons may have to work in a computer-oriented world, but usually enough different kinds of work are available to satisfy individual preferences. People and job matches won't be perfect, of course. But when supervisors show they are willing to make the effort, this act in itself helps counteract anxieties about computers depersonalizing the work.

4. **Help your employees see the benefits of MIS.** One of the greatest potential advantages is the creation of a *learning organization*. Here, organizations use their computer systems to catalog, systematically sort, and make available a wide range of evolving expertise and knowledge to other employees. As one person learns or creates something, the new knowledge is entered into an MIS, where it is instantly available to help others in the company. Cooperative learning takes place, and co-workers across the country are able to gain and apply new techniques almost instantly. Learning organizations have spawned the need for systematic *knowledge management* programs, where companies seek to gain a competitive edge by identifying what they don't know, need to know, and already know. In this way, employees with a question can benefit by using the MIS to search out others with valuable expertise. Additionally, as employees upgrade their skills, they receive the psychic benefit of being consulted (and praised!) by others throughout the organization. Supervisors need to train their employees to use the knowledge management system for the benefit of themselves and others.

Learning organization. A company in which new ways of thinking are nurtured, people are continually learning how to learn, and the results are widely shared and used at all levels.

Knowledge management. The process of creating and using human and technological networks to capitalize on a company's expertise, experience, and learning.

QUICK TEST 5	9	T or F	The effects of systematization of information handling are almost always clearly negative.
	10	T or F	Everyone plays a role in creating a learning organization, not just the corporate training department.

Practical Guidelines for Supervisors

1. Learn to *recognize—and even anticipate—problems* by comparing actual results against your prior expectations.

2. Carefully *practice the problem-solving process* until it becomes a mental habit, and discipline yourself not to skip any of the steps or fall prey to a "quick fix" mentality.

3. For every major problem you face, *choose how to approach it*: whether to solve it yourself, consult an individual, or involve a group of employees for their input and perspectives.

4. *Commit yourself to being an ethical supervisor* by learning your employer's standards, studying relevant policies, examining the actions of others, and sharpening your own moral perspectives.

5. *Sharpen your creativity* by breaking out of old mental ruts, using new and strange metaphors, and seeking inputs and help from employees.

6. *Expedite your decision process* by applying existing policies and procedures to routine, recurring, and programmed problems.

7. Always rigorously *consider the pros and cons* (costs and benefits) of any alternative you are considering to avoid being blindsided by surprises or questions later on.

8. *Learn to focus the bulk of your time on the big issues*—the ones that demand your attention and allow you to make an impact—and consider delegating the others to your employees.

9. Periodically *examine your decision-making success rate*; identify why you may have erred and be confident enough to admit mistakes and learn from them.

10. *Watch for the impact of management information systems on yourself and your employees*, and learn to see their merits and how they can be adapted to fit your needs.

Chapter 4 Review

Key Concepts to Remember

1. Problems: Cause and Effect. Effective supervisors are able to (a) recognize the existence of a problem or the need for a decision, (b) anticipate potential trouble spots, and (c) identify opportunities for improvement. Problems are caused by changes or other factors that disturb normal procedures or conditions. Problems can be recognized by a gap between what is expected (or planned) to happen and what actually occurs.

2. Systematic Problem Solving. Problems are solved by removing or correcting the cause of the disturbance, which, in turn, closes the gap in performance. Problem solving should always be approached systematically. The process can often be improved by seeking help from the individuals or groups of employees who are best informed and/or more closely involved in the problem and in implementing its solution.

3. Decision Making: Rational and Intuitive. Decision making is an inseparable part of the problem-solving process. It is the phase in which solutions, ideas, and new courses of action are examined critically and then chosen on the basis of their chances for success or failure in meeting related objectives. Decision making may be approached mathematically—using a variety of techniques, such as the decision tree—or intuitively. It is always

more effective, however, when based on firm objectives and sound information. Work groups can make useful contributions to problem solving and decision making, but their involvement must be genuine. Ethical standards and creativity are two key parts of supervisory decision making.

4. Information as a Raw Material. Effective problem solving depends on the quantity and quality of information upon which analysis and judgments are made. Increasingly, formal management information systems (MISs) provide operational information for decision-making purposes in a convenient form for managers and supervisors. Supervisors stand at both ends of the MIS. As end users, they receive computer outputs that provide them with operational and cost data. As prime sources of input, they collect and transmit all sorts of sales, production, quality, and cost data to the system.

5. Keeping the System Human. Computerized information gathering and monitoring pose a real or imagined threat to many employees. Supervisors should face these problems openly and try to reduce tensions and dissatisfaction by making job assignments as attractive as possible and accenting the benefits employees will receive.

Reading Comprehension

1. How would you recognize the existence of a problem?
2. What is the primary cause of most problems? Why do they occur?
3. Differentiate between problem solving and decision making.
4. Under what circumstances might it be better for supervisors to seek help in solving a problem than to handle it all by themselves?
5. If you were asked to decide which of five projects might be chosen for a public health

care program under your supervision, what technique might you use? Why?

6. Supply some examples of how a company's policies, rules, or standard procedures help "program" a decision for a supervisor.

7. What four requirements must be met if participation of a work group in the decision-making process is to be successful?

8. Describe a situation you have read about or experienced that involved an unethical action by a supervisor or manager. How could raising critical questions in advance have helped improve the outcome?

9. Which of the following are considered primary data for a supervisor's departmental MIS? Production tallies collected at the end of the day, inventory-status records retrieved from a company's central data file, a count of errors that have occurred in the department during the week, comparative cost data from the U.S. Department of Commerce.

10. The development of a learning organization may create both favorable and unfavorable working conditions. Describe these and explain what a supervisor might do to improve an employee's ability to adapt to these conditions.

Application

Self-Assessment

How Good Are Your Problem-Solving Skills?

Read the following statements carefully. Circle the number on the response scale that most closely reflects the degree to which each statement describes you. Add up your total points and prepare a brief action plan for self-improvement. Be ready to report your score for tabulation across the entire group.

	Good Description									Poor Description
1. I regularly monitor the actual performance in my department and compare it to expected levels to uncover variances.	10	9	8	7	6	5	4	3	2	1
2. When problems appear in my area, I can usually see them coming in advance.	10	9	8	7	6	5	4	3	2	1
3. I am aware that more problems than normal can be expected under conditions of rapid or frequent change.	10	9	8	7	6	5	4	3	2	1
4. As soon as a major problem appears, I try to create a clear statement of it that highlights the gap clearly and specifically.	10	9	8	7	6	5	4	3	2	1

	Good Description									Poor Description

5. When solving a problem, I generally try to brainstorm as many solutions as I can before selecting one.
10 9 8 7 6 5 4 3 2 1

6. I recognize the importance of differentiating between problem finding, problem solving, and decision making.
10 9 8 7 6 5 4 3 2 1

7. I usually follow a systematic process of choosing whether to decide alone, consult an employee, or involve a group of employees.
10 9 8 7 6 5 4 3 2 1

8. I consciously try to focus my attention on the 20 percent of problems that account for about 80 percent of my results.
10 9 8 7 6 5 4 3 2 1

9. I have a clear set of ethical standards that I can consciously apply to any situation that might arise at work.
10 9 8 7 6 5 4 3 2 1

10. I take systematic actions to ensure that my employees feel that they are part of a learning organization.
10 9 8 7 6 5 4 3 2 1

Scoring and Interpretation

Scoring

Add up your total points for the 10 questions. Record that number here, and report it when it is requested. _____

Also, insert your score on the Personal Development Plan in the Appendix.

Interpretation

81 to 100 points. You seem to have a basic set of problem-solving and information management skills.

61 to 80 points. Take a close look at some of your problem-solving and information management skills (those with lower self-assessments) and discuss them with a manager to see if they need improvement.

Below 60 points. Some of your skills may be substantially inconsistent with effective problem-solving and information management practices and could be detrimental to your success as a supervisor.

Identify your three lowest scores and record the question numbers here: _____, _____, _____.

Action

Write a brief paragraph detailing an action plan for how you might sharpen each of these skills. Then pay particularly close attention to the related material in the chapter as you review the relevant sections there.

Skill Development

Analyzing the Potential for Open-Book Management

Assume that your manager asked you to study the practice of open-book management, and make a recommendation regarding this question: "Should this organization implement open-book management at this time?" To prepare your report, you will likely wish to scan both of John Case's books on the subject (*Open-Book Management* and *The Open-Book Experience*), ask some employees for their reactions, scan the Internet for relevant information, and interview some managers for their reactions. In particular, you should identify the likely positive consequences of open-book management as well as the probable negative consequences on the worksheet below.

Positive Effects	Negative Effects
1. _____	1. _____
2. _____	2. _____
3. _____	3. _____
4. _____	4. _____
5. _____	5. _____
6. _____	6. _____
7. _____	7. _____

Action

Following your analysis of the effects of this change, state a conclusion that you would be comfortable supporting. (Note that this is an exercise that builds on the availability of timely financial and operating information, as well as the willingness of the organization to provide the MIS-generated data freely to all employees. The exercise also gives you an opportunity to demonstrate your cost-benefit analytical skills.)

Group Exercise

Problem Solving

Step 1: Form into groups of six. Select a problem to address, such as "How to make this course more exciting." Agree to follow the problem-solving steps outlined in the chapter.

Step 2: Be sure to generate an explicit analysis of both the costs and the benefits of your final recommendation.

Step 3: During the discussion, each person should note who plays each of the six roles, and how often they do so, by placing a check mark in the appropriate box below each time you note a contribution from that person.

Step 4: When the group is finished with its task, answer the following questions:

1. What role does each person think exemplified his or her primary contributions?
   Provide feedback to each person about your observational data on his or her role.
2. What role(s) seemed to be over/underemphasized in the group? Why?
3. Are there other types of roles that would be useful in a group such as this?

Member Roles	Group Members					
	A	B	C	D	E	F
Data gatherer						
Rational person						
Emotion injector						
Uplifter						
Devil's advocate						
Evaluator						

Cases for Analysis

Case 11

The Big Cookie Burnout

What seemed like a simple problem with an obvious solution turned out to be anything but that. It happened in the baking department of one of the nation's largest cookie makers. Too many batches of cookies, more than 10,000 dozen of them, were spoiled due to overheating. And when the finger-pointing was over, it was Arsenio, the department supervisor, who ended up being the fall guy.

Arsenio hadn't intended it to be that way. In fact, he was so sure that Joanna, the chief baker on the oven line, was at fault that he suspended her on the spot. It had seemed like an open-and-shut case. Chief bakers were supposed to monitor oven temperatures continuously, even though temperatures were automatically controlled by a sophisticated series of thermostats. The chief baker could override the automatic controls, however, if at any time she felt that the oven was getting hotter or colder than the optimum temperature. This was accomplished by switching the control to "Manual" and then manipulating a lever to increase or decrease the flame levels in the oven.

Monitoring was easily accomplished by observing a number of temperature-indicating devices. The main temperature indicator was an automatic recorder mounted at the chief baker's workstation at the front end of a 200-foot-long oven. It was there that the raw cookies entered the oven. The cookies had previously been formed by an extruding machine that squeezed the dough mixture through a battery of nozzles onto a stainless-steel conveyor belt. After entering the oven, the belt automatically carried the cookies through the oven at a predetermined speed. According to the kind of cookies being baked, it took from 12 to 18 minutes for them to move from one end of the oven to the other.

Besides the main temperature recorder, temperature indicators were mounted every 50 feet or so along the oven's side. The automatic temperature controls could also be switched to manual control at each of these points.

On the day of what came to be known as the Big Burnout, the cookies were not just "overdone," they were burned to a crisp. So, after first blowing his stack and shunting the spoiled cookies to the garbage truck, Arsenio demanded of Joanna, "How could you ever have let this happen?"

"I can't understand it," said Joanna. "I never left my workstation. I must have looked at the recorder a dozen times during that period. And while oven temperatures were nudging the high side occasionally, they always seemed to be within the control limits."

"So," said Arsenio, "you were too lazy to get off your duff and check the oven-side thermometers."

"That's not true. I can't remember whether I checked them because I was talking with the extruder-machine operator at that time about a problem he was having with his equipment. That distracted me."

"That's no excuse," said Arsenio, "and I don't believe for a moment you were talking about machine problems. You were probably arguing about last night's ball game. Anyway, your job is to watch the ovens, not to chat with every person in the shop. And no matter what the main recorder indicated, you're supposed to be monitoring the oven-side thermometers. It's obvious that somewhere along the line, temperatures got too high, and you should have been there to take over. By not doing your job right, you made a big mistake that cost the company a lot of money.

So I'm going to suspend you for a couple of days to give you a chance to get your head straight about this job."

To Arsenio's dismay, Joanna's suspension did not stick. The reason? After listening to Joanna's story, the bakery manager asked the plant engineer to examine the oven equipment. The plant engineer found that temperatures indicated by the main recorder were accurate, as were all the oven-side thermometers. He also checked the automatic temperature controls and found that they were functioning properly. He then asked the extruder-machine operator about the problems Joanna had spoken of. "The nozzles have been jamming lately," said the operator, "and I've had to shut the belts down from time to time to clean them."

"Don't you realize," said the plant engineer, "that when you shut the belt down, the belt in the oven stops, too? It's no wonder the cookies burned up. Next time you want to stop the belt, be sure to let the chief baker know in advance. Meanwhile, we'll see if we can't adjust the automatic temperature control system to avoid this problem."

Analysis

What do you think of Arsenio's approach to handling this problem? Of the five alternative opinions provided below, which do you think is most appropriate? Rank the alternatives on a scale from 1 (most appropriate) to 5 (least appropriate). You may add another alternative, if you wish. Be prepared to justify your ranking.

_____ a. Arsenio was justified in suspending Joanna because he had no way of knowing the whole story at the time.

_____ b. The suspension was justified because no matter what the extruder-machine operator had done, the chief baker should have discovered the belt stoppage before damage was done.

_____ c. Arsenio's only mistake was that he did not clearly identify and specify the problem to begin with.

_____ d. Arsenio's biggest mistake was to jump to a conclusion without having all the facts.

_____ e. Arsenio solved the problem as best he could under the circumstances.

Case 12

The Uncertain Reduction in Force

The commissioner of a federal agency sent this directive to its regional offices: "Due to an unanticipated reduction in funding, all offices will be expected to reduce their staffs by 10 percent by the quarter's end. We regret this decision, but we have been advised that due to improvements in our procedures, there should be a similar decrease in employee workloads. Please make your plans accordingly."

When this notice arrived on the desk of Kathy M., supervisor of a 10-person clerical unit of a regional office, she said to herself, "No problem." Kathy believed that the reduction could easily be reached by the transfer or separation of Joey, her least productive employee. She notified him of her decision immediately.

Unfortunately for Kathy, several things soon occurred to make the reduction in force (RIF) directive become a major problem: (1) Joey objected to the method used for selecting him to be RIFed, and he filed a grievance; (2) when queried, the agency issued a policy memo that pointed to the selection of an individual other than Joey for separation; (3) one clerk got sick and another quit before the quarter ended; (4) the workload did not diminish as promised; (5) the staff mounted a slowdown as its response to the threatened cuts; (6) at the last minute, the agency found additional funding and modified its directive to advise that the effective date of the RIF would be postponed until the end of the next quarter.

Analysis

a. Should Kathy have waited before telling Joey of her decision? Why or why not?

b. What should Kathy do now? In other words, how should she go about solving the potential problem, which will need a solution by the end of the next quarter?

Case 13

The Blue Jeans MIS

"What's that pile of papers on your desk?" asked Dora's friend, who supervised the department next door to Dora's.

"Oh, that!" answered Dora, who supervised the customer service section. "They're the latest batch of reports from the MIS department . . . and also last week's reports and the reports from the week before that."

"How can you get by without studying them?" asked her friend.

"A better question is how would I ever get time to look at them," said Dora. "They are more a nuisance than a help. Half the stuff in them doesn't even apply to my department. And most of the rest arrives too late to do me any good or doesn't tell me what I really want to know.

Besides, I'd rather fly this department by the seat of my blue jeans than get cross-eyed looking at an endless batch of figures."

"You're sure laid back," said Dora's friend, "but if I were you, I'd ask the MIS people if they couldn't do something to make your reports more useful to you."

Analysis

a. What is wrong with Dora's attitude toward the MIS reports she now receives?

b. What might the MIS people do to make the reports more useful to her?

ANSWERS TO QUICK TESTS	Quick Test 1	Quick Test 2	Quick Test 3	Quick Test 4	Quick Test 5
	1. F	3. F	5. F	7. T	9. F
	2. T	4. F	6. F	8. T	10. T

5

Organizing an Effective Department

LEARNING OBJECTIVES

After studying this chapter, you should be able to

- Describe the organizing process and its outcome, and differentiate between formal and informal organizations.

- Identify and differentiate among various organizational structures and formats, including functional, line-and-staff, divisional or product, matrix, and centralized and decentralized organizations.

- Define *authority, responsibility*, and *accountability* and explain their relationships.

- Understand the benefits derived from delegation and explain several effective approaches to it.

- Explain the concept of organizational culture.

Organizing for Effectiveness

What is an organization?

An *organization* is the structure derived from grouping people together so that they can work effectively toward a goal that members of the group want to achieve.

The goals of a business organization are primarily profits for stockholders, and salaries and wages for managers, supervisors, and employees. There are other important goals, of course, such as supplying goods and services valued by the general population. While the goals of nonprofit and public organizations do not include profit, members of such organizations expect them to provide compensation in addition to delivering valued services to others.

Members of an organization also look to it as a source of personal satisfactions, such as companionship, accomplishment, and status.

At a broader level, society expects organizations to act in ethically and socially responsible ways.

What is the distinction between organizing and an organization?

Organizing is the process of arranging the pattern of work relationships. An *organization* is the structure, or framework, that comes out of the organizing process.

Why organize in the first place?

Without an organization, we would have nothing but chaos in the workplace. We take organizations for granted because we have lived so long with them at home, in places of worship, and in the educational system. Little that we do together—anywhere—would be effective, however, if we didn't agree among ourselves on who should do what. We need look no further than team sports to see the extent of organizational structure that prevails. What would professional football be, for instance, without its highly organized structure of tasks for offense, defense, special teams, and special situations (first-down run, third-down pass, goal-line defense, etc.)?

The overriding value of an organization, then, is its ability to make more effective use of human resources. Employees working alone, and potentially at cross purposes, require the coordination and direction that an organization can provide. People working together within a sensible organizational structure have a greater sense of purpose and teamwork, and they accomplish vastly more than do people whose efforts are allowed to run off in any direction they choose.

Are all organizations formal?

No. In a good many of our activities, even in complex manufacturing plants, some people naturally take over responsibilities and exercise authority without anyone's ever spelling them out. Chances are that in a group of 15 employees who you might imagine are all at the same level, you'll discover some sort of *informal organization*. It may be that the person who sweeps the floors actually has the greatest influence in that group. This person is an informal leader. Acting as staff assistant may be the lift truck driver, who is the informant. The rest of the group may either work hard or stage a slowdown at a nod from a third member of the group, who has authority as surely as if the company president had given it.

Although you'll never see the informal organization on a chart, it exists as surely as barometric pressure in the atmosphere (which you can often feel but not see). Informal groups often have strong behavioral *norms* that prescribe and direct the behavior of group members. Supervisors should pay attention to these norms, study their compatibility with department goals, and strive to steer them in positive directions. The organizational system works best when the formal and informal organizations are blended together.

How does the organizing process proceed?

Organizing follows planning. The organizational structure must provide the framework for carrying out the plan. Suppose, for example, a supervisor plans to load a trailer by 5 P.M. The goal will be met if one employee is assigned to remove cartons from the stockroom, another to operate a fork-truck, another to stack cartons in the trailer, and another to verify and prepare the inventory and shipping documents.

Essentially, the organizing process moves from the knowledge of a goal or plan to a systematic *division of labor*, or *division of work*. Typically, the process follows these steps:

1. Making a list of all the important tasks that must be performed by the organization to accomplish its objectives.
2. Dividing these tasks into activities that can be performed by one person. Each person will then have a group of activities to perform, called a *job*. This specialization allows each person to become more proficient at his or her special job.
3. Grouping together related jobs (such as production jobs or accounting jobs) or sequenced jobs in a logical and efficient manner. This creates specialized departments or connected sections of the organization.
4. Establishing relationships between the various jobs and groupings of jobs so that all members of an organization will have a clear idea of their responsibilities and of either their dependence on or their control over people in other jobs or groups of jobs.

Which comes first, the organization or the work to be done?

If there were no job to do, there would be no reason to have an organization. So there is little reason to set up an elaborate organization just for the sake of having one. The best organization is a simple one that puts people together so that the job at hand gets done better, more quickly, and more cheaply than any other way. Good organizations are also flexible so that they can adapt to changing conditions.

QUICK TEST 1

1	T or F	An organization is the process of arranging the pattern of work relationships.
2	T or F	Planning comes first; then organizing helps carry out the plans.

2

Types of Organizational Structures

CONCEPT

Organizational structures follow several traditional patterns.

Functional organization. An organizational structure in which tasks are grouped according to a particular operating function, such as production, sales, information handling, and so on.

Which is the most basic organizational structure?

The *functional organization*. In it, each group of related activities is collected under one functional head. Thus, in Figure 5-1, the meats supervisor may have under her all the meat cutters, trimmers, and packers; the stockroom supervisor, all the receivers, inspectors, and pricing clerks; and so forth. The functional approach to organizing yields the simplest structure. It also provides the basic framework from which other types of structures are built. *It is, essentially, a line organization.*

How is a line-and-staff organization formed?

A *line-and-staff organization* adds to the basic features of functional (or line) organization *staff groups* that either give advice to or perform

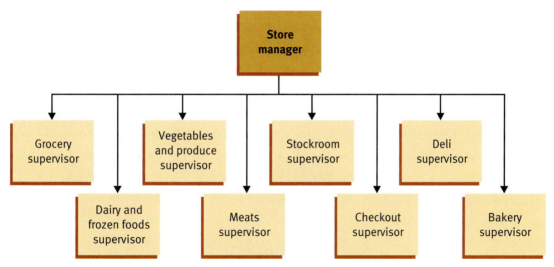

FIGURE 5-1

Example of a functional organization structure for a supermarket.
What are the advantages of this structure?

services for the line functions. A line-and-staff organization is illustrated in Figure 5-2.

What is the difference between line and staff groups?

An organization works best when it gets many related jobs done effectively with a minimum of friction. This requires coordination and determination of what to do and who is to do it. The managers and supervisors whose main job is to see that products and services are produced and delivered are usually considered members of the *line* organization. Other management people who help them decide what to do and how to do it, assist in coordinating the efforts of all, or provide service or special expertise are usually called *staff people.*

In manufacturing plants, line activities are most commonly performed by production departments, sales departments, and, occasionally, purchasing departments. The production supervisor is likely to be a member of the line organization.

Departments that help the line departments control quality and maintain adequate records are typically staff departments. Industrial engineering, maintenance, legal, research, MIS, and the human resource department are some examples of typical staff activities.

In service organizations such as banks and insurance firms, the line organization may represent the primary "action" operations (such as deposits, withdrawals, and record keeping, or premium collections and

Line-and-staff organization. The most common form of organizational structure, in which line managers hold accountability for results that most directly affect profits or institutional goals, and staff managers hold accountability for results that most directly affect the processes by which line managers accomplish their goals.

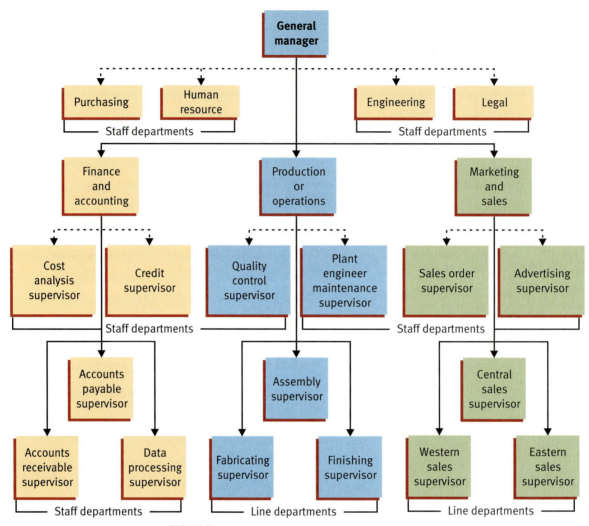

FIGURE 5-2

Example of a line-and-staff organization for a manufacturing company.
When does this structure work best?

claim settlements), and the staff organization may represent such support groups as computer departments and actuarial.

In hotel and motel chains, the line may be everything connected with the operation of a geographic unit, and the staff may be such home-office activities as advertising, accounting, and legal.

At the risk of oversimplifying, it may help you to think of line people as the doers, and staff people as the advisers. Each function—line and staff—is important in its own way, and collectively they help the organization achieve its goals. However, conflicts sometimes emerge between the two functions for a variety of reasons. The groups may compete for influence, be jealous of each other's status, question the limits of the other group's authority, want to claim credit for accomplishments, or be unclear

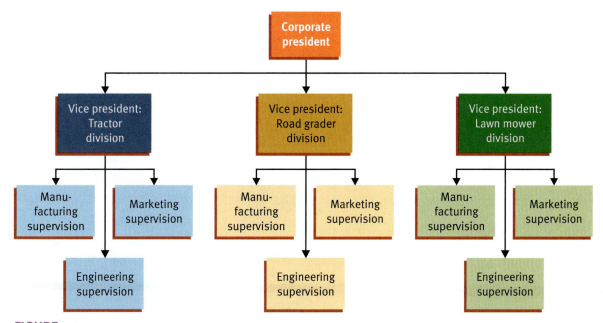

FIGURE 5-3

Example of a product, or divisional, organization structure for a manufacturing company.

What is the ultimate goal of any organization structure?

about areas of responsibility. These problems are often predictable and need to be addressed before they become detrimental to the desired working relationship.

In what other ways may organizations be structured?

The great majority of organizations combine some form of functional segmentation with a line-and-staff format. This allows for a great many variations. Among the most common are these:

Divisional or product. All functions needed to make a particular product, for example, are gathered under one highly placed manager. If a firm manufactures tractors for farmers, road graders for construction contractors, and lawn mowers for home use, it might "divisionalize" to make and sell each major product in its product line, as shown in Figure 5-3. Note that under each vice president each division is essentially a functional one; as a consequence, labels such as "functional" and "divisional" can be misleading.

Geographic. A firm may divide all of its activities, or only some, such as sales, according to the geographic region where those activities take place.

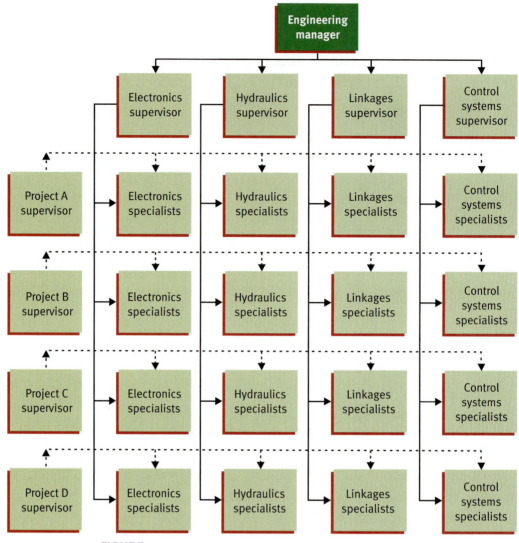

FIGURE 5-4

Example of a matrix organization structure.
What is the primary disadvantage of a matrix structure?

Customer. A company may also choose to organize some or all of its activities according to the types of customers it serves, such as farmers, contractors, and homeowners. This kind of organization is closely related to the product organization.

Regardless of organization type, always remember that the purpose of the organizational structure is to make a department's work fit together more closely with the work of other departments, while satisfying customer needs.

The matrix organization: What's it all about?

This is a nontraditional format that is especially suited for projects, task force work, or other one-of-a-kind enterprises. It is commonly used in research and development organizations and engineering firms for major projects or contracts. It allows a project manager to call upon—for a limited period—the time and skills of personnel with various functional specialties. When the project is completed, the specialized personnel return to their home units to be assigned to another project. Because project managers can exercise their authority horizontally across the basic organization while the specialists receive permanent authority from their functional bosses above them vertically on the chart (Figure 5-4), this form is called a *matrix* organization. The matrix organization has the drawback of requiring employees to report to more than one superior—a functional supervisor and one or more project supervisors. There is also some loss of control by both supervisors and the potential for communication breakdowns. Nevertheless, the format has proved to be effective in many of its applications.

How do you distinguish between a centralized organization and a decentralized one?

A *centralized* organization assigns decision-making authority to a few people at the top of an organization. It tends to have many levels of management, concentrate its facilities in one location, perform certain functions (such as engineering, labor negotiations, computer operations, and purchasing) from a single source, and gather together its power and authority at headquarters. A *decentralized* organization tends to have the opposite characteristics, especially when a company is divided into distinctly separate units with varying degrees of independence. These units may be set up along product lines, according to geography, or according to methods of marketing and distribution.

Centralized organizations tend to have more levels of management, have tighter controls, and allow employees less freedom to make their own decisions. Decentralized organizations have fewer levels of management, have looser controls, and allow employees greater freedom in their actions.

A decentralized approach pushes decision-making authority toward lower levels of an organization. As a result, it is more likely to release employee ingenuity in solving problems and pleasing the customers. Decentralization also provides opportunities for workers who enjoy contributing their knowledge and ideas, thus creating satisfied employees.

How wide should a supervisor's span of control be?

Authorities disagree on this point, and it depends on several key factors. A traditional rule of thumb suggests that no supervisor should have responsibility for more than five to eight separate activities. The span should be shorter when employees are geographically dispersed, the firm is centralized, the activities are specialized and complex, new problems are encountered frequently by employees, or the workforce is new and not well trained. Wider spans are more appropriate when several employees all perform similar activities in a single area, there are experienced workers close by to demonstrate proper methods, the organization is decentralized, and the supervisor can easily be contacted on short notice to respond to problems. More and more, organizations are finding that twenty-first-century employees can learn to work independently, can discover when to ask for advice or assistance, and will enjoy figuring out how to solve problems on their own. Under these conditions, spans of controls will invariably widen.

The **span of control** is defined as the number of people that a single manager directly supervises. It is not unusual for a supervisor to have a span of 30 or more employees, provided that they are engaged in only a few simple, related activities. However, corporate cost-cutting decisions (often eliminating layers of middle management) and a more highly trained workforce have increased some supervisors' spans of control, sometimes to as many as 100 employees.

Span of control. The number of activities or people that a single manager supervises.

In today's dynamic environment, organizations may have to downsize when business declines. **How would you, as a supervisor, feel about telling employees that they have lost their jobs?**

What purpose is served by charts of an organization's structure?

They help you understand organizational relationships. Such charts are really simple pictures of how one job or department fits in with others. Each box, or rectangle, portrays an activity or department. Boxes on the same horizontal level on the chart tend to have the same degree of authority or power and to have their work closely related. Departments in boxes on the next higher level have greater authority; those at lower levels have less authority. Clusters of boxes that enclose departments performing closely related functions (such as shaping, fabricating, assembly, and finishing in a manufacturing plant) are typically shown at the same level and report vertically above to the head manager of that particular function (such as the production manager).

Boxes containing line departments tend to descend from the top of the chart to the bottom (where supervisors' departments typically are) in vertical chains. Boxes that enclose staff departments tend to branch out to either side of the main flow of authority.

Organization charts can be drawn in any way that shows relationships best, even in concentric circles. For practical purposes, however, most charting is done in the manner just described and illustrated in the figures in this chapter. Two notes of caution: First, organizational structures and staffing change constantly. Accordingly, organization charts go out of date very quickly. Second, informal relationships, degree of centralization or decentralization, and actual communication patterns don't show up on organization charts. Therefore, they have a limited capacity to show "how things really get done."

What is restructuring? How does it relate to organizing?

Taken literally, restructuring would simply be a matter of changing the organization's basic arrangement of work into different departments, divisions, and so forth. That is only partially accurate, however. *Restructuring* is basically a euphemism (a word that hides an offensive truth) for downsizing—drastically reducing the number of employees on the payroll. Restructuring is often caused by forces such as mergers, product failures, massive lawsuits, and sharp changes in an organization's basic strategy and direction. But layoffs can also result from overhiring and a bloated workforce created during good economic times.

Restructuring. The process of laying off large numbers of employees to achieve greater cost efficiencies in the future.

Major downsizings do have an impact on an organization's structure, of course. Not only do individual employees lose their jobs or require retraining, sometimes whole product lines and departments are wiped out or consolidated. Therefore, an organization's structure may change dramatically when two firms merge. But the real

humanresources.about.com/od/layoffsdownsizing/a/downsizing.htm
Read about the toxic effects of downsizing and ways to avoid the pitfalls.

issues for supervisors lie in the impact at their level. Rumors may fly wildly, and communication needs to increase. Survivors of layoffs may look for other jobs, and you need to give them compelling reasons to stay. Employees may ask you how the layoffs will be made, and you need to have a decision process in place that they will understand and perceive as fair and consistent. A corporate restructuring—despite its obvious pain—should be viewed as an opportunity to reexamine and change the way things are done, evaluate the results, and learn from mistakes and failures.

You don't want your layoff survivors feeling as if they are the victims. Because in many ways, they may feel like victims.

Susan M. Heathfield

Are there ethical issues involved in restructuring?

Absolutely. At the broadest level, organizations are expected to be socially responsible—to act in the best interest of a collection of relevant *stakeholders*. These are any groups that affect, or are affected by, the actions of the company. Admittedly, it is usually impossible to fully satisfy all stakeholders (environmental groups, suppliers, governmental

Stakeholders. Groups who affect, are affected by, or deeply interested in, the actions of the company and its results.

agencies, customers, etc.). But organizations need to try to do so, and their actions are increasingly scrutinized by many social observers.

More specifically, a supervisor, when faced with the downsizing impact of restructuring, must face a number of ethical challenges. What do you tell employees who want a rumor confirmed or denied? What advice do you give someone who wants to know in advance the likelihood that cutbacks will take place? How do you choose between a competent employee with many years of experience and a newer one with greater potential? And pragmatically, how do you ever feel comfortable telling people that they are losing their jobs?

By their very nature, these issues are not easy to face or resolve. They often involve difficult choices and personal challenges in terms of finding a way to communicate the decisions to employees whose work lives, families, and emotional health are affected by them. The best approach is to have a clear set of standards to apply, a strong base of trust between you and your employees, a commitment to communicate on a timely and complete basis, and the greatest amount of empathy you can muster.

| QUICK TEST 2 | 3 | T or F | Staff groups give counsel and advice; line groups see that products and services are produced and delivered. |
| | 4 | T or F | Centralized organizations tend to have fewer levels in their hierarchy; decentralized ones have more. |

3 Authority, Responsibility, and Accountability

CONCEPT

The organizational structure provides the framework for the formal assignment of responsibility and delegation of authority.

Responsibility. The duty or obligation to perform a prescribed task or service or to attain a specified objective.

Are authority and responsibility the same thing?

No. Authority should go hand in hand with responsibility, but the two are no more alike than the two sides of a coin. Your *responsibilities* are those things you are held accountable for—such as costs, on-time deliveries, and accuracy. Responsibilities are also spoken of as your assigned *duties*—such as checking time cards, investigating accidents, scheduling employees, and keeping production records. *Authority* is the power you have been given to carry out your responsibilities. A supervisor's authority includes the right to make decisions, take action to control costs and quality, and exercise necessary discipline over the employees assigned to help carry out those responsibilities.

It's an axiom that you shouldn't be assigned a responsibility without enough authority to carry it out. If a supervisor is charged with responsibility for seeing that quality is up to specifications, that supervisor must also be given authority to stop the operation when the quality falls off or to take any reasonable steps necessary to correct the condition.

Authority. The legitimate power to issue orders to other people in an organization and to obtain resources from it.

Where does your organizational authority come from?

Authority, like responsibility, is usually handed down to supervisors from their immediate bosses. The bosses, in turn, receive their authority and responsibilities from their immediate superiors. And so it goes, on up to the company president or CEO, who receives assignments from the board of directors. This process of handing down authority is known as *delegation*.

The biggest chunk of authority rests with the company president, who may split this chunk into as few as 3 pieces (to vice presidents of production, sales, and financing) or as many as 20 (to vice presidents in charge of 20 different products). As the authority comes down the line to you, the pieces get smaller. But they also get much more specific.

Delegation. The assignment, or entrustment, to subordinates of organizational responsibilities or obligations along with appropriate organizational authority, power, and rights.

Organizations, and employees, operate best when clear systems of authority are in place.
Who probably has the most authority in this photo?

Your plant superintendent may have the responsibility of producing goods in sufficient quantities to meet sales requirements, whereas your responsibility may be to see that 10 milling machines are operated at optimum capacity so that 200,000 product units are produced each month. Similarly, the plant superintendent's authority may permit the exercise of broad disciplinary measures, whereas yours may be limited to recommending disciplinary action for employees who break rules or whose output is not up to production and quality standards.

Most companies try to make the responsibilities and authorities at each level of management fairly consistent. For instance, a supervisor in Department A should have the same general responsibilities as a supervisor in Department Z. And their authorities would be generally the same even though the specific duties of each might differ widely.

What other sources can you draw on for getting things done?

In addition to your organizational "right" to act, you may often need to draw on other, more personal sources. Your employer tries to establish your organizational rights by granting you a title or a rank, depicting you on an organization chart, and providing some visible demonstration of status, such as a desk or an office or some special privilege. Ordinarily, you must supplement this institutional authority with some of the following bases of power:

- Your job knowledge (expertise).
- Your personal influence in the organization (capacity to persuade others to help you or your team).
- Your interpersonal skills (caring, trustworthiness, or charisma).
- Your ability to get results (even doing some of the work, if necessary).
- Your empathetic and persuasive ability (communication skills).

All these sources are important because employees tend to discount your formal organizational authority over them. They expect you to earn your power and their respect. When employees voluntarily come to accept your authority as deserved or earned (referred to as the *acceptance* theory of authority rather than the *institutional*), you will find that your relationships with employees improve greatly.

Should a distinction be drawn among authority, responsibility, and accountability?

Yes. Although the distinction may appear to be only a technical one, it is not. As your boss, for example, I might be held accountable to higher management for the way in which operating supplies are conserved in my department. But I have the prerogative to assign this responsibility to you—if I also grant you the authority to take any steps needed to protect these supplies. If you were to misuse these supplies or to lose track of them, I might discipline you for failing to discharge your responsibility in this matter. But I'd still be held accountable to my boss (and would be subject to discipline) for what happened—no matter which one of us was at fault. My *accountability* is my nonassignable liability for the way my responsibilities are carried out. Therefore, when you assign a minor responsibility to one of your employees (together with the necessary authority to carry it out), you will still be held accountable to your boss for the way in which this responsibility is fulfilled by your subordinate. In other words, you can assign responsibility to others and delegate authority to them, but you will always remain accountable.

> **Accountability.** A nonassignable liability for the way in which an organizational obligation held by a supervisor is discharged, either personally or by subordinates.

How much leeway do supervisors have in taking authoritative action?

There is no hard-and-fast rule to follow. Generally speaking, a company may establish three rough classifications of authority within which supervisors can make decisions:

- **Class 1.** Complete authority. Supervisors can take action without consulting their superiors.
- **Class 2.** Limited authority. Supervisors can take action they deem appropriate as long as it fits within company policy, and the superior is told about the action soon afterward.
- **Class 3.** No authority. Supervisors can take no action until they check with their superiors and receive their approval.

If many decisions fall into class 3, supervisors become little more than messengers. To improve this situation, first learn more about your company's policy and then spend time finding out how your bosses would act. If you can convince them that you would handle matters as they might, your bosses are more likely to transfer class 3 decisions into class 2 and, as you prove yourself, class 2 decisions into class 1.

Note that the existing company policy would still prevail. The big change would be in permitting supervisory discretion. And this would be because you have demonstrated that you are qualified to translate front-office policy into front-line action.

How do staff people exert their influence?

More often than not, staff departments suggest, advise, or provide information. They may suggest a different, and improved, way of doing something, advise that your department is off target (on quality, for instance), or provide relevant information for your use and guidance.

If supervisors are smart, they will make every use they can of the staff department's knowledge. If you were building a house yourself for the first time and someone offered to give you the free advice of a first-rate carpenter, a top-notch mason, a heating specialist, and an experienced painter, you'd jump at the chance. The same holds true in accepting the advice and guidance available from staff departments and other specialists when you are tackling a management problem.

You should be alert, however, to the fact that in many organizations, staff units are granted functional authority. ***Functional authority*** entitles a staff department to specify the policies and procedures to be followed in matters within their specialties. For example, supervisors might be told they cannot hire a new employee unless he or she has been screened by the employment department; nothing can be ordered from outside the company without a completed purchasing requisition; maintenance repairs cannot be made without an approved work order; the production-control department will have final say on the scheduling of customer orders; and so on.

In still other variations, organizational policy may specify that while supervisors have final authority over a functional matter, they may be required either to consult with the functional specialist before taking action or to reach an agreement beforehand on the intended action.

Functional authority. The legitimate authority granted to a staff department to make overriding organizational decisions involving its particular functional specialty.

| QUICK TEST 3 | 5 | T or F | Authority means the duties that you have been assigned. |
| | 6 | T or F | Only line people have authority; staff personnel do not. |

Delegation for Leverage

CONCEPT
Delegation of selected tasks by supervisors can greatly add to their personal effectiveness.

When should you delegate some of your work?

Delegate when you find you can't personally keep up with everything you feel you should do. Giving minor time-consuming tasks to others will save your time for more critical tasks. Let one employee double-check the level of supplies, for example, and send another employee to see who wants to work overtime.

Arrange to have certain jobs taken over when you're absent from your department in an emergency or during vacation. Keep it to routine matters, if you will, and to those requiring a minimum of authority. But do try to get rid of the tasks of filling out routine requisitions and reports, making calculations and entries, checking supplies, and running errands.

How can you do a better job of delegating?

Start by thinking of yourself as primarily a manager. Recognize that no matter how good a person you may be, you'll always have more responsibilities than you can carry out yourself.

The trick of delegating is to concentrate on the most important matters yourself. Keep a close eye, for instance, on the trend of labor costs—that's a big item. But let someone else perform tasks for you that are less important.

Trouble begins when you can't distinguish between the big and the little matters. You may feel you can put off checking the production record; you may feel that it can wait until the day of reckoning at the end of the month. But in the long run, you'll be overwhelmed if you don't see that the small jobs must get done by someone else.

Be ready, too, to give up certain work that you enjoy. A supervisor must learn to let go of those tasks that rightfully belong to a subordinate. Otherwise, larger and more demanding assignments may not get done. And don't worry too much about getting blamed by your boss for delegating to an employee work that has been given to you. Generally speaking, supervisors should be interested only in seeing that the job is done the right way, not in who carries it out. See Figure 5-5 for a way to decide which jobs should be targeted for delegation.

What tasks should not be delegated?

As important as delegation is, don't go too far. Some things are yours alone. When a task involves technical knowledge or advanced skills that only you possess, it would be unwise to let someone less able take over. Of course, it's wrong to entrust confidential information to others. And

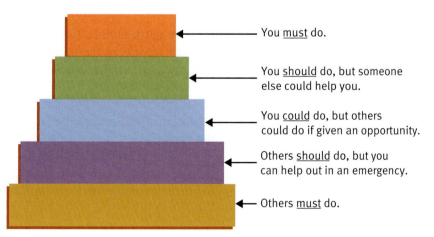

You <u>must</u> do.

You <u>should</u> do, but someone else could help you.

You <u>could</u> do, but others could do if given an opportunity.

Others <u>should</u> do, but you can help out in an emergency.

Others <u>must</u> do.

FIGURE 5-5
Supervisor's task and delegation chart.
Why do some supervisors find delegating difficult?

you wouldn't want to overload employees by delegating too much to them. Finally, you wouldn't normally allow one employee to appraise another. That's a task for you to retain.

What should you tell employees about jobs delegated to them?

Give them a clear statement of what they are to do, how far they can go, and how much checking you intend to do. Let employees know the relative importance of the job so that they can judge how much attention it should receive. There's no point letting an employee think that making a tally will lead to a promotion if you consider it just a routine task.

Tell employees why you delegated the job. It shows you have confidence in them, and they will try that much harder. But if they think you're pushing off all the dirty jobs onto them, they may deliberately rebel and make mistakes.

Don't mislead employees about their authority. You don't want them going far beyond your intentions. But do define the scope of the task and see that others in your department know that this new task isn't something an employee assumed without authorization. Let it be known that you gave the assignment and that you're seeking cooperation from the other workers.

Why should employees accept a delegated job?

Employees who accept a delegated job outside their own job responsibilities are really taking the job on speculation. They have a right to know what's in it for them:

- **Employees who take on an extra duty get a chance to learn.** If they have never seen how the individual records in the department are tabulated, here's a chance for them to get a better perception of what's going on.
- **Delegated jobs provide more job satisfaction.** Employees thrive on varied assignments. This is a chance to build interest by letting employees do something out of the ordinary.
- **Delegation is sometimes a signal of your confidence in others.** If you can truthfully say that you wouldn't trust anyone else with a certain delegated task, this will help build employee pride and a feeling of status.

- **Delegation provides direct preparation for a promotion.** An employee who performs well on a variety of delegated tasks demonstrates the competence needed when a supervisory position opens up.

You may also want to try the concept of "completed staff work." You assign a problem requiring judgment and common sense to a subordinate, and he or she is to provide you with a complete solution according to these specifications:

1. Consult other personnel who are affected by, or who can contribute to, the problem's analysis.
2. Provide concrete recommendations about how to proceed.
3. Work out all the details.
4. Avoid overly long and complex explanations.
5. Present a single, coordinated plan of action in written form.

When can delegating go wrong?

Delegation of personal tasks will invite trouble if you are tempted to engage in any of the following practices:

- Delegating only dirty work, trivial work, or boring work that cannot be justified as representing a genuine opportunity for self-development.
- Loading a subordinate beyond the limits of his or her time or ability.
- Failing to match responsibility with the appropriate authority to obtain the resources needed to complete the job successfully.
- Undercontrolling the subordinate. Part of your role is to keep on top of (major) aspects of your work responsibilities at all times. One danger is to delegate a task and then ignore the individual responsible until it is too late. Check in occasionally to see how things are going, and of course you will want to respond to requests for advice or guidance when it is requested.
- Overcontrolling the subordinate. This is known as ***micromanaging***, and most employees hate it. It often results from mistrust of an employee or from a supervisor's insecurities. Micromanaging involves looking over employees' shoulders constantly, giving them too much direction and no latitude, and specifying every little detail. Resist the urge to do this, and trust employees to perform properly once they have been trained and provided with appropriate guidelines.

Micromanaging. The act of overcontrolling employees' behaviors after delegating tasks to them, often causing resentment and dissatisfaction.

| 7 | T or F | Supervisors should concentrate on delegating the most important matters to others. |
| 8 | T or F | The sole purpose of delegating to others is to relieve yourself of unwanted tasks. |

What is the relationship of the chain of command to the structure of an organization?

The term *chain of command* is a traditional military phrase used to imply that delegation of responsibility and authority and of orders and information in an organization should originate at the top and proceed toward the bottom from each management level to the next lower level. In a rigid chain of command, you would neither skip any levels nor cross over to another chain of command. The same procedure would be followed regarding information and requests going up the line. Your direct manager is entitled to firsthand information about your work and its progress.

Are there any organizational practices you should avoid?

Yes, but not very many. Once an organization is set up, practicality ought to prevail. In fact, some odd—and informal—arrangements occasionally work out very well. For example, one leading manufacturing company has operated for years without a visual organization chart. Its maverick president believes that the staff will develop the most effective relationships without one, and apparently it has. Nevertheless, in the design stages, at least, there are a few hazards of organization that ought to be guarded against:

1. **Don't let the chain of command get too long.** Keep the number of responsibility levels at a minimum; otherwise, some information will never trickle all the way down to the bottom—at least not accurately!
2. **Don't ask one person to report to two bosses without previously clarifying priorities.** Anyone caught in this nutcracker knows the dilemma: Which boss's work comes first?
3. **Don't make fuzzy job assignments.** When there is a gray area between two positions, overlap, conflict, and duplication of effort are invited. Clarify each person's job.
4. **Don't be too rigid.** Try to retain flexibility for contingent situations—those problems that inevitably crop up and need handling by nonstandard assignments.

How does structure relate to organizational culture?

The formal organizing process creates the broad framework within which you operate. It arranges work into jobs and serves as a vehicle for defining authority relationships. But it also provides a clue to employees about the kind of work environment, or culture, they will encounter. An *organizational culture* is the underlying set of assumptions, beliefs, attitudes, values, and expectations shared by members of an organization. It tells members "the way things really are around here," providing important signals regarding acceptable behavior. An organization with many layers of management, rigid policies, and centralized decision making sets one tone for its employees. Another firm that embraces humor, creativity, and informality will be totally different.

Organizational culture. The underlying (often implicit) set of assumptions, beliefs, attitudes, values, and expectations shared by members of an organization.

How do you learn about the organization's culture?

Although all firms have a culture, these cultures are usually very different. Even within an organization, different cultures can emerge in different divisions or departments. But you can still identify the overall culture through close examination. Read about the company's history and its heroes and heroines, pay attention to popular slogans and stories and myths, watch the common rites and ceremonies, and examine the early actions of newly hired executives.

Most of all, ask for advice from a variety of peers about accepted practices and valued behaviors. In addition to learning about your own culture, you will discover that most cultures are

- Implicit and fuzzy, not explicit.
- Relatively stable, although they do change slowly over time.
- A product of top management beliefs and visions for the future.
- A powerful factor affecting employee behavior.

Your role as a supervisor is to help your employees understand the organization's culture and learn the norms governing their expected behavior and how to "fit in." You are a key link in shaping their attitudes and behavior (their socialization into the culture). If you communicate the culture clearly, they are more likely to avoid mistakes, while still being able to retain their individuality. Then both the company and the employees will be satisfied.

9	T or F	There are legitimate times when the chain of command doesn't need to be followed.
10	T or F	It is possible to discover an organization's culture through reading, observation, and inquiry.

QUICK TEST 5

Practical Guidelines for Supervisors

1. *Study the organization chart* of your organization to determine its primary structural basis. Determine why it is based on product, customer, geography, and so on.

2. *Determine whether you are in a line or a staff department.* Whichever you are in, identify how well you get along with your counterparts in the other roles.

3. *Examine the size of the span of control* at your level in the organization. Ask yourself if it should be larger or smaller, and what the consequences might be.

4. *Develop a contingency* (just in case) *plan for the possibility of downsizing.* What would you be prepared to do if you were told to cut expenses by 5 percent? By 10 percent? By 20 percent?

5. *Examine the authority you have been given to carry out your responsibilities.* Are your authority and responsibilities in balance? If not, discuss this with your immediate superior.

6. *Rate yourself (1 = poor, 10 = excellent) on your delegating skills.* What specific actions could you take to develop your abilities here?

7. *Rate the readiness (1 = low, 10 = high) of each of your employees to accept greater delegation.* Identify reasons why they might resist or welcome it, and how you could overcome any resistance.

8. *Assess the importance of the chain of command* in your organization. What does its apparent rigidity or flexibility tell you?

9. Seek feedback from your subordinates, peers, and boss to *determine if they think you are micromanaging.* Do some introspection to analyze why you might be guilty of this.

10. *Identify the "culture" of your organization*, noting specific elements that provide you with clues. What guidance does this give you about how to behave?

Chapter 5 Review

Key Concepts to Remember

1. Organizing for Effectiveness. The organizing process creates the organizational structure. This structure prescribes the way in which different individuals with different skills, and performing different tasks, can combine their efforts effectively into logical groupings (or departments) for the pursuit of common goals. Such structures also encourage order and harmony in the workplace.

2. Types of Organizational Structures. A variety of organizational structures can be built. The basic structure is the functional organization, which is often modified to incorporate staff, as well as line, departments. Other traditional forms are the divisional (or product), geographic, and customer organizations. The matrix organization is a newer form that is especially suitable to projects and task forces. When a great deal of authority is retained at the top, an organization is said to be centralized; when authority is pushed downward, an organization is said to be decentralized.

3. Authority, Responsibility, and Accountability. The formal organizational structure provides the framework—or chain of command—for determining accountability, and for the formal distribution of responsibilities and the authority needed to discharge them. Accountability is nonassignable liability for the way responsibilities are carried out; a responsibility is a duty or an obligation; authority is the power to carry out that obligation. When delegating a task to someone, it is imperative to transfer a proper amount of authority, too. Responsibility and authority should be balanced. A supervisor's authority is affected by the authority often granted to staff specialists. While their main responsibility is to advise or provide service, staff departments may also have functional authority in matters involving their specialties.

4. Delegation for Leverage. In addition to the formal allocation of job duties that occurs during the organizing process, there is an opportunity for supervisors to engage in the delegation of tasks to their subordinates. Such delegation, when fairly and prudently practiced, adds greatly to the amount of work a supervisor can accomplish.

5. Guidelines for Organizing. Certain principles prevail in the establishment of effective organizations. Among them are (a) an awareness of the chain of command and a respect for the channels it creates and (b) an adherence to the principle of an employee having only one boss. Organizations are more than just their structures, however. Their cultures (beliefs and expectations) can have a powerful impact on employee behavior.

Reading Comprehension

1. What features distinguish a formal organization from an informal one?

2. Explain the part that the division of work plays in the organizing process.

3. Jill is an assembly supervisor in a plastics novelty company. Her department receives maintenance services on its presses from a plant engineering department. A quality control department inspects the output of Jill's department and advises her when it is not meeting standards. What common form of organizational structure do these relationships imply? Identify the kinds of departments represented here.

4. Name three traditional kinds of organizational structures besides the functional and line-and-staff organizations. Why might they be used?

5. What is a major drawback of the matrix organization?

6. Distinguish between responsibility and authority, and explain how the two are related.

7. Discuss the pros and cons of restructuring.

8. In what way does the concept of accountability place restrictions on the delegation process?

9. What are some of the benefits a subordinate may gain from accepting a delegated task?

10. How can a supervisor learn about an organization's culture?

Application

Self-Assessment

How Good Are Your Organizational Skills?

Read the following statements carefully. Circle the number on the response scale that most closely reflects the degree to which each statement describes you. Add up your total points and prepare a brief action plan for self-improvement. Be ready to report your score for tabulation across the entire group.

	Good Description	Poor Description
1. I understand the differences between the formal and the informal organization.	10 9 8 7 6 5	4 3 2 1
2. I know when to use the chain of command, and when it is appropriate to use other channels.	10 9 8 7 6 5	4 3 2 1
3. I recognize the different implications of having a centralized or a decentralized organization.	10 9 8 7 6 5	4 3 2 1
4. I understand the need to balance responsibility with appropriate delegation of authority.	10 9 8 7 6 5	4 3 2 1
5. When delegating, I am careful not to either overcontrol (micromanage) or undercontrol.	10 9 8 7 6 5	4 3 2 1
6. I feel comfortable working with staff personnel who have substantial functional authority.	10 9 8 7 6 5	4 3 2 1

	Good Description									Poor Description
7. When I delegate, I am careful to explain not only what is to be done and how, but why.	10	9	8	7	6	5	4	3	2	1
8. I am aware of what organizational charts can and cannot portray.	10	9	8	7	6	5	4	3	2	1
9. I could make an effective case for either a wide or a narrow span of control.	10	9	8	7	6	5	4	3	2	1
10. I often pay attention to the visual, as well as the less visible, clues about my organization's culture.	10	9	8	7	6	5	4	3	2	1

Scoring and Interpretation

Scoring

Add up your total points for the 10 questions. Record that number here, and report it when it is requested. _____

Also, insert your score on the Personal Development Plan in the Appendix.

Interpretation

81 to 100 points. You seem to have a basic set of organizational skills.

61 to 80 points. Take a close look at some of your organizational skills (those with lower self-assessments) and discuss them with a manager to see if they need improvement.

Below 60 points. Some of your skills may be substantially inconsistent with effective organizational practices and could be detrimental to your success as a supervisor.

Identify your three lowest scores and record the question numbers here: _____, _____, _____.

Action

Write a brief paragraph detailing an action plan for how you might sharpen each of these skills. Then pay particularly close attention to the related material in the chapter as you review the relevant sections there.

Skill Development

Determining the Appropriate Span of Control

Assume that your manager asked you to review the factors affecting a span of control decision, apply them to your work unit, and make a recommendation regarding this question: *What is the best span of control for this unit?* To prepare your report, you probably will wish to review the text's discussion on span of control, scan the Internet for relevant information, and collect relevant information from within your department. In particular, you should recognize that even if you have an equal number of factors pushing in both directions, it is the *strength* and *relevance* of some forces that will determine your final conclusion. Record your findings on the worksheet below.

Forces for a Wider Span	Forces for a Narrower Span
1. _____	1. _____
2. _____	2. _____
3. _____	3. _____
4. _____	4. _____
5. _____	5. _____
6. _____	6. _____
7. _____	7. _____

Action

Following your analysis of the forces driving toward both wide and narrow spans in your unit, state a conclusion that you feel comfortable supporting. (Note that this exercise has no single precise numeric answer but should result in a strong directional conclusion. The exercise also gives you an opportunity to demonstrate your analytical skills.)

Role Play

Delegation

Pair up with two other persons. Designate one person as Pat, the second as Lee, and the third as an observer. Read your respective roles (do not read each other's until the role play is over) and engage in a conversation until you resolve any difference of opinion (or determine that you are unable to do so). Then discuss these questions:

1. What did Pat do well?
2. What could Pat have improved upon?
3. Were Lee's reservations/objections legitimate? Why or why not?
4. What lessons did you learn from this exercise?

Pat. You are first-line supervisor for a staff of mortgage lenders. Although several members of your team are capable, one in particular (Lee) seems destined to advance to managerial ranks. Your own workload has grown substantially in recent months, and the only way to stay ahead of deadlines is to delegate some assignments to your employees. In addition, you want to provide developmental opportunities for workers like Lee and keep them intellectually challenged. Therefore, you have decided to assign Lee the task of preparing a comprehensive statistical and analytical report on mortgage trends (within the bank, the local area, and nationally) over the last five years. You anticipate that the preparation of this report will require about 20 to 40 hours of effort (in addition to Lee's normal responsibilities). You are about to talk with Lee now to announce this opportunity.

Lee. You are one of eight mortgage lenders on the staff of a local financial institution. You all report to Pat, who is generally a first-rate supervisor. Work has been extremely busy for the past several months, and you hope things slow down pretty soon. Unfortunately, it always seems like you get additional projects dumped on you under the pretense of "developmental delegation," while the other lenders plod along at their normal pace. In addition, a major golf tournament is drawing celebrity pro golfers into the city in the near future, and you intend to ask Pat for several days off to attend this event. Pat has called you into the office, and you are about to speak to Pat now.

Cases for Analysis

Case 14

The Overworked Chorus Director

Dick was exhausted. A few months ago, he was asked by the company president to coordinate the firm's annual employee party. The event had grown from a simple summer picnic in the "good old days," to a complex musical extravaganza. He was put in charge of selecting a theme, renting an auditorium, choosing the music, choreographing the numbers, designing the sets, conducting auditions for the singers, and leading the rehearsals. All the work usually had to be done in the evenings, even though he had been promised release time from his job. It seemed as if there were people running everywhere, and there was a question, idea, comment, or complaint every minute. Dick had tried to get organized a few weeks ago, and had appointed four section leaders—one each for the sopranos, altos, tenors, and basses. Each section had 15 singers in it, including the section leader. Then he recruited three aides—a choreographer, a stage manager, and a publicity person. Finally, in desperation, he talked his friend Larry into being the assistant director, hoping that Larry could relieve him of some pressure by leading the chorus in rehearsals.

Analysis

a. What are Dick's organizational problems?
b. What is his span of control?
c. Draw his organizational chart.

Case 15

The New Quality Control Department

The Boonetown Electronics Company has never had a full-fledged quality control department. Until this year, the various functions have been carried out, irregularly, by the manufacturing and engineering departments. Recently, the company secured a large government contract and was told that it must set up a quality control department that could ensure proper product quality. Dan Crown, formerly a supervisor in the engineering department, was told that he could head the new department if he could come up with an acceptable organization. Dan got right to work, and after a few days this is what he wrote in his notebook:

The Need. Make sure that no products are shipped that do not meet government standards for size, weight, strength, and so forth.

Cost. Keep number of staff and cost of operating this department to a minimum, commensurate with the need for quality assurance.

Tasks to Perform

1. Implement design and engineering of product to conform to specifications.
2. Implement design and engineering of processes and equipment that can manufacture to specifications.
3. Specify, acquire, and maintain proper measuring instruments.
4. Inspect incoming raw materials and parts.
5. Inspect parts in process and assembly.
6. Inspect final products.
7. Establish and administer statistical control procedures for sampling of materials and for inspection.

Analysis

Dan has been told that, as the department's manager, he can appoint as many as three supervisors to assist him if he needs them.

Put yourself in Dan Crown's position, and draw up what you think would be an effective organization chart.

a. Divide the tasks into three logical groupings, or functions.
b. Decide which functions are most likely to be considered "line" for the quality control department's objectives and which should be "staff."
c. Construct a line-and-staff structure somewhat like that shown in Figure 5-2.
d. Decide which of the functions really requires a supervisor.

Case 16

Margaret's Delegation Decisions

The Metropolitan Planning Agency was set up to help the governments in a medium-size metropolitan area make plans for guiding future development in their area. The process carried out by the agency includes talking to local officials and members of the public to find out local goals; gathering and analyzing statistical information on population, economic growth, and so forth; and writing plans suggesting concrete steps the governments and citizens may take to reach their public goals. The plans may then be adopted by the governments and achieve legal status.

Margaret Walsh is a supervisor for the agency, overseeing nine employees who actually do the planning. Margaret used to be a planner, but now her work is entirely supervisory. The following list shows 10 activities, or duties, for which Margaret's department is responsible:

_____ 1. Assign sections of overall plan to individual planners.
_____ 2. Gather data on which the plans will be based.
_____ 3. Judge whether plan reports are of acceptable overall quality.
_____ 4. Decide what objectives will be included in plans.
_____ 5. Establish the number of planner-hours to be allocated to each project.
_____ 6. Meet with local officials to get their opinions for inclusion in plans.
_____ 7. Write community plans.
_____ 8. Work with governing bodies in their legal adoption of plans.
_____ 9. Present information about plans to the public.
_____ 10. Keep track of whether activities are being carried out within budget.

Analysis

Mark each activity on the list to show whether Margaret should or should not delegate it. Use one of the following lettered actions to indicate your decision.

a. She must do it.
b. She should do it, but someone else could help her.
c. She could do it, but others could do it if given an opportunity.
d. Others should do it, but she can help out in an emergency.
e. Others must do it.

ANSWERS TO QUICK TESTS	Quick Test 1	Quick Test 2	Quick Test 3	Quick Test 4	Quick Test 5
	1. F	3. T	5. F	7. F	9. T
	2. T	4. F	6. F	8. F	10. T

Staffing with Human Resources

After studying this chapter, you should be able to

- Know the factors that affect workforce requirements and understand the implications of overstaffing and understaffing.

- Identify the six steps of the staffing process and explain the extent of a supervisor's participation in each one.

- Discuss the critical aspects of the selection process and the role of application blanks, tests, and reference checks.

- Explain the main features of an employment interview and identify the types of questions that are most suitable and those areas that are restricted by equal employment opportunity legislation.

- Explain the importance of, and topics to cover in, employee orientation programs.

- Explain how careful selection and orientation can reduce employee turnover and absences, and discuss the primary causes of presenteeism.

1 Forecasting Workforce Requirements

CONCEPT

Effective staffing helps meet performance goals, but it depends on careful analysis of work requirements and needs for employees.

Why should supervisors be concerned about the staffing process?

People are an organization's most vital resource. They will make or break your department's performance. People are costly resources, however. They should be selected very carefully, just as you would do a thorough investigation before choosing an expensive piece of capital equipment. You must take equally good care of employees after their hiring, similar to the preventive maintenance schedule followed for new machinery.

A supervisor's primary goal is to achieve departmental performance results. This is a challenging task that extends across staffing and retention into training and motivation (the subjects of future chapters). It begins with estimating the number of workers needed to staff the department, playing an active and educated role in selecting the employees the organization hires, and maintaining the physical and emotional working conditions that attract and hold the best employees.

How do you engage in human resource planning for your department?

It's a matter of looking ahead, obtaining inputs, making assumptions based on past experience, working cooperatively with the human resource department, and remaining flexible. Here's a sketch of how it works.

1. Find out what your department is expected to produce—numbers of products or level of service—for the next week, month, quarter, or as far ahead as you can obtain input. Study the firm's sales and service projections.
2. Calculate how much the work schedule means in terms of total worker-hours for each type of job. Check your records for historical times for similar jobs, or carefully estimate the time required for each job.
3. Convert your total hours to worker-days by dividing by the number of hours in the standard workday for your organization. Then divide the total by the number of working days during the period to find the number of employees you'll need.
4. Make allowances for absences, training, and leaves. How many days of absences do employees in your department average per month? How many worker-days per month do all your employees combined lose due to workshops, parental leaves, and the like?

5. Search for other ways to meet your schedule. Many organizations today are concerned with "right-sizing"—rigorously examining their level of employment to identify the minimum number of employees they require. This places pressure on supervisors to search for creative alternatives to permanent employment. Options include the use of overtime, transfers, or borrowed employees from other departments, stretching the initial time lines for job completion, and using temporary or part-time employees to meet peak demands.

What are the implications of overstaffing or understaffing?

If you plan for too many employees, department costs will go up and your efficiency will suffer. Idle employees may become bored unless you can channel their free time into meaningful activities. The advantage of slight overstaffing, however, is that it allows you to cover varying demand (peak loads) and handle emergencies with greater flexibility. In addition, spare time can be a great opportunity for on-the-job coaching, informal training, and team-building activities.

Understaffing also has negative consequences. It can get you behind schedule and undermine an organization's effort to engage in time-based competition. Late deliveries may infuriate a customer and result in lost business. It can also give employees the feeling of being overworked and stressed out. And it doesn't give you much flexibility. But understaffing—at least in the short term—can stimulate your creativity to find and use alternative staffing techniques and also challenge employees to rise to the occasion. And a key advantage resulting from using either overtime for present employees or temporary-help agencies on a short-term basis to solve an understaffing problem is that you don't have to incur—at least directly—the additional benefits costs that are associated with new hires.

Your goal, then, is to balance the workforce. This means making sure that the number of employees on hand closely matches the workload, despite brief periods of staff shortages and excesses.

Neither overstaffing nor understaffing is desirable. **What are the problems associated with understaffing?**

| 1 | T or F | Proper staffing and retention can help a supervisor achieve departmental performance goals. |
| 2 | T or F | It is far better to be understaffed than to be overstaffed. |

QUICK TEST 1

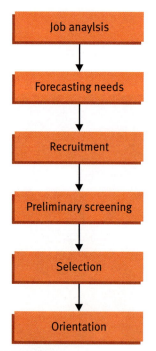

FIGURE 6-1

The staffing process.
Why should members of the work group be involved in the selection of new workers?

Application. A form used by an organization to legally and systematically gather and record information from a job applicant about his or her qualifications, education, and work experience.

References. People who give information on those seeking employment.

How is organization staffing accomplished?

It is done through a six-step procedure (see Figure 6-1). The first step is to specify the kinds of jobs and the characteristics of workers that will meet the production and service requirements. These jobs must fit within the organization structures described in Chapter 5. Then it is important to forecast the total number of different employees needed to complete a specific work schedule. Supervisors often play a key role in providing these estimates. Recruitment comes next; applicants are sought from inside and/or outside the company for unfilled job openings. Preliminary screening then takes place, usually by human resource department staff. They accept applications, administer employment tests, conduct reference checks, and keep legal files on the search process. Then the most appropriate individuals from among the candidates are selected. In many organizations, supervisors play a key role in the actual selection decisions. In addition, a contemporary trend is for work group members to be involved in the selection process. After one or more persons are hired, it is essential that proper orientation take place.

How can hiring decisions be improved?

Haphazard and discriminatory hiring practices have been exposed and condemned, and, one hopes, are becoming a thing of the past. They have increasingly been replaced with more formalized employment procedures, systematic data gathering, and well-trained personnel conducting the process. Modern organizations begin the hiring process with a careful *job analysis* that defines the knowledge, skills, and abilities needed by an employee to succeed. Hiring personnel then ask prospective employees to fill out an employment **application** (often on the Internet) that seeks relevant information about the nature and relevance of their work experience and education. This is usually followed by a preliminary screening interview conducted by the human resources department.

Employment **references** (relating to work history) may then be checked. A variety of *tests*—psychological, knowledge, honesty, performance, and medical—may be administered. Since many organizations are sharply reducing their corporate staff and decentralizing hiring authority to operating units, each of these procedures will be discussed briefly.

What information can be gained from the employment application?

Before examining any applications, you should develop a clear image of the kind of employee you want. Vague descriptions, such as "a good worker," are not very useful. Instead, specify the qualities you are looking for to suit the job that is open. Reflect on the better employees you've had in the past and their characteristics. Try making a checklist of qualifications, and indicate whether each one is necessary or just desirable. Consider factors such as the following:

- **Experience.** What type is best? How long should they have worked on similar jobs? Is related experience acceptable?
- **Specific skills.** Is it imperative that they be able to write creatively? Or is it sufficient that they be literate?
- **Speed and accuracy.** Does the job require dexterity? Is the pace likely to overwhelm some people? Is quality work expected on a consistent basis?
- **Initiative.** Will employees be working without close supervision? Will they need to make decisions on their own?
- **Teamwork.** Will new employees work alone, or in close interaction with others? Will there be a good "fit" with present employees? After these factors are identified, examine the application for relevant information. What skills do they list? How stable is their employment history? Have they worked in a team-oriented workplace before?

What kinds of tests can help you select better employees?

Properly chosen, administered, and interpreted, employment tests can be a big help in picking better workers *if* the tests are legally defensible. For example, *aptitude* tests may attempt to find out whether a person has the ability to learn a particular kind of job. *Personality*, *intelligence*, and job or career *interest* tests are widely used for applicants seeking higher-level management positions, but these tests are somewhat more difficult to justify as being job related. *Honesty* tests, which purport to measure applicant attitudes toward ethical behavior, have grown in popularity as employers try to hold down the costs of internal theft.

Tests may be simple and direct, such as those that show whether an applicant can read and write or perform the simple arithmetic that record-keeping on the job may demand. Of particular interest to supervisors are ***performance*** (work sampling) ***tests***, which measure the ability of applicants to do the major parts of the job for which they may be hired. Although it is possible only to sample work requirements and obtain limited data, at least these tests provide an opportunity to observe a candidate in action.

Performance test. An employment test that enables job applicants to demonstrate that they can actually perform the kind of work required by the job in question.

For instance, an applicant may claim competence at using the computer program Lotus 1-2-3. A 15-minute tryout on a specific task will provide powerful evidence whether that claim is valid. But remember: the test used must be relevant to the particular job you are seeking to fill.

Is it ethical to use a personality test to deny someone a job?

Personality tests come in many sizes and shapes, and should never be developed or used without professional guidance. But personality plays a large role in helping an organization assess an applicant's nature and predicting the jobs in which the applicant will (or won't) succeed. The better tests often focus on the relatively standard "big five" personality traits. These tests typically measure these dimensions: agreeableness, extroversion, conscientiousness, independence, and emotional stability. The tests should be job related, not discriminate against any group, not invade someone's privacy, and not be the only criterion for hiring or rejecting an applicant. Under those conditions they can be ethical, although still possibly intimidating to an applicant. Whatever the results, they should be used with caution.

What criteria do tests have to meet before they are used?

Validity. The proven ability of a test to measure what it purports to measure.

Reliability. The demonstrated ability of a test to yield similar scores for a candidate if the test were repeated (after a sufficient period of time to allow forgetting).

All tests used should be fully validated and their reliability established before they are used to screen applicants for jobs. This is done for two reasons—(a) to meet legal requirements and (b) to increase the likelihood of desirable selection decisions. *Validity* simply means that the test really measures what it is supposed to measure. *Reliability* means that it can do that consistently. For example, if an applicant were to take a reliable test repeatedly over several weeks, the scores would be nearly the same (unless the applicant learned the answers in the interim).

Underlying the challenges of validity and reliability is the requirement that any test given to applicants (a) should be directly related to the job's content, (b) should not discriminate unfairly against the persons taking it, and (c) should not unduly invade their privacy. In other words, it would not be right to require that an applicant for a data-entry job pass a test designed for an administrative assistant. Nor should the test explore issues of lifestyle that are the employee's own business.

What about physical examinations and disabilities?

Many employers no longer require physical examinations by a company nurse or doctor, at least not until *after* an employment decision has been made. At that point, applicants may be required to provide urine, hair, or blood samples to be tested for evidence of drug use. Since the Americans with Disabilities Act provides protection for the qualified disabled, the employer risks a charge of discrimination if it appears that a non-job-related disability has affected a hiring decision. Supervisors should ask only whether there is a physical or mental impairment that would make it impossible for the person to perform the job, or if there are specific positions for which the applicant should not be considered. Beyond that, supervisors should look for ways in which they can make reasonable accommodations that would allow differently abled persons to succeed on the job.

Should you check employee references?

Absolutely yes! It's foolhardy to hire anyone without checking with the last employer or two. You can at least find out the actual job the applicant held and verify the dates of employment. Most former employers will not tell you much more for fear of illegally prejudicing the applicant's chances. For this reason, it is wise to ask the job candidate to sign a *release*, which authorizes you to contact personal and employment references, as well as obtain verification of education and employment backgrounds. One good way to discover the applicant's views about his or her employment record is to ask, "What do you think your last employer would say about your performance, work habits, and attendance?"

3	T or F	The first step in the staffing process is to forecast future needs.
4	T or F	Employment tests can be helpful even if they lack validity and reliability.

QUICK TEST 2

Interviewing Job Candidates

3

What are the objectives of job interviews?

CONCEPT
Interview questions should be strictly job related and must be free from any implication of bias.

Simply stated, an ***employment interview*** has three broad purposes—to give information, to get information, and to "make a friend." In short, the interview is a face-to-face exchange during which you need to provide a candid overview of the job and work environment, obtain key data that allow you to decide which candidate is the best, and build a positive relationship with the applicants so that the persons who are rejected this time will apply again for future positions, and the person who is accepted will be "sold" on the job and the employer (and will accept your offer of employment).

Employment interview.
A face-to-face exchange of information between a job applicant and an employer's representative designed to develop qualitative information about the applicant's suitability for employment.

What information should you give to job candidates?

Realistic job preview.
A balanced presentation of positive and negative features about a job that allows a candidate to reach an informed judgment.

An important task is to provide applicants with a ***realistic job preview***. If you tell them about only the good features, or (worse yet) if you over-sell the job, the individual hired will likely be disappointed and soon quit. Your goal is to provide a realistic portrait—a healthy balance of both favorable and unfavorable job tasks. Specify the fixed requirements that are inescapable. Mention the job title, major tasks, relationships to other jobs, and degree of discretion allowed. Describe the job environment, equipment used, safety factors, physical demands, and working conditions. Better yet, show them the work site and job location.

It's especially wise to forewarn an applicant about any conditions that might be considered undesirable, such as job pressures, social isolation, and shift work. Don't scare the applicant, but be sure the key facts are known ahead of time. Better that the applicant turn down the job than walk off it after two weeks of costly training.

You should also describe the positive aspects of the job—opportunities for advancement, the organization's benefit programs, and so forth. This is the time to do some sound, factual selling, but don't make promises about raises, job security, or promotions. They can come back to haunt you later. And don't neglect to inform applicants that you are taking a few notes during the interview to help you remember their positive attributes. When it is presented in this way, most applicants will be pleased to see you stop to jot down a few things they have said.

Ethical Perspectives

Handling Revealed Information

During a series of employment interviews Candidate A mentions that she is pregnant, Candidate B reveals what year he graduated from high school, and Candidate C pleads that he desperately needs this job after being out of work for six months and having six children to feed. What should you do with this information?

How do you build a positive relationship with the candidates?

Your first task is to build rapport with them. Welcome them, extend a warm handshake, put them at ease, and possibly offer refreshments. Explain that your goal is to obtain enough information about them to make a sound judgment about their prospects of job success. Never turn the interview into a "grilling" by asking point-blank questions, or firing a series of questions at the candidates, or challenging their answers. Since job seekers are already on guard, this will only create greater caution and defensiveness. And when you are finished, thank them for their time and indicate clearly how and when they will hear about a decision from you.

What kinds of interview questions are most useful to ask?

You won't learn much from questions that can be answered with a simple "yes" or "no." For example, will you really gain much by asking a question such as "Did you get along well with your co-workers in the last place you worked?" Instead, ask a structured series of *open-ended questions* that begin with *what, where, why, when, how,* or *who.* These questions give applicants a chance to talk and, while talking, show you a lot about themselves. If the applicant does most of the talking and you do most of the listening, you'll have lots of time to gather data and form a reasoned opinion. And that's the primary purpose of the interview.

Ask open-ended questions such as the following:

- Tell me about your education. How do you feel that it would help you do the kind of work you are applying for?
- Where did you get your most valuable work experience? How did it prepare you for this job?
- When did you first decide to do this sort of work? What have you found most difficult about it? Most pleasant?
- Why did you leave your last job? Would you go back there if you could?
- How would you describe the nature of your relationship with your last supervisor?

Then follow up with a carefully prepared set of behavioral-based questions that elicit responses from the applicant in terms of what he or she would do (or has done) in specific work-related situations. For example, ask the applicant, "Tell me about a recent situation at your current

JOB TIP!

Cautions When Conducting a Job Interview

James Menzies Black, former director of human resources for a major railroad, offers this advice during interviews:

- **Don't be too formal.** When you are relaxed, the applicant will be, too.
- **Don't concentrate heavily on note taking.** Wait until the interview is over to capture your impressions and thoughts.
- **Don't high-pressure applicants.** Misled employees won't trust your word.
- **Don't hire overqualified applicants.** You want a close match between job requirements and employee qualifications.
- **Don't tell applicants why you rejected them.** It's not your job to do this, and you may say something

that becomes the basis for a subsequent lawsuit.
- **Don't make moral judgments or give advice.** An applicant's personal life is no concern of yours.
- **Don't ask trick questions that may embarrass them.** Be direct. Your job is to discover what you can about the individual's capacity to perform the job.
- **Don't give feedback on your reactions through facial expression, tone of voice, or gestures.** If an applicant sees a reaction, he or she may simply alter his or her answers to meet your preferences.
- **Don't be too impatient.** The best information often comes after you pause and invite further explanations.
- **Don't be misled by your prejudices.** Keep an open mind.

job when you had to deal with a conflict and how you went about it." The answers to these behavioral questions are a rich source of information that helps you better predict the applicant's future behavior based on past performance.

What kinds of interview questions should you avoid asking?

Be extremely careful. An ounce of prevention can save you a ton of trouble. Prepare your set of questions in advance, and follow them consistently with all candidates. Limit your deviations from the list to follow-up questions that probe for more complete responses. Before using the questions, consult someone from the human resources department to obtain his or her reaction. In particular, avoid these topics: race or color, religion, national origin, sexual preference, age, marital status, family intentions, employment of spouse, disabilities past or present, citizenship, arrest record, and any unnecessary probing of the candidate's privacy. Possible exceptions are asking about age if you need to determine if the applicant is old enough to work, asking about a person's legal right to work in this country, and convictions for major crimes if they are relevant to the job.

In addition, if an applicant *volunteers* any of the above information, be sure to avoid taking notes about it, and also inform the candidate that topics such as that will not be used in the selection decision.

| QUICK TEST 3 | 5 | T or F | A realistic job preview is a portrait of all the reasons why a candidate should accept the job. |
| | 6 | T or F | Open-ended questions are preferable to those answerable by a "yes" or "no" for getting candidates to talk. |

Making the Selection Decision

CONCEPT
Use the available information carefully to screen out the less-qualified candidates and find the ones with the greatest chance of success.

How do you use the information gained to make a sound decision?

First, recognize that there are no guarantees in hiring, only probabilities. No one has a perfect record of predicting success, but you do want continual improvement of your batting average. Second, remember that selection is more a process of screening out the poorer candidates than one of identifying the best one. You are looking for information that will disqualify some, while moving others higher on your list. Third, you are seeking corroborative evidence—information from two or more sources that confirms a tentative conclusion. That's why you don't rely on a single selection tool, but use multiple items such as the employment application, references, tests, and interviews.

Review the information you have gathered. Be especially alert to the following:

Desirable characteristics. Are the applicant's achievements well documented? Has the individual received some recognition in a previous job?

Problematic attitudes. Does the person engage in unnecessary boasting? Unnecessary criticism of a former employer or work colleagues? Failure to listen? Will those behaviors continue and affect work performance in the new job?

Work motivation. How willing is this person to work? To volunteer for extra assignments? To help out other workers? To seek creative solutions to technical problems?

Remember, most people looking for work are trying to put their best foot forward. And they may have been well trained to impress you with a smooth appearance. But if an interviewee can't show you something positive during the interview, there's a good chance that you won't see anything better on the job.

7	T or F	Selection is basically a process of screening out the less-qualified candidates.
8	T or F	It is reasonable to expect that supervisors will have a perfect record in hiring successful employees.

Orientation Training

⑤

Why do new employees need an orientation?

CONCEPT
New employees need an orientation to the job, co-workers, and work environment.

Providing an *orientation* for recently hired workers is a little like introducing friends at a club meeting where they are strangers. You'd want to introduce them to others and try to make them feel at home. You'd show them where to hang their hats and coats and where the rest rooms are. If you wanted to have them think well of your club, you might tell them something about its history and the good people who belong to it. If you had to leave them for a time to attend to some duty or other, you

Orientation. The process in which new employees are introduced to their jobs, co-workers, and work environment through tours, personal introductions, and explanations.

would come back occasionally to see how they were getting along. It's the same way with new employees who report to you. You want them to think well of you and to feel at home in your department from the beginning, so treat them accordingly.

What should be included in orientation programs for new employees?

Orientation has dual roles. You are *educating* employees about important things that they want or need to know, while also *socializing* them into the organization. Socialization is the process of shaping their thinking and behavior. It is designed to help employees fit in, adjust rapidly and smoothly, and learn how to get along with others in their work group. Effective socialization results in conformity to key rules and policies, innovative behavior where desired, high loyalty to the employer, and strong intentions to stay with the organization.

Orientation sessions should cover the major topics of probable interest to employees, as well as the items that you think are important to their success. These topics include the following:

- Pay rates, pay periods, when pay is first received, deductions from pay, and how pay increases may be earned.
- Hours of work, such as reporting and quitting time, lunch periods, and breaks.
- Information about the organization's vision, values, mission, and goals.
- Work-related policies, such as disciplinary procedures and harassment.
- Opportunities to use an alternative work schedule, such as four 10-hour days or telecommuting.
- Time reporting systems, availability of overtime and overtime pay, and premium pay for working shift schedules.
- Employee options under the company's benefit plans, such as group life, health, and dental insurance—and, especially, retirement plans.
- Procedure to follow when sick or late.
- Basic safety rules, the procedure for reporting accidents, the location of first-aid facilities, and the joint employee-company responsibility for identifying hazards under the Occupational Safety and Health Administration (OSHA) law.

Orientation should also include the following activities:

- Tour of the department and other areas of the company.
- Introduction to co-workers.
- Discussion of the organizational culture.

- Assignment to a work area and identification of initial tasks and necessary resources.
- Location of cafeteria and rest rooms.

This basic information is a lot for new employees to swallow at once. Don't be afraid to ask questions to gauge their understanding or to repeat what you tell them several times. Better still, give them some of the more detailed information in small doses. Give them some today, a little tomorrow, and as much as they can take a week from now.

Note that in many companies, new employees receive an orientation talk from the human resources department. As valuable as this talk may be, it won't help new employees half as much as an informal, one-on-one chat with their supervisor will. You are an important person in their eyes, and you also want to begin developing a healthy work relationship with them. Grab the opportunity to do so!

The first day on a new job can be difficult. **How can current employees help a new person "fit in"?**

How can you increase the chances that a chosen employee will succeed?

One powerful device is the *self-fulfilling prophecy*. This is the process of believing something to be true, and then acting in a way that makes it more likely to happen. You can use this in three ways. First, tell the chosen candidate that you were pleased to offer the job to your first choice—someone who really stood out over the others. Your statement of high expectations will set a challenging goal at which the new hire can aim. Second, tell your existing employees that you have selected a new worker with a strong track record and a high likelihood of success. Ask them to help the new employee "learn the ropes" and fit in. Third, remind yourself that your reputation is on the line with every new hire. Ask yourself what you can do to help the new employee become productive and then follow up by doing it.

9	T or F	Once an employee is selected, a supervisor's work in staffing is basically over.
10	T or F	The self-fulfilling prophecy can draw together expectations of success from co-workers, the employee, and the supervisor.

QUICK TEST 5

CONCEPT

The selection process should seek to minimize the employment of people whose unsuitability will result in excessive absences and/or turnover.

Quips&Quotes

Retention is corporate America's number one challenge.

Beverly Kaye and Sharon Jordan-Evans

What's the connection between the staffing process and high turnover and absenteeism among employees?

A high incidence of turnover and absenteeism among employees is a major indicator of an ineffective staffing and selection process or poor supervision. Other signs of ineffective staffing include excessive tardiness, poor quality of work, low productivity, poor customer relations, and missed deadlines. Experts also identify low creativity and poor teamwork as other symptoms.

It is difficult, costly, and time-consuming to recruit, select, relocate, and train new employees. For example, it may cost $50,000 to add an engineer or a systems analyst to the payroll. Even a conservative estimate of the cost of keeping a semiskilled worker on the payroll for a year is well over $30,000, when you consider salary, fringe benefits, training, overhead, and other costs. Consequently, each employee who works for you must return about $30,000 or more in productive effort before the company breaks even on his or her cost of employment. When the cost of hiring employees to replace those who quit or are discharged (turnover) is added to the losses of their costly services due to absenteeism, you can readily see why it is so important to hire people most suitable for the work in the first place, orient them well, and strive to retain them.

How do you measure employee turnover?

Employee turnover. A measure of how many people come to work for an organization and do not remain employed there, for whatever reason.

Employee turnover is the relationship between how many people come to work for you and how many don't stay (for any reason). Turnover includes employees who are hired or rehired, and employees who are laid off, quit, retire, die, or are discharged.

For consistency, the U.S. Department of Labor suggests that to determine the rate of turnover, compare only the *total* number of separations with the *average* number of employees on your payroll during a particular period. The *rate of turnover* is calculated as follows:

$$\frac{\text{Number of separations} \times 100}{\text{Average size of workforce}} = \text{Turnover percentage}$$

For instance, if you had an average of 50 employees during the month, but 1 quit and you laid off 2, the turnover would be 3. Your turnover rate would be $(3 \times 100)/50 = 6$ percent a month. While that doesn't sound so bad, you should realize that if that happened consistently, your turnover rate for the year would be a substantial 72 percent (6×12).

Turnover rates vary widely from department to department, organization to organization, and industry to industry. Therefore, it is important to find out what your employer's past turnover experience is, and what is considered "acceptable" in your situation.

Decisions about what *kinds* of separations and hires to include in turnover computations vary from organization to organization, too. For example, some firms distinguish between voluntary and involuntary separations, while others try to identify "functional" and "dysfunctional" separations (the loss of unproductive and productive employees, respectively). And some firms have aggressively sought to downsize their workforces by stimulating **attrition**—the use of natural events and causes such as resignations and retirements. Obviously, if certain kinds of separations or hires are excluded, the turnover rates will be lower. Thus, it's good to know exactly what the specifications are when comparing turnover rates, or when trying to control yours.

Attrition. The gradual reduction of a workforce by means of natural events and causes, such as retirements, deaths, and resignations, as opposed to reductions planned by management, such as discharges and layoffs.

What causes high turnover?

In general, employee turnover is considered the single best long-term measure of employee morale. High morale should contribute to lower turnover, and lower morale will be followed by higher turnover. Many other factors—such as an unusually high or low unemployment rate—may confound this relationship, of course. But one thing stands out: A highly dissatisfied employee has a higher *propensity* to think about quitting and is more likely to search for a new job. Then, when an opportunity arises, a dissatisfied worker will jump at the chance.

There are many causes of voluntary turnover decisions. Dissatisfaction with a poor supervisor, unhappiness with pay or benefits, lack of appreciation, a long commute, transfer of a spouse to another city, desire to seek a less stressful job, and a belief that greater job security lies elsewhere may all lead to employee resignations. Many times the problem leading to involuntary turnover, though, is simply having the wrong person in the job—the result of a poor staffing procedure. Something broke down, especially during the interviewing and selection stages. Even a potentially good employee may have been assigned to the wrong job during the placement process. Accordingly, high turnover rates can be greatly reduced by careful hiring and placement. And it is far easier to provide effective supervision for employees who are well matched to their jobs.

What are the negative effects of absenteeism?

Absences (like turnover) are costly, to the organization as well as to the employee. If it costs about $30,000 a year to keep a person on the payroll, then each day that a person is absent and receives pay can cost your department something like $125 (based on 240 working days a year) in lost effort. But there are other negative effects as well. Absences frequently

Quips & Quotes

More than one-third of U.S. workers say they played hooky from work over the last twelve months.

Kate Lorenz

Absenteeism rate. The average number of days absent per employee, or the percentage of scheduled worker-days lost.

Presenteeism. The productivity problem caused by employees who insist on trying to work even though they are troubled by physical or emotional ailments.

create a need for permanent overstaffing, or for hiring temporary employees, or for overtime caused by delays. And absent employees irritate both the supervisor and the co-workers who have to pick up an extra workload. In many cases, your **absenteeism rate** is one of the biggest obstacles you have in workforce planning—from day to day or from month to month.

There are two popular ways to compute absenteeism rates:

1. Absenteeism rate =
$$\frac{\text{total days absent}}{\text{average size of workforce}} = \text{average days absent per employee}$$

2. Absenteeism rate =
$$\frac{\text{total days absent} \times 100}{\text{worker-days worked} + \text{worker-days lost}} = \frac{\text{percentage of scheduled}}{\text{worker-days lost}}$$

Computation of these averages, when compared to norms for your industry, your geographical area, or comparable departments, can give you a good idea of whether you have a problem on your hands. Absences (and *tardiness*, which is simply short-term absenteeism) can usually be controlled by good supervision. Often all it takes is to monitor the data and share it with your workers, asking for their cooperation. Preferably, though, you can avoid many problems by screening out applicants who have displayed these undesirable characteristics in the past or are likely to develop them on the job in your organization—simply because they are unsuited for the work they were hired to do or were not given a realistic job preview.

Can your absenteeism rate ever be too low?

Curiously, the answer is yes. When supervisors place too much emphasis on lowering the department's absenteeism rate, another problem can emerge. *Presenteeism* occurs when employees come to work despite troublesome (and often recurring) health conditions that substantially affect their work performance. Presenteeism is a unique phenomenon—it is far harder to assess than absenteeism, it can reduce a worker's productivity by 33 percent or more, and it is driven by employees who are trying to do what is right by coming to work even when they don't feel like doing so. Common causes of presenteeism include migraine headaches, acid reflux disease, flu, depression, lower back pain, and arthritis. However, the most prevalent cause is sinus trouble or allergies.

How can you address this problem? The answers lie first in awareness by the supervisor of the existence and consequences of presenteeism. Then employees need to be counseled to manage their ailments through better diagnosis and medical treatment. Finally, supervisors need to be empathetic enough to encourage employees to stay away from work on occasion—especially if their ailments threaten to disrupt the work of co-workers or spread to them. The overall lesson here is to have a reasonable goal for your absenteeism rate—but not to push it to impossibly low levels.

How can better hiring reduce turnover and absences?

Selecting the proper person to fit first the company and then the available job opening hits the turnover and absenteeism problem at its source. With millions of people keeping an eye out for a better job, there is a substantial opportunity for upgrading the quality of your workforce as new hires are made. But knowledge of the causes and consequences of turnover and absenteeism should also drive supervisors to reexamine their own behavior, departmental working conditions, and other job factors for possible improvements.

Keep in mind that employees, too, are continually assessing the suitability of their employment after being hired. They ask themselves: "Is this still the right job for me? Is this an organization I want to continue working for?" An effective staffing procedure—coupled with effective supervision—is more likely to get these employees to answer "yes!" to these questions.

Internet connection

my.webmd.com/content/article/76/90290.htm
Refer to this site for a complete discussion of presenteeism from a medical perspective (but in lay language).

11	T or F	Employee turnover is best measured by the length of time a specific employee stays on the job after being hired.
12	T or F	Supervisors should be concerned with overall departmental absenteeism rates or presenteeism, but not both.

QUICK TEST 6

Practical Guidelines for Supervisors

1. *Set your human resource planning goal as right-sizing*—having the correct number of qualified employees in place at all times.

2. Make sure you *understand which steps in the staffing process you are directly involved in*, and which are more clearly the responsibility of the human resources department.

3. *Study all inputs to the selection process* carefully to corroborate the potential strengths and weaknesses of candidates before reaching an overall decision.

4. *Minimize your reliance on first impressions* of a candidate or assessments of the candidate's overall polish and likability; focus instead on actual qualifications.

5. Plan to *accomplish all three objectives in any employment interview*, and grade yourself afterward on how well you did.

6. *Develop a specific plan to follow regarding the questions you will ask interviewees*, and stick closely to it (using follow-up questions instead of spontaneous ones).

7. *Set a strong example for desired citizenship behaviors* from employees so that they will be clear on what you expect of them.

8. *View orientation programs as high-potential opportunities* not only to educate employees but to *socialize them* into desirable modes of future behavior.

9. Conduct ongoing investigations into why employees become turnover statistics, and then *seek to minimize unwanted departures*.

10. Understand why employees might choose not to show up for work, and *help them recognize the high costs and disruption that absenteeism produces*.

Chapter 6 Review

Key Concepts to Remember

1. Forecasting Workforce Requirements. Supervisors know they need to get results through people—good people. And supervisors, better than anyone else, should know the kinds of requirements the work in a department demands of employees—that is, what skills, aptitudes, and interests are required—and the number of such individuals needed to get the work done economically, on time, and well. Forecasts of the numbers of employees needed to staff a department are determined by workload projections, work schedules, vacations, and anticipated absenteeism rates. A proper balance should be struck so that a department is neither overstaffed nor understaffed.

2. The Staffing Process. Staffing of an organization is accomplished through a six-step procedure—(a) specifying the kinds of jobs and the characteristics of employees needed to attain work requirements, (b) forecasting the number of different employees needed, (c) recruiting those candidates for unfilled job openings, (d) preliminary screening of job candidates, (e) selecting the most appropriate individuals from among the candidates, and (f) proper orientation. Supervisors should participate in the selection of the right kind of people by fully describing jobs, specifying criteria for applicants, and interviewing candidates. A strong understanding of the legal requirements for fair treatment, and the need for valid and reliable selection tools, is essential.

3. Interviewing Job Candidates. Supervisors should remember the three objectives of job interviews, and be sure to provide applicants with a realistic job preview covering both favorable and unfavorable features. After establishing rapport, ask open-ended questions that focus on education, experience, skills, and job-related attitudes. All questions used should relate to a performance requirement of the job. Avoid questions that might generate information regarding race, color, religion, national origin, sexual preference, age, marital status, disability, or citizenship.

4. Making the Selection Decision. Effective selection is based on matching an individual's knowledge, skills, and abilities (or aptitude for learning) with those required by the job. In addition to checking demonstrable skills, look for evidence of past achievements, negative attitudes, and work motivation.

5. Orientation Training. New employees require special attention and are often receptive to any help received. Orientation is a valuable tool for sharing important information regarding pay, benefits, and safe work practices with workers and for developing a relationship with them. New employees should also be introduced to their co-workers as part of the overall socialization process.

6. Minimizing the Potential for Absences and Turnover. Careful selection of employees helps prevent a high incidence of absences and turnover later on. Employees whose capabilities and interests match those of the job tend to be better satisfied with their work and reflect this in better attendance and retention. It is costly to replace experienced employees with new ones all the time. Absences are costly, but so are sick employees who insist on working.

Reading Comprehension

1. What factors affect the determination of the optimal size of a department's workforce?

2. In which aspect(s) of the staffing process are supervisors *not* likely to play a major part? Which unit usually handles those aspects?

3. Gerry expects that his sales order department will have to handle peak loads during the spring and fall seasons. Should he plan to staff a year-round workforce large enough to handle these peak loads when they occur? Why or why not? What are his alternatives?

4. What is meant by the validity and reliability of selection tools?

5. What is meant by an "open-ended" question, as used during an employment interview? Provide some examples.

6. What kinds of information can generally be obtained from a job candidate without infringing upon rights guaranteed by equal employment opportunity legislation? What kinds cannot?

7. What are the risks of hiring a college graduate for a job that requires only a high school education, as long as the applicant is willing to take the job at the prevailing wage rate?

8. How can a supervisor use realistic job previews, orientation, and the self-fulfilling prophecy to increase the success of new employees?

9. Which factors are generally considered the main causes of excessive employee turnover?

10. How does presenteeism differ from absenteeism?

Application

Self-Assessment

How Good Are Your Selection Skills?

Read the following statements carefully. Circle the number on the response scale that most closely reflects the degree to which each statement describes you. Add up your total points and prepare a brief action plan for self-improvement. Be ready to report your score for tabulation across the entire group.

	Good Description		Poor Description
1. Before submitting a hiring request, I carefully specify the type of job to be filled and the kind of personal characteristics I am seeking.	10 9 8 7 6	5 4 3	2 1
2. I recognize that recruiting and selecting applicants should be a joint effort with the human resources department.	10 9 8 7 6	5 4 3	2 1
3. When I'm planning for an increase in the size of my workforce, I am careful to include estimates of absences, training, and leaves.	10 9 8 7 6	5 4 3	2 1
4. When interviewing applicants, I try to avoid asking questions that can be answered with "yes" or "no."	10 9 8 7 6	5 4 3	2 1

	Good Description		Poor Description
5. I can readily report my department's annual turnover rate and provide an explanation for it.		10 9 8 7 6 5 4 3 2 1	
6. When deciding on the proper staffing level, I am careful to avoid substantial understaffing or overstaffing.		10 9 8 7 6 5 4 3 2 1	
7. In a difficult job market with few applicants, I still feel the obligation to talk about the less pleasant aspects of an open job.		10 9 8 7 6 5 4 3 2 1	
8. Although it might be tempting to leave employee orientation up to the human resources department, I take those responsibilities very seriously.		10 9 8 7 6 5 4 3 2 1	
9. I am extremely careful not to ask questions about or make note of (or use) information about factors such as an applicant's age, race, and gender.		10 9 8 7 6 5 4 3 2 1	
10. I am fully aware of the meaning of and the need for all selection methods to have validity and reliability.		10 9 8 7 6 5 4 3 2 1	

Scoring and Interpretation

Scoring

Add up your total points for the 10 questions. Record that number here, and report it when it is requested. _____

Also, insert your score on the Personal Development Plan in the Appendix.

Interpretation

81 to 100 points. You seem to have a basic set of selection skills.

61 to 80 points. Take a close look at some of your selection skills (those with lower self-assessments) and discuss them with a manager to see if they need improvement.

Below 60 points. Some of your skills may be substantially inconsistent with effective selection practices and could be detrimental to your success as a supervisor.

Identify your three lowest scores and record the question numbers here: _____, _____, _____.

Action

Write a brief paragraph detailing an action plan for how you might sharpen each of these skills. Then pay particularly close attention to the related material in the chapter as you review the relevant sections there.

Skill Development

Interviewing Prospective Employees

Assume that you have an opportunity to interview several prescreened candidates for an important position in your department. Your overall goal is to answer the question, *Who is the best applicant for this job?* To prepare your questions, you will likely wish to review the text's discussion on effective interviewing, search the Internet for relevant guidelines, remind yourself to stay away from issues and topics that are illegal or inappropriate, and consult with staff persons in the human resources department for their advice. In particular, you recognize that it will be desirable to ask the identical (or very similar) questions of all applicants, so that you can directly compare their responses.

Action

Prepare a list of the 10 most useful questions you can, stated in the proper format. Include both open-ended and behavioral questions. Ask someone in the human resources department to review your questions.

1. _____
   _____
2. _____
   _____
3. _____
   _____
4. _____
   _____
5. _____
   _____
6. _____
   _____
7. _____
   _____
8. _____
   _____
9. _____
   _____
10. _____
    _____

Group Exercise

Evaluating Orientation Programs

Step 1: Form into teams of three persons. Each team should select a local company to explore. Contact that organization and request permission to interview someone there regarding his or her process for orienting new employees to the organization and their jobs.

Step 2: During the interview, obtain a specific list of topics covered and the approximate time allocated to each topic. See if you can determine how much time is spent on providing factual information versus how much is spent on making the new employee feel comfortable and helping him or her "fit in."

Step 3: Combine your results with those of other groups by completing the following matrix, showing time estimates for the various topics by each organization.

Step 4: Determine if there are differences across the organizations. If so, why? Which pattern seems to be the best from your perspective? What recommendation(s) could you make?

	Organization							
Topic (add time spent on each)	**A**	**B**	**C**	**D**	**E**	**F**	**G**	**H**
Pay								
Hours of work								
Alternative work schedules								
Time reporting system								
Benefit plans								
Sick leave								
Tardiness procedures								
Safety								
Physical facility tour								
Co-worker introductions								
Organizational culture								
Other								

Cases for Analysis

Case 17

The Biased Interview

"Nancy, the carpenter's position you're applying for is very demanding physically. We work outdoors in some of the coldest, wettest, windiest weather. And building forms with heavy, rough-cut lumber is a totally different ball game from trimming a few windows with clean, dried pine." That's Jake Barnes talking, site supervisor for the Jarvis Construction Company.

Nancy sat straight up in her chair and answered with pursed lips: "I'm strong, healthy, and an experienced backpacker. I haven't had a serious illness for years."

"I'm glad to hear that," said Jake. "Your application says that you have worked only indoors doing remodeling and trim work. I don't know whether you can stand this hard work."

"Mr. Barnes, I wouldn't have answered your ad if I were not sure of my physical capabilities," replied Nancy.

"We've had a lot of turnover here; I only want to hire carpenters who will stick with us. I see that you are married; do you plan to have children soon?"

Nancy crossed her arms. "I don't plan to, but I don't see how that would make a difference. During my last pregnancy, I never missed a day of work until right before the baby was born. I was back to work six weeks later."

Jake went on: "Another thing, Nancy. You would be the only woman in the crew. Can you handle that pressure?"

"Mr. Barnes, I'm interested only in doing good work and getting more experience. I've often worked with men; it's never been a problem. Wouldn't you like to know something about my work experience, about my training?"

"Oh, I already know you're a good carpenter. I called your last boss. It's just that this job is really demanding, and I don't know whether you can handle it."

That did it for Nancy. She said, "You're not giving me a fair chance at this job, Mr. Barnes, and I'd like to speak to the owner." Jake agreed to call in Mr. Jarvis. Nancy spoke to him with considerable heat. "This isn't fair. Mr. Barnes has assumed from the start that I can't handle this job. He implies that I'm not strong enough, that I might be unreliable if

I had another baby, and that I am unqualified because I'm a woman and the other carpenters are men. Won't someone listen to my qualifications? I'm a good carpenter, and I can do a good job for you."

Analysis

If you were Mr. Jarvis, how would you proceed? Of the following five alternatives, which do you think might be most effective? Rank the alternatives on a scale from 1 (most preferable) to 5 (least preferable). You may add another alternative if you wish. Be prepared to justify your ranking.

_____ **a.** Finish the interview with Nancy, but choose not to hire her. The issues Jake was raising, although delicate matters, are legitimate concerns for this position.

_____ **b.** Finish the interview and hire Nancy. It has been established that she has the carpentry and work skills that qualify her for the job. Plan a number of coaching sessions for Jake to improve his job-interviewing skills.

_____ **c.** Finish the interview and hire Nancy. Fire Jake Barnes because of the serious possibility of his involving the company in crippling legal action because of his illegal job interview questions.

_____ **d.** Tell Nancy that it was improper for her to insist on seeing you. Jake is an authorized management representative of the company. It is not always possible to bypass the organization's chain of command just because one fails to succeed at a lower level. Send the hiring decision back to Jake, with whom it legitimately rests.

_____ **e.** Finish the interview and hire Nancy. Sit down with Jake and Nancy in an effort to improve their personal attitudes toward each other.

Case 18

Who's the Best?

Patrick and Maria each run a separate shipping department, but they work for different divisions of the same company. In an attempt to improve communications between them and learn from each other's mistakes and successes, Patrick and Maria have agreed to meet once a month over a cup of coffee. They both have been told to monitor their absenteeism and turnover rates in an attempt to control costs. "Mine are the lower," said Maria. "No, they aren't," replied Patrick, "mine are." So they agreed to pull out their actual data for the past six months. Here's what they found:

	Maria	Patrick
Crew size	25	30
Working days	120	120
No. of separations/month	1	1
Attendance records of employees:		
working all 120 days	10	10
working 116 days	10	0
working 115 days	0	10
working 112 days	0	9
working 110 days	3	0
working 100 days	2	0
working 92 days	0	1

Analysis

Calculate their respective annual turnover percentages, the average days absent per employee, and the percentage of scheduled worker-days lost. Who has the better record, Maria or Patrick?

Case 19

The Superior Job Candidate

"At last," said Eduardo, "I've found the perfect stock clerk. Marcia has a wealth of experience. She has taken advanced courses in inventory planning and computerized controls. Compared to our other clerks, Marcia is far superior."

That was how Eduardo felt when he hired Marcia. Within a month, he felt less enthusiastic about her. Marcia could handle just about any assignment—perfectly. Trouble began, however, when it became apparent that the work of a stock clerk at Eduardo's company was mostly routine. In fact, Marcia found most of her work boring, and she let the other clerks know about it. In many ways, Marcia's superior attitude was disruptive, especially when she was asked to work along with others on group projects. Matters came to a head when Marcia confronted Eduardo on the Friday afternoon of her fourth week. "I'm extremely dissatisfied with my job," she said. "I've been here a month and there hasn't been a challenge in anything I've done. Can't you find more important assignments for me? Otherwise, I don't see much of a future in working here."

Analysis

a. What is the basic problem here?
b. How might it have been avoided?
c. Should Eduardo accommodate Marcia's request? Why?

ANSWERS TO QUICK TESTS	Quick Test 1	Quick Test 2	Quick Test 3	Quick Test 4	Quick Test 5	Quick Test 6
	1. T	3. F	5. F	7. T	9. F	11. F
	2. F	4. F	6. T	8. F	10. T	12. F

7

Training and Developing Employees

LEARNING OBJECTIVES

After studying this chapter, you should be able to

- Explain why employees need to be trained and what should be emphasized.

- Discuss the training roles of supervisors and their relationships with the training department.

- Understand how employees learn best and how those learning principles can be used in the four-step method of training.

- Choose appropriate training methods and aids to assist the learning process.

- Identify major ethical issues in training.

- Define transfer of training and explain the actions a supervisor can take to ensure that a payoff is received from training.

Training: Process and Purpose

How important is education and training today?

More important than ever before. For example, 15 to 20 percent of the workforce still comes to the job without a high school diploma. As a result, these persons are forced to accept lower-paying jobs and suffer a lifetime loss of earnings of over $100,000 for each year of education they are missing. More dramatically (see the Internet Connection), completion of a college degree can add about $1 million to one's lifetime income.

Within an organization, training can hold the key to productivity gains and improved customer service. Some companies, such as Motorola, have even required all managers to spend at least 1.5 percent of their payroll on training, and the overall average at that company is 2.4 percent. Employees in many firms are taking classes on quality, customer service, just-in-time inventory, process reengineering, and statistical process control. Trained employees who learn to use their heads as well as their hands hold the key to a company's future.

usgovinfo.about.com/library/weekly/aa072602a.htm
Read how college graduates earn nearly $1 million more in their lifetimes, on average, than high school graduates.

Will employees learn without being trained?

Yes. That's the danger. Whether employees are trained systematically or not, they will learn. What they learn may be good, or, more likely, it will be only partially correct. In some instances, what is learned may be downright wrong. A good illustration is the case of an assembler of tiny parts in an electronics plant. Her work was regularly judged to be of poor quality. Her supervisor wanted to get her off the job. The assembler insisted that she was doing her work exactly the same way as the others on the production line. On close investigation it was found that the assembler, who did her work with the aid of a binocular microscope, was looking through the microscope with only one eye at a time. No one had ever told her that to get the right depth of vision she had to use both eyes. As soon as she was instructed in this technique, which took only about three minutes, her work was as good as that of her colleagues.

The point is that there are four ways to provide training: hit-or-miss, sink-or-swim, trial-and-error, and structured and systematic. The only dependable way is the last one: structured and systematic. It is based on a careful study of what the job requires in terms of knowledge and skills. Then it involves an orderly period of instruction provided by an individual who is familiar with the job, well versed in training techniques, and aware of the learning process. Even then, supervisory follow-up is essential.

What are the key steps in a systematic approach to training?

There are six steps (see Figure 7-1). At a minimum, supervisors need to determine whether training is needed at all (other solutions include improved equipment, clearer performance expectations, and better supervisory support). Then they should specify exactly what the purpose (objectives) of the training will be. After this, they need to decide what the substance will be and what training method(s) should be used to produce the knowledge, skills, and attitudes necessary for improved performance. After the actual training experience occurs, two more steps remain: evaluating the effectiveness of the training and implementing an ongoing program for facilitating and encouraging trainees to use their new skills (transfer the training to the workplace) and perform well. Several of these topics will be discussed further in this chapter.

What is the primary purpose of training?

Historically, training programs have been presented for a variety of reasons, and not all of them stand up to close inspection. Employees have been sent to training as a reward for good performance, as an attempt to correct their bad habits, as a way to fill "down time" during slack periods, as an attempt to change their attitudes, and for a host of other reasons. However, *most good training is conducted to improve employees' present or potential job performance.* It is driven by a focus on customer wants and desires, and ways to meet those needs. It keeps a close eye on measurable performance outcomes and is often highly solution-oriented. As a consequence, good training is practical, efficiently presented, and directly relevant to trainee jobs. And trainees learn best when the employer's expectations are clearly defined, relevant models are demonstrated, constructive feedback is given, and useful materials are provided for later reference when needed.

How do you know that training is needed?

There are two major ways to identify **training needs**, which are gaps between expected and actual performance. Both ways—informal and formal—are potentially useful. Informally, you should be on the alert for any of these conditions: customer complaints, high turnover, repeated mistakes, subpar production rates, out-of-line operating costs, a high accident rate, excessive overtime, and even a general state of poor morale. Although these symptoms may indicate the need for training,

Identify need for training

↓

Set objectives

↓

Design training (content and methods)

↓

Deliver training

↓

Evaluate effectiveness

↓

Facilitate transfer

FIGURE 7-1
Typical steps in the training process.
What is the significance of the first step?

As a manager . . . first you have to understand that your number one job is developing people.

Jeff Howard, Senior V.P., Novations Group

Training need. A demonstrated gap between expected and actual performance.

they may also result from employee selection, motivational problems, or job-related conditions. As a result, interpretation of these symptoms is best supplemented by a formal analysis of needs.

Formal approaches to assessing training needs are more structured. They attempt to identify the people who need training and the type of training they need and even to determine whether training is a viable solution to performance problems. Common methods of assessing needs include the use of surveys, interviews, and skills tests, along with observation of employees at work. If these methods are employed regularly, they can be especially useful for identifying trends and for making comparisons with other employees or departments.

How can you keep track of an individual's training needs and achievements?

The overriding idea is to be systematic, both in recording prior skills that have been acquired and in planning future training on the basis of needs that have been identified. The record-keeping process can be a very simple one, like that shown in Figure 7-2, or it can be as detailed as you like. The important thing is to use it to (a) record what each worker can already do, (b) indicate what each worker doesn't need to be able to do, (c) plan ahead for what each worker has to learn and how that will be achieved, and (d) set definite dates for completing training in each part of the job.

An analysis such as the one illustrated in Figure 7-2 is sometimes called a *skills inventory*. It tells you what skills each worker has acquired as well as the total skills capability and training needs of your department.

	Answer telephone calls	File correspondence and reports	Handle routine inquiries	Handle customer complaints	File sales order forms	Prepare day-end report	Etc.
White	+	+	+	+	+	+	
Cruz	+	+	+	11-10	−	−	
Smith	11-1	11-20	−	+	+	12-1	
Klein	−	−	+	11-15	12-1	12-8	
Etc.							

+ means the worker can already do the job.
− means the worker doesn't need to know the job.
11-1, 11-15, etc., indicate the dates the supervisor has set to have the workers
trained to do the jobs required.

FIGURE 7-2

Sample skills inventory.
What are the ways in which a supervisor can use this information?

A Training Partnership

2

Why is a supervisor responsible for training employees?

CONCEPT
Supervisors are the primary source of employee training, but the training department, skilled co-workers, and the employees are also key partners.

Traditionally, supervisors have concentrated on planning, organizing, motivating, and controlling activities in their departments. But an emerging role in organizations calls for the supervisor also to be a teacher and

Long-term employee development may depend on the coaching skills of a supervisor.
What demands does this place on a supervisor?

Coaching. Helping employees learn through supervisory observation, demonstration, questioning, and timely feedback.

Teachable moments. The specific times when employees are most likely to learn.

JOB TIP!

Become a Better Coach

You can become a better coach if you follow some of these practical suggestions. When you engage in one-on-one coaching, make sure your comments are

• Personalized (tailored to the employee's unique needs).

• Specific (clear and detailed, with useful examples).

• Discreet (done in a private setting, to avoid embarrassing people).

• Timely (offered when the employee is ready to use the information).

• Performance-oriented (focused on ways to attain identifiable results).

• Regular (ongoing and continued across several occasions).

• Developmental (focused on improving the employee's future skills and abilities).

coach. Employees want to grow and take on new responsibilities, and supervisors must be there to show them how. This goes beyond teaching basic skills for task performance; it includes helping employees become lifelong learners who know how to analyze situations, solve problems, and integrate new ideas.

Coaching is an effective way to help employees learn. A supervisory coach alertly watches for improvement opportunities, demonstrates supportive behaviors (empathy and concern for worker needs), asks open-ended questions that stimulate employee thought, and gives timely feedback in a constructive manner. And the payoff will come. Just like collegiate athletes and their relationship to their coaches, workers are intensely loyal to their "coaches."

Make up your mind that coaching is one of your most important concerns. It is, or should be, part of the job description. Coaching needs to be done every day (see the suggestions provided in the Job Tip box), for training is the only surefire way to build a workforce that returns full value for every dollar invested. As a supervisor, you are judged by your ability to get the people who work for you to create a product or perform a service accurately and at a low cost. Employee training is your most powerful tool in accomplishing that end.

When does a good supervisor begin training an employee?

When a new employee is hired. There are two reasons for this. First, new workers who get off on the right foot by knowing what to do and how to do it are like a baseball team that builds a 10-run lead in the first inning. With a head start like that, there's a good chance of eventual success. The second reason revolves around the idea of the *teachable moment*. This involves sensing the times when new employees are most receptive to

instruction because they want to learn and succeed. Good supervisors respond to this need and begin training almost immediately.

Must supervisors do all the training themselves?

No. Two other parties can share in this responsibility. First, the organization's training department can prove extremely helpful in preparing individuals to conduct training. This department may offer *train-the-trainer* courses, in which they take highly knowledgeable or highly skilled persons (often called subject-matter experts) and turn them into capable trainers. The courses focus primarily on presentational skills, thus helping a qualified person communicate the key points and develop trainee skills without boring or overwhelming the trainees. In a nutshell, the training department provides information to the subject-matter expert on how to train. Train-the-trainer courses help a new trainer identify objectives, prepare appropriate course materials, determine the best pace at which to proceed, anticipate problems that may arise and ways to address them, and choose the best mix of information presentation and skill practice. Don't overlook the value of these courses for yourself or others; the training skills gained can be invaluable.

The second party who can play a role is the trainee. Many employees can take some responsibility for *self-directed learning*. They learn at

Self-directed learning. The process by which trainees learn at their own pace by consulting resources and asking for guidance when they think it is needed.

their own pace, asking for assistance only when it is needed. They refer to manuals (or ask co-workers) for explanations, and periodically submit the results of their initial efforts for supervisory evaluation. The feelings of accomplishment can be enormous when they realize, "I did it myself!"

Employees who are capable of self-directed learning may also wish to capitalize on the wealth of information that is becoming available on the Internet (Web-based training). They can do this independently through focused searches for relevant information, or they can take advantage of online courses (called *distance learning*) that are available at their fingertips. The existence of a wide array of electronic tools such as e-mail, whiteboards, and chat groups has created the possibility of a *virtual classroom* that can provide just-in-time training to workers.

Caution: Even if you have qualified job instructors in your department, you can never completely delegate your training responsibilities. It's also important to be aware of, and show a personal interest in, every employee's progress. This will stimulate employees to want to learn and become equal partners in the training process. In other words, even with the help of designated trainers and self-directed learners, you must continue to supervise the training and the trainees to be sure that they are meeting your expectations.

Internet connection

www.e-learningguru.com/gloss.htm
Check out this website for a comprehensive glossary of e-learning terms and their definitions.

Virtual classroom. The use of Web-based electronic programs to provide just-in-time training to employees.

If supervisors are responsible for training, what's the role of a company's training department?

The function of a company training (or human resources development) department is to identify training needs, specify and/or provide training programs and methods, conduct evaluations of training, and assist or supplement supervisors and other managers in meeting their training responsibilities. They may also centrally conduct training that needs to be standardized across departments, such as orientations on company history and new products, literacy training, team development, and statistical quality control.

Generally, the training department people are experts in teaching methods. For example, training specialists can be of real help in determining specific training needs. They can help you recognize and interpret the training symptoms mentioned previously. You'll want their help, too, in learning how to be a good instructor and in training some of your key employees to be trainers.

QUICK TEST 2	3	T or F	Effective supervisors should wait for a problem to occur before training a new employee.
	4	T or F	Self-directed learners should be encouraged to make use of Web-based training resources.

Factors in Learning

What's the difference between acquiring knowledge and learning a skill?

CONCEPT
Much is known about how employees learn best, and these ideas should be built into any training program.

Knowledge is information that can be learned from reading, listening to an expert, or keen observation. *Skill*, the ability to perform a job-related action, is a combination of relevant knowledge and physical or perceptual abilities. It is acquired through guided practice. For example, in operating a four-speed (manually shifted) sports car, you may be told that it is vitally important to reach certain minimum speeds before shifting from one gear to another. To apply this information, you will need to acquire a very special skill, a "motor" skill. Smooth shifting of gears will take place only after hours of practice in learning the "feel" of pushing in the clutch and coordinating that with a sense of how fast the auto is moving. And all this must tie in with a special movement of the gear shift by hand.

Knowledge. Job-relevant information.

Skill. The ability to perform a job-related action.

Almost all jobs in which an individual must place his or her hands, feet, or eyes on the material or equipment at the workplace require a unique combination of information and motor skills. In simple terms, then, the trainee on a job must not only acquire knowledge (knowing what to do and understanding why) but also learn a skill (being able to perform properly).

What can you do to make the job easier to learn and to teach?

Jobs that seem simple to you because you're familiar with them may appear almost impossible to a person who has never performed them. You may have heard the advice given to the diner faced with the overwhelming task of eating an elephant: "Just take one bite at a time!" Similarly, experience has shown that the trick to making jobs easier to learn is to break them down into simple (bite-size) steps. That way, employees need to learn only one step at a time, adding steps systematically, rather than trying to grasp the whole job in a single piece. At an early stage, however, it is useful to portray the entire task to the trainees so that they can see how each step fits into the larger picture.

Breaking down a job for training purposes (a *job breakdown analysis*) involves two elements:

1. You must observe the job as it is done correctly and divide it into its logical steps. (See Figure 7-3 for an example.)
2. For each step in a job breakdown, you must consider the second element: the key point. A *key point* is anything at a particular step that might make or break a job or injure the worker. Essentially, it's the knack or special know-how of experienced workers that makes

Job breakdown analysis. The segmentation of a particular job into important steps that advance the work toward its completion.

Key point. The essential element that makes or breaks the job.

Job breakdown sheet for training	
Task: Responding to customer complaints	Operation: Preparing written letter using computer
Important steps in the operation	**Key points**
Step: A logical segment of the operation during which something happens to advance the work	Key point: Anything in a step that might Make or break the job Injure the worker Make the work easier to do (i.e., knack, trick, special timing, bit of special information)
1. Read the customer's letter.	Knack—avoid defensive reactions.
2. Identify all issues raised.	Take notes using only key words.
3. Select a specific problem to be solved.	Identify the real complaint from a variety of frustrations expressed.
4. Consult the company policy manual.	Use the table of contents or index to find relevant material.
5. Determine acceptable response.	Knack—ask yourself how you would feel if you received that reply.
6. Pick appropriate standard paragraphs from computer files.	Refer to list of key words, and match with those in file paragraphs.
7. Tailor the letter to fit the individual.	Personalize letter by frequent use of customer's name and specific problem.
8. Proofread the product for errors.	Review letter once now; set it aside for a while; return to it when you are "fresh".

FIGURE 7-3
Sample job instruction breakdown.
What is the benefit of identifying key points for the trainee?

the job go easier or faster for them. The key point for one step in a customer relations representative's job would be to have the knack of sorting out the real complaint from a variety of frustrations expressed by the customer. For another step, it would be the capacity to personalize a standard solution to fit the unique problem and individual.

Figure 7-3 shows how this customer relations job might be broken down into several steps with their appropriate key points for training purposes. Key points in a product- or machine-oriented job might revolve around speed, timing, sequence, fit, temperature, appearance, alignment, noise, materials, tools, or safety. In professional and service-related jobs, key points often revolve around factors such as logic, courtesy, timeliness, and accuracy.

In what sequence must the parts of a job be taught?

The best way to teach a job is to present its elements in a logical order. Alternatively, you might start with the easiest part and proceed to the most difficult. This isn't always possible, of course. But if you can arrange your employee training in a systematic sequence, learning will go more smoothly and teaching will also be easier.

How skillful should you expect a trainee to become?

At one time, a supervisor expected employees to learn every facet of a narrowly defined job, and learn to do it well. Specialization was popular, and workers were expected to perform a few tasks skillfully for a particular job. Workers might receive additional pay as they progressed from minimum levels of competency to intermediate capabilities to a mastery level. But this approach had potential weaknesses—worker boredom, inflexibility across employees, and limited opportunities for advancement and wage increases.

A new trend has emerged—the idea of **multi-skilled employees** and *skill-based pay.* As employees acquire skills and demonstrate competency within a certain domain, they are certified as capable in that job and deserving of its pay. They are encouraged to *cross-train.* This means they learn new skills in another job or skill block, and by doing so qualify for a higher rate of pay. They are more valuable to the company because they can shift back and forth across multiple jobs, depending on production demands. They get better within a job and better at performing multiple jobs. The variety and challenge keep them interested. Employees are always learning something new, and so the need for training never ends.

Multi-skilling. The development of capacities to perform two or more key tasks by a single employee.

How do you get employees to want to learn?

The answer lies in three directions—personal payoff, challenge, and engaging their minds. Employees must see how training will pay off for them before they accept and embrace it. So show the younger employees, through examples, how training can help them to get ahead, build job security, and increase their incomes. Then show employees how learning new jobs or better methods makes the work more interesting. And be sure to explain why a job is done a certain way. Employees need to know not only *what* to do and *how* to do it but *why* it needs to be done. Your challenge is to involve all three dimensions of your employees—their hands, their heads, and their hearts.

How much should you teach at one time?

This depends on how quickly a trainee can learn and how difficult the job is. Each learner is different. Some catch on quickly; others are slower. It's better, therefore, to vary your training speed with each situation. If an

Job instruction training (JIT). A systematic four-step approach to training employees in a basic job skill.

JOB TIP!

Job Instruction Training

There are four cornerstones to systematic *job instruction training (JIT)*:

Step 1: Get the workers ready to learn. People who want to learn and are relaxed are the easiest to teach. Help them feel at ease. Explore their present knowledge, their experience, and their attitude toward learning. Let trainees know why the task is important and must be done right.

Step 2: Demonstrate how the job should be done. Begin by telling the employees how to perform the first step (and why). Then, demonstrate the procedure by doing it yourself. Next, check for their comprehension, and, finally, have them demonstrate it to you. This is a double process—tell and show (by you), followed by another tell and show (by the trainee).

Step 3: Try the workers out by letting them do the job. Let the employees try the job under your guidance. Observe for a while so that you will know how they are doing. Praise their success, and provide constructive feedback when they are wrong. Make sure they learn from their mistakes.

Step 4: Put the trainees on their own gradually. Every pilot must "solo" eventually, and employees are no different. Once you see that trainees can do the work reasonably well, turn them loose for a while. But check on their progress and performance regularly. And never assume they are completely trained. Not only might they forget, there is always something an employee can learn to do—or learn to do better.

employee has trouble learning, try to find out why. With new employees, for example, it may simply be that they are nervous and are trying so hard that they don't concentrate. So be patient. Help them relax. Make it easy for them to succeed. And when they complete even a small part of the new task successfully, be sure to praise them. Many companies use a systematic, four-step method of teaching employees a specific job skill (see the adjacent Job Tip).

How smoothly will the training process proceed?

The learning process doesn't go smoothly for most people. We all have our ups and downs, depending on the material to be learned and even the time of day. Expect progress to be slow at first as the trainees struggle to set aside old ways of doing things. They may learn quickly for a while and then taper off and stay at a plateau temporarily. They may even backslide a little. If this happens, reassure the trainees that their halt in progress is normal. Don't let them become discouraged. If necessary, go through the demonstration again so that they can get a fresh start. And pile on the encouragement.

How quickly do people forget what they have learned?

Rapidly. Research indicates that our learning disappears quickly unless we keep working at it. Therefore, for employees to become expert at the job you're teaching, you must keep repeating the important things you want them to retain. And they must practice new skills regularly under your supervision. It's not enough for them to qualify at a minimum level; they must overlearn a skill so that it becomes almost automatic. This is one reason why follow-up is so vital.

There are two other powerful ways to combat (prevent) the forgetting process. Each of them draws on research on how and when trainees learn best. First, the most important information should be previewed at the beginning of the training process; this builds on the **primacy principle** (people remember the first things they hear). Second, critical information should be reviewed and summarized at the end of the training process; this builds on the **recency effect** (people remember the last things they hear). The combination of primacy and recency is a bit like the two slices of bread that surround pieces of ham and cheese; without the bread you wouldn't have an effective sandwich!

5	T or F	Good training provides a balanced emphasis on both knowledge and skill.	
6	T or F	Most employees are extremely practical; they only want to know what to do and how to do it.	

QUICK TEST 3

Training Methods and Aids

What training methods should you use for instructing employees?

The key is to be aware of the many options available, recognize their unique strengths and weaknesses, and use the most appropriate one or ones. Training methods can be divided into those that primarily occur on the job (such as coaching and job rotation) and those that take an employee off the job (classroom lectures, for example). Other methods, such as apprentice training, combine elements of both settings. The key questions to ask in making a good decision about methods to use are these: What is my objective (knowledge acquisition or skill development)? How much time, space, materials, or special preparation is

CONCEPT
Effective training uses a variety of training methods and aids to facilitate employee learning.

TABLE 7-1 Three Unique Learning Styles

Visual (sight):
- Likes to visualize a process.
- Prefers dramatic demonstrations or charts and graphs.
- Wants to be able to refer to notes, manuals, handouts, and instructions.
- May respond by saying, "I *see* what you mean."

Auditory (sound):
- Likes to hear a presentation.
- Enjoys discussions and exchanges of ideas and positions.
- Doesn't mind listening to audiotapes.
- May even close eyes to shut out distractions.
- May respond by saying, "I *hear* what you are telling me."

Tactile (touch):
- Likes to learn by actively doing something; dislikes extensive sitting.
- Views himself or herself as being "hands-on."
- Enjoys working with tools and equipment.
- May give clues as to progress by saying, "I need to get a *feel* for this."

required? Will the method make trainees be active or passive? How many employees must be trained at one time? If new job skills are the desired product, supervisors will often use one-on-one methods, since they provide personalized attention and have a high impact on the trainees.

The best approach is to tailor the choice of training methods and support materials to the preferred learning style of each employee. Table 7-1 illustrates the key features of each dominant preference—the visual learner, the auditory one, and the tactile person. But remember, these are portrayed as "pure" styles, when in reality most employees learn best through a combination of approaches.

What's the purpose of visual aids?

A classic Chinese proverb states, "I hear and I forget; I see and I remember; I do and I understand." Training that only tells a worker how to do something may soon be forgotten. Visual aids, when used to supplement job instruction, demonstrate clearly that "one picture is worth a thousand words." Any device that helps trainees visualize what you're telling them speeds up the learning process and helps them retain the new information. Training that appeals to the visual senses will always be more effective.

Visual aids may include a variety of traditional devices, such as transparencies, slides, films, posters, or flip charts. However, many firms now rely extensively on PowerPoint presentations that are more dynamic and engaging. Visual aids may also be simple and inexpensive, such as writing key points on a chalkboard or distributing a diagram of the steps in a process. The best visual aid, of course, is actual demonstration on the equipment a worker will use.

Audiovisual instruction continues to upgrade the training field. Audiocassettes can present information to workers during their free time. Videos and DVDs can provide both information and realistic demonstrations right at the job site. And many forms of *computer-assisted instruction* (also called computer-based training) use interactive videodisks and CDs, which involve exciting graphic displays, realistic experiences, and even touch-screen responses.

A simple form of visual aid that is both inexpensive and useful is the *job aid*. These can be checklists, flow charts, worksheets, or listings of step-by-step instructions that remind a worker how to perform a task. They minimize the fear of forgetting something and are especially useful when a procedure is performed infrequently, a mistake would be costly, or a supervisor is not close by.

Job aids. Materials placed on or near the work area that help employees remember key points and perform effectively.

How good are off-the-job training methods?

Although individualized training is effective for developing job skills, it can be expensive and time-consuming for the supervisor. Some training can be conducted in small groups off the job at less cost per person with equal success. This is particularly true when new policies or procedures need to be explained to all workers or when employees need to know the theory and background behind an operation. But remember that most line employees are active individuals, and their attention span during a lecture is brief. The best training methods still draw on that Chinese proverb mentioned previously and *involve the participants actively in their learning.* As a result, many training programs use some form of experiential method where workers are performing a simulated task and drawing their own learning from it. They hear, see, and do, and they understand and remember.

Do any ethical issues affect training and trainers?

Yes. Whether you are a supervisor acting as a part-time instructor, a supervisor requesting external training for your employees, or a full-time trainer, there are many pitfalls to watch for and avoid. A few of these include the following:

- Competence—Does the instructor have the knowledge, skill, and background necessary to be a qualified trainer?

- Confidentiality—Does the trainer have the integrity necessary to know what personal information or class-related performance data should not be shared with others?
- Boundaries—Does the trainer adhere to a high set of moral standards to avoid crossing boundaries of propriety (e.g., taking advantage of one's power position or harassing trainees)?
- Prejudice—Is the trainer sufficiently aware of any personal biases or stereotypes to prevent them from unfairly affecting the treatment of any individual being trained?

These and many other issues can present themselves suddenly to naive trainers. It is most helpful if trainers have thought about them in advance and developed a planned response for each of them.

| QUICK TEST 4 | 7 | T or F | Training methods are used to deliver instruction; visual aids are used to supplement that instruction. |
| | 8 | T or F | Most trainees enjoy being passive during instruction; they are content to listen to the experts. |

5 Obtaining Results from Training

CONCEPT
Training is effective only if it has a demonstrable payoff and is transferred to the job.

What are the direct and indirect costs of training?

All training, structured or not, is costly. There are direct costs of training materials, visual aids, and outside instructors. Indirect costs include the time of both supervisor and trainees, the effects of errors made, and the productivity lost during training. But the alternative—not training—may be the most expensive of all. The key is to plan carefully for systematic training to avoid the need to repeat it later. And there are many ways to hold down costs, such as having a new employee learn while working alongside an experienced one.

What benefits can a supervisor expect from training?

In addition to making a better showing for your department in terms of improved quality and quantity of output or service, training puts you in a favorable light in other ways. Effective employee instruction:

- Smoothes the way for intradepartmental transfers.
- Allows you more time for other supervisory tasks, such as scheduling work.

- Provides a reserve of trained personnel in your department for expansion or emergencies.
- Wins the confidence and the cooperation of your workers.

Perhaps most important of all, training your employees makes *you* a prime candidate for promotion. To achieve this result, you should try to assess, and improve, the payoffs from training. Measure the productivity of an employee before training and again after it is over. Compare the performance of trained workers to that of untrained ones, and project the improvements for the whole year. This analysis will persuade you to continue your training efforts, and it also will justify the time and costs of training.

How will you know if training has been successful?

The only sure way is to measure some aspect of it; never *assume* that it was successful. All training—whether formal or informal, short or extensive—is expensive in some ways. Therefore, alert supervisors are always concerned about the benefit/cost ratio of the training they support. There are four classic indicators of the success of training:

1. **Trainee reactions.** Did they stick it out until the end? Did they feel something useful was being shared? Were they satisfied with the time spent and the materials received? If not, they will be less inclined to attend future sessions or to urge others to participate.
2. **Trainee learning.** Did they acquire new information? Can they pass knowledge-based tests after the training? Can they now explain a process or procedure that they were not aware of before training?
3. **Trainee behavior.** Did they acquire new skills? Can they demonstrate specific skills at a higher level than was previously possible? Can they now pass behavioral certification tests?
4. **Results.** Based on a combination of knowledge, skills, and attitudes, do the trainees now perform their jobs in ways that produce demonstrably better products or services than before the training? Has their speed increased? Quality improved? Mistakes declined? Complaints decreased?

All these indicators are important, but the biggest payoff lies in demonstrated results. Results "speak" best to upper management when you are requesting additional support of future training efforts, so be sure to focus your primary attention on results.

How can a supervisor increase the probability that training will transfer to the job?

Many supervisors are effective trainers. Many employees want to learn new skills. Yet evidence suggests that much training (especially in the

Quips & Quotes

The half-life of newly-learned material is three days; if learners don't use it immediately, they lose it.

Jay Cross and Tony O'Driscoll

classroom) doesn't result in improved job performance. Training has failed if it has not been transferred to the job. The reasons are diverse—lack of supervisory reinforcement, impractical training, or even peer-group norms that create barriers to its use.

Training is successful only to the degree that ***transfer of training*** takes place. This is the degree to which employees are able to transfer to their jobs the knowledge and skills they gain in learning sessions.

What can you do to aid the transfer of training? Discuss the objectives of training in advance with your new employees so that they will know what to expect. Point out effective workers to them so that they have successful role models. Have these skilled co-workers ***model***, or demonstrate, the performance of key job skills. Visibly monitor trainee performance; this lets the trainees know what you think is important. Praise successful behaviors regularly so that your new workers will feel good about their developing skills. Above all, consider training an important supervisory function and give it the attention it deserves.

How should you modify training for new entrants to the workforce?

Millions of people will enter the U.S. labor force in the next decade; a majority of them will be drawn from various ethnic, immigrant, or economically disadvantaged groups. How can they be trained to make them fully contributing workers? Training fundamentals do not vary much from situation to situation or person to person. It is more a matter of intensifying the fundamental techniques. Companies such as Daimler/Chrysler, Western Electric, Lockheed Martin, and the Equitable Life Assurance Society have found that the following guidelines need special emphasis:

1. **Make the training specific.** Avoid generalizations and abstractions. Talk about actions they should take or specific resources they should use. Show how each new subject relates to a job or a product.
2. **Rely on demonstrations.** Actions and illustrations, plus live demonstrations, communicate far more effectively than do words alone with an audience for whom speaking, reading, and other verbal skills may be underdeveloped. Repeat and repeat the demonstration until you are sure the trainee has understood what you are doing.
3. **Overtrain rather than undertrain.** Err on the side of providing more information and more skills than are needed for the work to be done. That way, trainees will be less likely to underperform on the job, and they'll have more confidence in their ability to do it well.
4. **Offer personal aid.** It may not seem germane to a training effort for a supervisor to help a trainee get a ride to work, wake up on time, or obtain childcare, but it helps keep the trainee's mind on what is being learned and, of course, builds confidence in the boss.

5. **Provide lots of follow-up.** In some cases, the most meaningful training takes place when a supervisor shows a trainee again on the job what may have already been shown in training. That's because it is on the job that learning becomes most relevant.

6. **Reassure and recognize frequently.** It may seem like pampering to assure a person constantly how well the work is going. However, people who are from culturally or linguistically diverse backgrounds, who have been economically disadvantaged, or who have developmental disabilities may benefit from an abundance of encouragement to reinforce their confidence in themselves.

7. **Use the buddy system.** Appoint a co-worker, preferably a person from a similar or sympathetic background, from whom the trainee can get private support. The first days on a new job are often full of hazing and mistakes. At one St. Louis plant, for instance, a trainee inadvertently was doused with oil on his first day in the shop. He would not have returned to the job after lunch, he said, if his buddy hadn't shown him that it was an accident and assured him that it wouldn't happen again.

How do training and development relate to the idea of performance management?

As discussed throughout this chapter, training and development focus on the preparation of employees to perform specific tasks or acquire skill sets. This process is often aimed at improving immediate job performance and is designed to remove deficiencies of knowledge or skills. **Performance management** (see Chapter 12) is much broader in scope and longer term in its orientation, while attempting to prepare employees for the changing nature of work and the workplace in the years ahead. A comprehensive performance improvement plan may include elements of goal setting, communications, motivation, job feedback, reinforcement, technical resources, and performance appraisal. Training, then, is only one component of the performance management process that attempts to examine and control all the factors that make employees effective or ineffective.

9	T or F	Once an employee has been trained, the supervisor's responsibility pretty much ends.
10	T or F	Training is training; supervisors should standardize their training efforts regardless of the backgrounds of their employees.

QUICK TEST 5

Practical Guidelines for Supervisors

1. Accept the fact that there is a substantial payoff for employee training, and *invest time, energy, and resources* in it.

2. *Follow the six steps in training systematically*, and don't neglect or downplay any of them.

3. *Commit yourself to being an award-winning coach*, developing your employees through guidance that is personalized, specific, discreet, timely, regular, and performance-oriented.

4. *Set time-specific goals* for employee training to make sure it is not relegated to "if we have the time available" status.

5. Remember that the ultimate goal of most training is to improve employee performance on the job; *ask how each method and each hour of instruction contributes* to achieving that goal.

6. *Increase the effectiveness of your training* by presenting information in a logical order, providing incentives for learners, using demonstrations, using visual aids, and sharing the most critical information at either the beginning or the end of a training session.

7. *Adapt your use of training methods* to the unique learning style of each trainee whenever possible.

8. Never guess at the outcomes of training; *evaluate at several levels and focus on results.*

9. Remember that forgetting diminishes the effectiveness of learning; *use a variety of methods to ensure that transfer of training takes place.*

10. Be patient with trainees from other cultural or ethnic backgrounds, *offering a variety of adaptive approaches* to support their desire to learn and succeed.

Chapter 7 Review

Key Concepts to Remember

1. Training: Process and Purpose. In the absence of sound training, employees learn their jobs haphazardly, inaccurately, or not at all. Only through careful assessment of needs, systematic instruction, and responsible follow-up can a supervisor be confident that employees will learn how to perform their work in the most effective manner. A skills inventory and training plan should be prepared for each employee.

2. A Training Partnership. Training is an important supervisory role, as well as a powerful tool for achieving bottom-line results. Although supervisors are ultimately responsible for the success of training, they can delegate some assignments to skilled employees. They should also call upon the training department for assistance in planning and designing training programs.

3. Factors in Learning. Learning—the acquisition of knowledge and the development of skills—can be accelerated in many ways. Identifying the key points through a job breakdown analysis, sequencing them logically, showing as well as telling,

repeating major ideas, and adapting to individual needs will all help the trainee. The four-step method of job instruction will also ensure that the process is systematic.

4. Training Methods and Aids. The process of instruction should use a variety of methods and aids, all carefully chosen to support the objectives of training. These methods and aids should be adapted to the preferred learning style of trainees, depending on whether they learn best by seeing, hearing, or touching. Supervisors also need to address a variety of ethical issues related to training.

5. Obtaining Results from Training. Training can be costly, both directly and indirectly. Fortunately, it can also produce tremendous benefits if it is planned and conducted well. To facilitate the transfer of training from classroom to work site, supervisors can use a number of methods, such as discussing objectives, providing role models, monitoring performance, and praising successful behavior. Overall, training should be viewed as one tool in the supervisor's performance management tool kit.

Reading Comprehension

1. Why is training an important supervisory function?

2. Mark's department is finally receiving the new computer terminals that other departments have had for several months. Would it be a good idea for Mark to let his employees learn about the operation of the new terminals by reading the manufacturer's instruction manual? Why or why not?

3. What information can you gain from a skills inventory?

4. What is the difference between training that focuses on knowledge and training that focuses on job skills? Why might both be important for a supervisor to accent?

5. Betty Jo, a checkout clerk in a discount store, has been told by her supervisor that she apparently understands how the cash register works but is too slow in operating it. Why does Betty Jo's acquisition of knowledge about her work differ from her skill development? How are these two factors related?

6. In a job breakdown, how do key points differ from important steps?

7. Why wouldn't a supervisor want to teach a job's sequence of steps rigidly in the same order they are performed?

8. Derek, a new supervisor, is worried that his employees will not be excited about the training he plans to conduct for them. What can he do to stimulate them to want to learn?

9. What guidelines can a supervisor follow to make training more successful?

10. Danielle, a recent immigrant to the United States, has just been hired for her first full-time job after several months of having temporary jobs while she worked on her English language skills. What advice do you have for her supervisor as she begins training Danielle?

Application

Self-Assessment

How Good Are Your Training Skills?

Read the following statements carefully. Circle the number on the response scale that most closely reflects the degree to which each statement describes you. Add up your total points and prepare a brief action plan for self-improvement. Be ready to report your score for tabulation across the entire group.

	Good Description								Poor Description
1. I am familiar with, and generally follow, the steps in the systematic approach to training.	10 9 8 7 6 5 4 3 2 1
2. I view training primarily as one approach to improving an employee's work performance.	10 9 8 7 6 5 4 3 2 1
3. I recognize the importance of carefully keeping a skills inventory for each employee.	10 9 8 7 6 5 4 3 2 1
4. I understand the tremendous importance of my role as a coach in helping employees succeed.	10 9 8 7 6 5 4 3 2 1
5. I am familiar with the ways in which an employee could engage in self-directed learning, especially by using the Internet.	10 9 8 7 6 5 4 3 2 1
6. I am capable of identifying and explaining the key points of a job to an employee.	10 9 8 7 6 5 4 3 2 1

	Good Description									Poor Description

7. I am fully aware that employees are as much interested in the "why" of training as they are in the "what."

10 9 8 7 6 5 4 3 2 1

8. I understand the unique value of providing job aids to employees.

10 9 8 7 6 5 4 3 2 1

9. When training a new employee, I would first concentrate on ways to produce a quality product or service, and then turn to speed.

10 9 8 7 6 5 4 3 2 1

10. I accept the need for, and importance of, actively supporting newly learned behaviors back on the job.

10 9 8 7 6 5 4 3 2 1

Scoring and Interpretation

Scoring

Add up your total points for the 10 questions. Record that number here, and report it when it is requested. _____

Also, insert your score on the Personal Development Plan in the Appendix.

Interpretation

81 to 100 points. You seem to have a basic set of training attitudes and skills.

61 to 80 points. Take a close look at some of your training attitudes and skills (those with lower self-assessments) and discuss them with a manager to see if they need improvement.

Below 60 points. Some of your skills may be substantially inconsistent with effective training practices and could be detrimental to your success as a supervisor.

Identify your three lowest scores and record the question numbers here: _____, _____, _____.

Action

Write a brief paragraph detailing an action plan for how you might sharpen each of these skills. Then pay particularly close attention to the related material in the chapter as you review the relevant sections there.

Skill Development

Identifying Barriers to Transfer of Training

Assume that the employees in your department will soon participate in a major training program to provide them with twenty-first-century job skills. However, you are concerned that some barriers might stand in the way of their learning and application. Review the following list of possible barriers, and select the three most relevant and powerful ones, marking them with an X.

Possible Transfer-of-Training Barriers	Most Critical (3)
1. Participants may lack knowledge of what the training is all about.	_____
2. Participants weren't involved in the design of the training.	_____
3. Participants don't want to take the training.	_____
4. Supervisor is reluctant to release employees for the training.	_____
5. Performance expectations haven't been shared with the trainees.	_____
6. The program as proposed overlaps heavily with information available from other sources.	_____
7. Top-level managers are unlikely to show their support for the training.	_____
8. The organization's culture doesn't support the results of training.	_____
9. Supervisors haven't been adequately briefed on the nature of the training.	_____
10. Participants are unlikely to see the benefits of being trained.	_____

Action

Prepare a report that suggests how you intend to prevent those problems or overcome them. To prepare your report, you will likely wish to review the text's discussion on transfer of training, scan the Internet for relevant guidelines, and consult with colleagues and staff persons in the human resources department for their advice.

Role Play

Determining the Costs and Benefits of Training

Pair up into sets of two persons. One of you will take the role of a supervisor (A), and the other will be the supervisor's manager (B). Read only your role, and when you are ready, engage in a discussion with the other party that reaches some balanced agreement.

A. Assume that you are a new supervisor. After an analysis of the current performance of employees in your department, you believe that they need a variety of training programs to meet future expectations.

You intend to propose these programs to your manager but first need to prepare the strongest rationale possible in support of such efforts. Brainstorm all possible benefits (both direct and indirect, short-term and long-term) that might accrue from training your employees. List them in the spaces below and be prepared to talk about them in a discussion with your manager.

1. _____   5. _____
2. _____   6. _____
3. _____   7. _____
4. _____   8. _____

B. Assume that you are the manager of a new supervisor. This person has requested a meeting, indicating that the purpose is to propose a considerable funding increase for new training programs for the supervisor's department. You are a strong believer in a balanced approach, looking at both the benefits and the costs of training. Since you expect the supervisor to focus on the probable benefits of training (while likely ignoring the considerable costs), you decide to prepare a set of counterarguments that identify all the likely costs (both direct and indirect, short-term and long-term) that might accrue from training these employees. List those points in the spaces below and be prepared to share them in a discussion with this supervisor.

1. _____   5. _____
2. _____   6. _____
3. _____   7. _____
4. _____   8. _____

After the initial presentation of each person's perspectives, combine your joint information into a *general model for benefit/cost analysis of training* that can prove beneficial in looking more objectively at future training proposals.

Cases for Analysis

Case 20

From Theory to Practice

Kelly McWhinny is the new manager of staffing and development for a large mining operation that employs nearly 2,000 people. As she began her new job, she reflected on some of the ideas a university professor had presented in a course on human resource development. As she recalled, he suggested that trainee learning was directly proportional to the number of human senses involved in the learning experience and the degree to which the trainee is active, not passive. This sounded similar to the Chinese proverb "I hear and I forget; I see and I remember; I do and I understand."

This simple theory made intuitive sense to Kelly, but she was still not sure how to use this information in the selection of training methods. Although she realized that each method currently under consideration varied in cost, she was equally concerned with the human side of each: Would the trainee be likely to *learn* as much from each method?

Analysis

Assist Kelly in her assessment of the following training methods by ranking them from 1 to 5 (1 = highest; 5 = lowest) according to the degree to which each method is likely to engage trainees' multiple senses and involve them actively in the learning process. In the next three columns, indicate with an X whether you feel the method clearly involves the sense of hearing, sight, or action.

Method	Rank	Hearing	Sight	Action
Listening to a lecture	_____	_____	_____	_____
Apprenticeship	_____	_____	_____	_____
Outside reading	_____	_____	_____	_____
Demonstration	_____	_____	_____	_____
Coaching	_____	_____	_____	_____

Case 21

The New Telephone Procedure

The supervisor of a rural office of a large electrical utility received a terse memo. It indicated that executives at headquarters were unhappy with the way some employees in the company were greeting customers when answering the phone. To avoid the possibility of problems in the rural office, the supervisor made a list of unacceptable practices and distributed the list to all the employees during the next staff meeting. He explained that "pressure from the home office" was the major reason for his preparation of the list. During the next several days, the supervisor made a point of listening in on at least two phone conversations of each employee to make sure that the workers were not engaging in the offensive practices.

Analysis

In the table that follows, put a check mark in the first column for each guideline for effective training that the supervisor apparently ignored or even violated; put a check mark in the second column for each guideline that the supervisor appears to have practiced or respected.

Guidelines for Effective Training	Ignored Guideline	Respected Guideline
1. Demonstrate how the job should be done.	_____	_____
2. Let the workers perform the job while being guided.	_____	_____
3. Periodically check on employee progress.	_____	_____
4. Explain why the procedure is to be used.	_____	_____
5. Break the job down into important steps and key points.	_____	_____
6. Present the parts of a job in a systematic sequence.	_____	_____
7. Provide a familiarization period for learning about the employee.	_____	_____
8. Assess whether the employee had a need for the training.	_____	_____

Case 22

It Sounds Good, But Will They Use It?

Your company's director of training and development recently contracted with a firm to present a workshop for all employees titled "Effective Time Management." As a member of the training committee, you have examined some of the materials and attended the pilot session. You are convinced the daylong program contains some good ideas and is skillfully presented but are concerned about the extent to which the employees will *use* these ideas on the job. If they don't use them, valuable production time will have been lost.

Analysis

Before suggesting ideas for improvement, you decide to assess those barriers that inhibit transfer of training. Of the following, which do you think is *most* likely to impede transfer? Rank the items on a scale from 1 (most likely) to 6 (least likely).

_____ **a.** Trainees usually dislike change and naturally resist it.
_____ **b.** Trainees want to change, but a lack of resources on the job prevents it.
_____ **c.** Trainees resist change because of negative peer pressure.
_____ **d.** Supervisors don't provide positive reinforcement for the new behaviors acquired in the workshop.
_____ **e.** Trainees are excited about change while attending a well-run workshop, but lose enthusiasm once separated from the trainer.
_____ **f.** The overall organizational climate doesn't support change.

ANSWERS TO QUICK TESTS	Quick Test 1	Quick Test 2	Quick Test 3	Quick Test 4	Quick Test 5
	1. F	3. F	5. T	7. T	9. F
	2. T	4. T	6. F	8. F	10. F

8

Leadership Skills, Styles, and Qualities

LEARNING OBJECTIVES

After studying this chapter, you should be able to

- Describe the essential skills of leadership, and explain the four parts of emotional intelligence.

- Differentiate between the assumptions of Theory X and those of Theory Y, and explain the importance of trust.

- Recognize the various leadership styles, and explain the benefits and prerequisites of a participative approach and the reasons for its potential failure.

- Discuss the factors a leader should consider when selecting a leadership style, and explain two models for choosing a style on a situational basis.

- Discuss the leader's responsibility for being an effective follower, actions for helping employees become self-leaders, and the impact of substitutes for leadership.

- Explain why good leaders see themselves as stewards and servants of others, and how there is a need to demonstrate caregiving behaviors.

Leadership Defined

Given certain characteristics, a supervisor may acquire and develop the skills required for effective leadership.

Leadership. The process of influencing and supporting others to follow you and do willingly the things that need to be done.

What is leadership?

Everyone will give you a different answer to this one—a set of traits (see the Job Tip), a certain behavior, a standard style. Our definition is this: *Leadership is the process of influencing and supporting others to follow you and do willingly the things that need to be done.* Obviously, the actions you request from others should be reasonable, relevant, and ethical. They should represent appropriate actions that will advance your department toward its goals of higher productivity, improved quality or service, and conservation of its resources. Two other factors stand out in this definition of leadership. First, employee responses need to be more than passive acceptance; you need willing and enthusiastic commitment. Second, as employees develop their skills and experience, they should begin to accept some of the responsibility for seeing what needs to be done.

Are good leaders born or made?

Most leaders must learn their skills. They do so by working at self-improvement, observing and studying effective leaders, obtaining useful

JOB *TIP!*

Important Leadership Traits

Several factors differentiate between effective leaders and ineffective leaders. The most important traits of good leaders are the following:

- **Energy.** Good leaders have a high level of personal drive and enthusiasm. They demonstrate a strong work ethic.
- **Desire.** Effective leaders have personal aspirations to rise to leadership positions, and the desire to guide others to greater achievements. They choose to be leaders.
- **Integrity.** Fidelity, strength of character, and credibility are their hallmarks. Good leaders set high ethical and moral standards for them-

selves, and live up to them conspicuously.
- **Self-confidence.** Leaders feel good about their past performance and future capabilities. They have appropriate levels of self-esteem and self-assurance.
- **Judgment.** Careful analysis and thoughtful consideration precede most actions by effective leaders. However, they can still be decisive when the situation calls for it.

Start *now* to develop your energy, desire, integrity, self-confidence, and judgment.

Source: "Leadership: Do Traits Matter?" by Shelley A. Kirkpatrick and Edwin A. Locke, *Academy of Management Executive*, May 1991, pp. 48–60.

feedback, and carefully analyzing their employees and the situations in which they do their jobs.

How much do a supervisor's personality and emotional intelligence have to do with leadership?

A good personality helps. Most employees react more positively to a supervisor who is optimistic, exhibits a sense of caring, and demonstrates personal warmth. But even an outgoing extrovert must be more than skin deep to be effective. Much more important is your real desire to understand and support the people who work for you. Fair play, interest in others, good decisions, and honesty will help make you a stronger leader than you would be if you relied solely on personality.

Leaders who are interested in the role of personality should consider their own level of **Emotional Intelligence (EI)**. This is the ability to identify and manage one's own emotions (personal competence) as well as the emotions of co-workers and employees (social competence). Emotionally intelligent leaders monitor their own feelings and regulate them so that they can respond appropriately in any situation. The four components of EI (see Figure 8-1) differ according to whether you are emphasizing passive awareness or active management, and whether you are focusing on yourself or on others. The four types of emphasis are:

Emotional Intelligence (EI). A challenging combination of self-awareness and self-management, plus social awareness and the ability to manage personal relationships with others.

- Self-awareness—knowing one's strengths and limits, having a sense of self-worth, and recognizing the impact of emotions on others.
- Self-management—keeping one's impulses under control, while also being transparent to others and demonstrating initiative and optimism.
- Social awareness—using empathy to sense other people's emotions, understand their perspectives, and take an interest in their priorities.
- Relationship management—being a catalyst for change, building bonds with others, inspiring them with a vision, and influencing them through a range of tactics.

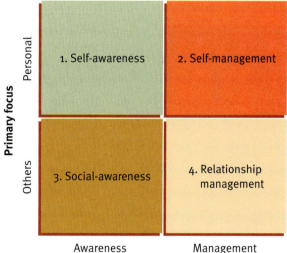

Primary emphasis

FIGURE 8-1

The four components of emotional intelligence. **Which ones might be most difficult to develop?**

Much has been written about charisma. Is that important in a leader?

Charisma is a leadership characteristic that can help motivate workers to take early and sustained action. Supervisors with charisma tend to have expertise, be assertive and self-confident, take moderate risks, and express high performance expectations for others. Their language, behavior, spontaneity, and personal energy seem to inspire others around them. Employees trust and respect leaders with charisma, accept their vision of needed departmental actions, and commit themselves to working hard to achieve results. Clearly, it is a trait that supervisors should work hard to achieve, for it is invaluable when changes must be introduced.

What personal skills does leadership require?

The list is almost endless. As specific keys to success, some would focus on time management (see Chapter 18) or on the way to run an effective meeting. Others would point toward problem solving or being a good teacher and communicator. Most people would agree, however, that good leaders have mastered the following three skills:

Persuasion. This is the ability to assemble and present to others a good case for what you think should be done. It works equally well with your boss and your employees. Persuasion relies both on a rational development of arguments and on a convincing presentation of them.

Influence. This is the ability to exert power over others. Many people possess or are given power, but few learn how to use it. Supervisors, for example, have the power and authority of their *position* and the prestige that accompanies it. They have the power of *expertise* in their greater knowledge of departmental and company operations than is normally possessed by their employees. They also have the power that comes from their capacity to administer or withhold *rewards* from others. But power is like the electrical energy that comes to a light socket—it is useful only when the switch is turned on. Similarly, your supervisory power will not make you a leader until you learn to use this power to move others.

Social skills. One of a supervisor's biggest tasks is creating in others a willingness to cooperate with each other. This requires a range of interpersonal skills, beginning with tact, diplomacy, a deep understanding of motivation, and the ability to perceive the needs of others. Leaders must first establish a firm foundation of rapport with their employees; then they can use their powers of influence and persuasion to motivate individuals and groups in the pursuit of worthwhile goals.

| 1 | T or F | Leadership is essentially a set of traits that one is (or is not) born with. |
| 2 | T or F | Supervisory influence can be derived from position, expertise, or reward power. |

QUICK TEST 1

Leadership Assumptions and Trust

2

Theory X, Theory Y. What's this all about?

To get along with people effectively, you must make a couple of fundamental decisions. First, you must recognize your responsibility for managing human affairs at work. Second, you must always weigh this concern against the practical urgencies of technical and administrative matters.

Douglas McGregor, late professor of industrial management at the Massachusetts Institute of Technology, had much to offer supervisors in his thoughtful work *The Human Side of Enterprise.* Most of today's management thinking was forged long ago to meet the needs of a feudal society, reasoned McGregor. The world has changed, and new thinking is needed for top efficiency today. That's the core of this unique philosophy of contrasting Theory X with Theory Y.

Theory X, the traditional framework for management thinking, is based on the following set of *implicit* assumptions about human nature and human behavior:

1. The average human being has an inherent dislike of work and will avoid it if possible.
2. Because of this human characteristic of dislike of work, most people must be coerced, controlled, directed, or threatened with punishment to get them to put forth adequate effort toward the achievement of organizational objectives.
3. The average human being prefers to be directed, wishes to avoid responsibility, has relatively little ambition, and wants security above all.

Do these assumptions make up a straw person for purposes of scientific demolition? Unfortunately, they do not. Although they are rarely stated so directly, the principles that underlie the bulk of traditional management action could have been derived only from assumptions such as those of Theory X.

CONCEPT
A leader's assumptions—explicit or implicit—guide his or her behavior, and the right assumptions help build a trusting relationship with employees.

Theory X. A set of assumptions in which a supervisor acts as if she or he believes that most people don't like to work and that they wish to avoid responsibility and prefer job security above all.

Did You Know

How Management and Leadership Differ

Management	Leadership
Get things done	Get right things done
Direct	Inspire
Cope with complexity	Initiate change
Organize and staff for task achievement	Communicate vision
Task achievement	Goal accomplishment

Theory Y. A set of assumptions in which a supervisor acts as if she or he believes that most people can set challenging goals and provide their own initiative and exert self-control to attain their goals.

Theory Y has its roots in recently accumulated and emerging knowledge about human behavior. It is based on the following set of assumptions:

1. The expenditure of physical and mental effort in work is as natural as play or rest.
2. External control and the threat of punishment are not the only— or the best—means for bringing about effort toward organizational objectives. Individuals will exercise self-control in the service of objectives to which they are committed.
3. Commitment to objectives depends on the rewards associated with their achievement. The most important rewards are those that satisfy needs for self-respect and personal improvement.
4. The average human being learns, under proper conditions, not only to accept but also to seek responsibility.
5. The capacity to exercise a relatively high degree of imagination, ingenuity, and creativity in the solution of organizational problems is widely, not narrowly, distributed in the population.
6. Under the conditions of modern industrial life, the intellectual potentialities of the average human being are only partially realized.

What makes Theory Y applicable today?

Under the assumptions of Theory Y, the work of the supervisor is to integrate the needs of employees with the needs of the department. Hard-nosed control (a Theory X–based approach) rarely succeeds today. In McGregor's words,

> [Supervisors] are dealing with adults who are only partially dependent. They can—and will—exercise remarkable ingenuity in defeating the purpose of external controls that they resent. However, they can—and do—learn to exercise self-direction and self-control under appropriate conditions. [The supervisor's] task is to help them discover objectives consistent both with organizational requirements and with their own personal goals.

In McGregor's mind, *the ability to help employees discover goals consistent with those of the organization is the essence of leadership.* When a genuine commitment to these objectives is secured, said McGregor, "supervision consists of helping employees achieve these objectives: to act as teacher, consultant, colleague, and only rarely as authoritative boss."

You can see that Theory Y, along with the leadership roles it implies, is far more in tune with today's employees than is Theory X and the autocratic style of leadership it implies. Good supervisors are willing and able to step back and examine periodically their implicit and explicit assumptions about the nature and motivation of the people they supervise. Some will find that they have been using styles of leadership based on inappropriate and outdated assumptions, and they will need to change those beliefs before they can change their behavior. The important thing is to identify and test your assumptions—would they hold up to close scrutiny by your peers? Your manager? Your own employees?

How important is it for employees to trust that their supervisor will act ethically?

Extremely important—especially in times of turmoil and change. Unfortunately, as one skeptic said, a "trusted leader" is an oxymoron; the two terms have almost become incompatible. This is most often true for Theory X leaders, who have a history of sending inconsistent messages, failing to deal with troubling behavior or painful issues, and allowing destructive rumors to circulate because they have withheld crucial information. **Trust** refers to the confidence employees have in a supervisor's integrity, ability, and character. It often develops slowly, can be dashed in an instant, and takes a long time to repair when it is damaged. Trust is the essence of ethical leadership behavior—acting on the basis of clear and accepted values, acting in ways that others will have confidence in, and doing so consistently. The consequences of low trust are costly—marginal loyalty and low morale, possible sabotage, withheld creativity and opinions, and high stress caused by feelings of insecurity.

Theory Y supervisors are much more likely to value trust. They assume that employees want to be trusted and respected, too. To accomplish this, they strive to assign work fairly, tell the truth candidly whenever possible, maintain confidentiality, honor agreements and promises, share credit with employees, and exhibit the characteristics of being consistent, predictable, and dependable. As a result, there is high consistency between their positive assumptions about people, their ethical behavior toward them, and the results they achieve from them. Remember—*your assumptions drive your behavior, and you usually get the results your behavior calls for.*

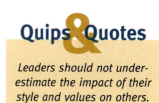

Quips & Quotes

Leaders should not underestimate the impact of their style and values on others.

Walter F. Ulmer, Jr.

3	T or F	Effective supervisors examine their assumptions about people and examine their implications for behavior.
4	T or F	One good thing about trust is that it can be developed rapidly but takes a long time to destroy.

QUICK TEST 2

CONCEPT
Leadership styles range widely from a job- or task-centered orientation, to a people- or relationship-centered one, with many other combinations. A participative style has special merit for consideration.

What is meant by "styles" of leadership, and which are the most basic?

A **style of leadership** refers to the total approach a supervisor uses in trying to direct, activate, or otherwise provide a motivational atmosphere for employees. It is a combination of the leadership traits, skills, attitudes, and behaviors that employees *perceive* their supervisor to have and consistently use. Leadership is in the mind of the beholder. A traditional way to distinguish among leadership styles was to divide them into three types:

Autocratic, or **directive, leadership.** Here, the leader independently sets goals, makes decisions, gives orders, and demands obedience from the people supervised. In some cases, this can produce short-run results, and it may even be appropriate when time is tight or a crisis is present. However, regular use of a highly directive style reflects assumptions consistent with Theory X. Most employees dislike—even fear—working for a rigid leader, feeling that they have more to contribute and deserve some respect. As a result, employee commitment may suffer, and absenteeism and turnover problems may arise (see Figure 8-2).

Democratic, or **consultative, leadership.** This style continues to be a popular approach. The

Internet connection
www.nwlink.com/~donclark/leader/leadstl.html
Positive and negative leadership behaviors are contrasted.

FIGURE 8-2
Clues that employees may fear you.
What happens when employees fear their leader?

leader presents problems to a group, consults with relevant individuals, or solicits ideas from those with expertise and interest in the issue before making a decision. This promotes involvement and strong teamwork. Some critics argue, however, that this approach delays decision making, weakens a leader's image, and results in compromises with less than optimum features.

Participative leadership. This style is the most difficult for a supervisor to learn and practice. It relies on the employee's sense of responsibility, training, experience, and good judgment, and the supervisor's capacity to "let go" of some authority. However, it is highly consistent with the need to empower employees and the assumptions of Theory Y. True participation gives one or more employees the right to explore a problem, gather relevant information, make a decision, and implement it. The positive result is that they are mentally and emotionally committed to its success. But there are risks, too—not all employees are immediately ready for it, and it can be threatening to a supervisor's desire to be in control.

A conductor is the leader of the orchestra.
How do conductors produce the results they are seeking?

Participative leadership. The act of fully involving employees in decision-making processes so that their ideas are used and they are fully committed to the solution's success.

What are the prerequisites to using a participative style?

Several conditions would ideally be in place before a participative approach could have the greatest chance of succeeding. There must be adequate time to consult with employees, the benefits of allowing participation must exceed the costs, and the issue must be sufficiently interesting to engage workers' minds and imaginations. It almost goes without saying that the problem must be within the supervisor's area of job freedom (latitude to make decisions). Consequently, not all problems lend themselves to a participative approach, and both the supervisor and the employees must understand this.

What formal programs can encourage employee participation?

Clearly, many supervisors can initiate a participative approach on their own. They need to recognize, however, that such an experiment may be nearly irreversible. Once they allow employee involvement in meaningful issues, it won't be relinquished easily. And it also changes their own role dramatically as they become facilitators of the work group—coaching, encouraging, and even "cheering" the employees' success.

On a more formal level, organizations have implemented a wide variety of participative programs, including the following:

- **Suggestion systems.** These programs invite individual employees to submit recommendations for work improvements. After careful evaluation of their practicality and probable cost savings, monetary awards may be made, sometimes amounting to thousands of dollars.
- **Quality circles and total quality management programs.** Some organizations set up voluntary groups of employees that receive training in problem solving, group decision making, and statistical techniques. Employees become involved in the idea of continuously searching for improvements in their operations and striving for quality and service improvements.
- **Employee ownership plans.** Sometimes called employee stock ownership plans (ESOPs), these systems allow employees to purchase shares of common stock in the company, becoming part owners. Employees thus are given a chance to share in profits (through dividend distributions), if there are any, or losses (if the stock's market price declines). The more substantive ESOPs actually give employees genuine opportunities to share in the management of their companies through formal involvement of representatives at a variety of organizational levels, possibly including a seat on the board of directors.

If participative management is so good, why does it sometimes fail?

Clearly, it's not for everyone, although most supervisors should thoroughly explore its potential benefits. When it breaks down, it is most often due to one—or more—of these factors:

- It may be uncomfortable for supervisors (or employees) to change old habits.
- It may be attempted in an insincere fashion, causing employees to see through the transparent attempt to manipulate them.
- Supervisors may fail to follow through on the implementation of employee inputs and decisions. When this happens, employees quickly decide it's not worth the effort when the next occasion arises.
- Intense performance pressure, coupled with widespread downsizings, may produce so much fear and insecurity in employees that they are literally "frozen" in their ability to think clearly and address critical problems, even when given the opportunity to do so.
- Perhaps most significantly, some supervisors fear that allowing their employees to participate results in a loss of power for themselves. Consequently, they cling to their "right" to make decisions in the face of demands from the workforce to be involved.

5	T or F	It doesn't matter much what supervisory style employees perceive. What matters most is what the supervisor intended to convey.
6	T or F	Participative leadership works well because all problems lend themselves to its use at work.

Selecting an Appropriate Style

4

What factors might affect the choice of a leadership style?

Situational leadership models maintain that leaders need to assess several key factors before making a decision on which style to adopt. This is in contrast to older models, which implied that the need for leadership should always be fully balanced between all-out concerns for both people and production. One situational approach, the **contingency model of leadership**, advanced by Professor Fred Fiedler and documented in many studies, identifies three critical factors. It asks the leader to examine (a) the quality of leader-member relations, or rapport and good feelings between the supervisor and those supervised, (b) the level of structure or precision in the job, in terms of how carefully procedures and specifications must be followed, and (c) the amount of real power given to the supervisor by his or her superiors. The model then relates this assessment to research results showing whether a task-centered (authoritative) or people-centered (democratic or participative) style is called for.

Contingency model of leadership. The belief that the leadership style that will be most effective in a given situation can be predicted by examining the intensity of three interacting factors.

What is the particular significance of the contingency approach?

It adds an important consideration when a supervisor is choosing a leadership style. As the term *contingency* implies, the style chosen depends on the conditions of the three factors in any given situation (see Figure 8-3). Surprisingly, the task-centered, or authoritative, approach, which uses forceful directing and controlling, is most effective in very favorable or very unfavorable circumstances. That is, it works best when relationships are either very good or very poor, job methods are either precisely defined or not defined at all, and the leader's true authority is either very strong or very weak. In the less

FIGURE 8-3

Choosing a leadership style according to the situation. **Which style is best?**

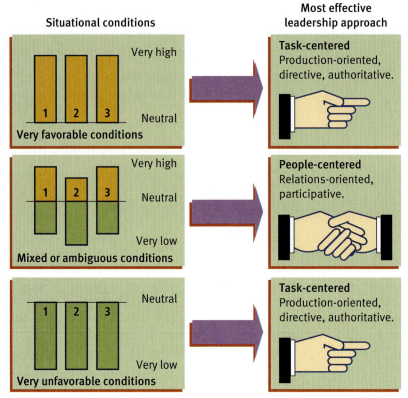

Situational conditions

Most effective leadership approach

Task-centered Production-oriented, directive, authoritative.

People-centered Relations-oriented, participative.

Task-centered Production-oriented, directive, authoritative.

Very favorable conditions

Mixed or ambiguous conditions

Very unfavorable conditions

1. Rapport   2. Job precision   3. Position power

clearly defined, or middle, situations, the participative approach is more likely to be successful.

In other words, an *authoritative style* works best (a) in situations where the supervisor has lots of real power, the process requires strong control, and rapport with employees is good, and (b) in situations where exactly the opposite conditions prevail.

A *participative style* is best in situations where the supervisor's authority hasn't been clearly spelled out by top management or acknowledged by the employees, the process and procedures are somewhat flexible, and the rapport between supervisor and employees is only moderately good.

The contingency approach tends to explain why directive supervisors can be effective in some situations and not in others. Similarly, it helps show where participative leadership may work best and suggest where it might fail. An authoritative approach may work for assembly-line workers or for labor crews cleaning up the area. A participative approach seems favorable on jobs for which exact procedures are hard to set or jobs that require creativity or initiative. These conclusions are contingent on the authoritative leader's having either high or low position power and high or low rapport, and on the participative leader's having moderate rapport and only a low degree of authority.

Which style of leadership, on average, will get the best results?

Surely the most difficult aspect of leadership involves the decision about when to lead and when to stand back. That is the value in employing the concept of situational leadership. Regardless of whether you accept the rather narrow prescriptions of Dr. Fiedler, the situational concept opens your mind to the wisdom of selecting a style that is most suitable for the individuals and circumstances involved.

Many successful managers will tell you that democratic leadership is the best method to use. The fact is, however, that whereas the democratic way may involve the least risk, you'll hamper your leadership role if you stick only to that method. You can play a round of golf with only a driver, but you'll get a much better score if you use a wedge in a sand trap and a putter on the greens. Select the best tool for the task.

A good way to consider such choices is to think of leadership as ranging along a ***continuum of leadership*** styles, as shown in Figure 8-4. At one extreme, a supervisor relies on complete authority; at the other, subordinates are allowed a great deal of freedom. Between the extremes are an infinite number of shadings of leadership styles from which to choose.

Continuum of leadership. A range of leadership approaches that progresses from the extremes of autocratic control by the supervisor to complete freedom for subordinates.

Should your leadership approach vary according to an employee's maturity level?

One school of thought believes that it should—provided that you are talking about a person's task-related maturity, not about chronological

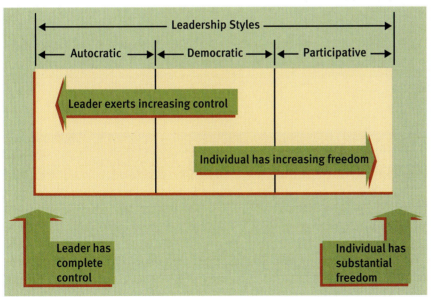

FIGURE 8-4
Continuum of leadership styles.
Where would *you* be on the continuum of styles as a leader?

Source: Adapted from "How to Choose a Leadership Pattern," by Robert Tannenbaum and Warren H. Schmidt, *Harvard Business Review*, March/April 1958, pp. 95–101.

age or emotional development. Paul Hersey's and Ken Blanchard's *situational (or life-cycle) model of leadership* suggests that employees vary in two important ways—their task-specific *competence (ability)* and their motivation to *perform (willingness,* or *commitment).* Supervisors can help employees develop along both dimensions of task-related maturity by providing appropriate guidance and feedback, offering a variety of job experiences, and clarifying the rewards for cooperative behavior.

Not surprisingly, any work group may have a mixture of members who are at a low developmental stage (low ability and low commitment), intermediate stages (low ability and high willingness, or high ability but low willingness), or a high level of development (high ability and high commitment). The Hersey-Blanchard model suggests that supervisors adapt their approach to *fit the development stage of each employee,* using a directive style for those at low levels, more supportive styles (or mixed directive and supportive) for those at intermediate levels, and a "delegating" style (low direction and low support) for employees who have demonstrated competence and commitment. The keys to success with this model lie in taking the time to analyze each employee's stage of development, working with the employees to move them upward, and matching your style to fit their current needs. This requires *behavorial flexibility* on your part.

7	T or F	According to the contingency model of leadership, a task-centered approach works well no matter what the situation calls for.
8	T or F	The Hersey-Blanchard model suggests that a supervisor may have to use different leadership styles with employees who are at different levels of task-related maturity.

5 Leaders and Followers

Can supervisors afford to focus exclusively on their leadership role?

No. Supervisors are leaders, but they are also *followers.* To be promoted in your organization, you may need to develop a reputation not only as an effective leader of your current work unit, but also as a loyal supporter of your boss. This requires a completely different orientation, in effect looking upward as well as looking downward. Effective followers avoid competing with their managers for the spotlight, act as team players, and feel comfortable disagreeing occasionally. They also take the initiative to raise penetrating (but useful) questions, constructively confront their manager's ideas and actions, and work hard to anticipate and prevent potential problems. Effective followership is an important role and needs to be balanced with the leadership job.

What responsibility do supervisors have toward helping their employees develop as leaders?

Some supervisors have been dismayed to learn that their career advancement was put on hold because higher managers felt that there was no one adequately prepared to take their place. Don't let that happen to you! In addition to providing job-related training (which was discussed in Chapter 7), good supervisors consider the opportunity to be a superleader for their employees. The *superleader*, according to authors Charles Manz and Henry Sims, Jr., is a person who places high priority on unleashing and expanding the capabilities of subordinates. A special focus is on encouraging them to practice self-leadership skills, including

Superleader. A supervisor who places a high priority on developing the skills of employees to manage themselves and engage in self-leadership.

Leadership often requires integrating the efforts of diverse team members to produce the greatest success. **Who gets the credit when things go well?**

self-observation, independent goal setting, rehearsal of desirable activities, self-administration of rewards, and self-criticism. Superleaders, then, create a win–win situation. Employees learn useful leadership skills that may qualify them for promotions, and the supervisor acquires a self-motivated group of employees who can be trusted to work toward organizational goals on their own volition. Theory Y assumptions play a large role in affecting one's decision to be a superleader.

I can't be present all the time. Are there substitutes for my leadership while I'm gone?

You have already learned one answer—create self-leading employees. Another simple response is that close and constant supervision can actually *inhibit* some productive employee behaviors. And believing that you are indispensable, or that employees will always fool around when your back is turned, may be an indication that you hold Theory X assumptions. But another fascinating set of alternatives lies in the idea of *substitutes for leadership*.

Substitutes for leadership. Factors in the task, organization, or employees that diminish the need for various kinds of supervisory leadership behaviors.

Have you ever considered the possibility that you can be replaced with factors already or clearly present in the task, the organization, or other employees? It's possible. Researchers have found that a supervisor's need to accent a production orientation may be diminished by the presence of strong subordinate experience, clear policies and rules, or a cohesive work group with a positive attitude. Similarly, there are potential substitutes for a supervisor's need to show a high concern for people and be supportive toward them. Intrinsically satisfying tasks, employees with a professional orientation, and individuals with a high need for independence can help relieve the supervisory pressure. The real lesson is that you should not cling to a rigid definition of your leadership role. The job has changed and probably will go on changing!

How do new attitudes in the contemporary workforce affect leadership behavior?

Much has been written about Generation X and the generation of employees already following it. The combination of a "new age" workforce and a dramatic influx of women, immigrants, and minorities into the labor force has created unique challenges for supervisors. Some new workers are less committed to their employers; they will readily quit for a better job—or no job at all. Some new workers don't want to work during "traditional" hours or wear "traditional" clothing at work. Others sharply protest the need to be subordinate to someone who may lack their level of technical expertise. Even simple and nonthreatening employee behaviors such as wearing decorative jewelry, displaying tattoos, and wearing extreme hairstyles can create challenges for supervisors, if they allow the behaviors to do so.

The key to adapting to these new forces lies in viewing one's job as that of a *steward*, according to noted author and consultant Peter Block. He suggests that good supervisory stewards retain their level of accountability for resources and results, while giving up their need to dominate, be right, or (always) be in control. Stewardship implies empowering others, building partnerships with others, and (most of all) having the humility to define one's role as being in service to others while building employees' capabilities and enhancing their performance. The supervisor-as-servant sets aside the idea of status and power differences while searching for ways to help others meet their goals and satisfy their needs through productive work. This type of leadership approach usually proves far more palatable to newer workers, who are less inclined to accept traditional, task-oriented supervision.

Can leaders always be popular with the people they supervise?

Probably not. The very best leaders seem to combine the knack of leading with the knack of winning friends. But most supervisors are not that successful. Instead, they must be satisfied with earning the respect of their followers. Why? Because many of the decisions you must make as a supervisor will not please everybody. Sometimes you will please nobody. The result is that you must often be satisfied with the knowledge that your leadership has been responsible, ethical, considerate, and equitable—regardless of how unfairly others may judge you.

However, there is room in the supervisor's leadership style to be a **caregiver** despite the pressures on the supervisor. This means demonstrating a supportive attitude toward employees whether you are in a business, school, hospital, or fast-food restaurant. To show that you care about someone else as a person, you must consider providing time and space for connecting with that person, inquiring about his or her emotional and physical needs, and listening attentively to his or her responses. Many employees appreciate a supervisor who shows compassion for their life challenges by displaying warmth, genuine affection, flexibility, understanding, and kindness. These responses can often go a long way toward building the trust and loyalty discussed earlier in this chapter.

Thoughts*to*ponder

Servant Leadership
A very different way of looking at leadership is provided by the *servant-leadership* model. Servant-leaders empower others to achieve their professional goals. They assist people in this process by treating them as equals, affirming their worth, and matching their own behavior to their espoused values. Servant leadership requires the courage to be vulnerable, admit mistakes, and ask for help, as well as to affirm the worth of each contributor. The goal is simple—to set up employees for success by supporting them at every opportunity.

Source: Max E. Douglas, "Service to Others," *Supervision,* March 2005, pp. 6–9.

Quips & Quotes

An effective leader is not someone who is loved or admired. . . . Popularity is not leadership. Results are.

Peter Drucker

9	T or F	A superleader is one who can step in and perform all of his or her employees' jobs if the need arises.
10	T or F	When substitutes for leadership exist, this removes the need to have a supervisor in that position.

QUICK TEST 5

Practical Guidelines for Supervisors

1. Candidly assess your personal characteristics (and seek feedback from others) to *determine the degree to which you have or need high levels of drive, desire, integrity, self-confidence, and analytical skills.*

2. Find ways to *increase your emotional intelligence* so that you will be both personally and socially competent in managing feelings at work.

3. Seek out opportunities (e.g., Toastmaster's Clubs) to *develop your skills at oral persuasion*, while also enriching your various sources of power and influence.

4. *Identify your implicit assumptions about people* (Theory X or Theory Y?), and test their validity.

5. *Set a goal of achieving a high level of trust* with your employees, and find ways to build this across time.

6. Determine your employees' interest in being involved in decision making, and then *find ways to capitalize on a participative leadership approach.*

7. Work to develop your flexibility to engage in a variety of leadership styles, and then *match your leadership style to fit the situation (employee and task at hand)* as well as your own comfort level.

8. Consider yourself not only a leader but a follower, and *find ways to help your manager be more successful.*

9. Ask yourself *what you would do differently* if leadership were defined exclusively as being a servant of those in your employ.

10. Find ways to *express your level of caring and compassion* for employees and peers at work by displaying warmth, understanding, and kindness.

Chapter 8 Review

Key Concepts to Remember

1. Leadership Defined. Leadership requires the ability to develop rapport with others and to apply appropriate persuasion and influence to obtain their willing cooperation in pursuing legitimate organizational goals. Given sound character in the supervisor, the skills of leadership—including the four elements of emotional intelligence—are not innate but can be acquired and developed.

2. Leadership Assumptions and Trust. Leadership involves providing conditions in the workplace that enable each person to satisfy his or her needs while also helping the organization attain its goals. It is important that the leader's assumptions concerning an employee's nature and needs are, in fact, correct. The two opposing sets of assumptions about employee motivation are characterized by Theory X (the desire to avoid work) and Theory Y (the desire to perform work that is challenging and worthwhile).

3. Leadership Styles and Concepts. Styles of leadership range from the autocratic approach (which is forceful and demanding) to the democratic, or consultative, approach to the participative approach (which encourages employee responsibility and initiative). A participative approach that empowers employees is recommended for obtaining high levels of commitment, although the conditions for its success must be evaluated first.

4. Selecting an Appropriate Style. The contingency model depends on an analysis of the state of three factors present in a situation: (a) leader–member relations, (b) task structure, and (c) position power of the leader. When the states of all three factors are either very favorable or very unfavorable, a more authoritative approach is recommended. When the states of the three factors are somewhere between favorable and unfavorable, a participative approach is recommended. A leadership approach can be selected from a continuum of styles that range from strictly autocratic to purely participative. The best choice of a style is one that is based on an analysis of a subordinate's task competence and motivation to perform. The more capable and committed the employee, the more likely that a participative style will be appropriate.

5. Leaders and Followers. Good leaders recognize their role as followers, and engage in a variety of behaviors that provide support to their own manager. These supervisors also attempt to fulfill their superleader role by helping their employees learn and practice self-leadership skills. Supervisors also learn that other factors can act as substitutes for their leadership behaviors, and that an emerging workforce demands that they act as servant-leaders and compassionate caregivers when appropriate.

Reading Comprehension

1. Which are the three personal skills most likely to be required of leaders? Can they be learned, or must a leader be born with them?

2. Some people have suggested that the four components of emotional intelligence are best developed in a particular order, as illustrated in the numbered quadrants in Figure 8-1. Explain why this order makes sense.

3. As supervisor of the catalog section of a direct-mail house, Mary has come to believe that without her close supervision, employees in her department would never get their work done. Which of McGregor's assumptions

about employees at work does Mary's view represent?

4. Describe what McGregor believed to be the essence of leadership.

5. Compare democratic leadership with participative leadership.

6. According to Fiedler's contingency model of leadership, what is likely to be the best approach in a situation where the supervisor has been newly appointed, relationships with the new group are strained, and the task to be performed requires great accuracy? Why?

7. In what ways are various leadership styles related to Theory X and Theory Y?

8. Provide examples of the use of leadership styles at three different points along the continuum of leadership styles.

9. Which kind of leadership style—autocratic or participative—is least likely to be effective with a relatively incompetent and uncommitted individual? Why?

10. Explain why it is important for a supervisor to manage upward (followership skills) as well as downward (leadership skills).

Application

Self-Assessment

How Good Are Your Leadership Skills?

Read the following statements carefully. Circle the number on the response scale that most closely reflects the degree to which each statement describes you. Add up your total points and prepare a brief action plan for self-improvement. Be ready to report your score for tabulation across the entire group.

	Good Description		Poor Description
1. I exhibit a high degree of energy, desire to help others succeed, integrity, self-confidence, and judgment.	10 9 8 7 6 5 4 3 2 1		
2. I am aware of the need to demonstrate a substantial level of charisma to induce others to make needed changes.	10 9 8 7 6 5 4 3 2 1		
3. I have a high level of emotional intelligence.	10 9 8 7 6 5 4 3 2 1		
4. I completely embrace the assumptions about people at work stated in Theory Y.	10 9 8 7 6 5 4 3 2 1		
5. I am comfortable playing the roles of teacher, coach, consultant, and colleague to my staff.	10 9 8 7 6 5 4 3 2 1		
6. I firmly believe in the value of participative leadership for involving employees.	10 9 8 7 6 5 4 3 2 1		

	Good Description	Poor Description

7. I understand why a task-centered leadership style might be effective in some situations and a people-centered style might work better in others.

10 9 8 7 6 5 4 3 2 1

8. It makes good sense to me to vary the style of leadership to fit the competence and level of commitment of each employee.

10 9 8 7 6 5 4 3 2 1

9. In addition to getting my employees to be productive, I accept the need to help them develop critical self-leadership skills.

10 9 8 7 6 5 4 3 2 1

10. I feel very comfortable viewing my role as a steward, servant, and caregiver to my employees.

10 9 8 7 6 5 4 3 2 1

Scoring and Interpretation

Scoring

Add up your total points for the 10 questions. Record that number here, and report it when it is requested. _____

Also, insert your score on the Personal Development Plan in the Appendix.

Interpretation

81 to 100 points. You seem to have a basic set of leadership attitudes and skills.

61 to 80 points. Take a close look at some of your leadership attitudes and skills (those with lower self-assessments) and discuss them with a manager to see if they need improvement.

Below 60 points. Some of your skills may be substantially inconsistent with effective leadership practices and could be detrimental to your success as a supervisor.

Identify your three lowest scores and record the question numbers here: _____, _____, _____.

Action

Write a brief paragraph detailing an action plan for how you might sharpen each of these skills. Then pay particularly close attention to the related material in the chapter as you review the relevant sections there.

Skill Development

Leadership Skills and Qualities

Assume that several high-level executives in your organization have indicated that they believe you have great potential for rapid advancement.

However, you are concerned that absence of (or weakness in) some leadership skills and qualities might prevent such advancement. Review the list of leadership characteristics below with a close colleague or friend, and select the three on which you need the greatest amount of development, marking them with an X. Then prepare a report that suggests how you intend to improve them. (For example, if you lack self-confidence and spontaneity, you might consider joining a Toastmaster's Club.) To prepare your report, you will likely wish to review the text's discussion on leadership, search the Internet for relevant guidelines, and consult with colleagues and staff persons in the human resources department for their advice.

Leadership Skills and Qualities	Most Deficient (3)	Action Plans
1. Personal warmth	_____	_____
		_____
2. Assertiveness	_____	_____
		_____
3. Self-confidence	_____	_____
		_____
4. Self-awareness	_____	_____
		_____
5. Persuasiveness	_____	_____
		_____
6. Risk-taking propensity	_____	_____
		_____
7. Sense of caring	_____	_____
		_____
8. Ability to influence	_____	_____
		_____
9. Social awareness	_____	_____
		_____
10. Interest in others	_____	_____
		_____

Role Play

Leadership Skills

Five individuals should be identified (through volunteering) for a leadership-development task. Ask each volunteer to select any work-related topic of his or her choice and propose a major change of some sort to the audience (his or her employees). It could be a new compensation system, a new work schedule, the introduction of new technology, or a new office layout, among other ideas. Have them step out of the room to prepare for a few minutes, and then return singly to give a brief, one-minute talk to the class in which they propose acceptance of the change. The other class members should rate each speaker (10 = very high; 1 = very low) on the dimensions shown. Collect and tabulate the information, and feed it back to each speaker privately for the purpose of individual development. Then engage the class in a discussion of leadership.

Leadership Dimension	Speaker				
	1	2	3	4	5
1. Charisma (expertise, self-confidence, assertiveness, spontaneity, high expectations for others)	____	____	____	____	____
2. Persuasion (rational arguments and convincing presentation)	____	____	____	____	____
3. Influence (use of position power, expertise, and rewards)	____	____	____	____	____
4. Social skills (tact, diplomacy, and perception/understanding of others' needs)	____	____	____	____	____

Cases for Analysis

Case 23

The New Supervisor of Nurses

This action took place on the general surgery floor of a small hospital in western New York State. For several months, the hospital trustees had debated the feasibility of building an addition that would move all critical-care facilities into a modern, fully equipped building. However, just last month, the decision was made not to expand but to modernize the present facilities. During this period of decision making, the administrative organization of the hospital changed markedly. A new administrator from a large city hospital took over and brought in a new nursing head and several new nursing supervisors.

The general surgery floor on this particular shift (3 to 11 P.M.) was staffed by eight longtime registered nurses, three licensed practical nurses, and two nurses' aides. Molly P., the new nursing supervisor for this shift, reported for the first time on Saturday night. She observed during the shift that there were several infractions of sterile procedures, that on two occasions practical nurses administered injections (which, by law, must be handled by the registered nurses), and that the nurses tended to congregate at the nursing station for long periods. The first thing Molly did when she went on shift Tuesday night was to call the entire staff together. She said that they should know that she expected all of them to adhere strictly to sterile procedures, that there must be no abrogation of R.N. responsibilities, and that "coffee klatching" at the nursing station must be kept to a minimum. It appeared that things improved on Wednesday and Thursday nights, but by the middle of the following week, Molly sensed a return to the general laxness that was evident when she first took over.

Molly waited until the next Monday. That night, she met with staff members individually in a quiet room. With each one, she reiterated her determination to "run a tight ship, medically," and then asked for cooperation. From most of the staff members, she got no meaningful replies. However, one of the older R.N.s looked her in the eye and said, "We've handled this floor in our own way for a number of years, and we've had no problems. Our record is as good as any in the hospital. We don't need your big-city ways here. And since the new addition won't be built, the chances are that you won't be here for long, anyway."

Analysis

If you were Molly, what would you do? Five approaches are listed below. Rank them on a scale from 1 to 5 in the order in which they appeal to you (1, most attractive; 5, least attractive). You may add another alternative if you wish. Be prepared to justify your ranking.

_____ **a.** Continue to insist on a high level of performance while taking steps to weed out those staff members who don't or won't measure up.

_____ **b.** Make changes after the staff is better unified under your leadership.

_____ **c.** Relax the rule about "coffee klatching," but stick to the letter of the procedures for sterile practices and R.N. responsibilities.

_____ **d.** Hold fast to your demands for a medically tight ship, but work with each person to find a way to convince him or her of the value of operating this way.

_____ **e.** Get together with the other nursing supervisors to make certain that the procedures set down are uniform from floor to floor.

Case 24

The Experienced Transferees

Due to the closing of several company plants, a number of employees have been transferred from other locations to your department. These are men and women reputed to have had good records elsewhere. Most of them have had extensive experience in other departments in the company. An examination of their employment records, however, shows that they have had little or no experience with the line of work performed in your department. However, they appear willing and cooperative.

Analysis

Which of the following approaches would you choose to make this group of transferees productive as quickly as possible? Why? Can you identify the leadership style of each alternative?

a. Hold a meeting with them to find out how they think the work should be handled; then proceed to make assignments.

b. Provide explicit directions for now, and accept no suggestions until the transferees have shown they can do the work properly.

c. Allow the transferees to find out through experience on the job the best way to handle the work.

d. Interview each transferee so that you can better understand his or her preferences, and then make assignments accordingly.

Case 25

Joe's "Pretty Good" Diner

Everything was, as the saying goes, "coming up roses." Joe had bought a small diner several years ago and worked hard to make it successful. Business had grown steadily through careful attention to costs and customer service. Joe had been able to stay on top of things for a long time, handling the ordering of supplies, payroll, and hiring and firing, and filling in for the cooks on their days off.

Suddenly, everything changed. A major electronics plant opened up a block away, providing hundreds of new customers daily at Joe's "Pretty Good" Diner.

Analysis

After expanding his seating area, upgrading his menu, changing his decor, and hiring three assistant managers to help out, Joe thought he could sit back and relax. However, on their first day, each new supervisor came to see Joe, asking which leadership style to use. What do you recommend for each of them?

- Mary had been promoted from her job as senior food server. She had received a warm recommendation from the other servers, and Joe put her in charge of the morning shift and told her that he would support almost anything she did. Trusting her completely allowed Joe an occasional morning off to go golfing, too.
- Danny was new to the diner and had received mixed reviews from the employee team that assisted in the selection process. Nevertheless, he seemed to be the best available candidate, and so Joe put Danny on probation for six months and sharply limited his decision-making authority.
- Tom was another story. He, like Mary, had been a food server, but his grating personality rubbed his co-workers the wrong way. Joe put him in charge of maintenance and supplies, and in addition gave him all the marketing responsibilities. But he put sharp financial controls on Tom, requiring him to clear in advance all expenditures over $25.

ANSWERS TO QUICK TESTS	Quick Test 1	Quick Test 2	Quick Test 3	Quick Test 4	Quick Test 5
	1. F	3. T	5. F	7. F	9. F
	2. T	4. F	6. F	8. T	10. F

9

Understanding and Motivating People at Work

LEARNING OBJECTIVES

After studying this chapter, you should be able to

- Recognize some of the factors that influence the development of each individual's unique personality.

- Describe the major needs that employees typically have, and explain how they influence motivation and behavior.

- Explain how goal setting helps satisfy employee needs.

- Explain the differences between satisfaction and dissatisfaction, and discuss how a supervisor can affect the contributing factors.

- Understand the concepts of expectancy theory; drives for achievement, power, and affiliation; and the impact of equity and inequity on employee motivation and morale.

- Discuss the ways in which money and recognition can be used to reinforce desirable employee behaviors.

- Identify the elements found in a people-centered approach to job design and explain how, when they are used to empower employees, they provide motivation and improve the quality of work life.

The Importance of Individuality

1

Why do people act the way they do?

If you mean, "Why don't employees act the way I wish they would?" the answer would be lengthy and probably not very useful to you. But if you are really asking, "Why do people sometimes act in such unpredictable ways?" the answer is simple: *People—their personalities and their behavior—are a product of their backgrounds.* Their actions at work, which may look irrational to someone who doesn't try to understand them, are in reality very logical—at least internally. If you could peer into people's backgrounds and into their psychological makeup, you'd be able to predict with surprising accuracy how one person would react to criticism or to a new task assignment. And this is a key part of the supervisor's job—seeking to understand employees before deciding how to motivate and lead them.

An example: The dog that's been scratched by a cat learns to steer clear of all cats. *It generalizes its past behavior*, perhaps more than it needs to. Workers who have learned from one boss that the only time they are treated with respect is when the workload is going to be increased quickly become suspicious when a new boss tries to be friendly. To the new boss such employee actions look absurd, but to the workers it's a logical thing to do.

Internet connection

agelesslearner.com/assess/motivationstyle.html
This site provides an opportunity to assess your motivational style.

What determines an individual's personality?

Just about everything. An individual's personality cannot be neatly pigeonholed (as we so often try to do) into simple categories. It is unfair and unwise to label people as pleasant or outgoing or friendly or ill tempered or unpleasant or suspicious or defensive. An individual's ***personality*** is the sum total of everything that person is today. It is exhibited in many ways—the clothing worn, the hairstyle chosen, the food preferred, the conversation enjoyed or avoided, the manners and gestures used, the methods of thought practiced, and the way situations are handled. All these are important cues, if you are alert enough to detect and interpret them.

Each person is the product of parents, home life, education, social life, peer pressures, and prior work experiences. And each person's personality is uniquely different from everyone else's. It results from heredity and upbringing, schooling or lack of it, neighborhoods, work and play experiences, parents' influence, religion—all the social forces around a person. From all these influences, people develop their individuality in a way that

Personality. An individual's unique way of behaving and of seeing and interpreting the actions of other people and events.

enables them to cope with life's encounters, with work, with living together, with aging, with success and failure. As a result, personality is the total expression of the unique way in which each individual deals with life. Consequently, when supervisors deal with employees, they are dealing with persons who have brought all their previous experiences with them to the job. The supervisor's task, then, is captured in the old saying "Seek first to understand others before you can expect to be understood by them."

Are all people different from each other?

Each person is, and has the right to be, a distinct individual. As a matter of fact, the differences inherent in any work group collectively bring a rich variety of assets to the job. But to predict and adapt to human behavior, you first have to understand the major work-related ways in which people are different—and there are many. The most significant personality traits (deeply ingrained ways in which people are inclined to think, feel, and act) are referred to as the *Big Five*. They include the following:

Big Five. The key personality traits that are exhibited to various degrees by all employees.

- **Extroversion** (positiveness). The degree to which an employee is assertive, talkative, friendly, and upbeat. These energetic people are often highly sociable, and enjoy work that brings them into frequent contact with others. Customer-contact jobs are a good fit for them.
- **Neuroticism** (criticalness). The degree to which employees are typically negative, are pessimistic, feel distressed, or get down on themselves. These persons may be tense, moody, or anxious. However, they may play a key role in adding critical thinking and objective assessment to a group's deliberations. The contrasting extreme of this dimension is emotional stability and high self-esteem, in which people feel good about their skills, believe they are capable, and can handle a variety of work challenges.
- **Agreeableness** (likability). The degree to which a person is kind and sympathetic, cares for others, is cooperative, and builds good relationships with co-workers. These employees are often good customer-contact persons because they are courteous, are sympathetic, and want to please others.
- **Conscientiousness** (thoroughness). The degree to which a person has self-discipline, is well organized, likes to plan, perseveres at tasks, and carefully follows directions. Conscientious people are also likely to be high *self-monitors*, persons who regularly assess how they are doing and are willing (and able) to make appropriate adjustments in their behavior. These employees are valuable because they require less attention and supervision.
- **Openness to experience** (risk taking). The degree to which employees are receptive to new challenges, are imaginative and

insightful, enjoy learning, and have a wide range of interests. These employees are often adventuresome and innovative, and are good candidates for assignments that provide a high degree of autonomy.

There are at least two important conclusions for supervisors who pay attention to personality traits among their diverse groups of employees. First is the recognition that although individuals will demonstrate more or less of these characteristics, all persons can be capable and productive workers if you are willing to adapt to *their* nature (and not impose your preference on them). The second conclusion flows from extensive research on personalities—employees with high conscientiousness and low neuroticism are consistently better job performers.[1] Dedicated, attentive, organized, upbeat people make the workplace a more desirable place! Once you understand the importance of personalities, the next step is to grasp the underlying reasons why employees choose to do anything at work. These reasons are called *needs* or *drives*.

QUICK TEST 1	1	T or F	To understand an employee's current behavior, it would be helpful to know about his or her personal background.
	2	T or F	A supervisor's first priority is to try to predict the behavior of employees.

2 A Powerful Pattern of Motivation

CONCEPT
Individuals strive to satisfy a hierarchy of five basic needs.

Motivation. The process that impels a person to behave in a certain manner in order to satisfy highly individual needs.

What do employees want from life—and work?

Most of us, including employees, seek satisfaction from life in relation to what psychologist A. H. Maslow called the "five basic needs." (See Figure 9-1.) And we seek a good part of this satisfaction from our work. Dr. Maslow outlined the basic needs as explained here and conceived of them as a sort of hierarchy, with the most initially compelling ones coming first and the more sophisticated ones later.

We Need to Be Alive and to Stay Alive. We need to breathe, eat, sleep, reproduce, see, hear, and feel. But in today's world these needs rarely dominate us. Real hunger among workers, for example, is rare. All in all, our first-level needs are often satisfied. Only an occasional experience—a couple of days without sleep, a day on a diet without food, a frantic 30 seconds underwater—reminds us that these basic needs are still with us.

FIGURE 9-1
Maslow's hierarchy of needs.
Which needs should be met first?

Self-actualization need
To do the work we
want to do

Esteem need
To be respected by others

Social need
To be with others we like

Safety need
To feel free from threats or harm

Survival need
To be alive and stay alive

We Need to Feel Safe. We like to feel that we are safe from accidents or pain, from competitors or criminals, from an uncertain future or a changing present. Not one of us ever feels completely safe. Yet most of us feel reasonably safe. After all, we have laws, police, insurance, lights, locks, social security, union contracts, and the like, to protect us.

We Need to Be Social. From the beginning of time we have lived together in tribes and family groups. Today, these group ties are stronger than ever. We marry, join clubs, and participate in recreational teams. Social need varies widely from person to person, just as other needs do. Few of us want to be hermits. Not everyone, of course, is capable of (or desirous of) intimate and deep relationships—even with a wife or husband and close friends. But, to a greater or lesser degree, this social need operates in all of us.

We Need to Feel Worthy and Respected. When we talk about our self-respect or our dignity, this is the need we are expressing. When a person isn't completely adjusted to life, this need may show itself as undue pride in achievements, self-importance, boastfulness—all signs of an inflated ego.

But so many of our other needs are so easily satisfied in the modern world that this need often becomes one of the most demanding. Look what we go through to satisfy the need to think well of ourselves, and have others do likewise. When a wife insists her husband wear a jacket to a party, she's expressing this need. When we buy a new sports car even though the old sedan is in good shape, we're giving way to our desire to show ourselves off.

Did You Know

Flow at Work

A researcher has identified a psychological state similar to self-actualization, which he calls *flow*. This, the researcher says, is the total immersion in a task and full involvement with life that provides an opportunity to grow and achieve happiness. Flow is most likely to occur when goals are clear, immediate feedback is received, opportunities for self-control are provided, and an individual is highly challenged—but not beyond his or her capacities. In a state of flow, employees lose track of time, concentrate only on the present, and pay no attention to their egos. The researcher suggests that it is possible for employees to experience flow at work if supervisors create jobs with meaning and value.

Source: Mihaly Csikszentmihalyi, *Good Business: Leadership, Flow, and the Making of Meaning.* New York: Penguin Putnam, 2003.

Challenging goals can often be achieved by properly motivated people.
What needs and drives probably motivate this person?

Ethical Perspectives

Motivating Mature Workers

Lee Iacocca said, "Management is nothing more than motivating people." But you are concerned about being able to motivate workers older than yourself. The older employees have mastered their job tasks. Is it normal for a supervisor to feel under-qualified or nervous in the managing and motivating of this sector of his or her team?

Goal setting. The process of providing clear objectives for employees to accomplish, often created on a cooperative basis.

We even modify our normal behavior to get the esteem of others. No doubt you've put on your company manners when out visiting. It's natural, we say, to act more refined in public than at home—or to cover up our less acceptable traits.

We Need to Become Very Good at Something—and Use Our Talents Fully. Some people get so immersed in their work that they lose track of time and don't mind working long hours. Those who don't like their jobs may turn to hobbies for self-expression and fulfillment, and craft beautiful pieces of furniture or art in their spare time. When people engage in behaviors that are largely an expression of their desire to fulfill themselves and maximize the development of their talents, they are demonstrating a strong need for what Maslow called *self-actualization*. This need is rarely fully satisfied, but it can be a compelling force for some people and an influencing factor for many.

Which employee needs are the most powerful?

The one or ones that are least satisfied. Maslow's greatest insight was the realization that once a need is satisfied, it no longer motivates a person to greater effort. If a person has what is required in the way of job security, for example, offering more of it, such as guaranteeing employment for the next five years, will normally not cause a person to work any harder. The supervisor who wishes to see greater effort generated will have to move to an unsatisfied need, such as the desire to be with other people on the job, if this employee is to be expected to work harder.

It should also be noted that people tend to move up and down the hierarchy as one of their needs is threatened. For example, rumors of downsizing and layoffs can shift attention quickly back to "safety and security."

How are needs related to goals?

Quite directly. Employees seek direction in their work lives; they don't want to wander aimlessly and have no purpose. *Goal setting*—providing clear objectives for employee behavior—provides a useful cue to employees, telling them what is expected of them. Goals also form the basis for comparing results to planned performance, and the discrepancies that are revealed are motivational to workers who want to feel good about themselves by removing the gaps. Effective goals should be specific, clear, measurable, jointly established, challenging, and accepted by employees. Most important, workers need to receive *performance feedback*, which is timely data on task-related results. This allows them to feel good about themselves (if deserved) and achieve satisfaction of their esteem needs.

3	T or F	According to psychologist A. H. Maslow, employees all have five basic needs of equal strength.
4	T or F	The most powerful motivational need may vary from person to person.

QUICK TEST 2

Satisfaction and Dissatisfaction

3

In what way can a job satisfy a person's needs?

CONCEPT
Supervisors are key forces in providing employees with need satisfaction.

It's a fact: Many people are happier at work than at home! Why? Because a challenging job with cooperative peers and a supportive supervisor goes a long way toward meeting one's needs. Even though all of us may complain about some parts of our jobs (or our bosses) from time to time, most of us appreciate having a good job in a solid organization. At home, the problems may pile up and seem insurmountable—a lazy spouse, sick children, aging parents, a barking dog next door, and a stack of bills to pay. But if one can find an appreciative supervisor at work, a stimulating job that is viewed as important, and the predictability of a decent paycheck and the possibility of future promotions, the average worker will enjoy coming to work.

Or look at it this way. Even an entry-level job with a thriving organization often provides satisfaction of the first two basic needs: (a) a livelihood that provides for food, shelter, and clothing and (b) a sense of safety from fears of job loss or accidents. Satisfaction of the other three basic needs—to have social contacts, to be respected by others, and to use one's talents—is often more a function of a person's supervisor than of the job itself.

A good supervisor can satisfy the *social need* by showing direct care and concern for employees, greeting them warmly, demonstrating empathy, and inquiring about their current activities. A supervisor can also help a worker break into a work group and acquire friends. For instance: "This is Paula Brown, our new records clerk. We're really glad to have her join the agency. I've told her what a great bunch of people you all are, and she's looking forward to meeting each of you. Since it's

Historically, supervisors used either a carrot (incentive) or a stick (punishment) to motivate workers.
Which approach would you prefer?

almost break time, how about taking Paula along to the vending area and showing her where she can get a cup of coffee?"

To satisfy the *esteem need*, a good supervisor will make sure workers know when their work is appreciated. For example: "Paula, I've looked over your report for August, and I couldn't find a single error in it. Not only did you point out some fruitful suggestions, but the report reads very well. I'm pleased with your effort."

To satisfy the *desire to do worthwhile work*, a good supervisor gives thought to assigning tasks that will stretch employees' minds and skills, while drawing on their aptitude and training. The supervisor might say to Paula, "We'll start you on this task until you get the hang of things. Then, in a couple of weeks, we'll give you a chance to broaden your experience by

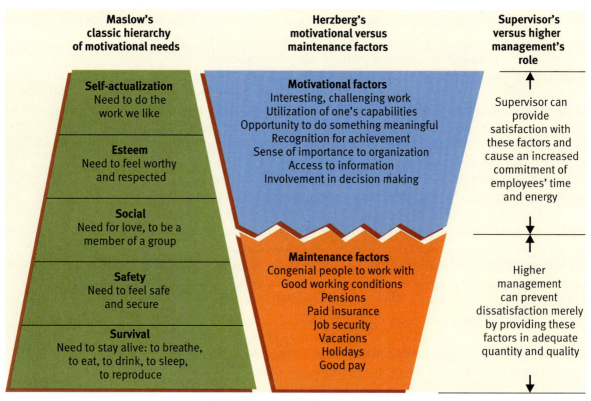

FIGURE 9-2

Employee needs that supervisors can satisfy.
Which task is more challenging—removing dissatisfaction or increasing satisfaction?

taking on some of Tom's responsibilities. And the more tasks you master, the more promotable you'll be."

How do the causes of satisfaction and dissatisfaction differ?

Behavioral scientist Frederick Herzberg made these distinctions between them:

Satisfaction for an employee comes from the presence of truly *motivating* factors (satisfiers) such as interesting and challenging work, utilization of one's capabilities, opportunity to do something meaningful, recognition of achievement, and responsibility for one's own work.

Dissatisfaction occurs when the following (maintenance) factors are *not* sufficiently present on the job: good pay, adequate holidays, long enough vacations, paid insurance and pensions, good working conditions, and congenial people to work with. These are called maintenance (hygiene) factors.

Whose responsibility is job satisfaction— the organization's or the supervisor's?

The employer has a huge stake in creating a productive work environment that helps attract, retain, and motivate good employees. The organization can do much to establish an overall climate, policies, and working conditions to make the supervisor's job easier. But a supervisor's day-to-day relationship with his or her employees is, ultimately, a very personal one. No amount of policies and procedures, cafeterias, generous fringe benefits, or clean rest rooms can take the place of a concerned supervisor who treats each employee with respect, and helps him or her feel needed and appreciated. Clearly, the responsibility for the dual tasks of removing dissatisfaction and increasing satisfaction is one that is shared by you and the parent organization (see Figure 9-2).

Satisfaction. The positive state that exists when truly motivating factors (satisfiers)—such as interesting and challenging work, full use of one's capabilities, and recognition for achievement—are provided.

Dissatisfaction. The state that exists when "maintenance" or "hygiene" factors such as good pay, job security, fringe benefits, and desirable working conditions are lacking.

| 5 | T or F | Satisfaction and dissatisfaction are basically two different feelings (positive and negative) about the same set of factors. |
| 6 | T or F | Supervisors are most directly responsible for affecting motivational, not maintenance, factors at work. |

QUICK TEST 3

Achievement, Expectancy, and Equity

CONCEPT

Employee performance is greatly influenced by workers' opportunities for personal achievement, their expectancy of what the job will provide, and their desire for equity in the workplace.

What important drives do employees typically have?

Researcher David McClelland discovered that people have varying degrees of drive toward achievement, power, and affiliation. Some people—those with *achievement* motivation—thrive on pursuing and attaining goals. Often they are the ones who aspire to supervisory and management careers. But many other people feel its strong pull, too. You can recognize achievement-driven persons, according to McClelland, if they:

1. Like to be able to control the situations in which they are involved.
2. Take moderate risks but not great chances.
3. Like to get immediate feedback on how they have done.
4. Tend to be preoccupied with a task orientation toward the job to be done.

Internet connection

www.accel-team.com/motivation
Seven key strategies for motivating people are presented in this concise discussion.

Achievement-oriented persons rise to challenges well, seek new horizons to conquer, and thrive on freedom of choice. But if left unchecked, they may be inclined to take off in an independent direction and balk at working closely with other employees.

Individuals who are *power* driven may see almost every situation at work as one in which they must seize control or dominate others. They love to influence others around them and change situations whether or not change is needed. Extreme power seekers tend to be abrasive and insensitive to others' feelings. They insist on doing a job their own way rather than admitting that your instructions may be more effective. But they are also willing to assert themselves when a decision needs to be made.

Employees who are strongly motivated by *affiliation* are usually friendly and like to socialize with others. They enjoy being with friends and value others whom they find compatible. This drive may even distract them from their performance requirements, but they will usually respond to an appeal for cooperation.

In contrast to basic needs that are felt instinctively, these three drives are usually acquired from life's experiences. The supervisor's task is to identify the strength of each drive in an employee, awaken the drive where appropriate, and then tap into its positive features by attempting to satisfy that dimension.

In addition to having their needs and drives satisfied, what other factors are important to employees?

Using their capabilities fully and being rewarded commensurately are other major concerns. An employee's *expectancy*—her or his judgment about the attractiveness and probability of a prospective reward—strongly influences that person's willingness to take on a new task. It is tempting, but too simple, to suggest that every employee is concerned with only one question—"What's in it for me?" Many employees *do* want to perform well and satisfy their supervisor's requests. They recognize that the organization's success and their need for satisfaction go hand in hand. To achieve these goals, however, they require answers to several questions, such as the following:

Expectancy. An individual's judgment about the attractiveness and probability of a reward.

1. Can I *do* what management is asking me to do? (Do I have the skills, resources, and time?)
2. If I do the job, will I be *rewarded*? (Will management recognize my work, be satisfied with it, and reward me?)
3. Will the reward I receive be *satisfactory* to me? (Will it be something I value, large enough to meet my needs, and received soon enough to be useful?)

As you can see, a person's effort will be greatly influenced by the answers received. But two factors stand out. First, the questions may be *implicit* in the employee's mind, suggesting that the supervisor has to stay one step ahead of the employee. You should anticipate such questions and be ready to raise them and offer solid answers. Second, the answers to *all* these questions must be positive, for employees will see no reason to exert their efforts if any of the factors are missing or unsatisfactory. As a baker knows when mixing a cake, all the ingredients are important to the overall product.

How important is it to treat different employees in a similar manner?

Extremely important, but this does *not* mean that all employees will receive the *same* rewards. Many employees are highly concerned about *equity*—the perception of fairness involved in rewards given by their supervisor to different employees. They are interested not only in their own efforts and rewards balance, but also in how that balance compares with the rewards received by others for their efforts. Here's how it works. Maria looks at the range of rewards (both satisfiers and maintenance factors) she receives, and compares this with the effort (talent, skills, and time) she contributes to her employer. Even if this ratio is initially satisfactory to her, she may still be unhappy if she senses that Nelson is contributing less or receiving more than she. When inequity exists, Maria is

Equity. An employee's perception of the fairness in the application of rewards to oneself and others for their efforts.

likely to withhold some of her contributions (consciously or unconsciously) to bring her ratio into a better balance. This has an important lesson for supervisors: They must manage not just objective reality (actual rewards given), but also the *perception* of fairness that exists in the mind of each employee. As you will see in Chapter 10, the task of communicating is never-ending!

A few other points about the distribution of rewards also deserve mention. It's a fact of life that the package of rewards given to one employee will differ from that given to another employee. This suggests that one role of a supervisor is to explain this fact—both in advance and at the time that rewards are given—to help employees understand the differential reward phenomenon and the reasons for it. One reason for this practice is that people are motivated by different needs (as discussed earlier in this chapter). The main principle to follow is this: Be consistent in what you reward so that employees will see the pattern and the rationale for it. Supervisors walk a shaky tightrope as they try to balance two objectives: consistency *within* rewards for an employee and equity *across* employees.

5. Motivation and Rewards

CONCEPT

Supervisors need to use money and other means to encourage and reward effective employee behaviors.

How does money relate to the motivational concepts discussed earlier?

Quite obviously, money is important to employees for several reasons. They use it to buy groceries, pay the rent or mortgage, contribute to charitable causes, and fund their children's education. It also serves as a status symbol, for it provides a clue about the value that organizations place on them and their jobs. Further, it demonstrates one's achievement in life, provides access to social organizations, and is a source of power and influence over others. Pay also satisfies lower-order needs (physiological and security) and helps remove the dissatisfaction associated with the absence of several maintenance factors in

Herzberg's motivational model. Finally, pay serves as a clear measure of equity when employees wonder if they are receiving rewards equivalent to their contributions and the rewards that their peers are receiving. Therefore, pay—and its careful administration—cannot be ignored as a means of motivation.

Should supervisors supplement pay with personal recognition?

Absolutely! Employees constantly ask themselves (and their employers), "What's in it for me?" So supervisors had better be ready with the answers. When money is tight, creative supervisors still have many options for recognizing employees. The process is straightforward:

1. **Specify the desired outcomes.** Is it better customer service? Is it more deliveries per day? Be sure to communicate your goals in terms of the behaviors you are expecting and the results that should appear from their efforts.
2. **Involve the employee in choosing the form of recognition.** Some people prefer public praise; some do not. Some will smile for a week after receiving a humorous T-shirt or coffee mug; some will not. Demonstrate that you care enough to ask, and the recognition will have a greater impact.
3. **Monitor the employee's performance.** Be observant, and gather evidence indicating how things are going. Then share the data with the employee.
4. **Immediately provide recognition for early evidence of results achieved.** Don't wait for "just the right moment," for that day may never come. Commend the employee now, and celebrate the results. Find creative ways to do this, and don't hesitate to rely on the element of surprise.

JOB TIP!

Top Ten Motivators

Employees across the land report that the top 10 ways supervisors can motivate them are as follows:

1. Personal and timely thanks.
2. Time to meet and listen.
3. Feedback on performance.
4. Fun climate.
5. Open communications.
6. Involvement.
7. Sense of psychological ownership.
8. Rewards based on performance.
9. Chance to learn and grow.
10. Celebrations of success.

How many of these are *you* using?

QUICK TEST 5

| 9 | T or F | One of the keys to motivation is the proper use of money and other economic rewards. |
| 10 | T or F | Personal recognition of employees should be reserved for extraordinary performance. |

6 Motivation in the Work Itself

CONCEPT

Employees can be greatly motivated by the design of their jobs and their involvement in work decisions.

How can work be tailored to provide the greatest motivation for the persons who perform it?

By redesigning jobs according to *people-centered* considerations. Most work is first designed according to process-centered constraints revolving around technology and natural work flows. That is, emphasis is given to the dictates of (a) product or service specifications, (b) tool, machine, and equipment requirements, (c) process-flow sequences, (d) computer-assisted controls, and (e) work space layout. Only by a subsequent redesign (sociotechnical) that considers social as well as technological factors will most work be made more satisfying and convenient to human beings.

Many present-day efforts are being directed at process *reengineering*. This approach challenges old ways of doing things and encourages the removal of unnecessary steps. Jobs are combined into one, information technology is put to work, and work is performed where it makes the most sense. At the same time, present-day ***job redesign*** efforts stress a better accommodation of the psychological, as well as the physiological, needs of workers. That is where supervisors enter the picture most actively.

Job redesign. The process of carefully restructuring a job to foster productivity and appeal to the interests of the employees who carry it out.

What are the basic dimensions on which job design focuses?

AT&T was a pioneer in experiments with work design. Authorities there and elsewhere identified five core dimensions of jobs. When all five dimensions are designed into a job, it is fully enriched and most likely to be motivational. As a result, high performance is expected, employees will be satisfied, and absenteeism and turnover will be lowered. The five dimensions are the following:

1. **Task identity** (whole job from beginning to end). This functional completeness enables an employee to start a task from scratch and see a definable product or service once the job has been completed.

2. **Task significance** (important work). This refers to the perceived impact the job has on other people, on a finished product, or on the customer.
3. **Skill variety** (different skills and abilities used). The need to employ more than one skill and accomplish more than one task in getting the job done helps relieve the sense of confinement and monotony.
4. **Autonomy** (freedom for self-direction). This is the reality as well as the feeling that an employee can make meaningful choices about how the work gets done, without direct interference or close supervision from others.
5. **Feedback** (direct information from the work itself). This is the possibility that an employee can tell immediately by looking at the finished product or service whether it has been done rightly or wrongly. The worker does not have to wait for hours, days, or weeks for a supervisor or inspector or an accounting report to provide this information.

Can employees be motivated by being involved in work-related decisions?

Absolutely. Most workers have the intellectual capability, and the desire, to be more involved in decisions about their jobs. What they have lacked in the past has been the opportunity and sometimes the specific information and skills to make a meaningful contribution. *Empowerment*— the autonomy and flexibility given to lower-level employees to examine problem situations and help resolve them as they arise—has become both a demand for a greater role by workers and a management practice responding to that demand. Sometimes supervisors drag their feet because they fear a loss of control, and sometimes employees try to exercise their new freedom too fast. But the potential motivational impact of empowerment is enormous, and the practice should not be overlooked by any supervisor.

Empowerment. Providing lower-level employees with the authority to examine problem situations and resolve them as they arise.

How are empowerment and job redesign related?

Maximum employee involvement is allowed in the design of each individual's job. Process considerations are not ignored. Instead, employees are trained to view technical demands and requirements as problems they are invited to help solve with the help of their supervisor. The major feature of the people-centered approach lies in its stress on genuine participation by employees, singly or in groups, in making their work more effective and their jobs more attractive.

An increasingly common example of empowerment is for organizations to provide employees with decision-making opportunities with

Quips & Quotes

The best motivators tend to be things that cost little or nothing. These can include a pat on the back, timely and sincere praise, a written note, a positive e-mail or voicemail, public praise, autonomy, flexibility, or learning opportunities.

Bob Nelson

vendors, customers, or clients. Not only can employees use and demonstrate their expertise, they gain valuable knowledge about product and service problems while gaining stature for being an important person who can solve problems. When done well, this creates a *high-involvement* organization.

How are jobs changed through redesign programs?

Two approaches—job enlargement and job enrichment—can each result in substantially changed jobs. Each has its merits, especially when it is tailored to the type of employee holding the job and his or her needs.

Job enlargement. Extends the boundaries of a job by adding differing tasks at the same level of expertise.

Job enlargement extends the boundaries of a job *horizontally* by adding differing tasks at the same level of expertise. The concept is to let employees be responsible for the steps just before and just after the one they currently are doing. It provides an opportunity to get away from a fixed place all day and a chance to converse for a minute or two with adjoining employees.

Job enrichment. Expanding a job vertically by adding higher-skill activities and delegating greater authority.

Job enrichment is very different from job enlargement. It expands a job *vertically* by adding higher-skill activities and by delegating greater authority. For example, employees might inspect their own work, order supplies, communicate with customers, and maintain their own output tallies.

Where does the biggest payoff come from in job redesign?

For the company or organization, it comes in greater output per employee; improved quality of the product or service; and—often most important— fewer absences, lower turnover rates, and greater cooperation from employees.

For employees, there can be little doubt that job redesign adds a number of attractive ingredients to their work. Experts say that it improves the *quality of work life (QWL)* itself. It offers greater freedom and flexibility and at the same time makes the work more challenging. Job redesign utilizes more of an employee's skills and does this more effectively than traditionally chosen methods.

What are some ethical issues in motivation?

There are many, as you might expect. People might argue whether it is appropriate to use an assessment of personality traits to select and place employees in certain jobs, for example. Others might question whether it is an invasion of privacy to explore the level of need satisfaction among employees to determine how to motivate them. Some people have argued that it is inappropriate to train employees to develop stronger achievement needs from which the organization will directly benefit.

Other issues arise in the area of job design. For example, is it fair to narrow one person's job responsibilities while enriching someone else's job? Finally, many delicate questions emerge regarding the administration of pay systems. Should employee pay be secret or open? Is it even possible to accurately differentiate the pay of two similar persons? What happens when a supervisor shows favoritism toward one employee over another? The overall lesson is simple—supervisors need to use their knowledge about employees and motivational approaches very carefully to avoid even the *appearance* of inappropriate action.

| 11 | T or F | Fully enriched jobs will likely result in higher performance, satisfaction, absenteeism, and turnover. |
| 12 | T or F | Job enlargement is likely to increase an employee's sense of skill variety; job enrichment is likely to increase an employee's task significance and autonomy. |

QUICK TEST 6

Practical Guidelines for Supervisors

1. *Identify the dominant personality trait(s) each employee exhibits,* and use that information to understand how each person's uniqueness can best help the organization.

2. *Examine which need level(s) seem to be driving each employee,* and find ways to offer satisfaction of that need to motivate that person. Recognize that these needs change over time.

3. *Set concrete and challenging goals with all employees*—preferably on a joint basis—so that they will know what is expected of them and how they are doing.

4. Strive to *remove as many dissatisfiers* from the workplace as you can, and then seek to add motivational factors to improve the overall climate.

5. Accept the fact that people may have different levels of drives for achievement, power, and affiliation; *work to increase their levels of achievement motivation.*

6. Remind yourself that rewards offered to employees are unlikely to be motivational unless the *employees value them and believe they are attainable.*

7. Recognize that it is not just the objective value of rewards given to employees that counts, but *the employees' perception of how equitable they are.*

8. Remember that many employees have an almost unlimited thirst for recognition, so monitor their performance and *find ways to praise and applaud them* when it is deserved.

9. Watch for ways to *redesign jobs* to increase the amount of identity, significance, variety, autonomy, and feedback in each of them.

10. Recognize that many (but not all) employees want to be involved in some decisions at work, so *provide opportunities to empower them.*

Chapter 9 Review

Key Concepts to Remember

1. The Importance of Individuality. Individual behavior is dependent on a vast heritage of background characteristics. One's personality is shaped by the forces of home environment, education, and work experience. This individuality causes people to behave as they do, even though such behavior often appears illogical to others who haven't taken the time to understand the person. Understanding five key traits can be helpful here.

2. A Powerful Pattern of Motivation. Most people are motivated to satisfy five basic needs, arranged in a hierarchy. The physiological needs of survival and safety are at the bottom. The psychological needs of being social, winning the respect of others, and performing well the work they want to do are at the top. Each individual places different priorities on these needs, and these priorities vary from time to time. Once a need has been satisfied, it no longer serves to motivate behavior, and a supervisor must appeal to the next level of unsatisfied needs. Goal setting should be tied closely to need satisfaction.

3. Satisfaction and Dissatisfaction. The two-factor theory says that the three lower-level needs—survival, safety, and social—do not provide motivation; they are "maintenance" factors that create dissatisfaction if they are not satisfied. Only the two higher-level needs—for esteem and for self-actualization—are genuine satisfiers.

Since supervisors often have little control over many of the dissatisfiers, their main motivational routes involve application of the satisfiers.

4. Achievement, Expectancy, and Equity. Employee motivation is also influenced by (a) the degree to which an individual seeks achievement, affiliation, or power, (b) the expectancy of rewards and the value placed on them, and (c) the desire to receive equitable treatment at work. In regard to all these factors, supervisors must be sensitive to the employee's perception of working conditions and rewards.

5. Motivation and Rewards. Employees need, want, and value money for a wide range of reasons, and that is a big part of the reason for working. They also desire recognition for their efforts and results, and that is an area where supervisors can have a powerful impact—if they are observant and systematic in rewarding employees.

6. Motivation in the Work Itself. When jobs are redesigned through a people-centered approach that blends individual needs and technology, the work becomes more nearly the kind that employees want to do. Job enlargement and especially job enrichment fulfill needs for variety, whole tasks, significance, autonomy, and feedback, thus providing its own motivational force. Work redesign is most successful when employees are empowered to make meaningful decisions about products and services.

Reading Comprehension

1. What sorts of things affect the development of an individual's personality?

2. Why is it possible for two employees to have entirely different reactions to the same boss?

3. If an employee's survival, safety, and social needs have been satisfied, which of Maslow's five needs should a supervisor appeal to next?

4. How might an individual's priorities of needs change with his or her growing maturity?

5. When worker motivation is low despite good pay, fringe benefits, and desirable working conditions, what can a supervisor do to increase motivation?

6. How does Herzberg distinguish between satisfiers and dissatisfiers (maintenance factors)?

7. Explain the three estimates an employee makes about a work assignment in deciding whether he or she will try harder.

8. An employee told her supervisor, "I'm being paid fairly for the work I do; it's just that others are getting more for doing the same thing!" Explain the source of her dissatisfaction, and then indicate how the supervisor should respond to her.

9. Name at least five factors that, if built into jobs, add to the potential of the work itself to motivate employees.

10. After some changes had been made in the job, an employee complained to the supervisor, "This is job enlargement, all right, but it sure isn't job enrichment." What did the employee mean?

Application

Self-Assessment

How Good Are Your Motivational Skills?

Read the following statements carefully. Circle the number on the response scale that most closely reflects the degree to which each statement describes you. Add up your total points and prepare a brief action plan for self-improvement. Be ready to report your score for tabulation across the entire group.

	Good Description									Poor Description
1. I believe it is wise to understand an employee's personality before trying to motivate that individual.	10	9	8	7	6	5	4	3	2	1
2. I understand the importance of removing dissatisfaction before trying to motivate an employee.	10	9	8	7	6	5	4	3	2	1
3. I believe that an employee's psychological needs are potentially as important as that individual's physiological needs.	10	9	8	7	6	5	4	3	2	1
4. I fully understand the difference in motivational impact between job enlargement and job enrichment.	10	9	8	7	6	5	4	3	2	1

	Good Description		Poor Description

5. I can see how I have to motivate individuals differently if they have strong achievement, affiliation, or power drives.　　10 9 8 7 6 5 4 3 2 1

6. I accept the role of the supervisor in making sure that employees perceive that their rewards are equitable.　　10 9 8 7 6 5 4 3 2 1

7. I believe in empowering people to the greatest extent possible, based on their abilities and interest.　　10 9 8 7 6 5 4 3 2 1

8. I understand the importance of building factors such as opportunities for variety, significance, and autonomy into jobs.　　10 9 8 7 6 5 4 3 2 1

9. I am the kind of supervisor who is quick to share a word of thanks or praise with employees.　　10 9 8 7 6 5 4 3 2 1

10. When I give feedback to employees, I usually focus on what they did well and the results that they achieved in relation to the goals they were given.　　10 9 8 7 6 5 4 3 2 1

Scoring and Interpretation

Scoring

Add up your total points for the 10 questions. Record that number here, and report it when it is requested. _____

Also, insert your score on the Personal Development Plan in the Appendix.

Interpretation

81 to 100 points. You seem to have a basic set of motivational attitudes and skills.

61 to 80 points. Take a close look at some of your motivational attitudes and skills (those with lower self-assessments) and discuss them with a manager to see if they need improvement.

Below 60 points. Some of your skills may be substantially inconsistent with effective motivational practices and could be detrimental to your success as a supervisor.

Identify your three lowest scores and record the question numbers here: _____, _____, _____.

Action

Write a brief paragraph detailing an action plan for how you might sharpen each of these skills. Then pay particularly close attention to the related material in the chapter as you review the relevant sections there.

Skill Development

Using Motivational Concepts

Assume that you have been promoted to be the supervisor of a dozen employees in your department. You are eager to develop a high-performing unit, and recognize the importance of motivating each employee to the highest level. You have decided to use what you know about motivational concepts. Indicate below how you would plan to obtain relevant information about each of the ideas listed for each employee. Then prepare a report that suggests how you intend to use that information to motivate your employees. To prepare your report, you will likely wish to review the text's discussion on various motivational concepts, scan the Internet for relevant guidelines, and consult with colleagues and staff persons in the human resources department for their advice.

Motivational Concept	Information Needed	Application
1. Maslow's need hierarchy	_____ _____	_____ _____
2. Goal setting	_____ _____	_____ _____
3. Herzberg's satisfaction and dissatisfaction model	_____ _____	_____ _____
4. McClelland's achievement, affiliation, and power drives	_____ _____	_____ _____
5. Employee expectancies	_____ _____	_____ _____
6. Perceptions of equity	_____ _____	_____ _____
7. Need for money	_____ _____	_____ _____
8. Need for personal recognition	_____ _____	_____ _____
9. Job design dimensions	_____ _____	_____ _____
10. Empowerment	_____ _____	_____ _____

Group Exercise

Motivational Debate

Careful reading and review of the chapter will suggest that many of the motivational tools available to supervisors can be classified as either extrinsic or intrinsic factors. *Extrinsic factors* are those that provide motivation from outside the employee (and are often more easily manipulated by supervisors); they include the lower-order needs (Maslow), dissatisfiers (Herzberg), and many others. *Intrinsic factors* are those that provide motivation from inside the employee; they include the higher-order needs (Maslow), satisfiers (Herzberg), and many job design dimensions.

Step 1: Form into two groups, and prepare yourselves for a debate.

Step 2: Team A will take the position that extrinsic factors are most important for a supervisor to use for motivation, while Team B will take the position that intrinsic factors are most important for a supervisor to use for motivation.

Step 3: Conduct the debate. Be prepared not only to present your side but to look for flaws in the other side's arguments. Make notes in the spaces below.

Arguments for Extrinsic Motivation	Arguments for Intrinsic Motivation
1. _____	1. _____
2. _____	2. _____
3. _____	3. _____
4. _____	4. _____
5. _____	5. _____
6. _____	6. _____
7. _____	7. _____
8. _____	8. _____
9. _____	9. _____
10. _____	10. _____

Cases for Analysis

Case 26

The Conflicting Coffee Breaks

Two employees, Janet and Martha, work side by side as bank tellers. For several months, they relieved one another for their coffee breaks. Janet took the first break from 9:45 to 10 A.M., and Martha took the second one, from 10 to 10:15 A.M. However, a new supermarket opened in the shopping center, and there was suddenly a large influx of shoppers coming in to cash checks right after 10 A.M. Accordingly, Jack Smith, their boss, asked Martha to postpone her coffee break until after 10:30 A.M. but told Janet she could continue taking the same break. Martha thought this request over, and when she came in the next day, she told Mr. Smith that the new arrangement was unfair. If anyone should postpone her break, it should be Janet, because she had had the early one for a long time. When Mr. Smith asked Janet her opinion, Janet said that she had been handling the peak load alone from 10 to 10:15 A.M. for a long while. Now she ought to get the choice because she is still going to be on duty during the extended peak period.

Analysis

If you were Mr. Smith, what would you do? Rank the following five alternatives on a scale from 1 to 5 in the order in which they appeal to you (1, most preferable; 5, least preferable). You may add another alternative if you wish. Be prepared to justify your ranking.

_____ **a.** Tell Martha that she is selfish for not going along with a simple adjustment, and insist that she comply with your request.

_____ **b.** Agree to Martha's suggestion, and tell Janet you expect her to cooperate.

_____ **c.** Point out that the morning hours are busy for only a very short time, and so this shouldn't be a factor.

_____ **d.** Ask Martha and Janet to resolve this problem between themselves, as long as there is double coverage from 10 to 10:30 A.M.

_____ **e.** Set up a rotating schedule.

Case 27

Putting Maslow into Practice

Hollie, who supervises the cassette reproduction room for a large audio manufacturer, made the following statements when talking to employees. Hollie is very aware of the five basic motivational needs described by A. H. Maslow: survival, safety or security, social, esteem or respect, and self-actualization.

Analysis

You can help Hollie by identifying the need she is appealing to and suggesting a way in which that need can be satisfied at work. On a separate sheet of paper, write the letters *a* to *e* to correspond to each of the following statements. After each letter on your list, write the number 1, followed by the need Hollie is appealing to, and then write the number 2, followed by your suggestion for satisfying this particular need at work. Use this example as a guide.

"Al, I know you're struggling on your present wages to meet expenses, but your work is good and you can expect regular pay increments."

1. Survival needs
2. Introduce merit pay programs

a. "If the boss approves, Marcie, I'm going to see that you get some free time to develop those product specification changes you suggested."
b. "I know that some of the organizational changes around here have bothered you, Bob, but you can be sure of having a good job here for as long as you want."
c. "Debbie, the boss asked me why the stripping bottleneck suddenly disappeared, and I told him it was mainly the result of your good work."
d. "Felix, you don't have to stop talking with the others whenever I come into the room. I don't mind if you talk, as long as it doesn't interfere with your work."
e. "You can relax about that rent payment now, Harry. Your job has been reevaluated, and you'll be getting a nice increase in salary."

Case 28

The "Disposable" Workforce

Ramon was in shock. Just two weeks ago, he had been promoted to the position of supervisor of security for a large electronics plant on the West

Coast. After 13 years in the profession, he was proud of his work record and looked forward to building a committed group of security officers. Then the bombshell hit. Corporate executives announced that the company was in severe financial difficulty, and "belt-tightening" measures would be implemented immediately. Ramon's boss directed him to lay off all 17 security personnel, and contract for plant security by hiring temporary and part-time workers as needed. Ramon had read something about the "new workforce"—millions of people working by the hour, day, or project and often receiving limited benefits. Now he would be supervising a loose-knit group of part-timers, leased employees, or "peripherals," as his boss was already calling them.

Analysis

a. How will this "new workforce" differ from the old?
b. What can Ramon do to motivate the part-time workers?

Quick Test 1	Quick Test 2	Quick Test 3	Quick Test 4	Quick Test 5	Quick Test 6
1. T	3. F	5. F	7. F	9. T	11. F
2. F	4. T	6. T	8. T	10. F	12. T

ANSWERS TO QUICK TESTS

Chapter Reference

1. T. A. Judge and R. Ilies, "Relationship of Personality to Performance Motivation: A Meta-Analytic Review," *Journal of Applied Psychology,* 2002, vol. 87, no. 4, pp. 797–807.

10

Effective Employee Communication

LEARNING OBJECTIVES

After studying this chapter, you should be able to

- Explain the process of communication, including the major steps essential for its success.

- Choose appropriate spoken and written methods for communicating with individuals and groups of employees.

- Assess the quality of your nonverbal communication skills and identify needed changes.

- Practice the rules for effective e-mails and active listening.

- List the major communication guidelines that help create positive working relationships.

- Use your knowledge of the communication process to make orders, instructions, and requests more acceptable to employees.

The Communication Process

Communication. The process of passing information and understanding from one person to another.

Quips & Quotes

The best strategy for communication may be this: Prepare to be misunderstood. And don't insist that your meaning is the right one. Sometimes what your listeners hear is more interesting than what you've actually said.

Don Moyer

What is the meaning and significance of the term *communication*?

Communication is defined as the process of passing information and understanding from one person to another. As a supervisory responsibility, the process is frequently called employee communication, although the communicating process is equally important between supervisors and between supervisor and manager.

The term *communications* is more narrowly used to describe mechanical and electronic means of transmitting and receiving information, such as newspapers, bulletin-board announcements, computer printouts, radios, telephones, e-mail, voice mail, teleconferencing, text messaging, and video screens. Employee communication has many of the qualities—and limitations—of these means, but it is infinitely more subtle and complex. Therefore, employee communication needs to be managed carefully.

How does communication affect results?

By providing the linking pin between plans and action. You may have a great set of plans and a fine staff, but until something begins to happen, you have accomplished nothing. Neither motivation nor leadership can bring about action without communication. This is what starts and keeps the whole plan in motion.

Good supervisors keep learning about employee communication. They recognize that employee perceptions of their leadership are affected by how they pass information on to others through the process of communication. Unless employees know how you feel and what you want, the best management ideas in the world go to waste. Good communication is especially important when a supervisor is trying to build team spirit or when employees are insecure because of rapid organizational changes or threatened cutbacks.

What is the communication process?

Communication process. The exchange of knowledge, skills, and feelings.

Noise. Any kind of distraction, physical or emotional, within an individual or the environment that distorts or obstructs the transmission of a message.

In a broad sense, the ***communication process*** is the series of steps that enables an idea in one person's mind to be transmitted, understood, and acted on by another person. This process is illustrated in greater detail in Figure 10-1. Clearly, it is an essential ingredient in all human relationships. To be effective, it requires that supervisors establish rapport with employees, be sensitive to how others perceive ideas and *information* (knowledge and feelings about tasks and people), and minimize the ***noise*** (physical

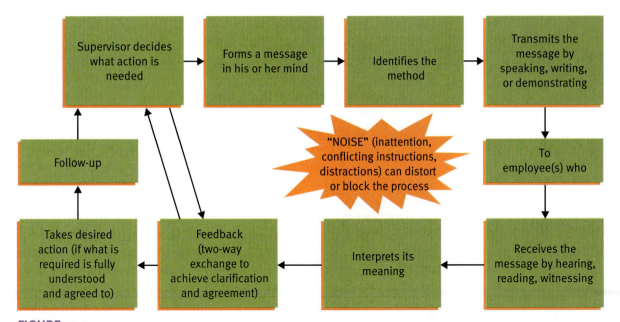

FIGURE 10-1

The communication process.

What are some distractions that can block the communication process?

or emotional obstructions to understanding) that can detract from the process. It also requires that supervisors have better-than-average skill in using the spoken word, the written word, and the nonverbal signals that the face and body send to others. Last, but far from least, it demands of supervisors that they be good at receiving communications from others. That is, they must be good listeners who are receptive to feedback and questions.

Some people talk about three-dimensional communication. What are they referring to?

Communication should not be a one-way street. For a complex, modern organization to function smoothly, communication must occur in three ways. First, not only must you furnish information downward to employees and upward to your manager, employees must communicate their ideas and feelings upward to you. Second, since interdepartmental cooperation among supervisors is extremely important, there also must be a horizontal flow of information. Third, there may also be a need to exchange information with "outside" sources, such as staff groups or external vendors, customers, and government agencies. In effect, this creates a challenging three-dimensional communication process—up/down, left/right, and in/out. All three dimensions involve transmitting, understanding and receiving *feedback*, information from the recipients that tells the sender how well the message was understood and received.

Feedback. Information provided by those engaged in the communication process that serves to clarify and/or verify understanding and to indicate either agreement or dissent.

Some supervisors report receiving 360-degree feedback. What is that?

Valid knowledge of your strengths and weaknesses is essential if you wish to continue improving your skills and preparing yourself for promotion. However, you may not have the capacity to assess your own behavior accurately. As a result, you should consider using some form of *360-degree feedback*. This procedure involves gathering data on your skills, abilities, and style from your manager, peers, subordinates, and even customers. Then you compare the results with organizational norms for a good supervisor, your own perceptions, or data from an earlier survey (to see if you have changed). Finally (often with the help of a "coach"), the supervisor prepares an action plan for personal change. The system works best when it is voluntary and is based on anonymous responses from the participants. The product is a rich set of feedback (both positive and negative) that, if used, can aid in your supervisory development.

Internet connection

www.hdinc.com/faqs/faq_change_man_11.html

A complete rationale for, and discussion of, 360-degree feedback is presented.

QUICK TEST 1			
1	T or F	Communication is the process of passing information and understanding from one person to another.
2	T or F	Communication is incomplete unless feedback is received.

2 Methods of Communication

CONCEPT

Effective supervisors select a communication medium on the basis of a careful analysis of situational factors.

How can you choose which communication method to use?

This depends on the specific task as well as on your objectives. If the task is a lengthy or highly technical message or one requiring a permanent record, you'll want to use a written form. However, if speed, informality, or personal impact is important, the spoken word is often preferred. Another supervisory choice revolves around whether to communicate with a single employee or the entire group. Person-to-person conversations allow you to control the flow of information, have a greater impact, and protect privacy. However, opening up communication among the entire department invites employee participation, develops commitment, and helps build team spirit. It demands that you become more of a facilitator, helping the group explore problems and make progress toward goals. All in all, wise supervisors employ a rich variety of methods.

How can person-to-person communication be conducted effectively?

A maximum of "custom tailoring" to an individual employee is not only feasible but definitely in order. This becomes increasingly important as you develop a sound working relationship with each person. That's because an individual who is addressed singly but in the same way as everyone else usually resents such treatment in proportion to the degree of previously assumed familiarity. *People are unique, and they like to be recognized for their differences.* Supervisors can choose among a variety of spoken or written communication methods.

Spoken communication. In spoken communication, the person addressed is immediately aware of the conditions under which the message is shared. Therefore, speed, tone, mood, gestures, and facial expressions may seriously affect the way the individual reacts.

1. **Informal talks.** These are still the most fundamental form of communication. They are suitable for day-to-day contacts, directions, exchanges of information, progress reviews, and some disciplinary sessions, and especially for maintaining effective personal relations. Even if the talks are brief, be sure they provide the opportunity for a two-way exchange. And if either party is likely to be emotionally involved in the subject, face-to-face communication should always be used (in preference to writing or using the telephone).

2. **Planned appointments.** These are appropriate for regular appraisal reviews, recurring joint work sessions, and so forth. The parties should be adequately prepared to make such meetings complete and effective by being up to date, providing adequate data and information, and limiting interruptions as much as possible. For extended projects or for some employees (especially new ones, those with problems, or those who travel extensively), many supervisors have regular daily (brief), weekly (longer), or monthly (extensive) appointments.

3. **Telephone calls.** These are useful for quick checkups or for imparting or receiving key information, instructions, or data. However, your telephone personality sometimes contradicts your real (face-to-face) self, and so you should examine how you sound when talking on the telephone. Also, since the impersonality of routine calls is sometimes resented, you should occasionally follow up with personal notes to confirm the message.

Voice mail. The use of electronic recording to capture, save, and transmit telephone messages.

A special concern with telephone calls arises when recipients are not present to receive the calls you make. *Voice mail* systems allow you to leave the desired messages anyway, and the other persons can listen to them at their convenience. These systems help alleviate the frustration of playing "phone tag" (repeated unsuccessful attempts to reach each other), and also give the recipients some control over when to listen to a set of messages. But don't forget some basic rules of phone etiquette when using voice mail: Speak slowly and clearly, identify yourself along with the time and date of your call, and clarify whether it is important to respond to your message (and when you plan to be available).

Written communication.   All messages that are intended to be formal, official, or long term, or that affect several persons in a related way should be written. Be sure that you use only a written communication to amend any previous written communication. Oral changes may be forgotten, may be recalled inaccurately, or may not be passed along to co-workers.

1. **Interoffice memos.** Used for recording informal inquiries or replies, interoffice memos can also be of value if several people are to receive a message that is extensive, or if data are extensive or complex. A memo can be a simple way of keeping your boss informed, and it can be read at his or her convenience. Memos should not be overused, or they will lose their impact and be ignored.

2. **Letters.** Usually addressed to individuals, letters are more formal in tone than memos. They are useful for official notices, formally recorded statements, and lengthy communications, even when the addressee is physically accessible. Letters are often valuable as a means of communicating involved thoughts and ideas for future discussion and development or as part of a continuing consideration of problems.

3. **Reports.** These are more impersonal than letters and often more formal. Reports are used to convey information, analyses, and recommendations to superiors and colleagues. They are most effective when based on the results of conferences, inspections, research, and careful thought. Reports should carefully distinguish objectively determined facts from more subjective guesses, opinions, impressions, and generalizations.

What can you do to communicate most effectively with groups of employees?

Employee groups that are uniform in status, age, sex, compensation level, occupation, and length of service provide a valid basis for highly pointed messages. This approach helps avoid the gradually numbing stream of form letters, memos, and announcements that are interesting to only a few. The establishment of such groups on a continuing basis helps build a sense of unity and group identity that fosters favorable group morale and group response. The appropriateness of different communication forms is summarized in the following paragraphs.

Spoken communication.

Effective spoken communication with groups calls for special skills. However, the skills that are useful in a committee of equals may be inadequate in a mass meeting. Nor does your ability to conduct a conference attended by your own staff mean that you will have equal ability to contribute effectively as a staff member in a conference called by your superior. You may be skillful at resolving conflicts of interest among participants in a meeting, but it is much more difficult to remain objective when, as a member, you are emotionally involved in the discussion of the topic.

1. **Informal staff meetings.** These meetings provide an opportunity for sharing useful information of common interest and developing strong group cohesiveness. Properly supplemented with individual face-to-face contacts, they are an outstanding means of coordinating activities and building mutual understanding. Hold brief, informal staff meetings regularly or as the need arises—at the beginning or end of the day or even during lunch or coffee breaks.

2. **Planned conferences.** These conferences are relatively formal affairs. A common error is to create an agenda without consulting those who will attend. Most participants appreciate being asked for their input and having sufficient time to prepare any needed data, information, reports, and recommendations. Properly conducted, a planned conference can be extremely useful. If improperly managed, it can waste time, antagonize people, and discourage future participation.

3. **Mass meetings.** Meetings of large numbers of employees or managers can be valuable for celebrating occasions such as the introduction of a new product, making emergency plans when a crisis occurs, sharing operational results in an "open-book" management context, and introducing new policies or key personnel. But because of the opportunity for emotions to flare and hostile questions to be asked, such "town hall" meetings require that the presiding individual have great patience, skill, and a forceful personality.

Written communication.

The effect of a single, isolated written communication to a group of employees is generally unpredictable. But a carefully planned program of written communications can have a desirable cumulative effect.

1. **Bulletin-board notices.** For lengthy or formal announcements of new policies or promotions, bulletin-board notices are appropriate. They are most effective when they are accompanied by illustrations, readers are constantly attracted to the area and interested in the topics, and out-of-date material is promptly removed. Most

Communication skills are an essential ingredient in supervisory success. **What does effective communication mean to you?**

bulletin-board announcements should be supplemented with other forms of written communications because there is no certainty that they will be seen or read by all employees.

2. **Posters, exhibits, and displays.** These can serve a useful purpose by visually catching the attention of workers. They are typically expensive, require considerable space, and must be properly prepared. The most common uses are introducing new company products, promoting quality production or service, increasing safety, cutting waste, and stimulating suggestions.

3. **Audio and visual aids.** Slides, flip charts, videocassettes, videodiscs, audiocassettes, and other visual materials such as PowerPoint (computer-assisted) presentations have great potential value, but only if they are used effectively. Many, such as DVDs and videos, require a thorough introduction and careful follow-up. Competent preparation and planning coupled with appropriate presentation skills should be applied to the use of all audio and visual materials.

E-mail. Use of the Internet or an intranet (local area network) to send and receive messages electronically.

4. Electronic communication, or *e-mail*, has added a whole new dimension to written messages in recent years. By drawing upon high-speed networks of interconnected computers, individuals can now transmit near-instantaneous messages to almost anywhere in the world.

TABLE 10-1 E-Mail Guidelines

1. Check your e-mail at least once a day, and respond promptly whenever possible; this shows that you care about the messages and the persons who sent them.

2. Keep your e-mail folder clean and up to date by screening items, deleting many, and moving important documents to folders.

3. Keep your messages short so that they are more likely to be read.

4. Help the reader by creating descriptive subjects for your messages and telling the recipient to pay particular attention to certain sections of longer documents.

5. Pay as much attention to grammar, punctuation, spelling, and sentence structure as you would in any other written message. Remember that every communication you send (internally or externally) is constantly being evaluated, and it tells the receiver much about you and your employer.

6. Do not send emotional or highly personal messages that you'll later regret. Stop and think.

7. Remove yourself from distribution lists that it is not necessary for you to be on.

8. Be cautious not to use the "reply to all" button by mistake.

9. Limit the use of "emoticons" (e.g., combinations of colons, brackets, and parentheses for smiles [:)] and frowns [:(] and other feelings). When using abbreviations and acronyms (e.g., BTW for "by the way" and EOM for "end of message"), make sure the recipients will understand their meaning.

10. Most important, be sure to familiarize yourself and your staff with your employer's policies on e-mail. Respect everyone's privacy, and don't send any materials that someone might perceive as creating an offensive atmosphere.

These e-mail transmissions can be rich forms of communication if they are timely, are carefully tailored to their recipients, and follow some commonsense guidelines (see Table 10-1). But don't let e-mail be a substitute for face-to-face communications—especially if the person you are writing to works close by!

Is any one method of communication better than another?

Each situation has its own best method or combination of methods. Some problems are urgent and demand an immediate response (an informal talk, telephone call, or handwritten memo). Some employees believe only what you put down on paper, and so time spent communicating face to face with them is virtually wasted. If the same message must be conveyed to a large number of people, a memo or a mass meeting is best. It seems that the most successful communicating is done by supervisors who (a) quickly analyze the situation they are encountering and (b) know and use many ways of getting their ideas, instructions, and feelings across to others.

Did You Know

The typical person at work receives about 20 e-mails a day. According to surveys, 86 percent of employees receiving e-mails respond within the same day—and many within the same hour.

Source: *Training*, April 2001, p. 88.

Should a supervisor use the company grapevine as a means of communication?

Listen to it, for it's one way of getting clues about what's going on. But don't depend on the *grapevine*, or informal communication network, to provide totally accurate information. And don't make a deliberate practice of leaking information to the work group through the grapevine, for employees will then rely even less on your formal communication methods.

The grapevine becomes most active in the absence of good communication about strategic changes, company rules, employee benefits, opportunities for advancement, and performance feedback. If you don't tell employees—promptly—about the things that interest or affect them, the grapevine will quickly emerge. However, much of the grapevine information will be based on incomplete data, partial truths, and outright lies. And surveys show that even though employees receive a lot of information from the rumor mill and enjoy participating in it, they'd much rather get the real story from a responsible party—their supervisor. You can prevent a lot of emotional upsets among your employees, and build a lot of goodwill, by spiking rumors as soon as they appear. Show employees you welcome the chance to tell the truth. They'll appreciate your candor and integrity.

Quips & Quotes

Subordinates are quick to comprehend your sincerity and honesty. They can smell a scam and a sham a mile away.

Orest Protch

QUICK TEST 2			
3	T or F	Supervisors should identify their favorite form of communication and rely on it heavily.	
4	T or F	Studies show that the grapevine is usually 100 percent accurate.	

3 Nonverbal Communication

CONCEPT
Nonverbal behaviors—actions, body language, and active listening—are vitally important communication skills.

What kinds of communications are likely to speak louder than words?

The messages transmitted by your actions. Talking and writing are the communication methods most frequently used, of course. But regardless of what you say, employees will be most affected by what you communicate to them by your actions. What you do—how you treat them—is the proof of your real intentions. Going to bat for an employee who needs help provides concrete evidence of how highly you value that person's contributions to your team.

Even on simple matters, such as training an employee to do a new job, the act of showing how to do it (demonstration) is eloquent even when no words are spoken. Similarly, going to an employee's work site to chat rather than always requesting that the employee come to your office helps project a supportive image. The best communications are generally those that combine spoken or written words with compatible actions.

What other forms of nonverbal behavior should I pay attention to?

You send messages every minute of the day in one form or another. Start to monitor—and work at improving—the clarity of your use of these forms:

1. **Time.** Do you arrive early for meetings or come late? Do you stick to your appointment schedule or keep people waiting? Do you make promises to return phone calls and then "forget"?
2. **Space.** Do you vary the physical distance between you and others, depending on whether the appropriate context is private or public, or whether you are close friends or spirited competitors? Do you consciously seek to eliminate physical barriers between you and your partner?
3. **Symbols and artifacts.** Is your work space devoid of personal mementos, or do you signal your "humanity" through the inclusion of photos and other objects? Is your desk cluttered or clean? Is there consistency in the symbolic messages you're sending, or a stark contrast (such as telling employees that there is "no money for raises this year" while ordering a new desk and equipment for yourself)?

What is the lesson here? Nonverbal cues are vitally important in the overall communication process, and you need to use them to your advantage. Don't just use words to communicate; think about your appearance, facial expression, and posture, and your use of time, space, and symbols, too.

Body language. What's that?

Nonverbal body movements or facial expressions that may convey to others what is really on your mind are referred to as ***body language***. These signals may be no more than a frown, a shrug of the shoulders, or a gesture with your hands. Unfortunately, they can be misinterpreted both within and across cultures. For example,

- Nodding the head up and down can imply agreement with the speaker; shaking the head from side to side can be perceived as disagreement.
- Drumming the fingers or tapping the foot can mean "Hurry up. I'm impatient for you to get to the point."
- Raising the eyebrows can signal doubt, surprise, or skepticism.
- Rolling the eyes often expresses disbelief.
- Tight-lipped frowning can indicate displeasure or even disgust.

Body language. Nonverbal body movements, facial expressions, and gestures that may project and reveal underlying attitudes and sentiments.

Active listening. The conscious process of securing information of all kinds (including feelings and emotions) through attention and observation.

Many body movements such as these are unconscious and deeply ingrained, and they would be difficult for you to change. But try to assess whether people are reacting primarily to your words or to your body language. Observe the nonverbal signals from others; they can often provide you with solid clues to what is on another person's mind—but test your interpretations for accuracy. If in doubt, ask for clarification!

How important is listening?

Listening should make up at least a third of your communications. *Active listening* requires good eye contact, an attentive expression, alert body posture, and the use of frequent verbal encouragement. It is a skill that must be continually practiced to be maintained. But it can provide great satisfaction both to you and to the speaker. Here are four basic suggestions regarding actions you should avoid:

1. **Don't assume anything.** Don't anticipate what someone will say. And don't let an employee think that you know what is going to be said, even if you do.
2. **Don't interrupt.** Let the individual have a full say. If you are busy, either set a time limit or schedule an appointment for a time when you can get the whole story.
3. **Don't guess about intentions.** Look for the real reason the employee wants your attention. Often this may be quite different from what first appears to be the purpose.
4. **Don't react too quickly.** Try not to jump to conclusions. Avoid becoming upset simply because a situation is explained poorly or an inappropriate word is used. Patience will produce a big payoff in terms of understanding the other person's viewpoint.

However, active listening shouldn't take the place of definite actions and answers on your part. If an employee is wrong on a point of fact or company policy, make that clear. When group discussions turn into purposeless rap sessions, you have an obligation to set talk aside and request (or take) action. And when an employee comes to you with a problem and truly wants you to solve it with your knowledge and experience, give a straightforward reply. Only if you—and the employee— are more interested in helping the individual develop problem-solving skills than in immediately solving the problem should you shift your emphasis to helping the person arrive at his or her own solution.

Under these conditions, active listening draws on the inquiry skills that form the basis for this book. Listening provides an opportunity—and a responsibility—to *ask questions.* These questions will tell the speaker that you are listening, are interested, and want to help him or her resolve the issue being presented. Open-ended questions (those that can't be answered with one word) are particularly useful not only for obtaining facts but for drawing out an employee's feelings. Questions also help the

How to Be a Better Listener

Effective listeners know that silence can be golden; they follow the ancient Asian prescription admonishing, "Seek first to understand, *then* be understood." Some suggestions for effective listening include the following:

- Select an appropriate time and place to hear a person out, based on the need for privacy and comfort. Eliminate distractions.
- Avoid, if possible, placing nonverbal barriers—such as a desk—between you and an employee when conversing.
- Be patient; use the "golden pause" to encourage further thought and sharing.
- Provide supportive cues: nod your head, offer a confirming remark, maintain eye contact, echo a few key words, or paraphrase a key thought.
- Listen for feelings expressed "between the lines"; demonstrate empathy; probe non-aggressively for additional thoughts; offer a tentative summary of what you've heard.

conversation stay on the subject and thus avoid time-wasting tangents. Finally, questions help you probe for hidden content and the "real agenda," and the responses give you the chance to paraphrase and summarize what you have heard. Supervisors *need* to be good listeners.

5	T or F	Many body language cues are expressed unconsciously.
6	T or F	Good listeners can usually guess what someone is about to say; they can save time by offering suggested words and phrases.

QUICK TEST 3

Communication Guidelines

4

What kinds of things should I tell my boss?

CONCEPT

Effective communication helps develop positive working relationships with both a supervisor's boss and his or her employees.

Your success as a leader depends on how freely employees will talk to you and tell you what's bothering them. Your superior, too, needs similar information from you. Make a point of voluntarily and regularly keeping your boss informed of the following:

1. **Progress toward performance goals and standards.** This covers items such as deliveries, output, and quality. If possible, warn your boss in advance about foreseeable performance problems, while there is still time to obtain help. Rarely do managers like negative "surprises."

Teamwork is almost impossible to achieve without some form of communication.
What do you think this supervisor is telling her employees?

2. **Matters that may cause controversy.** Arguments with other supervisors, a controversial interpretation of company policy, a discipline problem within your department—all are issues that should be brought to the attention of your superior. It's better to explain your side first and support it with the facts.

3. **Attitudes and morale.** Middle and top managers are relatively isolated from direct contact with the work group. This not only frustrates them but deprives them of needed information about how employees feel. Make a point of telling your boss regularly about both the general level of morale and employee reactions to specific issues.

4. **Constructive suggestions.** You can help your boss—and make yourself look good—by offering new ideas, suggestions for changes in policies or procedures, and cost-saving approaches for the organization to consider. This shows that you are going beyond minimum expectations and using your experience, insight, and intellect to improve operations. Most managers will be at least pleasantly surprised, if not delighted, to receive your inputs if they are offered in a positive manner.

How should I adapt my communications to fit my employees?

Research indicates that people often fall into one of three preferential categories—visual (relying primarily on what they see), auditory (relying primarily on what they hear), and kinesthetic (relying primarily on what they can touch or actively experience)—with regard to how they learn and how they like to communicate (see Figure 10-2). If you fail to identify their most comfortable pattern, your best communication efforts may miss the mark. Therefore, for *visual* learners, make sure to show them charts and diagrams, or give them backup materials in the form of written instructions and memos. For *auditory* learners, give them a chance not only to hear you but to hear themselves and others. Limit the background noise that might interfere with your message, and ask them to summarize what they heard you say. For *kinesthetic* learners, provide them with examples and illustrations; let them work "hands on" with tools and equipment; allow them to move around the work space. You'll soon find it easy to adapt your communications in this way, and the payoff from doing so will be remarkable!

Internet connection

www.employer-employee.com/comm101.htm
Communication differences in supervising females and males are explored.

Visual people

- Like to "see" an idea
- Love to use figures, models, and maps
- Enjoy concrete examples
- Appreciate visual consistency
- May express understanding in a form such as "I <u>see</u> what you mean."

Auditory people

- Like to "hear" an idea
- Thrive on discussion, argument, and debates
- Find themselves repeating ideas out loud (mostly to themselves)
- May express their understanding in a form such as "I <u>hear</u> what you are saying."

Kinesthetic people

- Like to "learn by doing"
- Are often active individuals, constantly in motion
- See themselves as "hands-on" learners
- Respond well to practice opportunities
- May express understanding in a form such as "I need to get a <u>feel</u> for this."

What can you do to help people understand what you mean?

To begin with, don't be afraid to occasionally repeat what you've stated. Repetition is a powerful aid to employee recall. You can also ask an employee to repeat to you what you've just said. Another practice is to get the employee to ask questions; this will give you an indication of areas of weak understanding. But the best advice is to be specific and avoid the poor understanding that stems from the unclear meanings of words. Instead of saying, "Speed up the machine a little bit," simply tell the operator, "I want this machine run at 2,100 rpm, not 1,900 rpm." And rather than ordering: "Type this up as soon as possible," say, "I need this letter typed by 2 P.M. today." Similarly, specific expectations can be identified for most quality, quantity, and time standards. But note that sometimes, in your attempt to be precise, you may select a brief but ambiguous word when a slightly *longer* explanation would provide greater clarity! For example, don't say "relocate these boxes" when you really want an employee to examine and sort a pile of boxes before moving only the more recently received ones to a new site. In short, always select your words carefully, and then check to see if they communicated your intent clearly.

Are there ethical issues that supervisors should consider in their communications?

The list is probably endless, but here are a few highlights. Supervisors need to be aware that they face possible ethical questions whenever

- They share information with some employees, but not others.
- They are tempted to disclose private information about others to any employee.
- They use their authority to force others to act in ways that violate their personal belief systems.
- They discipline one employee for abuse of e-mail privileges, but allow another violator to go unpunished.
- They disregard someone's cultural background and force that person to communicate on the supervisor's terms.
- They fail to disclose another individual's (or the organization's) violations of law.

As always, it pays for supervisors to be aware of the organization's communication policies, consult with others to assure understanding, and apply the rules consistently and fairly.

QUICK TEST 4	7	T or F	It is best to avoid telling your boss about potential problems or controversial issues for fear of arousing an angry response.
	8	T or F	Supervisors should determine whether they are visual, auditory, or kinesthetic persons, and stick to the communication style they use best.

Orders, Instructions, and Requests

CONCEPT
Supervisors make things happen by issuing orders, giving instructions and directions, and making requests.

How are orders and instructions linked to the communication process?

Orders—expectations that supervisors need to have obeyed—are the most direct, work-related kinds of communications. They can be supplemented with instructions, in which you provide directions and share job knowledge in a systematic way. Orders draw upon a supervisor's authority but may be disliked by employees who resent being told how to behave. *Instructions* are usually based on one's expertise and are designed to help workers perform their jobs better. There are appropriate moments for using each approach. Although it is desirable for employees to agree with your rationale for an order, it is absolutely imperative in some circumstances that employees *understand* what must be done and do it. Thus, as a supervisor, you can draw upon two tools: (a) orders to make sure that employees know *what* to do and (b) instructions to help them *do* it properly and tailor the guidelines to a specific situation. A sound understanding and application of the communication process will help you meet both of these responsibilities.

Orders. Commands given forcefully with the expectation of obedience to them.

Instruction. Furnishing knowledge or information in a disciplined, systematic way with the expectation of compliance.

How can you get the best results from the instructions and orders you issue?

By being sure that each instruction or order is the right one for the particular situation at hand and by being specific about what the employee is to do and what kinds of results you expect.

Your orders are even more effective when you exercise care in selecting the person most likely to carry them out correctly. And you add power to your orders by expressing confidence as you deliver them. If necessary, repeat or rephrase an order for additional impact. Finally, your orders will be most effective if you regularly check to make sure they are carried out at the time and in the manner you prescribe.

When should you request that an employee do something?

As often as possible. Many of today's employees resent being in positions where they must take orders. They dislike being in subordinate positions (implying that someone else is better than they are); they desire independence and autonomy; or they may have a wealth of experience or education that has prepared them to think for themselves. They want more consideration, they deserve increased respect, and asking for their cooperation signals your trust in them. Yet you may be torn between the need to have something done (now!) and the desire to treat employees in a proper manner.

The solution lies in making *assertive requests* for some tasks. A request is a courteous invitation to do something that will fulfill the organization's needs. It also implies that the employees have some discretion in how they respond and is a reflection of an attempt to empower them. Nevertheless, you may feel a strong need to get an employee to

Assertive request. To ask courteously; to make known your wishes with the implied expectation that they will be fulfilled.

JOB TIP!

Avoiding Trouble When Issuing Orders

How can a supervisor stay out of trouble when directing, ordering, assigning, or instructing an employee? There are no guarantees, but these 10 guidelines should help.

1. **Don't make it a struggle for power.** Avoid the appearance of relying on personal whims. Focus your mutual attention on the demands of the situation and the goals to be met.

2. **Avoid a casual manner.** It's all right to have fun occasionally, but be clear and firm about matters that are important to you.

3. **Watch your words and tone of voice.** Most employees accept your right to give orders, but they may object to your choice of words and the way in which you convey your thoughts.

4. **Don't assume that the employee understands.** Encourage employees to ask questions. Repeat the highlights of the order. Then watch to see if it is followed.

5. **Seek immediate feedback.** If the employee misunderstands or plans to resist, you might as well discover that right away. Then you'll still have time to iron things out.

6. **Don't give too many orders.** Be selective, or you'll fall prey to communication overload. Be brief, and to the point, and don't add new orders until the first ones are completed.

7. **Provide just enough detail.** Jobs differ in their complexity, and workers vary in their need for detail. Think about, and adapt to, the needs of the person you're addressing.

8. **Avoid conflicting instructions.** Check with other supervisors to make sure you're not telling your employees one thing, and they're sending a different message. Consistency is also key—both from day to day and from employee to employee.

9. **Carefully select the recipient.** Don't show favorites by picking on complainers or cooperative workers. Employees deserve to have work distributed fairly.

10. **Don't flaunt your authority.** Cracking the whip or letting your ego show won't earn you respect, and, more than likely, it will backfire on you. Act like one of the team (after all, you are).

cooperate, and adding a bit of assertiveness to the request may stimulate that. Supervisors demonstrate *assertiveness* when they describe a problem, express their feelings about it, request an action, and specify the consequences for positive or negative responses to the request. All this is best done, of course, in a direct, open, and confident manner. For example, a supervisor may say, "Please hold your coffee breaks down to 15 minutes," or "I'd greatly appreciate it if you would get your workplace cleaned up before you leave today." Properly phrased and delivered, assertive requests can convey to employees that they have some freedom of action while understanding that the desired behavior is important to the organization.

9	T or F	The difference between an order and an instruction is that an order states what to do, and an instruction explains how to do it.
10	T or F	Employees are more likely to respond positively to an assertive request than to an order.

Practical Guidelines for Supervisors

1. Practice ways of providing social support to employees by *showing them that they are valued individuals.*

2. Remember that the purpose of supervisory communication is usually to stimulate action; you'll need to *obtain feedback* to assure yourself that this has been accomplished.

3. Develop your capacity to use a wide range of oral and written communication methods, and *make conscious choices among them* to fit the situation.

4. Accept e-mail as a useful tool, but remember to *apply a series of guidelines* so that you'll never have to apologize for your messages or explain them to others.

5. Obtain feedback from others (peers, managers, employees) and use it to *become a world-class active listener.*

6. *Practice the art of asking good questions* (either targeted or open-ended ones); they will express interest in others and help you learn something.

7. *Be a courteous communicator*; demonstrate the nearly lost art of saying "please" and "thank you."

8. *Pay close attention to your nonverbal signals* (use of time, space, symbols, and body language) to make sure that those signals are consistent with your verbal message and intentions.

9. *Recognize that the recipients of your communications may be defensive*; find ways to assure that they understand the *why* as well as the *what* of your messages.

10. Make sure that both you and your employees *know the differences between orders, instructions, and requests*, and use each of them wisely.

Chapter 10 Review

Key Concepts to Remember

1. The Communication Process. Communication is the process of passing information and understanding from one person to another. Supervisors rely on it daily to give orders and instructions, build team spirit, obtain results, and receive feedback. Communication relationships must be maintained with employees and bosses, other supervisors, and important groups outside the organization.

2. Methods of Communication. Supervisors have a wide array of spoken and written methods—both traditional and electronic—to choose from when communicating with individuals or groups. Successful communication depends on analyzing each major situation and choosing the methods that best match the recipient and the specific objectives the supervisor wishes to accomplish.

3. Nonverbal Communication. Although spoken and written words are generally the most visible element in communication, information exchange is greatly influenced by nonverbal factors. An employee's attitude, personality, tone of voice, and gestures are all important. Accurate receiving of messages is influenced by both observation and listening. Supervisors can reap huge benefits from active, attentive listening and effective questions.

4. Communication Guidelines. Supervisors can make many errors when communicating with employees. Many of them can be prevented by staying informed, being sensitive to employee feelings, and anticipating what employees are interested in hearing. Similar guidelines apply to communication relationships with one's superior. It is especially fruitful to analyze the visual, auditory, and kinesthetic preferences of the recipient.

5. Orders, Instructions, and Requests. Issuing orders and giving instructions is a fundamental part of most supervisors' jobs. Orders are more likely to be effective if they are clear, delivered confidently, repeated, and followed up to make sure action has occurred. But much employee cooperation can be obtained by phrasing most orders as assertive requests and providing explanations for them.

Reading Comprehension

1. Why is it important for an organization to have effective communication?
2. Discuss the pros and cons of the grapevine.
3. How can supervisors develop high levels of credibility among their employees?
4. If you are unable to complete a project on schedule, is it preferable to inform your boss about it immediately or to wait until it is done and then provide a detailed explanation?
5. With all this emphasis on communication, isn't there a danger of overcommunicating? Is it ever possible to overcommunicate?
6. Suggest three or more different techniques for helping supervisors listen more effectively.
7. How would you communicate differently with employees who are primarily visual, auditory, or kinesthetic?
8. Are there any conditions under which a supervisor should refrain from giving orders? If so, what are they?
9. Does listening have any role in the process of giving orders?
10. Discuss the pros and cons of using e-mail for employee communications.

Application

Self-Assessment

How Good Are Your Communication Skills?

Read the following statements carefully. Circle the number on the response scale that most closely reflects the degree to which each statement describes you. Add up your total points and prepare a brief action plan for self-improvement. Be ready to report your score for tabulation across the entire group.

	Good Description										Poor Description
1. I understand the communication process, and I pay attention to every step within it every time I communicate.	10	9	8	7	6	5	4	3	2	1	
2. I recognize the value of 360-degree feedback and actively solicit it from my manager, my peers, and my employees.	10	9	8	7	6	5	4	3	2	1	
3. I am alert to the differences in situations and select a communication method to fit each one as best as I can.	10	9	8	7	6	5	4	3	2	1	
4. I am aware of the special demands of voice mail and adapt my approach to fit it.	10	9	8	7	6	5	4	3	2	1	
5. I find e-mail communication to be beneficial, and I carefully follow the guidelines for its proper use.	10	9	8	7	6	5	4	3	2	1	
6. I am careful to point out to my employees the shortcomings of the grapevine.	10	9	8	7	6	5	4	3	2	1	
7. I am confident that I demonstrate most of the characteristics of an effective listener.	10	9	8	7	6	5	4	3	2	1	
8. I feel very comfortable communicating upward to my boss regarding progress issues, controversial matters, morale problems, and constructive suggestions.	10	9	8	7	6	5	4	3	2	1	
9. I recognize the differences in communication preferences among my employees, and adjust my style to their visual, auditory, or kinesthetic preferences.	10	9	8	7	6	5	4	3	2	1	

	Good Description								Poor Description
	10	9 8	7	6	5	4	3	2	1

10. I consciously try to minimize my use of commands, and prefer to seek voluntary cooperation through assertive requests.

Scoring and Interpretation

Scoring

Add up your total points for the 10 questions. Record that number here, and report it when it is requested. _____

Also, insert your score on the Personal Development Plan in the Appendix.

Interpretation

81 to 100 points. You seem to have a basic set of communication skills.

61 to 80 points. Take a close look at some of your communication skills (those with lower self-assessments) and discuss them with a manager to see if they need improvement.

Below 60 points. Some of your skills may be substantially inconsistent with effective communication practices and could be detrimental to your success as a supervisor.

Identify your three lowest scores and record the question numbers here: _____, _____, _____.

Action

Write a brief paragraph detailing an action plan for how you might sharpen each of these skills. Then pay particularly close attention to the related material in the chapter as you review the relevant sections there.

Skill Development

Listening Skills

Poor listening skills are one of the most common downfalls of supervisors. Absence of these skills can imply arrogance, insensitivity, and a lack of concern for employees. You are concerned that your listening skills might need improvement, but you really don't know. Review the list of listening skills below and select the three about which you feel the most confident (mark those with a +). Then identify the three on which you believe you need the greatest development, marking them with a −. Next, engage a close colleague or friend in an extended discussion (e.g., one hour) on a topic of vital interest to you, and then solicit that person's assessment of your listening skills (three strengths and three weaknesses). Compare that assessment to your own evaluation.

Listening Skills	My Assessment		Other's Assessment	
	+ (3)	− (3)	+ (3)	− (3)
1. Positive eye contact	_____	_____	_____	_____
2. Paraphrasing key thoughts	_____	_____	_____	_____
3. Paying attention to feelings	_____	_____	_____	_____
4. Probing nonaggressively	_____	_____	_____	_____
5. Being patient	_____	_____	_____	_____
6. Using pauses	_____	_____	_____	_____
7. Demonstrating empathy	_____	_____	_____	_____
8. Making confirming remarks	_____	_____	_____	_____
9. Echoing key words	_____	_____	_____	_____
10. Showing strong interest	_____	_____	_____	_____

Action

Prepare a report that suggests how you intend to improve those items which you both agree need improvement. To prepare your report, review the text's discussion on active listening, scan the Internet for relevant guidelines, and consult with colleagues and staff persons in the human resources department for their advice.

Role Play

Are You Listening?

Identify two volunteers from the class. One should take the role of Khrystyne, and the other the role of Elana. After both persons have had an opportunity to read their respective roles, ask them to come to the front of the room to engage in whatever conversation arises. The rest of the class should act as observers.

Khrystyne. You work in Elana's department of 11 employees, where you have been employed for the last seven years. Although you have always enjoyed your job, things seem to have deteriorated badly in recent months, and you are very upset about that. To the best of your knowledge, five new employees have been hired at salaries higher than yours; they have been given their choice of cubicle spaces (nearer the windows so that they have a view and you do not); they have received state-of-the-art computer systems, while yours is almost archaic; and they seem to be receiving much more attention from Elana than you do. You have thought about these things for two weeks and have finally decided to have a heart-to-heart conversation with Elana to "air out your laundry" with her.

Elana. You are the supervisor in a department of 11 employees, including Khrystyne. You have always viewed her as a cooperative, productive employee until the last few weeks. Her recent behavior, however, has caused you to seek a heart-to-heart conversation with her to "air out your laundry." She has acted rather coldly to the five new employees hired recently, made several curt comments to you, and started taking the maximum number of personal leave days during each pay period. You realize that times have been tense with the unusual amount of turnover your department has experienced and the necessity of paying higher salaries to attract new employees, but you had hoped that Khrystyne would be a role model for the new hires. Since she has not offered to help them, you have had to spend a large amount of time helping them learn how to operate their new computer systems. You are about to have a conversation with Khrystyne now.

Observers. Pay attention, in particular, to the listening skills demonstrated by the two parties as they interact with each other. Rate both of them (10 = high; 1 = low) on the degree to which they exhibit each of the following behaviors and characteristics:

	Khrystyne	Elana
Attentive	_____	_____
Concerned	_____	_____
Courteous	_____	_____
Empathetic	_____	_____
Eye contact	_____	_____
Paraphrased	_____	_____
Patient	_____	_____
Probed	_____	_____
Respectful	_____	_____
Summarized	_____	_____

What constructive suggestions can you give to each person?

Cases for Analysis

Case 29

The Man Who Wouldn't Move

Rachel Fields was at her wit's end. Office space was in heavy demand at the research laboratory where she was supervisor of the environmental monitoring section. Program funding had grown gradually over the last five years, but no new buildings were constructed to house the newly hired scientists. This was not a problem until this year, when Rachel reached the absolute limit of her imagination in shuffling people around and even creating offices out of other work spaces. There was literally nothing left but an old work table in the space next to the noisy area where the coffeepot was located. And there was absolutely no construction money forthcoming.

But the problem would have been manageable even this year if it weren't for Dick Lansford. Dick had been with various units of the laboratory for 43 years and loved every minute of it. He never would have retired, except that his family insisted on it. At first, Rachel thought Dick's announcement of retirement was the answer to her dreams, as she could allocate Dick's office to the newest scientist the laboratory had just hired. Then the bombshell dropped when Dick walked into Rachel's office.

"Rachel, I've been down to the human resource office, and the people there reviewed the policy on retirements for me," Dick said. "They discovered that I'm automatically eligible for status as a scientist emeritus."

"Yes, I believe that's true," Rachel replied cautiously.

"Furthermore," continued Dick, "the policy says that I may be granted office space to support the continuation of my work projects. So I just wanted to tell you how elated I am that I won't have to move out of my office after all!" With that, Dick turned on his heel and went back to his office, whistling happily all the way.

Rachel called the human resource manager for additional details. She discovered that Dick was right, except he had left out one important detail—the granting of an office to a scientist emeritus was a *privilege* subject to availability of space. Now Rachel didn't know what to do. On the one hand, Dick had been a loyal and valuable employee for many years and would be heartbroken to be forcibly moved from his office. On the other hand, the laboratory desperately needed to assign Dick's space to the new scientist arriving in one week.

Analysis

If you were Rachel, which of the following actions would you select to resolve this dilemma? Rank the alternatives on a scale from 1 (most preferable) to 5 (least preferable). You may add another alternative if you wish. Be prepared to justify your ranking.

_____ **a.** Write a memo to Dick, telling him that you're sorry but he simply must be out of the office within one week and that there is no other space available for him.

_____ **b.** Hold your announcement of his eviction from the office until Wednesday, when you can make it at the weekly staff meeting, where it is less likely that an argument will take place (due to the presence of other scientists).

_____ **c.** Place an announcement of the new office assignments on the department's bulletin board, which most employees check daily.

_____ **d.** Don't bother with a formal announcement; simply have the building and grounds staff box up Dick's belongings over the weekend so that they will be ready for him to pick up on Monday.

_____ **e.** Go to see Dick in his office, explain the problem to him, and ask for his assistance in solving the dilemma you face; then follow up the decision with a short memo of confirmation.

Case 30

Now That I've Got It, What Do I Do with It?

Jay Pierce was a 15-year employee at the Great Lakes marine biology laboratory. About a year ago, he had only reluctantly accepted a promotion to supervisor of the freshwater studies group—he really wanted to continue with his research. This promotion required that he give up nearly two-thirds of his research projects and take on the administrative responsibilities for the lab's eight technicians. He warmed to the job slowly, but after several months he began to take it more and more seriously. Of course, he made a few errors along the way, but he was learning.

After a year, Jay was curious about his success to date. He even volunteered to participate in the laboratory's "360-degree feedback" program—a systematic process of data gathering from key people all around (above, beside, and below) a supervisor regarding his or her performance and needs for improvement. After four other supervisors were identified as his relevant peers, questionnaires were sent to them, his boss, and his eight technicians. Jay also completed the forms himself, rating his performance in six categories on a five-point scale (5 = excellent; 1 = poor).

Analysis

Now the results from all areas of the 360-degree feedback program were back, and he was unsure how to interpret them. What conclusions would you draw from the data?

		Respondents		
Category	Jay	Jay's Boss	Peers	Technicians
Oral communications	3	3	4	3
Written communications	4	4	2	5
Decision making	5	4	5	3
Planning and budgeting	2	2	3	4
Leadership	4	2	4	2
Employee development	3	3	3	1

Case 31

Modifying the Method

In a classic case of overnight success, Ted's business has grown by leaps and bounds. Starting with a small camera shop, he has recently expanded to a complete line of photographic goods and related developing services in three locations in the city. He used to be able to communicate with his three employees by using a very informal "Hey, you!" approach, simply calling across the aisle to ask about a price, provide advice on the location of a display, or tell a clerk when to take a coffee break. Now, however, he has 26 employees working two different shifts in the three retail outlet–service center establishments. The "Hey, you!" approach just doesn't work anymore.

Analysis

The following situations arise for Ted during the course of the current week. What communication method should he use to handle each of them?

a. Mary has been late for work twice this week. She is a new employee, still in her probationary period with the firm, and Ted decides to let her know that she will have only one more chance.
b. One of the developing machines broke down, and a backlog of work to be done on a short schedule has developed. Ted is anxious to discover whether either of the other two shops can handle the overload.
c. Ted is concerned about providing high-quality customer service. Twelve employees have face-to-face contact with customers, and Ted

wants to tell these workers how to greet the customers, take their orders, and handle their problems.

d. Ted's accountant has announced that the firm set dramatic records last year for its level of profits. Ted would like to share his joy with his employees.

e. While attending a camera manufacturer's conference, Ted learned that one of last year's models has a defect in it which, if not corrected, will result in damage to each roll of film used. He feels obligated to tell both prior and future purchasers of that camera model about the defect.

ANSWERS TO QUICK TESTS	Quick Test 1	Quick Test 2	Quick Test 3	Quick Test 4	Quick Test 5
	1. T	3. F	5. T	7. F	9. T
	2. T	4. F	6. F	8. T	10. T

11

Appraising and Developing Employees

LEARNING OBJECTIVES

After studying this chapter, you should be able to

- Explain the main purposes and benefits of an employee performance appraisal.

- Identify a number of factors that may cause poor employee performance.

- Describe the kinds of factors that are evaluated and some of the formats used, suggest ways of reducing bias, and recognize the influence of the halo effect.

- List the main steps in an appraisal interview and discuss techniques for making it more effective.

- Discuss ways of handling sensitive problems that may arise during or after the appraisal interview, and point out how to focus on employee development.

- Explain the legal implications of a performance appraisal, recognize its limited relationship to financial rewards, and identify ethical issues in the process.

Purposes of Appraisal

1

Did You Know

What are the primary purposes of an appraisal?

There are four basic reasons for making an appraisal of employee performance:

1. **To encourage good behavior or to correct and discourage below-standard performance.** Good performers expect positive reinforcement, even if it is only praise. Poor performers should recognize that continued substandard behavior will, at a minimum, stand in the way of advancement. At the most drastic, poor performance may lead to termination.

2. **To satisfy employees' curiosity about how they are doing.** People have a fundamental drive to want to know how well they are doing in the eyes of their organization. Employees may dislike being judged by others, but the urge to know is very strong.

3. **To provide an opportunity for developing employee skills.** It is not enough to tell employees about their weaknesses; they must also know how to overcome their shortcomings. A powerful role for the supervisor is to coach employees on ways to improve in the future.

4. **To provide a firm foundation for later judgments that concern an employee's career.** Such matters as pay raises, promotions, and transfers can be handled more smoothly if the employee is aware of the possibilities (and probabilities) beforehand. And in an era of downsizing, appraisals can create a basis for making tough decisions about who must be terminated.

Won't employees resent being evaluated?

The biggest fear in most supervisors' minds is that an employee will dislike being judged. Surprisingly, this fear is often unfounded—if the appraisal is based on facts (rather than on opinion only), if you have sought input from the employees and their peers, if the appraisal is consistent with the pattern of feedback you have previously provided, and if you are flexible enough to change ratings if an employee can show you that you're wrong. People want to know where they stand, even if it isn't at the top of the heap. But don't interpret this to mean that appraisal interviews are free from stress for either of you, or that employees will make it easy for you. Some will, but others won't.

Don't treat your employees as you would grade-school children. Mature adults resent that and will resist your suggestions. Instead, use a constructive tone, clarify the purpose, invite their participation, and explore barriers to their performance. And be sure to let them know that you want them to succeed and will help them do so.

How often should you evaluate an employee?

Twice a year for a formal *performance appraisal* is a happy medium. If you rate too often, you're likely to be too impressed by day-to-day occurrences (as well as being burdened with paperwork). If you wait too long, you're likely to forget many of the incidents that ought to influence your appraisal. Even if your company has a plan that calls for rating only once a year, it's good practice to make appraisals of your own—informally, perhaps—more often. This means that you should observe employee performance routinely and compliment or criticize it on a timely basis. You should do this, of course, regardless of formal appraisal sessions. In other words, *don't wait* for formal appraisals to reinforce good performance or curb poor performance.

Performance appraisal. A formal and systematic evaluation of how well a person performs his or her work and fills the appropriate role in the organization.

What is the relation of performance appraisals to job evaluation, compensation rates, and merit raises?

This is a sensitive question that often is asked by employees. You should approach this issue carefully, since much depends on your company's policies toward it. *Job evaluation* is a systematic method for appraising the worth of a particular job, *not* the individual who performs it. The compensation range set for a particular job is the result of a job-pricing decision based on the job's evaluation and market factors, and should have little or nothing to do with the person who actually performs the job. *Merit raises* are salary increases based on merit, or the quality of an individual's performance. Most organizations strive to separate the performance appraisal session from decisions regarding the issuance of merit raises. The purpose is to keep the focus of the appraisal on past and future performance, not salary. This distinction is not always clear to employees.

It is a cardinal mistake, then, for a supervisor to stress the relationship of performance to pay raises during the appraisal interview. It is only human for persons who have been told that their work is good to expect an increase in pay (or other rewards) to follow. If your company's compensation plan doesn't work that way, you may have a very red face when an employee tells you later on, "You told me my good work would bring a raise or a promotion—and it didn't." The best

Job evaluation. A systematic technique for determining the worth of a job, compared with other jobs in an organization.

Merit raises. Increases in an employee's salary based on the supervisor's assessment of an individual's job performance.

advice is to keep appraisals and pay raises separate by following two different time schedules.

Some employees try very hard, but their performance remains below par. What is the reason for this? What can be done about it?

If there is a weakness in performance-appraisal programs, it is that management assumes that employees have only to try harder in order to measure up to standards. This is often not the case. Many factors can contribute to problems with employee performance. For example:

1. **Individuals may be assigned to work that does not match their capabilities.** The work may be too easy or too difficult. One solution is a transfer to a more suitable job. Or the job might be redesigned to provide a better fit for the employee. An employee may not be able to handle the paperwork required. Perhaps it can be done by someone else. Or the job may require too little judgment for a highly intelligent person. Perhaps it can be rearranged to provide options that use this person's analytic ability.

2. **Employees may not have received proper training.** In any case of continued poor performance, the supervisor should first reexamine the training program and find a way to review the job procedure with the employee from start to finish. A key operating point may have been missed or forgotten.

3. **Individuals may be victims of pressures from the work group.** An employee may be trying to conform to your job standards, but co-workers may be giving him or her a hard time. To correct this situation, you may need to approach it from the group's point of view to change or modify the co-workers' position.

4. **Workers may not be up to the job requirements, physically or emotionally.** A checkup by the company nurse or doctor may be in order. If there are persistent or significant family problems (such as divorce, death, or severe illness), you may try gentle counseling. Your objective should be to show that you are sympathetic but that there is a limit to how long the related poor performance can be accepted.

5. **Your own supervision may be at fault.** It takes two to tango, and poor performance may be related to a supervisor's failure to provide clear-cut standards, train employees effectively, or help with problems and changes as they arise.

6. **Mechanical or procedural problems may exist.** Possibly there is a hitch in the operating process—such as improper tools, materials, or equipment—or a conflict in prescribed paperwork procedures. You may want to review these problems with your own boss or with the appropriate staff departments.

| 1 | T or F | The primary purpose of appraisals is to provide a basis for merit increases. |
| 2 | T or F | Employees should be appraised—at least informally—about twice a year. |

QUICK TEST 1

Factors and Format

2

How formal will the performance rating procedure be?

CONCEPT
Appraisals evaluate, in a systematic way, an individual's job-related traits and behavior as they affect performance.

Because of legal implications, most organizations now carefully specify and monitor their performance-appraisal programs. Most appraisal formats incorporate some form of "graphic rating scale." A simple version is shown in Table 11-1. Typically, these formats provide a choice of ratings for each factor, ranging from "superior" or "outstanding" to "expected level" and down to "unsatisfactory." Numerical weights attached to each factor show its relative importance. Upon completion, a total score for the overall appraisal can be obtained.

A variation of this is the "forced-choice" format. This provides a series of paired descriptive statements for each factor being rated. One statement is always more positive or less negative than its opposing member. Thus, in making judgments, a supervisor is forced to choose

TABLE 11-1 **Example of a Weighted Graphic Rating Scale**

Factor	Rating*					Score
	A	B	C	D	E	
1. Quality of work	20	16	12	8	4	_____
2. Quantity of work	20	16	12	8	4	_____
3. Dependability	20	16	12	8	4	_____
4. Attitude	10	8	6	4	2	_____
5. Initiative	5	4	3	2	1	_____
6. Housekeeping	10	8	6	4	2	_____
7. Attendance	10	8	6	4	2	_____
8. Potential for advancement	5	4	3	2	1	_____
Total rating score						_____

*A: superior; B: very good; C: at expected level; D: below expected level; E: unsatisfactory.

the most accurate phrase very carefully. Regardless of the format, supervisors need to demonstrate objectivity, impartiality, and honesty.

What factors should you consider when appraising an employee?

These factors can vary from plan to plan. What you are trying to answer about an employee's performance, however, are these questions:

- What has the individual done since last appraised? How well has it been done? How much better could it be?
- In what ways have strengths and weaknesses in the individual's job approach affected this performance? Are these factors ones that could be improved? If so, how?
- What is the individual's potential? How well could the employee do if really given a chance?

Factors that are judged in an appraisal also tend to fall into two categories: objective judgments and subjective judgments. *Objective factors* focus on hard facts and measurable results—quantities, quality, attendance. *Subjective factors* tend to represent opinions, such as those about attitude, personality, and adaptability. Distinguish between the two. Be firmer about appraisal of objective factors than about those involving opinion only. But even subjective factors can be rated with confidence if they are supported by documented incidents. The sample performance rating form shown in Table 11-1 includes both objective (e.g., numbers 1, 2, and 7) and subjective (e.g., numbers 3, 4, and 5) factors. Figure 11-1 on pages 282 and 283 presents a rating scale that includes descriptions for each factor.

How can you make sure your standards are consistent from employee to employee?

Before we answer this question, it should be stressed that one employee's rating is not usually measured against another's—except in forced ranking systems. Performance is always compared with the stated responsibilities and standards established for a particular job. If there is a variety of skills and experience among your employees, however, you may find it helpful to double-check your ratings to make sure that you are not favoring one employee or making an unsupported judgment about another. Accordingly, try this approach:

1. List the name of each employee down one side of a sheet of paper and the factors to be rated across the top.
2. Work down the columns, looking at only one factor at a time. Take quality, for instance. If you have rated Tom only "fair" and Pete and Nicosha "good," ask yourself if you are using the same standards for each one. Perhaps upon reconsidering, you'll want to drop

Pete's rating to "fair" because Pete and Tom produce the same quality of work, whereas Nicosha's quality is demonstrably better than either Pete's or Tom's.

You may also want to consider whether you are rating *all* employees either too high or too low. In most workforces, there is some sort of variation in performance levels. The performance of some employees will be exceptionally high and that of some others exceptionally low, with that of the remainder somewhere in between. Keep in mind, however, that every employee can rate near or at the top on one or more job factors if he or she performs well against the stipulated responsibilities and standards.

Doesn't an employee's rating represent only the supervisor's opinion?

A good performance rating includes more than just a supervisor's opinion. It should be based on facts. In considering quality of performance, what is the employee's error record? As to quantity, what do the production records show? As for dependability, what's the absence and lateness record? Can you cite actual incidents in which you have had to discipline the employee, or speak about the quality or quantity of output? Answering such questions makes your rating less opinionated and, consequently, more valid.

Such documented incidents become examples, called ***critical incidents***, of an employee's performance. These incidents should represent the quality—good or bad—of an employee's work. It is a good practice to make notes about such occurrences and place them in the employee's file. At appraisal time they serve to illustrate what you consider good or subpar performance and to support the ratings you make.

Critical incident. An actual and specific occurrence, either favorable or unfavorable, that serves to illustrate the general nature of an employee's performance.

What is the halo effect, and how can it be avoided?

Nearly all appraisers have a tendency to let one favorable or unfavorable incident or trait color their judgment of an individual as a whole. This is called the ***halo effect***. A range of biases can be introduced this way. Among the most insidious are these eight:

1. **Recency.** Relying too heavily on what happened last week or last month.
2. **Overemphasis.** Placing too much weight on one good or poor factor.
3. **Unforgiveness.** Not allowing an employee's improved performance to outshine a poor record in a prior appraisal period.
4. **Prejudice.** Allowing an individual's contrary personality to affect the appraisal of his or her good work.

Halo effect. A generalization whereby one aspect of performance, or a single quality of an individual's nature, is allowed to overshadow everything else about that person.

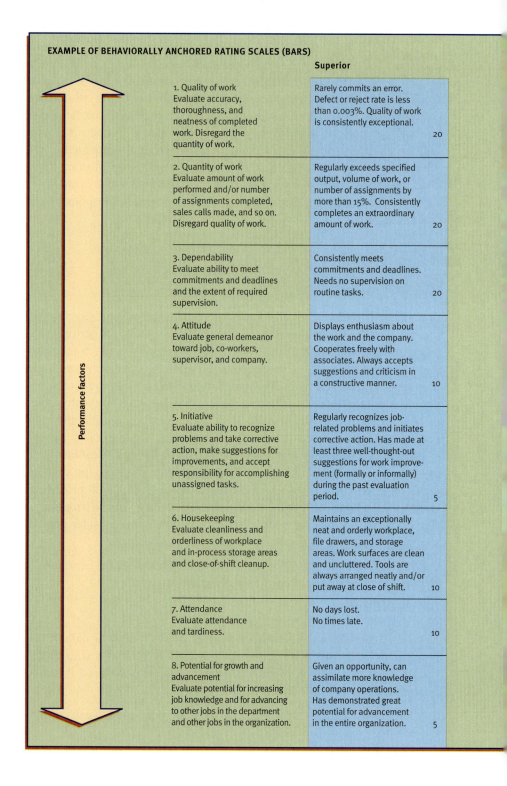

EXAMPLE OF BEHAVIORALLY ANCHORED RATING SCALES (BARS)

Performance factors

	Superior
1. Quality of work Evaluate accuracy, thoroughness, and neatness of completed work. Disregard the quantity of work.	Rarely commits an error. Defect or reject rate is less than 0.003%. Quality of work is consistently exceptional. 20
2. Quantity of work Evaluate amount of work performed and/or number of assignments completed, sales calls made, and so on. Disregard quality of work.	Regularly exceeds specified output, volume of work, or number of assignments by more than 15%. Consistently completes an extraordinary amount of work. 20
3. Dependability Evaluate ability to meet commitments and deadlines and the extent of required supervision.	Consistently meets commitments and deadlines. Needs no supervision on routine tasks. 20
4. Attitude Evaluate general demeanor toward job, co-workers, supervisor, and company.	Displays enthusiasm about the work and the company. Cooperates freely with associates. Always accepts suggestions and criticism in a constructive manner. 10
5. Initiative Evaluate ability to recognize problems and take corrective action, make suggestions for improvements, and accept responsibility for accomplishing unassigned tasks.	Regularly recognizes job-related problems and initiates corrective action. Has made at least three well-thought-out suggestions for work improvement (formally or informally) during the past evaluation period. 5
6. Housekeeping Evaluate cleanliness and orderliness of workplace and in-process storage areas and close-of-shift cleanup.	Maintains an exceptionally neat and orderly workplace, file drawers, and storage areas. Work surfaces are clean and uncluttered. Tools are always arranged neatly and/or put away at close of shift. 10
7. Attendance Evaluate attendance and tardiness.	No days lost. No times late. 10
8. Potential for growth and advancement Evaluate potential for increasing job knowledge and for advancing to other jobs in the department and other jobs in the organization.	Given an opportunity, can assimilate more knowledge of company operations. Has demonstrated great potential for advancement in the entire organization. 5

Very good	At expected level	Below expected level	Unsatisfactory
Makes only an occasional error. Defect or reject rate is consistently less than 0.010%. Quality of work is high grade, but not exceptional. **16**	Errors are only occasionally troublesome. Defect or reject rate rarely exceeds standard of 0.010%. Quality of work is average. **12**	Errors are frequently troublesome. Defect or reject rate often exceeds standard of 0.010%. Quality of work is below average. **8**	Errors are frequently troublesome. Defect or reject rate regularly exceeds standard of 0.010%. Quality of work is unsatisfactory. **4**
Regularly exceeds specified output, volume of work, or number of assignments. Consistently turns out a good volume of work. **16**	Usually meets the specified output, volume of work, or number of assignments. Amount of work completed is about average for this job. **12**	Often fails to meet specified output, volume of work, or number of assignments. Amount of work completed is about 10% less than average for this job. **8**	Regularly fails to meet specified output, volume of work, or number of assignments. Amount of work is almost always greater than 11% less than average for this job. **4**
Meets commitments and deadlines 95% or more of the time. Needs minimum supervision on routine tasks. **16**	Meets commitments and deadlines 90% or more of the time. Needs occasional supervision on routine tasks. **12**	Meets commitments and deadlines less than 85 to 90% of the time. Needs constant checking, even on routine tasks. **8**	Meets commitments and deadlines less than 85% of the time. Work and progress must be checked all the time. **4**
Appears to be happy at his or her work. Cooperates freely with associates. Usually accepts suggestions or criticism in a constructive manner. **8**	Accepts most assignments without complaint. Cooperates with associates when requested to do so. Follows instructions. **6**	Frequently questions suitability of assignments. Complains regularly about the nature of the work. Cooperates with associates when requested to do so. Often rejects suggestions or criticism. **4**	Constantly complains about the work and the company. Regularly voices objection to assignments. Does not cooperate with co-workers. Is always negative toward suggestions and criticism. **2**
Usually recognizes job-related problems and initiates corrective action. Has made at least one well-thought-out suggestion for work improvement during the past evaluation period. **4**	Occasionally recognizes and acts upon job-related problems. Occasionally makes well-thought-out suggestions for work improvement. **3**	Fails to recognize job-related problems or to initiate action to correct them. Usually waits to be told what to do. **2**	Fails to recognize job-related problems or to initiate action to correct them. Needs to be told what to do. Never displays any kind of initiative. **1**
Maintains a neat and orderly workplace, file drawers, and storage areas. Work surfaces are usually clean and uncluttered. Tools are put away at close of shift. **8**	Maintains a reasonably neat and clean workplace. Work surfaces are acceptably free from soil or debris that would interfere with work. Only occasionally does not put tools away. **6**	Often fails to maintain a reasonably neat and clean workplace. Work surfaces are often cluttered and not conducive to quality craft. Often fails to put tools away. **4**	Consistently fails to maintain a neat and clean workplace or work surface. More often than not, fails to clean up or put tools away at close of shift. **2**
1 to 2 days out sick, or 1 day absent of own accord, or 1 time late. **8**	2 to 3 days out sick, or 2 days absent of own accord, or 2 times late. **6**	3 to 5 days out sick, or 3 days absent of own accord, or 3 times late. **4**	More than 5 days out sick, or more than 3 days absent of own accord, or more than 3 times late. **2**
Given an opportunity, can assimilate more knowledge of company operations. Has demonstrated good potential for advancement in the department. **4**	Has pretty much acquired as much knowledge here as he or she can assimilate. Has demonstrated some potential for advancement in the department. **3**	Has difficulty in acquiring knowledge and skills here. Has demonstrated only limited potential for advancement. **2**	Has great difficulty in acquiring knowledge and skills here. Has demonstrated no potential for advancement here. **1**

5. **Favoritism.** Being positively influenced by a person's likableness, despite a poor performance.
6. **Grouping.** Tarring all employees in a substandard work group with the same brush, despite individual differences.
7. **Indiscrimination.** Being too critical or too generous; no one gets a good rating, or everyone does.
8. **Stereotyping.** Basing judgments on preconceived notions about such things as race, gender, color, religion, age, and national origin.

The halo effect can be minimized by (a) being aware of the pitfalls, (b) rating all employees on one factor before proceeding to ratings of the next factor, and (c) discussing your ratings with peer supervisors and inviting their questions.

Are all appraisal formats the same?

No. One popular format, which is shown in Figure 11-1, is an example of a **behaviorally anchored rating scale (BARS)**. Its various items, or standards, are described or illustrated in the form of the behavior expected of an employee. These descriptions are usually based on critical incidents judged to be characteristic of the various levels of performance. This helps provide greater objectivity in rating, as well as greater consistency across supervisors. The BARS's weakness is that it tends to focus on activity rather than results. Nevertheless, the BARS is generally considered the best and the most effective means of appraisal.

Many of the older formats emphasize an individual's traits, such as "initiative," "dependability," and "cooperation." The weakness with the *trait format*, however, is that the evaluation becomes almost unavoidably subjective. As such, trait evaluations are difficult to defend, especially in the courts.

Management by Objectives (MBO) provides a unique form of *results-oriented appraisal*. This approach is sometimes used for supervisors and other highly motivated employees. It requires that specific objectives, in the form of measurable results, be agreed on beforehand by both superior and subordinate. These objectives become the appraisal factors to be evaluated. The MBO approach is not particularly suitable for employees who rely heavily on their supervisors to plan and control their work.

At the core of all successful appraisal formats, however, are clearly defined and explicitly communicated standards (or expectations) of employee performance on the job. Without these standards, appraisals become vague or contentious, are difficult to support, and lose their value as developmental tools. A good, up-to-date job description can be an invaluable tool that forms the basis for a performance appraisal.

3	T or F	Graphic rating scales often provide not only a choice of levels of assessment, but a weighting showing the relative importance of each factor.
4	T or F	The halo effect occurs only when you let one positive factor color your appraisal of the individual as a whole.

QUICK TEST 2

The Appraisal Interview

3

What is the best way to handle the appraisal interview itself?

Although there are any number of approaches you might use, there are seven steps that form a very good path toward understanding and acceptance of the appraisal.

Step 1. Prepare the employee, as well as yourself, to come to the meeting expecting to compare notes. That way, you have your facts at hand, and the employee has the same opportunity to recall and document performance during the previous period.

Step 2. Compare accomplishments with specific targets that you both previously agreed upon—and invite the employee to share a self-assessment with you. Don't be vague or resort to generalizations. Be specific about what was expected and how close the employee has come to meeting those expectations. Then discuss any differences of opinion that arose.

Step 3. Be sure to give adequate credit for what *has* been accomplished. It is a temptation to take for granted those things that have been done well and to concentrate only on the deficiencies.

Step 4. Review the things that have *not* been accomplished. Emphasize where improvement is needed, and explore together with the employee how this can be done and why it is necessary for the employee to improve.

Step 5. Avoid the impression of your sitting in judgment. If there is responsibility to be shared, acknowledge it. Don't talk in terms of mistakes, faults, or weaknesses. Never compare the employee with a third person. Stick to a mutual exploration of the facts and what they imply to both of you.

Step 6. Agree on targets to be met during the period ahead. Be specific about them. Relate them to what has not been accomplished during the current period. This sets the stage for a more objective appraisal discussion next time.

CONCEPT

The *appraisal interview* is a developmental exchange between supervisor and employee, aimed at reinforcing appropriate—or correcting unsatisfactory—performance.

Appraisal interview. A meeting held between a supervisor and an employee to review the performance rating and, using that evaluation as a basis, discuss the overall quality of the employee's work and methods for improving it, if necessary.

Quips & Quotes

The primary purpose of appraising and coaching employees is to instill in them the desire for continuous improvement.

Gary P. Latham

Step 7. Explore what you can do to be of greater help. Then follow through and do it. Improvement is almost always a mutually dependent activity. An employee who knows that you share responsibility for it will approach the task with greater confidence and enthusiasm.

Where should you conduct performance-appraisal interviews?

Do it privately, in your own enclosed office (not in a cubicle!) or in a private room. You'll want to be able to give the interview your undivided attention. And you won't want to be within earshot of other employees, either. Allow yourself enough time—at the very least a half hour. Otherwise, the whole procedure will be too abrupt.

How should you combine feedback on the favorable and unfavorable aspects of an employee's performance?

Traditionally, supervisors were told to "sandwich" unfavorable comments between favorable comments, as shown in Figure 11-2. For example, say, "I've been pleased with the way you've stepped up your output by 7 percent. You've made a real improvement there. I am a little disappointed, however, by the quality of what you produce. The records show that your error rate is twice as high as the standard. So I hope you'll work as hard to improve quality as you did quantity. I feel sure you will, since your attitude toward your work has been just fine."

The same technique is a helpful guide to the entire appraisal/review discussion. Use it by starting off the talk with a legitimate compliment. Then discuss the work that must be improved. Finish by finding something else good to say about the employee's work.

FIGURE 11-2
The "sandwich" technique.
What are the pros and cons of this approach?

Begin with recognition of work well done

Discuss unsatisfactory areas of performance and plans for improvement

End with summary of favorable performance

How are employees likely to respond to an appraisal?

All people, when presented with negative feedback, want to *save face*—to restore their self-image and regain their self-esteem. Some (the really good ones) will do this in the months ahead by simply working harder and performing better. Others, however, will give a variety of explanations for their behavior, which may or may not be valid. Foremost among common excuses for poor performance are "unfair standards," "bad luck," and "inadequate tools, materials, training, and/or equipment."

Saving face. Employees' actions taken to restore their self-image and regain their self-esteem after receiving criticism during an appraisal.

Most employees will be quick to respond to your appraisal comments. Give them every chance to tell you what obstacles stand in the way of their performance. Don't interrupt them or dismiss their feelings with "That's just an excuse." Instead, be patient. Let the person talk. Probe for additional explanations. Often the first reason given isn't the real one. Above all, don't get angry, regardless of what remarks the employee makes. Only if you listen carefully will you discover underlying causes for poor performance from the employee's perspective. Then you can work together to solve the problems. Be sure to negotiate an action plan for future improvements before ending the session.

Internet connection

www.beyondintractability.org/m/face.jsp
Read a discussion of face-saving and how it differs in various cultures.

Why don't employees initiate a request for feedback? How can they be encouraged to do so?

Many employees engage in what is described as *feedback-avoiding behavior*.[1] They almost never ask for performance-related information from their supervisors, and they may even try to avoid most contacts with them. Despite having a valid urge to gain useful information, these avoiders have a stronger drive to manage the impression they give to others. They also prefer to receive positive feedback, and they want to maintain their self-esteem. This places the burden for appraisal on the supervisor.

Here are some suggestions for overcoming this avoidance tendency. Start by empathizing with these employees, indicating that you understand their reluctance. Encourage them to become *feedback seekers* who actively invite useful critiques from others. Praise them when they initially ask for feedback, and tell them how much easier that makes your job. Reserve your negative feedback for moments of privacy. Help them

Performance appraisals have been called the "job supervisors love to hate."

Why do you think this appraisal session seems to be going well?

consider their failures and shortcomings as opportunities to learn, while emphasizing the importance of outside perspectives. These actions will help you develop an open, trusting dialogue with your employees.

Should you discuss one employee's rating with another employee?

Never! Always avoid comparisons. And be sure that each employee knows that you treat each rating as confidential. Try to establish the entire procedure on the basis of confidentiality.

5	T or F	The last typical step in performance appraisal is to set targets for the next rating period.
6	T or F	Providing negative information to employees during an appraisal often creates the need for them to save face.

QUICK TEST 3

Special Considerations

4

How do you handle charges of bias or favoritism?

Unfavorable criticism stings an occasional employee so hard that it's not unusual for that person to react by charging bias or favoritism. Don't try to argue the employee out of it. Your direct denial probably won't be accepted anyway. Instead, point out that you are rating the employee against job *standards*, not against other employees. But be prepared to document your reasoning, and explain the entire appraisal process.

CONCEPT
Supervisors must be prepared to handle a variety of sensitive issues that may arise from the appraisal as well as change the emphasis to employee development.

Isn't it dangerous to give employees a high rating? Won't they expect to get an immediate raise or a promotion?

Knowledge of where an individual stands with the supervisor is every bit as important to a top-notch performer as it is to a mediocre employee—maybe more so. If you fail to show your recognition of a good job, an employee is likely to think, "What's the use of doing a good job? No one appreciates it."

Good workers are hard to come by, and they find it relatively easy to locate other jobs. They should know how you feel, even when you can't provide an immediate reward. Remember, people work for lots more than what they get in their paycheck—for challenge, accomplishment, social satisfaction, and feelings of competency.

How can you tell poorly performing employees their work is way below par?

First, be especially sure that you have previously asked for and supported the best kind of performance. Otherwise, they may believe that their poor showing is more your fault than their own.

Your guides should be these: Be candid and clear and direct. If the work has been bad, say so. Then stick with the statement.

Be specific. For example: "We've been over this before. During the last six months I've made a point of showing you exactly where you have fallen down on the job. Remember the rejects we had on the X-56 job? And the complaints on your work? It looks to me as if you just aren't performing acceptably. So I'm recommending that you be transferred out of this department. If there's no other suitable work available, you may have to look for work elsewhere."

Don't rub it in, though. Leave the employee with some self-respect. End the discussion by summarizing what you have found satisfactory as well as the things that are unsatisfactory. Then wish the employee well in a new job.

How soon should you appraise a new employee?

Don't wait for the end of the probationary period or the formal appraisal time. Constructively criticize new employees as soon as a problem arises. Identify the cause of any poor performance. Ask whether the unsatisfactory performance was due to forgetfulness, carelessness, lack of skill, a gap in their training, or failure to understand the standards expected. Offer whatever assistance is needed. With new employees, you should document the conversation right away by sending them a memo and placing a copy in their personnel file. If the problem occurs a second time, immediately confront the employee and repeat the documentation. Otherwise, a poor start may deteriorate into an unsatisfactory, but permanent, employee.

How can the appraisal process become focused on employee development?

By changing one's mind-set away from being a judge, and switching it to that of a *coach*. As the opening section of this chapter pointed out, one of the objectives of appraisals is to develop employee skills. This is becoming the overriding purpose in many

organizations. Aside from the obvious benefits for employees, it turns the "job managers love to hate" into one that supervisors enjoy and thrive on.

As a coach, guide, and mentor, supervisors help employees see the connection between what they do and the results they achieve. They set challenging expectations but also instill an "I can do it" mind-set and raise self-confidence in specific tasks. They identify weaknesses and offer training to overcome them. They make sure that desired behaviors are under the control of employees. They communicate the organization's vision and strategy, and help employees see how they fit in. They point out role models for newer employees to observe and interact with, and they provide richly descriptive behavioral statements to focus employees on preferred practices. As a result, employees know what is expected of them, and appreciate the support provided to them as they strive to improve.

Can employees be trusted to appraise themselves?

Some organizations have experimented with *self-appraisal* systems. Employees are asked to evaluate their own performance, just as they are

Appraisals often require a supervisor to act as both a judge and a coach. **Can you tell which role is being played here?**

When we ask employees what they want from the people above them, they mention more coaching, more guidance, clearer goals, more constructive criticism, and more recognition for achievements.

Bruce Tulgan

Self-appraisal. The process of allowing employees to take responsibility for evaluating their own performance.

increasingly being allowed to act as their own quality control inspectors. They are told the criteria, given the performance standards, and asked to complete the rating forms. Most employees respond in a highly mature manner, often being even more critical of themselves than their supervisor would have been. Of course, the organization must endorse this procedure first, training must be provided to employees before starting it, and the results of such an approach need to be monitored. If this self-appraisal process proves successful, it may help eliminate one of the most frustrating supervisory tasks.

5 Legal, Financial, and Ethical Aspects

CONCEPT
The appraisal represents a critical, legal communication to an employee and should be supported by objective reasoning and documentable evidence.

What are the legal implications of a performance appraisal?

There are several. Most of them are derived from the following legal doctrines:

- Equal pay for equal work.
- Absence of discrimination on the basis of age, gender, religion, race, color, or national origin.
- Accommodation of the physical and mental needs of the disabled and of veterans of the Vietnam era.
- Equal employment opportunity.

To minimize accusations of noncompliance with these legal requirements, try to do the following:

1. Make certain that your appraisals are based on what the job actually requires employees to do, not on a comparison with other employees and not on what you'd like them to be able to do. That's the value of job analysis, a detailed job description, and specific performance standards.
2. Be especially cautious in making subjective judgments. Ask yourself, "Could I back them up if challenged?" Focus on observable *behaviors*.

3. Stick to facts that can be documented. When in doubt, keep a record of an occurrence that might be disputed.
4. Never say anything, even in the spirit of "leveling" with an employee, that could possibly be interpreted as meaning that your appraisal was based on a favorable or unfavorable reaction to the individual's race, color, religion, age, gender, national origin, disability, or veteran's status. It is difficult, of course, to be so neutral in your judgments, but you must do everything possible to avoid even the *appearance* of prejudice or discrimination. Doing otherwise might bring you and your employer into court.

Should a supervisor keep a written record of what transpires during an appraisal interview?

Ask your employer or human resources department for advice on this one. In general, you *should* keep a written record. For one thing, your memory may fade over time or you may be transferred to another position. If either of these things happens and the employee needs a recommendation from your unit, written documentation of successful performance will be extremely useful.

Even if your appraisal has been negative and you expect that improvement may not be forthcoming, it's wise to make a written record that summarizes the interview, especially what you expect from the employee in terms of improved performance in the future. If you make such a record and place it in the employee's official file, you will be expected by law to give a copy to the employee. That's the problem. You'll have documentation if you need it later on, but you may irritate the employee (or at least make him or her wary).

It is also a good idea to collect in an employee's official file some sort of documentation of critical incidents. This might include regularly kept reports that show the level of and/or quality of output, written complaints or compliments from customers or internal staff members, and examples of very good or very poor work, such as a report filled with arithmetic or factual errors.

Ethical Perspectives

Inconsistencies

Your supervisor heaped praise on you during your annual performance appraisal, and then—three months later—gave you the lowest raise of any employee in the department. You feel that this inconsistent treatment is unethical, because the praise implied a hefty salary increase. What do you do?

How do you convert employee performance ratings to money?

This is strictly a matter of your company's policy. About the only generality that can be drawn is that employees whose ratings are less than satisfactory should not be recommended for pay increases. Where a company has a rate range (maximum and minimum wage rates) for each job, many people believe that only workers who are rated "very good" or "exceptional" should advance to the maximum rate for the job.

Internet connection

www.performance-appraisal.com/intro.htm
Explore the pros and cons of linking performance appraisal with reward systems.

What ethical issues are involved in appraisal?

There are four key traps that supervisors must watch out for. The first is *confidentiality*—the need to maintain the privacy rights of each person despite the occasional temptation to discuss an employee's performance with other employees. The second potential trap is *inconsistency*—the danger of using one set of standards for one employee and another (higher or lower) set for another employee. The third trap is *egoism*—the assumption that you know everything and can sit in supreme judgment of everyone. The final issue is simple *fairness*—the need to treat all persons being appraised without regard to factors unrelated to behaviors and results. Falling into any of these traps can spell doom for a supervisor.

| QUICK TEST 5 | 9 | T or F | It is generally advisable to create and keep a written record of the highlights of a performance appraisal discussion. |
| | 10 | T or F | It is acceptable—even desirable—to discuss an employee's performance appraisal with other employees. |

Practical Guidelines for Supervisors

1. *Be clear on what your primary and secondary objectives are* for conducting an appraisal, and tailor your approach to those objectives.

2. Remember that an employee's performance is a function of many factors, not just effort; *explore other explanations* before blaming an underachieving individual.

3. Be aware of the many errors you can make in conducting performance appraisals, and *work to avoid or minimize their impact.*

4. Formally or informally, use a BARS system to *provide all employees with clear descriptions of desirable and undesirable work behaviors*; they'll appreciate the clarity.

5. *Follow a systematic (seven-step) process in conducting appraisal interviews*, remembering that two very important steps are the preparation and the follow-up.

6. Recognize that you and your employees may have different objectives in the appraisal: They want to receive a favorable evaluation, whereas you hope for future improvements. *Make sure they have heard what you are trying to say to them.*

7. *Encourage employees to replace their feedback-avoiding tendencies with feedback-seeking behaviors*; this will help create an open and ongoing dialogue on performance.

8. Remember that the best way to obtain repeated favorable behaviors is to reinforce them the first time; *give praise in a variety of ways to employees who have earned it.*

9. Don't wait for the annual or semiannual performance appraisal time; *give frequent and informal feedback to employees* throughout the year.

10. Try to minimize the judgmental aspects of appraisal by involving employees in conducting their own self-appraisals and by *focusing on their development through work-related coaching.*

	Good Description									Poor Description
6. I believe that being candid with employees during an appraisal is more likely to give them valid information from which to improve.	10	9	8	7	6	5	4	3	2	1
7. I recognize the value of confidentiality of appraisals, and would not disclose one employee's data to another.	10	9	8	7	6	5	4	3	2	1
8. I think it is important (and fair) to disclose to an employee the purpose(s) of an appraisal discussion.	10	9	8	7	6	5	4	3	2	1
9. I recognize the necessity of including both objective and subjective ratings in most appraisals.	10	9	8	7	6	5	4	3	2	1
10. I am aware of all the types of halo effect biases, and consciously work to eliminate them from my ratings.	10	9	8	7	6	5	4	3	2	1

Scoring and Interpretation

Scoring

Add up your total points for the 10 questions. Record that number here, and report it when it is requested. _____

Also, insert your score on the Personal Development Plan in the Appendix.

Interpretation

81 to 100 points. You seem to have a basic set of performance feedback skills.

61 to 80 points. Take a close look at some of your performance feedback skills (those with lower self-assessments) and discuss them with a manager to see if they need improvement.

Below 60 points. Some of your skills may be substantially inconsistent with effective performance feedback practices and could be detrimental to your success as a supervisor.

Identify your three lowest scores and record the question numbers here: _____, _____, _____.

Action

Write a brief paragraph detailing an action plan for how you might sharpen each of these skills. Then pay particularly close attention to the related material in the chapter as you review the relevant sections there.

Skill Development

Employee Appraisal Skills

Many supervisors struggle with finding a good way to deliver an appraisal to employees and find it to be a difficult task with few rewards. This responsibility can become even more complex when the employee group contains representatives from the Baby Boomers, Generation X, and subsequent generations. Nevertheless, the task cannot be ignored, and (if done well) can produce very positive outcomes for both the appraisee and the organization.

Interview a number of supervisors to obtain a sampling of their experiences with performance appraisal. Record their suggestions of things to do and things not to do in a performance appraisal.

Things to Do	Things Not to Do
1. _____	1. _____
2. _____	2. _____
3. _____	3. _____
4. _____	4. _____
5. _____	5. _____
6. _____	6. _____
7. _____	7. _____
8. _____	8. _____
9. _____	9. _____
10. _____	10. _____

Action

Prepare a report that succinctly presents a set of action guidelines that you can follow in the future. This report should contain lists of both what to do and what not to do. To prepare your report, review the text's discussion on employee appraisal, search the Internet for relevant guidelines, and consult with colleagues and staff persons in the human resources department for their advice.

Role Play

Performance Appraisal

Identify two volunteers from the class and assign each of them a role to read. Do *not* allow them to read the other person's role description.

Collegiate Dean (Dr. Kim). You are the dean of a college that employs about 30 full-time faculty members. Each year you conduct a performance appraisal interview with each faculty member. This year you are particularly anxious about communicating your assessment of Pat, who is an assistant professor. Pat has been here for three years and from what you have observed has a messy office, dresses too casually for your taste, smokes cigarettes (outside the building, of course), and seems to be trying too hard to relate to the students by matching their language and musical interests. In addition, Pat's grade distributions at the end of the semester are always higher than those of departmental colleagues; you wonder if Pat is just "too easy." You grudgingly admit that Pat has already published several articles and seems to be well liked by students but wonder if this is the right place for Pat to build an entire career. Pat is about to enter your office now for the appraisal discussion.

Assistant Professor (Pat). You are an assistant professor in this college and have been on campus for three years. You have invested an enormous amount of energy in your job here but feel that your accomplishments have gone largely unnoticed until now—presumably because you have been so new on campus. You work long hours, have published several notable articles, and spend enormous amounts of energy trying to "connect" with students. For example, you play contemporary music in your office, dress much the way students do, try to speak their "language," and talk to them about issues with which they are concerned. You have been especially pleased about the student learning demonstrated in your classes, and this has shown up in the unusually high grades that you have given them. You are looking forward to the annual appraisal discussion with your dean and hope that not only a pay raise but possibly an early promotion might be on the agenda today. You are about to speak with the dean (Dr. Kim) now.

Observers. Observe the interaction between Dr. Kim and Pat closely, listening especially for not only what is said but how it is received. Watch specifically for opportunities to praise the dean (Dr. Kim) for what is done well and reflects the lessons in this chapter, as well as for possible errors that Pat makes. Be prepared to provide constructive feedback to the dean when the role-play is over.

Cases for Analysis

Case 32

The Downgraded Performance Appraisal

Norma Jean has worked for three years as a buyer in the purchasing department of the Barnwell Company. Her supervisor, Mr. Morgan, consistently rated her performance as "very good," with a point total of 85 out of a possible 100. Typically, Norma Jean got top ratings for her knowledge of the job and the quality and dependability of her work. The only reason her aggregate score did not move her into the "excellent" range was that her rating for "Quantity of Work Produced" was never better than "fair." Six months ago, Mr. Morgan left the company and was replaced by the dynamic young Ms. Conti. When the semiannual evaluations were filed, Ms. Conti judged Norma Jean's overall performance as only "fair," with a score of 70 points. Yesterday, Ms. Conti called Norma Jean into her office for the appraisal interview.

The news that her present rating was only "fair" upset Norma Jean. "How can that be?" she asked. "I'm working as hard as I always have. My previous supervisor was always more than satisfied with my work."

"I'm sorry, Norma," said Ms. Conti. "That's the way I see it. The amount of work you turn out is deplorably low. If you can't pick up speed, I'm going to have to put you on notice. As it is, I certainly won't be recommending you for a raise when that time comes around."

"That's not fair," said Norma Jean. "I work on purchases that need very precise specifications and quotations. You can look at my record and see that I make hardly any mistakes. No one else in the department is as reliable as I am."

"You're placing emphasis on the wrong thing," said Ms. Conti. "You slow everything down with your nitpicking on every requisition. There is no need for precision on 90 percent of what you do, yet you triple-check every 5-cent item as if it were golden. Either you learn to pick up speed, or you'll be looking for work elsewhere."

Analysis

Obviously, there is something wrong with the past and present evaluations of Norma Jean's performance. Of the following five possibilities, which seems most likely to you? Rank them on a scale from 1 (most likely) to 5 (least likely). You may add another alternative, if you wish. Be prepared to justify your ranking.

_____ **a.** Ms. Conti dislikes Norma Jean and is "out to get her."

_____ **b.** Mr. Morgan's standards for Norma's job emphasized quality and dependability rather than output, although even Mr. Morgan had reservations about the quantity of work Norma Jean produced.

_____ **c.** As an entrenched employee, Norma Jean is resisting any change in performance standards applied to her job.

_____ **d.** Ms. Conti and Norma Jean will have to have a meeting of the minds about the job's demands before Norma Jean's performance will change and her evaluation will improve.

_____ **e.** Ms. Conti's threats will shift Norma Jean's concept of her job so that she emphasizes quantity rather than quality in the future.

How might Ms. Conti have improved this interview?

Case 33

Polishing the Halo

David was given an assignment to study and improve the company performance-appraisal system. Specifically, the vice president for human resources gave him a list of different types of halo-effect biases, and asked him to consider the various effects and make recommendations to his colleague supervisors in the company for preventing the occurrence of these problems.

Analysis

Examine David's list of halo-effect biases, shown below. Review the definition and text discussion, if necessary. Then match each halo-effect bias with its most appropriate guideline for prevention.

Halo-Effect Biases	Guideline for Prevention
_____ **1.** Recency	**a.** Use only current performance data as a foundation for employee appraisal.
_____ **2.** Overemphasis	**b.** Treat employees as individuals; be alert to their unique strengths and weaknesses.

_____ **3.** Stereotyping   **c.** Collect periodic performance information; rely on critical incidents over time.

_____ **4.** Unforgiveness   **d.** Assign weights to each appraisal factor and use.

_____ **5.** Grouping   **e.** Examine your biases; share them with peers and ask them to provide feedback if they sense discrimination.

Case 34

Betty's Carpet-Cleaning Service

Betty Morrison started a small carpet-cleaning service five years ago. (Her motto: "Love your carpet, love your wife; when we shampoo, it'll enrich their life!") The demand for her service has grown so rapidly that she added one employee, then another, until she reached her present staff of four employees. Now she does less and less cleaning herself, spending her time instead on task scheduling, billing and payroll, obtaining and dispensing supplies, and handling advertising and customer relations. She has always used a simple performance-appraisal system, evaluating her cleaners on the following criteria: speed, quality, customer satisfaction, equipment repairs, and overall attitude.

This year, after attending a local half-day workshop on performance appraisal, Betty decided to assign weights to the five appraisal factors for the first time. Then she assessed each employee on each of the five factors, using her usual scale from 1 to 5 (1 = unsatisfactory; 5 = exceptional), and gave the results to each employee.

| Factor | Weight | Employee Ratings | | | |
		Maria	Trang	Kent	Terry
Speed	.40	4	5	1	3
Quality	.30	4	4	2	3
Customer satisfaction	.20	4	3	3	3
Repairs	.05	4	2	4	3
Attitude	.05	4	1	5	3

When Betty checked the appraisal records from last year, she found that she had rated all four employees precisely the same as she had a year ago. Yet, when she gave the table of ratings to Maria, Trang, Kent, and Terry in individual meetings with them, she got a variety of reactions.

Analysis

a. Calculate the weighted ratings for each employee and the unweighted ratings from a year ago.
b. Predict the reaction of each employee.
c. What should Betty have done differently, if anything?

Case 35

The Dissatisfied Mechanic

Shawn was very unhappy. He had just discovered that raises had been handed out to several other mechanics in the maintenance shop of the Flyaway Aviation Co., a regional commuter airline. As soon as his shift ended, he stormed into the office of his boss, Myra Maxwell, the shop supervisor.

"What happened to my annual raise?" Shawn demanded.

"Let's get one thing straight," said Myra. "There is no such thing as an annual pay raise at Flyaway."

"That's the first I've heard about it," said Shawn. "I got one last year when everyone got theirs. Now I find that everyone else just got a raise this year, and I didn't. Why was I passed over?"

"Not everyone got a raise," said Myra. "Raises were given only to those mechanics who I considered were doing outstanding work in the shop."

"Since when has my work not been outstanding?" asked Shawn.

"For a long time," said Myra. "I did speak to you about it at your last performance-appraisal interview. I suggested then that your work warranted improvement."

"But I didn't think that it had anything to do with my annual merit increase," said Shawn. "I work as hard as anyone else out in the shop."

"I don't think you do," said Myra. "Several times I've noticed you taking a break when the shop was jammed up. And when things are slow, I never see you pitch in with some of the standby, shop-cleanup work I've set aside for off-peak times."

"You never made that clear to me," said Shawn. "I have always thought that shop-cleanup work was voluntary around here. And I don't see anything wrong in taking a break from time to time."

"Then that makes two things you don't seem to know much about," said Myra. "Both affect your performance, and that's enough to keep your work from being considered outstanding."

"That's downright unfair!" said Shawn. "I think that you have discriminated against me in not giving me my annual raise, and these are only excuses you're giving me now."

Analysis

a. Do you agree or disagree with Shawn? Why?

b. What do you think has been wrong with the way Myra has conducted Shawn's appraisal interviews in the past?

c. What would you suggest Myra do in the future to avoid confrontations like these?

ANSWERS TO QUICK TESTS	Quick Test 1	Quick Test 2	Quick Test 3	Quick Test 4	Quick Test 5
	1. F	3. T	5. F	7. F	9. T
	2. T	4. F	6. T	8. F	10. F

Chapter Reference

1. Sherry E. Moss and Juan I. Sanchez, "Are Your Employees Avoiding You? Managerial Strategies for Closing the Feedback Gap," *Academy of Management Executive*, 2004, vol. 18, no. 1, pp. 32–44. See also Jay M. Jackman and Myra H. Strober, "Fear of Feedback," *Harvard Business Review*, April 2003, pp. 101–107.

12

Counseling and Performance Management

LEARNING OBJECTIVES

After studying this chapter, you should be able to

- Describe problem performance and identify the symptoms of a troubled employee.

- Explain the general approach to employee counseling, explain its rules and limitations, and know when a troubled employee should be referred to a professional counselor.

- Identify the various kinds of absenteeism and know the recommended remedial approaches for each one.

- Recognize alcoholism and illegal substance abuse among employees, and know how to respond appropriately.

- Explain the goals of performance management, the most common types of offenses that require disciplinary action, and the range of employee responses to it.

- Differentiate between constructive and progressive discipline, know the four elements of the "hot-stove" rule, and recognize the necessity of due process and having a just cause when firing an employee.

Problem Performers

Problems with employee performance can often be attributed to troubling personal factors that arise from conditions not related to the job.

How would you define problem performance?

Problem performance encompasses (a) job performance that does not measure up to established standards of output or quality and (b) behavior that is distracting or disruptive to the normal conduct of operations. The former is routinely dealt with during performance appraisals. The latter problem is far more difficult to identify and deal with, yet it often leads to the former. This chapter will focus on problem performance of the latter kind.

What kinds of employees become problem performers?

Internet connection

http://www.opm.gov/er/poor/understanding.asp

Differentiate between misconduct and poor performance—both of which are causes for supervisory intervention—at this site.

Most people experience brief periods in their lives when they are troubled by problems away from their place of employment. At such times, their performance at work may suffer. This is usually a temporary condition (either the problem disappears or they learn to cope with it), and their performance soon returns to normal.

There are other people who are especially susceptible to stress, and their resulting performance lapses are more pronounced and more prolonged. They may be troubled by continuing personal problems that make adjustment especially difficult. Examples in today's society include marital discord, personal debts, and addiction to gambling. These people can be described as "troubled." When this state persists, there is a good chance that the troubled person is suffering from a problem with an emotional, rather than a physical, cause.

Adjustment is the process by which people modify their feelings and behavior to accommodate the stress of life and work. Individuals adjust to situations with different degrees of difficulty and success.

Adjustment. The process by which healthy as well as disturbed individuals find a way to fit themselves to difficult situations by modifying their feelings and their behavior to accommodate the stresses of life and work.

Supervisors must learn to deal with employees whose difficulty in adjusting to emotional problems is only temporary and those whose adjustment problems are chronic. More severely disturbed employees should be referred to the organization's *employee assistance program (EAP)*. There, more serious problems can be diagnosed and treated by appropriate professionals.

Who are these troubled employees, and how do they appear?

Psychologists believe that about one in five workers is subject to emotional upsets that visibly disturb his or work. Troubled employees may appear as the chronic absentee, the willful rule breaker, the antagonist, or the troublemaker. They may also appear in a more sympathetic form as the employee with almost-imaginary ailments, the person who has lost confidence in work-related skills, the alcoholic, and even the work-obsessed individual. Symptoms of emotional upsets may even emerge unexpectedly in the most normal and stable individuals. Some may demonstrate their emotional distress through *hostility*, the aggressive expression of anger on the job. In extreme cases, this may be exhibited in various forms of workplace violence. By contrast, other disturbed employees may demonstrate *withdrawal*, in which they retreat from social interaction and confrontation.

Many problem employees fall into these categories. They are perpetually dissatisfied, are given to baseless worries, tire easily, are suspicious, are sure that superiors unfairly withhold promotions, or believe their associates gossip maliciously about them. Some are characterized by drinking sprees, are given to drug abuse, are insubordinate, or have an uncontrolled temper.

Among themselves, problem employees differ widely, just as more normal people do. But within the framework of their symptoms, they are surprisingly alike in their reactions.

When do the personal problems of employees become a concern of the supervisor?

The most important rule is this: Intervene when the *performance* of a troubled employee becomes unsatisfactory. (Note the emphasis on performance.) Although some stress can serve to stimulate and challenge individuals, employees under severe stress often function far below their capabilities, or they may disturb the work of others. When either condition occurs, these employees become problems to themselves and to their supervisors. Ultimately, many of these troubled employees, if not helped, become the subject of disciplinary action.

For many workers, the distinction between problems arising from their personal lives and those associated with their work becomes increasingly blurred. Sometimes an alert supervisor can play a timely role in helping employees sort out their problems. And, difficult as it may be, supervisors have a continuing responsibility to confront employee behavior that affects productivity.

Many supervisors also find that employees voluntarily look to them for assistance even when their work performance isn't affected. Sensitive supervisors can provide invaluable aid during these times if they project a sincere sense of caring and take the time to practice their listening skills.

Hostility. An aggressive expression of anger displayed by problem employees as an unconscious, unwitting relief from fears about their security or other feelings of inadequacy.

Withdrawal. A passive way for emotionally disturbed employees to cope with their anxieties, in which they retreat from confrontations, appear unduly preoccupied, discourage social overtures, and keep very much to themselves.

Thoughts*to*ponder

Guiding Employees through a Crisis

Many factors can cause an employee to become distracted—or even emotional—at work. The illness or death of a loved one, difficulties with children or parents, a romantic breakup with a significant other, a household fire, and an environmental disaster such as a hurricane, flood, or tornado can produce a powerful distraction and greatly diminish one's productivity. The best bet for a supervisor is to acknowledge the crisis, support the individuals, empathize with them, listen patiently, and reassure them. Identify corporate resources and policies that will help these troubled persons, and develop a transition plan that will enable them to return gradually to an acceptable level of usefulness.

Why must supervisors pay so much attention to troubled employees?

Mainly because there are so many of them. Hardly a week goes by in which a supervisor does not deal with problems created by a troubled employee. Happily, most of these problems are minor. If left unattended, however, they can begin to demand a major portion of a supervisor's time and attention.

There are also many sociological and humanitarian reasons for being concerned about problem workers. One big reason is that a problem employee is probably also a problem husband, son, daughter, or wife. But industry's concern, admittedly, is primarily an economic one. Problem employees are expensive to have on the payroll since their productivity suffers. They are characterized by excessive tardiness and absences. They are difficult to supervise. And they have a tendency to upset the morale of the work group. Consequently, a supervisor should be concerned about (a) hiring potential problem employees in the first place, (b) handling them on the job so that they reach an acceptable level of productivity with the least disruption of the company's overall performance, and (c) determining whether these employees have become so seriously troubled that they need professional attention.

| QUICK TEST 1 | 1 | T or F | Supervisors should intervene at the first sign that an employee is experiencing emotional difficulty. |
| | 2 | T or F | Employee withdrawal refers to those persons who leave the organization. |

2 | Employee Counseling

CONCEPT

Counseling—within carefully prescribed limits—offered by a supervisor to a troubled employee may improve performance by providing a degree of relief from anxieties.

What can you do about troubled workers?

Let's make this clear. We are not talking here about persons with serious personality disorders. *They need professional help.* Nor are we talking about routine performance appraisals, where it can be assumed that criticism will be received and suggestions for improvement will be discussed rationally and objectively. What follows here applies mainly to counseling efforts with mildly troubled employees.

You can help troubled employees toward better adjustment only after establishing an empathetic atmosphere. You must first reassure them that you are trying to help them keep their jobs or enjoy their work more. You are *not* looking for ways to punish them or for an excuse to get rid of them. No approach will do more harm to a troubled person than adopting an attitude that says, "Better get yourself straightened out or you'll lose your job." Emotionally upset people are fearful or angry enough without feeling additional pressure from their supervisors. You must genuinely want to help them, and you must project this conviction to them.

Empathy requires sensitivity and effort. It is the ability to view a situation from the other person's perspective and see it through that person's eyes. You must be able to understand people's beliefs and values, their backgrounds, their hopes and dreams, and, most of all, their personal concerns, pains, and fears. Some people refer to it as emotional bonding—at least temporarily. When you do this successfully, you can gain insight into their problems, broaden your understanding of their perspectives, win their trust, and defuse potentially explosive situations. But remember, the purpose of empathy is to give troubled employees a better opportunity to help themselves, not for you to solve their problems for them.

Empathy. Building an emotional bond with others by establishing trust and understanding their problems, perspectives, and fears.

Employee counseling is essentially a problem-solving technique. It is ultimately task-oriented; that is, it deals with a specific, job-related condition. The supervisor's role is a facilitating one. You do not direct or control the session; the employee does. The counselor listens rather than talks. You do not criticize or argue, nor do you offer "evaluative" opinions. You do not "judge" an employee's personal problems. Instead, you try to act as a "sounding board" to help release the pressures that are adversely affecting performance. If the counseling is successful, the employee—not the supervisor—solves the problem.

Employee counseling. A task-oriented, problem-solving technique that features an empathetic, interactive discussion—emphasizing listening—aimed at helping an employee cope with some specific aspect of his or her work life.

It cannot be overemphasized, however, that supervisors have great limitations in their counseling roles. *They are not psychologists or social workers*, and they can do more harm than good if they attempt rehabilitation beyond their training and experience. They cannot be "fix-it persons" for employees' personal problems. If they try to do so, they often spend large amounts of time and energy, and their own performance may suffer. Supervisors should be, of course, experts at recognizing these problems and be understanding about them. Beyond that, their counseling roles should be restricted to facilitating safe emotional release and providing support for the employees' efforts to solve their problems.

How, exactly, should you approach employee counseling?

First, take a close look at your attitudes and assumptions. Do you believe that people can be, and must be, responsible for their own actions? Do you agree that employees should solve their own problems (after obstacles are removed)? Do you think it is important for the solution to employees' personal problems that they conform to *their* beliefs and values, not yours? Do you appreciate, and convey, a profound respect for the importance of the other person's feelings? Positive answers to all these questions provide a strong foundation for the type of counseling a supervisor must often engage in.

You need to remember that a troubled employee has a very important need to release pent-up feelings, emotions, and stresses. This process, which psychologists call *catharsis*, relieves bothersome pressure, just as lifting the lid off a pan of boiling water prevents a scalding accident. As a supervisor, you can best counsel employees if you follow these 10 rules:

1. Let the employee control the direction of the session.
2. Give your undivided attention to the employee who is talking.
3. Listen patiently to what the employee has to say before making any response.
4. Convey through words, posture, eye contact, and facial expression your attentiveness, receptivity, and empathy.
5. Don't argue, interrupt, criticize, or offer advice about the employee's problem.
6. Look beyond the mere words in what the employee says and attempt to capture his or her feelings. Listen to see if he or she is trying to tell you something deeper than what appears on the surface.
7. Use silence—an extended pause before responding—to encourage the employee to provide an expanded explanation of a brief remark.
8. Don't express surprise or judgment at anything the employee discloses to you.
9. Polish your skill at *reflecting feelings*—feeding back to an employee the emotional essence of what she or he has conveyed to you. This confirms to the employee that you accept feelings as a legitimate topic; it builds trust between the two of you, and it encourages the employee to probe her or his own thoughts at a deeper level.
10. Encourage the employee, through gentle open-ended questions, to take the initiative in deciding what the next appropriate action should be.

How do you start a counseling session?

Find a reasonably quiet place where you're sure you won't be interrupted or overheard. Try to put the employee at ease.

You may be helpful simply by letting the employee know how much the current distress is affecting the job—and how much of this the company will tolerate. Above all, a troubled person may add to his or her problem materially with fears of what the company might do if and when it discovers the condition. If you offer some rule of thumb, you at least provide something concrete to guide the employee's actions.

Catharsis. The relief that follows release of accumulated feelings, emotions, and frustrations that comes through their expression in a harmless fashion.

(For example: "We understand the fact that you have something bothering you. And we're willing to go along with your present performance for a couple of weeks or so. But if it doesn't improve after that, we'll have to find a solution.")

If the employee voluntarily brings the problem to you, you can help most by listening. This is more difficult than it appears. Listening must mean truly *nonevaluative* listening—no interruptions, advice, prescriptions, solutions, or preaching.

How many counseling interviews should you have with a problem employee? How long should a counseling interview last?

These are questions that lack clear-cut answers. For a less serious case, one interview might clear the air for a long time. With employees whose emotional problems are more serious, it may take several conversations just to gain confidence and identify the issues.

You can readily see that counseling can be time-consuming. That's why it's so important to spot worried workers early and take corrective action while you can help them with the minimum use of your time.

How long should an interview last? You can't accomplish much in 15 minutes, but that's a lot better than nothing. At the very least, it shows the employee you're interested in the person and the problem. Ideally, an interview should last no more than an hour.

What results should you expect from counseling an employee?

Recognize what you are counseling an employee for, and don't look for immediate results. Never mix the counseling interview with some other action you need to take, such as an appraisal or employee discipline.

A counseling interview is aimed at helping employees unburden themselves—get worries off their chests. Whether the conversation is related to the problem they create for you at work is not initially important. The payoff comes as they get confidence in you—and consequently don't vent their hostility and frustration on the job. This takes patience and time.

Some of the results you can expect include greater employee confidence in handling future problems, a more relaxed (and rational) individual, and one who is capable of clarified thinking and redirected energy. But don't necessarily expect appreciation in return, for if the counseling is done well, the employees will feel that they have solved their own problems.

JOB TIP!

The Dos and Don'ts of Employee Counseling

Nancy Hull, a former chemical-abuse counselor and an authority on the subject, cautions supervisors about the legal aspects of counseling. She suggests a conservative approach to what an employee may otherwise consider a confrontation. Hull's prescriptions for counseling follow.

- **Performance orientation.** Do let the employee know that the company is concerned about work performance.
- **Deterioration.** Do be aware that personal problems generally get worse, not better, without professional help.
- **Confidentiality.** Do emphasize that anything said will not be passed along to others.
- **Exemptions.** Do explain that going for help does not exempt the employee from standard disciplinary procedures and does not open the door to special privileges.
- **Improvements needed.** Do explain in very specific terms what the employee needs to do to perform up to the company's expectations.
- **Diagnosis.** Don't analyze what the problem is; you are not an expert.
- **Responsibility.** Don't probe personal problems during counseling unless they occur on the job or are raised by the employee.
- **Moralizing.** Don't impose your values on the employee; restrict the confrontation to job performance.
- **Sympathy.** Don't be swayed by emotional pleas or "hard-luck" stories.

Source: Adapted from "The Dos and Don'ts of Confrontation," by Nancy Hull, in *The Troubled Employee*, a film produced by Dartnell Corporation, Chicago. Used with permission of the copyright holder.

How can you recognize when an employee needs professional help?

Dr. Harry Levinson, a nationally recognized authority and founder of the Levinson Institute, advises adhering to the following basic steps (Figure 12-1) in assessing an employee's needs:

1. Recognize the emotional disturbance.
2. Relieve acute distress by listening (counseling).
3. Refer cases beyond your limits to professional help.

Step 1	Recognition
Step 2	Relief
Step 3	Referral

FIGURE 12-1

Levinson's three-phase guideline for supervisors to follow in counseling troubled employees.
How would you, as a supervisor, prepare for such a session?

Dr. Levinson offers this rule of thumb: *If after two listening sessions you seem to be making little headway in establishing confidence, you should refer the case (in confidence, of course) to an appropriate staff person or professional.* Some possibilities include a physician, a psychologist, a psychiatrist, a social worker, or a financial planner—all depending on the nature and degree of the underlying problem.

Dr. Levinson also advises that your approach in making a referral should be that of opening another door for additional help.

What do the professionals do for troubled employees that supervisors can't do?

Professionals offer at least two kinds of assistance that may be beyond the scope of a supervisor's capabilities. First, they are likely to have a reservoir of specialized expertise and experiences that they can draw on to help solve a particular problem (e.g., excessive credit card bills). Such persons can more likely diagnose what an individual's trouble is and prescribe the proper kind of solution or treatment.

Second, the extensive training these professionals have often gives them the ability to listen with great sensitivity to an employee's account of problems and then probe them in depth with their questioning and reflective skills. Further, because these persons don't present a threat of disciplining the employee, they often have a greater chance of winning an employee's confidence and stimulating the emotional release that often precedes constructive problem solving.

3	T or F	In good counseling sessions, the employee determines the focus of the discussion and the topics to be discussed.
4	T or F	One effective way to help employees relieve stress is to provide them with an opportunity for catharsis.

QUICK TEST 2

Reducing Absenteeism

Absentees are a special kind of problem people. How should you handle them?

CONCEPT
Certain forms of absenteeism can be materially reduced by employee counseling.

It depends on the reasons for absence. Professor P. J. Taylor of London University, who was formerly medical director of Shell (U.K.) Ltd., observes that 60 percent of all absentees have serious or chronic illnesses; 20 percent have acute, short-term illnesses such as the flu; 10 percent complain of minor illnesses such as colds and do or don't report to work according to their attitude about their jobs; and the final 10 percent are completely well but fake illness to enjoy a day off.

It is the group of absentees who make up the bottom 20 percent who are suspect. Industrial psychologists call their problem *voluntary absence*. In many, this is deeply rooted. They may lack an appreciation for the value of hard work. There is an inevitable conflict between the desire for more leisure and the desire for more work. This tug is especially evident among some workers who reflect an attitude of "entitlement." They feel that somehow the job is owed to them and that they have no responsibility for delivering a fair day's work in return. Regardless of the reason, you can help reduce absenteeism by doing the following:

- Firm up your rules about it—and remind employees periodically.
- Be consistent in applying penalties.
- Try to get at the reasons why an employee is frequently absent.

The last method requires the use of the counseling technique. It is important to promptly follow up each individual case. In your discussion of the problem with employees, be sure to permit them to explain their reactions to the job itself, the people they work with, the working conditions, their tools and equipment, and the kind of training they receive. You thus avoid making them feel that you are placing all the blame on them. And if they are specific in their reactions, you have specific complaints, rather than vague dissatisfactions, to deal with.

Don't overlook, however, the power of job satisfaction in luring absence-prone workers back to the job. Surprisingly, however, physical working conditions seem to have little effect. In company after company, attendance figures show little variation between the dirty, unpleasant areas and those that are clean and well lighted. Even most incentive schemes aimed at reducing absences are relatively ineffective. Closeness of the work team, its homogeneity, and the state of its morale seem to have the greatest effect.

How effective is counseling in reducing absenteeism?

Success depends on the root cause of individual absences. See how the patterns and the motivations differ in the following groups:

1. **Chronic absentees.** The people who have little capacity for pressure, either on the job or off, may be prime candidates for counseling. But first they must be made fully aware of the consequences of poor attendance. Theirs is a habit, usually of long standing, and correction requires pressure to attend as well as supervisory support.
2. **Vacationing absentees.** The people who work only so long as they need the cash and who then treat themselves to a day or two off are difficult cases. These employees are often extremely capable on the job, but they feel no deep responsibility for it. "Vacationers" make a conscious choice to be absent and are rarely helped by counseling.
3. **Directionless absentees.** Some younger employees who have as yet found no real purpose in work may simply follow the lead of the vacationer, who appears to lead a footloose, exciting life. A candid, direct talk with a directionless absentee may be more effective than counseling.

4. **Aggressive absentees.** The persons who willfully stay away from work in the hope that their absence will cause an inconvenience for you are probably emotionally troubled. This kind of behavior, however, requires professional counseling to correct it, not the kind of ordinary counseling a supervisor can provide.

5. **Moonlighters.** The persons who hold more than one job are often either too tired to come to work or are faced with conflicting schedules. Straight talk, rather than counseling, is prescribed. When attendance is affected, a moonlighter must be forced to make a choice between jobs.

6. **Occasional absentees.** The persons who seem to have slightly more absences than the rest of your staff are probably prime candidates for counseling. Their absences are legitimate. Their illnesses are real. Their problems often seem temporarily insurmountable. These people deserve a mixture of sympathy, understanding, and sometimes outright advice. This might also be the time for you to take a look in the mirror. For example, are you contributing to the absenteeism by not providing support and training?

In summary, you can probably help people who are absent for the following reasons:

1. Getting to work is a problem, real or imagined.
2. Off-job pressures are so strong that they weaken the employee's resolve to get to work.
3. The employee is easily led or misled by friends and peers.
4. The work appears boring, disagreeable, or unattractive.
5. Working relationships are unpleasant.
6. There are in fact off-job problems—child care, serious illness, court appearances—that need immediate attention.
7. Absence or lateness has become a habit.

You will have difficulty, however, helping people who are absent because of the following reasons:

1. The work or the pay associated with it does not hold a strong attraction.
2. Off-job pleasures have a greater appeal than work.
3. The employee is willfully absent in order to disrupt or inconvenience the organization.

| 5 | T or F | Employee counseling works best at reducing absenteeism in employees who have chronic illnesses. |
| 6 | T or F | Firm rules, consistency in applying penalties, and exploration of causes are all useful methods in combating voluntary absences. |

QUICK TEST 3

The Problems of Substance Abuse and Illness

What is the difference between alcohol abuse and drug abuse?

In principle, there may be very little difference between them. In practice, there are significant differences, especially legal ones. Many of the counseling approaches, however, are the same for both problems.

What can you do for alcoholic employees?

Whatever you attempt, proceed slowly and cautiously. Not all heavy drinkers are alcoholics. And the more they drink, the less likely they are to admit to anyone (even themselves) that their ability to handle liquor has gotten out of their control.

An alcoholic employee is really just another kind of problem employee, except that the case is an aggravated one and may need the help of a professional. Nevertheless, many alcoholic workers have rescued themselves with the aid of Alcoholics Anonymous (AA). This is an association of recovering alcoholics who, because they don't preach and because they emphasize the individual's need to face weaknesses, have perfected the art of listening without being either sympathetic or critical.

Your best bet, however, is to recognize an alcoholic in the early stages. Watch for these characteristic symptoms:

Some employees consume alcohol or drugs while at work. **How would you respond if you walked into this employee's office?**

- Sharp rise in absenteeism rate.
- Absenteeism spread throughout the week (to disguise it).
- Frequent partial-day absenteeism (employee works half a day and then leaves).
- Employee inexplicably leaves work for short periods during the day.
- Employee's actions and behaviors change (deteriorate) as the day progresses.

Then you can apply the same techniques to gain the person's confidence that you would with any other problem employee. Your objective is to provide security at work and to help the employee with talking out problems. If these employees can be helped to recognize that excessive drinking is a problem they aren't handling, you can refer them to an employee assistance program, which, in turn, may be able to persuade them to look into Alcoholics Anonymous or visit a professional counselor, a physician, or a special clinic for alcoholics.

How should you approach counseling an employee you believe is an alcoholic?

Alcoholism requires a special form of counseling, according to those who have coped most effectively with it. For example, the U.S. Department of Health, Education, and Welfare (HEW) in its *Supervisors' Guide on Alcohol Abuse* offers these hints to supervisors who are faced with this problem among their employees:

1. Don't apologize for confronting a troubled employee about the situation. Your responsibility is to maintain acceptable performance among all your employees.
2. Do encourage the employee to explain why work performance, behavior, or attendance is deteriorating. This can provide him or her with an *opportunity* to mention the use of alcohol. Recognize, however, that some alcoholics deny that they have a problem.
3. Don't discuss a person's right to drink. Don't make a moral issue of it. Alcoholism is a progressive and debilitating illness, which, if untreated, can eventually lead to significant health, family, and social problems.
4. Don't suggest that the employee use moderation or change his or her drinking habits. A person who is an alcoholic is usually unwilling or unable to voluntarily control drinking habits.
5. Don't be distracted by the individual's excuses for drinking (a difficult spouse, problem children, financial troubles, and so on).
6. Don't be fooled by the employee's assertion that a physician or a psychologist is already being seen and does not consider the drinking a problem. Therapists probably wouldn't say that if they knew an employee's job was in jeopardy because of alcohol abuse; they would attach great significance to the drinking habits.
7. Do remember that an alcoholic, like any other sick person, should be given the opportunity for treatment and rehabilitation.
8. Do emphasize that your major concern as a supervisor is the employee's poor work performance, attendance, or behavior. You can firmly state that if there is no improvement, administrative action—such as a suspension or discharge—will be taken.
9. Do state that the decision to seek and accept rehabilitative assistance is the employee's responsibility.

Give an employee every chance to get treatment, but make it clear that he or she must cooperate or lose the job.

How should an organization respond to drug abuse among employees?

You need only read the headlines of the daily newspapers to know that drug abuse is pervasive in many areas. Without discounting the terrible impact

Quips & Quotes

Drug testing has always been an intelligence test. What you're really measuring is whether someone is smart enough and strong enough to stay clean while they are conducting a job search.

Eric Greenberg, Director of Research for the American Management Association.

of drugs on society, the problem is usually less severe in work organizations (but this varies widely by geographical region and even by occupation). Why has drug abuse been slow to achieve notoriety at work? For one thing, many companies attempt to screen out hard-drug users before their employment begins, based in part on conviction records or preemployment drug tests. Second, the trend has been for many organizations to establish much tougher ongoing random drug screenings, security systems, and policies that enable them to dismiss drug abusers. Third, it is difficult for many abusers at work to conceal the symptoms of their habits.

Internet connection

http://workplace.samhsa.gov/DrugTesting/ReasonForTesting/index.html#PreempTest

Read about a variety of valid reasons for workplace drug testing.

Symptoms of drug use are well known. At work, drug use shows up as poor or erratic performance, tardiness, absenteeism, requests to leave early, forgetfulness, indifference to deadlines and safety, and, in many instances, theft of company property.

Treatment and rehabilitation for drug users are as difficult and complicated as they are for alcoholics, and the treatments are somewhat similar. Company policies against drug addiction, however, tend to be firmer than those against drinking and alcoholism. For one thing, an addict is different from an alcoholic because many addicts try to involve other people in drugs or endanger their safety. The risk of an alcoholic's inducing another employee to begin abusing alcohol is slight. Then, too, drug use is illegal; in most instances, use of alcohol is not.

Here again, a supervisor's responsibility should be limited to the detection of drug use, prevention of the use or sale of drugs on company property, and counseling of drug users, including referral, if indicated, to the appropriate company authority.

Supervisors also need to remember that both alcohol abuse and drug abuse fall under the auspices of the Americans with Disabilities Act (ADA) of 1990. This act protects the needs of persons with mental and physical disabilities from discrimination at work. Consequently, supervisors who recognize employee abuse problems should immediately consult the human resource department for their advice and counsel in handling a situation so that no discrimination takes place.

What sort of responsibility do supervisors have for counseling employees with major illnesses?

Much has to do with your own sense of compassion, tempered by your company's policies. Increasingly, supervisors must cope with employees who are suffering from life-threatening illnesses, such as cancer or AIDS. The presence of these employees can affect others on your staff as well. In general, the advice seems to run this way:

- Allow the affected employee to choose whether, when, and how to tell other employees about his or her condition.

- Develop some sort of transitional role for the employee. It should be one that matches the individual's capacity for work and still reflects her or his value to the company.
- Within these limits, expect the employee to follow established rules and maintain standards of performance. That's what most ill people who choose to keep working prefer. This enhances their sense of worth as adults who are still 100 percent alive and capable of contributing their talent and experience.

| 7 | T or F | Supervisory counseling can be highly appropriate for problems of either alcohol or drug abuse. |
| 8 | T or F | If an employee has a life-threatening illness, you should disclose it to other employees as soon as possible to prevent rumors. |

QUICK TEST 4

Performance Management

5

What is the real purpose of performance management?

In comparison to the multiple goals in counseling, the real purpose of *performance management* is quite simple. It is to encourage employees to meet or exceed established standards of job performance and to behave sensibly and safely at work. Most employees recognize the legitimate need to keep everyone working toward the same organizational goals and standards. Many employees are capable of self-control—planning their own workday, obtaining necessary resources, coordinating with others, monitoring the results of their effort, and correcting errors.

Employees who observe the rules and meet work standards may be rewarded by praise, financial rewards, job security, and advancement. Those who do not stay in line or measure up to performance standards are possibly subject to discipline. *Discipline* is the imposition of a penalty by management on an employee for breaking a rule. A *penalty* is a specific punishment or forfeiture, such as suspension, loss of pay, demotion, or, in extreme cases, loss of job. It is not designed to be punitive toward employees, but to act as a form of training so that they can clearly learn what acceptable performance and behavior are. Because the use of penalties represents an admission by management that it may share in the blame for failure, a supervisor should resort to disciplinary action only after all other attempts at performance management fail. Discipline should never be used as a show of authority or power on the supervisor's part.

CONCEPT
Properly administered performance management systems serve to guide future behavior in constructive directions, while developing self-control among employees.

Performance management. The ongoing process of clarifying and communicating performance expectations to employees, and then providing coaching and feedback to ensure the desired actions.

Discipline. The imposition of a penalty by management on an employee for the infraction of a company rule, regulation, or standard in such a manner as to encourage more constructive behavior and discourage a similar infraction in the future.

What sorts of infractions typically trigger the need for disciplinary action?

This varies among companies, and sometimes among departments within a single company. Supervisors, however, are most interested in the specific type, frequency, and degree of the infraction. Some employee behaviors, though frowned upon, may not be prohibited by company policy. And occasional (if rare) infractions of some standard or rule may be tolerated because they are offset by exemplary behavior in another domain. But when the breach becomes large or persistent, the need for discipline becomes obvious and urgent.

In addition to poor performance—either of output or of quality—infractions that most commonly result in disciplinary action include excessive absenteeism, insubordination, carelessness, negligence in following procedures, horseplay or fighting, dishonesty or falsification of company records, abusive or obscene language, intoxication, and sexual harassment.

When do employees resent discipline?

Most employees recognize the need for some rules and regulations at work; many welcome the clarity that they provide. They are more likely to object to specific rules that defy logic or tie their hands; they may criticize the organization for adhering too closely to a set of archaic rules; and they may be unable to separate their dislike for discipline received from a supervisor from their general regard for the supervisor who administers it. As a result, effective administration of discipline requires impartiality, good judgment, and courage.

When discipline is not administered fairly, it is likely to threaten employees' pride in who they are and their achievements—their level of *self-esteem*. And sometimes it doesn't take much to do this. For example, the following actions can lower employees' self-esteem:

- Criticizing an employee in front of peers.
- Talking down to workers.
- Assigning work unevenly.
- Not praising adequately when it is deserved.
- Implying that a worker is incompetent.
- Ignoring people or not asking for their input.

When self-esteem is threatened or damaged, the consequences may include distrust, defensiveness, reduced commitment, resentment, and unnecessary conflicts. When these problems deteriorate further into decreased productivity or excess absenteeism, discipline is called for. But this just continues a negative cycle consisting of problem → discipline → damaged self-esteem → problem → discipline, and so on.

When do employees embrace discipline?

Three major factors affect positive attitudes toward a disciplinary system. First, employees are more likely to support discipline when they participated in its development, which makes a strong case for employee involvement. Second, their support is almost assured when they can see the reasonable logic for it (as when worker carelessness threatens their own safety). Third, when groups (such as semiautonomous teams) administer their own justice system, they are more likely to support the process (and, incidentally, take some of the heat off the supervisor).

Why do employees break the rules?

As in most personnel problems, only a small percentage of workers (perhaps less than 10 percent) cause disciplinary problems. People who break rules do so for a number of reasons, including being in the wrong job, having an overdemanding and unsupportive supervisor, and non-job-related problems that are causing stress in their lives. But the contributing factor often resides in their personal characteristics—dislike of authority figures, carelessness, lack of desire to cooperate, a poor work ethic, dishonesty, or failure to adjust to the employment world. The supervisor's job, as a result, is to help employees better adjust to their jobs and employers.

Supervisors may have to discipline their employees for infractions of key rules. **How do you turn a disciplinary situation into a developmental one?**

What kind of handling do employees expect from a supervisor in the way of discipline?

Justice and equitable treatment. "Let the punishment fit the crime," is the advice in Gilbert and Sullivan's *Mikado.* No one likes to be treated worse than anyone else for the same fault.

People are less inclined to break rules when the supervisor is a good leader, when sincere interest and real caring are shown toward employees, and when employees get satisfaction from their work. After all, if an employee finds the work uninteresting and the supervisor unpleasant to deal with, is it surprising that the employee will find reasons for being late or for staying away from work altogether? And is it a large step from those withdrawal behaviors to more aggressive forms of resistance and sabotage?

Thus, when an employee breaks a rule, make discipline your last resort. Use inquiry to discover the real reason the employee acted that way. Then see what you can do to remove the reason.

6 Administrative Guidelines

CONCEPT

Discipline is most effective when applied constructively, progressively, and in accordance with the "hot-stove" rule.

What is meant by constructive discipline? By progressive discipline?

If a supervisor accepts the goal of getting employees to behave acceptably and perform appropriately, the purpose of discipline becomes primarily positive. From this perspective, you focus on setting performance objectives, coaching for skill development, providing resources, and sharing *constructive criticism*. This requires taking the time to investigate a troublesome situation and compose one's thoughts, carefully selecting the words to use, and stimulating new insights in the employee about how to do the job better. Constructive criticism tries to redirect employee energy and behavior into productive channels by offering feedback and observations, making useful suggestions, and clarifying goals and steps to perform. It requires sensitively protecting an employee's self-esteem and dignity, while simultaneously indicating the urgency for change. A supervisor may say, "Let me show you an easier way to do that," or "I think there'd be less risk of problems if you went through that more slowly the first few times."

Progressive discipline, however, means that the penalties for substandard performance or broken rules get increasingly harsh as the condition continues or the infraction is repeated (see Figure 12-2). Progressive discipline usually begins with the employee receiving a **warning**, a formal notification of the consequences of further infractions. Typically, a first offense, unless it is a dramatic one, may receive an oral warning. A second offense elicits a written warning. A third infraction may bring a temporary layoff or a suspension. The final step occurs when an employee is discharged for the fourth (or a very serious) infraction. This system gives any employee adequate warning of the eventual consequences of repeated violations.

Warning. A reprimand worded so as to give formal notice to an employee that repetition of a particular form of unacceptable behavior, such as infraction of a rule, will draw a penalty.

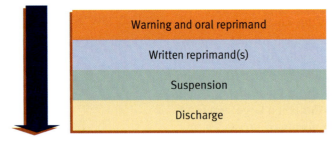

FIGURE 12-2

Example of steps in progressive discipline.
Is progressive discipline primarily positive or primarily negative?

FIGURE 12-3

"Hot-stove" rules for discipline. **Which principle is the most important?**

1. Advance warning
2. Immediacy
3. Impartiality
4. Consistency

What is the "hot-stove" rule of discipline?

This is a metaphor used to illustrate the four essentials of a good disciplinary policy (see Figure 12-3). If the stove is red-hot, you ought to be able to see it and to know that if you touch it, you will be burned; that is the principle of *advance warning*. If you touch the hot stove, you get burned (penalized) right away; that is the principle of *immediacy*. Everyone who touches a hot stove will get burned because it plays no favorites; that is the principle of *impartiality*. Every time you touch a hot stove, you will get burned; that is the principle of *consistency*.

What should you do when an employee willfully refuses to do what you ask?

The first piece of advice, and the toughest to follow, is not to fly off the handle. Review the order's fairness, the selection of the person to carry it out, and the probability that you were understood. If you think you've done your part, find out what the employee objects to and the reasons for the objection. Ask for specifics: "What is it you object to? Why do you think it's unreasonable?" Chances are, a nonthreatening exploration of the situation will let both of you cool down and help you clarify the real problem. Perhaps you can even modify the order so that it will be accepted.

But if the employee continues to resist a reasonable request, you're faced with a disciplinary problem. Find a private place where you can talk calmly but firmly. Let it be known that you will take disciplinary steps if the problem isn't resolved. But try to avoid a showdown situation in which one (or both) of you will wind up losing. Resist making threats if you can.

The primary purpose of any disciplinary action is to have the employee make a permanent and positive change in their behavior.

Gary Bielous

If You Snooze, You Lose

A survey by the National Sleep Foundation stated that employee sleep deprivation—whether minor or major—costs employers an estimated $18 billion a year in lost productivity. Although the reasons are highly diverse (including late-night TV watching, tending to sick children, working two jobs, and physical causes such as sleep apnea), the results can be the same—productivity loss, safety issues, anger by co-workers, and even sleeping on the job. Should an employee who falls asleep repeatedly on the job be terminated? What do you think?

Under what conditions can an employee be fired?

That depends on your company's management policy, the autonomy granted you by your manager, and the labor agreement (if your employees are unionized). More specifically, the right to fire an employee does not extend to termination at will (discharge without a valid reason). Instead, the principle of *just cause* governs most discharge situations—there must be a substantive rationale for the action. Possible just causes for firing include stealing, willful destruction of property, fighting, threats against fellow employees or the supervisor, poor-quality work, and altering one's time record. In judgmental situations, a labor agreement usually provides workers with the right to *grieve,* or appeal, the results when discipline has been unfairly applied. Wise supervisors often consult with a union representative as well as a human resources person before taking severe disciplinary action.

How, exactly, do you go about firing someone?

First, bring him or her to a quiet place where privacy is assured. If possible, invite a colleague to serve as a witness. Bring along whatever documentation you have regarding the compelling problem. Present your rationale, the relevant policy, and your decision. Expect that the person to be discharged may deny the behavior, exhibit extreme anger, or break into tears. Avoid being argumentative, while remaining tactful and assertive. And be sure to provide details of his or her residual rights to employee benefits, if any. Handle any questions, or promise to obtain the answers. As soon as the meeting is over, make sure you have a plan for communicating the action to the rest of your department, to minimize rumors.

What are the most common pitfalls in discipline?

Employee discipline is difficult, and so supervisors should avoid making the following mistakes:

- **Failure to establish a clear-cut breach of rule.** Many areas of enforcement remain "gray" despite efforts to clarify standards of behavior. Although supervisory judgment is always called for, the violation must be clear.
- **Inadequate warnings.** Even the presence of clear rules and guidelines in an employee manual may not be enough; workers need a personal warning that their conduct will not be tolerated.
- **Insufficient evidence.** A spot check, a random observation, or a little bit of information is not enough. The data gathered must be thorough and complete.
- **Violation of policy or labor contact.** This should be one of the first priorities for supervisory consideration. Discipline imposed after an

infraction should accurately reflect an organization's established policies and/or, if a union is present, provisions of the labor contract.

- **Prejudice.** Discrimination or favoritism casts a shadow over disciplinary action. Don't let personal attitudes affect your treatment of a worker.
- **Unequal enforcement of policy.** Because judgment is involved and the supervisor is busy, rules sometimes get applied to one worker but not another. Make sure policies are applied consistently across the board.
- **Inadequate records.** The value of written records documenting an accumulation of offenses over time cannot be overemphasized. Keep a detailed record in the employee's personnel file.
- **Overly severe punishment.** Don't let momentary anger color your judgment. Assess historical records and move only to the next disciplinary step needed.

Supervisory handling of disciplinary actions is always subject to someone else's review—by a manager, the human resource department, the union, an arbitrator, or someone in the legal system. Consequently, supervisors must eliminate all of the above mistakes if they expect their disciplinary actions to stand up to external scrutiny.

How can you make disciplinary action stick?

By carefully planning it and gathering sound documentation to support it. Actions must be based on genuine evidence, free from bias and discrimination. Avoid impulsive, spiteful actions, for they will surely backfire. Arbitrators, as well as representatives of the EEOC and other investigatory agencies, are quick to spot weak cases and reject them.

How can you make sure that your records will support a disciplinary action?

Take care to make the proper records at each step of a progressive disciplinary action. Follow carefully your organization's policies and procedures in this matter. The legal concept of *due process* is important in all areas of employment, especially those involving job security. This means that all employees, regardless of union representation, are entitled to a fair and just hearing. Under such circumstances, a supervisor's opinions and vague recollections will not carry much weight. Conclusions have to be supported by specific documentation. Records that help provide this documentation include the following:

Due process. An employee's entitlement to a fair hearing before discipline can be meted out. Often, the hearing is conducted by an impartial party, allows appropriate representation, and involves presentation of available evidence.

- Regularly kept records, such as time cards showing absences and lateness, production and quality control reports, and the like.
- Written complaints from customers, suppliers, or other contacts that can be identified without qualification with the individual who is to be disciplined.

- Examples of unsatisfactory or careless work, including sloppy reports, incorrect tabulations, and damaged goods, all marked in such a way that they identify the culpable individual.
- Written summaries of appraisal and/or disciplinary conferences, which should contain specific rather than general statements, including dates, figures, and clearly described incidents. But remember that copies of these reports (which are retained in personnel records) must be given to the individual at the time they are written.
- Documentation of information collected from co-workers and others while investigating the events leading to disciplinary action. The important thing to remember here is that these records should be developed on an ongoing basis over time, not reconstructed from memory at the time of a crisis or just before a hearing. The stream of incidents thus recorded and all key details will be very useful in making and supporting your decision.

| QUICK TEST 6 | 11 | T or F | Constructive discipline and progressive discipline are basically the same thing. |
| | 12 | T or F | When firing someone, it is important that supervisors follow the guidelines of due process. |

Practical Guidelines for Supervisors

1. *Focus your efforts primarily on employee performance* and the factors that interfere with or contribute to it.

2. *Stay alert for signs that employees may be experiencing a personal crisis* and find supportive ways to help them work through the experience constructively.

3. Recognize that *supervisory counseling of troubled employees often requires empathy*—seeing a situation through other people's eyes and values.

4. *Practice sharpening your listening skills* (patience, attentiveness, reflecting feelings) to provide troubled employees with an opportunity to experience catharsis.

5. Don't be afraid to *refer an employee to a professional counselor or expert* if the problem is more complex than you can handle.

6. *Study the different types of absenteeism* to determine which ones can be improved through counseling and which ones require other approaches.

7. *Learn about the telltale symptoms of an alcoholic employee* (often revolving around unexplained absenteeism) and focus on the performance effects of the individual's behavior as well as rehabilitative opportunities.

8. Commit yourself to *building employee self-esteem* in legitimate ways, while avoiding conscious or unconscious actions that can diminish it.

9. *Take a positive approach to discipline* by focusing on constructive criticism where possible, while holding the steps in progressive discipline in reserve.

10. *Reserve the tool of firing for those disciplinary situations that provide a legitimate just cause*; be sure to adhere to due process rules and document all actions thoroughly.

Chapter 12 Review

Key Concepts to Remember

1. Problem Performers. Supervisors have a legitimate interest in employee performance that either (a) does not measure up to established standards or (b) is disruptive to the normal conduct of operations. Such problem performance is often a reflection of temporary emotional problems stemming from an inability to adjust to the stress of life or work. This failure to cope sometimes causes employees to behave unproductively or erratically on the job and interrupt the regular harmony of the workplace. Troubled employees can be recognized by such disharmonious conduct as sudden changes in behavior, preoccupation, irritability, increased accidents or absences, unusual fatigue, irrational anger, and hostility.

2. Employee Counseling. Constructive counseling by a supervisor can help a great many troubled employees improve their performance or control their behavior, provided that the degree of their maladjustment is slight and the underlying causes are not intense. The objectives of the counseling process are to (a) recognize the symptoms of a troubled employee, (b) provide relief if the symptoms and causes are minor (to ease the employee's return to satisfactory performance), and (c) *refer the employee to a professional counselor* if the conditions are more than minor.

3. Reducing Absenteeism. Constructive counseling can also reduce absenteeism among chronic and occasional absentees. Other forms of absenteeism respond better to a three-part program involving (a) clear-cut rules, (b) consistent penalties, and (c) counseling to determine—and confront—the reasons for the absences.

4. The Problems of Substance Abuse and Illness. Alcoholism and drug abuse are found among special kinds of problem employees. Counseling by the supervisor, combined with insistence that performance standards be met, may be helpful. In anything but minor cases, professional assistance or advice from groups such as Alcoholics Anonymous should be sought.

5. Performance Management. When supervisors use performance management correctly, discipline is seldom needed. Most employees prefer to stay out of trouble. Only a few employees find it difficult to (a) meet work standards or (b) conform to the rules imposed by an organized activity. Accordingly, effective discipline is aimed not so much at punishing bad performance as at encouraging and rewarding good performance. The objective of discipline is to train erring employees to develop their own self-control so that they are not drawn over the line that separates acceptable from unacceptable behavior.

6. Administrative Guidelines. Effective discipline should be an essentially positive effort. Its three hallmarks are (a) punishment that is suitable to the importance of the offense, (b) penalties that become progressively severe (e.g., warnings, suspension, discharge) as offenses are repeated, and (c) discipline that is consistent with the "hot-stove" rule (that is, discipline should be given only if there has been adequate warning, and it should be immediate, impartial, and consistent). Severe violations may result in suspension or firing for just cause, but only if the supervisor has carefully thought through and documented the process in advance. Employees are entitled to, and expect, due process; without it, labor unions, the EEOC, and other federal, state, and local agencies may intervene on behalf of the employee.

Reading Comprehension

1. Why is it so important for supervisors to identify and attempt to help troubled employees in their workforce?

2. When a supervisor is thinking of counseling an employee, should the emphasis be placed on behavior, performance, or attitude? Why?

3. Explain what it means for a supervisor to be empathetic.

4. Describe the characteristics of the counseling approach.

5. List five specific counseling skills that you could use in counseling a troubled employee.

6. Discuss the difference between valid absences that result from bona fide illness and absences that psychologists describe as *voluntary* absences. What is a supervisor's role in minimizing the latter?

7. Why might a company have policies for confronting drug abuse that are different from those for dealing with alcohol abuse?

8. Summarize these four arguments: why a well-behaved employee and another employee prone to bending the rules would like and dislike the presence of disciplinary regulations in the workplace.

9. Progressive discipline suggests a sequence of four steps. What reasons can you suggest for *not* using all four, such as starting at step 1 and jumping to step 3, or starting directly at step 2?

10. The "hot-stove" rule is meant to help supervisors remember four important points about discipline. Briefly describe each one.

Application

Self-Assessment

How Good Are Your Counseling and Performance Management Skills?

Read the following statements carefully. Circle the number on the response scale that most closely reflects the degree to which each statement describes you. Add up your total points and prepare a brief action plan for self-improvement. Be ready to report your score for tabulation across the entire group.

	Good Description	Poor Description
1. I recognize that any employee can develop emotional problems occasionally that might negatively affect performance.	10 9 8 7 6 5 4 3 2 1	
2. I am generally alert to sudden changes in a person's normal behavior at work.	10 9 8 7 6 5 4 3 2 1	

	Good Description	Poor Description
3. I have the patience to recognize that most employee problems won't be solved in a single counseling session.	10 9 8 7 6 5 4 3 2 1	
4. I have the necessary skills to develop empathetic relationships with troubled employees at work.	10 9 8 7 6 5 4 3 2 1	
5. I am skillful at allowing catharsis by using silence and listening skills, using non-verbal responses, and reflecting feelings.	10 9 8 7 6 5 4 3 2 1	
6. I feel comfortable confronting chronic absentees and occasional absentees about their disruptive behaviors.	10 9 8 7 6 5 4 3 2 1	
7. I am aware of the common symptoms of alcoholic employees.	10 9 8 7 6 5 4 3 2 1	
8. I actively use the practice of performance management to help employees become more productive.	10 9 8 7 6 5 4 3 2 1	
9. I am acutely aware of the ways in which my behavior can affect employee self-esteem.	10 9 8 7 6 5 4 3 2 1	
10. I am conscious of the important steps in progressive discipline, and I practice the four essentials of the "hot-stove" rule.	10 9 8 7 6 5 4 3 2 1	

Scoring and Interpretation

Scoring

Add up your total points for the 10 questions. Record that number here, and report it when it is requested. _____

Also, insert your score on the Personal Development Plan in the Appendix.

Interpretation

81 to 100 points. You seem to have a basic set of counseling and performance management skills.

61 to 80 points. Take a close look at some of your counseling and performance management skills (those with lower self-assessments) and discuss them with a manager to see if they need improvement.

Below 60 points. Some of your skills may be substantially inconsistent with effective counseling and performance management practices and could be detrimental to your success as a supervisor.

Identify your three lowest scores, and write the question numbers here: _____, _____, _____.

Action

Write a brief paragraph detailing an action plan for how you might sharpen each of these skills. Then pay particularly close attention to the related material in the chapter as you review the relevant sections there.

Skill Development

Counseling

Many employees go through periods of substantial stress in their lives, caused by work-related or nonwork problems (or both). When they find it desirable to "let off steam" at work, supervisors need to take the time—and demonstrate the skills—to allow for their catharsis in a psychologically safe setting. This requires the acquisition and development of some basic counseling skills, as outlined in this chapter. When done well, this type of counseling can produce very positive outcomes for both the stressed employee and the organization.

Pair up with another person. Assume that this person has asked to speak with you on an urgent basis. The problem he or she presents to you may be of any kind (e.g., family crisis, alcohol abuse, financial difficulties, temporary depression around the holidays, frustration with another employee at work). Spend several minutes counseling this person until it appears that she or he is more relaxed and in control emotionally. (To prepare yourself, you will likely wish to review the text's discussion on employee counseling, scan the Internet for relevant guidelines, and consult with colleagues and staff persons in the human resources department for their advice.) When you are finished, ask the other person to provide constructive feedback to you on the following dimensions:

1. Degree to which you let the person control the direction of the conversation.
2. Degree to which you gave your undivided attention.
3. Degree to which you listened patiently.
4. Degree to which you were attentive, receptive, and empathetic.
5. Degree to which you refrained from arguing, interrupting, or offering advice.
6. Degree to which you were alert to underlying feelings.
7. Degree to which you used silence to draw out the other person.
8. Degree to which you refrained from expressing surprise or judgment at anything that was said.

9. Degree to which you appropriately reflected the other person's feelings.
10. Degree to which you used gentle, open-ended questions.

Action

Based on the feedback from your partner, make a list of the ways in which you can improve your counseling skills.

Group Exercise

Performance Management

Step 1: Form groups of three to five persons. Viewing the classroom as an organization, your task is to develop a performance management system for it.

Step 2: Decide what your goals are in several areas—safety, room cleanliness, attendance, participation, learning, and so on. Be as specific as possible. Then anticipate what types of (student) problems might arise in each of these areas.

Step 3: Create a model set of policies for addressing potential problems, incorporating the text's guidelines for progressive discipline. Prepare to present your report to the class, anticipating members' reactions and criticisms.

Step 4: After class presentations are completed, compare and contrast the various approaches, followed by a discussion of these issues:
1. How difficult was this task?
2. What additional information would be desirable? Where might you get it?
3. What is the likely response if you implement such a performance management program in this classroom?
4. How did your model program differ from the others? What have you learned by listening to the class presentations?

Cases for Analysis

Case 36

The Irrational Documents Clerk

Benny was not exactly a knockout as a documents clerk for the Northern Empire Power and Light Company, but he was reasonably dependable. He got most of his work done on time, and his error rate on document coding was no worse than the average clerk's rate. His manner was generally pleasant, although he was considered somewhat of a loner by his associates.

That has all changed during the last three months. Benny's output has deteriorated markedly. He no longer meets his deadlines, and his boss, Aretha Ford, keeps discovering costly miscodings in the documents Benny prepares. Benny appears to be working hard, but his results are no longer satisfactory. When approached by other clerks to make corrections in the documents he sends them, Benny flares up. On some occasions, he has been downright insulting.

Yesterday, Aretha asked Benny to come to her office to talk about this problem. She opened the discussion by saying: "Your error rate on document preparation has become entirely unacceptable lately. So has your output. This can't keep on. What can you do to bring your work back into line?"

Benny was silent for a few minutes, and so Aretha repeated her question. Then, without warning, Benny slammed his fist down on the desk. He shouted obscenities and heaped abuse on Aretha: she was unfair, played favorites, expected too much of him, didn't understand his situation; if she wanted him to quit, why didn't she say so; and so on.

Analysis

If you were Aretha, what would you do now? Of the following five alternatives, which do you think would be most appropriate? Rank the alternatives on a scale from 1 (most preferable) to 5 (least preferable). You may add another alternative if you wish. Be prepared to justify your ranking.

_____ **a.** Don't say anything for the time being; allow Benny to continue talking.

_____ **b.** Advise Benny that he isn't making sense; tell him that when he is ready to talk rationally, you'll resume the discussion.

_____ **c.** Carefully show Benny why his accusations are not justified by the records.

_____ **d.** Wait a while; then tell Benny that you want to help him if he's suffering from some sort of emotional problem.

_____ **e.** Tell Benny that you understand how he feels, but say that it would be better if he faced up to his problem now.

Case 37

A Difference of Opinion

Twenty-two supervisors, all from different local companies, met for an all-day workshop on "Effective Supervision for the 21st Century." They heard presentations about, and engaged in discussions on, a range of topics, including communication, motivation, leadership, and counseling. During the afternoon refreshment break, Josie, a supervisor who had been rather quiet all day, directed a question toward the instructor and another workshop participant who was standing close by.

"I have a problem with an employee," said Josie. "One or two days a week one of my drivers comes to work with liquor on his breath. Although he's not had an accident yet, I'm afraid that if he gets stopped by the police for any reason, they'll ticket him for DWI (driving while intoxicated). That could be bad for the company's reputation in the community and for our insurance rates. What should I do?"

Before the instructor could reply, the other supervisor said, "Your role as a supervisor is to identify and solve problems, isn't it?" Josie nodded.

"Well, then, tell the employee you think he's an alcoholic. Say he'd better control himself right now. Threaten him with immediate discharge if he doesn't shape up. You've got to take prompt action on these matters, or you lose all control."

Josie turned to the instructor. "I guess he's got a good point there," she said. "What do you think?"

Analysis

Respond to Josie, commenting on both the other supervisor's perspective and any ideas you have for a different approach.

Case 38

She's a Charmer, But . . .

Julie Garvo is 23 years old and serves as a paralegal clerk in a large law firm. She's been employed there for six months. Julie is charming and energetic, and is very popular with the office staff and the lawyers.

Julie, however, is frequently late for work. She takes long lunch hours and has been absent from work an average of two days a month for the last three months. She apologizes when she saunters in late but seems unconcerned about this or her absences. To her co-workers, Julie readily admits that she doesn't have a great deal of interest in her work. The best thing about the job, she says, is that it pays well enough for her to do some of the things she enjoys in her off-hours.

Analysis

Julie's supervisor, the office manager, notes, "She's a charmer, but she's become a problem." If you were her supervisor, what would you do?

a. Encourage Julie to improve. Sympathize with her lack of interest and try to make the job less boring for her.
b. Have a shoulder-to-shoulder talk with Julie, pointing out the importance of her creating a good work record.
c. Have Julie seek professional help to "get her head on straight."
d. Tell Julie to stop the lateness and absences, or she will be fired.

Can you make any other suggestions to Julie's boss?

Case 39

"That Was the Week That Was"

It was finally Friday afternoon, and Martina breathed a big sigh of relief. It had not been, in anyone's eyes, a very good week. As the supervisor of a large crew working on clearing a mountain trail for hikers, she had a challenging job. She was responsible for the efforts of 24 workers, organized into four teams of six people each. The teams were spread out over nearly one-half mile, with team A cutting large trees, team B removing stumps, team C clearing smaller brush, and team D building footbridges across small streams and swampy areas.

Unfortunately, Martina was having trouble controlling several of her crew members. This was probably due, she reasoned, to the fact that she had split her time across the four crews, and she couldn't be everywhere at once. Just this week, she had to discipline several individuals for a variety of infractions:

- She gave an oral reprimand to Andrea, because when Martina walked up to one crew, she thought she saw Andrea quickly jump up and grab her tools to start working.
- Jackie had been coming to work late almost every other day for the last two weeks. "This can only set a bad example for the entire crew," reasoned Martina one night. Finally, on Thursday, Martina had put up with enough of Jackie's tardiness and fired her when she arrived at work.

- Mickey was one of those workers who moved so slowly that Martina sometimes wondered if she should check his pulse to see if he was even alive. "He's just lazy," concluded Martina. "Maybe a written reprimand will stimulate him to work a little faster!"

Analysis

Will Martina's disciplinary actions hold up if they are challenged? Should her manager support her? What errors in discipline did she make?

Quick Test 1	Quick Test 2	Quick Test 3	Quick Test 4	Quick Test 5	Quick Test 6	ANSWERS TO QUICK TESTS
1. F	3. T	5. F	7. T	9. T	11. F	
2. F	4. T	6. T	8. F	10. F	12. T	

Building Cooperative Teams and Resolving Conflicts

LEARNING OBJECTIVES

After studying this chapter, you should be able to

- Explain the formation, roles, and influence of formal and informal groups in an organization.

- Discuss the use of participatory management with groups of employees, and know how to conduct a group meeting.

- Identify the clues to good and bad teams, and explain how teams develop over time.

- Identify the most common sources of conflict in an organization and describe some effective ways to resolve conflict.

- Discuss ways in which cooperation can be obtained from associates, staff people, individuals, and groups.

Group Dynamics

Group dynamics. The interaction among members of a work group and concurrent changes in their attitudes, behavior, and relationships.

Formal work group. A group or team of employees who are assigned by management to similar activities or locations with the intent that they work together in a prescribed way toward goals established by management.

Why are group relations so important today?

Business, industrial, service, and government enterprises are often large and complex. As a result, they depend on the effectiveness of group effort. Modern jobs involve great interdependence among individuals and among departments, and demand close cooperation among all parties.

As Casey Stengel, the eccentric but immensely successful manager of baseball's Dodgers, Yankees, and Mets, observed: "It's easy to get the players. Gettin' 'em to play together, that's the hard part."

Which groups take priority: the formal or the informal ones?

Formal groups do, such as your own department or assigned work teams within your department. *Formal work groups* have been set up by management to routinely carry out the work in the best fashion. But informal groups require your attention and consideration, too. A supervisor must be realistic about the emergence of informal groups within the department because:

1. **Informal groups are inevitable.** They form at the water fountain and in the locker room. They are made up of carpoolers and those with common interests in sports or politics. You find them everywhere.
2. **Informal groups can be very powerful.** They strongly influence your employees. To enforce compliance among group members, such groups often establish sanctions (penalties) that run counter to a supervisor's formal authority. Most informal groups, however, will work with you if you develop good relationships with them.
3. **Informal leaders tend to emerge within these groups and to guide opinion within them.** Supervisors should be aware of such leaders and be prepared to draw upon their influence. Strive to win their support and cooperation.

What causes employees to create their own informal groups?

There are a number of causes. The most powerful is a common specialty or skill. For example, the customer service representatives in a telemarketing office are naturally going to find things in common to talk about. Other common experiences, backgrounds, or interests also serve to pull parts of a formal grouping of employees into "cliques." Proximity plays a role, too. Workers who are physically close tend to form close relationships to the exclusion of others in the department who are in more remote locations.

Membership in *informal work groups* develops gradually. Over a period of time, an individual begins to feel accepted (or rejected) by the others. In return for acceptance, the individual begins to accept—and carry out—the interests and behavior of the group. The bonds are tighter when the attraction is fostered by a desire for protection or support (often with regard to the company or management). Groups are less cohesive when the common bond is more casual, as with hobbies and sports.

A supervisor must be careful in his or her relationships with informal groups. They can't be ignored; often they can be helpful. However, giving these groups too much attention, especially to the exclusion of those outside the groups, will surely bring about dissension, feelings of favoritism, and lack of cooperation.

Informal work group. A group that forms spontaneously among employees who work near one another, have common personal interests, or work toward common job goals.

How do informal groups compare to "in" groups?

Most supervisors tend—consciously or unconsciously—to have favorite employees. These workers may have been there longer and thus are better known, may be better performers, or may simply share some recreational and social interests with the supervisor. These favorite employees become part of the *"in" group*, while other employees in the same department are excluded and can be loosely called an "out" group.[1] The primary difference between an "in" group and an informal group is that the supervisor has chosen the "in" group members, whereas the members of the informal group have chosen themselves. The consequences are powerful, however. "In" group members have higher social status, often learn about new developments sooner, and may receive special treatment from the supervisor. Obviously, this can cause resentment among the "out" group workers. The lesson for supervisors is clear—strive to be objective and impartial in dealing with your employees.

How does a group of employees differ from a single employee in the group?

Take a group of 10 employees who work in a food-packing plant. This group is respected by its supervisor as one of the most productive in the plant. It also has a collective reputation for advocating work stoppages over many issues. Yet in the group there are three people who, polled separately, are strongly against a walkout. And there are another three who, when working with other groups, are low producers. This is typical. Each person in a group may be a fairly strong individualist when working alone. But when people work in a group, the personality of the group becomes stronger than that of any single individual in the group. The group's personality will reflect the outlook and work habits of the various individuals, but it will bring out the best (or worst) in some and will submerge many individual tendencies of which the group does not approve.

Group norms. Beliefs held by a group about what is right and what is wrong as far as performance at work is concerned.

Furthermore, each group sets the standards of conduct—or *group norms*—for its members. Norms are accepted ways of doing things, an accepted way of life within the group. The group's ways may not be the best ways. Group norms may even stand in the way of doing things the way the company and the supervisor want them done. But the group will support the group standards. Individuals who don't conform will be cut off from the group's break sessions, playful bantering, informal rewards, and social activities. It's not uncommon for the group to ridicule those who don't "play ball" or to purposely make it difficult for outsiders to get their own work done.

What makes some groups stronger than others?

Cohesiveness. The degree to which team members are attracted to the group, feel a part of it, and wish to remain in it.

It all revolves around *cohesiveness*—the members' desire to join, remain a part of, and participate in the group and its activities. In a cohesive group, members are attracted to the group, willing to make personal sacrifices for the good of the group, and enthusiastic about what the group is doing. They enjoy a common sense of identity and feel close to each other. And a cohesive work group tends to have greater similarity of output among its members and higher productivity *if* the group's norms support the organization's goals. However, high cohesiveness also has its limitations. It could lead to less risk taking by individuals, withholding of unpopular views, failure to confront areas of conflict, and suppression of unique perspectives from individual members. Supervisors can predict with high accuracy whether a group will become cohesive. Table 13-1, based on a review of research, presents two sets of factors that allow a supervisor to estimate how cohesive a group will be.

Morale. A measure of the extent (either high or low) of voluntary cooperation demonstrated by an individual or a work group and of the intensity of the desire to meet common work goals.

The key to determining whether a cohesive group will be for or against the organization's goals lies in its level of *morale*. Often defined as a group's collective job-satisfaction level, morale is a measure of the team's voluntary cooperation and desire to meet common work goals. If a group's morale level is high, its members are more likely to cooperate with management and contribute to its goals. But if it is low, watch out!

A fascinating by-product of group activity is the experience of *synergy*. This is the supplemental energy, creativity, and productivity that emerges when a group of individuals "click" together to produce a better product than the sum of their individual efforts would have predicted. It doesn't occur in all groups, and it doesn't emerge automatically, but when it happens, it is nearly magical to observe. It is almost the collective

TABLE 13-1 Major Factors Affecting Group Cohesion

Contributors	Detractors
• Opportunity for frequent interaction.	• Favoritism shown by supervisors toward some group members.
• Prior group attractiveness (e.g., past successes, enjoyable experiences by early members).	• Domination of the group by one or more members.
• Similar attitudes, values, and backgrounds of members.	• Absence of interpersonal attractiveness (liking) among members.
• Presence of a superordinate goal (one that can be reached only through cooperative efforts of the members).	• Actions by members that prevent or destroy trust within the group.
• Existence of a common "enemy" or threat (such as an authoritarian supervisor, risk of job loss, or even physical danger).	• Disagreement over goals or standards of performance.
	• Large groups (often those with more than 10 members).
• Competition with other groups.	• Scarce resources, leading to competition within the group.

Source: Allan R. Cohen et al., *Effective Behavior in Organizations* (5th ed.). Homewood, IL: Irwin, 1992, pp. 105–120.

parallel to the term athletes use to describe their feelings when everything goes perfectly for them—they are in a *zone.*

In what ways are informal groups most likely to cause problems?

By ganging up to present collective resistance (spoken or silent) and by pressuring individual members to conform to the group's standards. Strong work groups stick together. They will protect one of their loyal members, and they will force a nonconformist to go along with the majority. The pressure can be so strong that even a high performer or a loner can be made to fall in line—or to quit. Groups are powerful. Their support is to be cherished. Their antagonism or hostility can be awesome. For these reasons, prudent supervisors seek a group's help in establishing and accomplishing attainable work goals.

What are work groups likely to do best?

Solve work problems. Groups, formal or informal, have an uncanny knack for unsnarling complex work situations. In a few minutes, they can straighten out overlapping procedures between employees. They often know causes of difficulty hidden from the supervisor. Typically, they are acutely

Quips & Quotes

Synergy is the highest activity of life; it creates new untapped alternatives; it values and exploits the mental, emotional, and psychological differences between people.

Stephen Covey

Participation. The technique in which a supervisor or manager shares work-related information, responsibilities, decisions, or all three with the work group.

aware of personality conflicts between their members. Thus, a group's ability to put together jointly held know-how in a constructive manner is one that experienced supervisors need to tap. The technique of securing group aid this way in solving departmental problems is called *participation*.

QUICK TEST 1

1	T or F	Informal groups are inevitable, are usually weak, and have informal leaders.
2	T or F	Cohesive groups with organizationally supportive norms are usually more productive.

2   Group Participation

CONCEPT
A participative approach tends to enhance a supervisor's effectiveness with employee groups.

How can a supervisor set goals with the work group and invite its involvement?

Unless the people you supervise believe that what you want them to do is to their advantage as well as to yours, you'll have little success as a supervisor. The solution lies in permitting the members of the work group to set their goals along with you. Then you need to show them that these goals are attained through group action: teamwork.

You may initially feel that to permit the group to get into the decision-making act will be hazardous to your authority. It needn't be. First of all, you'll always retain a veto power over a group decision (but don't exercise it unless absolutely necessary). Second, establish ground rules for the group's participation beforehand. Explain what's negotiable and what's not. Make areas of freedom, as well as limitations, clear. Finally, provide enough information for the group so that its members can see situations as clearly as you do. It's when people don't have enough facts that they rebel against authority or go off on tangents.

In dealing with work groups, try to make your role that of a coach. Help employees see why cost cutting, for instance, is desirable and necessary to prevent layoffs. Encourage them to discuss ways to cut costs. Welcome their suggestions. Try to find ways of putting even relatively insignificant ideas to work—at least on a trial basis. And report the team's achievements frequently. Emphasize that good records are the result of the team's united effort, not your own bright ideas.

Of course, it goes without saying that certain decisions, such as those concerning work standards or quality specifications, may be beyond the group's control or even yours (see Figure 13-1). Consequently, you should make it clear at the start what areas and problems are off limits as far as group participation is concerned.

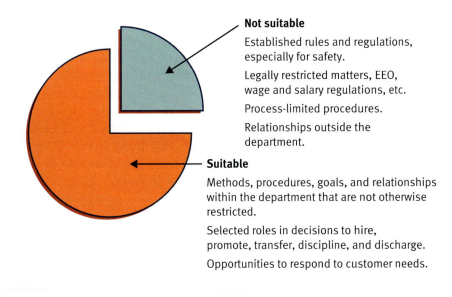

Not suitable

Established rules and regulations, especially for safety.

Legally restricted matters, EEO, wage and salary regulations, etc.

Process-limited procedures.

Relationships outside the department.

Suitable

Methods, procedures, goals, and relationships within the department that are not otherwise restricted.

Selected roles in decisions to hire, promote, transfer, discipline, and discharge.

Opportunities to respond to customer needs.

FIGURE 13-1

Areas suitable for and areas usually not suitable for participatory management methods.
What is the supervisor's role in the areas where participatory management methods are suitable?

What makes group participation so effective?

You've probably heard about many forms of participation, ranging from simple and time-honored methods such as suggestion systems to dramatic experiments with self-managing work teams. Both Japanese and European organizations have successfully introduced systems of consensus management, quality circles, and industrial democracy. Each of these programs has its advocates, and the results have been widely acclaimed. They all tap into two important phenomena—(a) widespread desire on the part of many employees to be more actively involved in their work organizations and (b) the predictable joint products of such participation, which are a *better quality* of decisions and *employee commitment* to carrying them out successfully. As a result, participative techniques have been very useful in developing harmony and attaining common goals in the organizations that have made a sincere effort to use these methods from top to bottom.

Participation is an amazingly simple way to inspire people. And its simplicity lies in its definition: "to share in common with others."

Sharing, then, is the secret. You must share knowledge and information with others to gain their cooperation. You must share your own experience so that employees will benefit from it. You must share the decision-making process itself so that employees can do some things the way they'd like to. And you must share credit for achievement.

How often can you expect group participation to work in your behalf?

Only as often as the group's perception of a situation leads the members logically or emotionally, or both, to the conclusion that their efforts

will pay off—for them. Self-interest is a powerful force! Keep in mind that merely permitting participation will not necessarily produce decisions similar to those you would have made—nor should it! And the larger the group, the more forces are at work in it that complicate the process.

There are two rules of thumb to guide you: (a) Without group support your chance of achievement is slim, and (b) your best chance for winning group support is to let the forces within the group itself work toward a decision with minimal interference from you. This isn't to say you must stand by helplessly while the group strikes off in the wrong direction or struggles to solve a problem while lacking appropriate skills. You can still apply sound direction by providing facts that might otherwise be overlooked; you can ask the group to weigh the pros and cons of various alternatives; and you can provide training so that the group members know how best to capitalize on the group process.

What are the keys to conducting successful group participation meetings?

The first is *preparation.* Select a good time and place to meet—one that will be convenient for most, as well as clean, comfortable, and free of distractions. Then decide exactly which people should attend, based on their interest, expertise, and availability. This is the time to create and distribute an agenda so that everyone invited will know the key issues—and their background—in advance. Arrange for refreshments, if appropriate.

The second key is *running the meeting in a fair and efficient manner.* Set a time limit so that the participants know the meeting won't drag on forever. Review the issue, its background, the importance of the problem, and ground rules for deciding (e.g., majority rule). Intervene if necessary to prevent tensions from escalating. And make sure everyone has the opportunity to be heard, while firmly limiting anyone who tries to dominate the process. Avoid reaching premature closure by consciously soliciting from the group the possible pitfalls and weaknesses of a proposal. Then check for the level of commitment to the solution.

The final key lies in *ending the meeting and preparing for future actions.* Stick to the time limit as closely as possible. Give credit to key individuals and the group as a whole for the roles they played. Summarize the major conclusions, and make specific assignments for further action. Try to end the meeting on a positive note. If possible, send out a brief summary of the agreed-upon decision to all who attended plus others who need to be informed. Finally, be sure to follow up to assure yourself that all actions are taken.

What is the major difference between a group and a team?

In one sense, a **group** is simply a collection of individuals. They may be located in the same area, they may hold similar job titles, they may have the same supervisor, they may aim for the same goals, they may interact occasionally to achieve them, and they may even refer to themselves as a team. But none of this guarantees that they *will* be a team.

Teams generally have a compelling common objective that pulls them together intensively to achieve it. They are so committed to success that they are willing to devote the extra energy—not only to the overarching goal, but also to the interpersonal processes—necessary to attain it. In short, they *work* on becoming more effective, and this often results in more open communication, occasional conflict, and higher levels of cohesiveness.

Group. Two or more people who are aware of one another and interact with one another.

Teams. Groups of people who must work together to achieve common goals.

3	T or F	Group participation generally produces both higher-quality decisions and higher commitment among employees to their success.
4	T or F	The key to running a successful meeting is to let the group members know what solution you want them to select.

QUICK TEST 2

Developing Cooperative Teams

3

CONCEPT
Supervisors can apply the methods and skills of organizational development to improve the operation of their work teams.

What are the signs that a group of workers is not acting as a team?

They're usually pretty obvious, if you're paying attention. A simple sign may be the absence of laughter and friendly banter among workers. You may overhear one employee bad-mouthing another one frequently, or you may notice increasing friction among factions. Individual efforts may be fragmented. Incidents of littering, graffiti, complaints, and insubordination may increase. When you ask an employee help out another one, you may hear a variety of excuses for not doing so. At the extreme, employees may request transfers out of your unit, while asserting that it is nothing you did that caused them to leave. All these are clues to low morale and the absence of teamwork, and they demand your attention.

Members of corporate teams need to know the goal, contribute their talents, and coordinate their efforts. **What unique challenges do they face?**

What are the indicators that teamwork is present?

The differences will be as clear as the contrast between the darkest night and the sunniest day. Workers will show up on time with a positive attitude most days. They'll volunteer for tasks, willingly tackle assignments, exhibit pride in their performance, and pitch in when others need help. The whole atmosphere will be different, with employees having fun and engaging in good-natured teasing. And perhaps most important, a sense of *community* will emerge, with co-workers genuinely caring about each other. As a result, the teamwork will pay off in terms of increased quality, efficiency, and morale.

What can supervisors do to create more effective work units?

Organizational development (OD). A set of values and assumptions about individuals, groups, organizations, and their environments that suggests they must embrace change and find ways to deal more effectively with each other.

They can apply some of the techniques of *organizational development (OD)*. OD is a set of approaches to creating and sustaining high-involvement, high-performance organizations and their subunits. It assumes that employees have much to offer, want to do so, and will grow and mature through various activities. It assumes that highly effective teams are essential to organizational success, while recognizing that teamwork does not develop overnight. Also, OD assumes that most organizations have been autocratically controlled, filled with detrimental conflict, and too rigid to respond to their dynamic environments. As a result, they *need* to change.

OD typically consists of a series of steps, as shown in Figure 13-2. A manager, often working with an OD consultant, makes an initial diagnosis that a problem exists. For example, employees may be confused about their roles, or priorities may conflict, or groups may be competing with each other. Then some perceptual data are collected to serve as a basis for understanding and discussion. The data are fed back to the interested parties so that they are forced to confront the issues. Action plans are developed and implemented, and after they have been given a chance to work, the results are evaluated.

A key feature of OD is its use of one or more forms of *interventions*, which are a variety of activities designed to make individuals, groups, or the entire organization more effective. Typical interventions include the following:

- **Process consultation**—helping *others* see their behavior more clearly by observing, asking probing questions, and confronting them with new information about their impact on others.
- **Feedback mechanisms**—collection of data and perceptions from others that are then provided to an individual or group, allowing the members to see *themselves* as others see them and take action on that data to improve.
- **Encounter groups**—unstructured small-group interactions, often with some degree of stress, designed to get participants to understand themselves and others more clearly and confront each other candidly and constructively.
- **Job design and strategic approaches**—a range of methods that may focus on job enrichment, Management by Objectives, career planning systems, or organizational transformations.

FIGURE 13-2
Typical steps in the OD process.
What assumption about employees underlies OD?

Interventions. A variety of activities designed to make individuals, groups, or the entire organization more effective.

What can you do to help a collection of individuals work as a team?

A popular OD intervention is known as ***team building***. In situations where employees must work closely with each other, share resources, and act to achieve overall goals, it is imperative that they become a team. Team-building interventions take many forms but generally involve an activity that encourages members to explore how they work together, identify the nature and intensity of their problems, and develop more effective ways of interacting with one another. Trust is often a key ingredient in effective teams, and members are encouraged to take risks, share

Team building. Activities designed to help group members develop more effective ways of problem solving and interacting with each other.

TABLE 13-2　Shared Leadership Roles in Groups and Teams

Task-Oriented	Relationship-Oriented
• Providing problem definition and goal clarity	• Soliciting and encouraging involvement
• Seeking and giving key information	• Harmonizing and compromising
• Using logic, creativity, and critical thinking	• Modeling trust, openness, and flexibility
• Clarifying and interpreting	• Building bridges of support
• Organizing the meeting and recording the results	• Modifying positions and admitting errors
• Testing for consensus	• Suggesting positive norms for the team

significant information with one another, and provide support and encouragement to other members.

A key part of team building is the process of getting team members to be aware of, and actively play, various *leadership roles.* These roles can be divided into two major types—task and relationship. Task roles emphasize the importance of getting a project done efficiently and achieving a collective goal. Relationship roles are oriented toward minimizing conflict and maintaining healthy interactions among the members of a team. Both sets of roles (see Table 13-2 for illustrations of each) are needed, and will produce huge payoffs for the team. Most significantly, not all of these roles need to be played by the supervisor, but can be *shared* among all the team members.

Can teams develop to the point where they don't need active supervisory leadership?

Self-managing team. A group of employees who perform most managerial activities themselves, thus dramatically changing the roles of a traditional supervisor.

Yes. When they do this, they become ***self-managing*** (self-directed or self-reliant) ***teams***. And the best ones produce productivity gains and cost savings ranging from 30 to 70 percent compared to traditional systems.

How are these self-managing teams different from others? They keep their own time records, analyze quality problems, assign jobs to each other, train team members, redesign production processes, set team goals, and analyze internal performance and quality results. Some teams maintain their own inventory control, adjust schedules, prepare annual budgets, and resolve internal conflicts. They elect their internal team leaders, administer competency tests to each other, and make selection decisions regarding the hiring or transfer of new members. They truly assume many "management" roles!

The results may include leaner staff units, fewer job classifications, lower absence and turnover rates, higher commitment and job satisfaction, and improved efficiency and customer service. These gains are possible only if employees are willing to learn multiple skills, substitute pay for knowledge for seniority-based compensation, and be perpetually in a learning mode. But supervisors must give up their traditional roles based on authority, giving directions, disciplining, appraising, and controlling resources. The new roles for a supervisor may include being a mentor, buffer, champion, counselor, and coach.

Virtual teams. What are they?

In most teams, the members interact in the same location. This allows them to see each other, read body language, and listen to the tone of another person's voice. *Virtual teams*, by contrast, may have their members scattered across the globe but still need to work interdependently for a shared purpose. Problems can emerge because the team members are drawn from different cultures, have no shared background, may speak different primary languages, and are on different time schedules. Because they cannot meet face to face frequently, they rely on technology to facilitate their communications and enhance their collaboration. Virtual teams create special challenges for supervisors, who need to define roles carefully, develop norms for communication, keep people on task, identify and resolve conflicts, and keep the focus on team goals.

Virtual team. A group of people who have a shared goal and must work together to achieve it despite being separated by space, time, or organizational boundaries.

Internet connection

www.businessballs.com/tuckmanforming
stormingnormingperforming.htm
For further discussion of the stages of group development, refer to this site.

Are there any predictable patterns in the evolution of a team?

Bruce Tuckman, a noted researcher, has found that most teams go through five key stages as they develop (see Figure 13-3). In the *forming stage*, members are concerned about their own "fit" with the group. Will they be accepted? Do they have adequate competence to make a contribution? And who are all these other people? In the *storming stage*, predictable conflicts arise as the group struggles to create an identity and develop a mode of operation. As they move toward the *norming stage*, members examine their goals and resources, and develop fairly explicit statements about their beliefs and values (e.g., what is and is not acceptable to the group). In the *performing stage*, members start to take risks, step into predictable roles, empower each other to change, and become action-oriented. Finally, most teams eventually disband (after achieving the goals, of course!) in the *adjourning stage*. Here, they engage in retrospective reviews to document and celebrate their accomplishments, record what they have learned, and relive what they have struggled through, as well as look to the future to see what lies ahead of them. Often the process begins anew as members are assigned to other teams.

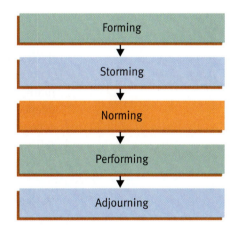

FIGURE 13-3
Typical stages in team development.
What might happen if a group tried to skip a developmental step?

The supervisor of a self-managing team faces many new challenges. While the team is developing its new skills, the supervisor must learn to embrace a broad set of new values. These values include recognition of the need for continual change, collaboration with others, open communications, shared power, and constructive confrontation. One of the new values lies in looking at conflict as both predictable in its emergence and potentially useful in bringing issues into the open.

4 Resolving Conflict in Groups

CONCEPT

A limited amount of conflict within or between groups is to be expected; intense or disruptive conflict, however, should be resolved without delay.

Is conflict in teams good or bad?

It's not necessarily either. It is natural for people to disagree, see things differently, and even complain about each other. Conflict results from disagreements about goals to achieve, values to embrace, definitions of problems and the relevance of facts, or methods for resolution. The thing to remember is that when many people work together under high-pressure conditions, *some conflict is inevitable.* However, conflict can be either constructive or destructive, depending on how a supervisor manages it, how much conflict exists (too little or too much), and how readily it can be set aside by the participants.

On the positive side, conflict can lead to stimulation and excitement, innovative ideas, and mutual benefits for both parties. Negative consequences include hard feelings if inappropriate comments are made, a perception that there are winners and losers, and even blind spots if people refuse to examine their own positions objectively. All parties need to develop better conflict-management skills if the team is to survive.

Where are the main sources of conflict in an organization?

There are many. People with different ideas about what should be done and how to do it are a common source. Departments that are sometimes at cross-purposes—such as production and maintenance, production control and sales, sales and credit, accounting and retailing, and purchasing

Employees with different personalities or contrasting goals may "butt heads" with each other. **How can a supervisor turn this conflict into a cooperative situation?**

and engineering—cause intergroup difficulties. But most of the causes of conflict in a supervisor's department are closely related to the work itself: how it is laid out and the way in which the supervisor manages the employees. In particular, a supervisor should be on guard against the following:

- **The appearance of an unfair allocation of equipment, materials, supplies, and other resources.** There is seldom enough of everything to go around equally. The supervisor must often make hard decisions about who will have what, how much, and when. When these decisions are made openly and fairly, employees are more likely to accept them without quarreling with one another. If allocations are made behind the scenes or on the basis of favoritism, trouble will brew.

- **Expressed disagreements about what is and is not important.** If these disagreements are the result of lack of information or misinformation, they should be cleared up right away. If the disagreements arise because individuals see things differently, the supervisor must try to get to the root of the problem. For example, one individual sets priority on output, the other on quality. The supervisor must find an answer to this question: Are these priorities (or goals)

Coming together is a beginning.

Keeping together is progress.

Working together is success.

Henry Ford

merely a reflection of each individual's values—or are they related to the department's established goals and standards?

- **Changes in work flow or conditions that imply a change in status.** If in the past Anita handled incoming orders before passing them on to Jack for posting, Anita may regard her work as more valued than Jack's. A change in the order of flow so that Jack handles the orders first may disturb Anita's sense of status. And she may begin finding fault with everything Jack does. Experienced workers tend to develop "territorial rights." Hence, they feel that they should resist outside forces such as a new supervisor, new employees, or any changes in which they have not participated.

- **A growing sense of mistrust among employees.** This is liable to occur when things in the department are generally going wrong. If business is bad, or if the department has been criticized for mistakes or low productivity, employees may look around for others on whom to place the blame. The production department, for example, will blame poor-quality products on the maintenance people, suggesting that the equipment was faulty. The floor salesperson may blame the cashier for a lost sale. The nurse may blame the nurse's aide for upset patients.

- **Lack of stability in departmental operations.** Change is so threatening to many people that they take out their fears and anxieties in quibbling and complaints. Many times, change is something beyond the supervisor's control. But as a supervisor, you can calm troubled waters simply by maintaining open channels of communication. You can, for example, alert employees to impending change and talk with them about the reasons for the change, how long it will last, and how it will affect—or not affect—normal operating conditions.

Internet connection

www.intractableconflict.org/m/competitive_cooperative_frames.jsp
Read about five major conflict-management styles on a continuum from competitive to cooperative.

How does competition differ from conflict?

Competition. A relatively healthy struggle among individuals or groups within an organization to excel in striving to meet mutually beneficial, rather than individual, goals.

Conflict. A disruptive clash of interests, objectives, or personalities between individuals, between individuals and groups, or between groups within an organization.

The former is usually productive; the latter is often counterproductive. The right kind of *competition* can stimulate a healthy, controlled discussion between two individuals. Informal contests allow employees to try to excel at meeting departmental goals that are mutually beneficial. When this is carried too far, however, the contestants may lose sight of the common good and become antagonistic. *Conflict* tends to pit individuals and groups against one another in trying to control the department's resources in pursuit of their own goals. For example, a salesperson may demand the major portion of the section's travel expenses because he perceives that his customers are the most important.

What's a good way to handle conflict in your department?

First, be alert to its potential or its presence. Next, seek out its causes. Then meet it head-on. A basic approach involves five steps:

1. **Decide what it is that you want to have accomplished.** Do you want peace and quiet at any price? Or do you want better quality? Greater productivity? A project finished on time? Fewer mistakes? An end to delays caused by quarrels between two software developers? Nothing will be resolved unless you make up your mind what the desired outcome should be.

2. **Call together the people who can best settle the issue.** If the conflict is strictly between you and an individual, limit the confrontation to the two of you. If others are involved, invite them to the discussion. If a disinterested party, such as someone from the quality control department, can shed light on the subject, ask for that person's participation. If a referee or someone who can speak authoritatively about the company's viewpoint is needed, get your boss into the act.

3. **Be ready to bargain; don't hand out edicts.** Conflicts are settled by negotiation. A short answer tends only to put off the problem, which will keep recurring. If you keep your eye on the objective you have set, there are usually many ways to attain it. Remember that each individual has an objective, too. If the maintenance department, for example, can provide the necessary repairs while still keeping its costs in line, and dependable repairs are your objective, let the maintenance people do it their way.

4. **Don't be distracted by personalities.** Whereas some people do rub one another the wrong way, most conflicts have a much more tangible basis. That's the value of keeping the eyes of all concerned on the main objective. It tends to push personality conflicts into the background. Finally, try not to get emotionally involved. Most important, don't choose sides.

5. **Focus attention on mutually beneficial outcomes.** Above all, don't make performance comparisons between individuals. This will only heighten competition and stress. Instead, hold up total organizational results as the criterion for success. If Kevin insists that Sharon takes up more than her share of the keyboard time, for example, try to reach a solution that makes the most effective use of the keyboard. That way, both Sharon and Kevin can contribute to departmental effectiveness, even though both may have to give in a little while doing so.

| 7 | T or F | Some conflict in teams is inevitable. |
| 8 | T or F | Competition always leads to disruptive conflict. |

QUICK TEST 4

Securing Cooperation

Thoughts*to*ponder

Conflict Issues
Many questions arise in considering conflict and the supervisor's role in managing it. Consider, for example, the following:

• What are the consequences of *avoiding* all conflict?

• What role do *perceptions* play in creating conflict?

• Are most conflicts about facts or about underlying *feelings*?

• Is compromise the same as *collaboration*?

• How can a supervisor best remain *nonjudgmental, supportive, problem-oriented, and sensitive to everyone's needs* in the face of conflict?

Transactional Analysis (TA). A way of improving relationships between people that is based on an understanding of each individual's (mature) attitudes and behavior toward one another.

Why do some people not cooperate?

For a very natural reason: They see no personal advantage in doing so. Is this a terrible attitude? Not at all.

Not one of us does anything for nothing. We do some things for money, others for lots of other reasons. Joe works well because he likes the feeling of being with a group of people. Jane works hard because she gets a sense of accomplishment from what she is doing. Louise puts in top effort because her job makes her feel important.

Hardly anyone works for money alone. We all expect different satisfactions in different proportions from our work. Therefore, don't be annoyed when a worker's attitude when asked to cooperate seems to say, "What's in it for me?" That's your signal to get busy and find a way of providing satisfaction for that person on the job.

How can your view of a relationship help build cooperation?

Transactional Analysis (TA) helps provide insights because it simplifies some of the apparently complex interactions that take place between people. This analysis maintains that there are four possible views of a relationship that can be held by the employee, the supervisor, or both:

1. **I'm not okay. You're not okay.** This is a negative view that implies an employee's dissatisfaction with her or his own behavior but also, in effect, says that the supervisor's actions are just as bad. It is somewhat like the attitude of a rebellious child quarreling with a parent. At work, it might arise when an employee accused of pilfering materials says that the boss does the same thing.

2. **I'm not okay. You're okay.** This is often the mark of a person who has lost self-respect or a person who places all the responsibility on the boss's shoulders. This person often feels unable to do the job without continual assistance from the supervisor. Supervisors should strive to get out from under this kind of dependence.

3. **I'm okay. You're not okay.** This is the parental kind of role that many supervisors traditionally displayed. Essentially it means treating the employee like a child. Such an attitude invites rebellion or loss of any hope the employee may have that the job can be done to the supervisor's satisfaction.

4. **I'm okay. You're okay.** This is the mature, or healthy, way to handle conflicts. It assumes that each individual has value and respects the other. Starting from a point of mutual respect, each person tries

to understand—without necessarily agreeing with—the other's point of view. The supervisor says to the employee: "I understand why you may think I'm taking advantage of your good nature, but listen to me long enough so that you understand my point of view. Once we're sure we understand one another, maybe we can come to some sort of agreement that gives you some satisfaction while making sure that the job gets done."

Any one of the first three approaches tends to drive people apart. The fourth approach, which encourages *positive stroking* (recognition and appreciation for employees), can be very effective if carried out honestly. It helps provide a solid basis for cooperation and compromise.

How do you best get cooperation from your associates?

The secret of getting along well with other supervisors is much the same as that of winning cooperation from your employees: *Find out what they want most from their work and then satisfy those desires.* With your peers, though, it's not so much a problem of providing satisfaction as it is of not blocking their goals and ambitions.

Face up to the fact that, to a degree, you and your associates are competing—for raises, promotions, praise, popularity, and a host of other things. If you compete too hard or compete unfairly, you won't win much cooperation from the other supervisors. And your chances of getting ahead depend on your ability to run your department in harmony with the departments that interface with yours.

Winning friends among other supervisors requires intelligent sacrifice. Occasionally you'll have to put aside your wish to make your department look good so that you don't make the supervisor of the next department look bad by comparison. Be willing to lend a hand when

JOB TIP!

Managing Conflicts

There are many useful skills that supervisors can use to help prevent and resolve interpersonal conflicts. These skills include the following:

- Observing unobtrusively to gather information and gain insights.
- Negotiating so that all parties feel that they "won" something.
- Stimulating deeper explorations of issues through effective questions.
- Facilitating new insights by providing feedback on behaviors.
- Encouraging others to accept uncertainty in their lives.
- Showing concern and empathy for people.
- Soliciting commitment to objectives.
- Coaching individuals to become more sensitive and skillful.

another supervisor falls behind, don't blame others for your own problems, and avoid hairsplitting when allocating interdepartmental charges and responsibilities.

Above all, let other supervisors run their own shows. Don't try to give orders in their departments or encourage disputes between your workers and theirs.

How can you get along with staff people?

Generally speaking, staff people in your organization are almost entirely dependent on the cooperation of you and other supervisors. And in this case, cooperation will breed cooperation. When you cooperate with staff people, their jobs are made infinitely easier. Their superiors judge them by their success in giving you assistance and by the degree to which you accept and act on their advice. When you cooperate with staff people, you're actually helping them get more satisfaction from their work. And you can be pretty sure that they'll go a long way toward helping you excel in *your* job.

What's the best way to avoid misunderstanding and gain willing cooperation?

The starting place is respect for other people's points of view, no matter how much they vary from your own. For a manager, this implies an appreciation of subordinates for what they really are. It's wishful thinking—and downright harmful—to measure someone against a mythical ideal such as the perfect person for the job.

Try to remind yourself that by definition you, as a supervisor, deal in other people's lives. An order to take any action in the company is interpreted all down the line in terms of its personal effects on people. And the effectiveness of the implementation of any order is a matter of approval or disapproval on the part of your subordinates and your associates.

Many managers never learn that their subordinates are constantly evaluating the manager's actions and varying their efforts accordingly. It's certainly the rare subordinate who will risk telling the boss when he or she is making mistakes, particularly if the boss isn't one who takes criticism willingly. Thus, many supervisors never get any critical feedback about themselves. Fortunately, if you can take the first step, you'll find yourself becoming a new and better kind of supervisor. You'll gain a new awareness that there are more consequences to any action involving people than those on the surface. And those consequences often interfere with productivity because people who are working on their own frustrations have less energy to devote to the job.

Of course, it isn't always possible to solve the human problems that can result from a necessary and unpleasant management action.

But sensitive supervisors enjoy two distinct advantages over their less sensitive counterparts:

1. An awareness of other people's needs aids in avoiding the unnecessary human problems that ordinarily seem to crop up each day.
2. A pattern of awareness of other people's needs in itself tends to blunt the edge of problems and conflicts that cannot be avoided because subordinates and associates know that the supervisor has tried.

| 9 | T or F | Gaining cooperation from others is usually a function of satisfying their desires. | **QUICK TEST 5** |
| 10 | T or F | Many supervisors are virtually starved for constructive feedback on their performance. | |

Practical Guidelines for Supervisors

1. Identify informal groups, recognize their underlying norms, and *solicit the cooperation of their leaders*.

2. Recognize the sensitivity of employees to "in" group and "out" group status, and strive to *minimize the perception that you show favoritism* to some employees.

3. Study how cohesive groups form and ascertain whether their norms are favorable to the organization; if they are, take action to *facilitate greater cohesiveness*.

4. Study the process and benefits of group participation, and *find ways to gain from the improved quality and acceptance of group decisions*.

5. *Commit yourself to conducting highly effective group meetings* by preparing for them, running them efficiently, and following up to be sure that the promised actions were taken.

6. Study the differences between a group and a team, and use a variety of measures to *determine (and improve) the level of teamwork your employees exhibit*.

7. Explain the significance of task-oriented and relationship-oriented roles to team members, and *encourage them to share the responsibility for playing those roles* in team meetings.

8. Accept the fact that new groups move through a series of stages of team development, and *help members understand the importance of the early stages* as they move toward high performance.

9. Face the fact that although some conflict is inevitable, *you can help it become either destructive or constructive* for the participants, depending on how you handle it.

10. Examine your attitude toward conflict; *consciously choose an "I'm okay—you're okay" perspective* in handling conflicts with your employees and staff.

Chapter 13 Review

Key Concepts to Remember

1. Group Dynamics. Since supervision is involved with organized human effort, group dynamics—group relationships—are present in every situation. Work groups may be either formal (established by management) or informal (spontaneously created by their members because of mutual interest). Because groups can exert a tremendous influence in work situations, supervisors must weigh the characteristics of a group's norms and behavior just as carefully as those of an individual.

2. Group Participation. With groups especially, the principle of participation presents an effective approach. By recognizing a group's ability to attain (or block) goals, a supervisor who invites participation encourages the group to direct its influence in a productive manner. While respecting the power, valued inputs, and legitimate interests of work groups, supervisors should not abandon management's responsibility to the group or relinquish their ultimate authority.

3. Developing Cooperative Teams. A new model of supervision is emerging, stressing collaboration, sharing of power, and open communication. These values can be demonstrated and instilled through the use of various organizational development (OD) intervention methods. Team building is a method that most supervisors can use to build trust and a cooperative spirit within their departments. Teams develop through a series of five stages, and some teams may be "self-managing" or even "virtual."

4. Resolving Conflict in Groups. Conflicts are natural in any organization. The supervisor's responsibilities are to try to understand the causes of conflicts and resolve them in a way that will contribute to meeting the objectives of the work group and the organization. Conflict is best resolved by focusing on mutually beneficial goals, seeking areas of compromise, examining facts and feelings, and keeping personality differences out of the discussion.

5. Securing Cooperation. Listening to an employee's point of view and the reasons for it can be one of the most effective ways for a supervisor to obtain cooperation. Transactional Analysis (TA) can be a useful tool for understanding different points of view and taking a positive perspective.

Reading Comprehension

1. Describe a situation in which you might be a part of both a formal group and an informal group at the same time.

2. Give an example of how a group's norms may differ from the standards of performance set by the company.

3. Why would an experienced supervisor encourage group participation in solving a work problem?

4. What are the primary benefits of allowing employees to be involved in decision making?

5. What areas of supervision are not usually appropriate for participatory management? Is it possible that more of those areas could be candidates for involvement?

6. What accounts for the current interest in OD?

7. Examine the new skills and values for a supervisor under conditions of self-managing teams and team building. How do they compare?

8. Distinguish between competition and conflict in an organization.

9. John and Mary are quarreling over who should have the use of a lift truck first while loading cartons into a truck for shipment.

What steps would you take to settle this dispute?

10. Can cooperation be forced on others? Why or why not?

Application

Self-Assessment

How Good Are Your Team and Conflict-Management Skills?

Read the following statements carefully. Circle the number on the response scale that most closely reflects the degree to which each statement describes you. Add up your total points and prepare a brief action plan for self-improvement. Be ready to report your score for tabulation across the entire group.

		Good Description									**Poor Description**
1. I am aware of the presence and power of informal groups in my organization.	10	9	8	7	6	5	4	3	2	1
2. I avoid doing the things that detract from work group cohesiveness, and practice the actions that contribute to it.	10	9	8	7	6	5	4	3	2	1
3. I can see multiple opportunities for work groups to be involved in participative decision making.	10	9	8	7	6	5	4	3	2	1
4. I consciously practice at least 10 of the text's ideas for running effective meetings.	10	9	8	7	6	5	4	3	2	1
5. I could identify at least three clues that a group is not functioning effectively as a team.	10	9	8	7	6	5	4	3	2	1
6. I could identify at least three indicators that a group is functioning effectively as a team.	10	9	8	7	6	5	4	3	2	1
7. I could feel comfortable with the new roles required of the supervisor of a self-managing team.	10	9	8	7	6	5	4	3	2	1
8. I can envision specific things I could do to help a team at each stage of its development process.	10	9	8	7	6	5	4	3	2	1

	Good Description									Poor Description
9. I am comfortable helping others resolve their interpersonal conflicts.	10	9	8	7	6	5	4	3	2	1
10. I actively seek to avoid creating perceptions that there is an "in" group and an "out" group.	10	9	8	7	6	5	4	3	2	1

Scoring and Interpretation

Scoring

Add up your total points for the 10 questions. Record that number here, and report it when it is requested. _____

Also, insert your score on the Personal Development Plan in the Appendix.

Interpretation

81 to 100 points. You seem to have a basic set of team and conflict management skills.

61 to 80 points. Take a close look at some of your team and conflict management skills (those with lower self-assessments) and discuss them with a manager to see if they need improvement.

Below 60 points. Some of your skills may be substantially inconsistent with effective team and conflict management practices and could be detrimental to your success as a supervisor.

Identify your three lowest scores, and write the question numbers here: _____, _____, _____.

Action

Write a brief paragraph detailing an action plan for how you might sharpen each of these skills. Then pay particularly close attention to the related material in the chapter as you review the relevant sections there.

Skill Development

Group Meeting Skills

Most organizations hold meetings, and sometimes it seems that supervisors spend the whole day in meetings! But supervisors also must conduct frequent meetings, and these meetings represent opportunities to demonstrate one's effectiveness at getting results while leaving the participants satisfied with their contributions. This requires the acquisition and development of some basic group meeting skills, as outlined in the chapter. When done well, these group leadership skills can produce very positive outcomes for both the participants and the organization.

Pair up with another person, who will be your observer. Identify a small group of individuals who are willing to attend a short meeting to discuss and decide on a key problem or issue (such as how to lower college tuition rates by 30 percent!). (To prepare yourself, you will likely wish to review the text's discussion on conducting group meetings, search the Internet for relevant guidelines, and consult with colleagues and staff persons in the human resources department for their advice.) When you are finished, ask the other person to rate you on a 10-point scale (1 = poor; 10 = great) and provide constructive feedback to you on each of the following dimensions:

1. Degree to which you created and shared an agenda in advance.
2. Degree to which you set a reasonable time limit for the meeting and then stuck to it.
3. Degree to which you reviewed the background and importance of the problem.
4. Degree to which you clearly established how decisions were to be made.
5. Degree to which you gave everyone the opportunity to be heard.
6. Degree to which you avoided reaching premature closure.
7. Degree to which you checked for the group's level of commitment to the decision.
8. Degree to which you successfully exhibited both task and relationship roles.
9. Degree to which you gave appropriate credit to individuals who contributed input.
10. Degree to which you summarized conclusions and ended on a positive note.

Action

Based on the feedback from your partner, make a list of the ways in which you can improve your meeting skills.

Role Play

Resolving Conflict

Form groups of three individuals, and assign one of the following roles to each person. Do *not* read each other's roles. When everyone is ready, hold a conversation among the three, with Amber playing the role of a mediator who is trying to help Bobbi and Carl reconcile their differences.

Amber. You are a mutual friend of Bobbi and Carl, who are two co-workers in your office. They have been squabbling for several days, and you have asked them to meet with you to iron things out. Before the session begins, you review the five suggestions for handling conflict presented in the text. You vow to yourself to give these principles an honest effort today, as your goal is to eliminate the conflict between Bobbi and Carl.

Bobbi. Sometimes, it seems, some of your co-workers just rub you the wrong way, and Carl is one of those persons. He's actually a pretty decent person, but he has some peculiar habits, too. Whenever he comes to your work area to chat about something, he always picks up your personal objects (such as family photos), examines them, and then sets them back down in a different position. And he's always rubbing your nose in the fact that he has more seniority than you do, even if it is by just a few weeks. You've also noticed that he spends a lot of time in the supervisor's office, and you assume that he is just "polishing the apple" to get on the good side of your boss. You really want to get along with him, but Carl can be pretty irritating sometimes. Amber—a mutual friend and co-worker—has asked you to meet with her and Carl today. You hope that Amber can get Carl to see things your way. You are about to meet with both of them now.

Carl. You have worked here for several years, and see yourself as one of the senior people in the department. As a matter of fact, you were hired several weeks before Bobbi came on board, and you like to tease her about it once in a while. Your supervisor also consults with you quite a bit to obtain your opinions and tap into your experience, and it gives a big boost to your ego to spend time in the "corner office." You hope, however, that others haven't noticed this, as it might be interpreted differently. Lately, you've noticed that Bobbi has acted irritably and even snapped at you as you chatted with her at her desk. You suspect that something is causing her to be stressed out, and speculate that it must be some kind of problem at home. Another co-worker, Amber, has commented on the shaky relationship between you and Bobbi and asked the two of you to meet today to iron things out. You agreed that a meeting was needed and are about to meet with both of them now.

Discussion Questions

1. What issues arose during the conversation?
2. What did both parties learn about the other that they were not aware of before?
3. Why did the conflict come about? How could it have been prevented?
4. What actions taken today by Amber were helpful in resolving the relationship? What else could Amber have done?
5. Will Bobbi and Carl get along better in the future, based on this conversation? Discuss.

Cases for Analysis

Case 40

Problems, Problems, Everywhere!

Addie's emotional state had gone from low to high in less than a week. Before she left for the workshop on "Organizational Development for Supervisors," she felt overwhelmed by the problems her employees seemed to cause for her. Every day it was something new, and there were issues including bickering, jealousy, scarce resources, and misunderstandings. At times, it seemed like a lost cause, and Addie wished she'd never accepted supervisory responsibility for her group.

Then, in just three days, Addie's hopes were lifted. She was introduced in the seminar to a wide range of OD interventions, and each of them seemed to have some merit. "Now," she thought as she flew home from the workshop, "if I could just figure out which one to use with each of my employees, I might make some progress."

Addie has identified the following five key problems and placed them in priority order. (She believes that Ahmad's problem requires immediate solution; the "retreat" issue can be confronted last.)

1. Ahmad's morale has been steadily sagging for months, and several symptoms of boredom and monotony have appeared. For example, she was absent three times in the last month alone. When asked for the cause, Ahmad blurted out, "I hate to keep doing the same reports over and over again each month!"

2. Addie's department consists of three sections, A, B, and C, each with about seven employees. The B section never gets into trouble, but people from the A and C sections always seem to be fighting with each other, and nobody seems to know why.

3. Frans has been a technical star—a real whiz at his job—but when it comes to interacting with others, he is a total bomb. Frans seems totally unaware of his impact on other employees, and it is beginning to affect their cooperation with him. As Marissa said, "Frans just doesn't get it, does he?"

4. The members of the B section get most of their work done on schedule, but problems seem to arise whenever the members have to communicate with each other. No one tells anyone else what he or she is doing or when he or she needs something until the last minute, and then tempers flare.

5. Once a year, Addie calls all members of sections A, B, and C together for a one-day "retreat," in which she attempts to share vital information, obtain ideas for improvements, and encourage empathy for problems in each other's sections. However, in each of the last two years, the meeting has deteriorated rapidly after the first hour. People go off on tangents, break into small cliques, ignore the speaker, and interrupt each other.

Analysis

Each of Addie's problems may lend itself to the application of at least one OD intervention. Of the following five possibilities, which one should she use first (with Ahmad)? Second? Rank them on a scale from 1 (immediate use) to 5 (delayed use for the "retreat" issue).

_____ **a.** Team building
_____ **b.** Process consultation
_____ **c.** Job enrichment
_____ **d.** Encounter group
_____ **e.** Feedback mechanisms

Case 41

Tell Them to Lay Off Me!

Deep in the Ozarks is a knitting mill that moved there from New England during the Great Depression of the mid-1930s. The mill has grown during the last decade, however. From being essentially a subcontracting facility, manufacturing its goods for large eastern apparel firms, the mill now operates independently. It produces its own line of sportswear under its own, well-known brand name. Its sales representatives call directly on major department stores and retail chains throughout the country. The mill, now known nationally as Linda Kay Fashions, could be considered a major success story.

Inside the home office at Linda Kay Fashions, however, a small drama is unfolding, with many of the aspects of a soap opera. Nevertheless, it is a very real situation to its participants.

Here is what is happening. In a group of seven Linda Kay employees who work as a team to receive, record, and process sales orders, Stella is the least productive. Typically, she takes the most time at coffee breaks and spends more time in the lounge than any of the other employees. Yesterday, she complained to the group's supervisor that others in the group were "petty and impossible."

"What makes you say that?" asked the supervisor.

"Because they continually harass me and pressure me for more production."

"Perhaps they are right about your production," said the supervisor.

"Right or wrong," said Stella, "tell them to lay off me. Who is running this department, anyway? You or them?"

Analysis

a. What do you think about Stella's complaint?
b. What is the problem here?
c. How should the supervisor handle it?

Case 42

Inviting Participation

Oprah is the newly appointed supervisor of the clients' records department of a large commercial service firm in California. She is to supervise 17 workers; nearly all of these employees have been with the company for some time and have established lasting friendships and informal groups. Oprah wants to invite the employees to participate in decision making at regular meetings she plans to hold. She wants to be sure to use good practices in conducting these meetings.

Analysis

Your assignment is to prepare a checklist of important ideas for Oprah to review before each meeting. These ideas should help Oprah achieve her goals of productive participation. Use the guidelines given in concepts 2, 3, and 5 in this chapter.

Factors That Encourage Participation

a. Extent of authority: _____
b. Information available: _____
c. Topic areas to cover: _____
d. Suggestions to make: _____
e. Teamwork to stress: _____
f. Credit to be given: _____
g. Other factors: _____
h. Other factors: _____
i. Other factors: _____

ANSWERS TO QUICK TESTS

Quick Test 1	Quick Test 2	Quick Test 3	Quick Test 4	Quick Test 5
1. F	3. T	5. F	7. T	9. T
2. T	4. F	6. T	8. F	10. T

Chapter Reference

1. Art Kleiner, "Are You In with the In Crowd?" *Harvard Business Review,* July 2003, pp. 86–91.

14

Control: Keeping People, Plans, and Programs on Track

LEARNING OBJECTIVES

After studying this chapter, you should be able to

- Understand the dual nature—judgmental as well as problem solving and decision making—of the supervisor's role in carrying out the control function.

- Define and recognize a control standard, and explain and evaluate the sources of those standards.

- Discuss the four steps of the control process, be alert to the dangers of overcontrol and undercontrol, and explain the three major types of controls.

- Identify the seven major areas of organizational control that guide supervisory actions and explain the technique of management by exception.

- Discuss employee resistance to controls, explain some of the ways to reduce it, and explain the relationship of Management by Objectives to the control process.

A Dual Role

Controls. The rules, regulations, standards, and specifications that enable a supervisor to measure performance against a department's goals and to determine causes and take corrective action when necessary.

What is the basic purpose of a supervisor's control function?

To keep things in line and make sure your actions hit their planned targets. In the restrictive sense, you use **controls** to make sure that employees are at work on time, materials aren't wasted or stolen, and persons don't exceed their authority. These controls tend to be the don'ts of an organization, the rules and regulations that set limits of acceptable behavior. In the more constructive sense, controls help guide you and your department to achieve your service or production goals and quality standards.

How much does control rely on the information system, and how much on the supervisor?

That depends. In a large, well-managed organization with performance information constantly available, the supervisor may play only a small part in the control system. That's the exception, however. Most supervisors are an integral part of the control system, and it won't function without their participation, informally as well as formally.

Day-to-day control means that most of the time supervisors should be on their feet—walking around—observing, listening, counting, taking nothing much for granted. In other words, the supervisor's desk is only a part-time workstation. Especially regarding clerical and customer contact work, much that goes on is not detailed by a master control system. There are daily and seasonal fluctuations in employee workloads, for example. Only an alert and observant supervisor can provide standards and enforce controls for these conditions.

What is control, and what are the supervisor's roles in the control process?

Control always begins with the establishment of some *standards*, which are advance expectations for something (e.g., quality of raw materials received). Next, actual conditions, activities, or results are *measured* to determine their real characteristics. In the critical third step, the measurements are *compared* to the standards to see if there is a significant difference between them that warrants action. In the fourth step, *corrective action* is taken (if necessary). These steps will be explained further in section 3. Now let's see how two supervisory roles relate to the major steps in the control process (see Table 14-1).

Supervisors fulfill two principal functions. In the first role, a supervisor acts somewhat like a *judge*, watching what happens in the department to see whether activities, conditions, and results are occurring as they are supposed to. In the second role, supervisors act as *problem solvers* and *decision makers*. They do this to find out why something is going (or has gone) wrong and then to decide what to do about it.

Even little problems need to be monitored to make sure they don't turn into big ones. **How are these firefighters engaging in the control process?**

TABLE 14-1	Roles* of the Supervisor in the Control Process		
	Stages of a Process		
Control Steps	**Inputs**	**Conversion**	**Outputs**
1. Standards set	P	P	P
2. Measurement	J	J	J
3. Comparison	J	J	J
4. Corrective action	P-S	P-S	P-S

*P = planning; J = judgmental; P-S = problem solving/decision making.

In their *judgmental role*, supervisors observe what is happening (or has happened) throughout the conversion process and then compare these observations (or measurements) with the standards for what was supposed to happen. These standards are derived from, or may be exactly the same as, the goals that were set during the planning process. Here are two examples of how the judgmental role is handled: In the first, a supervisor in a check-processing unit of a bank expects that all 10 operators will be at their stations within five minutes after the lunch break (a standard she has set for the operators). Now she observes that only eight operators are regularly at their stations when they should be. The supervisor knows that a standard condition is not being met; it is temporarily out of control. In the second example, an assembly supervisor in a video game factory has set a goal of completing 300 assemblies a day. At the end of one day, the production report tells her that only 255 games were assembled. The supervisor knows that her department is 45 assemblies below standard; production is temporarily out of control.

In their *problem-solving* and *decision-making role*, supervisors not only must find out why conditions or results are below standard but also must correct conditions and bring results up to expectations. Here's how the supervisors might handle the two control problems in the last paragraph: In the first case, the supervisor makes certain that the word processing equipment is in good operating order and that there is plenty of work available for all 10 operators. Then she speaks to the latecomers to find out if any extenuating circumstances are preventing them from being at their stations immediately after the lunch break. She then outlines the need for promptness and the penalties for being late. Finally, she continues to watch for late arrivals to keep this condition in line with her standard. In the second case, the assembly-line supervisor conducts a similar problem-solving search to find the cause of the missed standard. She might find a number of conditions: faulty assembly tools, shortages of parts, changed specifications, employee absences, lack of training, or failure of one or more employees to apply themselves to their work. Once the true cause has been identified, the supervisor decides what to do and takes the steps needed to correct the problem and bring the conditions and/or results back under control.

Controlling or coaching? Which orientation should be taken?

Increasingly today, the two are inseparable. Many employees view control as a negative thing, akin to criticism or scolding, regardless of how necessary it may be. They respond more positively to coaching, in which

Thoughts*to*ponder

Confronting Behavioral Deviations

Some employees, while meeting all their performance expectations, engage in behaviors that "drive their coworkers crazy," according to research by Mary J. Nestor. Examples include playing the radio too loudly, not refilling an empty coffeepot, borrowing supplies and not replacing them, spamming co-workers' e-mail systems, "cruising the office" to visit others and disrupting them, not returning messages promptly, and talking on cell phones for personal reasons. At a minimum, these actions are discourteous to others; in some cases, they also violate company policies (standards). How can alert supervisors use their knowledge of control systems to bring these employees back into line?

Source: Mary J. Nestor, "Top 10 Things That Drive Co-Workers Crazy," *Training and Development*, January 2001, pp. 58–59.

the control is offered in the form of constructive advice and suggestions for improvement. At AT&T, for instance, a spokesperson recently said, "While we haven't yet attained our goal of having managers and supervisors less control minded, we are working toward a redefinition of a leader from a controller to a coach." The trend seems clear: To be an effective controller, a supervisor should, as often as possible, approach control problems as a coach rather than a critic. Why? Because criticism looks backward, whereas coaching looks forward.

In what way are controls linked to plans?

Controls are directly related to the goals that are set during the planning process. In many instances, controls (or control standards) are actually goals that have been sharpened to make them more detailed and specific. Suppose, for example, you are the supervisor of the commercial office of a telephone company and your office has been given a goal of handling 2,000 service calls for the next month. For a month with 20 working days, that goal can be converted into a control standard of 100 service calls a day. If your office handles 100 calls a day, it has met the target and you need no corrective controls. If, however, your office handles fewer than 100 calls a day, it is performing below the control standard. If this persists, your office may not meet the goal planned for that month. You must take some sort of action to improve this performance, to "bring it into control."

Control Standards

2

What is a control standard?

CONCEPT
Effective controls are based on sound standards.

A control standard, usually called simply a **standard**, is a specific performance goal that a product, a service, a machine, an individual, or an organization is expected to meet. It is usually expressed numerically: a weight (14.00 ounces), a rate (200 units an hour), or a flat target (four rejects). The numbers may be expressed in any units, such as inches, gallons, dollars, or percentages.

Many companies also allow a little leeway from standard, called a **tolerance**. This implies that the performance will be considered to be in

Standard. The measure, criterion, or basis—usually expressed in numbers and/or other concrete terms—for judging performance of a product or service, machine, individual, or organizational unit.

Tolerance. The permissible deviation, or variance, from standard.

control if it falls within specified boundaries. A product, for instance, may be said to meet its 14.00-ounce standard weight if it weighs no less than 13.75 ounces or no more than 14.25 ounces. The control standard would be stated as 14 ounces, ± 0.25 ounce. The tolerance is the ± 0.25 ounce.

Where do control standards come from? Who sets them?

A great many standards are set by the organization itself. They may be set by the accounting department for costs or by the industrial engineering department for wage-incentive (or time) standards. They may be issued by the production-control department for schedule quantities or by the quality improvement people for inspection specifications. It is typical for control standards in large organizations to be set by staff specialists. In smaller companies, supervisors may set standards themselves. But even in large companies, the supervisor may have to take an overall, or department, standard and translate it into standards for each employee or task.

On what information are control standards based?

Standards are based on one, two, or all three of the following sources:

> **Past performance.** Historical records often provide the basis for controls. If your department has been able to process 150 orders with three clerks, this may be accepted as the standard. The weakness of this historical method is that it presumes that processing 150 orders represents good performance. Perhaps 200 would be a

better target. This might be especially true if improvements have recently been made in the equipment, layouts, or job design.

High hopes. In the absence of any other basis, some supervisors reach for the moon. They set unreasonably high standards for their employees to shoot for. Whereas it is a sound practice to set *challenging* goals, standards should always be *attainable* by employees who put forth a reasonable effort. Otherwise, workers will become discouraged, or will rebel, and won't try to meet them.

Systematic analysis. The best standards are set by systematically analyzing what a job entails. This way, the standard is based on careful observation and measurement, as with time studies. At the very least, standards should be based on a consideration of all the factors that affect attainment of the standard, such as equipment, training of the employee, absence of distractions, and clear-cut instructions and specifications.

The Control Process

3

How is the control process carried out?

The control process follows four sequential steps. The first step, setting performance standards, often takes place "off camera." That is, the standards may have been set before the supervisor arrives on the scene. Other times, it is up to the supervisor to set the necessary performance standards for his or her department. Steps 1, 2, 3, and 4 of the control process were outlined in Table 14-1. Following are the four process steps in order:

1. **Set performance standards.** Standards of quantity, quality, and time spell out (a) what is expected and (b) how much of a deviation can be tolerated if the person or process fails to come up to the mark. For example, the standard for a grocery store's checkout counter might be that no customer should have to wait in line more than five minutes. The standard could then be modified to state that if only 1 out of 10 customers had to wait more than five minutes,

no corrective action needs to be taken. The standard would be stated as "waiting time of less than five minutes per customer with a tolerance of 1 out of 10 who might have to wait longer." The guideline is that the more specific the standard, the better, especially when it can be stated with numbers as opposed to vague terms such as "good performance" and "minimum waiting time."

2. **Collect data to measure performance.** Accumulation of control data is so routine in most organizations that it is taken for granted. Every time a supervisor or an employee fills out a time card, reports on productivity, or files a receiving or inspection report, he or she is collecting control data. Whenever a sales ticket is filled out, a sale rung up on a cash register, or a shipping ticket prepared, control data is being recorded—often with a computer-related terminal. Of course, not all information is collected in written form. Much of what a good supervisor uses for control purposes is gathered by observation, by simply watching how well employees carry out their work.

3. **Compare results with standards.** From top manager to first-line supervisor, the control system flashes a warning if there is a substantial gap between what was expected (the standard) and what is taking place or has taken place (the result). If the results are within the tolerance limits, the supervisor's attention can be turned elsewhere. But if the process exceeds the tolerance limits—if the gap is too big—action is called for.

4. **Take corrective action.** You must first find the *cause* of the gap (called *variance*, or deviation from standard). Then you must take action to remove or minimize this cause. If shoppers are waiting too long in the store's checkout line, for example, the supervisor may see that there is an unusually high degree of shopping because of a holiday. One possible corrective action is to open another lane. If, however, the supervisor observes that the employees are taking extra-long coffee breaks, this practice will have to be stopped as soon as possible.

Variance. The gap, or deviation, between the actual performance and the standard, or expected performance.

JOB TIP!

Measure Performance

Many motivational experts have long argued, "The things that get rewarded are the things that get done"—and we agree. But we can also modify this statement to fit this chapter with equal validity: "The things that get *controlled* (measured and analyzed) are the things that get done."

Try to get better results by informing your employees of what you will be monitoring, and then follow through and actually measure their performance in those domains. You'll be surprised how a little bit of emphasis will pay off!

How much control should be applied to a process, and where?

There are two major dangers in designing and applying control systems. *Overcontrol* suggests that standards are too tight, that monitoring takes place too frequently, and that even trivial deviations receive major attention. This is equivalent to oversteering an automobile to avoid an obstacle in the road (and possibly causing a tragic accident as a result). *Undercontrol* is just the opposite; it implies that measurement and adjustment do not take place frequently enough (or in time) to prevent a serious situation from arising. Accordingly, supervisors should look for key places—make-or-break points—in their operations where control makes the most sense. These are often called **strategic control points** because measurement, comparison, and correction take place early enough in a process that the impact of an error does not reach significant proportions.

Strategic control points. Key places where it makes the most sense to measure performance and take corrective action.

The selective locale of observation points can also provide three distinct types of control opportunities. Refer to Table 14-1 as you read their explanations.

> **Preventive controls.** These take place at the input stage before the conversion process begins. Materials are inspected. Machinery undergoes examination and preventive maintenance. The proper kinds of employees are selected for each assignment and trained beforehand. By catching problems before they can affect later operations, preventive controls have the greatest potential for savings.

Preventive controls. Controls applied, primarily to an examination of resources, before the conversion process begins.

> **Concurrent controls.** These are controls that take place during the conversion phase of a supervisor's operations. In manufacturing and processing plants, pressures and temperatures are checked and online inspections are made as partially converted products flow through the process. In offices and retail shops, supervisors monitor output and the quality of employee performance during the workday. Concurrent controls make their biggest contribution by catching and correcting problems while there is still time to act.

Concurrent controls. Controls applied to conditions to be maintained and results to be obtained during the conversion process.

> **Corrective controls.** These controls take place at the output stage after an operation is completed, a product is finished, or a service is delivered. Such "final inspections" occur too late to do much good for what has already happened. Their value lies in alerting supervisors to ongoing performance problems to be avoided in the future.

Corrective controls. Controls applied, mainly to results related to products or services produced, after the conversion process has been completed.

To what extent is control automatic?

Feedback. The process of relaying the measurement of actual performance back to the individual or unit causing the performance so that action can be taken to correct, or narrow, the variance.

Increasingly, operating processes depend on automatic, or computer-driven, control systems. These systems try to minimize the human element. We expect *feedback* from a thermostat, for example, to tell the furnace to keep the room warm. In many automobiles, we expect a buzzer or a bell to let us know whether a seat belt is not fastened. Many processes in industry are controlled according to the same principle. A worker feeds a sheet of metal into a press, and the machine takes over. A clerk slips a sheet of paper into a copying machine, and the machine automatically reproduces the number of copies the clerk has dialed onto the control mechanism. There will be much more of this automatic control in the future.

Computer monitoring of employee performance is the latest phase in this trend. The computer, by sensing a terminal at which an employee works—or any mechanism related to an employee's output—automatically counts, times, and records an employee's performance. Such objective and continuous computer measurement, while viewed as a boon to management, arouses resentment in the minds of many employees because they feel they are being closely "watched." It also raises social issues that are under continuing debate and attacks from labor unions and others that believe the practice is an invasion of privacy.

4 Control Targets

CONCEPT
The primary targets of supervisory control are output, quality, time, materials, equipment, costs, and employee performance.

What specific kinds of organizational controls are most likely to apply to supervisory actions?

These controls depend largely on the nature of the organization in which the supervisor works. The following controls, however, are the most common:

Output controls. These relate to the demand of almost every organization for some standard of output or production. The quantity of production required is often the basis for all other aspects of control. In other words, a supervisor must first make sure that output quantities measure up. Then the supervisor's attention can turn to controls that specify a certain quality or time, for example.

Quality controls. If, in meeting the production standard, a department sacrifices the quality of its work, there will likely be trouble.

Quantity and quality go hand in hand. The inspection function is intended to make sure the final product or service lives up to its *specifications*, its quality standards. As a supplement to routine inspections, many companies practice *statistical quality control*, a way of predicting quality deviations in advance so that a supervisor can take corrective action before a product is spoiled.

Time controls. Almost every organization must also meet certain deadlines or live within time constraints. A product must be shipped on a certain date. A service must be performed on an agreed-on day. A project must be completed as scheduled. Such time standards point up the fact that it is not enough just to get the job done if it isn't also finished on time.

Material controls. These are related to both quality and quantity standards. A company may wish to limit the amount of raw or finished materials it keeps on hand; thus, it may exercise *inventory controls.* Or an apparel firm may wish to make sure that the maximum number of skirts is cut out of a bolt of cloth so that a minimum amount of cloth is wasted—*a material-yield standard.*

Equipment controls. These include those that the manufacturer builds into the machinery and also those that are imposed on the operator to protect the equipment or the process. The most common controls are for speed, pressure, temperature, and loads.

Cost controls. Another crunch in exercising controls involves costs. A supervisor may meet the quantity and quality standards, but if in so doing the department has been overstaffed or has been working overtime, it probably won't meet its cost standard.

Employee performance controls. These cover a wide spectrum and are often inseparable from all the controls discussed above. The difference is that employee performance controls focus on individuals or groups of employees themselves. Such controls may be concerned with employee absences, tardiness, and accidents as well as with performance directly related to the quantity or quality of the employees' work.

Where do budgets fit into this picture?

Many controls and control standards are often incorporated in a single control document—a budget. A ***budget*** is typically cost- or expense-related, since it is usually prepared by an accounting or finance department. The budget is not limited to cost items, however. It may also include allowable items for quantities of materials to be used and units of product or service to be produced, as well as any other quantifiable activity or condition an organization may wish to control.

Do supervisors spend all their time controlling?

It would appear that way. But through the use of a simple principle called management by exception, time taken by a supervisor for control activities can be held to a reasonable level. ***Management by exception*** is a form of delegation in which the supervisor lets things run as they are as long as they fall within prescribed (control) limits of performance. When they deviate from the limits, the supervisor steps in and takes corrective action.

Figure 14-1 shows how a supervisor can use the management by exception principle as a guideline for delegating much of the control work to subordinates.

Let's look at the example in Figure 14-1, a broiler chef in a fast-food restaurant. The supervisor says that the chef should expect to broil between 180 and 200 hamburgers an hour. This is control zone 1. As long as results fall within the prescribed limits, the chef is completely in charge.

If the requests for hamburgers, however, fall below 180 but above 150, the chef keeps the grill hot but puts fewer hamburgers into the ready

Management by exception.
A principle of control that enables a supervisor to delegate corrective action to a subordinate as long as the variances in performance are within specified ranges.

Did You Know

Make No Mistakes!

Some organizational control systems are set up to allow *no* errors, not just an acceptable number of errors. These firms—called *high-reliability organizations*—work hard to recognize and manage relatively unpredictable events that could destroy them. Examples include nuclear power plants, hospital emergency departments, and aircraft carriers. The key supervisory element is *mindfulness*—a kind of supersensitivity to extremely weak control signals that something might be wrong. Then the supervisor must react quickly to those deviations from standards.

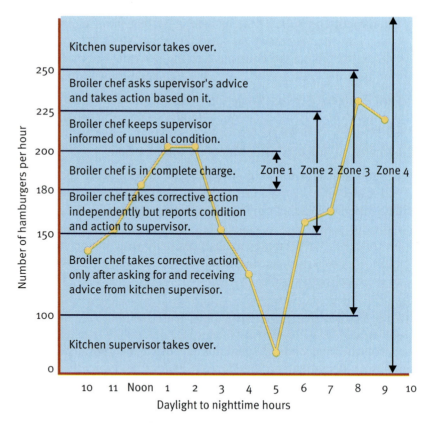

FIGURE 14-1

Use of a management by exception chart for controlling the operation of a hamburger grill.
How does this principle benefit both the kitchen supervisor and the broiler chef?

Zone 1: Expected or planned conditions.
Zone 2: Unusual but acceptable conditions.
Zone 3: Undesirable or highly unusual conditions.
Zone 4: Unacceptable conditions.

position; or, if requests build up to 225, the chef moves more hamburgers to the completed stage. This is zone 2. The chef takes this action without first checking with the supervisor but tells the supervisor what has been done.

If business falls below 150 but is more than 100 hamburgers an hour, the chef may ask the supervisor whether part of the grill can be turned off for a while; or, if the requests build up to 250 an hour, the chef may ask if one of the counter clerks can help. This is zone 3.

If conditions now move to either extreme—hamburger requests drop below 100 or exceed 250, the chef calls this to the supervisor's attention. This is zone 4. The supervisor may in the first instance (below 100) decide to shut down the grill, or in the second instance (above 250) decide to start up an auxiliary grill.

7	T or F	The first kind of control a supervisor should use relates to outputs.
8	T or F	In a management by exception system, supervisors only monitor and react to the very best levels of performance—those that are truly exceptional.

Handling Employee Resistance

5

The human element in the control process: How important is it?

It is probably the most critical element. Regardless of management's efforts to automate the control system, human activities remain the vital factors. Supervisors provide the eyes and ears for the system. They must continually find ways to make sure that employees meet (or exceed) job standards. Especially sensitive is performance relating to (a) attendance, (b) speed and care in feeding or servicing automatic operations, and (c) relationships with other departments and with customers or client organizations.

As was noted earlier, organizations are moving toward greater employee participation in decision making. As this occurs, it becomes essential that a supervisor—through observation—determine which employees can work with little supervision (or control) and which ones cannot. This should determine the degree of personal control a supervisor exerts in each particular case. It is a fact of life that many employees will resist control from their supervisors, yet willingly provide self-control on their own.

Airline pilots working in the cockpit of a sophisticated aircraft spend much of their time controlling.
What are the controls that they are likely to engage in?

What key characteristics of the control process are important to include?

We've already talked about a couple of these: acceptance by the people being controlled and identification of strategic control points. But there are several others that ideally should be considered, too. They include the following:

- **Timeliness.** Since controls are designed to identify problems in time for them to be fixed before too much damage is done, the best control systems provide key information to supervisors as soon as possible.
- **Accuracy.** In many processes there is little room for error, and therefore the data reported must be valid and trustworthy or the resulting actions could make matters worse.
- **Conciseness.** Too much information can overwhelm a supervisor. Usually, the best data are brief and easily understood, with additional information readily available if more analysis is necessary.
- **Beneficial in comparison to cost.** All controls cost money, directly or indirectly. Therefore, don't measure more often than necessary or you'll spend too much time controlling and not enough on the other important tasks that are facing you.

Two other features are also critical. The control process must be *understood* by the people (supervisors or employees) who use it. Without clear understanding, they will at best be confused by it, and possibly even resist it. The other feature relies on the element of *causality*. Simply put, this means that when things go awry, the user of a control system must be able to determine what caused the deviation and how to fix the problem. Without that feature, the control system only produces useless data that will frustrate the recipient.

How can you soften employee resistance to controls?

Many people do not like to be "controlled." They don't like to be told what to do, and they feel boxed in when faced with specific standards. Few persons like to be criticized or corrected. Yet that is what control often comes down to. When correction means discipline or termination (see Chapter 12), controls can seem very harsh indeed. For this reason, a supervisor should be realistic about controls. Controls can have a very negative effect on employees, to say nothing of what they may do to the supervisor.

The negative aspects of controls, however, can be minimized. Supervisors should consider the following more positive approaches.

Emphasize the value of controls to employees. Standards make it possible to provide employees with feedback that tells them whether they are doing well. Standards actually minimize the need for the supervisor to interfere and often allow an employee to choose a way to do the job as long as standards are met. It's like telling the employee, "You do the job, and I will stay out of your way."

Avoid arbitrary or punitive standards. Employees respond better to standards that can be justified by past records that support the standards. "Our records show that 150 a day is a standard that other workers have consistently met." Standards based on analysis, especially time studies, are even more acceptable. "Let's time this job for an hour or two so that we can be sure the standard is reasonable." Compare this with "We'll have to step up our production rate to 175 units each day."

Be specific: Use numbers if possible. Avoid such expressions as "improve quality" and "show us better attendance." Instead, use numbers that set specific targets, such as "fewer than two days' absence in the next six months" or "decrease your error rate from 7 out of 1,000 to 3 out of 1,000."

Aim for improvement rather than punishment. Capitalize on instances of missed standards to try to help employees learn how to improve their work. "Your output was below standard again last month. Perhaps you and I ought to start over to see what is preventing you from meeting standards. There may be something I haven't shown you about this particular operation."

Make the penalty for nonconformance absolutely clear. A supervisor must balance rewards with punishment. Most employees respond to positive motivation. Some do not. All employees, however, good and poor alike, want to know what the "or else" is about their jobs. The guiding rule is to hold off punishment if you can, but to make it clear to everyone that the most critical standards must be met. Specify in advance what the penalty will be for those who don't meet them—and when it will occur.

Avoid threats that you can't or won't back up. If you must discipline an employee for failing to meet a quota or a standard of quality, be specific about the nature and timing of the discipline. "If you don't get your production up to 150 a day by the first of April, I will recommend that you be laid off for good." Don't say, "If you don't shape up soon, your head will be in a noose." If you do make a specific threat, it is good to make certain in advance that the company will help you make it stick.

Be consistent in the application of controls. If you have set standards that apply to the work of several employees, it should go without saying that you will be expected to make *everyone* measure up to them. If you do feel that exceptions can be made, be prepared to defend that position. In the main, however, standards should be the same for everyone doing the same work. Similarly, rewards and punishment should be the same for all those who meet or fail to meet these standards.

Is it feasible to encourage self-control?

Self-control is beautiful for those who can exert it. Douglas McGregor, a notable pioneer in human relations research, insisted that many people need only be given the targets for their work—the standards. After that, he said, they wish to be left alone and to be judged on the basis of their results in meeting or not meeting those targets. Many employees will, McGregor said, provide their own control and do not need a supervisor to threaten them or cajole them into meeting standards.

Try to give an employee the benefit of the doubt. Give more freedom to those who demonstrate their job-related maturity. Keep the reins on those who soon show that they need, or expect, the control to come from the supervisor.

When do management goals become control standards?

Very often, as was shown when we discussed the link between planning and controlling. More specifically, however, many companies convert their organizational goals into control programs by using a system of Management by Objectives. ***Management by Objectives (MBO)*** is a participative planning and control process that provides managers at each organizational control point with a set of goals, or standards, to be attained. It is presumed that if all supervisors reach their goals, the organization will also reach its goals. In companies where MBO is practiced to its full extent, the supervisors' goals literally become the standards of performance that must be met. The assumption is that the supervisors are capable of finding, and will exert, their own controls in striving to meet these objectives. The MBO system also presumes that the supervisors have been given enough freedom of action to meet these goals with the allocated resources. In essence, MBO is simply a formalization at managerial levels of the principle of self-control. Typically, the goals in MBO are jointly set by the boss and the subordinate, with the subordinate taking the leading role.

Management by Objectives (MBO). A planning and control technique in which a supervisor and his or her immediate superior agree on goals to be attained and standards to be maintained.

9	T or F	There is little a supervisor can do to counteract employee resistance to controls.
10	T or F	Self-control is not always appropriate for all employees to engage in.

QUICK TEST 5

Practical Guidelines for Supervisors

1. *Accept the fact that control is a major part of the supervisor's job*—and it will probably consume more time and energy than planning or organizing may take.

2. *View your control responsibilities as being primarily a problem finder and a problem solver*; this will enhance your personal reputation while making your job challenging.

3. *Remind yourself that planning and controlling are inseparably linked*; plans provide goals and standards for you to aim at, while controls allow you to measure your success.

4. *Communicate your performance expectations (standards) to your employees in advance*; they not only will appreciate the information but will be better able to achieve the goals.

5. *Exercise control at the earliest possible time, when the payoffs are greatest*; focus on preventive controls, then concurrent ones, and—as a last resort—corrective controls.

6. *Don't limit your control efforts to one or a few areas*; find a balance among a variety of control areas (output, quality, time, materials, equipment, costs, etc.).

7. *Adopt the spirit and practice of management by exception*; *focus your attention on the few things that can make a real difference*—for better or for worse—in your department.

8. *Remember that controls can have many positive features* (e.g., timeliness, accuracy, conciseness, a favorable cost/benefit ratio), but unless they are *accepted* by employees, they will not work as well as you would like them to.

9. *Remember that the very word control may have a negative connotation for employees*; soften their resistance by *focusing on improvements and the resultant benefits to them.*

10. *Involve employees in the creation of goals and standards and their subsequent measurement and interpretation*; they are more likely to support the results of their own self-control efforts.

Chapter 14 Review

Key Concepts to Remember

1. A Dual Role. The control function is inseparably linked to planning, in that planning goals are converted to control standards. Good control requires that a supervisor keep continuous track of progress toward departmental goals so that corrective action can be taken as soon as possible. In exercising control, supervisors (a) apply judgment in determining whether deviations from standards are significant and (b) engage in problem solving and decision making when taking corrective action.

2. Control Standards. Good controls are based on reliable, attainable standards of performance. The best standards are those that are based on historical data, current information, and, especially, systematic analysis.

3. The Control Process. The control process entails four steps, usually taken in sequence: (a) setting standards, (b) measuring performance, (c) comparing performance with standards, and (d) taking corrective action. To avoid overcontrolling, supervisors should place controls selectively at key, make-or-break points in the process. Preventive controls are those exerted before the conversion process begins; concurrent controls take place while operations are under way; and corrective controls occur after the conversion process is completed.

4. Control Targets. The most frequently used organizational controls are targeted at output, quality, time, materials, costs or budgets, and employee performance. Supervisors must take advantage of the management by exception principle to delegate some of the decisions regarding corrective controls to qualified employees.

5. Handling Employee Resistance. Key characteristics of good control systems include acceptance, strategic control points, timeliness, accuracy, conciseness, cost-benefit, understanding, and causality. While employee resistance to controls is a natural human reaction, too much of it will disrupt the control system. Controls should (a) be fair, (b) be specific and numerical, (c) motivate rather than coerce, (d) be consistently applied, and (e) encourage the greatest degree of self-control possible. Management by Objectives (MBO) is a method of control that higher management sometimes extends to supervisors to give *them* an opportunity to exercise the greatest degree of self-discipline in controlling their own work.

Reading Comprehension

1. What is the ultimate purpose of the control process?

2. Explain the difference between a supervisor's judgmental role in organizational control and his or her problem-solving and decision-making role.

3. Which do you think is better: to overcontrol or to undercontrol a process?

4. Of the three chief ways of setting standards, which is the best? Why? What's likely to be wrong with the other two?

5. If a supervisor has been given the standards for her or his department, what three other steps in the control process will she or he still have to deal with?

6. Tammy relies mainly on checking merchandise just before it is shipped from her department. What kind of control is she relying on? What are the dangers in waiting until then to exercise control?

7. Briefly describe the seven areas of organizational control that warrant the most supervisory attention.

8. How are management by exception and control-standard tolerances related?

9. How should supervisors approach the issue of self-control for their employees?

10. What technique, involving self-control or self-discipline, is sometimes made available to supervisors for controlling their own performance?

Application

Self-Assessment

How Good Are Your Controlling Skills?

Read the following statements carefully. Circle the number on the response scale that most closely reflects the degree to which each statement describes you. Add up your total points and prepare a brief action plan for self-improvement. Be ready to report your score for tabulation across the entire group.

	Good Description									Poor Description
1. I feel equally comfortable playing either the judgmental role or the problem-solving role in the control process.	10	9	8	7	6	5	4	3	2	1
2. I consciously and systematically follow the four-step model of control.	10	9	8	7	6	5	4	3	2	1
3. I strive to emphasize coaching in my controlling actions.	10	9	8	7	6	5	4	3	2	1
4. I tell each employee what the desired standard is for each major task, and I make this as specific as possible.	10	9	8	7	6	5	4	3	2	1
5. I make sure that employees know how much tolerance is allowed around the standards I set.	10	9	8	7	6	5	4	3	2	1
6. I regularly check with my employees to make sure that I am neither undercontrolling nor overcontrolling them.	10	9	8	7	6	5	4	3	2	1
7. I do *not* place all my emphasis on corrective controls; I pay considerable attention to using preventive and concurrent controls also.	10	9	8	7	6	5	4	3	2	1

	Good Description	Poor Description
8. I make sure that my employees are involved in the control process by practicing management by exception with them.	10 9 8 7 6 5 4 3 2 1	
9. I carefully monitor my employees' resistance to controls and follow several of the guidelines to minimize their negative effects.	10 9 8 7 6 5 4 3 2 1	
10. I seek to make the control feedback I give timely, accurate, and concise.	10 9 8 7 6 5 4 3 2 1	

Scoring and Interpretation

Scoring

Add up your total points for the 10 questions. Record that number here, and report it when it is requested. _____

Also, insert your score on the Personal Development Plan in the Appendix.

Interpretation

81 to 100 points. You seem to have a basic set of controlling skills.

61 to 80 points. Take a close look at some of your controlling skills (those with lower self-assessments) and discuss them with a manager to see if they need improvement.

Below 60 points. Some of your skills may be substantially inconsistent with effective controlling practices and could be detrimental to your success as a supervisor.

Identify your three lowest scores, and write the question numbers here: _____, _____, _____.

Action

Write a brief paragraph detailing an action plan for how you might sharpen each of these skills. Then pay particularly close attention to the related material in the chapter as you review the relevant sections there.

Skill Development

Self-Control Skills

The opportunity—and the need—to engage in control is everywhere, both at work and in our personal lives. And since many of us tend to resist being controlled by others, we need to practice and demonstrate our self-control skills. When we can provide strong evidence of our capacity for self-control, others around us will see that they can practice management by exception with greater confidence. As a result, both parties will feel more comfortable.

Select an area of your life in which you would like to make a change. (This might include weight reduction, smoking cessation, cursing less, exercising more, etc.) Follow the control model's four steps, and lay out a plan for engaging in self-control that incorporates many of the guidelines for effective control. (To prepare yourself, you will likely wish to review the text's discussion on control, scan the Internet for relevant guidelines, and consult with colleagues and staff persons in the human resources department for their advice.)

Action

Invite another person to monitor your attempt at self-control across the next several weeks or months, and then rate you on a 10-point scale (1 = poor; 10 = great) on each of the following dimensions:

1. Degree to which you set a specific standard (goal) for yourself.
2. Degree to which you allowed exceptions for variation within control limits.
3. Degree to which you regularly measured your own behavior and progress.
4. Degree to which you reacted only to major deviations from the standard.
5. Degree to which you gave constructive feedback to yourself.
6. Degree to which you demonstrated both judging and problem-solving roles.
7. Degree to which you took responsibility for your success and failure.
8. Degree to which you stuck to the original standard despite possible setbacks.
9. Degree to which you gave yourself rewards for short-term progress.
10. Degree to which you demonstrated independent thought and action.

What does your overall score tell you about your capacity for self-control?

Role Play

Implementing Controls

Assume that you are part of a management team that is in charge of designing and implementing a control system. Your organization is just about to begin hiring employees who will apply their skills to the assembly of key components for a computer manufacturer. These components must conform to the customer's specifications for quality and performance.

Anne-Marie, the company's CEO, has asked two of the team members to take different sides of a "mini-debate" in order to raise all relevant issues before setting up a control system.

Tomas. You have been asked to argue for *more* and *tighter* controls. Pull together all the major arguments you can as to why this is appropriate and useful, and prepare to present them in front of your boss.

Vang. You have been asked to argue for *fewer* and *looser* controls. Pull together all the major arguments you can as to why this is appropriate and useful, and prepare to present them in front of your boss.

Anne-Marie. You will soon listen to two sets of arguments (one each from Tomas and Vang), designed to bring up key issues regarding the control system you will implement in the near future. Listen to both sides and be prepared to provide feedback to both presenters regarding the effectiveness of their arguments. Then lead a brief discussion in which the three of you reach a resolution regarding the degree of control to implement in your new assembly operations.

For Discussion

1. What arguments were raised on each side?
2. Which ones were the most important in deciding the outcome?
3. What makes this a difficult issue to resolve?
4. How might the final decision be different in a different company or industry?

Cases for Analysis

Case 43

The Overworked Copying Machine

Bill Blake was the first to admit it. Use of the copying machine at the Regional Water Board, where he was office manager, had gotten out of control. Employees were indiscriminately making copies of everything, not only of official documents but also of personal items. This put Bill's office way over its paper budget. Not unexpectedly, word came down from state headquarters to "get things under control."

Bill's first effort was to post a notice over the copying machine, reminding employees that the machine could be used only for official business. At the end of the month, however, the number of copies was as high as ever.

Bill fumed over this development. He called his employees together and read the riot act to them. "The next person I find using that machine to copy personal items will be suspended on the spot," he threatened. Only a day later, Bill saw two employees laughing as they came away from the copier. When he asked to see what they had been copying, they held out a dozen or so sheets of paper. They had been copying a slightly off-color limerick that someone in the office had typed. "Aw, Bill," one said, "we were just having a little fun. After all, what's a few sheets of paper to the government? Why, only last week, we ran off dozens of copies of a report that the state board later canceled."

"That's not the point," said Bill. "In the future, nothing personal goes on that copying machine. Do you hear me?"

"We hear you," said the employees.

At the end of the month, however, the situation had not improved, and so Bill decided to take firmer action. He posted a log sheet next to the copier. It instructed employees to record their names and the date, time, number of copies, and purpose each time the machine was used. "Anyone I find cheating on this new system *goes*!" Bill announced.

Two weeks later, Bill checked paper usage and found that the rate of consumption had dropped only a fraction. This month, the regional office would again exceed its budget.

That did it! Bill got the key to the copying machine and locked it. Next, he posted a sign over the machine that read: "From this time forward, anyone who wishes to use the copying machine must fill out a request form and present it to me. The individual will also show me exactly what has been run off when the key is returned."

With this measure, Bill thought he had gained control of the situation. However, Bill now found that he was interrupted several times a day to hand out the key and to check paper use when the key was returned.

Analysis

If you were Bill, which of the following actions would you select to attain a more effective form of control? Rank the alternatives on a scale from 1 (most preferable) to 5 (least preferable). You may add another alternative, if you wish. Be prepared to justify your ranking.

_____ **a.** Explain to state headquarters that it costs more to exert control over copier usage than the extra paper is worth.

_____ **b.** Post the monthly paper use next to the machine. Ask one employee to check each day's use and post the cumulative totals daily. Explain that when the budget total is reached, the machine will be inoperative until the beginning of the next month.

_____ c. Meet with employees to explain the budget and the resulting control problem. Ask for their ideas about control procedures that might work. Try to follow their suggestions.

_____ d. Call your employees together and tell them that the copy machine problem has gotten ridiculous. You have been too soft so far. You are going to unlock the machine and use the original log-sheet method. From now on, however, you will act on your threat to suspend anyone using the machine for personal items.

_____ e. By means of a log sheet, analyze use during the next month. On the basis of what you find, set up an allotment system for the various legitimate uses needed for official work. If there is too little paper in the budget, ask state headquarters to increase the paper allowance.

Case 44

Seven Situations Under Control

Supervisors are especially concerned with the seven areas, or types, of organizational control presented in the alphabetic list that follows the numbered list. The numbered list contains examples of control situations related to these areas.

Analysis

Your assignment is to match the correct organizational control (a–g) with each of the numbered situations (1–7). Next to each number on the list below, write the letter of the appropriate organizational control. (You may decide that some examples illustrate more than one type of organizational control. If this is the case, enter more than one letter for that numbered item, but be prepared to justify your choices.)

The Situations

_____ 1. At Metro City, the city purchasing director instructs the city's department supervisors that they should not order new supplies of computer paper until the supply level in their department drops below five boxes.

_____ 2. At Crystal Soft Drinks Co., the bottling supervisor sets a production quota of 5,000 bottles each day for the capping machine operator.

_____ 3. At the Seaside Warehouse, employees must "keyboard" into a data recorder the starting and ending times for each order pulled.

_____ 4. At JR's Chicken-in-the-Rough fast-food restaurant, the counter help has been told that the fried potato servings should weigh between eight and nine ounces each and should be discarded if the fries have been on the holding rack for more than a half hour.

_____ 5. At Handy Home Builders, construction workers who do not intend, for any reason, to report to work on a given day must notify the building-site office by 8:00 A.M.

_____ 6. At WMQQ, a local radio station, the station manager states as policy that travel expenses cannot exceed $500 per month for each news person.

_____ 7. At Western Utilities, power plant operators are advised to hold steam-turbine temperatures between 220 and 235 degrees F.

The Kinds of Organizational Control Exercised

a. Output, or quantity, controls
b. Quality controls
c. Time controls
d. Cost, or expense, controls
e. Material controls
f. Equipment controls
g. Employee performance controls

Case 45

The Wayward Bus Line

Things had gotten out of hand for Manuela M., the bus dispatching supervisor at the Hometown Transit Authority. Drivers were arriving late for their shifts. Buses were not running on time. There was an inordinate number of breakdowns on the road, which required that the maintenance department send out special buses to continue the route and to tow the disabled bus back to the dispatching shed. There were also frequent reports of buses not following their specified routes and skipping scheduled stops on their return trips. On the other hand, many drivers who started their trips on time returned to the garage late from their runs, with unsubstantiated excuses. Nevertheless, they still had to be paid the extra monies that their union contract guaranteed them. In a disturbing number of cases, too, a driver's cash receipts did not conform to the normal expectation of fare collections for a scheduled run.

Manuela had been puzzling for some time over what to do about this deteriorating performance, when the situation was brought to a head by a call from the transit commissioner. "The mayor and I have been receiving far too many complaints from bus riders this year. The complaints include just about everything, including the rudeness of our drivers, being deliberately passed by at a bus stop, and unreliable timetables. For my part, I've reviewed the expense reports for the last few months, and your department is way over budget, especially for overtime. Fare collections are down, too.

"I know that you can't be responsible for everything that's happened, but I do want you to come up with a plan that can put a stop to these irregularities."

"I'll do my best," said Manuela.

Analysis

1. What can you suggest in the way of control measures that would help Manuela correct these conditions? On a separate sheet of paper, write the following headings: (a) preventive controls, (b) concurrent controls, and (c) corrective controls. Under each heading, enter the problems or conditions in the case that might be solved best by the particular type of control. Then, for each problem or condition, write the ideas you have for correcting it.
2. Discuss the problems Manuela may encounter when instituting these controls and what she might do to overcome these problems.

ANSWERS TO QUICK TESTS	Quick Test 1	Quick Test 2	Quick Test 3	Quick Test 4	Quick Test 5
	1. T	3. F	5. F	7. T	9. F
	2. T	4. F	6. F	8. F	10. T

15

Stimulating Productivity and Quality

After studying this chapter, you should be able to

- Calculate productivity ratios and percentages, and know what factors contribute to rising or falling productivity rates.

- Understand and describe the various approaches to work measurement and improvement, including reengineering and value analysis.

- Explain the meaning of quality, and discuss a number of ways to carry out a supervisor's responsibility for quality improvement.

- Understand the concepts of statistical quality control, make use of frequency-distribution and quality control charts, and explain a reliability measure.

- Describe the main features of zero-defects, quality circle, and Total Quality Management programs and explain the value of participative approaches for solving quality problems.

Understanding Productivity

Productivity. The measure of efficiency that compares the value of outputs from an operation with the cost of the resources used.

What is productivity? How is it measured?

There are many definitions, and most of them are complex. Yet *productivity* is a very simple and vital concept. Technically, productivity is a measure of how efficient a person or work activity is; it is determined by comparing (a) the value of the output result with (b) the cost of the input resource. It is usually expressed as a ratio (or rate):

$$\text{Productivity} = \frac{\text{output}}{\text{input}}$$

Take a simple example. The productivity of a telephone salesperson might be stated as 10 sales completed per salesperson hour. That would yield a productivity rate of 10:1. A productivity rate can also be established by comparing the dollar costs of output and input. Suppose the dollar value of each sale averaged $25, for a total of $250. If the telephone salesperson is paid $10 per hour, then the financial productivity rate would be $250 divided by $10, or 25:1.

Once a productivity ratio has been established as a standard for a work activity, it is very helpful to compare current productivity with that standard. This comparison is usually expressed as a percentage increase or decrease. Take the preceding example of the 10:1 ratio. Suppose the salesperson increased this productivity ratio next year to 12 completed calls per hour, or 12:1. It would then be correct to state that productivity had improved by 20 percent. Here's how it is calculated:

New rate minus Old rate, divided by Old rate = Percent change
$$(12 - 10) \div 10 = 2 \div 10 = 0.20 = 20 \text{ percent}$$

Note that when one uses the dollar-based productivity rate, the productivity improvement comes to the same 20 percent. Here's how this is arrived at:

The value of the new output is 12 calls × $25, or $300, while the cost of the input remains the same $10 per hour. Hence, the new ratio is $300:$10 = 30:1. The comparison is calculated as before:

$$(30 - 25) \div 25 = 5 \div 25 = 0.20 = 20 \text{ percent}$$

What you'll hear most about productivity is not the standard or basic rate, but whether the actual level has improved or deteriorated.

How can supervisors tell how good their departmental productivity is?

Only by comparing it with the standard rate or an industry rate for the particular work activity, if either one is available, to see if yours is better or worse. Otherwise, you must base the judgment on a comparison of your current rate with a previous one. In most ongoing organizations, your productivity performance will be judged by whether it is rising or falling.

A simple concept should guide you here. Productivity will increase if the new number or value of the outputs increases *relative* to the new number or value of the inputs. When the reverse occurs, productivity will decrease. Said another way, if the size of your output goes up while the size of the input remains the same, productivity will increase. Conversely, if the size of your output goes down while the size of the input remains the same, productivity will decrease. This concept is illustrated in Figure 15-1.

Graphic display	Units	PRODUCTIVITY		
		Ratio	Movement	Percent change $\dfrac{\text{latest} - \text{original}}{\text{original}}$
	$\dfrac{10}{10}$	= 1.00 : 1	Original	
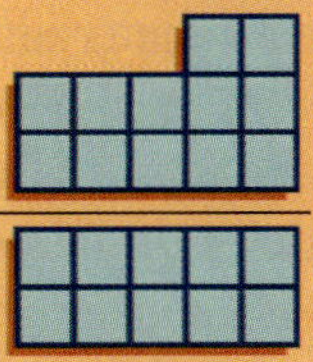	$\dfrac{12}{10}$	= 1.20 : 1	Increase	$\dfrac{1.20 - 1.00}{1.00} = +0.20 = +20\%$
	$\dfrac{10}{8}$	= 1.25 : 1	Increase	$\dfrac{1.25 - 1.00}{1.00} = +0.25 = +25\%$
	$\dfrac{8}{10}$	= 0.80 : 1	Decrease	$\dfrac{0.80 - 1.00}{1.00} = -0.20 = -20\%$

FIGURE 15-1

How productivity ratios are computed and interpreted. **How might supervisors use productivity measures when making decisions for their units or departments?**

Can productivity measurements be made anywhere?

Just about anywhere. It used to be thought that productivity was only a concern of the manufacturing industries. Today, productivity measures are applied to government work, educational and charitable institutions, hospitals, and almost every kind of service operation. A word processor's productivity, for example, would be measured by the number of lines or pages of copy keyboarded, or forms completed per hour worked. A supermarket checkout counter clerk's output would be the number of items checked (or dollars taken in) a day. A bank teller's productivity would be the number of transactions handled an hour, day, week, or month.

The main limit to the application of productivity is the need to obtain a valid and relevant measurement of output. It is difficult, for example, to measure the value of a nurse's output, although many hospitals talk about the number of patients tended by one nurse per shift as a measure of productivity.

Another factor to watch is the impact that quality demands have on productivity. If quality requirements are raised, the quantity of output may drop accordingly. Or, if product specifications are loosened, output may rise solely because of this change and not represent a real improvement in productivity.

What factors should supervisors focus on to obtain productivity improvements?

Quips & Quotes

You cannot mandate productivity; you must provide the tools to let people become their best.

Steve Jobs

Supervisors can work on two basic ingredients to improve productivity—technology factors and human factors. The technological factors usually include product or service design, facilities and equipment, automation, computer controls, robots, process layout and methods, better materials, more efficient power usage, and rapid access to job-related information. The relatively obvious human factors include ability, knowledge, motivation, education, experience, levels of aspiration, work schedules, training, organizational groupings, human resource policies, and pay practices. In addition, an easily overlooked factor is supervisory leadership and its role in contributing to employee job satisfaction.

What role does employee job satisfaction play in improving productivity?

It is the most important factor not yet fully exploited. In high-technology industries—such as petroleum refining—job satisfaction may be a smaller, though still vital, factor than technology. In most work, however, there is an ever-important need to place major emphasis on the role of job satisfaction. In the long run, people control the work pace. They can be devilishly clever in thwarting machines if their work-related attitudes are poor.

Supervisors must try to match jobs with each person's own kind of job satisfaction. Productivity gets its strongest boost from the human side when supervisors support employees in their individual search for job satisfaction. The trick, of course, is to balance employees' needs for satisfaction with the organization's need for productivity and cost control.

Methods Improvement

2

What does work measurement have to do with productivity improvement?

CONCEPT
The systematic way to increase productivity is to analyze, and then improve, the methods used for performing work.

It is the foundation stone of productivity improvement. Work—human effort especially—is the basic input in a great many processes. Unless you have a good idea of how much work is entailed, it is almost impossible to know where to look for productivity improvements or to tell whether you've accomplished anything when you're through. **Work measurement** is the term generally applied to any method of determining how long it would take an individual (or group of individuals) to perform a specific task.

Work measurement. The determination, by systematic and (ideally) precise methods, of the time dimension of a particular task.

TABLE 15-1   Example of Work-Sampling Study of Office Employees

Observation Sheet
Random Observation Times

	9:09	9:57	11:18	1:15	2:43	3:11	3:52	4:21	4:39
Chavez	7	8	1	1	3	5	6	3	1
Yost	2	1	6	4	1	3	7	6	2
Albers	7	4	5	1	8	1	1	3	8
Dowdy	7	8	7	4	1	1	2	1	8
Rozetti	4	1	2	5	7	5	1	4	1

Activity Category Code Numbers

1. Keyboarding	5. Away from desk, but in office
2. Copy machine	6. Telephoning
3. Attending meetings	7. Personal
4. Writing at desk	8. Not in office
Date: 7/21	Supervisor (Observer): F. Diehl

Summary of 990 Observations

Category	Number of Observations	Percentage of Observations
1. Keyboarding	487	49.2
2. Copy machine	23	2.3
3. Attending meetings	86	8.7
4. Writing at desk	71	7.2
5. Away from desk, but in office	36	3.6
6. Telephoning	68	6.9
7. Personal	113	11.4
8. Not in office	106	10.7

What are the main ways in which work is measured?

Historically, engineers made *time studies* of the actual job as it is performed. The crudest measures involve simply looking at past records that show how much an employee has produced in a day, week, or month.

The most elaborate approach uses tiny building blocks of time units based on *motion studies*. Experts add the time for every motion required on a job (lifting, pulling, straightening, etc.) to find the total time needed. The measuring units are called *predetermined elemental time standards.*

Work sampling is a simple approach to work measurement. It has some shortcomings, but it is especially suitable for supervisors who wish to get a quick idea of the productivity of their departments.

Work sampling is accomplished by making random observations of various activities in the work area (see Table 15-1). It enables a supervisor to find the proportion of delays and interruptions that occur in relation to the total time required to do a job.

Whatever work-measurement technique is used, the times that are found become time standards, or simply **standards**. These standards for various jobs are accumulated in a company's record files.

What is implied by the term *methods improvement*?

Any change in the way a task is performed so that it lowers the cost, shortens the time, or improves the quality of the product or service provided by the task is called a **methods improvement**. The *process* of methods improvement is simply the organized use of careful analysis and common sense to find better ways of doing work.

Methods improvement has many names and takes many forms. It may be known as work simplification, work study, time-and-motion study, operations analysis, methods engineering, systems engineering, methods and systems analysis (especially for clerical and service work), waste reduction, motion economy, or even quality circles.

Methods improvement has been applied by experts and novices alike to such diverse fields as construction, supermarkets, and endless paperwork systems in offices. While the methods-improvement process has many variations, it usually involves observing each minute segment of a job and then examining those segments for ways to do the job better as a whole.

Which elements of a work activity are more highly valued than others?

During a work activity, five distinct things can happen, but only one of them adds directly to the value of the product or service. The other four elements may be necessary, and are often costly, but they do not add value. See Figure 15-2(a). Here's how experts separate the "valued" element of a work activity from the nonproductive or "wasteful" ones.

The valued element. An *operation* occurs when the subject (object, person, or service) is changed in any of its physical characteristics, is assembled or disassembled or provided, or is arranged in a special way. An operation also occurs when a person is served or when information

Work sampling. A technique for finding out what proportion of employees' time is used productively on job assignments, compared with the proportion that is not.

Standard. The normal or expected time required to perform an operation or process or make a product, computed on the basis of past performance, estimates, or work measurement.

Methods improvement. Any of many systematic methods of work analysis aimed at finding simpler, faster, less physically demanding ways of accomplishing a given task while at the same time increasing productivity and reducing costs.

FIGURE 15-2

How to break down a work activity for analysis and improvement.
What is the primary difference between the valued element and the auxiliary element?

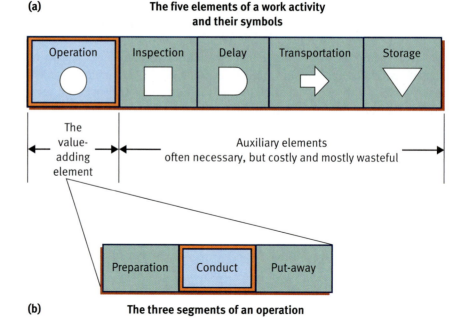

(a) **The five elements of a work activity and their symbols**

| Operation | Inspection | Delay | Transportation | Storage |

The value-adding element

Auxiliary elements often necessary, but costly and mostly wasteful

| Preparation | Conduct | Put-away |

(b) **The three segments of an operation**

is given, received, or processed. What really makes an operation unique is that it *does* something to improve and/or add value to the object. All other elements of a work activity add costs and are potentially wasteful, no matter how necessary they may at first appear.

The wasteful elements. These are the four troublesome auxiliary elements of a work activity:

1. **Inspection.** This occurs when an item is checked, verified, reviewed, or examined for quality—and nothing is done at that time to change it.
2. **Delay.** Also called *idle time*, this occurs to an object while it is waiting to be worked on, equipment that is available for work but is not operating for any reason, or a person who waits for materials, instructions, a customer, or available equipment.
3. **Transportation.** Also called *movement* or *transfer*, this occurs when an object is moved from one place to another, or a person moves from one place to another—not as the key operation, as with bus or plane travel—but solely to support another element in the work activity.
4. **Storage.** This is a special kind of delay, mostly purposeful, in which something remains in one place for a measurable amount of time. Typically, such storage is not a part of a regular process and occurs while an item is awaiting further action at a later date, often in a storage area, file cabinet, data bank, stockroom, or warehouse.

Where should you begin your attempt to improve methods?

The wasteful elements should get your attention first. Once each of them has been broken out of the pack as a separate element, examined, and improved, you can then concentrate on the value-adding operation.

How do you go about improving the value-adding operations?

Think of an operation as consisting of three distinct segments, as illustrated in Figure 15-2(b).

Preparation. This includes the effort and time that go into setting up the particular job, such as arranging equipment and materials beforehand. A painter, for instance, prepares to paint a house by mixing paint, raising the ladder, spreading the drop cloths, and so forth. A word processing employee turns on the computer, obtains and stacks the batch of reports to be keyboarded, and adjusts the copy holder.

Preparation, as necessary as it often is, adds no value to the product or service that is being produced by the job. It is a prime target for combining, reducing, or elimination.

Conduct. This is the segment of the operation that actually adds the value. The painter adds value to the house by applying the paint. The word processing employee adds value to the service by placing the data into the computer, where it will be automatically processed into a more useful format. A bank teller adds value to the checking operation by verifying the endorsement, stamping it with a new endorsement, and either exchanging it for cash or preparing a deposit slip. A machinist adds value to a piece of iron rod by cutting it into two-inch lengths for bolts.

Since the actual operations are the essential ones, they are hard to eliminate. They do, however, lend themselves to speeding up and simplifying or to combining with another operation. Furthermore, the great advantage of eliminating a conduct segment is that it simultaneously eliminates both the "preparation" and the "put-away" associated with it.

Put-away. This segment covers anything that's done after the operation is finished. It includes unloading, disposing, storage, transfer, and cleanup. The painter takes down the ladder, removes the drop cloth, cleans up spots on the floor, washes brushes, and stores material and equipment. In like manner, the word processor closes down the computer, puts a protective cover on it, and files away the completed and uncompleted source forms. And the bank teller, for each task, sets aside the canceled check and enters the transaction on a computer. The machinist, also after cutting the rod, sets aside the bolt for the next task operation.

The preparation and put-away segments are often the choicest targets for improvement. They are prime candidates for (a) elimination, (b) combination either with the task segment itself or with the preparation of the next task segment, or (c) for handling automatically, since these segments normally require the least skill and attention from human hands.

How can you develop new and better methods?

Uncovering delays and finding out what's wrong with a work activity or job operation are valuable accomplishments, and their worth shouldn't be minimized. But this effort doesn't pay off until you've devised a better way to perform the job. There are many approaches from which to choose.

Eliminate.   First look for the chance to drop out a part of or the entire operation. There's no point wasting time improving methods if the job doesn't have to be done at all.

Combine.   Doing two or more things at once saves time. Often it saves additional time by eliminating the transportation, storage, and inspection that previously took place between operations.

Change the sequence.   Frequently you can do things more easily or cheaply by changing the order in which they are done. For example, it is best to finish a part only after the shaping operations have been completed.

Simplify.   After you've followed the first three approaches in this list, look for ways of doing the job in a simpler manner. Here's where you try to cut down on wasted motions or replace hand operations with mechanical ones. But remember, don't try to simplify until you've first tried to eliminate, combine, or change the sequence.

In what ways does motion economy help improve productivity?

Motion economy is the use of the human body to produce results with the least physical and mental effort. It's been the subject of study by methods engineers and physiologists. Here are principles of motion economy that are generally agreed on as aids to getting a job done with the least labor:

- **Motions should be productive.** Every motion a person makes should be concentrated on actual operations that bring the job closer to a finish.
- **Motions should be simple.** The fewer parts of the body used, the better. Motions should be along curved paths rather than straight lines.
- **Motions should be rhythmic.** Arrange the work so that it's easy to do with smooth motions.
- **Make workers comfortable.** The work site, the keyboard, and the chair should all be arranged so that the operator feels comfortable, whether the work requires sitting or standing or walking.
- **Combine two or more tools.** It's quicker to reverse a tool with a working edge on either end than to pick up and lay down two separate tools.
- **Pre-position equipment and materials.** Have things arranged so that they are conveniently available for employees to use.
- **Limit stretching.** If an employee has to reach or stretch beyond the normal work area, turn around, bend, or stoop, it takes time and is fatiguing. *Ergonomics* is the name given to the study of how workers react to their physical environment. Its goal is to create more comfortable, and therefore more productive, workstations. In current terminology, workplaces should be ergonomically sound.

Who takes care of high-tech improvements?

The highly engineered and/or large-scale approaches to improving productivity are usually the responsibility of engineering specialists and computer systems people. *Automation*, once thought of as simply a form of stepped-up mechanization with a degree of self-control in the process, has exploded in some industries. In fact, hundreds of thousands of fully automatic devices, called *robots*, are already in place in hundreds of manufacturing plants. But it is the computer that has made the biggest difference. It has enabled engineers to look at an entire process—department-sized or even plant-sized—and tie the scheduling and operation of dozens of separate machines and subprocesses into a whole.

Similarly, *office automation* links together by means of computers any number of previously independent clerical and administrative activities. "Workflow automation" goes even further in that many such activities are programmed to be performed within the computer network itself. One unanticipated result is the shrinking not only of office staffs in some circumstances, but also of the work space allotted to the employees themselves.

Reengineering. A top-down, broad-based approach to improvement that can lead to sweeping changes in goals and methods throughout an organization.

On an even broader scale, *reengineering* is seen by some authorities as a major source of companywide methods improvement. The reengineering approach asks the same questions of the entire organization that improvement-oriented supervisors ask about work activities within a department:

Why are we doing this?

How can we do it better?

How can we achieve more with less?

The net effect is that the organization may redefine its purpose, its customers, and the very way a department functions.

Whatever the approach, whenever high-tech improvement takes place, supervisors should be alert to changes such as these:

- **Accelerated time frames.** That is, there will be shorter leadtimes for making changes, much faster-paced operations, and the need to provide quicker answers.
- **Less forgiving monitoring of output.** Control of a process won't be considered satisfactory unless the results are acceptable, too.
- **Closer coupling with outside forces.** The activities of an internal department are likely to be linked with customers and clients, suppliers, and distributors.

Overall, supervisors may or may not have an opportunity to participate in these high-tech decisions. One thing is certain, however: Supervisors are the ones who will be charged with making these improvements work. As a consequence, supervisors will be expected to ease the problems associated with workplace changes, counsel employees about relocations and displacements, and train them to handle the new systems.

Where does value analysis fit into this picture?

Value analysis (also called *value engineering*) is simply a productivity improvement that focuses on a product rather than on a process. It has another unique aspect in that it studies the value of the functions a product or service performs *from a customer's or client's point of view.* Functions for analysis are classified two ways, *use* and *esteem*:

- The *use* function provides the action that customers want from the product. An automobile's use function is to provide transportation. A hotel's use function is to provide lodging.
- The *esteem* function pleases a customer and stimulates the purchase. An auto's esteem function might be its styling and optional features such as a multidisc CD player or GPS guidance system. A hotel's esteem function might be its attractive lobby and the decor of its rooms.

The objective of value analysis is not only to retain the use and esteem functions that customers want, but also to provide them at a lower cost. As a consequence, value analysis focuses on (a) simplifying a product's design features and (b) minimizing the amount and cost of materials used in that product.

| 3 | T or F | Work-measurement methods typically result in time standards. |
| 4 | T or F | Productivity improvements are best sought through a focus on the inspection of a job. |

QUICK TEST 2

Quality and the Supervisor

3

What exactly is meant by quality?

Quality is a measure of the degree to which a process, product, or service conforms to the requirements that have been established for it. This means that quality is not merely a descriptive term; to have meaning, quality must be defined in highly specific terms. For example:

- "This product (a box of cereal) must conform to the requirement that it weigh no more than 16¼ ounces and no less than 16 ounces."
- "This service (recording of telephone sales orders) must conform to the requirement that *all* prices be exactly as they appear in the published catalog."

CONCEPT
Supervisors have a major responsibility for making an organization's quality assurance effort successful.

Quality. The measure of the degree to which a process, product, or service conforms to the requirements that have been established for it.

How do you differentiate among the many terms that are associated with quality?

Unfortunately, many quality-related terms have evolved without precise definition. It helps, however, to classify them as either conceptual terms or operational terms. The paragraphs that follow will clarify the generally accepted usage of some of the more important terms.

Conceptual terms include:

Quality control (QC) is the basic term. Unfortunately, its emphasis on control projects a narrow, negative, or corrective connotation. Its usage would benefit from the use of broader, more positive and preventive concepts of quality assurance and total quality performance.

Quips & Quotes

Today's highly competitive worldwide marketplace and advances in information technology have created greater customer demand for quality than ever before.

Armand and Donald Feigenbaum

TABLE 15-2 International Standards for Quality Management

The most widely accepted international standards for judging systems that organizations use to manage quality are the ISO 9000 and ISO 14000 series. These were set by the International Standards Organization of Geneva, Switzerland. The ISO 9000 standards serve to identify and certify a supplier's ability to meet a customer's product, service, and regulatory requirements. This is increasingly important for companies that participate in global markets. The ISO 14000 standards are concerned primarily with environmental management. This refers to what the organization does to minimize harmful effects on the environment caused by its activities, and to achieve continual improvement of its environmental performance.

To become certified, a company must pass an audit against the appropriate quality management standard. The 9000 series consists of four parts:

ISO 9000 is a guide to the selection and use of total quality management and quality assurance standards.

ISO 9001 is a standard for quality assurance in design and development, production, installation, and servicing of products. This is the most important standard.

ISO 9002 provides additional details on the standard for quality assurance in production and installation.

ISO 9003 elaborates on the assurance standards for final inspection and test activities.

The Malcolm Baldrige National Quality Awards, while having no direct connection with ISO 9000, recognize U.S. companies that excel in quality management and quality achievement. These awards are sponsored by the National Institute of Standards and Technology of the United States Chamber of Commerce and are administered by the American Society for Quality Control.

Quality assurance.
An approach to quality control that encompasses all the efforts made by an organization to ensure that its processes, products, and services conform to the requirements set for them.

Total Quality Management (TQM). An approach to quality control that focuses on customer satisfaction and embraces not only all the internal functions of an enterprise, but also external contributors.

Internet connection

http://www.quality.nist.gov/Improvement_Act.htm
Learn about the law establishing the Baldrige National Quality Award and its goals.

Quality assurance encompasses *all* the efforts made by an organization to ensure that its processes, products, and services conform to the requirements set for them. This concept has gained general acceptance, and companies around the world are likely to insist that their suppliers maintain active quality assurance programs. See Table 15-2 for an international standard for such programs.

Total Quality Management (TQM) is an even broader concept than quality assurance. TQM implies that all the constituents of an enterprise (suppliers and distributors as well as the internal members of the organization) must (a) accept responsibility for the quality of the goods and services that are linked to providing customer and client satisfaction, and (b) become involved in the process that produces them.

Return on Quality (ROQ) is a modification of TQM and is similar to value analysis (discussed earlier). It forgoes quality for quality's sake alone and focuses on providing only the degree of quality that a customer or client values highly and is willing to pay the price to obtain.

Operational terms include the following:

Acceptable Quality Level (AQL) is an expression of the limits of deviation from a specified quality characteristic of a product or service that is accepted as having met the quality requirement. A required dimension or characteristic of quality is called a *specification*. The allowable limits of a deviation from a specification are called the *tolerance*. Despite the practicality and wide use of AQL, many purists do not like the concept that underlies the term because it implies acceptance of less-than-perfect performance. In fact, many Japanese firms have adopted the *Taguchi Method*, which sets specifications with no tolerance. They believe that the presence of an AQL inevitably leads to faulty products and services. Worldwide, however, most organizations find the AQL approach to be effective. Any deviation in a product (or service) from its specified quality characteristics (or AQL) constitutes a *defect* or an error. The consequences of a defect or an error are that the product or service may either (a) require *rework* such as repair, adjustment, or repetition of all or part of the process that produced it, or (b) be classified as a *reject* to be discarded or destroyed.

Inspection is the process of examining a process, product, or service to determine whether it conforms to the established requirements and, if it does not, the extent of the deviation. Inspections can be made before, during, or after a product is finished or a service is delivered.

Nondestructive testing is an inspection that does not break, distort, or otherwise damage the product being made. A farmer who candles an egg is applying nondestructive testing. Industry techniques include X-rays, sound waves, temperature flow patterns, magnetic fields, and ultraviolet rays. Some of these techniques— such as ultrasound and CT scans—are widely used in the medical field to determine the internal conditions of the body without damaging the tissues.

How great is a supervisor's responsibility for quality assurance?

It is a very large, but shared, responsibility. First of all, it should be made clear that the attainment of quality does not reside in a single person or even a single department. Every activity of an organization contributes to, or detracts from, the quality of its products or services. These activities include, especially, such functional departments as product design, methods engineering, purchasing, and maintenance and repair.

Many foreign auto manufacturers have historically produced very high-quality vehicles, such as this British-built 1980 MGB. **What is the secret to their success?**

Return on Quality (ROQ). A modification of TQM in that it focuses on providing only the degree of quality that a customer or client values highly and is willing to pay the price to obtain.

Acceptable Quality Level (AQL). A general form of specification that tells a supervisor the kind of tolerance limiting that will be judged as acceptable performance.

Specification. The definitions of expected performance of a product (or quality of a service).

Tolerance. A statement of precision that establishes limits within which the product or the service must meet the specification.

Defect. Any variation (in the product or service) from specifications that falls outside the prescribed tolerances.

Reject. A product that needs to be discarded or destroyed.

The functions that receive the greatest amount of heat, however, are (a) the inspection and quality control departments and (b) the supervisor's own operations. Inspection and QC are expected to catch errors and defective work before they leave the department. Supervisors are expected to make certain that the errors and defects do not occur in the first place.

There is a long-standing guideline that should govern any supervisor's approach to the responsibility for quality: *Quality must be built into the product. No one can inspect it in.*

Why do employees make errors?

Generally speaking, employees make mistakes for six reasons—and most begin with *management* inadequacies rather than with employee shortcomings. The experience of companies that have improved their productivity and quality shows the following potential causes of errors:

- Lack of training
- Poor communication
- Inadequate tools and equipment
- Insufficient planning
- Incomplete specifications and procedures
- Lack of attention or concern

In what ways does poor quality add to costs?

Poor quality costs industry billions of dollars each year. It is most obvious in the form of product liability suits (a million claims for a total of $50 billion in damages in a year is not unusual) and manufacturers' recalls to repair defective goods. Billions of dollars are lost to poor quality, however, in two other ways.

Corrective costs.   These costs include money down the drain for any of the following: (a) damaged parts and materials that must be scrapped or, at best, reworked; (b) the time and effort of redoing poor work; (c) the cost of warranties that presume errors will be made that must be corrected later; and (d) the cost of handling customer complaints. Corrective quality is by far the most costly approach to quality problems.

Preventive costs.   These are the costs of trying to prevent poor workmanship or defective goods in the first place. They include routine (a) inspection, (b) testing, and (c) quality control procedures, including education and motivation programs. Obviously, prevention is less costly than cure.

How can you make your own checks of quality?

Keep in mind these 10 points:

1. Set up specific quality standards, such as dimensions and appearance. Keeping examples of acceptable and nonacceptable work on exhibit helps.
2. Put quality specifications or standards in writing. See that your employees get a copy to guide them.
3. Allocate some of your own time for inspection. The total amount isn't as important as doing a certain amount each day.
4. Pick the spots where quality can best be made or lost. There is no point spending time checking operations where nothing much can go wrong.
5. Make inspection rounds from time to time. Change the order of your trips frequently.
6. Select at random 5 or 10 percent of the output produced (for example, letters typed) at a particular station. Inspect each one carefully.
7. Correct operating conditions immediately when your inspection shows material to be problematic or equipment to be faulty.
8. Consult with employees to determine the reason for poor workmanship or unacceptable products. Seek their cooperation in correcting conditions and improving quality.
9. Check the first piece on a new production run or a new assignment. Don't permit production to proceed until you are satisfied with the quality.
10. Post quality records, scrap percentages, and so forth, to keep employees informed of the department's performance.

5	T or F	Quality control and quality assurance mean basically the same thing.
6	T or F	The responsibility for quality basically resides in a single department assigned those duties.

QUICK TEST 3

Statistical Quality Control

4

What is meant by statistical quality control?

Statistical Quality Control (SQC) simply means that numbers—statistics—are used as a part of the overall approach to controlling quality. Statistics are tools and in no way relieve supervisors or employees of concern with quality. Used properly, however, statistics can be of considerable aid.

CONCEPT

Statistical quality control makes valuable use of mathematical techniques for monitoring and controlling the quality of processes, products, and services.

In many industries, it is only the techniques of SQC that make rigid specifications economically attainable. For example, JC Penney Co., Inc., orders millions of knitted garments each year. It uses various inspection and statistical methods to screen the thousands of samples submitted to the company for purchase. As a consequence, the company often rejects 30 percent of the submissions, thus preventing subsequent disasters at the sales counters.

In Japan, the practice of SQC is so widespread that a great many employees, including truck drivers and workers of all kinds, prepare and maintain their own quality control charts.

What are some of the tools of Statistical Quality Control, and how do they affect the supervisor's job?

Greatly increased demands for precision parts have increased the need for better methods to measure and record the accuracy with which manufacturing people meet product specifications. Statistical methods speed up this measuring process, and many companies in all kinds of industries use them in some form.

Three statistical quality control tools are most commonly encountered:

1. **Frequency-distribution chart.** Hold on. It isn't as bad as it sounds. Probably you'll recognize it by its more popular name—a tally card. If you were asked to place an X in the appropriate space for every shaft diameter you measured in a certain sample of parts, chances are that you'd come up with a tally that looks something like Figure 15-3.

   In this case, the expected shaft diameter was 0.730 inch with a tolerance of ±0.002. This tally gives you a picture of just what and where the shaft variations are instead of merely recording whether a

FIGURE 15-3

A simple frequency-distribution chart (histogram) used in statistical quality control.
What is its purpose?

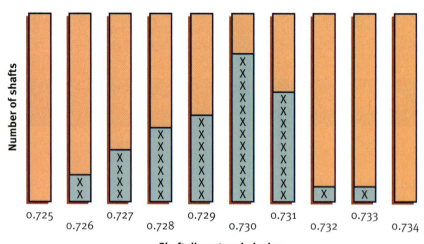

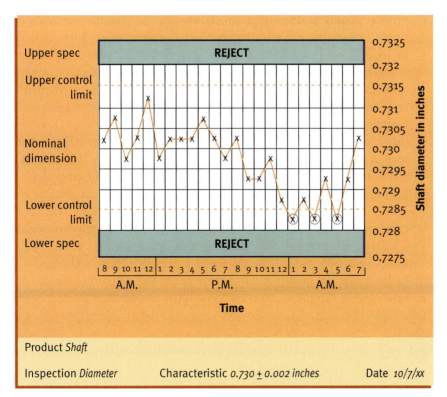

FIGURE 15-4

A quality control chart.
What does it mean to be "on the highway"?

shaft is good or bad. This frequency-distribution chart (or histogram) helps tell you the extent of the variation. The wide distribution in this case indicates a problem and suggests that the setup must be adjusted.

2. **Quality-control chart.** This is an hour-by-hour, day-by-day graphic comparison of actual product quality characteristics. On the chart are limits that reflect the person's or the machine's ability to produce, as shown by past experience. Statisticians make use of their knowledge of shop tolerances and analysis of previous frequency distribution tallies to establish these limits. Whenever the inspections plotted on the control chart show that the product is going outside the predicted control limits, that's a signal for the supervisor or the operator to correct what is being done so that the product can be brought back into specification.

   In Figure 15-4 the part being made is supposed to measure 0.730 inch. The tolerance is ±0.002, or from 0.728 to 0.732 inch. The quality control statistician has predicted in advance from a frequency-distribution diagram that most production will vary within these control limits—the 0.7285 and 0.7315 lines. When quality stays within these limits, it is said to be "on the highway." It is to be expected that a few products will fall outside the limits, into the "shoulder." But when the trend of measurements indicates that product quality is drifting progressively into the shoulder area, it's time to check the process. Any product that goes beyond the upper or lower specification limits (goes "into the ditch") is rejected.

The value of the chart lies in its visual ability to tell the supervisor and the operator whether they are within bounds or whether they are losing control of the process, before the process goes completely haywire.

3. **Sampling tables.** The trend today has been away from 100 percent inspection, which is costly and often misleading. (In a 100 percent check of a load of oranges, this might mean that each orange has been inspected for color, ripeness, thickness of skin, and appearance.) The first solution to less than 100 percent checking was spot checking, but this proved unreliable. Today, most sampling is done according to the size of the lot of goods produced and according to tables designed by statisticians for this purpose. These sampling tables guide the quality-control manager in the determination of how large a sample to take and how often to take it.

Is there a connection between reliability and Statistical Quality Control?

Reliability. A measure (usually a statistical estimate) of the probability of a product's performing specific functions, under given conditions, for a specified time without failure.

Yes, indirectly, and it often has a direct relationship to product liability claims. *Reliability* is defined as the probability of a product's performing a specific function, under given conditions, for a specified time without failure. It must measure up specifically, therefore, to (a) what it's supposed to do (such as, for a bolt, hold 500 pounds of direct pull); (b) the circumstances under which it will be used (such as temperatures up to 185°C in an acid atmosphere); and (c) the length of time it should perform before it breaks or stops working (such as 25,000 fastenings or 39 months). Reliability can be determined either by direct test (using the product until it fails) or by statistical computation (based on assumptions about the design and work characteristics of the product). Reliability is usually expressed as the (mean) time expected between failures, for example, 500 hours.

Because the assumptions made vary in terms of the degree of confidence the estimator has in them, reliability figures are often qualified as having, say, 85 percent confidence (being 85 percent sure to last as long as predicted, with a 15 percent risk of not lasting that long).

Reliability enters Statistical Quality Control considerations when you are deciding on the tolerance limits of variation, on how far from standard the product can be without being rejected. Obviously, the tighter the variable limits, the greater the reliability of the product. However, this does not mean that a perfect part will be reliable forever. It will be reliable only as long as it was designed to be under the specified operating conditions.

7	T or F	Statistical Quality Control is too complex for all but the most sophisticated experts to use.
8	T or F	Quality control charts rely on previously set tolerances to indicate when a system is in or out of control.

Toward Total Quality Management

5

CONCEPT

The ultimate in quality achievement depends on complete commitment and maximum participation by the entire organization.

Commitment to quality? How inclusive must it be?

When it comes to succeeding with quality, commitment must involve every member of an organization, as well as constituents outside the enterprise. Originally, it was thought that a good inspection team was all that was needed to ensure acceptable quality. Then, with the introduction of the zero-defects approach, commitment from top to bottom became the guideline. Broad commitment led to participation at all levels, together with deep involvement by the workforce. Gradually there emerged the belief that customer satisfaction must be drawn into the quality planning, as well as a commitment from suppliers and distributors. This principle formed the basis for Total Quality Management (TQM). And TQM is now being fine-tuned by the idea of benchmarking, as explained later in this section. Figure 15-5 illustrates this evolution.

What is the zero-defects program, and why did it work so well?

Philip Crosby, a quality control expert intimately involved with the NASA space program and later corporate vice president for quality for ITT Corporation, removed the emphasis on Statistical Quality Control and expert inspectors and placed the responsibility for quality in the hands of the employees. *Zero defects (ZD)* stressed personal motivation. It attempted to instill in each individual a pride in his or her work. It was the first quality program to put quality on a personal basis. ZD techniques were aimed at stimulating everyone involved to care about accuracy and completeness, pay attention to details, and improve work habits. In this manner, everyone worked toward reducing his or her own errors to zero.

Zero-defects techniques got great results for three good reasons:

1. **The quality standard was very explicit: Do it the right way from the start.** As Philip Crosby said, "What standard would you

Ethical Perspectives

Taking Credit

Indira Gandhi said, "There are two kinds of people, those who do the work and those who take credit. Try to be in the first group; there is less competition there." What do you think of employees who reach their goals at the expense of others? Is this ethical?

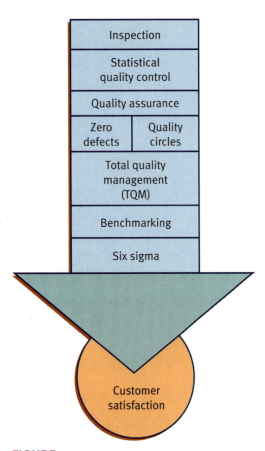

FIGURE 15-5

The evolution of quality management techniques.
What is the primary target of quality management?

set on how many babies a nurse should be allowed to drop?"

2. **There was complete commitment by everyone.** From sweeper to top executive, from production worker to clerical employee, everyone was encouraged to spot problems, detect errors, and prescribe ways and means for their removal.

3. **Action was taken immediately to change behavior and remove conditions that cause errors.** Crosby maintained that 90 percent of all causes of errors could be acted on and fully removed by first-line supervisors. In other words, top management had to do its part to improve conditions, but supervisors and employees could handle most problems at the operating level.

If ZD was so good, what caused all the excitement about quality circles?

If you agree with the participative aspect of ZD, you'll probably agree that the quality circle movement is the next logical step forward. Both programs are based on the belief that quality cannot be produced or controlled by a single individual or department. Both programs conceive of quality as the result of dozens, perhaps hundreds, of interactions. These interactions take place between the designer and the manufacturing department, between manufacturing and purchasing, between sales and production, between the data-entry operator and the computer programmer, and so on. Quality is the end result of a complex system. The quality circle concept accepts quality as a starting point (as with ZD) and *then* concludes that only by bringing together the people who are directly involved in the system will the obstacles that block good quality and error-free performance be removed.

Quality circles were conceived of by an American statistician, W. Edwards Deming (abetted by Joseph M. Juran, a noted quality consultant), and introduced in Japan in the 1950s. Gradually, firms in the United States, such as General Motors and Westinghouse Electric Corp., got wind of the idea. Those companies formed small groups of 10 to 15 employees to meet regularly to examine and suggest solutions to common problems of quality. The number of U.S. firms using these circles has grown into the thousands. Circles are found just about anywhere, in small companies as well as large, in hospitals as well as banks, in government agencies, and in offices as well as factories.

How does a quality circle operate?

Since the quality circle concept is based on maximum—and voluntary—involvement of employees from the top to the bottom of an organization, quality circle programs are almost always initiated at the executive level. If the program doesn't get all-out support at that level, it probably won't work at any level. Next, the quality circle idea is fanned out into the total organization. It is typically spearheaded by a "facilitator" or "coordinator." That person helps organize the departmental and interdepartmental circles. He or she also provides the necessary training in problem and opportunity identification and in methods improvement and problem solving.

Each circle is made up exclusively of volunteers, who meet on company time. They place personnel and labor relations problems off limits. Also prohibited are discussions about the performance or lack of performance of specific individuals. Typically, a new quality circle will focus on simple workplace problems. Early achievements build confidence and experience. Later, the circle will tackle more ambitious problems, ones that extend beyond its own control and involve other departments and other circles. As its expertise grows, the circle will shift gears from problem solving to problem preventing.

Supervisors should be cautioned that under current labor law in the United States, an employee team such as a quality circle must function in such a way that it does not encroach upon labor union prerogatives or employees' rights to union representation and collective bargaining. *Generally speaking, a quality circle must stick to its charter: investigating problems involving quality and productivity and the like, and suggesting ways to improve them.* This means that team leaders and members should avoid appearing to represent or negotiate for employees in matters such as wages, hours of work, working conditions, and grievances.

Is quality the only focus of a quality circle?

It started that way, but most circles have found that quality is inevitably involved with every imaginable kind of operating problem. As a consequence, most circles will turn their attention to any troublesome problem. And most organizations with a quality circle program cite example after example of productivity improvement.

You may have observed by now that all quality improvement approaches have much in common with productivity- and cost-improvement programs. There is a great deal of desirable overlap. Many of the techniques of quality improvement have been borrowed from work simplification, for example. The reason for these similarities is that at the heart of all improvement programs are the problem-solving and decision-making

techniques described in Chapter 4. The effective quality circle program makes special use of all the approaches associated with problem solving and methods improvement (see Figure 15-5).

Where does Total Quality Management fit in?

A simple answer is that TQM is bigger than either zero defects or quality circles. To begin with, TQM focuses on ultimate customer or client satisfaction. Satisfaction in this context applies not only to the primary goods or services contracted for, but also to the way in which they are delivered and serviced. And it doesn't stop there. Under TQM, the customer must be satisfied with the manner in which all contacts with the provider are conducted. This means no "brush-offs" or buck-passing when a customer or client seeks information or registers a complaint. Obviously, this is a tall order and a difficult one for an enterprise to fill. Nevertheless, that is the main idea of TQM.

The implementation of TQM typically involves some aspects of both ZD and quality circles. For instance, TQM adheres to the belief that attitudes, education, and motivation can play a large part within an organization as its various functional departments strive for quality. That's the ZD way. The quality circle approach is reflected in the emphasis TQM places on teamwork and on specifications-oriented, systematic, problem-solving programs.

Benchmarking? What's that?

The secret to many firms' success is to provide excellent customer service. **How does this customer feel when she is pampered in unexpected ways?**

In a way, **benchmarking** is much like TQM, but with an added twist. It, too, is vitally concerned with customer satisfaction. Benchmarking often begins with finding out exactly what customers and clients really want in the product or service. This establishes the "customer benchmark." That way, productive efforts can be devoted to giving customers what will satisfy them, rather than wasting time producing something that isn't valued much. Once the customer benchmark has been set, its impact may be felt (in the form of changed specifications and procedures) all the way back to the supervisor's department.

A related phase of benchmarking focuses on the quality of competitors' products and services—and the way they provide these services. The guideline is "Identify the best there is in your field . . . and do it that way yourself." This phase of benchmarking may also look not only to competitors, but also to any company that has a reputation for doing something very well. It may be order processing, inventory control, or any phase of manufacturing or providing a service. Here again, the objective is to identify the best way of doing something and copy it. These "competitor" or "external" benchmarks, too, may change the way things are done in a supervisor's department.

Finally (although many companies begin with this phase), there is a search for "internal" benchmarks, which are usually cost- and/or quality-related. In this phase, the idea is to locate the place in the organization where a particular work activity is best performed. The procedures used there then become the benchmark (or model) for all departments that perform similar work.

Ultimately, the goal of a benchmarking program is to establish a set of benchmarks in the form of goals, standards, or specifications (a) for products and services that will provide the optimum in customer satisfaction and (b) for internal methods and procedures that will be most cost- and quality-effective.

Benchmarking. A quality management technique based on finding the best product, service, process, or procedure and adopting it as the standard of quality performance.

Internet connection

http://www.tutor2u.net/business/production/quality_circles_kaizen.htm
Read about kaizen—its characteristics and guidelines—at this site.

How does the Six Sigma approach to quality work?

Some organizations (notably Motorola, Allied Signal, and General Electric) have "raised the bar" for quality to new heights. They set a demanding challenge for themselves—to produce products of such high quality that fewer than 3.4 per million would not pass inspection. This is **Six Sigma**—six standard deviations away from the mean. In addition to the extremely high quality standard, Six Sigma is a philosophy that strives to reduce variation and to make data-based decisions that will benefit and retain customers. It accomplishes this goal by focusing on a highly structured problem-solving process, following the steps of DMAIC (Define quality, Measure it, Analyze it, Improve it, and Control it). Six Sigma programs have proved to be systems worth benchmarking for other companies that are striving to improve quality.

How can you get employees more interested in productivity and quality?

It has been popular to complain about the "I don't care" attitude of some employees. Your viewpoint should be that if employees don't care about quality, it's because you have failed to convince them of its importance.

To get a worker to become performance-conscious, start right from the first day by stressing quality as well as output. Emphasize that the two must go hand in hand in your department. Whenever you show an employee how to do a job—especially a new employee or a new job—be specific about what kind of work is acceptable and what kind will not meet specifications. Explain the reason behind product- or service-quality limitations, and try to teach your employees the little tricks of the trade that help make productivity and quality standards easy to attain.

Thoughts*to*ponder

Winning Devoted Customers Through Quality
Professors Robert Ford and Cherrill Heaton, in their book *Managing the Guest Experience in Hospitality*, offer 14 principles for managing service organizations in ways that will produce a "wow" experience. The whole idea is to minimize negative experiences for customers while managing their expectations and experiences to create loyal, enthusiastic, devoted fans who love the company. Harley-Davidson, Disney, Starbucks, Volvo, and many other firms are passionate advocates of *guestology*. In these firms, supervisors hire people who love to serve, train employees to provide seamless service delivery and pursue perfection relentlessly, encourage workers to make the connection with guests a magical one, and empower guests to create their own satisfying experiences. The results include customers who return again and again, while recommending (even insisting) that others do business with you.

Practical Guidelines for Supervisors

1. Practice the principle of empowerment; *involve employees in decisions* regarding the improvement of productivity and quality.

2. *Remember that control is the key* to productivity and quality improvements; measure results, compare them with standards or benchmarks, and make appropriate corrections.

3. *Devise measures of productivity* that are unique to your department, and inform employees in advance how they will be assessed.

4. *Reduce or eliminate the nonproductive activities* of employees (and yourself) by closely examining inspections, delays, transportation, and storage.

5. When training new employees, start them off right by *demanding high quality at the beginning* and then expecting improvements in quantity later.

6. Don't forget that employee satisfaction is an excellent predictor of customer satisfaction; *find ways to make each employee's job more satisfying.*

7. *Interact with your customers or clients*; discover how they will use your product or service and what functions of it are most important to them (high value).

8. *Preach—and practice—quality daily*; set high standards; inspect before, during, and after major steps; and try to prevent problems and errors from arising.

9. *View statistics as your friend*; use various statistical quality control methods to produce products that have high reliability and meet customer needs.

10. Look "outside the box" to *study what your competitors are doing to achieve quality*; benchmark the very best of them and then strive to exceed their quality levels.

Chapter 15 Review

Key Concepts to Remember

1. Understanding Productivity. Productivity is akin to efficiency. It compares (a) the output value of the product or service produced with (b) the costs of the input resources (labor, materials, equipment) that are used to make the product or provide the service. Productivity is the "bottom line" for supervisory performance evaluation. Productivity increases whenever the output rises faster or falls slower than the input; it decreases when the opposite occurs. Productivity improvement is affected by the contributions of two types of factors: technological and human.

2. Methods Improvement. The time needed to perform a task is directly proportional to the way in which the job is performed. The time needed can almost always be reduced through the application of various techniques for methods improvement and motion economy that simplify work procedures and utilize work-assisting devices, tools, and machinery. Large-scale productivity gains are achieved mostly through the introduction of automation, robots, and computers using such techniques as workflow automation and reengineering. Value analysis is a form of productivity improvement that focuses on the customer's expectations for a product, rather than on the process by which it is made.

3. Quality and the Supervisor. Quality is a measure of the degree to which a process, product, or service conforms to the requirements that have been established for it. The cost of correcting defects and errors is high compared with the cost of preventing poor quality in the first place. Concerns for quality extend far beyond the manufacture of products into every kind of service that is provided internally, as well as externally, to customers. The first-line supervisor is in a key position to see that quality is built into the product or service as it is produced.

4. Statistical Quality Control. Statistical Quality Control (SQC) provides a valuable method for monitoring and controlling quality performance. The three principal tools of SQC are frequency-distribution charts, quality control charts, and sampling tables. Reliability is a special concept that establishes the probability of a product's performing a specific function, under given conditions, for a specified number of times (or period of time) without failure.

5. Toward Total Quality Management. The concepts of zero defects and quality circles have been especially effective in quality assurance programs. They both illustrate that most errors of workmanship can be eliminated if each individual is properly motivated and supported throughout the organization. The success of quality circles is highly dependent on group participation techniques applied to solving problems of quality and productivity. Both approaches usually are incorporated now into Total Quality Management (TQM), which enlarges the scope of quality management to focus on customer satisfaction and include suppliers and distributors. Benchmarking is a related technique for finding the best there is in a product, service, process, or procedure and adopting that as the standard of quality performance.

Reading Comprehension

1. What two factors determine the productivity measurements of an operation? Why is higher productivity so greatly valued by an organization?

2. A collection agency estimated that each transaction a clerical worker recorded contributed 25 cents to the total value of the agency's services. The average clerk receives

$8.00 per hour, and can record 800 transactions during an eight-hour day. What is the productivity rate stated in units per hour for an average clerk? Express this rate as a ratio. What is the productivity rate stated in dollars per hour for an average clerk? Using dollars for calculating both outputs and inputs, what is the productivity ratio for an average clerk? Why are the two ratios different? Which is the correct one? Why? For what purpose might each be used?

3. Name the five elements used in analyzing a work activity for methods improvement and explain why one of these is considered value-adding and the others are considered wasteful.

4. Compare, for the sake of value analysis, the use function and the esteem function.

5. What are some of the things supervisors should do for themselves in seeking to ensure quality performance in their departments?

6. Besides poor workmanship, what are some of the things that can contribute to defects and errors?

7. How does Statistical Quality Control differ from inspection?

8. In what way are zero-defects programs and quality circle programs alike?

9. Prepare a frequency-distribution chart for an activity you are familiar with, such as the time at which students in your class or seminar show up (compared with the formal starting time). What do the results tell you?

10. Some employees focus on how hard (or how long) they work instead of on how much they produce. Suggest ways to change their attitude toward productivity.

Application

Self-Assessment

How Good Are Your Productivity/Quality Improvement Skills?

Read the following statements carefully. Circle the number on the response scale that most closely reflects the degree to which each statement describes you. Add up your total points and prepare a brief action plan for self-improvement. Be ready to report your score for tabulation across the entire group.

	Good Description	Poor Description
1. I understand how the basic productivity ratios are determined.	10 9 8 7 6 5 4 3 2 1	
2. I am open to exploring both technological and human avenues for productivity improvements.	10 9 8 7 6 5 4 3 2 1	

	Good Description									Poor Description

3. I am continuously on the alert for potential productivity improvements in the areas of inspection, transportation, delays, and storage.

10 9 8 7 6 5 4 3 2 1

4. I can, in my mind, see the useful distinction between the use function and the esteem function in the product or service for which my unit is responsible.

10 9 8 7 6 5 4 3 2 1

5. I can explain the difference between quality control and quality assurance to employees.

10 9 8 7 6 5 4 3 2 1

6. I fully understand the value of exercising preventive control versus corrective control when it comes to achieving quality.

10 9 8 7 6 5 4 3 2 1

7. I feel comfortable with my ability to use a variety of statistical quality control tools, such as histograms and quality control charts.

10 9 8 7 6 5 4 3 2 1

8. I fully endorse the three underlying principles of zero defects: explicit standards, complete commitment, and immediate action to improve conditions affecting quality.

10 9 8 7 6 5 4 3 2 1

9. I would strongly support the use of employee participation for identifying and solving both productivity and quality problems.

10 9 8 7 6 5 4 3 2 1

10. I can explain at least three ways to improve quality.

10 9 8 7 6 5 4 3 2 1

Scoring and Interpretation

Scoring

Add up your total points for the 10 questions. Record that number here, and report it when it is requested. _____

Also, insert your score on the Personal Development Plan in the Appendix.

Interpretation

81 to 100 points. You seem to have a basic set of productivity/quality improvement skills.

61 to 80 points. Take a close look at some of your productivity/quality improvement skills (those with lower self-assessments) and discuss them with a manager to see if they need improvement.

Below 60 points. Some of your skills may be substantially inconsistent with effective productivity/quality improvement practices and could be detrimental to your success as a supervisor.

Identify your three lowest scores and record the question numbers here: _____, _____, _____.

Action

Write a brief paragraph detailing an action plan for how you might sharpen each of these skills. Then pay particularly close attention to the related material in the chapter as you review the relevant sections there.

Skill Development

Productivity/Quality Improvement

Opportunities for productivity and quality improvement are almost everywhere if we are alert to them, creative enough to address them, and receptive to the inputs of others to assist us in this process. But supervisors must also be humble enough to recognize that not all good ideas need to come from within themselves; many employees can generate amazingly useful suggestions for change, too. The trick lies in soliciting their ideas in a fashion that convinces them that you are serious about using the best of the suggestions.

Identify a productivity problem or quality issue in your educational institution or employer that lends itself to a fresh look from a variety of perspectives. Create a team of 10 or more people to participate in attacking the problem, and establish them as a quality circle. Explain their function and their assignment to them, and (acting as their recorder) develop a set of suggestions for solving or reducing the problem addressed. List these suggestions in the spaces provided.

Productivity/Quality Improvement Suggestions from the Quality Circle

1. _____

2. _____

3. _____

4. _____

5. _____

6. _____

7. _____

8. _____

9. _____

10. _____

Action

After assessing all the ideas produced, prepare a brief report that summarizes the group's 10 best suggestions for productivity or quality improvement. If possible, share the results of your study with someone else and obtain his or her reactions.

Group Exercise

Role Reversal

Assume that your instructor for this course has asked you, the students, for help in improving the instructor's productivity, quality, and innovativeness. In short, *you* are the expert consultants, and your instructor is the client for your services (a reversal of the usual relationship). Your task is to help your instructor examine the roles she or he performs, identify barriers to high quality, and begin to shape a strategy for productivity improvements in the service she or he provides to students.

Step 1: Divide into groups of four to five persons. Prepare a set of interview questions designed to explore with your instructor the following topics:
   a. *Nature of his or her job* (major duties and responsibilities; key outcome measures for assessing productivity and quality).
   b. *External reasons* (obstacles and barriers) that work to prevent a higher level of performance.
   c. *Internal factors* (within the instructor) that work to prevent a higher level of performance.

Step 2: Ask the questions, and gather the results.

Step 3: Scan Chapter 15 to identify relevant concepts and tools that potentially could be applied to your instructor's situation to attain productivity improvements.

Step 4: Present a brief report to your instructor, and assess the reaction to your suggestions. How relevant are the concepts and tools to a professional occupation? How likely is it that your instructor will implement some of your suggestions? Why or why not?

Cases for Analysis

Case 46

As the Wheels Turn

This actually happened in a British lawn mower factory.

Regina, a methods engineer, was timing the work of an employee who was attaching wheels to a lawn mower body. The job instruction card read: "Mount 5-inch black wheels with red inserts, half-inch nuts, two spring washers and two flat washers, torque to 28 pounds." First, however, the workman rolled a dolly of 10 bodies from the painting room to his workbench. Then he went to the tool room for a torque wrench. Next, he went to the stockroom to pick up wheels and parts. He then set up a jig, or holding fixture, to simplify the handling of the lawn mower body. To do the actual work that Regina was timing, the workman placed each body in the jig, inserted the wheels onto the body's axles, placed the washers and nuts, and tightened them to a torque of 28 pounds. When he had fitted the wheels to 10 bodies, he inspected his work, rejecting one of the bodies because of paint drips, and placed the remaining bodies on a dolly to be moved to the next operation.

Regina checked her watch: It had taken the workman only 75 minutes from start to finish. But the workman had clocked in at 8:00 and it was now 9:45, so that made a total of 105 minutes for nine bodies, and he was about to go on tea break. That meant 105 minutes for 36 wheels.

As Regina was thinking about this, she noticed an inspector in a white coat measuring the gap between the wheels and the body on the nine finished assemblies. The inspector then put a pink tag on two of those bodies, and they were set aside to be reworked. Another inspector also came along, and he was checking the torque settings on the wrench that the workman had used. He saw that the torque measured only 22 pounds, and he adjusted it up to the prescribed 28 pounds.

When Regina went back to her office, she spoke to the assembly supervisor. "I watched a fellow spend 105 minutes working this morning, but he spent only 75 minutes of that time actually screwing 40 wheels onto 10 lawn mower bodies. Worse still, three of these bodies were rejected and will have to be reworked. That's really only 28 wheels in 105 minutes."

"Wait a minute," said the supervisor. "The standard for the wheel mounting job is 1.88 minutes, or about 2 minutes per wheel. If all 10 bodies had been okay, that would have been 40 wheels in 75 minutes actual time taken, or about two minutes per wheel. That's right on target!"

Analysis

a. What's wrong with the supervisor's argument?

b. How do you explain the difference between the 75 minutes the employee spent actually mounting the wheels and the 105 minutes he was on the job?

c. What other problems that affect productivity do you see in this case?

Adapted from "A Changing View of Factory Labor," by J. Roger Morrison, *The McKinsey Quarterly*, Spring 1988, p. 79.

Case 47

The Hard-to-Meet Quality Standards

Rhonda is the housekeeping supervisor for a 200-room motel located near the airport in a major southwestern city. Ten full-time and 15 part-time room cleaners report to her. Hours are staggered to allow for housekeeping services throughout the day, although most room cleaners report at 9 A.M. and finish by 5:30 P.M. Some night coverage is provided, and of course service must be provided on the weekends, too. Because of the nature of the work and the hours, turnover among housekeeping employees has traditionally been high.

The motel, which is a franchise of a national chain, has been given standards that not only specify the amount of work to be done by a room cleaner during a shift, but also provide a long list of quality conditions that a serviced room should meet. Typically, a room cleaner should service 3 rooms per hour, or 24 on an 8-hour shift. Exceptions to this standard can be made when the cleaner encounters unusual conditions in the room. Generally speaking, the room cleaners meet this standard.

Where Rhonda has trouble is with the room cleaners' ability to meet the quality standards. These standards specify such details as the way a finished bed must look, arrangement of furniture, replacement of stationery in the desk, and placement of soaps and towels in the bathroom.

There are over 20 of these details per room. Each is demonstrated in a training video shown to new employees and is also reproduced on an illustrated poster mounted in the housekeeper's office. Nevertheless, a day never goes by that Rhonda doesn't have to send a cleaner up to one or more rooms that haven't been properly serviced.

There is an even bigger quality problem, too. This has to do with the less definable conditions of quality, such as how completely the wall-to-wall carpet has been vacuumed, whether the drapes and curtains have been dusted, and the degree of cleanliness of the tub and shower, tile flooring, and mirrors in the bathroom. Verifying the quality of these conditions is difficult and subject to debate, at which Rhonda has learned her employees are expert.

Here are some of the arguments Rhonda has heard from the room cleaners:

"The last cleaning person didn't do the job right, and it would have taken me another 10 minutes to get it in shape."

"The mops we're using need replacement. It's a wonder I can get the tile floors clean as it is."

"You're scheduling too many rooms early in the day. Many times, I've got to slip in and out while a lodger is still shaving."

"They must have had some party in that room last night. You should be happy I got it ready in time for the couple who were checking in."

"The vacuum cleaner on my floor is faulty and has needed maintenance for two weeks now."

"I did a super job of cleaning that room. You just show me where I didn't do it right."

"The supply man was late with the linens and towels, so I had to rush through several rooms in order to catch up."

"I can't clean three rooms an hour if you expect me to cover every one of the 20 details and still do a first-rate job of vacuuming and mopping."

Analysis

What do you think Rhonda should do to improve the level of cleanliness and conformance to detail specs in the rooms her staff services? Of the five alternatives provided below, which do you think would be most appropriate? Rank them on a scale from 1 (most appropriate) to 5 (least appropriate). You may add another alternative, if you wish. Be prepared to justify your rankings.

_____ **a.** Agree that the room-cleaning job is difficult, but urge the cleaning persons to "do the best you can."

_____ **b.** Ask the maintenance department to examine all vacuum cleaners, mops, and other equipment to make sure that these are in good operating order.

_____ **c.** Take her employees' complaints seriously, investigate them one by one, and take action on those that have merit.

_____ **d.** Post this notice on the employees' bulletin board: "From now on, all rooms will be spot-checked for cleanliness. Employees with more than one room a week that doesn't meet cleanliness standards will be subject to dismissal."

_____ **e.** Notify the national chain headquarters that the room-cleaning standards are unreasonable and should be adjusted.

Case 48

The Dried-Out Burger

"I can't eat this hamburger," declared the irate customer. "It's completely dried out!"

"I'm sorry," said the assistant manager of the fast-food restaurant. "We'll make you a fresh one."

"I don't have time to wait," said the customer. "This will be the last time I eat here."

When Gilda, the assistant manager, spoke to the counter person, he said that he had served the customer a wrapped hamburger that the fry cook had placed on the serving rack. "I assumed that it was okay," he said. "That customer seemed like an old crab. Nothing would have satisfied her. The hamburger wasn't that bad. She must have just gotten tired of waiting till we could get around to her."

The fry cook, when asked for her explanation of the dry hamburger, said, "We had been very busy earlier, and I made up an extra-large batch so that I could stay ahead."

"You know," said Gilda, "that our standard says that you should never put more than 10 hamburgers up at a time. From the look of things, you must have had a couple of dozen in the serving rack. When they dry out, we can't serve them; they must be thrown away."

"Maybe I did," said the fry cook, "but I can't see what difference an occasional dry hamburger is going to make."

Analysis

a. What do you think of the counter person's view of the situation?
b. How valid was the fry cook's explanation?
c. If you were Gilda, what would you do to prevent the serving of dried-out hamburgers in the future?

Case 49

The Best and the Worst of It

On the quality-control chart for the production of a high-priced facial lotion, the pH specification is 7.0, with tolerance limits of ± 0.02. The control of pH is very important, because it measures acidity, with 7.0 being neutral. The manufacturer wishes to maintain this reading to avoid

FIGURE 15-6

A pH specification quality control chart.

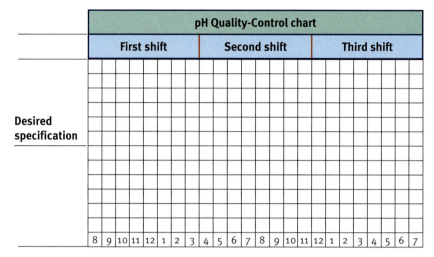

potential skin irritation, which could mean possible product liability suits from customers. Operators make check readings of the pH meter on the lotion flow line once each hour and record them on a chart like the one provided in Figure 15-6.

Here are the readings made by operators on the first, second, and third shifts:

8 A.M. to 4 P.M.: 7.00, 6.99, 6.98, 7.00, 7.01, 7.02, 7.01, 7.00

4 P.M. to 12 A.M.: 6.98, 7.00, 7.02, 6.99, 7.02, 7.03, 6.99, 6.98

12 A.M. to 8 A.M.: 6.99, 7.00, 6.98, 6.97, 6.98, 6.96, 6.97, 6.95

Analysis

a. Using the information supplied, complete the quality control chart in Figure 15-6. (Refer to Figure 15-4 for guidance.)
b. Which shift operator has the best control of the operation?
c. Which shift operator appears to have lost control of the operation?
d. Which operator appears to have more consistent control, the one on the first shift or the one on the second?

ANSWERS TO QUICK TESTS	Quick Test 1	Quick Test 2	Quick Test 3	Quick Test 4	Quick Test 5
	1. F	3. T	5. F	7. F	9. F
	2. T	4. F	6. F	8. T	10. T

16

Managing a Diverse Workforce

LEARNING OBJECTIVES

After studying this chapter, you should be able to

- Discuss the nature and workplace implications of a culturally diverse society.

- Identify and interpret the major equal employment opportunity legislation, explain the intent of affirmative action plans, and describe the role of the Equal Employment Opportunity Commission.

- Discuss the special problems of disadvantaged workers and suggest ways to integrate these employees into the workplace.

- Discuss the importance of women in the workplace and their difficulties in advancing from their traditional roles, including related subjects such as job evaluation, comparable worth, and sexual harassment.

- Discuss the unique values and characteristics of each generation of workers.

- Explain the legal and social aspects of an employee's right to privacy and the impact this has on a supervisor's right to manage.

Cultural diversity. The recognition that society and the workforce are composed of a variety of groups, each of which has, in addition to similarities with other groups, unique differences in beliefs and experiences that can be assets at work.

What is the general makeup of the workforce today?

It has changed dramatically in the last few decades. Just 25 years ago, half the members of the labor force were native-born white men. Today, although they still constitute a major segment of the existing workforce, only 15 percent of *new* workers are native-born white men. In contrast, about 40 percent of the new entrants are white women. Other significant groups entering the labor force include immigrant men, native-born nonwhite women, and native-born nonwhite men. In addition, the number of young workers (ages 16 to 24) has dropped slightly. Today, about 60 percent of all women of working age are employed. Clearly, the labor pool is richly heterogeneous from many perspectives—gender, race, and age.

Good supervisors will seek a workforce reflective of these changes in the labor pool. They will also recognize that they must understand and accept *cultural diversity*, the cultural differences between ethnic and racial groups, in order to be completely effective supervisors. For example, members of many Native American cultures do not make eye contact when speaking to a superior. They do this as a gesture of respect, but it is often misunderstood as failure to pay attention or as disrespect. Participation in cultural awareness and cultural diversity workshops can give supervisors a better understanding of the range of people they will encounter as supervisors and provide helpful suggestions to assist them in managing that diversity.

Diversity such as that portrayed here can either divide a group or produce rich payoffs.
What are the potential gains from cultural diversity in the workplace?

Is workforce diversity limited to ethnic and gender differences?

Definitely not. In addition to differences of race and gender, supervisors should also be aware of differences resulting from marital status, disability, age, sexual orientation, veteran's status, and religious belief. It is not the supervisor's responsibility to have a professional opinion on the correctness of the differences that they will note in the workforce. Pay attention to work performance, knowing that part of managing people is understanding their needs and focusing their attention on work goals and objectives. The better you understand people and what motivates them, the more effective you will be in your supervisory responsibilities.

GLBT. What's this acronym all about?

An increasing number of individuals with alternative lifestyles (gays, lesbians, bisexuals, and transgenders) have "come out" to their friends, families, employers, and work colleagues. Formerly marginalized by an intolerant society, they increasingly have begun to stand up for their rights—and are slowly making progress and gaining acceptance. Some employers now offer health benefits to same-sex couples; others encourage the creation of support groups for gays and sensitivity training classes for supervisors to debunk homosexual stereotypes. Progressive supervisors may need to rethink and update their attitudes toward members of GLBT groups, and be especially alert to signs of discrimination against members of those groups in the workplace.

| 1 | T or F | From a diversity perspective, the workforce has stayed about the same for the last half century. |
| 2 | T or F | The idea of a diverse workforce focuses exclusively on having proportionate representation of gender and racial minorities. |

QUICK TEST 1

The Legal Basis

2

In the eyes of the law, who is a minority employee?

Just about everyone who is not under 40 years of age and a white male of European heritage. The generally more useful term applied to minorities today is *protected groups*. A **protected group** consists of people who, historically, have encountered discrimination in the American workplace. **Discrimination** is defined as any managerial action or decision that either favors or penalizes individuals on the basis of characteristics that are not related to their work performance or professional qualifications. Most of the relevant laws specifically identify these people as ethnic and racial minorities (African Americans, Hispanics, Asians, and Native Americans, in particular), women, disadvantaged young persons, disabled workers, veterans of the Vietnam War era, and persons over 40 years of age.

CONCEPT
A strong body of law has established the rights and privileges of all job applicants and employees, regardless of race, color, national origin, gender, disability, or age.

Protected groups. Certain minority and/or disadvantaged groups in the population that warrant special protection in employment matters.

Discrimination. Any managerial action or decision based on favoring or disfavoring one person or member of a group over another on the basis of race, color, ethnic or national origin, gender, age, disability, Vietnam-era war service, or union membership.

The basic equal employment opportunity laws say that an employer cannot discriminate because of race, color, religion, gender, sexual orientation, national origin, or age. In trying to make these laws work, various agencies of the U.S. government have interpreted them to apply to all victims of prejudice and discrimination.

What has caused this intensified concern for minorities?

Stereotype. The characterization of an individual on the basis of a standardized, over-simplified view of the characteristics believed (often wrongly) to be held in common by the group to which the individual is assumed to belong.

Great social forces at work in the last 50 years have altered the values of many people. What were once widespread *stereotypes* (oversimplified and often unfounded group characteristics applied indiscriminately to individual members of a group) of blacks and women, for example, are no longer tolerated, either by law or by society in general. Family lifestyles and marriage patterns have radically changed. And with them, our notions of what are appropriate occupations and behavior for women—and men—have changed, too. A great many people make relatively affluent and privileged livings. This makes for harsh comparisons with those who do not have jobs or who are relegated to less-skilled work and often poverty-level pay. The power of television and instant communication intensifies the awareness of these differences. People—especially those who believe that their lesser status is a result of discrimination (as it often is)—are impatient for improvement. The newer laws are a direct expression of the public's general dissatisfaction with these conditions and its wish to provide equal employment opportunities for all.

What is the legal basis for equal employment opportunity programs?

There is a great body of federal, state, and local laws. These laws have been reinforced by a number of significant rulings in the courts. The laws are further supported by guidelines laid down by the Equal Employment Opportunity Commission (EEOC), the federal agency charged with enforcing the law.

Equal employment opportunity (EEO). A system of organizational justice, stipulated by law, that applies to all aspects of employment and is intended to provide equal opportunity for all members of the labor force.

A discussion of the legal basis for nondiscriminatory legislation is beyond the scope of this text. A synopsis of the major federal laws, popularly referred to as the *equal employment opportunity (EEO)* laws, is provided for your review in Table 16-1. Most importantly, these laws specify that the great majority of business firms and public institutions cannot do any of the following:

- Make any distinctions based on race, gender, or national origin in any condition of employment, including hiring, setting wages ("equal pay for equal work"), classifying, assigning or promoting,

TABLE 16-1 Synopsis of Major Federal Laws Enacted Since 1960 That Affect Equal Employment Opportunity

LAW

Equal Pay Act (1963)

PROVISION

Prohibits job discrimination in all employment practices on the basis of race, color, sex, religion, or national origin. This includes recruiting, selecting, compensating, classifying, assigning, promoting, disciplining, and terminating, as well as eligibility for union membership. The EEOC administers these laws and monitors related affirmative action programs.

LAW

Executive Order 11246 of 1965 as amended by Executive Order 11375 of 1967

PROVISION

Prohibits discrimination in employment in organizations having contracts of $10,000 or more with the federal government. The orders require that these organizations institute affirmative action programs and recruit and promote women and minorities where necessary.

LAW

Age Discrimination in Employment Act (1967) as amended in 1975

PROVISION

Prohibits discrimination in hiring and employment of workers over 40 years of age unless BFOQ can be established.

LAW

Rehabilitation Act of 1973 and Executive Order 11914 of 1974

PROVISION

Prohibits discrimination by federal contractors of applicants and employees with physical and mental disabilities.

LAW

Vietnam Era Veteran's Readjustment Assistance Act of 1974

PROVISION

Prohibits discrimination—by federal contractors—in employment of disabled veterans and veterans of the Vietnam War; also specifies certain affirmative actions in the employment of veterans.

LAW

Americans with Disabilities Act of 1990

PROVISION

Prohibits discrimination by all governmental units and private employers with 15 or more employees in the employment of qualified applicants or employees with a disability if reasonable accommodation to a job or a work environment is possible.

LAW

Family and Medical Leave Act of 1993

PROVISION

Requires public and private employers with 50 or more employees to provide eligible employees with the opportunity to take up to 12 weeks of unpaid leave per 12-month period for specifically defined family and medical situations.

Thanks partly to affirmative action programs, many members of minority groups have been given opportunities to demonstrate their talents. **Why do some affirmative action programs fail to produce the desired results?**

and allocating the use of facilities, and in training, retraining, and apprenticeship programs.

- Distinguish between married and single people of one sex and not of the other.
- Deny employment to women with young children unless the same policies apply to men with young children.
- Penalize women because they require time away from work for childbearing.
- Maintain seniority lists based solely on gender or race.
- Establish jobs as either men's or women's. The only exceptions allowed are jobs for which the employer can prove that there is a bona fide occupational qualification (BFOQ).
- Discriminate against workers 40 years of age or over in hiring, firing, promoting, classifying, paying, assigning, advertising, or determining eligibility for union membership.
- Similarly discriminate against qualified disabled persons. The law defines persons with disabilities as individuals who (a) have a physical or mental impairment (many prefer the terms *challenged* or *differently abled*) that substantially limits one or more major life activities, (b) have a record of such impairments, or (c) are regarded as having such an impairment.

Obviously, EEO legislation was designed to protect minority groups of any definition from discrimination. Its principal intent, however, was to encourage utilization of all the potential and talent of all minority groups in the workforce. Note that the law is not a labor-management law: It is directed at employers, and they must comply without obstruction from labor unions.

Affirmative action. An in-company program designed to remedy current and future inequities in employment of minorities.

Where does affirmative action apply?

In enforcing the provisions of the equal employment opportunity laws, the EEOC and its state and local equivalents have encouraged firms to engage in affirmative action programs. An ***affirmative action*** program consists of action taken to ensure nondiscriminatory treatment of all groups that are protected by legislation that forbids discrimination in employment because of race, religion, gender, age, disability, Vietnam-era war service, or national origin. The EEOC emphasizes that results count, not good intentions. If company statistics on pay and promotion, for example, show that the current status of protected groups is inferior to that of most other employees in that company or geographic area, the company may be directed to set up an affirmative action program. Companies with federal contracts over $50,000 and with more than 50 employees have no choice. They must have a written program in place and follow it.

In investigating EEO discrimination charges, what areas are most sensitive?

The EEOC will look for three possibilities:

1. *Differential treatment.* This occurs when a member of a protected group is treated differently from a nonmember in the same situation.
2. *Disparate effect.* When a job requirement acts to exclude a protected group, it creates a disparate (unfair) effect. The employer must demonstrate that the requirement is a "business necessity" and thus a BFOQ.
3. **Evil intent.** This is present, for instance, when an employer or supervisor is "out to get" a member of a protected group.

These infractions are most likely to occur in recruiting, interviewing, selecting, assigning, appraising, training, promoting, and disciplining employees. Supervisors are intimately involved in all these areas. Accordingly, they bear a great deal of the responsibility for carrying out the spirit, as well as the requirements, of the law.

Differential treatment. The act of treating a member of a minority, or protected group, differently from other applicants or employees in a similar situation.

Disparate effect. The existence of job requirements that have the effect of unfairly excluding a member of a protected group.

What is meant by *reverse discrimination*?

Reverse discrimination is what many believe happens to men, or to Caucasians in general, when preference in employment is shown to women, minorities, or both. In *Bakke v. University of California Board of Regents* (1978), the U.S. Supreme Court said in effect that it is wrong to use quotas designed to accommodate women and minorities in such a manner as to withhold employment from eligible men and whites. At the same time, however, the Court upheld the principle of affirmative action programs.

As you can infer, supervisors must act in a very unbiased manner in this matter. They must be sure to support the principle of equal employment opportunity and affirmative action, yet they must also be careful not to use these guidelines unfairly to discriminate against nonminorities.

Reverse discrimination. The notion that implementing affirmative action programs deprives qualified members of nonprotected groups from their rightful opportunities.

What is the ADA, and how does it affect my job?

The Americans with Disability Act of 1990 (ADA) applies to private employers with 15 or more employees. State and local governments of any size are also included. ADA prohibits discrimination in all employment practices, including job application procedures, hiring, firing, advancement, compensation, and training, and in other terms, conditions, and privileges of employment. It applies to recruitment, advertising, tenure, layoff, leave, fringe benefits, and all other employment-related activities.

ADA defines an *individual with a disability* as a person who has a physical or mental impairment that substantially limits one or more

major life activities, has a record of such an impairment, or is regarded as having such an impairment. Individuals with minor nonchronic conditions of short duration, such as sprains, infections, or broken limbs, generally would not be covered.

If persons with a disability meet the legitimate requirements of a job and can perform the essential functions of that job, they should be accepted as candidates for employment without considering their disability. In fact, it is expected that an employer will make *reasonable accommodations* to a job or a work environment to enable a qualified applicant or employee with a disability to perform the essential job functions. An employer is not required to make accommodation if that would impose an undue hardship on the employer's business. In most cases, accommodations for employees covered by this act are possible within the economic resources of most employers. The act also requires that physical barriers to facilities be removed when this is readily achievable.

Examples of barrier removal measures could include installing ramps, making curb cuts; modifying sidewalks and entrances; rearranging tables, chairs, and other furniture; widening doorways; installing grab bars in toilet stalls; and adding raised letters or Braille to elevator control buttons. Before a supervisor makes any specific change, the ADA accessibility guidelines should be consulted to be sure that the alterations meet those requirements.

Who is covered by the Family and Medical Leave Act (FMLA) of 1993?

All public and private employers with 50 or more employees are covered by the FMLA. Part-time employees are counted as long as they are on the payroll for each day of the workweek. To be eligible for a leave, an employee must work at a work site with 50 employees or for an employer who has 50 or more employees within 75 miles of that work site; have worked for the employer at least 12 months; and have worked at least 1,250 hours (about 24 hours per week over the previous 12-month period). Eligible employees may take up to 12 weeks of unpaid leave per 12-month period for the birth of a child and to care for a child; for the placement of a child with the employee for adoption or foster care; to care for an immediate family member, spouse, child, or parent, if such immediate family member has a serious health condition; or in response to a serious health condition that makes the employee unable to perform the functions of his or her position.

After completing the leave, employees must be restored to their former position or an equivalent position. If the need for a leave is foreseeable, an employee must give 30 days' notice to the employer before taking it. FMLA does not supersede state laws or collective bargaining agreements that require more generous leave policies, including provisions that may provide for paid leave for all or a portion of the 12-week leave period.

Who are the hard-core unemployed?

The majority of unemployed persons are people who move in and out of the workforce temporarily as they lose or quit one job and seek another. There are millions of other unemployed persons, however, who are out of work more of the time than they are employed. These are the especially disadvantaged, or the *hard-core unemployed.* Typically, they have the following characteristics that make them a challenge to their supervisors when they finally find what they hope will be good jobs:

- They are school dropouts, usually with only a sixth- or seventh-grade education. Many are functionally illiterate, and do not speak or write English. As many as 30 percent have less than fifth-grade reading and arithmetic skills.
- They are single heads of households, men and women with large family responsibilities that tend to overwhelm them with problems.
- They have poor work histories. Few have worked at anything but day labor or in casual service as dishwashers or porters, for example. They have not been prepared for work by their families, their communities, or their schools.
- They are plagued by personal problems, such as undependable transportation to work. They have little experience in managing a regular income and may need help in handling credit, balancing a budget, or even learning how to cash a paycheck.

Recently employed hard-core or disadvantaged persons are troubled by job and business conditions that others accept as routine. They may have difficulty in getting along with the boss or with their co-workers. For example, one 24-year-old ghetto youth said that he reacted at first to orders from his supervisor the way he'd react to being pushed around by a street-gang leader: "I had to learn not to take orders personally. When someone told me to get this or do that, I'd get mad. Finally, I learned that the boss was reacting to the pressure of his job and had nothing against me." In like fashion, many of the disadvantaged view work rules and regulations as something devised to harass them, not as reasonable guidelines for organized behavior that everyone has to follow.

What is the role of testing in preventing discrimination?

In 1971 the U.S. Supreme Court *(Griggs v. Duke Power)* handed down a decision barring "discriminatory" job testing. Few tests, however, are

Quips & Quotes

Success is to be measured not so much by the position that one has reached in life as by the obstacles which he has overcome while trying to succeed.

Booker T. Washington

intentionally discriminatory; it is just that most tests have been built around cultural models of white, middle-class people. As you can see, by definition, such people are not typical of the hard-core unemployed, and tests, when used indiscriminately, screened out the latter. Nevertheless, as a result of the Supreme Court decision, testing for selection, placement, or training in industry has been modified to identify the aptitudes and skills of disadvantaged persons rather than unwittingly separating out from the labor force people with untapped potential.

Federal guidelines for employment testing require that tests be validated (if adverse impact is present). This means that they have been analyzed and revised to be sure that a test really measures what it says it measures and does not discriminate against protected groups. Tests must be *validated* on two counts:

1. **Content validity.** This means that the test content appropriately represents all the key elements of the job. It would be unfair to use only the results of a keyboarding speed test for the selection of an individual when keyboarding represents only 20 percent of that job. Clearly, the other job requirements also need to be assessed.
2. **Construct validity.** This means that the test is put together in such a way that it does not screen out applicants who could pass the content part if only they could understand the test questions themselves. For example, applicants might be able to demonstrate mechanical aptitude if they could read the questions. Perhaps the test should be administered orally rather than in writing.

| QUICK TEST 2 | 3 | T or F | Reverse discrimination occurs, for example, when a minority supervisor discriminates against a minority employee. |
| | 4 | T or F | To demonstrate that they are nondiscriminatory, tests should have both content and construct validity. |

③ Women in the Workplace

Women have traditionally been denied equal opportunities in the workplace, and their rights must now be protected and enhanced.

How important are women to national productivity?

They are absolutely essential. Out of every five persons working in the United States, nearly half are women, and this number is growing rapidly. Women now occupy more than 40 percent of all managerial and professional positions; nearly two-thirds of all technical, sales, and administrative support jobs are filled by women.

The increase in the proportion of women working has been nothing less than spectacular, as illustrated in Figure 16-1.

But what about compensation for women?

Unfortunately, that's another story, and it is one that makes many women justifiably unhappy. Estimates vary, but it would appear that, on average, women receive only about three-quarters of the pay that men do in the labor market. How can that happen? Mainly because women have traditionally held lower-paying, lower-status jobs and then been blocked from advancement into higher ones, a condition referred to as the *glass ceiling*.

Why doesn't job evaluation put an end to this discrimination in pay?

It does, but only for work that is performed and compensated for under a job-evaluation plan. Even then, it does not close all the possible loopholes. And, of course, it can do nothing to remedy the lack of opportunities, which is the role of the EEO legislation.

The relevant law of the land (the Fair Labor Standards Act as amended by the Equal Pay Act of 1963 and again by Public Law 92-318 in 1972) stipulates that all employees, regardless of gender or other discriminatory identification, should receive the same pay for the same kind and amount of work. *Job evaluation* is the basic means for making sure that this occurs. The "equal pay for equal work" standard, like job evaluation, requires scrutiny of the job as a whole. Its intention is that job titles be ignored and attention be focused on actual job requirements and performance. The law examines four factors in particular: equal skill, equal effort, equal responsibility, and similarity of working conditions. Whereas the law does acknowledge some exceptions, it will not permit the concepts of "women's jobs," "men's jobs," "job lists for nonwhites," and the like. However, the law does permit the use of merit pay plans that recognize, within a job pay range, different levels of performance among individuals or different levels of seniority.

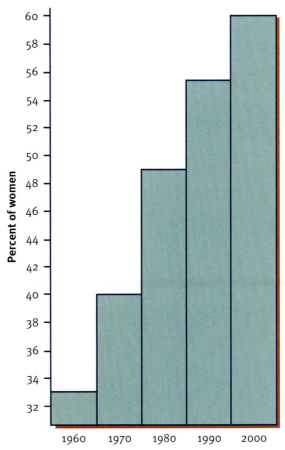

Percentage of all women of working age who are in the labor force

Source: U.S. Department of Labor

FIGURE 16-1

Growth in the percentage of women who work.
Will that percentage continue to increase, or will it plateau? Why?

Quips & Quotes

More women are shattering the proverbial glass ceiling, and many more are chipping holes in it.

Cari Dominguez

What is meant by *comparable worth*?

This is a concept used for evaluating widely dissimilar jobs. The Equal Pay Act of 1963 charges discrimination if women aren't given pay equal to men's pay for equal work. In a great many instances, however, women perform work that is radically different from the work performed by men in the same organization. Nevertheless, these women often feel, with justification, that their pay is still not equal, all things considered. The concept of *comparable worth* is an effort to rectify this kind of situation. It makes it possible for the work and pay of a toll collector, for example, to be compared with that of, say, a nurse. Typically, this approach involves examination and comparison of four factors: level of know-how required, problem solving entailed, accountability, and working conditions.

For most women, what appears to be the main ingredient missing in the labor market in general and in their jobs in particular?

Women need an opportunity equal to that of men for securing intellectually challenging employment and a chance for advancement based on their performance and capabilities. Too often in the past, the traditional or stereotypical attitude of management and supervision was essentially protective. The question asked was, "Is the work fitting for a woman?" not "What is she capable of?" Accordingly, women generally found themselves restricted to secretarial and clerical routines in the office and to lesser-skilled jobs in the plant.

Supervisors and managers must open, rather than block, the way outward (in terms of job scope) and upward (in terms of training, status, and financial opportunity) for the women who work for them. A supervisor who is progressive and liberated in the management of women will find that *all* employees are more highly motivated and have a greater loyalty and devotion to the company's objectives.

How differently from men should you treat women at work?

There should be no basic difference in how you supervise women and men. The principles of sound, equitable, and supportive management should apply just as fully to the supervision of women as to the supervision of men. Simply stated, a person is a person is a person, regardless of gender—and color and national origin and religious preference. A good supervisor will recognize and adapt to each person's unique individuality, with the conviction that he or she will respond most favorably when treated fairly with respect and thoughtfulness.

What is sexual harassment?

The Equal Employment Opportunity Commission has defined *sexual harassment* as "unwelcome sexual advances." Requests for sexual favors and other verbal or physical conduct of a sexual nature constitute sexual harassment when (a) submission to such conduct is made, either explicitly or implicitly, a term or condition of an individual's employment, (b) submission to or rejection of such conduct by an individual is used as the basis for employment decisions affecting such an individual, or (c) conduct has the purpose or effect of unreasonably interfering with an individual's work performance or creating a perception of an intimidating, hostile, or offensive working environment.

The supervisor's role in preventing sexual harassment is a crucial one. In fact, according to EEOC guidelines, if you as a supervisor know or should have known about an act of sexual harassment and respond in an inappropriate way, including failure to act, you may be placing yourself and your employer at significant risk of personal and corporate liability.

How should I respond to a complaint of harassment?

The precise answer to this question depends to a large extent on your company's policy with regard to handling an accusation of sexual harassment. In any case, you must know who to contact and who will conduct the investigation. Often cases of sexual harassment are initially investigated by the human resource department or an affirmative action officer of the Equal Opportunity Employment Office. It's also possible that you will be the first source of intervention. In those cases, be sure to document all the actions you take, including any contacts you have with the victim, the alleged perpetrator, and other company officials. After a full investigation of the facts related to a case, it is important to consider appropriate discipline, up to and including termination. Remember, sexual harassment is not primarily about sex; it is about *power*. Victims often endure the pain of harassment for long periods until they have the courage to come forward and express their anger, frustration, and outrage. It is also much more prevalent than most males believe. Several reputable national studies have suggested that more than 50 percent of all women in the workforce, at some point in their work lives, have been the victims of sexual harassment. Encourage the victim to participate in whatever employee assistance programs are available.

The message sent to employees must be clear. Men, and women, who want to play games or seek favors with sexual implications must not do so at work. Supervisors have the responsibility for preventing those actions

Sexual harassment. Repeated or unwarranted verbal or physical advances or sexually explicit remarks that are offensive or objectionable to the recipient.

Ethical Perspectives

Sexual Harassment

How would you respond to the following statement? "The problem with sexual harassment is all these women the company has hired. If they would loosen up and learn to talk like the guys, there would be no more problems."

Begin your response with the definition of sexual harassment, and keep in mind that business ethics is coming to *know* what is right or wrong in the workplace and *doing* what's right.

by maintaining the proper levels of sexual decorum, including the treatment of employees by suppliers and customers.

How can I prevent the harassment of my employees?

1. One important way is by stating clearly that you will not tolerate sexual harassment and that any case reported to you will be investigated completely and, if proved, dealt with promptly and severely. Make sure your employees know your organization's sexual harassment policy by offering periodic training sessions on the topic.

2. Review your department's physical environment. Suggestive photos, offensive humor, and physical sexual intimidation cannot be tolerated.

3. Encourage employees to report acts of sexual harassment they experience or overhear. The victims of sexual harassment need to know that they will be supported by their employer. If they have that confidence, they are more likely to use the internal investigation process for the resolution of sexual harassment complaints. If not, they may, and will be encouraged to, have recourse to the state or federal agencies that will investigate these complaints on their behalf. A sensitive, caring, alert supervisor can make all the difference in resolving harassment complaints and creating a climate where it is clear that harassing behavior is unacceptable. Perhaps one major employer gave the best advice to its employees when advising them to evaluate their behavior with co-workers and determine whether they would act in that manner with that individual in front of their spouse, parents, or children. If not, a reevaluation of that behavior is probably in order.

JOB TIP!

Affirmative Defense

Organizations that wish to achieve two objectives—preventing sexual harassment and protecting themselves in court if a lawsuit is filed against them—are well advised to establish an "affirmative defense," according to the Society for Human Resource Management. Here are some of the key ingredients of an affirmative defense:

- Develop a zero-tolerance policy on harassment.
- Disseminate the policy widely and frequently.
- Provide multiple avenues for reporting alleged violations.
- Conduct relevant training for all employees and managers regarding what the likely judgment of a "reasonable person" might be with regard to various actions.
- Investigate allegations promptly and thoroughly; take swift disciplinary action where it is appropriate.

Source: *Workforce* magazine's website at *www.workforceonline.com*.

| 5 | T or F | Comparable worth suggests that women must be paid the same as men, regardless of differences in their job responsibilities. |
| 6 | T or F | Supervisors have the responsibility for preventing, as well as investigating and resolving, sexual harassment at work. |

Younger and Older Workers

4

What differences in the workforce are a function of age?

There are actually four distinct generations of people in the workplace,[1] according to when they were born and raised:

- **Veterans** were born in the two decades before World War II. Because of their exposure to the Great Depression and several wars, they often believe in hard work, sacrifice, patriotism, respect for authority, and law and order. Veterans are often financially conservative, logical, and oriented toward the past (the "good old days").
- **Baby Boomers** were born from about 1943 to 1960. They experienced greater prosperity, the emergence of television, and defining events such as the civil rights movement, the birth of women's liberation, and the Cold War. Boomers value personal growth and self-gratification, teamwork and involvement, and their own health and wellness. They are often driven to succeed and are willing to expend the time and effort to do so.
- **Gen Xers** were born and raised during the next two decades. The development of computers had a profound impact on them, along with MTV and the dramatic increase in AIDS worldwide. They tend to be skeptical, informal, pragmatic, technologically literate, and risk taking. They also accept diversity readily and think globally, while being focused on their families.
- **Nexters** emerged in the most recent two decades. They have witnessed school violence, terrorism, and highly candid TV talk shows. Nexters are often highly self-confident, achievement-oriented, Internet-savvy, upbeat, impatient, and tenacious. They often love to learn and enjoy flexibility and autonomy at work.

The similarities *within* each group unite them around music preferences, historical events, economics, and politics. By contrast, the age and attitudinal differences *across* these groups often stand out in regard to their members' views on leadership, the work ethic, balance between work life and home life, and especially technology. Unfortunately, conflict sometimes arises between groups as they polarize into an "us" versus "them" mentality, with each group feeling that "we" know better than "they" do. The existence of distinct age groups presents unique challenges for supervisors of mixed-age employees in terms of recruiting, training, motivating, communicating, and team building.

What can a supervisor do to better motivate and manage young workers?

Supervisors should take their cues from the values and complaints of Gen Xers and Nexters. Specifically, a supervisor must be mindful of the following:

1. **Exert authority only from reason.** Dependence on power invites rebellion. A supervisor's authority ought to make sense in terms of its conservation of effort and resources, its recognition of the humanness of employees, and its understanding of the value in change as well as that in conformity.

2. **Learn to move faster in making changes.** The twenty-first century will move ever faster in its development of knowledge and technology. Tradition has lost much of its value and meaning. It should be tested constantly against current needs. Learn to let go of the old. Neither progress nor capable young workers will wait very long for you to embrace the new.

3. **Convey the meaning of each assignment.** There is nothing unique about the younger worker's cry for relevance. Men and women have wished to gain this from their work since time began. To apply oneself, one needs to know *why* a job must be done a certain way, why it must be done at all, and how it relates to what is going on around one.

4. **Make sure the younger workers know what results are expected of them.** Vague and critical admonitions ("use your head") rather than specific goals and targets will sound too much like a parent speaking—and probably induce a comparable response. Make certain, too, that the wage system is clearly understood—exactly how pay will be related to accomplishment.

5. **Provide support and assistance.** Especially in job training, a supervisor's desire to help employees become proficient is welcomed as an expression of respect and confidence.

6. **Praise freely when it is deserved.** Younger people without experience may be less confident of their performance and need frequent feedback on its quality. Conversely, when you criticize, it is important to be tactful. Similarly, discipline must be reasonable rather than arbitrary.

7. **Enrich the nature of the work.** Monotony stems from repetition that allows no room for improvisation and ingenuity. Give employees the freedom, should they choose it, to provide their own variety while they are still committed to a specific, demanding goal.

When is a worker considered older?

The Age Discrimination in Employment Act categorizes people over 40 years of age as older. These Veterans and Boomers are mature, settled, experienced, and usually well trained. But they already have family responsibilities, often heavy ones, and signs of both physical aging and emotional wear will soon become evident.

It is important to keep in mind that age affects each person differently. Its effect depends on a large number of factors: heredity, durability, physical condition, exposure to weather, extreme living or working conditions, climate, indulgence in food or drink, drug abuse, and emotional and psychological strains. Consequently, it is a good rule of thumb for a supervisor to monitor signs of change due to age in any employee over 50 years old. Changes may be physical or mental, slight or marked. Changes may affect the older worker's performance for better or for worse—or not at all. Just keep your eyes open for changes.

What are the chief assets of older workers?

Older workers have many assets. According to Dr. William A. Sawyer, formerly medical director of the Eastman Kodak Company and later medical consultant to the International Association of Machinists, AFL, older workers take these and other assets to work:

Safety. They have far fewer accidents.

Attendance. They have a better absence record and take fewer "discretionary" days off. They are sick less often, although their illnesses tend to last longer than those of younger people.

Judgment. The variety of their work and social experiences tends to improve older workers' judgment and familiarize them with a variety of work situations.

Loyalty. Broad experience has helped older workers recognize good supervision when they get it—and to reward that supervision with the loyalty and cooperation deserves.

Skill. Once acquired, job skills rarely start to fade before a person reaches 60, often not until much later.

Did You Know

An Underutilized Resource

Older workers often represent a substantially underutilized resource, according to Drexel University's Center for Employment Futures. For one thing, older workers are growing in numbers; workers age 55 and older now represent approximately 25 percent of the workforce. Further, many workers of traditional retirement age (65 and older) still work full- or part-time. The reasons? They like to be with other people, they like to feel productive, and—for some—they need the money to supplement their retirement pensions (especially since full Social Security benefits don't begin for some workers until years after the "normal" retirement age).

What are the potential drawbacks of older workers?

Older workers have one or more liabilities. But their experience and skills often permit them to compensate for their limitations. On the whole, older workers may exhibit one or more of the following limitations:

Slower. Age slows athletes and workers alike. But whereas older people work more slowly, they may make fewer mistakes.

Weaker. Their strength fades, too, although by now they may have learned to work more intelligently, not harder.

Less resilient. Older workers often don't have the endurance they once had. Fatigue—mental and physical—sets in faster. And illnesses and accidents keep them off the job longer than they would a younger person. But remember, older workers are less likely to have accidents happen.

Suffer from poorer eyesight. Near vision may suffer; older workers may need bifocals to correct it. But if "vision" also includes the ability to understand work situations within a broader context, older workers are at least as well off as their sharper-eyed children.

Under what conditions do older workers have the most difficulty in learning a new job?

Older adults have the most trouble learning a new skill when that skill conflicts with one they have already learned. Experience grows strong roots. When learning a new skill means cutting off those roots, older workers may not be psychologically ready to learn something new.

To make a difficult learning task easier, it's wise to demonstrate to older workers the similarities between what they have been doing and what you're asking them to do now. For instance, the supervisor could show that the procedures for performing a new task are basically the same as those for the previous one and that the differences are mainly a matter of degree. It's always easier for any person to learn if the move is gradual from the familiar to the unfamiliar.

How can you best motivate older workers?

By understanding them and helping them understand themselves. As all of us grow older, the gap widens between what we are and what we'd like to be. It's only natural for us to adopt an "I am what I am" attitude—especially when someone asks us to improve or to change our ways. In fact, the very stability that makes older workers an asset also makes it harder for them to change, since this stability is based on their having found contentment with their present lot. Thus, the problem of getting them to want to change, or to do better, resolves itself in your ability to get them to try.

To get older persons to try, you must help them be less critical and less self-conscious. Show them what other older workers are doing—in your company, if possible. Urge them to talk to others who have changed.

A word of caution: Keep performance standards high for both output and quality for older workers. There should be no rewards for age in terms of relaxed requirements.

QUICK TEST 4

| 7 | T or F | There are few meaningful differences between younger and older workers today. |
| 8 | T or F | From a legal standpoint, any worker over 40 years of age is considered to be older. |

Special Problems in a Changing Environment

5

What are the ways in which an employee's rights to privacy may be threatened?

The explosion in applications of technology has unleashed a wide array of devices that allow employers to monitor some aspects of employee behaviors. These include:

- Viewing interpersonal e-mail messages.
- Monitoring voice mail messages and websites visited.
- Observing images on computer monitors.
- Overhearing conversations in a variety of work and nonwork areas.
- Counting the number of keystrokes at a computer terminal.
- Electronically monitoring employee movement around the work facility.
- Watching employees on video.
- Running background checks.

The frequency of such practices has risen sharply in recent years, such that two-thirds of large firms now report some forms of such "snooping" being used.

CONCEPT

Changes in both the social and legal environments create special problems of supervision in handling sensitive issues of privacy and other employee rights.

Internet connection

http://www.privacyrights.org/fs/fs7-work.htm
Find intriguing questions and straight answers on monitoring and workplace privacy at this site.

TABLE 16-2	The Employee Privacy Bill of Rights

Companies are urged to provide employees with these rights:

- The opportunity to provide informed consent before being monitored.
- The chance to learn about the presence of surveillance devices at work.
- No unauthorized use or release of employee personal or medical information.
- Maintenance of a boundary between work and home (e.g., for telecommuters).

Source: Frederick S. Lane, *The Naked Employee*, New York: Amacom, 2003.

Employers defend themselves, arguing that they have the right to check employee backgrounds as well as monitor productivity. Employers routinely engage in drug testing, criminal record examinations, and credit checks. But employees are becoming more vocal about their rights to privacy, too. Unfortunately, the law regarding privacy at work is not as clear as it might be. It varies from state to state, too. In general, however, three things stand out: (1) Employees are entitled to know what information is on file about them, (2) employees should be informed in advance about what activities will be monitored, and (3) supervisors are restricted in their efforts to find out confidential information about their employees or to pass on to others outside the company information that has been gathered about an employee. See Table 16-2 for an example of proposed employee rights.

In addition, the Federal Electronic Communications Privacy Act places one key restriction on employers—it bans them from deliberately eavesdropping on purely personal conversations between employees while they are at work. However, workers should be made aware that some courts have allowed employers to break their promises about not monitoring employee behavior. The net effect, says Kevin Conlon, district counsel for the Communication Workers of America, is that "there is no such thing as privacy in the workplace."[2]

When can lie detectors and drug tests be used?

The use of lie detectors is severely restricted to specified occupations (such as security guard) and particular situations. They can no longer be randomly used. In general, such tests (including testing for drug use) are acceptable only if it can be clearly demonstrated that they are needed

(a) to protect the business itself or its customers from damage or theft or (b) to protect employees from interference or harm. Most organizations adopt and publish a policy on these matters. It is the supervisor's responsibility to assist in the dissemination and enforcement of this policy.

Does privacy extend to sensitive issues such as AIDS?

To a large extent, the answer is yes. In most instances, supervisors must rely on policies adopted by their employers and comply with them. This must be done regardless of how employees view the matter. It is important to support the letter of whatever law applies and your company's policy for implementing it. With regard to the specific issue of AIDS, it is now clear that those with this disease can have long, productive work lives. As a supervisor, you should be prepared to offer reasonable accommodations if changes in the illness require them. If other employees express concerns about working with a person who has AIDS, get the facts about the illness and share them with your employees.

To what extent does the concern for protected employees and for employee rights affect a supervisor's right to manage?

It complicates a supervisor's life, for sure. But it can be handled if you follow these priorities:

1. First things should come first. It's a supervisor's job to deal promptly and firmly with subordinates whose performance is unsatisfactory, who act in an unsafe manner, or who are uncooperative or abusive. This is consistent with laws about management and labor relations. Furthermore, it matches what most employees expect of their supervisor.
2. Thereafter, full respect and attention should be given to equal employment opportunity laws and other legislation intended to protect the rights and welfare of people at work. This should include an attitude of accommodation toward social concerns that are increasingly reflected in workplace practices, such as family leaves and child care or parental-assistance programs.

9	T or F	Supervisors need to be sensitive to, and protect, employee rights to privacy.
10	T or F	A supervisor's primary responsibility is to ensure a safe, fair, and productive workplace.

QUICK TEST 5

Practical Guidelines for Supervisors

1. *Review your employer's policies regarding diversity*, and communicate them periodically to your employees.

2. Continually "look in the mirror" to explore your attitude toward persons from protected groups; make sure you *do not treat any employee unfairly*, either consciously or unconsciously.

3. Whenever you are unsure about a potential discrimination issue or practice, *consult the human resource department* to obtain expert and objective advice and guidance.

4. Practice placing yourself in the shoes of protected group employees; *ask yourself how you would like to be treated* if you were one of them.

5. *Study the federal (and state) laws* affecting equal employment opportunity; be aware of both the letter of the law and its spirit.

6. Identify individuals who may have physical or mental disabilities, and *make every reasonable effort to accommodate them* in your workplace.

7. Study the job responsibilities of your female employees and their pay in comparison to that of males; *take aggressive action* to remedy any unexplained differences.

8. Closely monitor both your own behavior and that of other employees to *guarantee that there is no sexual harassment* (or the perception of it) at work.

9. *Analyze the employees in your department by age* to see if they fit into the Veteran, Boomer, Gen Xer, or Nexter generations; adjust your treatment of each accordingly.

10. Become aware of all the ways in which your organization monitors the behavior of its employees; advise them of their rights and *encourage them not to risk a violation*.

Chapter 16 Review

Key Concepts to Remember

1. A Diverse Workforce. The composition of the workforce is changing, and it is doing so at a dramatic pace. The number of white males as a percentage of the total workforce is getting smaller. The vast majority of new job holders are now women, minority men, and immigrants. With these changes come increased responsibility for a supervisor to understand effective and productive ways of managing that diversity.

2. The Legal Basis. A large body of equal employment opportunity (EEO) legislation has been enacted to protect and enhance the rights of protected groups, including women, African Americans, Native Americans, Hispanics, Asians, disabled workers, older workers, and Vietnam-era veterans. This places great responsibility on supervisors to make sure that these laws are effective in the workplace.

The federal agency charged with enforcing EEO laws is the Equal Employment Opportunity Commission (EEOC). The EEOC encourages, and often requires, the formation of affirmative action programs to ensure a more equal representation of minorities in a company's workforce. The EEOC looks, especially, for evidence of differential treatment, disparate effect, or evil intent. Disadvantaged workers represent a special kind of supervisory problem in that they often enter the workforce poorly prepared in terms of education and job skills. For this reason, it is essential that employment and advancement tests demonstrate their content and construct validity.

3. Women in the Workplace. Women are a major and valued portion of the workforce. Nevertheless, the quality of their participation continues to need protection and enhancement. This is evident in the difference between women's compensation and that of men, despite the efforts of job-evaluation programs to equalize pay. Most women ask only that their worth be judged on their merits and that they be given opportunities equal to those given to men for higher-paying and higher-status jobs. Sexual harassment in the workplace also continues to be a threat to a woman's dignity, welfare, and opportunities. Supervisors share a direct responsibility with higher management to prevent such harassment.

4. Younger and Older Workers. Workers can be viewed as Veterans, Boomers, Gen Xers, and Nexters, depending on the era in which they were born and raised. Younger workers represent a special kind of supervision problem in that they bring to work very high expectations but very little self-discipline. However, older workers may begin to suffer limitations caused by deterioration in pace, strength, eyesight, and resilience. These limitations are more than counterbalanced, however, by older workers' experience, skills retention, superior attendance, steadiness, safe working habits, and loyalty to their company and supervisors.

5. Special Problems in a Changing Environment. Increasingly, both the law and society in general believe an employee's right to privacy should be protected. This view has many ramifications in the areas of drug testing, lie detectors, and workplace monitoring, and in policies toward employees with life-threatening illnesses, such as AIDS. Nothing in any of the laws designed to protect the rights, or enhance the opportunities, of employees deprives supervisors of their fundamental right—and responsibility—to manage.

Reading Comprehension

1. What changes are occurring in our workforce today and are likely to continue into the future?

2. What is meant by affirmative action, and how does it tie in with EEO legislation?

3. In seeking to ensure conformance to EEO laws, what evidence of discrimination does the EEOC look for? In which areas of management is this most likely to occur?

4. Lupe's mother has just been involved in a serious car accident. Lupe has asked her supervisor for an extended period of time away from the job to care for her mother. How should the supervisor respond? If a leave is approved, can Lupe be transferred to a different, lower-paying job when she returns? Why?

5. Distinguish between the content validity and construct validity of employment tests.

6. Which approach do you think would motivate the company's "hard-core" van driver more: offering the driver membership in the company's recreational club or allowing the driver to take the keys of the van home at night? Why?

7. The men in Jane's work group repeatedly— but jokingly and admiringly—address her as "Pam," an obvious reference to her physical resemblance to Pamela Anderson. Jane doesn't particularly like this and complains to her supervisor. What should the supervisor do?

8. If 19-year-old Pete is dissatisfied with his job and blames his unrest on the meaninglessness of his work, what is the possibility of this charge being justified? What might Pete's supervisor do about this situation?

9. Why might an employee who works at a computer keyboard object to the number of her keystrokes being counted electronically as a measure of her performance? Do you believe that her employer has a right to make these measurements?

10. If, as a supervisor, you suspected an employee of drug dealing, would it be all right to inspect that employee's locker? Why?

Application

Self-Assessment

How Good Are Your Diversity Management Skills?

Read the following statements carefully. Circle the number on the response scale that most closely reflects the degree to which each statement describes you. Add up your total points and prepare a brief action plan for self-improvement. Be ready to report your score for tabulation across the entire group.

	Good Description	Poor Description
1. I am aware of, and sensitive to, the need for, cultural diversity.	10 9 8 7 6 5 4 3 2 1	
2. I take special care not to discriminate against the members of any minority group.	10 9 8 7 6 5 4 3 2 1	
3. I make a conscious effort to eliminate the use of stereotypes by me and my co-workers.	10 9 8 7 6 5 4 3 2 1	
4. I have a clear understanding of the various laws affecting equal employment opportunity.	10 9 8 7 6 5 4 3 2 1	
5. I understand and support the nature and purpose of affirmative action.	10 9 8 7 6 5 4 3 2 1	
6. I would feel comfortable making reasonable accommodations for a person with a disability.	10 9 8 7 6 5 4 3 2 1	
7. I understand and support the intentions of the Family and Medical Leave Act.	10 9 8 7 6 5 4 3 2 1	
8. I fully support equal pay for women and men who are performing similar or comparable jobs.	10 9 8 7 6 5 4 3 2 1	
9. I understand what constitutes unwelcome sexual advances, and would feel comfortable intervening immediately to stop them if I were aware of them happening.	10 9 8 7 6 5 4 3 2 1	
10. I understand the ways in which I need to relate differently to younger and older workers.	10 9 8 7 6 5 4 3 2 1	

Scoring and Interpretation

Scoring

Add up your total points for the 10 questions. Record that number here, and report it when it is requested. _____

Also, insert your score on the Personal Development Plan in the Appendix.

Interpretation

81 to 100 points. You seem to have a basic set of diversity management skills.

61 to 80 points. Take a close look at some of your diversity management skills (those with lower self-assessments) and discuss them with a manager to see if they need improvement.

Below 60 points. Some of your skills may be substantially inconsistent with effective diversity management practices and could be detrimental to your success as a supervisor. Identify your three lowest scores, and write the question numbers here: _____, _____, _____.

Action

Write a brief paragraph detailing an action plan for how you might sharpen each of these skills. Then pay particularly close attention to the related material in the chapter as you review the relevant sections there.

Skill Development

Diversity Management Improvement

Some organizations and some communities are rich melting pots of various racial and ethnic groups, but others are not. However, despite a possible absence of cultural diversity, almost all work organizations contain a mixture of male and female employees. Although many major organizations (e.g., Avon Products, Colgate-Palmolive, Coopers & Lybrand, Dow Chemical, and Motorola) have made major strides in creating a healthy environment for the advancement of females, others have lagged and still have a glass ceiling.

Select an organization and gain access to it to chat with some of its employees. Solicit their reactions to the problems they have encountered or observed, and the specific actions their employer could take to break down the glass ceiling. (To prepare yourself, you will likely wish to review the text's discussion of the glass ceiling, search the Internet for relevant guidelines, and consult with colleagues and staff persons in the human resources department for their advice.)

Problem Areas

1. _____
2. _____
3. _____
4. _____
5. _____

Suggestions for Improving Opportunities for Women

1. _____
2. _____

3. _____
4. _____
5. _____
6. _____
7. _____
8. _____
9. _____
10. _____

Action

After talking to several different people and assessing all the ideas produced, prepare a brief report that summarizes the problems and your 10 best suggestions for improvement in opportunities for women. If possible, share the results of your study with a responsible person in the host organization and obtain his or her reaction.

Role Play

Dealing with Diversity

Five persons are asked to volunteer to play the role of one of five supervisors who are about to hold a meeting with their employees. Each volunteer is assigned one of the supervisory roles shown below and asked to prepare a brief statement to be delivered orally to a group of his or her employees. Then each supervisor will have the opportunity to receive feedback from the employees.

First Supervisor. You have recently attended a supervisory development workshop on various aspects of diversity. At the end of the workshop, you decided that it would be appropriate to share some of your feelings with your employees as a way to ensure that everyone acts in a consistent manner and doesn't cause either intentional or inadvertent difficulties. You have chosen to make a brief statement on the topic of older workers—their unique characteristics, the challenges they present to co-workers, their right to be different, and the importance of tapping into their strengths and attributes.

Second Supervisor. You have recently attended a supervisory development workshop on various aspects of diversity. At the end of the workshop, you decided that it would be appropriate to share some of your feelings with your employees as a way to ensure that everyone acts in a consistent manner and doesn't cause either intentional or inadvertent difficulties. You have chosen to make a brief statement on the topic of the younger generation—their unique characteristics, the challenges they present to co-workers, their right to be different, and the importance of tapping into their strengths and attributes.

Third Supervisor. You have recently attended a supervisory development workshop on various aspects of diversity. At the end of the workshop, you decided that it would be appropriate to share some of your feelings with your employees as a way to ensure that everyone acts in a consistent manner and doesn't cause either intentional or inadvertent difficulties. You have chosen to make a brief statement on the topic of ethnic minorities—their unique characteristics, the challenges they present to co-workers, their right to be different, and the importance of tapping into their strengths and attributes.

Fourth Supervisor. You have recently attended a supervisory development workshop on various aspects of diversity. At the end of the workshop, you decided that it would be appropriate to share some of your feelings with your employees as a way to ensure that everyone acts in a consistent manner and doesn't cause either intentional or inadvertent difficulties. You have chosen to make a brief statement on the topic of the GLBTs—their unique characteristics, the challenges they present to co-workers, their right to be different, and the importance of tapping into their strengths and attributes.

Fifth Supervisor. You have recently attended a supervisory development workshop on various aspects of diversity. At the end of the workshop, you decided that it would be appropriate to share some of your feelings with your employees as a way to ensure that everyone acts in a consistent manner and doesn't cause either intentional or inadvertent difficulties. You have chosen to make a brief statement on the topic of monitoring employee behaviors—the fact that your organization feels it is necessary and appropriate to keep tabs on employee behavior, and the various ways in which it does so.

All Others (the Employees). Listen attentively to each of the supervisory talks. When each one is finished, you should react to what you heard and respond with questions, expressions of support, statements of concern, and so forth (expressing your honest reactions to the supervisor). Respond as you think typical employees might respond upon hearing such a talk.

Questions (Answer after all five talks have been delivered.)

1. What did the supervisors say or do that was highly effective?
2. What did the supervisors say or do that might be viewed as inappropriate or offensive?
3. How could information such as that heard today be presented in such a way that it is well received and adhered to by the employees?
4. Based on the feedback received, the five supervisors should indicate how they might have improved upon their presentations.

Cases for Analysis

Case 50

Jackrabbit Jokers

Dave's Jackrabbit Delivery Service is a small local package delivery service in the Midwest. Three of the 15 truck drivers are women. At the start of every day, it was common for all the drivers to get together in the lunchroom for a morning cup of coffee and a chance to discuss the day's events before going out on the run. After work, they would gather at the Cueball Bar for a couple of drinks before going home. The crew had no turnover in the last five years. It was a close-knit group whose members enjoyed one another's company. It wouldn't be uncommon when they got together for them to tease one another about an unusual or distinctive habit—their weight, their bodies, or even their love lives. They all seemed to enjoy themselves.

Eight months ago, one of the women, Theresa, got married to someone not well known to the rest of the group. The before- and after-work routine continued, much as before Theresa's wedding. One day, as Theresa came into the lunchroom, Hector said, "Hey, Theresa, you look like you had a real workout last night." Marty commented that if his wife had a body like that, he'd be "coming to work with bags under his eyes."

Everyone laughed, and why not? It was typical of the type of interplay that they had had with each other over the years. You can imagine their surprise when Dave came into the lunchroom the next day and announced that Theresa had filed a charge of sexual harassment against Hector and Marty. Someone responded to Dave, "I don't get it. We've always been able to kid each other like this."

Analysis

Based on the information presented above, prepare a brief response to each of the following statements:

a. Sexual harassment did not occur because no requests for sexual contact or physical touching occurred in this case.
b. No sexual harassment occurred because, whether we like it or not, this kind of behavior had gone on for years and Theresa had never complained about it before.
c. Theresa has a good case for sexual harassment because the environment in which she worked was clearly hostile, intimidating, and offensive.
d. Hector and Marty should receive no discipline for their action because Theresa never told them she found their behavior offensive.
e. This entire work group was looking for trouble, and some action needs to be taken to ensure this behavior doesn't continue in the future.

Case 51

Upward on Cannery Row

In a West Coast cannery, Luis Valdes, a 45-year-old ex-migratory worker, was hired into the steam-pack operation. For his first few weeks on the job, Luis performed general labor, helping the operator load the vats and mop up spills. He was eager and attentive, and, although his English was not particularly good, he seemed to get the idea of what was wanted from him. Accordingly, the steam-pack supervisor suggested that Luis might swing over to the second shift as a number two operator.

Analysis

In preparation for this move, the supervisor should do which of the following?

a. Assemble a series of operating manuals for Luis to study.
b. Ask the day-shift operator to tell Luis exactly what will be expected of him.

c. Show, by demonstration, how each step of the steam-pack operation is performed, and have Luis repeat each step while the supervisor watches him.

d. Tell Luis that he should clear up any questions he has about the steam-pack operation now, before he swings over to the second shift.

Case 52

Banking Jobs for All Ages

If you were the branch manager of a bank in a booming industrial area where it was very difficult to attract and hold younger people, how might you suggest to your various supervisors that they adjust their job openings and work assignments to accommodate and make the most valuable use of the larger supply of older people in the local labor market? You know that business at the tellers' windows has a great deal of variety: some is routine, such as accepting deposits and cashing checks; other transactions are more complex, such as making out certified checks, selling traveler's checks, and opening up new accounts. Then, too, at some hours of the day, business is hectic and fast-paced; at other times, it is relatively slow. In the cashiers' department, keypunching is generally a "high-production" job, whereas resolving and verifying balances is a more painstaking one.

Analysis

What are your suggestions for making the most of the younger and older workers in the local labor market?

Think first about the characteristics of younger workers: their attitudes toward their work, what they expect and enjoy most, and what they like least. Then think about what the text says about older workers and their strengths and their weaknesses. With this knowledge in mind, what might be done to modify and restructure work at the bank to make it more appealing and more effective for both younger and older workers? Consider, especially, changes that affect the following:

- Work schedules
- Division of work
- Employee training
- Job progression

Quick Test 1	Quick Test 2	Quick Test 3	Quick Test 4	Quick Test 5
1. F	3. F	5. F	7. F	9. T
2. F	4. T	6. T	8. T	10. T

Chapter References

1. Ron Zemke, "Here Come the Millenials," *Training*, July 2001, pp. 44–49.
2. Sarah Boehle, "They're Watching You," *Training*, August 2000, pp. 50–60.

17

The Supervisor's Role in Employee Safety and Health, and Labor Relations

LEARNING OBJECTIVES

After studying this chapter, you should be able to

- Discuss the extensive list of factors in addition to human error that contribute to occupational injuries and illnesses.

- Explain various facets of the Occupational Safety and Health Act, compute occupational accident incident and severity rates, and understand the procedures for investigating and analyzing an accident.

- Evaluate several common approaches to accident prevention—including the three Es of *engineering, education,* and *enforcement*—and discuss the effectiveness of safety committees.

- Explore the role of wellness programs, identify the negative consequences of employee obesity, and specify the warning signs for workplace violence.

- Discuss a supervisor's responsibilities in labor-management relations, as affected by significant provisions of the main labor-management relations laws.

- Explain the collective-bargaining process and the supervisor's role in implementing a labor agreement and handling grievances.

Safety at Work

Accident. An unplanned or uncontrolled event in which action or reaction of an object, material, or person results in personal injury or property damage, or both.

Hazard. A potentially dangerous object, material, condition, or practice that is present in the workplace to which employees must be alert and from which they must be protected.

What causes accidents?

People do, mostly. In fact, study after study shows that approximately 91 percent of accidents can be attributed to unsafe acts, compared to about 9 percent caused by environmental factors or faulty equipment. Of course, people don't have accidents on purpose. An **accident**, by definition, is an unplanned or uncontrolled event, usually one that results in personal injury or property damage. Accidents happen for a variety of reasons. Sometimes, it's just plain carelessness. Sometimes, people haven't received proper instructions or have not been alerted to a **hazard**, a known, potentially dangerous object or condition associated with their work. Sometimes, the person's attitude is to blame. Sometimes, equipment fails. Sometimes, machines are not properly guarded. But almost always, there is a person, usually the person who gets injured, who could have prevented the accident by taking proper protective or control action.

This does not remove the responsibility from the company, institution, or agency involved. Ownership and management must be committed to the principle of accident and health protection. This often means a sizable investment as well as costly and time-consuming safety and health measures.

How costly are work-related accidents?

Very costly, indeed. The annual bill to industry is over $50 billion, and it is rising. The human costs, however, are even greater. Nearly one worker in the United States is killed every hour of every day on the job. That's more than 5,000 deaths each year. And it doesn't stop there. Every 5 to 10 seconds, another worker is injured on the job, or some 4 million a year. Consider the physical pain and suffering, the loss of self-esteem that can accompany becoming dependent on others, and the disruption to a family when the breadwinner loses his or her normal source of income.

How much of the blame can be placed on accident-prone employees?

Some blame belongs there, but it would be wrong to overemphasize their presence. Examination of safety records often shows that just a few employees account for the bulk of accidents. This suggests that the great majority of employees rarely have accidents. The people who get injured frequently are spoken of as *accident prone*. This means that for one reason or another, they have a tendency to have accidents and hence are prone to injury. Psychologists have shown, however, that only a small percentage of so-called accident-prone employees are truly accident prone. Most of these habitual sufferers can actually be made accident free by proper job placement, training, and encouragement. If one or more of your workers appear accident prone, don't assume it is not your responsibility. Instead, encourage the development of work habits that will protect these employees from themselves.

Where else, then, does the blame lie?

Finger-pointing doesn't prevent accidents. There are many commonly recognized causes of accidents besides those immediately attributable to employee carelessness or inattention. Among them are the following:

- Absence of, or faulty, protective devices.
- Ineffective specifications for safety clothing.
- Inadequate ventilation or the presence of fumes.
- Presence of hazardous or unauthorized materials.
- Wrong tools, materials, or supplies issued for the job.
- Absence of a safety standard for the operation.
- Lack of safety training for a specific task.
- Inadequate or improper instructions.
- Safety rules or procedures not enforced.
- The wrong person placed in an unsuitable task.
- Poor housekeeping or sanitation at the workplace.
- Pressure from supervision to disregard safe procedures in the interest of faster movement or greater output.

Do not disregard the fact, of course, that each of these causes is directly or indirectly related to the faulty performance of an individual or group of individuals somewhere along the line.

Which industries experience the most accidents?

They have their greatest frequency and severity in the manufacturing, mining, food processing, construction, transportation, and hotel industries. They occur less frequently in banks and insurance companies.

It bears repeating here that accidents *can* be prevented. Du Pont Co. has an exemplary safety record despite the fact that the company manufactures explosives and heavy chemicals, which can be extremely hazardous processes. In one recent year, Du Pont had a lost-time incident rate of 0.04 when the national average for its industry was over 70. The company is justified in asserting that its employees are safer at work than at home.

Did You Know

Gangs in Corporate America

Gangs have begun to infiltrate many industries and organizations in corporate America. According to some estimates, as many as 400,000 gang members work in corporations, and they regularly engage in a wide variety of activities, including theft, extortion, drug sales, and hijackings. Some even stage workplace accidents to cover up gang-related injuries so that they can collect huge reimbursements from health insurance companies. What can organizations do? Supervisory actions include the following:

- Don't assume that any workplace is immune from gang activity.

- Carefully screen prospective employees.

- Watch for clues that gang members may be present in your workforce.

- Install—and use—a variety of security measures (e.g., video cameras).

- Strictly enforce existing policies for security and behavioral violations.

Where are ergonomic hazards most likely to occur? How can they be minimized?

Ergonomic hazard. A workplace condition that requires the job holder to repeat or sustain a fixed motion or stress pattern over an extended period of time, and that may include a repetitive strain injury (RSI).

Increasingly, organizations are paying close attention to risk factors arising from **ergonomic hazards**. These are workplace conditions that have the potential for inducing injury from an occupational activity that involves repetitive motion and stress. The technical term for such an injury is a *repetitive strain injury (RSI)* or *musculoskeletal disorder (MSD)*. These injuries include carpal tunnel syndrome, tendinitis, and back injuries. Employers are most concerned with ergonomic hazards associated with

- Performance of the same motion pattern for a prolonged period, such as at a computer keyboard.
- Use of vibrating or impact (jarring, jolting) tools.
- Using forceful hand, leg, or foot exertions repeatedly.
- Maintaining a fixed or awkward posture for an extended period.

The incidence of RSI can be minimized in three important ways:

1. By stretching, changing position, alternating tasks, moving about, or otherwise interrupting the muscular routines.
2. By redesigning the workplace so that it can be adapted to the needs and size of the workers (an ergonomic workplace). Examples: a desktop that can be raised or lowered at will, a fully adjustable chair, positioning devices to hold the work, glare-free illumination.
3. By the use of special tooling, machinery, and accessories intended to help the body accommodate to the routines imposed by the work assignment.

| **QUICK TEST** 1 | 1 | T or F | Basically, a hazard and an accident are the same thing. |
| | 2 | T or F | Accident-prone employees have usually just been in the wrong place at the wrong time. |

2 OSHA's Mandated Safety Standards

CONCEPT

The federal government establishes and monitors (through OSHA) strict standards for the protection of safety and health at work.

What role does the federal government play in the prevention of accidents?

A major one. In earlier times, the safety of an employee at work was largely the result of efforts by state governments, insurance companies, independent safety organizations such as the National Safety Council, and the employer. Passage of the Williams-Steiger *Occupational Safety and Health Act* of 1970 (effective April 1971) and the creation of the *Occupational Safety and Health Administration (OSHA)* put the federal government and the Department of Health, Education, and Welfare (HEW) squarely into the safety act in every significant plant and office in the United States. The purpose of OSHA is to establish safety and health standards with which every employer and every employee must comply. And to make sure that there is compliance, OSHA makes thousands of inspections annually.

What do the OSHA standards specify?

The General Duty clause states that each employer

1. Shall furnish to each employee, employment and a place of employment that is free from recognized hazards causing, or likely to cause, death or serious harm to employees.
2. Shall comply with occupational safety and health standards set forth by the act.

The standards specify just about everything imaginable. They include specifications for guarding walks and walking surfaces, means of egress, powered platforms, environmental controls, noise, radiation, hazardous materials, sanitation, first-aid services, fire protection, compressed gases, material handling, machine guards, portable tools, welding, and electrical installations. OSHA pays particular attention to paper, textile, laundry, sawmill, and bakery operations.

To what extent does OSHA specify accident record keeping?

It insists that every company or separate establishment maintain a log of illnesses and accidents as they occur. The OSHA log (Form 200) is used to record each occupational injury or illness and identify whether it has caused a fatality, a lost workday, a permanent transfer to another job, or a termination of employment. Since your company will probably specify what records must be kept and who will maintain them, the supervisor—as in so many other areas—is a pivotal person in collecting the data.

How are accident rates classified and measured?

OSHA and the U.S. Bureau of Labor Statistics have worked together to establish (a) what constitutes an incident (or accident case) and (b) how to measure the incident rate (frequency rate) and severity rate.

A *recordable incident* (or *accident case*) is one that involves occupational injury or illness, including death. Not recordable are (a) first-time ailments that involve one-time treatment and (b) minor cuts, scratches, or

Occupational Safety and Health Act. Comprehensive legislation that establishes standards and calls for the inspection of safety and health conditions and the investigation of all serious accidents and alleged safety or health hazards. Created Occupational Safety and Health Administration.

burns that do not ordinarily require medical care, even if such treatment is provided by a physician or registered nurse.

Accident rates are measured by two very similar formulas. The first formula measures an *incident rate* (also called *frequency rate*) by comparing the number of accident cases that have occurred with the total number of hours worked by all employees during the same period. The second formula measures a *severity* rate by comparing the number of lost workdays that have occurred with the total number of hours worked by all employees during the period. For consistency's sake, all rates are computed using a standard based on the expectations of 100 employees working 2,000 hours per year, or 200,000 hours.

To illustrate the use of these formulas, suppose that plant XYZ has 200 employees each averaging 40 hours a week for 50 weeks (or 2,000 hours per year each). During the year, 12 accident cases are recorded, and a total of 88 workdays are lost as a result.

Incident rate (Frequency rate)

$$= \frac{\text{number of recordable cases} \times 200{,}000 \text{ hours}}{\text{total hours worked by all employees during the year}}$$

$$= \frac{12 \text{ cases} \times 200{,}000 \text{ hours}}{200 \text{ workers} \times 40 \text{ hours/week} \times 50 \text{ weeks/year}}$$

$$= \frac{2{,}400{,}000}{400{,}000}$$

$$= 6 \text{ incidents per 100 full-time employees}$$

Using the data provided, the severity of these accidents, as gauged by the total lost workdays they caused, is measured in the following way:

$$\text{Severity rate} = \frac{\text{number of workdays lost} \times 200{,}000 \text{ hours}}{\text{total hours worked by all employees during the year}}$$

$$= \frac{88 \text{ workdays lost} \times 200{,}000 \text{ hours}}{200 \text{ workers} \times 40 \text{ hours/week} \times 50 \text{ weeks/year}}$$

$$= \frac{17{,}600{,}000}{400{,}000}$$

$$= 44 \text{ workdays lost per 100 full-time employees}$$

Similar incident and severity rates can be calculated for disabling injuries only or for illnesses only.

How do you investigate an accident?

If an accident happens in your department or to an employee under your supervision, one of the best ways to prevent its happening again is to investigate the accident to find out exactly why it happened. Once you have determined this, you can establish safeguards to protect individuals from any unnecessary dangers. When you are checking on accidents, your primary goal is to find causes, not to fix blame. Look for answers to such questions as these:

- **What happened?** Who got hurt? How badly? What material was spoiled? Was any equipment damaged? Does it need repair before being put into operation again? Who, besides the injured individual, was involved?
- **Why did it happen?** Was it solely human error? If so, was it due to a lack of skill? Of knowledge about key points? Was it mainly carelessness? How about the equipment involved? Was it in good working order? Did the individuals involved know how to operate it properly?
- **What needs to be done to prevent this from happening again?** Does it require special training? A specific new rule or regulation? A change in process or procedure? Different kinds of equipment? Additional safeguards?
- **What steps have you taken to prevent recurrence?** How much of the above have you put into practice with improved training and instruction? Have you worked out a prevention plan?
- **What still needs to be done?** Do you need further assistance from your boss or from the appropriate staff departments? Should you enlist the help of the safety committee? Have you set up a follow-up procedure?

What happens to a company when it doesn't meet the OSHA standards?

It receives a citation. A severe penalty and fine will follow if the problem is not corrected. More specifically, the citation is issued to the manager in charge of the facility. It may even be issued, for example, to a supervisor who failed to make certain that protection was in place. A company and an individual may seek a temporary variance from the standard, but in most instances the only recourse is to take corrective action as soon as possible. In many cases, heavy fines and even jail sentences have been imposed on companies and managers who failed to comply promptly with the citation.

How has OSHA affected safety training?

It has made it mandatory. Supervisors are expected to make certain that safe procedures are taught not only to new employees but also as an ongoing program.

General safety training applies to the proper observance of safety regulations, routing for emergency egress in case of fire or other common

danger, accident and injury treatment and reporting, and fire and explosion emergency activities.

Specific employee training required by OSHA applies to occupational health and environmental controls, hazardous materials, personal protective equipment, medical and first aid, fire protection, material handling and storage, and machine guarding.

Where do employees fit into the OSHA picture?

The law insists that they, too, act safely within established standards—provided that employers live up to their responsibilities. In other words, an employee who refused to wear the safety glasses provided by the employer in prescribed areas could be cited. A bearded employee might be required to shave to make his respirator fit. Specifically, OSHA states, "The Williams-Steiger Act also requires that each employee comply with safety and health standards, rules, and orders issued under the Act and applicable to his conduct."

Employees have several important rights under OSHA, however. For example, they may do the following:

1. Request an inspection if they believe an imminent danger exists or a violation of a standard exists that may cause physical harm.
2. Have a representative (such as a union steward) accompany an OSHA compliance officer during the inspection of a workplace.
3. Advise an OSHA compliance officer of any violation of the act that they believe exists in the workplace, and question, and be questioned privately by, the compliance officer.
4. Have regulations posted to inform them of protection afforded by the act.
5. Have locations monitored to measure exposure to toxic or radioactive materials, have access to the records of such monitoring or measuring, and have a record of their own personal exposure.
6. Have medical examinations or other tests to determine whether their health is being affected by an exposure, and have the results of such tests furnished to their physicians.
7. Have posted on the premises any citations made to the employer by OSHA.

QUICK TEST 2	3	T or F	OSHA requires organizations to record *any* injury to or illness of its employees.
	4	T or F	The accident incident rate focuses on the frequency of accident cases, whereas the severity rate focuses on the number of hours lost as a result of accidents.

Accident Prevention: The Basics

CONCEPT

Supervisors play the key role in accident prevention by emphasizing safety awareness, education, and enforcement.

With whom does accident prevention begin?

Good supervision is the starting place for an effective accident-prevention program. No amount of protective devices or safety rules will stop accidents from happening if supervisors aren't absolutely sold on the fact that it can be done—and that it's their responsibility.

Shouldn't employees have a responsibility for safety?

By all means! People failure is at the heart of most accidents. Supervisors cannot be everywhere at once, and they shouldn't want or need to be. In the long run, it will be your employees who cause—or prevent—accidents in your department. But you've got to take the lead in showing them how prevention is achieved.

1. **Instill in employees the belief that they are the most influential source of accident prevention.** Discuss the particulars of the accidents that have occurred in your organization. Seize every opportunity to let employees see cause and effect for themselves.
2. **Show employees how to develop safe working habits.** People have to be trained to work safely just as they must be trained to work accurately. Few persons are naturally cautious, or know instinctively where danger lies. After training, remind them frequently to help them maintain safe habits and to integrate those habits into their work routines.
3. **Pay special attention to new employees.** Statistics show that a majority of accidents involve first-year employees. The first day on the job isn't too early to start this indoctrination.
4. **Be specific about prevention techniques.** Often a demonstration is needed to supplement the clear instructions. For example, you might begin by saying, "Stack boxes carefully on this shelf and not too high; otherwise, they may fall and hurt someone." Then *show* the employee how to stack cartons safely, and also make a mark on the wall above which they must not be stacked.
5. **Enlist safety suggestions from employees.** When an accident happens close to home, for instance, talk it over with one or many of your employees. Get their ideas on how it could have been prevented. Ask them if similar situations could arise in their areas. Continually bring the conversation around to the role of the human element.

Health and safety should be a paramount concern for both employers and employees. **What indicators of safety equipment can you see here?**

6. **Set a good example.** Supervisors should go out of their way to observe the letter of every safety rule themselves. Never—*never*—yield on safety in favor of your own convenience.

7. **Firmly enforce job safety standards.** Many employees think of safety as a matter of "Don't do this or that," or as just so many rules and regulations. Let employees know immediately the danger to themselves—and your dissatisfaction—when they don't follow the safety guidelines you've outlined for them. Reason and encourage first, but penalize if you don't get the necessary conformance.

What is the basis for accident prevention?

Accident prevention requires a balanced, three-pronged attack. For years, the National Safety Council has stressed the three Es: engineering, education, and enforcement. (See Figure 17-1.)

You can observe the three elements of accident protection in the workplace, too. For instance:

- To *engineer* a job for safety is to design the equipment, lay out the work, plan the job, and protect the individual—all with accident prevention as a primary ingredient.
- To *educate* for safety is to show employees where, why, and how accidents can happen and develop in them safe work habits and the desire to avoid injury. Help workers analyze the danger spots in their jobs and train them to build a defense against each one.
- To *enforce* safety is to make an actuality of the slogan "Safety first." Employees need guidance in the form of regulations and discipline to protect safe workers from those who would cause accidents through unsafe acts.

FIGURE 17-1
The three E's of safety and accident prevention.
What role does each of them play in worker safety?

What can be done to make safety committees more useful?

If you or your company has organized departmental safety committees, see that the committee has a real job to do. Don't let meetings turn into nonproductive rap sessions. And don't use them solely as a sounding board for your inspirational appeals for safety. Treat the safety committee as a business organization:

Assign specific problems. If you discover a pattern of injuries, get the committee to investigate this condition to find out what the facts are, where the injuries occur, and to whom. Then ask for a specific recommendation on how to correct the situation.

Expect results. Make it clear that being on a safety committee entails more than sitting in on a meeting. Assign area safety responsibilities to the members. Let them assist with inspections.

Reward Safety

Reward employees for safe work practices and accident-free results. Why? Because, in general, every dollar spent on safety-recognition programs saves about $10 in injury costs (lost time, medical expenses, and workers' compensation). But the real art lies in *how* to reward employees, especially if the rewards are combined with safety-awareness programs and safety training. In general, follow these rules:

- Don't provide cash awards to employees for good accident records (the amount is too low to be meaningful).
- Set targets for employees to achieve (e.g., six-month or yearly goals).
- Provide a variety of company-related items as rewards (e.g., inexpensive coolers, hats, or flashlights) with the company's safety slogan imprinted on them.
- Provide team rewards for a team's safety achievements.

Ask for a report on the minor accidents in each area. Have the members tell what improvements have been made and what more can be done.

Have members participate in investigations. Talking about safety isn't as effective as having employees get out on the floor to see what's being done about it. Use this opportunity to demonstrate the company's efforts and expenditures for safe working conditions. Emphasize that unsafe practices are just as important to watch out for.

Delegate duties. If the committee plans a safety competition, let it handle the publicity, the method of making awards, and the establishment of rules. Committee members know their co-workers better than anyone else does and can guess what will work best.

Safety inspections: Are they useful, or are they another example of window dressing?

Safety and sanitation inspections are an essential part of a successful accident prevention and control program. It is important, however, that they (a) be conducted regularly, (b) be based on verifying compliance with the company's and OSHA's rules and standards, (c) seek also to detect new areas of necessary coverage, and (d) be followed up quickly by rigorous action to correct unsatisfactory conditions.

How prevalent are wellness programs?

Increasingly, prevention programs extend beyond safety to health and wellness. For example, the U.S. Department of Health and Human Services

The number of Americans who are obese is increasing, obesity-related chronic conditions are increasing, and obesity drives up health-care costs.

Camille Haltom

reported that the following wellness programs were most common in industry: smoking control, health-risk appraisal, back care, stress management, exercise and physical fitness, off-the-job accident prevention, nutrition education, blood-pressure control, and weight control. They indicate how broad an employer's concern for safety and health enhancement can grow.

What about obesity? Is that a supervisor's concern?

Overweight employees—particularly obese ones—can have substantial consequences for both themselves and their employers. For example, their annual medical expenses often are four times higher than those for normal-weight individuals. Also, on a national scale, 300,000 deaths annually are directly linked to the epidemic of obesity and the pervasiveness of physical inactivity.[1] Despite the sensitivity of the issue and the difficulty of addressing it with an individual, supervisors play a key role in at least making employees aware of the employer's concern and the opportunities available. Many firms provide weight-management programs, healthy food alternatives in their cafeterias, "10,000-step programs," and fitness centers to aid employees in achieving their health and weight-loss goals.

Is workplace violence a safety issue too?

Absolutely, based on the figures. One million employees are assaulted at work every year, and 700 of them die; nearly 2 million days of work are missed because of violence or stress-induced hostility. Unfortunately, many employers still don't have effective violence-prevention programs.

Violence at work includes intimidation and bullying, threats of bodily harm or property damage, and actual destruction of people or equipment. Supervisors should be alert to some of the reliable warning signs, especially when they appear in combination—suddenly withdrawn personalities, drug or alcohol abuse, mood swings, refusal to accept criticism, feelings of persecution or paranoia, antagonistic relations with others, fascination with weapons, and of course a deterioration in productivity. In addition, sudden job loss or even dramatic loss of face at work can trigger violent responses. Clear company policies dealing with violence should be in place, pre-employment checking should be done, employee assistance programs can be established, outplacement counseling can be offered, and violence-prevention training can be implemented for all employees. Because of the explosiveness of the issue, this is a prime opportunity for being proactive and *preventing* this type of problem.

| 5 | T or F | Supervisors represent the first line of defense in preventing accidents. |
| 6 | T or F | The three Es of accident prevention focus on engineering, education, and elimination. |

Labor Unions and Labor Law

4

What role does the first-line supervisor play in labor matters?

Many organizations do not have unions. In fact, only about 12 percent of all employees are formally represented by a union. Nevertheless, unions are powerful in some industries (e.g., auto manufacturing, steel production, mining, and airlines). Further, the results attained by unions in those industries often set a precedent for internal practices in other, nonunionized organizations. Unions, or the possibility of unions, cannot be ignored.

In the eyes of the law, supervisors are responsible agents of their organizations. Your employers are held responsible for any action you take in dealing with employees or with labor unions, just as if they had taken the action themselves. For this reason, if for no other, it is essential that a supervisor be familiar with the legal aspects and terminology of labor relations. This is especially true for two particular points: (a) Your actions may be considered violations of laws, and may affect a union's attempts to gain or retain bargaining rights for employees, and (b) the ***labor agreement*** that your organization has signed with a union (a mutually binding contract stipulating wages and benefits, hours, and various working conditions) can have a powerful impact on policies, practices, and procedures that make for effective operation of the organization as well as constructive employee-employer relations.

CONCEPT
Supervisors are considered legal representatives of management in matters affecting labor union recognition and contracts: therefore, they need to be aware of relevant labor laws.

Labor agreement. The written agreement that binds a company's management and its employees' organization (labor union) for a stipulated period of time to certain conditions of pay, hours, work, and any other matters the parties deem appropriate. (Also called *union agreement* or *labor contract*.)

Why do employees join labor unions?

Employees join labor unions for at least three reasons:

1. **The union offers bargaining power and takes risks through collective activity that many individuals cannot, or do not wish to, provide by acting alone.** That's the underlying purpose of labor (or trade) unions; to promote, protect, and improve—through joint action—the job-related economic interests of their members.
2. **Membership is often compulsory.** In three-quarters of labor agreements (but not in all states), an individual must join or at least pay

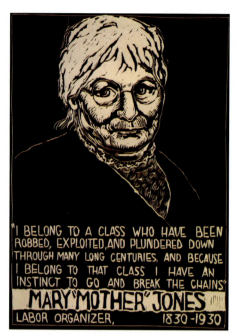

"I BELONG TO A CLASS WHO HAVE BEEN ROBBED, EXPLOITED, AND PLUNDERED DOWN THROUGH MANY LONG CENTURIES, AND BECAUSE I BELONG TO THAT CLASS I HAVE AN INSTINCT TO GO AND BREAK THE CHAINS"

MARY"MOTHER"JONES
LABOR ORGANIZER, 1830-1930

Some employees still perceive that they have been "robbed, exploited, and plundered" in the workplace. **Is it any wonder that they seek union representation?**

dues if she or he wants to keep a job. The idea behind compulsory membership is that everyone should pay his or her fair share of the cost of benefits derived from unionism and that no one should get a free ride.

3. **Membership provides both a real and a perceived countervailing power to management's power to hire, promote, or fire at will.** No matter how fair-minded an organization's management may try to be, many individuals feel helpless in today's increasingly large and complex organizations. Others may believe they have received unfair or arbitrary treatment. For these individuals, union membership provides a feeling of strength and security that is otherwise lacking.

What should your attitude be toward an existing union?

Adopt the attitude that if your company has made an agreement with a union, your best bet is to work as hard as you can to get along with it. Don't try to undermine the union. Instead, put your efforts into making your department a better place in which to work. It's more important than ever, when your company has a union, to show employees that you still consider them your department's greatest asset. If you abandon their interests, you're likely to find employees looking to their union representatives rather than to you for leadership.

How should you react when your employees display strong loyalties to their union?

Don't feel hurt. An extensive study of employees' loyalties showed rather conclusively that it's natural for workers to have dual loyalty—to their supervisors and to their union leaders. Employees look to their boss for sound business judgments and for the satisfactions that come from doing a purposeful job under good working conditions. But employees look to their union for the social prestige of belonging to an influential group and as a protector of their economic interests and job security. An employee who works for a good company and a considerate supervisor and who also is represented by an honest, active union enjoys both relationships.

What is the impact of the Wagner Act?

The Wagner Act (formally called the National Labor Relations Act) describes the conditions under which workers can organize and bargain collectively through their authorized representatives. It does not set out any specific working conditions that employers must give to their employees, nor does it concern itself with the terms of the union agreement. All it does is guarantee that employees may act in a group together—rather than as individuals—if they so desire, in bargaining for three key items: wages, hours, and working conditions.

Supervisors have learned that they need to be especially careful to avoid *interference* during a union's organizing drive or representation election. They must avoid (a) any actions that affect an employee's job or pay, (b) arguments that lead to a dispute over a union question, (c) threats to a union member through a third party, or (d) interactions without advice from top management with any of the organizing union's officers. These could all be deemed **unfair labor practices** under the Wagner Act.

How did the Taft-Hartley Act change the Wagner Act?

The National Labor Relations Act (the Wagner Act) was amended by the Taft-Hartley Act (Labor-Management Relations Act) in 1947. The Taft-Hartley Act clarified and added to the list of unfair practices that could be charged against management. But more significantly, the act provided a better balance between the parties by imposing on unions certain restrictions on their organizing activities and ability to make use of certain types of boycotts.

Under the amended law, unions and their agents are forbidden to engage in the following unfair labor practices:

- Attempt to force an employer to discharge or discriminate against former members of the union who have been expelled for reasons other than nonpayment of regular union dues or initiation fees.
- Attempt to force an employer to pay or deliver any money or other things of value for services that are not performed. This outlaws featherbedding and other make-work practices.
- Restrain or coerce other employees into joining or not joining a union.
- Require excessive or discriminatory fees from employees who wish to become union members.

In addition, the act made clear that employees are protected in their desire to bargain or not to bargain collectively. For example, they may take up a complaint directly with management—but only when the issue and the settlement do not involve issues covered by a union contract. However, a union representative must be given an opportunity to be present.

Closed shop, union shop—what are they?

In a *closed shop*, a prospective employee had to belong to the union before being hired. The closed shop was outlawed by the Taft-Hartley

Unfair labor practices.
Practices engaged in by either management or labor unions that are judged by the federal labor law (National Labor Relations Act) to be improper, especially in that they (a) interfere with the rights of employees to organize or (b) discriminate against employees for labor union activities.

Act. The *union shop* is still a form of compulsory unionism, but with a big difference: The person need not be a union member at the time of hiring. But a new employee (usually after a 30- or 60-day trial period) must *become* a member of the union to stay on the payroll. Of course, the union shop is not automatic in all collective bargaining cases—it must be negotiated and agreed on contractually by the union and management.

What is a right-to-work law?

Right-to-work laws. Legislation passed in nearly two dozen states that makes it illegal to negotiate for a union shop after a union gains recognition.

When the Taft-Hartley Act outlawed the closed shop, it also permitted the individual states to pass laws making the union shop illegal. Such laws, enacted in 21 states, are called ***right-to-work laws***. In these states, compulsory membership in a labor union is illegal. Then, when unions do gain recognition in an organization, it is illegal to negotiate for a union shop. Thus, it is possible for 51 percent of a company's bargaining-unit employees to be union members and 49 percent to be nonmembers because they have the right to choose their own status and still work.

What other labor-related laws should a supervisor know about?

Two important laws are the Walsh-Healey Public Contracts Act and the Fair Labor Standards Act. Generally, your company will watch for compliance, but since the laws influence decisions that affect you, here's a fast rundown.

Walsh-Healey Public Contracts Act.   Walsh-Healey sets the rules for any company that works on a government contract in excess of $10,000. The act sets minimum ages for the hiring of teenagers, and limits the basic hours of work to 8 per day and 40 per week. The employer must pay time and a half for overtime hours on a daily basis. The act also sets up strict standards for safety, health, and working conditions. A very important feature is the right to establish a minimum wage for a particular industry.

Fair Labor Standards Act.   Also known as the Wages and Hours Law, this act regulates methods of wage payment and hours of work for any industry engaged in commerce between two or more states. The law restricts the employment of children over age 14 and under 16 to non-manufacturing and nonmining positions and prohibits the employment of children between 16 and 18 in hazardous jobs, including driving or helping a driver of a motor vehicle. The law sets the minimum wage (periodically adjusted by Congress) and prescribes that time and a half must be paid for all hours worked over 40 in a week.

The Fair Labor Standards Act also sets guidelines for determining which supervisors and other employees must be paid overtime and which should not. To be classed as an *exempt* employee (and thus not subject to the provisions of the act), a supervisor must meet the following requirements:

- Have as a primary duty the management of a recognized department or subdivision.
- Customarily and regularly direct the work of two or more other employees, exercise discretionary powers, and have the power to hire or fire or make suggestions and recommendations that will be given particular weight in the hiring, firing, and promotion of subordinates.
- Not perform nonexempt (clerical, nonadministrative) work more than 20 percent of the time (40 percent in retail trade).
- Receive a minimum level of weekly salary specified by federal law.

Nonexempt employees (those who are directly covered by the act) include almost all hourly paid people; overtime provisions of the law apply to them. Professional employees who require advanced knowledge, customarily acquired through prolonged instruction and study of a specialized field, are usually considered exempt.

What is the purpose of the Landrum-Griffith Act?

Officially designated as the Labor Management Reporting and Disclosure Act of 1959 (also known as the Landrum-Griffith Act, for its primary sponsors), it compels employers to report the following types of financial items:

- Payments to labor union officials, agents, or stewards (for purposes other than pay for work).
- Payments to employees (other than regular wage payments) or to groups or committees of employees for purposes of persuading other employees regarding the choice of a union or other union matters.
- Payments to a consultant on labor union matters.

Payments that must be reported also include reimbursed expenses. More important, the law also compels a labor union to make a more complete disclosure regarding the sources and disbursement of its funds. The law also strictly regulates the internal affairs of unions and clearly defines the rights of individual union members.

The law is aimed primarily at (a) preventing unethical collusion between a company and a union or other interference with the due process of collective bargaining, (b) preventing the misuse of a union's funds by its leaders, and (c) otherwise minimizing the possibility of labor "racketeering."

Ethical Perspectives

Employees are often hired, and paid, for 40 hours a week. But with intense corporate drives for additional profitability, some supervisors have been pressuring workers to "voluntarily" work extra hours after punching out for the day. In some cases, the supervisor has even promised that the extra "off-clock" effort will pay off in future promotions. Aside from the legal issue of not paying overtime for hours worked, what do you think about the ethical implications of this practice?

| 7 | T or F | Not all employees have freedom of choice about whether they will join the union. |
| 8 | T or F | Unions commonly—and legally—coerce employees into joining a union. |

5 Collective Bargaining and Grievances

CONCEPT

Collective bargaining sets the organizational context for labor relations, but supervisors are the primary implementors of labor contracts and handlers of grievances.

Collective bargaining.
The process of give-and-take engaged in by the management of an organization and authorized representatives of its collective employees (a labor union) to reach a formal, written agreement about wages, hours, and working conditions.

What does collective bargaining include?

Collective bargaining takes place only after a labor union has won a representation election. When authorized representatives of the employer and authorized representatives of the employees bargain together to establish wages, hours, and working conditions, this process is called *collective bargaining*. Various labor laws have determined what are fit matters for collective bargaining and what are not. Generally speaking, however, the term *working conditions* is so broad that almost anything that affects employees at work or the manner in which they carry out their jobs can be included.

The mere fact that a matter, such as wage rates or pensions, is a fit subject for collective bargaining doesn't necessarily mean that the union can control the way it is handled. The union can bargain for its position, and both sides must bargain in good faith over the issue. But the company does not have to accept the union's position. Several considerations will determine the issue's final disposition: the reasonableness of the union demand; the desirability of the demand to employees, management, and stockholders; the ability of the company to pay for its cost; the judgment of management as to its worth; and, finally, the relative bargaining strength of the union and the company.

Internet connection

http://www.socialstudieshelp.com/Eco_Unionization.htm
See this site for a history of labor unions and explanations for their recent and continuing decline in membership and influence.

What happens after the signing of the contract?

Collective bargaining usually starts with the negotiation of the labor agreement. But it doesn't end there. Supervisors, managers, employees, and union stewards must live with the agreement for the duration (or term) of the contract—usually one, two, or three years. Applying the contract and interpreting its meanings from day to day are what make collective bargaining effective—and exciting. The labor agreement, like any other contract, is rarely changed during its life. But there are dozens, sometimes hundreds, of occurrences between supervisor and employees that require astute judgment on how the situation should be handled to carry out the meaning of the contract. It is such interpretation and differences of opinion between management and unions that make labor relations a key supervisory headache and responsibility. This is also the source of many grievances, as we shall discuss later in this chapter.

What is a supervisor's authority in labor relations?

Your primary responsibility to your organization in labor matters is to protect the interests and the rights of management. How far supervisors can exercise authority in carrying out this responsibility depends on the extent to which upper management feels that supervisors can act without first checking to see if their decisions are in line with company policy.

The first-line supervisor is usually the first contact between employees and management and between union representatives and management. Since what you do and say in labor matters has such vital consequences to your company's overall relationship with employees and their representatives, you must be knowledgeable about the major provisions of the contact and your company's labor practices. Your actions are not confined only to yourself and a single employee; they could very well have companywide impact. Under certain circumstances, your actions could cause your employer to be charged by the union with violating the contract or even with breaking the law.

Supervisors have been charged with unfair labor practices of discrimination. What is that all about?

One supervisory unfair labor practice—interference—was discussed earlier. Another one—discrimination—is also governed by the Wagner Act. *Discrimination* applies to any action (such as discharge of an employee, layoff, demotion, or assignment to more difficult or disagreeable work) taken by any member of management because of an employee's union membership or activity.

There is an easy way to avoid charges of discrimination. Simply disregard completely an employee's union membership, activism in union affairs, or general attitudes toward the union when you make decisions regarding job assignments, discipline, and promotions. Before you act, make sure in your own mind that you have separated ability, performance, and attitude toward the job from the employee's stand on unionism or zeal in supporting it.

How far does a union shop steward's authority go?

A *steward* is to the union what you are to the employer. It's a union steward's job to protect the rights of union members just as it's yours to protect the rights of management. But in protecting those rights, a union shop steward has no authority to run your department or to tell you or any employee what to do about work.

You may get the impression that a steward is telling you what to do. A new steward may even feel that it is his or her job to do so. All the steward has authority to do, however, is to advise you or employees about his or her understanding of how the contract limits your actions and decisions. It goes without saying that you are the department supervisor, and you are not obligated to share your responsibility with anyone.

It is good practice, however, to keep stewards informed of your actions—so that they can make their position known. Better yet, if you wish to build a strong working relationship with the steward under an overall atmosphere of company-union cooperation, you may occasionally even wish to ask the steward's input in advance of making a decision. The steward's job experience—and worker perspective—could prove invaluable.

Why is there a grievance procedure? Wouldn't it be better to settle gripes informally?

Grievance procedure. A formalized, systematic channel for employees to follow in bringing their complaints to the attention of management. Typically, it prescribes a progression of appeals from lowest to highest authority within the company and the employees' organization. It often has arbitration as a final step.

Most union contracts establish a step-by-step *grievance procedure*. Experience has shown both management and labor that it's best to have a systematic method of handling complaints. Without a formalized procedure, management (in dealing with unionized employees) would find it difficult to coordinate labor and personnel practices from department to department.

The formal procedure provides an easy and open channel of communication for employees to bring complaints to the attention of management, and guarantees that those complaints won't be sidetracked or allowed to fester without corrective action being taken. Good supervisors and wise higher managers know that an unsettled grievance, real or imaginary, expressed or hidden, is always a potential source of trouble. The grievance machinery helps uncover the causes and get the grievance out into the open.

Does the law dictate a standard grievance procedure?

No. The actual grievance procedure varies from organization to organization. It depends on what the employer and the union have agreed on and have written into the labor contract.

A typical grievance procedure has from three to five steps, as shown in Figure 17-2, and usually originates after an employee is dissatisfied with a supervisor's actions or initial response to a complaint.

Step 1. Supervisor discusses the complaint with employee and union steward.

Step 2. Superintendent and labor relations manager discuss complaint with union grievance committee.

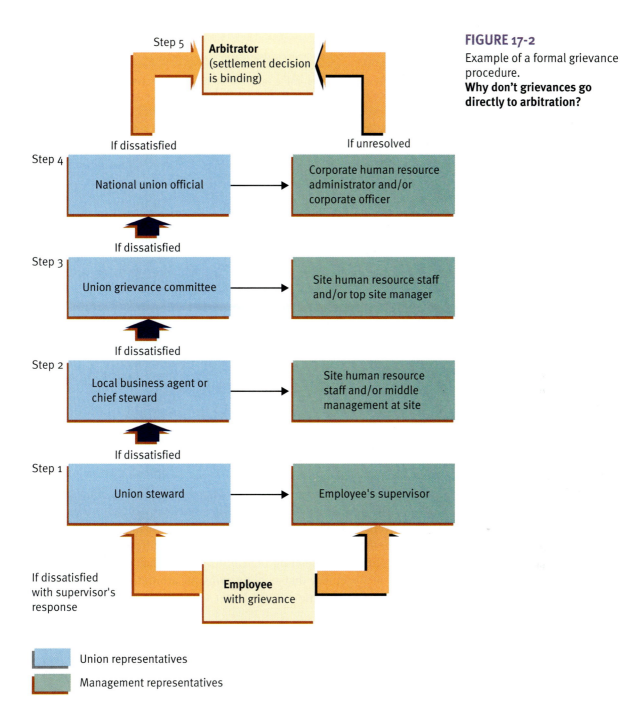

FIGURE 17-2

Example of a formal grievance procedure.
Why don't grievances go directly to arbitration?

Step 5 — Arbitrator (settlement decision is binding)

If dissatisfied — If unresolved

Step 4 — National union official → Corporate human resource administrator and/or corporate officer

If dissatisfied

Step 3 — Union grievance committee → Site human resource staff and/or top site manager

If dissatisfied

Step 2 — Local business agent or chief steward → Site human resource staff and/or middle management at site

If dissatisfied

Step 1 — Union steward → Employee's supervisor

If dissatisfied with supervisor's response

Employee with grievance

Union representatives

Management representatives

Step 3. Site manager and labor relations manager discuss complaint with union grievance committee.

Step 4. General company management discusses complaint with national union representative and union grievance committee.

Step 5. Dispute, if unresolved, is referred to an impartial arbitrator for decision.

JOB TIP!

T. L. Stanley offers several useful suggestions for supervisors facing a grievance:

- Familiarize yourself with the grievance steps, the contract, and the facts in the case.

- Know how many days you have to respond to each step.
- Enlist higher management's support for your decision in advance.
- Stay calm. Stay focused. Stay current. Act professionally.

It should be emphasized that a serious and prolonged effort should be made by both parties to settle the grievance at each step—including the first. As a matter of fact, many companies appraise their supervisors on a number of relevant criteria, such as the number of grievances filed per employee per year, or the proportion of grievances resolved at the first step. Prompt action by supervisors has been shown to be effective in solving as many as 75 percent of all grievances at the first step.

Why don't grievances go right to the arbitrator in the first place?

Arbitration. The settlement of a labor dispute or employee grievance by an impartial umpire selected by mutual agreement of the organization and the union.

Arbitration, the settling of labor-management disputes by a mutually acceptable, impartial third party, is not popular among members of either unions or management. They seem to agree on this point: They'd both rather settle their household quarrels between themselves than invite a stranger in to settle disputes. Both parties reason, and rightly, that they know more than anyone else about their affairs. In the long run, union and management must learn how to settle their differences themselves without continually depending on a third party. It has been said by both union and management that nobody wins an arbitration. But when it's needed, peaceful arbitration is far better than strikes or lockouts.

Why might an arbitrator overrule the supervisor?

Most supervisors make a strong effort on a regular basis to be sure their decisions and actions are in line with their employer's interpretation of the union contract. Nevertheless, they are sometimes overruled at subsequent steps of the grievance process. Why? Experience shows it may be due to any of five major reasons:

1. **Bad information.** The supervisor may have acted on insufficient or incorrect information.
2. **Reinterpretation.** The supervisor may occasionally be made the sacrificial lamb when the company realizes at the third or fourth

step of the procedure that its interpretation of the contract won't stand up to the union's position.

3. **Arbitration decision.** The supervisor and the company may be overruled by the arbitrator, who saw greater merit in the union's case.

4. **Rigidity.** The supervisor may be too concerned about saving face (sticking with an earlier decision to maintain an image of never making a mistake) to back down.

5. **Overindependence.** The supervisor may have failed to consult with other colleagues or the human resource department on issues of contract interpretation. Sometimes a bit of insight, a word of caution, or a shared lesson from another's experience can be invaluable.

9	T or F	A formal grievance procedure is usually advantageous for both labor and management.	**QUICK TEST 5**
10	T or F	Historically, about 75 percent of all grievances advance to the level of an impartial arbitrator before they are resolved.	

Practical Guidelines for Supervisors

1. Remember that accidents have tremendous personal, social, and financial consequences; *do everything in your power to prevent them*.

2. *Familiarize yourself with OSHA*, and *keep accurate records* of every occupational illness or injury.

3. Build cooperative responsibility for safety by *involving employees in accident-prevention programs*; invite them to submit ideas and then use those ideas that are practical.

4. Be especially alert to the warning signs for possible workplace violence; *intervene at the earliest feasible moment* to prevent intimidation, threats, harm, or destruction from taking place.

5. Study the relevant history of labor laws; *be careful not to violate any of their guidelines* to prevent charges of unfair labor practices.

6. *Do not interfere* with unions or their formation, and do not interfere with employees who act in accordance with the labor agreement.

7. Within the context of a labor agreement, *maintain your right* to make job assignments, hold employees to performance expectations, and train, appraise, and discipline employees.

8. If a union exists, *study the labor agreement carefully* so that you can make appropriate supervisory decisions within its context.

9. *Develop a healthy relationship with the union steward*; consult with him or her where appropriate while recognizing that the steward's job is to represent the employees under the contract.

10. *Don't take it personally* when a grievance is filed against you; study it carefully, review the background, and consult with others before responding to it.

Chapter 17 Review

Key Concepts to Remember

1. Safety at Work.   An accident is evidence of something wrong in the workplace—with an employee, a machine, methods, materials, or a supervisor. Although there is evidence that some people are accident prone, the great majority of accidents are attributable to human error by ordinary people somewhere along the line. Only aware and responsible people can recognize these wrongs—and correct, guard against, and avoid them.

2. OSHA's Mandated Safety Standards.   The Occupational Safety and Health Act of 1970 created a large body of standards for safe working conditions, sanitation, and the handling of hazardous materials. The law is enforced by the Occupational Safety and Health Administration (OSHA), which places a great deal of responsibility for its implementation on supervisors. OSHA specifies that a great many accident records be maintained in a prescribed fashion. Calculation of accident incident (frequency) and severity rates is a helpful way to measure the effectiveness of safety programs. Supervisors are directly involved in the investigation and analysis of accidents and their causes.

3. Accident Prevention: The Basics.   Accident prevention is a major supervisory responsibility that is shared with employees. Most accidents can be prevented by a unified program that encompasses (a) engineering—proper job and equipment design; (b) education—effective employee communication and training; and (c) enforcement—consistent adherence to, and enforcement of, the prescribed safe practices. Employee obesity has become an issue of national concern that greatly affects employees' lives and the health-care costs of their employers. Workplace violence, too, has reached epidemic proportions and demands careful supervisory attention.

4. Labor Unions and Labor Law.   In dealing with employees and labor unions, courts view supervisors as responsible agents of the organizations for which they work. Regardless of a supervisor's attitude toward organized labor, she or he is bound to behave in accordance with labor laws and to abide by the agreements that may be derived from collective bargaining.

The basic labor-management law in the private sector is the National Labor Relations Act, or Wagner Act (which protects the rights of employees to bargain collectively for wages, hours, and working conditions), as amended by the Taft-Hartley Act. Other related legislation includes the Labor Management Reporting and Disclosure Act, the Walsh-Healey Public Contracts Act, and the Fair Labor Standards Act.

5. Collective Bargaining and Grievances.   Collective bargaining between management and a labor union takes place only when a union legally represents the employees. The end result of a collective-bargaining negotiation is a labor contract. Supervisors play vital roles in administering the labor contract. Accordingly, it is important that supervisors (a) maintain their own interest in, and responsibility toward, the well-being of their employees and (b) protect their own authority and rights as managers to motivate and control their staffs—modified only by contractual limitations. Supervisors need to refrain from discrimination at all times, but especially during contract administration. Supervisors also have a special interest in employees' grievances. It is in the supervisor's interest to listen to, understand, and resolve them at the first level of management rather than have them move beyond his or her control into the formal channels of referral specified by the grievance procedure.

Reading Comprehension

1. Many accidents are caused by the ever-present human factor. Name at least six other possible causes of accidents.

2. Vivian, the housekeeping supervisor in a state mental institution, devotes time each day to safety training for her employees. This activity fits into which phase of the three Es of accident prevention? What are the other two phases?

3. Distinguish between an accident incident (or frequency) rate and an accident severity rate.

4. What can a supervisor do to instill safety consciousness in employees?

5. Why should a supervisor want to investigate an accident?

6. Suggest two good reasons why a supervisor should know about the basic principles of labor-management relations.

7. Compare the objectives of the Wagner Act with those of the Taft-Hartley Act.

8. How do the closed shop and the union shop differ? Which is more closely associated with right-to-work laws?

9. Contrast a union steward's responsibility with that of an employee's supervisor.

10. Describe a typical grievance procedure. What role does a supervisor play in the process?

Application

Self-Assessment

How Good Are Your Safety And Labor-Relations Management Skills?

Read the following statements carefully. Circle the number on the response scale that most closely reflects the degree to which each statement describes you. Add up your total points and prepare a brief action plan for self-improvement. Be ready to report your score for tabulation across the entire group.

	Good Description									Poor Description
1. I believe that I can improve the safety record of "accident-prone" employees by working closely with them.	10	9	8	7	6	5	4	3	2	1
2. I understand and appreciate the positive role that OSHA plays in encouraging safe working conditions.	10	9	8	7	6	5	4	3	2	1
3. I understand the difference between accident incident rate and severity rate.	10	9	8	7	6	5	4	3	2	1

	Good Description		Poor Description

4. I feel comfortable approaching a safety problem from the perspectives of the three Es: engineering, education, and evaluation. 10 9 8 7 6 5 4 3 2 1

5. I know several warning signs that might predict workplace violence. 10 9 8 7 6 5 4 3 2 1

6. I can explain several reasons why employees might join a labor union. 10 9 8 7 6 5 4 3 2 1

7. I can explain the difference between a closed shop and a union shop. 10 9 8 7 6 5 4 3 2 1

8. I understand the four prerequisite conditions that define an exempt employee. 10 9 8 7 6 5 4 3 2 1

9. I understand the role of a union steward as it relates to that of a supervisor. 10 9 8 7 6 5 4 3 2 1

10. I can explain a number of reasons why my decision on a grievance might be overturned at a higher level of the process. 10 9 8 7 6 5 4 3 2 1

Scoring and Interpretation

Scoring

Add up your total points for the 10 questions. Record that number here, and report it when it is requested. _____

Also, insert your score on the Personal Development Plan in the Appendix.

Interpretation

81 to 100 points. You seem to have a basic set of safety and labor-relations management skills.

61 to 80 points. Take a close look at some of your safety and labor-relations management skills (those with lower self-assessments) and discuss them with a manager to see if they need improvement.

Below 60 points. Some of your skills may be substantially inconsistent with effective safety and labor-relations management practices and could be detrimental to your success as a supervisor.

Identify your three lowest scores, and write the question numbers here: _____, _____, _____.

Action

Write a brief paragraph detailing an action plan for how you might sharpen each of these skills. Then pay particularly close attention to the related material in the chapter as you review the relevant sections there.

Skill Development

Safety and Labor-Relations Management Improvement

No matter how hard an organization tries, there are often some overlooked or temporary safety hazards present in its operations. As a result of negligence during internal safety inspections, careless actions by employees, or lack of familiarity with relevant laws, even the best organizations sometimes receive citations when an OSHA inspector makes a surprise visit. Nevertheless, a prepared organization can do much to minimize such problems.

Select an organization, and gain access to it. Conduct a personal walk-around inspection, identifying the unsafe conditions (problem areas) that you encounter or observe, and the specific actions (unsafe practices) that employees are demonstrating that could lead to an accident. (To prepare yourself, you will likely wish to review the text's discussion on the safety investigations, search the Internet for relevant guidelines, and consult with colleagues and staff persons in the human resources department for their advice.)

Problem Areas

1. _____
2. _____
3. _____
4. _____
5. _____

Unsafe Practices

1. _____
2. _____
3. _____
4. _____
5. _____

Suggestions for Creating a Safer Work Environment

1. _____
2. _____
3. _____
4. _____
5. _____
6. _____
7. _____
8. _____
9. _____
10. _____

Action

After studying your findings, prepare a brief report that summarizes your 10 best suggestions for making the work environment safer. If possible, share the results of your study with a responsible person in the host organization and obtain his or her reactions.

Role Play

Making Task Assignments

Background. Many supervisors make task assignments to employees on a daily, or even hourly, basis. On the positive side, this provides great flexibility to shift resources where needed and to respond to fluctuations in the demand for human resources. On the negative side, this practice might result in undertrained employees being assigned to tasks, uncertainty in the minds of employees about where they will work next, and a limited ability to enjoy sustained social relations with co-workers. This role-playing incident deals with such an incident of task assignments and the employee's reaction to it. Class members should break into groups of three persons, with one each assigned to the role of Olga, Daryl, or Mickey. After they have read (only) their own roles, they should hold a three-way meeting among themselves.

Olga. You are a word processing operator in a state agency whose employees are represented by a union of government workers. You work in a word processing pool made up of employees with low seniority. You have no regularly assigned job but report each morning to the pool's supervisor, Daryl Dowd, to find out where you will work that day. Sometimes you work in the same area you did the day before, but other times Daryl pulls you out of a job to place you on a particularly demanding or short-deadline job. When the workload is relatively light, Daryl lets you and the other operators pick the job each wants to work on. When the calls for operators from various departments are frequent, however, Daryl makes all the assignments and is not receptive to counterarguments.

Lately, you have begun to feel that Daryl is taking advantage of your good work and your good nature. You rarely get to stay on the same assignment (which is desirable because it means a chance to get a feel for the work and the people in a particular department) more than one day at a time. Besides, many of the jobs Daryl gives you are unattractive ones. The work is especially painstaking; for example, it has to be done under pressure, or the people in the department are largely unfriendly.

This morning, Daryl wants to send you up to the tenth floor to work in the budget-review department. Suddenly, you boil over. "Send someone else up there to do their kind of picky work today," you tell him. "I won't take another assignment like that until every other operator in the pool has been rotated to as many rotten jobs as I've had." Then Daryl replies, "You've got to work any assignment that is legitimate, so get going!" With that, you storm off to talk to Mickey, the union steward. After briefing the steward on the interaction with Daryl and your frustrations, the three of you agree to meet. You hope that with Mickey on your side, the two of you can persuade Daryl to be more fair about task assignments.

Daryl. You are the supervisor of a group of word processing operators in a state agency whose employees are represented by a union of government workers. You head up a word processing pool made up of employees with low seniority. They have no regularly assigned job but report to you each morning to find out where to work that day. Sometimes they work in the same area they did the day before, but other times you have to pull them off a job to place them on a particularly demanding or short-deadline job. When the workload is relatively light, you let the operators pick the job they want to work on. When the calls for operators from various departments are frequent, however, you must make all the assignments and you don't feel any reason to be receptive to counterarguments.

Lately, the pressure to provide operators to various departments has been particularly intense. You rarely get to keep an operator on the same assignment (which is desirable because it means a chance for him or her to get a feel for the work and the people in a particular department) more than one day at a time. Besides, many of the jobs the operators do are unattractive ones. The work in some departments is especially painstaking; for example, it has to be done under pressure, or the people in the department are largely unfriendly.

This morning, you assign Olga, one of your operators, to the tenth floor to work in the budget-review department. Suddenly, she boils over. "Send someone else up there to do their kind of picky work today," she tells you. "I won't take another assignment like that until every other operator in the pool has been rotated to as many rotten jobs as I've had." Then you reply, "Olga, you've got to work any assignment that is legitimate, so get going!" With that, she storms off to talk to Mickey, the union steward. The steward calls and says that Olga has reported on the interaction with you and her frustrations, and asks that the three of you meet now to resolve the situation. You are about to talk to them and hope to convince Mickey and Olga that what you said and did was clearly within your rights as a supervisor.

Mickey. You are the union steward, representing several dozen word processing operators in a state agency. Your job is to make sure that employees are treated fairly and the union contract is followed by supervisors. A little while ago, Olga came storming in to see you and related her story in the following fashion.

"I have begun to feel that Daryl is taking advantage of my good work and my good nature. I rarely get to stay on the same assignment (which is desirable because it means a chance to get a feel for the work and the people in a particular department) more than one day at a time. Besides, many of the jobs that Daryl gives me are unattractive ones. The work is especially painstaking; for example, it has to be done under pressure, or the people in the department are largely unfriendly.

"This morning, Daryl wants to send me up to the tenth floor to work in the budget-review department. Suddenly, I just boil over. I tell him to send someone else up there to do their kind of picky work today. I won't take another assignment like that until every other operator in the pool has been rotated to as many rotten jobs as I've had."

"What did Daryl say?" you ask Olga. "He told me in no uncertain terms that I had to work any assignment that is legitimate, so I'd better get going! That's when I came up to see you; I just don't think it's fair!" said Olga.

You think it over for a few minutes and then call Daryl to arrange a three-way meeting. Somehow you have to get this problem resolved before Olga decides to quit her job, or Daryl starts to treat all employees this way.

Questions for Discussion

1. What is the outcome in each group (what is decided)?
2. Will Olga take the assignment Daryl gave her? Why or why not?
3. What basic issues are presented in this incident?
4. What is the appropriate way to resolve the disagreement before it deteriorates further?
5. How can further incidents such as this be prevented?

Cases for Analysis

Case 53

Their Aching Backs

"Not another one!" moaned Jerry, supervisor of the shelf-stocking unit at the SuperDuper Mart, a 60,000-square-foot discount hardware and lumber supply store. He had just received a call from the company doctor, reporting that one of his crew had suffered a severe strain in the lumbar region of his back. Not only would this employee be off duty for a week or two, the injury would also be recorded as a lost-time accident. Jerry would hear lots about that from his boss, especially since the company's insurer had been threatening to raise its premium due to the high incidence of back-related injuries at SuperDuper Mart.

To forestall further incidents, Jerry immediately toured the facility, stopping to admonish each of his crew. His message was essentially the same for everyone:

"Too many of you are going to the company doctor complaining about your aching backs. When you were hired, you knew you had to lift 50- to 70-pound cartons on a regular basis.

"There's no excuse for all these back injuries if you will only be more careful when you're lifting heavy cartons.

"Furthermore, I'm ordering a batch of those new back-support belts so everyone will have one. Don't let me catch you not wearing it.

"Remember, from now on around here, it's going to be safety first."

Analysis

Despite these admonishments, employees in Jerry's department continued to have frequent back injuries. What might Jerry have done to be more effective in reducing back injuries in his department? Of the five alternatives listed below, which do you think might be most effective? Rank them on a scale from 1 (most effective) to 5 (least effective). You may add another alternative, if you wish. Be prepared to justify your rankings.

_____ **a.** Post a summary of his message on the bulletin board and hang "safety first" signs throughout the shop.

_____ **b.** Be sure to wear the new back-support belt himself.

_____ **c.** Hold regular safety meetings with his crew so that he can keep emphasizing his safety message.

_____ **d.** Train or retrain all employees in proper lifting techniques.
_____ **e.** Appoint an employee safety committee to study the lifting problems in the store and recommend appropriate safety equipment and protective clothing.

Case 54

Mary's Pinched Ring Finger

While filing computer reports in a steel filing cabinet, Mary McDonald pinched the knuckle of her ring finger. It happened when the sleeve of her jacket caught in the steel drawer as she slammed it shut. Her supervisor examined the operation of the drawer and declared that the accident should not have happened. Other file clerks, however, observed that the opening and closing of the file drawers was a constant hazard. In fact, many of the clerks declared that they had torn a blouse or had a finger pinched.

Analysis

a. To what extent do you think that these accidents were caused by the file clerks rather than by the design and operation of the drawers in the file cabinets?

b. Using the three Es of accident prevention, what sort of safety program would you recommend for this particular hazard?

Case 55

Nine Who Did Wrong

Each of the following nine labor actions is a violation of one of the principal labor and employment laws. On a separate sheet of paper, write the name of the law that is violated by each action.

Analysis

a. The Jasper Company refuses to talk about its wage scale to a union agent duly selected by employees.

b. A labor union insists that the Axe Construction Company discharge Tony, one of its employees, because he was expelled from the union for disagreeing with its policies.

c. The supervisor of the receiving department insists that a worker uncap a tank car of chemicals even though a needed safety respirator is not available.

d. A company refuses to hire Audrey Hill solely because she is married and her future supervisor thinks she will quit soon to have a baby.

e. Torger Branson, who works for National Distributors, did not receive time-and-a-half pay for the hours over 40 that he worked last week.

f. Astro Metals Manufacturers hires 17-year-old George Cone to work on a job connected with a large government contract it has recently acquired.

g. A union prohibits one of its employees from speaking up on a complaint she has against the company's management.

h. Stan's supervisor assigns Stan to a very unpleasant task to discourage him from asking other employees to sign union membership cards.

i. The Texto Company fails to report to the government its arrangement for reimbursing shop stewards for their expenses while attending union conventions.

Quick Test 1	Quick Test 2	Quick Test 3	Quick Test 4	Quick Test 5	ANSWERS TO QUICK TESTS
1. F	3. F	5. T	7. T	9. T	
2. F	4. T	6. F	8. F	10. F	

Chapter Reference

1. Maryann Hammers, "The Fight Against Fat Goes on the Offensive in the Workplace," *Workforce*, October 2003, pp. 74–76.

18

Achieving Personal Supervisory Success

LEARNING OBJECTIVES

After studying this chapter, you should be able to

- Identify a set of supervisory time wasters and tactics for better time management.

- Explain the negative effects of stress on employees, the relationship of stress to productivity, and methods for minimizing or adapting to stress.

- Increase your creativity through the free association of ideas, and differentiate between creativity and brainstorming.

- Discuss the role of a mentor (both downward and upward), describe the benefits of mentoring others, and differentiate mentoring from coaching.

- Understand why some managers engage in unethical behavior, explain their rationales for bending the rules, and identify ways to help yourself act ethically in the face of challenges to your integrity.

Managing Job-Related Time

CONCEPT
Supervisors need to acquire and apply good time-management skills.

Time management. The process of analyzing one's use of time, dividing it into controllable and uncontrollable categories, and using various tactics to make the best use of your time.

Time is a precious resource that is squandered by many. **How can a simple calendar help improve time management?**

Is it really possible to manage time?

One of the major challenges facing supervisors—especially early in their careers—is *time management*. Although you can't control time itself (hours and minutes and seconds), you can often manage what you do with the time you have. The first key step in time management, then, involves dividing your time into two compartments: (1) the time that you *can* control and (2) the time that you *can't* control. When your manager expects you to present a report at a meeting, for example, that is usually time that you can't control. So is the time you spend in an emergency or dealing with a customer or supplier who wants an answer now. In your own situation, there are probably a number of other demands placed on your time, not at your convenience but at that of someone else. It's a good idea to make a list of these potentially uncontrollable occurrences right now. This is important because you'll want to think about them differently from the way you think about time demands that

you *can* control. As a consequence, your approach to time management can be guided by two general rules:

1. Systematize and prioritize the management of your controllable time.
2. Minimize the amount of your uncontrollable time. This has to be done in bits and pieces, and probably over a long period of time. Also, since this time is often controlled by others, you'll have to work out ways to gain some concessions from them in the interests of your own flexibility while still accommodating their needs.

What are the major time wasters for supervisors?

Many experts on time management have identified these time wasters, and the critical ones are summarized in Table 18-1. New supervisors are especially guilty of continuing to do tasks that they handled previously, and failing to switch their time emphasis to managerial tasks. Other supervisors are unconsciously "people pleasers" who have a hard time turning down requests for various types of assistance (company tours, advice) or rejecting unnecessary interruptions. Finally, some supervisors fail to delegate—a process discussed later in this section. The point is that time-wasting activities are seductive; they make you feel that you are accomplishing something, but they seldom produce a direct result.

Quips & Quotes

Our observation is that managers spend time performing unproductive, time-wasting activities to avoid or escape job-related anxiety.

Ronald Askenas and
Robert Schaffer

TABLE 18-1   **Top Ten Time Wasters for Supervisors**

1. "Hovering" over employees when they don't need your help
2. Jumping into tasks without proper preparation
3. Failing to block out interruptions (phone calls, noise, and social chats)
4. Procrastinating (delaying the start or completion of a project)
5. Investing excessive effort in low-importance tasks
6. Shuffling papers (rereading material or recategorizing files)
7. Waiting for others and having nothing to do while you wait
8. Participating in poorly run meetings (including your own!)
9. Surfing the Internet
10. Having too many goals, goals that aren't clarified, or no plan for the day

Sources: Adapted from Don Farrant, "Tighten Your Control on Time," *Supervision*, March 2005, pp. 17–19, and Robert D. Ramsey, "15 Time Wasters for Supervisors," *Supervision*, June 2000, pp. 10–12.

What can you do to manage your time better?

Here are seven guidelines to follow:

1. **Make up your mind fast.** This is not to advocate snap judgments, but it's a fact that 85 percent of the problems you face aren't worth more than a few minutes of your time. Learn to say "yes" or "no," "we will" or "we won't." Employees and associates like working with decisive people—even when they aren't right all the time. And few things save time like a decisive answer—time saved for you and your employees.

2. **Be specific about dates.** You promise to get out an order "sometime next week." What happens? You're likely to find several deadlines coming due at the same time. If you're specific—Wednesday for Triangle and Thursday for Superior—you've started to systematize your thinking.

    Or let's say Pete calls you. Can he drop by to see you? Any time, you say. So Pete drops by just when you're up to your ears in a last-minute project. Pete doesn't get much attention, your project gets the "good enough" treatment, and your time budget suffers. Instead, tell Pete that the best time to see you would be between 2:00 and 2:30.

3. **Control the telephone.** It's a monster to supervisors in some departments. But it needn't be (if your boss will cooperate). If you can get someone else to answer it for you, do. Otherwise, let your voice mail take a message. Then call back when you have the time. Avoid using the telephone for routine messages that can be forwarded through the interoffice mails or by e-mail. And watch yourself so that you don't develop telephonitis and bother others unnecessarily.

4. **Write down reminders.** Don't trust yourself to remember things to do. Use a surefire reminder system, such as jotting down important jobs to be done on your desk calendar or in a personal digital assistant.

5. **Limit chitchat.** Conversation, with employees and other supervisors, is vitally important to your role as supervisor. But you've got to keep it under control or it will eat up all your spare time. Limit casual conversation to a few pleasantries when you can. Nothing ruins your day as well as a couple of 20-minute conversations with your associates about the fish they didn't catch or the status of a do-it-yourself project.

6. **Set up a time budget.** Try preparing a time budget beforehand like the one charted in Figure 18-1, by which you plan to distribute your daily time usage into four scheduled categories:

    a. *Routine work*, such as checking time sheets, answering mail, and handling normal paperwork.

    b. *Regular job duties*, such as the important ones of supervising, training, controlling, and appraising.

	MONDAY	TUESDAY	WEDNESDAY	THURSDAY	FRIDAY
8					
	ROUTINE	ROUTINE	ROUTINE	ROUTINE	ROUTINE
9	Inspection and supervision of operations REGULAR	Individual work with staff REGULAR	Inspection and supervision of operations REGULAR	Individual work with staff REGULAR	SPECIAL WORK
10		Inspection and supervision of operations REGULAR		Control studies and reports REGULAR	Inspection and supervision of operations REGULAR
11					
12			Division staff meeting REGULAR		Our staff meeting REGULAR
1	L	U	N	C	H
	Interviews and contacts REGULAR	Interviews and contacts REGULAR	Interviews and contacts REGULAR	Interviews and contacts REGULAR	CREATIVE WORK
2					
3	Planning and organizing REGULAR	Inspection and supervision of operations REGULAR	SPECIAL WORK	Inspection and supervision of operations REGULAR	
4					
5	ROUTINE	ROUTINE	ROUTINE	ROUTINE	ROUTINE

FIGURE 18-1
Example of a supervisor's weekly time budget.
Is there a danger of a supervisor's time being *too* well planned?

    c. *Special work*, such as serving on committees or assisting on special projects.

    d. *Creative work*, such as developing new methods to improve your department's quality or productivity.

7. **Begin each workday with a plan.** Each day will present a new set of problems, so take five minutes to tailor your plans before the workday begins. List the things you plan to do that day.

How can you use ABC analysis to control time?

ABC analysis is a concept that suggests that 80 percent of your time is best spent on only 20 percent of your problems. To make this idea pay off for you, the 20 percent of the problems that you work on should be rated as class A—the **vital few**. The president of a major appliance firm, for example, begins his day by labeling each task ahead as A, B, or C. Class B items aren't quite as important as A items. And class C problems are very small fish, even though there are lots of them. The president goes after A items first and then tries to get to the Bs.

Invariably, says the president, a surprising thing happens. When he gets to the Cs, he can "wipe out a lot of them in one sweep." These are the tasks, of course, that can be disposed of quickly with a telephone call, a jotted note, or a brief instruction to employees as you walk through the department. Happily, some of these Cs will have disappeared on their own!

How can you judge a problem's importance so as to concentrate on the vital few?

Experience will provide a good basis. You may waste a couple of hours the first time around on what turns out to be an inconsequential problem. The next time it comes up, however, either you will know how to dispose of it quickly or you will know that you should put it far down on your priority list.

There are other ways, too, of judging a problem's importance. For example, ask yourself any of these questions:

Where did it come from? If the problem arose as a directive from your boss or a request from the sales department, it may need top priority. If it came from a lesser source, perhaps you can delay it. In organizational matters, you must be realistic and hardheaded politically.

What is its potential for trouble? Some unsolved problems can cause other problems to pile up elsewhere. Suppose there is a machine that needs a minor repair. You put it off. But that machine is in the main line of flow in your operation. It is in a position to cause quality problems, and if it breaks down altogether, it will hold up production. The repair problem is minor, but its potential for trouble is great. Get to it sooner rather than later.

Is it aimed at results rather than activity? Dr. George Odiorne, who popularized MBO, warned that supervisors and managers devote too much time going through motions that are essentially trivial. On paper, their efforts may look good; they write reports, keep their files up to date, and attend all the meetings. But they don't get results in terms of greater output, better quality, or lower costs. Odiorne said that these managers have wasted their time by falling into the "activity trap."

How quickly can it be disposed of? Watch your answer on this one. It is what R. Alec Mackenzie calls the "time trap." Many problems look as if they could be handled quickly. It is a temptation to jump into them without thinking. But what was supposed to be done with a three-minute phone call turns into several phone calls, a meeting, and a follow-up report. What should have taken only a minute or two of discussion grows into a major hassle. Tasks that can truly be handled quickly—such as responding to the day's e-mail messages—should be grouped together and finished in one block of time. Problems that need a major effort should be budgeted for your undivided attention, with enough time allotted for their solution.

Where does delegation fit into time management?

Delegation is an essential ingredient of good management. And, to be painfully frank, it's often the only way you'll be able to keep your head above water. The average managerial job is so fraught with responsibilities that you could worry yourself into an 80-hour, jam-packed week just checking up on every detail yourself. If you allow yourself to fall into that trap, you're on your way out as a supervisor.

Delegation means, of course, that you've got to trust and train others on your staff to do the job nearly as effectively as you'd do it yourself—and sometimes better. And if you can steel yourself to leave them alone, they usually will. There is a big difference, however. Others won't do the job exactly the way you'd do it yourself. They'll also regard some factors as more important than you think they are. Worse still, they'll overlook or ignore other factors that you think demand top priority. That's the by-product of delegation. Learn to accept the fact of less-than-perfect results and to delegate just the same. Without delegation, you won't be able to make the grade as a supervisor and still maintain your peace of mind.

In delegating to make better use of your time, there are three good rules of thumb to follow:

1. Try not to spend time working on tasks that are below your capabilities. These are things that you can do, of course, but that others should be doing for you.
2. Don't give your priorities to a series of minor jobs while putting the big job on "hold." It's important that you take on the big job first. If the lesser jobs are urgent, you should delegate them right away to the most qualified subordinates.
3. Follow up on your delegation of tasks. You are still responsible for results!

| 1 | T or F | Effective time management literally puts more hours into the workday for you than you had before. |
| 2 | T or F | Consultants in time management suggest that you ought to do an A task first, then a B, then a C, then an A, and so on, so that you'll have variety in your day. |

Coping with Stress

Stress. The experience of mild or severe psychological and physical reactions to pressures and frustrations that may have arisen over time or appeared suddenly.

What is stress?

Poor time management often leads to stress. A supervisory job is the kind of position in which, by its nature, you are asked—or expected—to do more than most people can in a normal workday. When you find that you are not accomplishing what you believe you should be, you may become frustrated. Frustrations exert pressure on your mind and eventually on your nerves and body. Such pressure is popularly known as *stress*. In its exaggerated state, it is often called "burnout." As a matter of practical fact, almost everybody suffers from some stress. It is when stress places a load on the body or mind beyond a point that can be tolerated that stress becomes a medical problem.

To understand stress better, you should identify both the typical *causes* of stress in life in general and the *symptoms* that indicate that something may be wrong. Table 18-2 gives you an opportunity to assess the products of stress in your life.

Twenty stress indicators are listed in the table. For each condition, circle the number of the answer at the right that best describes the frequency with which that condition occurs in you. Add the numbers you have circled. Then use the scoring key at the end of the table to assess your apparent ability to manage stress.

Internet connection

http://www.rd.com/stresstest
This classical self-scored stress test rates the importance of various life events on a total scale of 18 to 123.

Why do some individuals thrive on pressure, whereas others don't handle it very well?

Probably because those who don't show signs of wear and tear (a) have learned their stress limits, (b) have kept their stress load within those boundaries, or (c) have learned how to manage their stress. Your mind and body flex freely under tolerable stress, somewhat like the way a steel beam flexes under a heavy load. If the load is within its stress limits, the beam will snap back into line when the load is removed. If, however, the beam is severely overloaded, it will be bent out of shape. Loads that are too heavy for *you* to carry will bend your mind or body out of shape, too. There is always a limit beyond which the mind or body will flex no longer. At that point, you show some of the signs indicated in Table 18-2. Accordingly, you "manage" this stress by finding ways of relieving it, redistributing it, or removing it.

For example, you shift some stress to others by delegating. You remove some of it by obtaining additional resources (people, technology,

TABLE 18-2 Stress Indicator Barometer

Conditions	Frequency or Degree		
	Never, or Absent	Sometimes, or Mild	Frequently, or Severe
1. General irritability	1	2	5
2. Difficulty in getting along with others	1	2	5
3. Feelings of guilt	1	2	5
4. Worry about seemingly small matters	1	2	5
5. Depression, or lack of enthusiasm	1	2	5
6. Concern that nothing gets done on time	1	2	5
7. Overeating	1	2	5
8. Insomnia	1	3	10
9. Substance abuse, excessive use of alcohol, or use of illegal drugs	1	5	10
10. Use of prescribed sleeping pills, pain-killers, or pep pills	1	3	10
11. Increased use of tobacco	1	3	10
12. Feelings of weakness or dizziness	1	5	10
13. Difficulty in concentrating	1	2	5
14. Loss of appetite	1	2	5
15. Increased occurrence of cuts, bruises, falls, or minor accidents	1	3	10
16. Stomach cramps, upsets, diarrhea	1	3	10
17. Temper tantrums	1	5	10
18. Impatience with delays	1	2	5
19. Changes in bodily functions	1	3	10
20. Unusual pattern of lost personal objects such as keys, glasses, and notebooks	1	3	10

Scoring: 20 to 50, *normal.* Indicates good tolerance of, or management of, stress.
51 to 99, *marginal.* Indicates greater-than-average difficulty in coping with stress.
100 or above, *watch out!* Indicates very low tolerance and/or severe difficulty in managing stress.

information, and the like) to help out in your department. You can also make sure that stress doesn't all come at once by planning and controlling your personal time more effectively. The steel beam, for example, can carry a load of 100 tons in 24 hours, *provided* that no more than 5 tons is placed on it at a time. That's why so many bridges bear signs that read "Maximum load is 10 tons." You can't go around wearing such a sign; employees and associates often have little sympathy for one's limits,

This man is showing signs of severe stress.
What would you do if he were your employee?

anyway. Instead, you must learn exactly how much stress you can bear before you suffer a strain, and then you must develop a plan for managing stress so that it never exceeds that limit.

Where is stress likely to come from?

Career counselors tell us that stress at work originates from three sources:

1. **The work environment.** This includes just about everything, from malfunctioning machinery, faulty materials, tight schedules, reduced budgets, and pressure-cooker deadlines to your overdemanding boss, your uncooperative associates, and your disinterested employees.

2. **Your inner self.** This includes such things as a loss of self-confidence, sensitivity to criticism about your performance, fear of failure, and doubts about your ability to cope with stress, wherever it originates.

3. **Interpersonal relationships.** This combines the worst elements of the first two. Most work situations involve some sort of interpersonal transaction. For example, stress often arises when another worker's personality conflicts with yours and a flexible compromise cannot be reached.

What role does stress play in creating problem employees?

Stressors. Environmental, psychological, or psychosocial factors that produce stress within employees and often detract from their work performance.

Resilience. The capacity of an employee to handle short-term stress, and bounce back from its distractions.

Burnout. The inability of employees to handle major incidents of, or sustained, stress.

Psychologists suggest that "to be alive is to experience stress; it is inevitable in most jobs as well as home lives." Stress refers to the pressures that people feel in life caused by *stressors*—the physical or human environment (noise, odors, discrimination, boredom), psychological factors (anxiety over job security), or psychosocial factors (interpersonal friction with co-workers). The resulting stress can appear in the form of headaches, upset stomachs, skin disorders, and distractedness. Some employees have greater *resilience*, or capacity to handle short-term stress. They have learned to handle minor irritations, to find a balance between work and home life, and to set realistic goals. They may even find some degree of stress to be a stimulus to their performance (see Figure 18-2). But when major stressors appear, or stress is sustained for long periods of time, some employees with lesser resilience experience *burnout*. This condition is characterized by severe alienation, inability to accept responsibility for errors, sharp declines in work performance, and (sometimes) abrupt resignations. Supervisors need to be aware of the entire range of stress-induced symptoms, and rely on their counseling skills to help employees work through their problems before they become unmanageable.

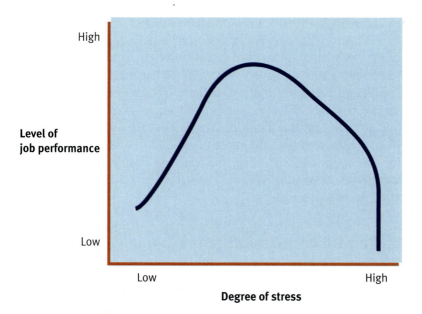

High

Level of
job performance

Low

Low   High

Degree of stress

FIGURE 18-2

Relationship between stress and performance.
What are the consequences of stress that is too low? Too high?

Did You Know

Avoid Burnout

Psychologists Christina Maslach and Michael Leiter have found that if you provide the following six factors for employees at work, they are much less likely to experience burnout:

- A manageable workload.
- A sense of control.
- The opportunity for rewards.
- A feeling of community.
- Faith in the fairness of the workplace.
- Shared values.

In regard to job-related stress, what are the main opportunities for improvement?

Former U.S. President Harry Truman was partly right when he said, "If you can't stand the heat, stay out of the kitchen." The supervisory job is, by its nature, stressful. That's what makes it so invigorating and challenging. As another wise person once said, "If there were no stress, you might as well be dead." But there is a great difference between an invigorating amount of stress and too much stress. A basic goal in stress management, therefore, is to try to eliminate persistent but unnecessary stress. There's enough of the other kind already to make many of your days hectic. Among the basic sources of stress that should be corrected are the following:

- **Ambiguity about the results for which you are held responsible.** If your organization provides a job description for your position, make sure that it is specific about vital results such as output expected, the acceptable percentage of rejects or errors, allowable expenses, and tolerance for employee absences, tardiness, and accidents. Be wary about performance expectations in these and any other areas that are described with such loose terms as *good, better, soon*, and *improved*. Ask, politely but firmly: "How good?" "How much better?" "How soon?" "How big an improvement?" These are reasonable questions, and they will do much to take the vagueness—and stress—out of the measurements by which you will be judged.
- **Inadequate resources for the job at hand.** Few things are more frustrating than being pressed to get results without having been given the resources to get the job done properly. You want to try to make certain that the performance demands that are made of you

are matched from the start with adequate labor, equipment, materials, and supplies. Supervisors often make their biggest mistake by saying "yes" to a request before carefully sizing up the situation. Sometimes you may have to say "no" or bargain for a delay.

- **Conflicting demands and instructions.** These often stem from having two bosses. This situation shouldn't happen, of course, but it does. And as matrix organizations increase in number, it will happen more often. When faced with the stress of conflict in orders or instructions, don't let it pass. Instead, make the results of such a conflict clear to both parties as soon as you can. Show them how it affects productivity, costs, or customer relations.

What can be done about non-job-related sources of stress?

So far, we've talked about how to avoid or minimize stress at work, especially stress arising from time pressures. You should not overlook the very important matter of stress sources outside work. These sources are often just as hard to avoid or reduce. The same principles prevail, however. You must do the following:

1. Alter or change the conditions of your personal environment to reduce stress, if you can.
2. Be realistic about your personal ambitions and capabilities, but don't undersell yourself to yourself.
3. Identify those necessary interpersonal transactions where your performance is unsatisfactory, and do something to improve your skills in those areas. Admittedly, none of this is easy to do. Accordingly, if the strain you feel—from stress at work or elsewhere—is great, you'll need to consider professional counseling. This might be obtained from a variety of professionals, including doctors, lawyers, and accountants; marriage counselors, psychologists, and clinical social workers; and religious or spiritual advisers.

What can you do personally to lessen or manage the impact of stress?

The three fundamental approaches to the management of stress, no matter what its origin, were outlined in the last section. In a more specific context, however, there are several other constructive things you can do to lessen the impact of stress on your system:

1. **Understand your limitations and live within them.** This calls for you to (a) be realistic about your true capabilities, (b) exploit them only as far as they'll carry you, (c) try not to move too far too fast, and (d) accept the fact that it's usually more satisfying to do well at

Quips & Quotes

The phrase, "Don't work harder, work smarter," really means, "We're going to give you more work, and you'd better do it."

Patricia Farrell

a lesser job than to feel relentlessly pressured at one slightly above your capacity.

2. **Break away, if necessary, before you break yourself.** Don't run away from every crisis, but if you find yourself crumbling, do make time to remove yourself physically from the stressful situation. Take 15 minutes or more to think, meditate, pray, relax—so that you can get a fresh perspective.

3. **Get more genuine exercise.** It's a fact that tensions are reduced when the blood circulation rises. Even if you're not athletically inclined, find a half hour each day to loosen up your body in some relaxing form of exercise. The activity need not be too vigorous— walking, bike riding, bowling, or lawn mowing may do you as much good for relaxation purposes as jogging, tennis, or swimming.

4. **Select and pursue at least one diversion.** Most important, this should be something you truly enjoy doing, not something you feel is a matter of obligation. Let it be stamp collecting, woodworking, local politics, gardening, gourmet cooking, card playing, or needle- point. If it's a true diversion, you will find that you are totally absorbed in it, that time flies and cares are forgotten during your involvement. The purpose of the diversion is to give your mind a rest from stress so that it can recharge its psychological energy cells.

5. **Take time to look at—and help—the world around you.** Most people who are troubled by stress tend to turn their vision inward. This is like trying to climb out of a pit by digging downward. The escape from pressure usually lies in the other direction, outside one- self. Simply taking five minutes to look at the morning or evening sky helps place personal matters in perspective. Similarly, the act of getting concerned about other people's problems or volunteering in your community has a tension-relaxing effect. Immerse yourself in coming to the aid of others.

How does spirituality at work tie into stress management?

One of the factors that create stress for some employees is their percep- tion that work lacks meaning and fails to provide fulfillment. They may also see a lack of harmony between their personal values and the orga- nization's actions. As a result, employees increasingly are searching for a sense of *spirituality* at work. Although it is defined in many ways, spir- ituality is basically the search for a greater good or higher purpose in one's life. It is a quest for a sense of significance, a feeling of hope, a search for a sense of soul, and the opportunity to use one's talents fully. As one corporate trainer put it, "helping people link their spirit with their work may be the most rewarding task you can undertake."[1] And when people are given opportunities to do so—whether it be through medita- tion or discussion of values—their stress levels may decrease.

3   Developing Personal Creativity

CONCEPT

Supervisors can solve problems and increase their managerial stature by using their creativity and that of others.

Free association of ideas. The ability of the mind to unconsciously visualize relationships between seemingly different objects and ideas.

Exactly what is creative thinking?

It is simply the ability to apply your mind to a problem that hasn't been solved by a routine method and come up with a brand-new solution or batch of solutions. Many experts think that the secret of creativity lies in *free association of ideas*, that is, the mind's ability to make a connection between two vastly different objects or ideas. Take this example: A factory was spray painting bedsprings automatically. Drips and "teardrops" were a big problem. The engineer tried all the obvious ideas. He speeded up the spraying and then slowed it down; he changed paint consistency, surface preparation, drying heat, and airflow. No luck. Then the supervisor of the operation came up with the bright idea of whacking the painted springs automatically with a rubber hose. It worked! Paint flew off like the dust from a rug she had seen her grandmother beat with a rug beater. Not only was the drip problem solved, but enough paint was collected in gutters beneath the springs to paint twice as many springs as before.

The free association of ideas led to linking the painting problem with getting dust out of a rug.

What isn't creative thinking?

Critical, negative thinking tends to discourage the flow of ideas. Alex Osborn, the advocate and popularizer of brainstorming, always advised innovators to think the "green-light" way. When the green light is on, you don't stop to judge the merit of the ideas that emerge. The time to apply "red-light" thinking is after you've created a batch of ideas and want to evaluate their potential for solving the problem under review.

What is the best way to generate innovative ideas on your own?

There is no one best way, but successful innovators follow a systematic approach something like this:

1. **Narrow down the problem or the target.** It's easier to think of ideas for changing the way reports are filed, for example, than to redesign the entire filing system.
2. **Learn to concentrate.** Try writing the problem on a sheet of paper and keeping it in front of you to focus your attention.
3. **Persevere.** Good ideas don't always come quickly. If you can't produce a workable solution today, try again tomorrow. Keep your mind focused on it.
4. **Preserve.** When you come across good ideas, write them down before they're forgotten. Put them in a special file (an "idea bank"), and search it occasionally for possible applications.
5. **Build your confidence.** Look for early breakthroughs on small matters; then raise your sights to more difficult challenges.
6. **Use your unconscious mind.** Remove blockages by sleeping on a problem, letting your mind wander, or taking a break.
7. **Keep ideas flowing.** When you're hot, don't stop generating ideas just because it's quitting time.
8. **Take action.** Ideas may strike you in a sudden burst of inspiration. Nothing much will come of them, however, unless you convert them to practical uses.

What's the difference between brainstorming and creative thinking?

Brainstorming is the group approach to idea generation. The term was coined by Alex Osborn, an advertising executive, and he set four rules for a successful brainstorming session:

1. **Don't criticize ideas.** There's a time for judicial thinking, but not while brainstorming.
2. **Welcome new ideas freely.** That is, the wilder the idea, the better. A "can you top this?" attitude is encouraged. Participants use others' ideas as jumping-off places for their own.
3. **Strive for quantity.** Experience shows that the more ideas there are, the better they are likely to be. A seemingly remote idea from one person may trigger a more valuable idea from another.
4. **Combine and improve.** Ideas are like building blocks. Brainstorming participants are encouraged to suggest how an idea can be expanded upon or how two ideas can be combined into a single idea that is better than either idea alone.

Brainstorming. A group approach to idea generation that encourages free association of ideas among participants, while forbidding negative judgments, in order to generate a maximum number of ideas in a short period of time.

| 5 | T or F | It is best to critique new ideas immediately, before the brainstorming discussion moves on. |
| 6 | T or F | A key principle in brainstorming is to strive for quality ideas. |

QUICK TEST 3

Becoming a Mentor and Coach

Mentoring. What is that?

Employees learn job skills and other valuable information from job descriptions, orientation sessions, training programs, their peers, and informal on-the-job supervisory instruction. Yet there are many things that remain for people to learn that will help their career development—career paths, political savvy, and the organization's hidden culture. A **mentor**—someone with unique experience, expertise, and power who guides, provokes, and counsels another—can provide these additional professional and personal skills. The mentor is a role model for the other person, who is usually called a *mentee, protégé, or partner*. Mentors act as sounding boards for possible actions, act as sponsors to advance another person's career, and encourage, guide, coach, and advise interested employees.

The benefits of mentoring programs include increased employee loyalty, more productivity, higher upward mobility, and the capacity to deal successfully with stress and change in the workplace. But mentoring programs can be costly, time-consuming, poorly organized, and discriminatory if they aren't provided equally to all employee groups.

What does it mean to mentor upward?

Supervisors—especially early in their careers—need one or more mentors to help them get established and "learn the ropes." As they gain more and more experience, they may be called upon to be mentors to employees from other areas of the organization. But some organizations are also establishing *reverse mentoring* programs. These programs match up younger, tech-savvy employees with older (and sometimes much more senior in status) employees to help spread new product knowledge or information technology expertise upward throughout the

JOB *TIP!*

The Ideal Mentor

Searching for a potential mentor? Appraise possible candidates against these criteria: relevant knowledge, skills, and expertise; influence in their field; a track record of success; sensitivity to the organization's politics; willingness to help others and the time to do so; personal characteristics that you admire and trust; and excellent coaching skills. Then approach them with an offer that is specific, focused, and mutually beneficial.

organization. Here, the senior mentees require healthy self-confidence, openness to learning, and a certain amount of humility to gain the most from these relationships. Being a reverse mentor can be especially rewarding, as it publicly acknowledges one's expertise and provides recognition to the mentor.

How does mentoring relate to coaching?

Not all supervisors are mentors to others (or are mentored by others), but many supervisors report that they spend as much as 50 to 60 percent of their time coaching employees. Also, personal coaches sometimes come from outside the organization. Either way, the role of a *coach* in athletics or in business is to help "players" prepare for and play the game to the best of their abilities. How do they do this? They question, listen, probe, cajole, prod, inspire, and support others in their attempts to set challenging goals, identify obstacles, and choose a plan of action. Good coaches are sometimes tough and demanding, and sometimes they are warm and encouraging cheerleaders and facilitators. Coaches, then, are usually more directly involved in daily activities—and more assertive—than are mentors, who typically let the protégé set the agenda and initiate interactions. But both roles help employees stretch themselves to be the best they can be. And even great executives (and coaches) such as Jack Welch, former CEO of General Electric, admit that they could have used some coaching. Welch said, "I've learned in a hundred ways that I rarely regretted acting but often regretted not acting fast enough."

7	T or F	A mentor usually focuses specifically on developing a mentee's job skills.	QUICK TEST 4
8	T or F	A mentor and a coach are essentially the same thing.	

Personal Actions at Work

5

What kinds of ethical problems are likely to arise?

CONCEPT
Supervisors need to decide—and act—on their own ethical standards and take steps to promote their own career advancement.

Anyone with eyes and ears is aware that some corporate executives have been guilty of errors in judgment and major ethical mistakes in the last decade. Supervisors should be careful *not* to use these managers as role models. But crime doesn't pay, and unethical behavior usually comes back to haunt the perpetrator. Nevertheless, co-workers may be found who falsify reports, pad their expense accounts, pilfer supplies, make inflated estimates to win project approval, or take credit for the work of their subordinates. One contributing factor is the apparent absence of ethical values within individuals and across organizations. *Ethics*, at the personal level, is a code of conduct that specifies guidelines and principles for acting with integrity. Many people profess to be ethical, but some ignore their own values when faced with ethical choices.

Why do some people bend the rules for personal or organizational gain?

Many reasons exist. Sometimes they haven't thought about and clarified their values in advance of a crisis. Sometimes their values simply differ from the societal norm. Sometimes the opportunity for personal gain is so large and tempting that they ignore their own values. Other reasons include pressure from superiors, a self-centered belief that "rules are for others," the presence of ambiguous or outdated policies, the excitement of "getting away with something," the perceived need to pay back a favor, and the ever-present but false arguments that "everyone else is doing it" and "it won't hurt anyone." Regardless of the rationalization used, these arguments and the dishonest behaviors that stem from them are damaging to an organization's reputation and represent a malignancy that can cause absenteeism and turnover to skyrocket while productivity and job satisfaction plummet. The organizational costs, both direct and indirect, are enormous. Surveillance costs increase, tensions rise, trust disappears, and employees resent the imposition of controls and loss of autonomy. It is far better for supervisors to speak their values at every opportunity and then live them openly.

How can you cling to high ethical standards in the face of temptation?

Find others who are clearly ethical and use them as role models. Consult with respected peers or staff specialists for their advice when you are faced with ethical issues. Periodically review your employer's guidelines and your own ethical and moral beliefs. Try to avoid putting yourself in positions where temptation is likely to occur. And don't succumb to the claim that "everyone is doing it." Choose the high road and it will be its own reward.

What sort of attitudes should you avoid?

Always keep in mind that an organization is a group of people working together toward common goals. Large organizations are made of many smaller, overlapping organizations. These are groups within groups. As a consequence, at any one time at work you'll be a member of many organizations. What you say and do to make you a hero in one organization may make you an outcast in another. If you're strong enough and right enough often enough, you can say and do just about anything you please and few people will take sides openly against you. Most of us, however, are not like the eight-foot bear who can "sleep anywhere he pleases." We've got to be more politically astute. This means that it's not wise to take extreme positions. You needn't always be in the middle of the road, but you don't want to get so far away from the consensus that you can't make a compromise when good judgment dictates one. Here are some additional points to remember:

- It's important to show others that you are willing to pull your weight in the total organization. There are always a number of unpleasant assignments; make sure to take your share.
- You can't go far—or for long, either—with a win-lose attitude toward your peers. Resource allocations can spark battles between departments. Each department wants the new clerk, the extra lift truck, first access to the computer upgrade, and the like. If you insist on getting the most or the best every time, you'll inevitably make enemies. Organizations create mutual dependencies. You'll need to learn when to fight for a particular resource and when you will contribute more to the organization's goals by letting another department have the resource without a quarrel.
- It's also wise to avoid being characterized as a "negative," a person who resists every change. Try to check yourself before you think or say: "We've tried that before and it didn't work." "It isn't practical in the shop." "We're too busy with more important matters to be bothered right now."
- Finally, don't hog all the credit. Most of your accomplishments depend on the contributions of others. When reporting progress, give others the credit they deserve, and then some. Go out of your way to tip your hat (in your reports to your superiors) to anyone who can reasonably be said to have been a party to success. It costs very little to be generous, and it goes a long way toward defusing any potential undercutting of your organizational ambitions.

How can you put your best foot forward in an organization?

You will succeed as a supervisor not only because of the extent of your basic competencies but also to the degree that you learn to fit into and master the organization you serve. Call it politics, organizational sensitivity, or just plain practicality—you must learn to go with the flow most of the time rather than swimming upstream.

There are many ways to gain personal acceptance in an organization, but here are some that have been particularly effective.

1. **Demonstrate your job competence.** Few things gain as much respect as an individual's ability to do a job well. Your job is supervision. Show that you can run your operation like a clock, that company-wide problems never have their origin in your department, and that you've got your employees well motivated and under control.

2. **Become an integral part of the information network.** Almost all organizations, public and private, derive a great deal of their power from the information they assemble and control. By becoming a part of the information network of an organization, you become an integral part of the organization. Accordingly, make an early effort to know (a) the extent of unique information the organization possesses, (b) how to gain access to it, (c) how to contribute to it, and (d) how to use it in your operation. This means that you should know how to obtain and exchange the data you need to improve productivity and smooth out operations in your department.

3. **Go with the flow of the organization.** That is, try to find a way to go along with the organization's standards and general style of management. A maverick has a hard time proving his or her worth. It's better to give up a little of your independence in return for the support you'll eventually need if you are to be fully effective in any organization. After all, that's what an organization is—a cooperative effort. Loyalty, too, plays a part here. If you disagree with some of the things that are going on, don't stand aside and criticize; try constructively to improve them.

4. **Build a personal support system.** It can be awfully lonely in an organization without friends, especially influential friends. Accordingly, it is wise to be somewhat selective about the people in the organization with whom you develop special rapport. Be cordial and courteous to everyone, of course. These qualities provide the lubrication that enables interpersonal contacts to thrive. But it is important to go beyond that by *networking*. This means making friends (business friends, not necessarily personal friends) with those people who are—or whose positions make them—influential in the organization.

   A first step is to develop a good relationship with the key person in the department that precedes or follows yours in the product or service flow. If you make things reasonably comfortable for that person, he or she may be expected to come to your aid when you need help. A next step is to establish contacts in key staff departments (if you're a line supervisor, or in line departments if you're a staff supervisor). You'll want to be able to get confidential advice, and perhaps a little extra cooperation, from those in a position to do you good in payroll, accounting, sales order, field service, inventory, production control, and information systems, for example. In a great many instances, you will be able to develop this network only by first demonstrating that you will discharge your own responsibilities in a way that, at the very least, does not create problems for these key people. *People for whom you do favors are more likely to do you favors.* People about whom you say good things speak well of you. That's based on the principle of *reciprocity*, and it's a fact of organizational survival and success. Make no mistake: your personal support network depends on such trade-offs.

9	T or F	Supervisors should observe other people's ethical or unethical behavior and pattern their own behavior on that of their peers.
10	T or F	Networking is a valuable activity for supervisors interested in enhancing their careers.

QUICK TEST 5

Practical Guidelines for Supervisors

1. *Study your own use of time*, both now and periodically in the future. Monitor the proportions of your work time spent on routine, regular, special, and creative activities.

2. *Identify the major time wasters* in your life (both at work and at home); resolve to reduce or eliminate some of them in the next week.

3. *Select and implement three time-management tactics* of your own choosing; monitor your success and make a mental note of their effectiveness.

4. *Delegate something (anything) to another person*; follow up to assess how well that person did and then solicit a critique from him or her on your delegation skills.

5. *Assess your stress level* on a 100-point scale daily for the next month, noting the sources of your major stressors (both at work and at home).

6. *Identify three people who seem to be highly resilient* (either resistant to stress or capable of handling it well); interview them to obtain their secrets.

7. Seize an opportunity to *engage a small group in structured brainstorming*; critique the process afterward to assess what went well and what needed improvement.

8. *Enlist the assistance of a mentor* in some aspect of your life; commit energy to capitalizing on the opportunity, and assess the objective results after six months.

9. Commit yourself to *coaching someone else in work-related activities*; evaluate your success in using a variety of coaching skills and develop a plan for improvement.

10. *Develop a list of the 10 most important "commandments"* you have learned from this book; share them with others to obtain feedback on their practicality and importance.

Chapter 18 Review

Key Concepts to Remember

1. Managing Job-Related Time. An awareness of time, its incredible value, and its fleeting elusiveness, together with an ability to utilize and conserve it, is what distinguishes an outstanding supervisor from an ordinary one.

It takes self-discipline and conscious control to prevent personal time from being frittered away on nonessential, nonproductive activities. Inevitably, wasted time leads to job stress.

Capable supervisors are tempted to consume too much of their own time by doing too much themselves, retaining too many responsibilities instead of delegating time-absorbing routines to their subordinates.

2. Coping with Stress. An overload of stress can come from (a) the work environment, (b) your inner self, and (c) poorly handled interpersonal relationships. Job stress is often magnified by (a) ambiguity concerning responsibilities and results, (b) resources that do not match responsibilities, and (c) conflicting demands and instructions. Individuals manage stress by (a) understanding their limitations and living with them, (b) breaking away to regroup when pressures become extreme, (c) getting the proper amount of exercise, and (d) developing outside interests that distract and relax them. Acceptance and acknowledgment of spirituality at work can help ease the effects of stress.

3. Developing Personal Creativity. Supervisors and their employees, because of their nearness to the work, can be especially creative in suggesting new ways to improve productivity. Such innovation is related to an individual's ability to obtain a free association of seemingly unrelated ideas. When this process is carried out in group sessions, it is called *brainstorming*.

4. Becoming a Mentor and Coach. Supervisors need to find a mentor for themselves, and also play a mentoring role for others to aid in their career development. This may include reverse mentoring—helping others higher in the organization with matters that require technical expertise. More directly job-related, coaching draws on a variety of skills (questioning, probing, listening) to help employees become more effective and satisfied.

5. Personal Actions at Work. Few people rise far in management without having found a way to harmonize their personal goals and actions with those of their superiors and the organization as a whole. To do so requires a strong set of ethical beliefs, tact, and a degree of compromise, but it does not mean that you must sacrifice your independence or integrity.

Your acceptance and support by the organization depend in large measure on (a) how well you demonstrate competence in your work, (b) the readiness with which you accommodate group goals and consensus, (c) your contribution to, and use of, the information network, and (d) the power and influence of the personal support system that you build.

Reading Comprehension

1. What are the major ways in which you currently waste time? How do these ways compare to supervisory time wasters?

2. Talk to several colleagues and ask them for their most potent ideas for utilizing time more efficiently. Would these ideas work for you?

3. Consider delegation as a time-management tool. Should you delegate A, B, or C tasks to others?

4. If stress is a regular part of supervisory jobs, how well have you been prepared to handle stress? Where have you learned stress management?

5. Which stress-management activities do you already engage in? Which ones do you think you ought to start using?

6. What are your feelings about discussing spirituality at work? Would you be comfortable doing it yourself? Listening to other people's perspectives?

7. Why do brainstorming sessions strive for large quantities of ideas? Wouldn't it be better to stress the quality of ideas?

8. Who has been the primary mentor in your life? What have you learned from him or her? What mentoring skills did you observe that would be useful to you?

9. Some people are highly resistant to being mentored or coached by others. Why might they object to receiving such valuable assistance?

10. Some observers contend that the level of ethics has declined in our society. State five major reasons why this might have happened.

Application

Self-Assessment

Managing One's Own Career

Read the following statements carefully. Circle the number on the response scale that most closely reflects the degree to which each statement describes you. Add up your total points and prepare a brief action plan for self-improvement. Be ready to report your score for tabulation across the entire group.

	Good Description									Poor Description
1. I waste very little time on a daily basis.	10	9	8	7	6	5	4	3	2	1
2. I consciously practice a variety of time-management techniques.	10	9	8	7	6	5	4	3	2	1
3. I have learned the benefits of delegation very well.	10	9	8	7	6	5	4	3	2	1
4. Every day I divide my tasks among A, B, and C priorities and work on the As first.	10	9	8	7	6	5	4	3	2	1
5. I have stress well under control in my life.	10	9	8	7	6	5	4	3	2	1
6. I regularly practice thinking "out of the box" by engaging in free association of ideas.	10	9	8	7	6	5	4	3	2	1

	Good Description									Poor Description

7. I meet regularly with a mentor to obtain feedback on my ideas and comments on my behavior.

10 9 8 7 6 5 4 3 2 1

8. I believe that most employees would like to have more active coaching in their work lives.

10 9 8 7 6 5 4 3 2 1

9. I have consciously examined my values and could quickly tell another person what guides my ethical behavior.

10 9 8 7 6 5 4 3 2 1

10. I am aware of the value of reciprocity, and I regularly seek to do favors for others.

10 9 8 7 6 5 4 3 2 1

Scoring and Interpretation

Scoring

Add up your total points for the 10 questions. Record that number here, and report it when it is requested. _____

Also, insert your score on the Personal Development Plan in the Appendix.

Interpretation

81 to 100 points. Your attitudes and beliefs are appropriate for supervisory positions.

61 to 80 points. Examine your attitudes and beliefs and discuss them with current supervisors and managers to determine need for revision.

Below 60 points. Your attitudes and beliefs may be substantially inconsistent with current organizational practices. They could be detrimental to your career.

Identify your three lowest scores and record the question numbers here: _____, _____, _____.

Action

Write a brief paragraph detailing an action plan for how you might change your beliefs and practices. For example, if you scored low on item 1, you may wish to obtain additional training in the skill of time management. Include a target date for mastering that skill.

Cases for Analysis

Case 56

"Get Your Priorities Straight!"

Tomas was deep into his review of the week's time sheets when the phone rang. It was a call from the plant manager's office advising him that there was a productivity committee meeting for all supervisors at 11:00 that morning. Tomas looked at his desk calendar. He was supposed to deliver his time sheets to the payroll office by noon, and it was 10 A.M. already. Just then, the chief inspector walked into Tomas's office. "There's a small problem developing out there on the assembly line right now. If you don't get it straightened out soon, it may end up with having to shut down the line." Tomas dropped everything and went out into the shop. The quality problem was a sticky one, and it was 11 A.M. before it was corrected.

When Tomas got back into his office, the phone was ringing. "Where are those time sheets?" queried the payroll supervisor.

"I'll get them up to you in a few minutes," Tomas said. And he set to work on them again.

At noon, the phone rang again. This call was from a very angry plant manager, who wanted to know why Tomas had not attended the productivity meeting. Tomas explained the quality control problem and the need to get the time sheets into payroll. The plant manager was not sympathetic. He said, "You'd better get your priorities straight in the future."

Analysis

a. Should Tomas have gone to the meeting? Why?

b. How would you have advised Tomas to arrange his priorities for handling the problems he faced that morning?

Case 57

The Unfaceable Day

"I can't face this day," said Vito to his wife as he drank his third cup of breakfast coffee.

"What's wrong?" asked his wife.

"Just about everything," said Vito. "We just got through laying off a third of the office staff to cut costs. That was bad enough. Telling people they'd be going on unemployment, with no hope of their being called back. Now, we've got a big surge of orders to process. And my boss says that we've got to make do with the help we have. No temporaries. No callbacks. How am I ever going to press the remaining help to do more than normal? As it is, they've all slowed down the pace to stretch out the work."

"You'll manage, somehow," soothed Vito's wife.

"Maybe," said Vito as he chewed on a couple of antacid tablets before he lit up his first cigarette of the day. "I guess I'll have to put more pressure on to get everyone back into line!"

Analysis

a. What's wrong with Vito's approach to his staff?
b. How would you suggest he handle this situation?
c. What kind of advice can you give Vito, generally, to enable him to cope better with his stress?

Case 58

Passed Over Again

"I work hard," complained Connie to a fellow supervisor over coffee, "but I don't get much for it. Oh, sure, I get an occasional merit increase or pat on the back. But that's not enough. I feel like I'm just marking time here. I'm really down now. Last week, when my boss retired, I thought for sure that I'd get his job. But I was passed over again. And that's the third good job that's passed me by."

"What reason did they give this time?" asked the other supervisor. "Was it the old 'glass ceiling' treatment?"

"No, I can't say that," said Connie, "As you must know, Mary from Department C got the job. But I did hear some of the old excuses."

"Like what?" asked the other supervisor.

"Like they didn't think I was really interested, that I was satisfied where I am. That Mary was better qualified. That the new information-control system needed someone who had advanced training. Mainly, but without being specific, they thought I hadn't demonstrated that I have the skills the new job would require."

"What really bothers me," continued Connie, "is that I *am* interested in moving ahead. I'd have liked advanced training if someone had offered it to me. And I do have a lot of skills that I haven't been asked to use on my present job. The system is so unfair. Why can't they see that?"

Analysis

a. How unfair has the system been to Connie? Whose fault is it?
b. What might Connie do to improve her chances for advancement in the future?

Chapter Reference

1. William David Thompson, "Can You Train People to be Spiritual?" *Training & Development*, December 2000, pp. 18–19.

Appendix A

Personal Development Plan

Self-awareness is a crucial first step toward self-improvement for any aspiring supervisor or potential manager. You can develop a comprehensive self-portrait by returning to the Self-Assessment application exercises that appear at the end of each chapter, and recording your scores below.

CHAPTER	SCORE
1. The Supervisor's Role in Management	_____
2. Creating a Positive Workplace Within a Dynamic Environment	_____
3. Setting Goals, Making Plans, and Improving Costs	_____
4. Problem Solving and Managing Information	_____
5. Organizing an Effective Department	_____
6. Staffing with Human Resources	_____
7. Training and Developing Employees	_____
8. Leadership Skills, Styles, and Qualities	_____
9. Understanding and Motivating People at Work	_____
10. Effective Employee Communication	_____
11. Appraising and Developing Employees	_____
12. Counseling and Performance Management	_____
13. Building Cooperative Teams and Resolving Conflict	_____
14. Control: Keeping People, Plans, and Programs on Track	_____
15. Stimulating Productivity and Quality	_____
16. Managing a Diverse Workforce	_____
17. The Supervisor's Role in Employee Safety and Health, and Labor Relations	_____
18. Achieving Personal Supervisory Success	_____

If you are vitally interested in an overall "score," you can add up all the chapter-by-chapter scores and then divide that total by 18. Record that number here: _____

What should you do with this information? *Don't* just set it aside and think that you'll "get back to it later." Here are four suggestions. First, you can use this information productively when you apply for jobs; it will impress an interviewer when you pull out a *portfolio* of evidence that shows you have taken a hard look at yourself and candidly assessed your strengths and weaknesses! This suggests that you are looking ahead beyond your first or second job and planning for much more than that—a *career* in management.

Second, it would be wise to *obtain a "second opinion,"* just as a person with a major illness checks with another medical professional to corroborate a diagnosis before undergoing treatment. Find one or more friends (or, preferably, work colleagues) who know you well, and ask them to assess you by using blank forms for each of the chapter self-assessments. Then compare their information with your own (but don't take offense at what they said). This is a process of triangulation—"seeing" yourself from a variety of perspectives for a more complete (and, one hopes more accurate) overall picture, similar to the contemporary process of "360-degree assessment and feedback" that many organizations use for their managers.

Third, you are urged to create a *concrete action plan* to guide your self-improvement efforts. This should reference a specific item (e.g., "question 3 from Chapter 7"), and then identify exactly what you are going to do to improve yourself by a certain deadline. For example, if you need help in becoming a better listener, you might commit yourself to actions such as turning physically toward the other person, practicing good eye contact, not interrupting people until they are finished, pausing before responding, limiting the use of the word *but* to start your response, and shutting out major distractions (such as turning off the radio or iPod while interacting with people). You could even keep a journal that records your efforts and the results you experience.

Fourth, set a target date for when you will *conduct another self-assessment* after you have had sufficient time to make substantial changes. Be brutally candid with yourself; have you *really* made meaningful changes? (Remember, it does little good to tell yourself that you are better, if others wouldn't agree with that.) Give yourself praise for measurable improvements; commit yourself to new changes; promise yourself not to "backslide" and return to old habits. You'll soon be on your way to a lifetime of effective supervisory behaviors—and a deeply engrained cycle of self-improvement!

Appendix B

Your Career in Supervision and Management

The success—or shortcomings—of your career will depend largely on the skills you acquire and develop by yourself and the programs you devise to capitalize on them. Other people may offer advice and guidance—and even an occasional assist—but, in the main, advancement in supervisory and management careers is a bootstrapping operation.

Starting from scratch

If you are just beginning to seek a career in supervision and management, it is important to find a starting point that best suits your aptitudes and potential. Your first place of employment will probably not be your last, but some places provide a better springboard than others. These are some of the more important aspects of employment to consider:

Blue collar or white collar? Do you prefer activities associated with production or construction, working close to tools and machinery? Or is your preference for clerical, desk-related, and administrative operations?

Inside or outside? Do you like to be close to your support system, along with the comfort of daily routines that are clearly set? Or do the independence and challenge of sales and other field-related activities exert a greater appeal?

People relationships versus technical expertise? Do you favor activities in which interpersonal relationships play a large part? Most supervisory and management positions place greater emphasis on interpersonal skills than on technical expertise.

Line versus staff? Line jobs often carry with them the authority and visibility that lead to advancement. Work in line activities also tends to provide more action and a sense of being at the heart of an operation. Staff activities, in contrast, may be less stressful and more rewarding from a creative and intellectual point of view.

Manufacturing or services? The downtrodden manufacturing industries are experiencing a rebirth, with opportunities for advancement growing again. The major economic growth, however, continues to be in service-related industries such as banking and finance, food service, and hotel and restaurant management, and in wholesaling and retailing.

Large or small company? Relative job security, good working conditions, and opportunities for advancement make work in many large organizations attractive. There are drawbacks, of course, with the pressure to conform, reels of red tape to put up with, and responsibilities that are narrowly specialized. Work for smaller organizations, in contrast, presents an opposing set of advantages and disadvantages. Pay and benefits are often less attractive, as are job security and chances for advancement. Responsibilities in small companies, however, are usually more varied and challenging, with a minimum of red tape and a great deal of informality.

Private or public employment? Risks of employment in private industry are generally considered to be greater, but with the possibilities of greater financial rewards. Public employment, while usually less remunerative, is more secure and may provide a greater sense of social contribution.

An awareness of the flames. The better positions in supervision and management are always challenging and demanding. Some jobs, however, are characterized by too much heat. These are the ones that cause "burnout"—since they often demand the impossible. This kind of pressure isn't always apparent at the start, and so it pays to explore advancement opportunities carefully before pursuing them. You should expect a good job to demand much of you, but not so much that you can't do it well every day without feeling exhausted.

Planning a career search inside or outside your present organization

The competition for good jobs in supervision and management is more intense than ever. This is especially true of the higher-paying, more interesting positions. Curiously, neither the available positions nor the better ones necessarily go to the most qualified candidates. In a great many instances, these jobs are won by the people who plan and carry out the most appropriate search. Whether you are exploring opportunities for advancement with your present employer or somewhere else, your career search should combine at least five essential elements: (a) a seek-and-search timetable, (b) a realistic list of job factors that you consider necessary to make a job attractive and appropriate for you, (c) a résumé that clearly and concisely demonstrates your most valuable qualifications, (d) preinterview research and preparation, and (e) a strategy for handling interview questions to favorably differentiate you from other candidates.

Elements (d) and (e) will be discussed in detail later. Suffice it to say about elements (a), (b), and (c) that diligence is required in making out applications and seeking interviews. Résumés should be carefully prepared and error-free. Persistence is a strong tool for prying open the best positions in supervision and management. However, you should also be ready to accept something less than the perfect assignment to get a foothold in the area or field that is attractive to you. Most people have to perform work that has menial, tedious, and unattractive facets so that they can show their potential. Good supervisory and management positions are obtained by building on a record of sound performance in lesser assignments.

Preparing for a career-advancement interview

Many a good position is lost before the candidate walks in the door for an interview. A successful advancement interview requires planning, research, and rehearsal—even for jobs within your own company. Days before your interview, you should do the following:

1. **Find out more about your potential employer, department, or boss.** Consult the company's annual report, published reports about it found in a library, or someone who is working there now. You want to know something about the background of the company or department, its financial condition, and its products, services, and personnel along with any problems it is seeking to solve. After all, your application will have told the interviewers something about you; it will give you an equivalent edge to know something about the company or department that is interviewing you.

2. **Review your strengths and weaknesses.** Plan to put your strongest qualities forward, as they relate to the job in question. Be prepared also to defend your weaknesses. You must be ready to acknowledge, for example, that you may have little experience in a particular line of work. If you are prepared, however, you can counter with a reply that this has not been a serious problem in the past since you are an attentive and diligent learner.

3. **Anticipate the kinds of questions you might be asked.** Generally speaking, interview questions fall into two categories:

   - **Substance questions.** These questions seek out concrete information about you, your education, and your work history. Reply to them in short, specific sentences. Be concise: you'll want to guard against rambling. Typical questions are: "Tell me about your background." "What are your major accomplishments?" "How does your education or experience qualify you for this position?" "Why should we hire you for (or promote you to) this position?"
   - **Poise questions.** These questions are asked by interviewers to judge your personality, your ability to reply under stress, and the extent to which you would fit in with the people at that company

(or department) and its philosophy. There are usually no "right" or "wrong" answers to these questions, so try to answer directly and honestly. Often, the interviewer doesn't care so much about what you say as about *how* you answer. Obviously, don't get angry. Don't allow yourself to become too negative. Your objective is to project a pleasant, enthusiastic, and positive outlook. Typical questions here are: "What kind of people do you enjoy working with?" "What kinds of situations have you found most unsatisfactory?" "How would you handle a disagreement between you and one of your employees?" "Tell me about your worst boss."

4. **Rehearse your interview beforehand.** Like an actor before a play or a golfer practicing her swing, it helps to rehearse beforehand what your answers and behavior will be during the interview. Have a friend ask you the questions outlined above. Try out your answers by speaking them aloud. Record them on tape to see how they sound and whether the tone of your voice reflects confidence. Think through what you want to say and revise your answers so that you can make the most concise and effective replies.

Your interview strategy

Some authorities describe the job interview as "the 60 most critical minutes of your life." That may be an exaggeration, but it points up the wisdom of having a preplanned strategy for making the most of a brief period of time. You won't be able to control the interview; the interviewer will. Nevertheless, you can contribute greatly to its success by following a strategy that places you and your capabilities in the best possible light. For example, a winning strategy can be based on the following nine points:

1. **Have a good appearance.** Neatness in dress and care in grooming are absolutely necessary. Generally speaking, your clothing choice ought to be conservative so as to distract neither from your person nor from what you are saying.
2. **Be on time.** It is even better if you arrive a few minutes early. This gives you a chance to catch your breath and become comfortable in strange surroundings. If you are kept waiting for the interview, don't be impatient or demonstrate nervousness. It's not unusual for someone to observe, and report on, your behavior while you're waiting.
3. **Take advantage of the "warm-up" period.** Most interviewers use the first few minutes to get a "feel" for your personality before they proceed to the substance questions. During this period, try to relax yourself and tune your ear to the voice and manner of the interviewer.

4. **Be pleasant and cordial.** As in most human exchanges, a smile goes a long way in gaining acceptance. As a job candidate, you are a guest, even when applying for advancement in your own company. Your behavior should indicate appreciation for the opportunity to present yourself for consideration. Don't approach the interview as an imposition placed on you or as an opportunity to debate.

5. **Project a positive image.** This is especially true in applying for a supervisory or managerial position, which implies that you would be representing the employer, both to employees and to the community. A positive image can be projected in a number of ways. Shake hands firmly. Look the interviewer in the eye in a friendly fashion. Listen attentively. If you miss a question or don't understand it, ask that it be repeated: this demonstrates your interest. Don't be afraid to display enthusiasm. Take your time, if needed, to think through what you want to say before answering difficult questions. Try to keep your replies short. Don't smoke, eat food, or chew gum during the interview.

6. **Ask the interviewer questions.** If you have done your homework, you can ask questions that demonstrate the validity of your interest in the position. Don't dwell on pay or benefits. Do ask about the company's or department's product or service line, its plans for growth, and what the normal promotion paths might be for a person with your qualifications.

7. **Differentiate yourself from other candidates.** Your career-search preparation should help here. Try to focus on the two or three things that you do best, such as: "I have a strong sense of commitment." "I meet my objectives." "I work well with people." "I can handle, and am ready to perform, a variety of assignments." Show how these things can contribute to a solid performance as a supervisor. In replying to questions, don't be afraid to repeat these qualifications.

8. **Close the interview firmly.** Most employment interviewers will control the close of the interview. Nevertheless, it is appropriate and it makes a good impression if you also sum up clearly and confidently your understanding of what has transpired and your concluding view of the job opening. Say something like this: "I understand that you will be interviewing several other candidates, but I do wish to emphasize how interested I am in filling this position. I believe that my qualifications, by reason of education, experience, and motivation, would enable me to perform this job very well. You would find me an excellent employee and supervisor." When the interview is concluded, thank the interviewer. Shake hands if possible. Leave in a businesslike fashion.

9. **Follow up.** Regardless of the outcome of the interview, it makes a good business impression if you write a brief note, thanking the company or department head for the interview and expressing your continued interest in the position. (If the job no longer appeals to you, write anyway, asking that your name be removed from the list of active candidates.) It is also appropriate to telephone the interviewer periodically to determine the status of the job opening and ask that your application be kept active. Don't, however, persist to the point of becoming a nuisance, especially if you are told that the job has been filled. As an applicant, you will "lose" many interviews before you "win" one. Approach each as an opportunity for improving your job-advancement skills, and be appreciative of the company or department that gave you the chance. Persistence in your career search and maintaining a positive outlook will eventually pay off.

A strategy for survival and advancement

Once you have secured the particular position in supervision and management that you want, you'll have to work just as hard to succeed in it. Don't let this phase be accidental. It requires a plan and policies, too, for your personal guidance.

1. **Be a team player.** The big difference between academic pursuits and those of business or other real-life occupations is that you will be able to accomplish very little at work without the support of your co-workers, whether they are supervisors, managers, or other professionals. Almost everything productive that happens in organizations requires the combined and coordinated efforts of many people with many different skills. Trouble lies ahead if you try to go it alone. It is far better to acknowledge your interdependency with others.

2. **Establish credibility.** Your previous achievements won't be mounted on a plaque and hung on a wall in your office. Your new boss will judge you not by what you say or may have done before, but by what you accomplish now—and every day thereafter. *It is performance that counts.* Performance means discharging your responsibilities productively and with a minimum of complaints or callbacks. It also means being dependable, showing that you can meet your obligations by the designated times. Your reputation for performance will be established, or discredited, within your first few months on a new assignment. If it is good, you are on your way upward. If it isn't so good, you may be heading toward a dead end—or even be on your way out.

3. **Do right by your boss.** Will Rogers, the cowboy philosopher, once said, "I never met a man I didn't like." The reason for these almost unbelievably happy words is that Rogers found a way of finding something in everybody to like. It may seem too much to ask for you to like every boss you have. It is almost certain, however, that your bosses will always like you a little better if you try to perform your job so that it helps them meet their performance goals, too. Few bosses will exploit you. Most will want you to succeed. Many bosses may seem unreasonably demanding at times, but this is usually in response to the pressures imposed by the organization on them. It is counterproductive to set yourself against your boss. Instead, try to cultivate a productive, friendly relationship. Put yourself on the boss's side, for example, by asking about the direction the company is moving in and what your department can do to help cope with upcoming changes.

4. **Dress appropriately.** Advising women or men about what to wear at work is a sensitive issue, so find out from your employer what is acceptable.

   Some companies today are permitting employees to wear casual business attire. In such cases, the company must define for employees what clothing is acceptable.

5. **Build a network.** Networking is now an accepted dynamic of business and organizational life. At its simplest, networking is just another name for making friends. Among these friends, however, should be people who are supportive of you careerwise as well as personally. Your work associates will provide an important part of this network. Most important, you should try to make business friends of people at higher levels of management in your own organization.

   The main purpose of such a network, however, is to use these friends not as a way to seek advancement, but as a means of exchanging information, contacts, and resources. A good way to expand your network is to join a professional association related to your field and volunteer your time to it. That way, you can establish credibility based on your service and can exchange useful information as a result.

6. **Observe these guidelines.** Management development experts generally agree on these 10 fundamental guidelines to help keep your supervisory and management career on an upward path:

   - Know where your job fits into the organization.
   - Put your efforts into tasks that your boss values.
   - Don't be afraid to ask questions, and learn where to go for answers. Develop your inquiry skills.
   - Learn to communicate—with the right people.
   - Always share credit; never spread blame.

- Let others know when you've done a good job. It's not enough to be good; influential people have to know about it.
- Be sensitive to office politics.
- Cultivate a career-support network.
- Don't let emotions control your actions; try to stay cool and reasonable.
- Learn how to manage stress before you need to.

Glossary of Terms

Absenteeism rate The average number of days absent per employee, or the percentage of scheduled worker-days lost.

Acceptable Quality Level (AQL) A general form of specification that tells a supervisor the kind of tolerance limiting that will be judged as acceptable performance.

Accident An unplanned or uncontrolled event in which action or reaction of an object, material, or person results in personal injury or property damage, or both.

Accountability A nonassignable liability for the way in which an organizational obligation held by a supervisor is discharged, either personally or by subordinates.

Active listening The conscious process of securing information of all kinds (including feelings and emotions) through attention and observation.

Adjustment The process by which healthy as well as disturbed individuals find a way to fit themselves to difficult situations by modifying their feelings and their behavior to accommodate the stresses of life and work.

Affirmative action An in-company program designed to remedy current and future inequities in employment of minorities.

Application A form used by an organization to legally and systematically gather and record information from a job applicant about his or her qualifications, education, and work experience.

Appraisal interview A meeting held between a supervisor and an employee to review the performance rating and, using that evaluation as a basis, discuss the overall quality of the employee's work and methods for improving it, if necessary.

Arbitration The settlement of a labor dispute or employee grievance by an impartial umpire selected by mutual agreement of the organization and the union.

Assertive request To ask courteously; to make known your wishes with the implied expectation that they will be fulfilled.

Attrition The gradual reduction of a workforce by means of natural events and causes, such as retirements, deaths, and resignations, as opposed to reductions planned by management, such as discharges and layoffs.

Authority The legitimate power to issue orders to other people in an organization and to obtain resources from it.

Behavioral management A management approach that seeks to stimulate cooperation on the basis of an understanding of, and genuine concern for, employees as individuals and as members of a work group.

Behaviorally anchored rating scale (BARS) A performance-appraisal format that describes and provides examples of behavior that can be rated along a scale from outstanding to unsatisfactory.

Benchmarking A quality management technique based on finding the best product, service, process, or procedure and adopting it as the standard of quality performance.

Big Five The key personality traits that are exhibited to various degrees by all employees.

Body language Nonverbal body movements, facial expressions, and gestures that may project and reveal underlying attitudes and sentiments.

Brainstorming A group approach to idea generation that encourages free association of ideas among participants, while forbidding negative judgments, in order to generate a maximum number of ideas in a short period of time.

Budget A planning, reporting, and control document that combines standards for various departmental operating conditions with allocations for operating expenses. Also a plan, or forecast, especially of expenses that are allowable in the operation of a department.

Bureaucracy An organized system of work characterized by policies and rules, a chain of command, an emphasis on organizational goals, and many written records.

Burnout The inability of employees to handle major incidents of, or sustained, stress.

Business ethics Having a set of moral values that one consciously develops, examines, and applies to business issues to produce fair decisions.

Caregiving Demonstrating a supportive relationship toward employees by providing time and space for interation, inquiring about their needs, and listening attentively.

Catharsis The relief that follows release of accumulated feelings, emotions, and frustrations that comes through their expression in a harmless fashion.

Chain of command The formal channels in an organization that distribute authority from top to bottom.

Coaching Helping employees learn through supervisory observation, demonstration, questioning, and timely feedback.

Cohesiveness The degree to which team members are attracted to the group, feel a part of it, and wish to remain in it.

Collective bargaining The process of give-and-take engaged in by the management of an organization and authorized representatives of its collective employees (a labor union) to reach a formal, written agreement about wages, hours, and working conditions.

Communication The process of passing information and understanding from one person to another.

Communication process The exchange of knowledge, skills, and feelings.

Competition A relatively healthy struggle among individuals or groups within an organization to excel in striving to meet mutually beneficial, rather than individual, goals.

Concurrent controls Controls applied to conditions to be maintained and results to be obtained during the conversion process.

Conflict A disruptive clash of interests, objectives, or personalities between individuals, between individuals and groups, or between groups within an organization.

Contingency management The selection and use of a management practice that is most appropriate for a particular problem or situation, based on prior research.

Contingency plans Special-purpose plans that anticipate crises and specify the probable responses to them.

Contingency model of leadership The belief that the leadership style that will be most effective in a given situation can be predicted by examining the intensity of three interacting factors.

Continuous improvement The ongoing process of searching for cost reductions (and process improvements) by taking a critical view of the present situation.

Continuum of leadership A range of leadership approaches that progresses from the extremes of autocratic control by the supervisor to complete freedom for subordinates.

Controls The rules, regulations, standards, and specifications that enable a supervisor to measure performance against a department's goals and to determine causes and take corrective action when necessary.

Corrective controls Controls applied, mainly to results related to products or services produced, after the conversion process has been completed.

Cost-benefit analysis A technique for weighing the pros and cons of alternative courses of action.

Creativity The generation of new solutions to existing problems by using techniques to encourage "out of the box" thinking.

Critical incident An actual and specific occurrence, either favorable or unfavorable, that serves to illustrate the general nature of an employee's performance.

Cultural diversity The recognition that society and the workforce are composed of a variety of groups, each of which has, in addition to similarities with other groups, unique differences in beliefs and experiences that can be assets at work.

Decision making The part of the problem-solving process in which alternatives are evaluated and a choice is made.

Decision tree A graphic portrait of the possible outcomes of alternative solutions.

Defect Any variation (in the product or service) from specifications that falls outside the prescribed tolerances.

Delegation The assignment, or entrustment, to subordinates of organizational responsibilities or obligations along with appropriate organizational authority, power, and rights.

Differential treatment The act of treating a member of a minority, or protected group, differently from other applicants or employees in a similar situation.

Discipline The imposition of a penalty by management on an employee for the infraction of a company rule, regulation, or standard in such a manner as to encourage more constructive behavior and discourage a similar infraction in the future.

Discrimination Any managerial action or decision based on favoring or disfavoring one person or member of a group over another on the basis of race, color, ethnic or national origin, gender, age, disability, Vietnam-era war service, or union membership.

Disparate effect The existence of job requirements that have the effect of unfairly excluding a member of a protected group.

Dissatisfaction The state that exists when "maintenance" or "hygiene" factors such as good pay, job security, fringe benefits, and desirable working conditions are lacking.

Division of work The principle that performance is more efficient when a large job is broken down into smaller, specialized jobs.

Downsizing A reduction in the number of people employed by an organization, usually in order to respond to unfavorable economic conditions or in an attempt to improve efficiency.

Due process An employee's entitlement to a fair hearing before discipline can be meted out. Often the hearing is conducted by an impartial party, allows appropriate representation, and involves presentation of available evidence.

E-mail Use of the Internet or an intranet (local area network) to send and receive messages electronically.

Emotional intelligence A challenging combination of self-awareness and self-management, plus social awareness and the ability to manage personal relationships with others.

Empathy Building an emotional bond with others by establishing trust and understanding their problems, perspectives, and fears.

Employee-centered supervision Emphasis on a genuine concern and respect for employees, and on the maintenance of effective relationships within a work group.

Employee counseling A task-oriented, problem-solving technique that features an empathetic, interactive discussion—emphasizing listening—aimed at helping an employee cope with some specific aspect of his or her work life.

Employee turnover A measure of how many people come to work for an organization and do not remain employed there, for whatever reason.

Employment interview A face-to-face exchange of information between a job applicant and an employer's representative designed to develop qualitative information about the applicant's suitability for employment.

Empowerment Providing lower-level employees with the authority to examine problem situations and resolve them as they arise.

Entitlement The perception by employees that they ought to receive certain benefits, protections, and privileges from their employer.

Equal employment opportunity (EEO) A system of organizational justice, stipulated by law, that applies to all aspects of employment and is intended to provide equal opportunity for all members of the labor force.

Equity An employee's perception of the fairness in the application of rewards to oneself and others for their efforts.

Ergonomic hazard A workplace condition that requires the job holder to repeat or sustain a fixed motion or stress pattern over an extended period of time, and that may include a repetitive strain injury (RSI).

Ethics Both a belief system and a set of behaviors. It is often stated as a code of conduct that specifies guidelines and principles for acting with integrity.

Executive A top-level manager in charge of a group of subordinate managers; this person establishes broad plans, objectives, and strategies.

Expectancy An individual's judgment about the probability of receiving a valued reward.

Facilitating An approach to management in which a supervisor assists and guides employees in their efforts to perform their jobs rather than emphasizing orders, instructions, and control.

Feedback Information provided by those engaged in the communication process that serves to clarify and/or verify understanding and to indicate either agreement or dissent. Also the process of relaying the measurement of actual performance back to the individual or unit causing the performance so that action can be taken to correct, or narrow, the variance.

Feedback-avoiding behavior Actions by employees to not seek and even avoid performance-related information from their supervisors.

Feedback-seekers Employees who actively encourage and invite useful critiques from others.

Flexible work schedule A system by which employees can choose—and periodically change—the blocks of time in which they work.

Flow The total immersion of an employee in a task and full involvement with life that provides an opportunity to grow and achieve happiness.

Formal work group A group or team of employees who are assigned by management to similar activities or locations with the intent that they work together in a prescribed way toward goals established by management.

Free association of ideas The ability of the mind to unconsciously visualize relationships between seemingly different objects and ideas.

Fun workplace A work unit in which both employees and the organization benefit from the inclusion of playful and humorous activities.

Functional authority The legitimate authority granted to a staff department to make overriding organizational decisions involving its particular functional specialty.

Functional organization An organizational structure in which tasks are grouped according to a particular operating function, such as production, sales, information handling, and so on.

GLBTs Employees who are gay, lesbian, bisexual, or transgender.

GenXers Employees who were born and raised in the period from 1960–1980.

Goals Short-term and long-range targets (objectives) toward which an organization strives.

Goal setting The process of providing clear objectives for employees to accomplish, often created on a cooperative basis.

Grapevine The informal communication network that employees use to convey information of interest to them.

Grievance procedure A formalized, systematic channel for employees to follow in bringing their complaints to the attention of management. Typically, it prescribes a progression of appeals from lowest to highest authority within the company. It often has arbitration as a final step.

Group Two or more people who are aware of one another and interact with one another.

Group dynamics The interaction among members of a work group and concurrent changes in their attitudes, behavior, and relationships.

Group norms Beliefs held by a group about what is right and what is wrong as far as performance at work is concerned.

Halo effect A generalization whereby one aspect of performance, or a single quality of an individual's nature, is allowed to overshadow everything else about that person.

Hazard A potentially dangerous object, material, condition, or practice that is present in the workplace to which employees must be alert and from which they must be protected.

High reliability organization Firms that work hard to recognize and manage relatively unpredictable events that could destroy them.

Hostility An aggressive expression of anger displayed by problem employees as an unconscious, unwitting relief from fears about their security or other feelings of inadequacy.

"In group" A set of employees who are favored by the supervisor and spend more time with her/him.

Indirect costs Variable costs that are essential to the production of goods or rendering of services but which do not clearly add value to them, or do not do so in an easily measurable way.

Informal work group A group that forms spontaneously among employees who work near one another, who have common personal interests, or who work toward common job goals.

Information Data that has been selected, arranged, and analyzed to make it useful for supervisory decisions. Also the knowledge, skills, and feelings that are exchanged in the communication process.

Instruction Furnishing knowledge or information in a disciplined, systematic way with the expectation of compliance.

Interventions A variety of activities designed to make individuals, groups, or the entire organization more effective.

Japanese management The participative practice of seeking consensus of agreement from employees and other managers before choosing or implementing a course of action.

Job aids Materials placed on or near the work area that help employees remember key points and perform effectively.

Job breakdown analysis The segmentation of a particular job into important steps that advance the work toward its completion.

Job enlargement Extending the boundaries of a job by adding differing tasks at the same level of expertise.

Job enrichment Expanding a job vertically by adding higher-skill activities and delegating greater authority.

Job evaluation A systematic technique for determining the worth of a job, compared with other jobs in an organization.

Job instruction training (JIT) A systematic four-step approach to training employees in a basic job skill.

Job redesign The process of carefully restructuring a job to foster productivity and appeal to the interests of the employees who carry it out.

Job sharing The process of taking one job and splitting its duties into two so that the combined time and efforts of two persons will satisfy all the work demands.

Key points The essential elements that make or break the job.

Knowledge Job-relevant information.

Knowledge management The process of creating and using human and technological networks to capitalize on a company's expertise, experience, and learning.

Labor agreement The written agreement that binds a company's management and its employees' organization (labor union) for a stipulated period of time to certain conditions of pay, hours, work, and any other matter the parties deem appropriate. (Also called *union agreement* or *labor contract*.)

Leadership The process of influencing and supporting others to follow you and do willingly the things that need to be done.

Learning organization A company in which new ways of thinking are nurtured, people are continually learning how to learn, and the results are widely shared and used at all levels.

Line-and-staff organization The most common form of organizational structure, in which line managers hold accountability for results that most directly affect profits or institutional goals, and staff managers hold accountability for results that most directly affect the processes by which line managers accomplish their goals.

Management The process of obtaining, deploying, and utilizing a variety of essential resources in support of an organization's objectives.

Management by exception A principle of control that enables a supervisor to delegate corrective action to a subordinate as long as the variances in performance are within specified ranges.

Management by objectives (MBO) A planning and control technique in which a supervisor and his or her immediate superior agree on goals to be attained and standards to be maintained.

Management information system (MIS) A system (usually computerized) which collects, analyzes, exchanges, and delivers information in a way that helps managers make timely and valid decisions.

Management principles A set of guidelines established by Henri Fayol and others for carrying out the management process.

Management process Covers the five key functions of planning, organizing, staffing, leading, and controlling organizational resources for the attainment of results.

Manager An individual who plans, organizes, directs, and controls the work of others in an organization.

Merit raises Increases in an employee's salary based on the supervisor's assessment of an individual's job performance.

Methods improvement Any systematic methods of work analysis aimed at finding simpler, faster, less physically demanding ways of accomplishing a given task while at the same time increasing productivity and reducing costs.

Micromanaging The act of overcontrolling employees' behaviors after delegating tasks to them, often causing resentment and dissatisfaction.

Middle manager A person who reports to an executive and who directs supervisory personnel toward the attainment of goals and the implementation of plans of an organization.

Mission statement A statement that clarifies the nature and purpose of a business.

Modeling The process in which a skilled coworker or supervisor explains and demonstrates the performance of a key job skill.

Morale A measure of the extent (either high or low) of voluntary cooperation demonstrated by an individual or a work group and of the intensity of the desire to meet common work goals.

Motivation The process that impels a person to behave in a certain manner in order to satisfy highly individual needs.

Multi-skilling The development of capacities to perform two or more key tasks by a single employee.

Nexters Employees who were born and raised since about 1980.

Noise Any kind of distraction, physical or emotional, within an individual or the environment that distorts or obstructs the transmission of a message.

Nonmanagerial employees (often referred to as "employees" or "associates"). Workers who receive direction from managers and then perform specific, designated tasks.

Obesity The condition describing employees who are substantially overweight for their age, height, and build to the point of inhibiting their successful work performance.

Occupational Safety and Health Act Comprehensive legislation that establishes standards and calls for the inspection of safety and health conditions and the investigation of all serious accidents and alleged safety or health hazards. Created the Occupational Safety and Health Administration.

Open-book management The practice of sharing extensive information with employees, training and empowering them to use it, and rewarding them for the results.

Orders Commands given forcefully with the expectation of obedience to them.

Organization The structure derived from systematically grouping the tasks to be performed and from prescribing formal relationships that strengthen the ability of people to work more effectively together in pursuing common objectives.

Organizational citizenship roles Voluntary acts by employees that go above and beyond the call of duty.

Organizational culture The underlying (often implicit) set of assumptions, beliefs, attitudes, values, and expectations shared by members of an organization.

Organizational development (OD) A set of values and assumptions about individuals, groups, organizations, and their environments that suggests they must embrace change and find ways to deal more effectively with each other.

Orientation The process in which new employees are introduced to their jobs, co-workers, and work environment through tours, personal introductions, and explanations.

Participation The technique in which a supervisor or manager shares work-related information, responsibilities, decisions, or all three, with the work group.

Participative leadership The act of fully involving employees in decision-making processes so that their ideas are used and they are fully committed to the solution's success.

Penalty A punishment or forfeiture imposed by management on an employee as a form of discipline. Typically, such penalties include suspensions, loss of time and/or pay, demotion, or loss of job—that is, firing.

Performance appraisal A formal and systematic evaluation of how well a person performs his or her work and fills the appropriate role in the organization.

Performance management The ongoing process of clarifying and communicating performance expectations to employees, and then providing coaching and feedback to ensure the desired actions.

Performance test An employment test that enables job applicants to demonstrate that they can actually perform the kind of work required by the job in question.

Personality An individual's unique way of behaving and of seeing and interpreting the actions of other people and events.

Policies Broad guidelines that must be followed in pursuit of goals.

Presenteeism The productivity problem created by employees who insist on trying to work even though they are troubled by physical or emotional ailments.

Preventive controls Controls applied, primarily to an examination of resources, before the conversion process begins.

Primacy principal The tendency for trainees to remember best the things that they heard first.

Problem solving A process of systematically analyzing gaps between expected and actual conditions to find and remedy their causes.

Productivity The measure of efficiency that compares the value of outputs from an operation with the cost of the resources used.

Programmed decision A solution to a recurring problem that can be established for continual use every time the problem reappears.

Protected groups Certain minority and/or disadvantaged groups in the population that warrant special protection in employment matters.

Quality The measure of the degree to which a process, product, or service conforms to the requirements that have been established for it.

Quality assurance An approach to quality control that encompasses all the efforts made by an organization to ensure that its processes, products, and services conform to the requirements set for them.

Quality of work The idea that work can—in addition to being productive in a material way—be rewarding in a psychological way to the person who performs it.

Quality of work life (QWL) The extent to which the work itself provides motivation, satisfaction, and the chance for personal growth.

Quantitative management A management sciences approach to management that emphasizes the use of advanced mathematics and statistics and the application of information theory.

Realistic job preview A balanced presentation of positive and negative features about a job that allows a candidate to reach an informed judgment.

Recency effect The tendency for people to remember best the things that they heard last.

Reengineering A top-down, broad-based approach to improvement that can lead to sweeping changes in goals and methods throughout an organization.

References People who give information on those seeking employment.

Reject A product that needs to be discarded or destroyed.

Reliability The demonstrated ability of a test to yield similar scores for a candidate if the test were repeated (after a sufficient period of time to allow forgetting). Also a measure (usually a statistical estimate) of the probability of a product's performing specific functions, under given conditions, for a specified time without failure.

Resilience The capacity of an employee to handle short-term stress, and bounce back from its distractions.

Responsibility The duty or obligation to perform a prescribed task or service or to attain a specified objective.

Restructuring The process of laying off large numbers of employees to achieve greater cost efficiencies in the future.

Return on quality (ROQ) A modification of TQM in that it focuses on providing only the degree of quality that a customer or client values highly and is willing to pay the price to obtain.

Reverse discrimination The notion that implementing affirmative action programs deprives qualified members of nonprotected groups from their rightful opportunities.

Right-to-work laws Legislation passed in nearly two dozen states that makes it illegal to negotiate for a union shop after a union gains recognition.

Satisfaction The positive state that exists when truly motivating factors (satisfiers)—such as interesting and challenging work, full use of one's capabilities, and recognition for achievement—are provided.

Saving face Employees' actions taken to restore their self-image and regain their self-esteem after receiving criticism during an appraisal.

Schedules Detailed date-and-time indications of how facilities, equipment, and employees are to be used to accomplish organizational goals.

Self-appraisal The process of allowing employees to take responsibility for evaluating their own performance.

Self-directed learning The process by which trainees learn at their own pace by consulting resources and asking for guidance when they think it is needed.

Self-esteem The degree of self-confidence that employees have, often based largely on their personal expectations and prior levels of performance.

Self-managing team A group of employees who perform most managerial activities themselves, thus dramatically changing the roles of a traditional supervisor.

Sexual harassment Repeated or unwarranted verbal or physical advances or sexually explicit remarks that are offensive or objectionable to the recipient.

Six Sigma Efforts by firms to greatly reduce variation in their processes and products and make data-based decisions that will benefit and retain customers.

Skill The ability to perform a job-related action.

Span of control The number of activities or people that a single manager supervises.

Specification A collection of standardized dimensions and characteristics pertaining to a product, process, or service. Also the definitions of expected performance of a product (or quality of a service).

Spirituality at work The search for a greater good or higher purpose in life.

Stakeholders Groups who affect, are affected by, or deeply interested in, the actions of the company.

Standard The measure, criterion, or basis—usually expressed in numbers and/or other concrete terms—for judging performance of a product or service, machine, individual, or organizational unit. Also the normal or expected time required to perform an operation or process or make a product, computed on the basis of past performance, estimates, or work measurement.

Statistical quality control (SQC) Numbers are used as a part of the overall approach to controlling quality.

Stereotype The characterization of an individual on the basis of a standardized, oversimplified view of the characteristics believed (often wrongly) to be held in common by the group to which the individual is assumed to belong.

Stewardship The view that supervisors are stewards of resources and must play the role of servant-leader to help others achieve their goals.

Strategic control points Key places where it makes the most sense to measure performance and take corrective action.

Strategies The major methods for achieving an organization's vision and mission.

Stress The experience of mild or severe psychological and physical reactions to pressures and frustrations that may have arisen over time or appeared suddenly.

Stressors Environmental, psychological, or psychosocial factors that produce stress within employees and often detract from their work performance.

Substitutes for leadership Factors in the task, organization, or employees that diminish the need for various kinds of supervisory leadership behaviors.

Superleader A supervisor who places a high priority on developing the skills of employees to manage themselves and engage in self-leadership.

Superordinate goal An objective that requires cooperation from others to achieve and appeals to both heart and mind.

Supervisor A manager who is in charge of, and coordinates the activities of, a group of employees engaged in related activities within a unit of an organization.

System An interrelated set of elements functioning as a whole.

Systematic management The traditional approach to management that emphasizes the functions performed in the management process as well as systematic measurement.

Task-centered supervision An emphasis on the job or task that employees are expected to perform so as to produce results.

Teachable moments The specific times when employees are most likely to learn.

Team building Activities designed to help group members develop more effective ways of problem solving and interacting with each other.

Teams Groups of people who must work together to achieve common goals.

Telecommuting Working at one's home, while being connected electronically to the employer's office.

Theory X A set of assumptions in which a supervisor acts as if she or he believes that most people don't like to work and that they wish to avoid responsibility and prefer job security above all.

Theory Y A set of assumptions in which a supervisor acts as if she or he believes that most people can set challenging goals and provide their own initiative and exert self-control to attain their goals.

Time management The process of analyzing one's use of time, dividing it into controllable and uncontrollable categories, and using various tactics to make the best use of your time.

Tolerance The permissible deviation, or variance, from a standard. Also a statement of precision that establishes limits within which the product or the service must meet the specification.

Total quality management (TQM) An approach to quality control that focuses on customer satisfaction and embraces not only all the internal functions of an enterprise, but also external contributors.

Training need A demonstrated gap between expected and actual performance.

Transactional analysis (TA) A way of improving relationships between people that is based on an understanding of each individual's mature attitudes and behavior toward one another.

Transfer of training The process in which trainees effectively apply to their jobs knowledge and skills gained in off-the-job training.

Trust The confidence that employees have in a supervisor's integrity, ability, and character.

Unfair labor practices Practices engaged in by either management or labor unions that are judged by the federal labor law (National Labor Relations Act) to be improper, especially in that they (a) interfere with the rights of employees to organize or (b) discriminate against employees for labor union activities.

Unity of command The principle that each individual should report to only one supervisor.

Unity of direction The principle that there should be a single set of goals and objectives that unifies the activities of everyone in an organization.

Validity The proven ability of a test to measure what it purports to measure.

Values What an organization believes in and guides its practices by.

Variance The gap, or deviation, between the actual performance and the standard, or expected, performance.

Virtual classroom The use of Web-based electronic programs to provide just-in-time training to employees.

Virtual team A group of people who have a shared goal and must work together to achieve it despite being separated by space, time, or organizational boundaries.

Vision A statement of an organization's ideal future.

Voice mail The use of electronic recording to capture, save, and transmit telephone messages.

Warning A reprimand worded so as to give formal notice to an employee that repetition of a particular form of unacceptable behavior, such as infraction of a rule, will draw a penalty.

Withdrawal A passive way for emotionally disturbed employees to cope with their anxieties, in which they retreat from confrontations, appear unduly preoccupied, discourage social overtures, and keep very much to themselves.

Work An activity involving physical or mental effort to perform tasks and overcome difficulties to attain valued organizational results and a means of personal livelihood.

Work distribution chart A visual device for allocating tasks equitably among the members of a department, according to time required and skill levels available.

Work measurement The determination, by systematic and (ideally) precise methods, of the time dimension of a particular task.

Workplace bullies Employees who insult others, make unreasonable job demands, falsely blame others, verbally harass others, and steal credit from deserving persons.

Workplace violence Acts of intimidation, bullying, threats of bodily harm or property damage, or actual destruction to people or equipment.

Work sampling A technique for finding out what proportion of employees' time is used productively on job assignments, compared with the proportion that is not.

Photo Credits

Index